TM 9-802
WAR DEPARTMENT TECHNICAL MANUAL

GMC DUKW-353 "DUCK" AMPHIBIAN TRUCK TECHNICAL MANUAL TM 9-802

by War Department

©2012 PERISCOPE FILM LLC
ALL RIGHTS RESERVED
ISBN #978-1-937684-87-7
WWW.PERISCOPEFILM.COM

WAR DEPARTMENT • FEBRUARY 1945

DISCLAIMER:
This manual is sold for historic research purposes only, as an entertainment. It contains obsolete information and is not intended to be used as part of an actual DUKW operation or maintenance training program. No book can substitute for proper training by an authorized instructor. The licensing of operators is overseen by organizations and authorities such as the state Department of Motor Vehicles and other entities. Operating a commercial vehicle without the proper license can result in criminal prosecution.

This book has been digitally watermarked to prevent illegal duplication.

©2012 PERISCOPE FILM LLC
ALL RIGHTS RESERVED
ISBN #978-1-937684-87-7
WWW.PERISCOPEFILM.COM

WAR DEPARTMENT TECHNICAL MANUAL
TM 9-802

GMC DUKW-353 "DUCK" AMPHIBIAN TRUCK TECHNICAL MANUAL TM 9-802

2½-TON, 6x6

WAR DEPARTMENT • FEBRUARY 1945

©2012 PERISCOPE FILM LLC
ALL RIGHTS RESERVED
ISBN #978-1-937684-87-7
WWW.PERISCOPEFILM.COM

WAR DEPARTMENT
Washington 25, D. C., 23 February 1945

TM 9-802, 2½-ton, 6x6, amphibian truck (GMC DUKW-353) is published for the information and guidance of all concerned.

BY ORDER OF THE SECRETARY OF WAR:

[A. G. 300.7 (24 Mar 44)]

G. C. MARSHALL
Chief of Staff.

OFFICIAL:

J. A. ULIO,
    Major General,
        The Adjutant General.

DISTRIBUTION: AAF (10); AGF (10); ASF (2); AAF Comds (2); S Div ASF (1); Arm & Sv Bd (2); Dept (10); Tech Sv (2); Sv C (10); P C & S (1); PE "Mark for Ord-O" (5); H & R (5); Dist O. 9 (5); Dist Br O, 9 (3); Reg O, 9 (3); Establishments 9 (5); Decentralized Sub-O, 9 (3); Gen & Sp Sv Sch (10); USMA (2); A (10); CHQ (10); D (2); AF (2). T/O & E 1-907 (2); 1-911 (2); 9-7, (3); 9-9 (3); 9-37 (3); 9-57 (3); 9-65 (2); 9-67 (3); 9-76 (2); 9-127 (3); 9-197 (3); 9-317 (3); 9-325 (2); 9-327 (3); 9-328 (3); 9-377 (3); 55-37 (3).

(For explanation of symbols, see FM 21-6)

TM 9-802

CONTENTS

PART ONE—INTRODUCTION

			Paragraphs	Pages
Section	I.	General	1-2	5-7
	II.	Description and data	3-4	7-17
	III.	Tools, parts, and accessories	5-8	17-25

PART TWO—OPERATING INSTRUCTIONS

Section	IV.	General	9	26
	V.	Service upon receipt of equipment	10-13	26-32
	VI.	Controls and instruments	14-17	33-42
	VII.	Operation under ordinary conditions	18-28	42-60
	VIII.	Operation of auxiliary equipment	29-41	60-85
	IX.	Operation under unusual conditions	42-47	85-94
	X.	Demolition to prevent enemy use	48-49	94-96

PART THREE—MAINTENANCE INSTRUCTIONS

Section	XI.	General	50	97
	XII.	Special organizational tools and equipment	51	97-98
	XIII.	Lubrication	52-53	98-16
	XIV.	Preventive maintenance services	54-60	116-144
	XV.	Trouble shooting	61-83	144-172
	XVI.	Engine description, data maintenance, and adjustment on vehicle	84-92	172-186
	XVII.	Engine removal and installation	93-95	186-197
	XVIII.	Ignition system	96-102	197-207
	XIX.	Fuel and air intake system	103-112	207-225
	XX.	Exhaust system	113-115	225-230
	XXI.	Cooling system	116-122	230-241
	XXII.	Starting system	123-125	241-244
	XXIII.	Generating system	126-128	244-249

TM 9-802

CONTENTS

			Paragraphs	Pages
Section	XXIV.	Battery and lighting system	129-134	249-258
	XXV.	Wiring, harnesses, and circuits	135-137	258-269
	XXVI.	Radio noise suppression system	138-142	269-274
	XXVII.	Instruments, gages, and switches	143-151	275-287
	XXVIII.	Clutch and controls	152-156	287-292
	XXIX.	Transmission	157-159	293-294
	XXX.	Axle transfer case and controls	160-163	294-300
	XXXI.	Power take-off and controls	164-168	300-307
	XXXII.	Front axle	169-176	307-320
	XXXIII.	Rear axles	177-180	320-324
	XXXIV.	Propeller shafts, housings, and pillow block	181-184	324-340
	XXXV.	Service brake system	185-198	340-361
	XXXVI.	Hand brake system	199-203	361-367
	XXXVII.	Spring suspension	204-209	367-376
	XXXVIII.	Wheels, tires, and hubs	210-215	377-391
	XXXIX.	Steering system	216-224	392-409
	XL.	Hull	225-238	410-431
	XLI.	Forward bilge pump system (Oberdorfer type)	239-244	431-442
	XLII.	Forward bilge pump system (Gould type)	245-249	442-449
	XLIII.	Rear bilge pump system (Higgins)	250-253	449-456
	XLIV.	Water drive system	254-258	456-476
	XLV.	Tire pump system (early type)	259-263	476-482
	XLVI.	Central tire pressure control system	264-271	482-498
	XLVII.	Winch and controls	272-278	498-508
	XLVIII.	A-frame	279-281	508-511
	XLIX.	Compass	282-284	511-518

PART FOUR—AUXILIARY EQUIPMENT

Section	L.	General	285	519

APPENDIX

	LI.	Shipment and limited storage	286-288	519-523
Section	LII.	References	289-291	524-525
		Index		526-332

General

PART ONE
INTRODUCTION

Section I
General

1. SCOPE.

a. These instructions are published for information and guidance of personnel to whom this equipment is assigned. They contain information on operation and maintenance of the equipment as well as description of major units and their functions in relation to other components of this vehicle. They apply only to the *Truck, 2½-Ton, 6x6, Amphibian (GMC Model DUKW-353)* and are arranged in four parts: Part One, Introduction; Part Two, Operating Instructions; Part Three, Maintenance Instructions; and Part Four, Auxiliary Equipment.

b. The appendix at the end of the manual contains instructions for shipment and limited storage, and a list of references including standard nomenclature lists, technical manuals, and other publications applicable to the vehicle.

c. The stock and part numbers which appear throughout the manual are extracted from ORD 7, SNL G-501.

2. RECORDS.

a. Forms and records applicable for use in performing prescribed operations are listed below with a brief explanation of each.

(1) W.D., A.G.O. FORM NO. 7360, ARMY MOTOR VEHICLE OPERATOR'S PERMIT. This form will be issued by commanding officers of posts, camps, stations, or organizations, to all operators of military vehicles who have passed the driver's examination (TM 21-300) and are qualified to drive the particular vehicles noted on the permit.

(2) WAR DEPARTMENT LUBRICATION ORDER. War Department Lubrication Order No. 9-802 prescribes lubrication maintenance for this vehicle. A lubrication order is issued with each vehicle and is to be carried with it at all times.

(3) STANDARD FORM NO. 26, DRIVER'S REPORT—ACCIDENT, MOTOR TRANSPORTATION. One copy of this form will be kept with the vehicle at all times. In case of an accident resulting in injury or property damage, it will be filled out by the driver on the spot, or as promptly as practical thereafter.

(4) WAR DEPARTMENT FORM NO. 48, DRIVER'S TRIP TICKET AND PREVENTIVE MAINTENANCE SERVICE RECORD. This form, properly executed, will be furnished to the driver when his vehicle is dispatched on non-tactical missions. The driver and

TM 9-802

Introduction

the official user of the vehicle will complete in detail appropriate parts of this form. These forms need not be issued for vehicles in convoy or on tactical missions. The reverse side of this form contains the driver's daily and weekly preventive maintenance service reminder schedule.

(5) W.D., A.G.O. FORM NO. 478, MWO AND MAJOR UNIT ASSEMBLY REPLACEMENT RECORD. This form, carried with the vehicle, will be used by all personnel completing a modification or major unit assembly (engine, transmission, transfer case, tracks, etc.) replacement to record clearly the description of work completed, date, vehicle hours, and/or mileage, and MWO number or nomenclature of unit assembly. Personnel performing the operation will initial in the column provided. Minor repairs, parts, and accessory replacements will not be recorded.

(6) W.D., A.G.O. FORM NO. 460, PREVENTIVE MAINTENANCE ROSTER. This form will be used for scheduling and maintaining a record of motor vehicle maintenance operations.

(7) W.D., A.G.O. FORM NO. 6, DUTY ROSTER. This form, slightly modified, will be used for scheduling and maintenance operations until W.D., A.G.O. Form No. 460 is available. It may be used for lubrication records.

(8) W.D., A.G.O. FORM NO. 461, PREVENTIVE MAINTENANCE SERVICE AND TECHNICAL INSPECTION WORK SHEET FOR WHEELED AND HALF-TRACK VEHICLES. This form will be used for all 1,000-mile (monthly) and 6,000-mile (semiannual) maintenance services and all technical inspections performed on wheeled or half-track vehicles.

(9) W.D., A.G.O. FORM NO. 9-70, SPOT-CHECK INSPECTION REPORT FOR ALL MOTOR VEHICLES. This form may be used by all commanding officers or their staff representatives in making spot-check inspections on all vehicles.

(10) W.D., A.G.O. FORM NO. 9-68, SPOT-CHECK INSPECTION REPORT FOR WHEELED AND HALF-TRACK VEHICLES. This form will replace W.D., A.G.O. Form No. 9-70 for making spot-check inspections on wheeled and half-track vehicles when existing stocks of W.D., A.G.O. Form No. 70 are exhausted.

(11) W.D., A.G.O. FORM NO. 9-69, SPOT-CHECK INSPECTION REPORT FOR FULL-TRACK AND TANK-LIKE WHEELED VEHICLES. This form will replace W.D., A.G.O. Form No. 70 for making spot-check inspections on full-track and tank-like wheeled vehicles when existing stocks of W.D., A.G.O. Form No. 70 are exhausted.

(12) W.D., A.G.O. FORM NO. 468, UNSATISFACTORY EQUIPMENT REPORT. This form will be used for reporting manufacturing, design, or operational defects in materiel with a view to improving and correcting such defects, and for use in recommending modifications on materiel. This form will not be used for reporting failures, isolated materiel defects, or malfunctions of materiel resulting from fair wear and tear or accidental damage, nor for the replacement, repair or the issue of parts and equipment. It does not replace currently authorized operational or performance records.

Description and Data

(13) W.D., A.G.O. FORM NO. 9-81, EXCHANGE PART OR UNIT IDENTIFICATION TAG. This tag, properly executed, may be used when exchanging unserviceable items for like serviceable assemblies, parts, vehicles, and tools.

Section II
Description and Data

3. DESCRIPTION.

a. General. The vehicle described in this manual is known as TRUCK, 2½-TON, 6x6, AMPHIBIAN (GMC Model DUKW-353). The vehicle (figs. 1 and 2) has the automotive characteristics of a conventional 2½-ton, 6x6 truck and, in addition, is equipped with an integral watertight hull, marine propeller, bilge pumps, and rudder. For land operation, vehicle utilizes six driving wheels powered by a six-cylinder valve-in-head engine through transmission, transfer case, and propeller shafts. For water operation, vehicle is propelled with marine type propeller powered from the engine through the transmission and a water propeller transfer case. The vehicle is commonly known as a "duck," receiving the name from the model designation "DUKW."

b. General Characteristics.

(1) HULL. The welded steel hull is built to accept chassis frame and power plant. The spring suspension and driving axles are attached to and through the bottom of hull to the frame, with attaching parts at the hull adequately sealed. The hull is decked forward of driver's compartment, to the rear of rear wheels, and along both sides.

(2) DRIVER'S COMPARTMENT. The two-man driver's compartment is open type with removable canvas top and open back. The windshield, either vertical (fig. 1), or sloping (fig. 2), can be positioned for ventilation and visibility. Driver's compartment, with entrance from the rear, has driver and co-pilot seats.

(3) CARGO SPACE AND COMPARTMENTS. Cargo space to rear of driver's compartment is provided with removable flooring, permitting access to the bilge and to driving units installed below level of cargo space floor. Hatches in rear deck provide access to tool and stowage holds, and also to the rudder linkage. Two hatches in bow permit access to power plant and forward compartment. Entire cargo space can be covered with a one-piece tarpaulin which is supported on conventional removable bows.

(4) POWER PLANT. The engine, with accessories, is mounted on the frame, and is accessible for service through main hatch in the front deck. The power plant is removable through the hatch.

(5) POWER DRIVE. The main transmission is conventionally mounted to engine. A power take-off mounted to transmission operates winch on all vehicles, and tire pump on early vehicles. The axle transfer

Figure 1 — Truck, 2½-Ton, 6x6, Amphibian (GMC Model DUKW-353) — Prior to Chassis Serial No. 2006

Legend for Figure 1

A ENGINE HATCH COVER
B WINDSHIELD SURF BOARD
C AIR SCOOP DOOR
D DRIVER'S COMPARTMENT
E CO-PILOT'S SEAT
F AIR EXHAUST GRILLE (RIGHT)
G AIR INTAKE GRILLES
H REAR DECK HATCH COVER
I LIQUID CONTAINER BRACKETS
J B O STOP AND TAILLIGHTS
K WINCH
L B.O. TAILLIGHT AND SERVICE STOP AND TAILLIGHTS
M SPARE WHEEL AND TIRE
N FUEL TANK FILLER CAP
O DRIVER'S SEAT
P AIR EXHAUST GRILLE (LEFT)
Q HORN
R FRONT DECK HATCH COVER
S BLACKOUT DRIVING LIGHT
T HEADLIGHT (LEFT)
U FRONT SURF BOARD
V WINCH CABLE CHOKE
W HEADLIGHT (RIGHT)
X REFLECTOR (FRONT)
Y FRONT LIFTING EYE
Z WINDSHIELD

AA DRIVER'S COMPARTMENT DOOR (LEFT SHOWN)
AB DRIVER'S COMPARTMENT TOP COVER
AC FRONT BILGE PUMP DISCHARGE
AD MOORING EYE
AE REAR BILGE PUMP DISCHARGE
AF REFLECTOR (CENTER)
AG TARPAULIN
AH REAR LIFTING EYE
AI REFLECTOR (REAR)
AJ FUEL TANK DRAIN PLUG
AK FRONT BILGE PUMP BLEEDER STRAINER
AL REFLECTOR (REAR LEFT)
AM REAR SURF BOARD
AN REFLECTOR (REAR RIGHT)
AO PINTLE HOOK
AP RUDDER
AQ WATER PROPELLER
AR BLACKOUT FRONT MARKER LIGHT (RIGHT)
AS RIGHT REAR VIEW MIRROR
AT HAND OPERATED WINDSHIELD WIPER
AU VACUUM WINDSHIELD WIPER
AV LEFT REAR VIEW MIRROR
AW BLACKOUT FRONT MARKER LIGHT (LEFT)
AX TOW HOOK SHACKLE (UPPER)
AY TOW HOOK SHACKLE (LOWER)

RA PD 33

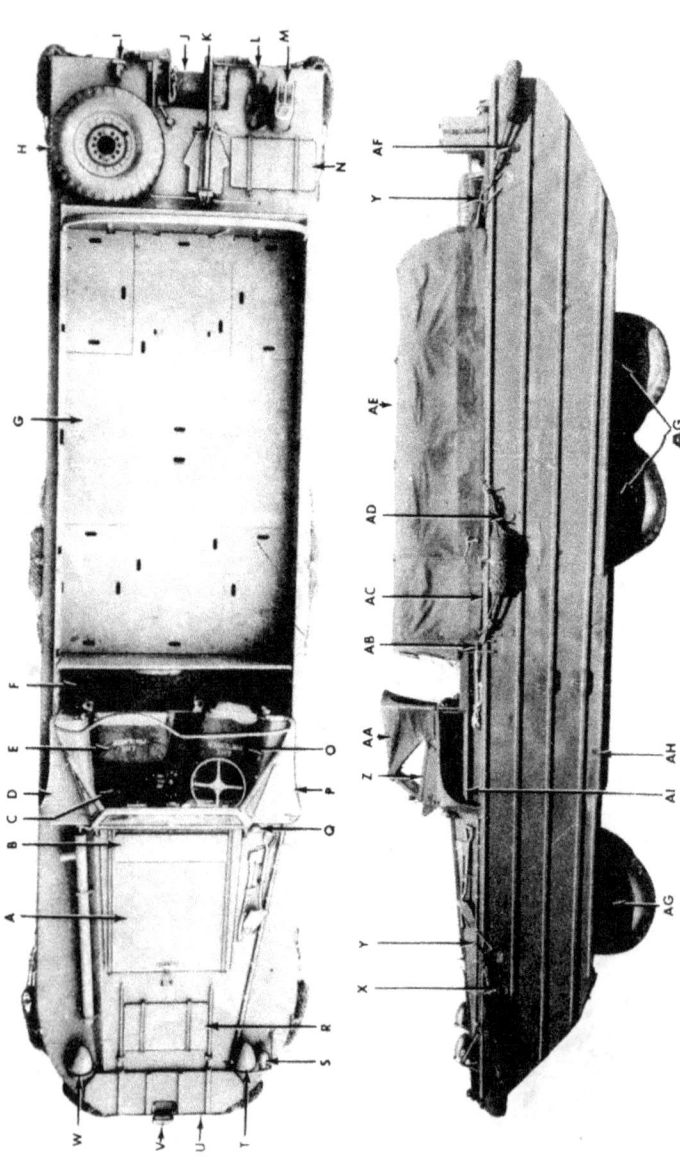

Figure 2 — Truck, 2½-Ton, 6x6, Amphibian (GMC Model DUKW-353) — After Chassis Serial No. 2005

- A ENGINE HATCH COVER
- B AIR SCOOP DOOR (NOT USED ON LATER VEHICLES)
- C DRIVER'S COMPARTMENT
- D AIR EXHAUST GRILLE (RIGHT)
- E CO-PILOT'S SEAT
- F AIR INTAKE GRILLES
- G CARGO SPACE
- H SPARE WHEEL AND TIRE
- I B.O. STOP AND TAILLIGHTS
- J WINCH
- K ANCHOR
- L B.O. TAILLIGHT AND SERVICE STOP AND TAILLIGHTS
- M LIQUID CONTAINER BRACKET
- N REAR DECK HATCH COVER
- O DRIVER'S SEAT
- P AIR EXHAUST GRILLE (LEFT)
- Q HORN
- R FRONT DECK HATCH COVER
- S BLACKOUT DRIVING LIGHT
- T HEADLIGHT (LEFT)
- U FRONT SURF BOARD
- V WINCH CABLE CHOKE
- W HEADLIGHT (RIGHT)
- X REFLECTOR (FRONT)
- Y FRONT LIFTING EYE
- Z WINDSHIELD
- AA DRIVER'S COMPARTMENT COVER
- AB MOORING EYE
- AC REAR BILGE PUMP DISCHARGE
- AD REFLECTOR (CENTER)
- AE TARPAULIN
- AF REFLECTOR (REAR)
- AG TIRE INFLATING DEVICES
- AH FRONT BILGE PUMP BLEEDER STRAINER
- AI FRONT BILGE PUMP DISCHARGE
- AJ REFLECTOR (REAR LEFT)
- AK RUDDER
- AL WATER PROPELLER
- AM PINTLE HOOK
- AN REFLECTOR (REAR RIGHT)
- AO REAR END CURTAIN (AFTER CHASSIS SERIAL NO. 420) OR REAR SURF BOARD (PRIOR TO CHASSIS SERIAL NO. 4202)
- AP WINDSHIELD WIPERS
- AQ REAR VIEW MIRROR
- AR BLACKOUT FRONT MARKER LIGHT (LEFT)
- AS TOW HOOK SHACKLE (UPPER)
- AT TOW HOOK SHACKLES (LOWER)
- AU BLACKOUT FRONT MARKER LIGHT (RIGHT)

Legend for Figure 2

RA PD 337

TM 9-802

Introduction

case permits drive of rear axles, or front and rear axles in two power ranges. Axles are driven through propeller shafts and universal joints, which operate in watertight housings under hull.

(6) WATER DRIVE. The water propeller transfer case, mounted in drive line between the transmission and axle transfer case, permits engagement and disengagement of water propeller. The water propeller is driven through propeller shafts and universal joints. Shafting is equipped with a marine type stuffing box to prevent water leakage where it passes through hull into the propeller tunnel.

(7) STEERING. Vehicle is steered on land in conventional manner. A rear mounted rudder, linked to the steering gear column, steers the vehicle in water when steering wheel is turned.

(8) BRAKES. Conventional vacuum-hydraulic operated service brake system is used to brake vehicle on land. In addition, a hand brake operating on propeller shaft is used as a parking brake, or to assist in an emergency stop.

Figure 3—Vehicle Nomenclature and Publication Plates

Description and Data

(9) ACCESSORY DRIVE.

(a) Winch. The shaft driven winch, mounted at rear, is driven by the transmission power take-off. The winch is controlled by a shift lever in the driver's compartment and a jaw clutch at the winch. Chocks and guides for front or rear operation of winch cables are provided on the hull.

(b) Tire Pumps. On vehicles prior to chassis serial No. 2006, the tire pump (air compressor) is mounted under driver's compartment, and is chain driven from power take-off. On later vehicles, the tire pump is mounted directly in front of radiator in front compartment. This tire pump, connected to engine crankshaft with a drive shaft and coupling, constantly operates when engine is running.

(c) Bilge Pumps. Forward bilge pump is operated by belt from water propeller shaft, and is connected through a manually controlled selector manifold to the lowest parts of hull. The rear bilge pump, also power driven by propeller shaft, pumps from the main part of the hull when the bilge water exceeds the capacity of the forward pump. Both pumps operate constantly when water propeller is engaged.

c. Identifications. The vehicle nomenclature plate (fig. 3), located to right of co-pilot on early vehicles or on right end of dash panel on

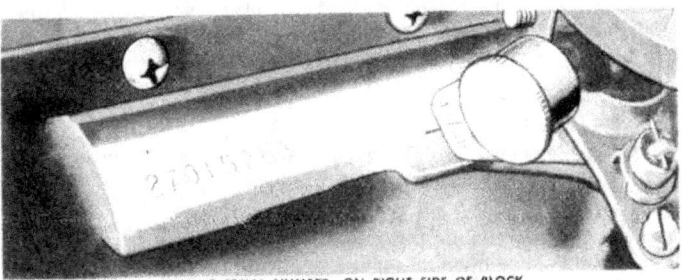
ENGINE SERIAL NUMBER—ON RIGHT SIDE OF BLOCK

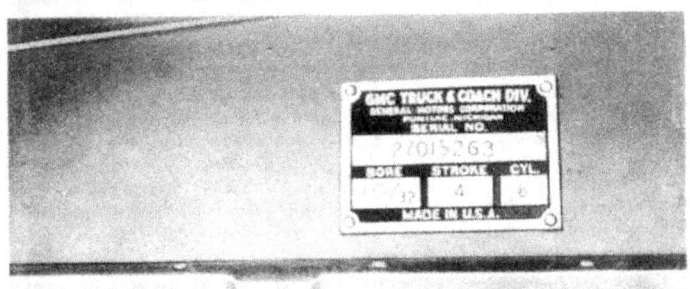
ENGINE SERIAL NUMBER—ON LEFT SIDE OF BLOCK   RA PD 333186

Figure 4—Engine Serial Number Locations

Introduction

later vehicles, includes vehicle name, serial number (chassis), weight, payload, etc. The publication plate (fig. 3), directly under nomenclature plate, indicates correct Technical Manuals and parts lists applying to vehicle. The engine serial number plate (fig. 4) is mounted on left-hand side of engine. The engine serial number is also stamped on lower part of cylinder block (fig. 4).

d. Differences in Design. This manual covers all vehicles from chassis serial No. 006 to approximately 14500. Briefly, vehicles prior to chassis serial No. 2006 (fig. 1) can be identified by vertical windshield, left-side rear mounted spare tire, and midship mounted tire pump. Vehicles after chassis serial No. 2005 include sloping windshield (fig. 2), central tire pressure control system, and right-side rear mounted spare tire. The two-speed water propeller transfer case started on chassis serial No. 2506. Operation and maintenance instructions in this manual deal briefly with design prior to chassis serial No. 2006, consistent with proper maintenance instructions. Design changes throughout the manual will be identified by chassis serial numbers whenever possible so that proper operating and maintenance instructions can be applied.

e. Maximum Utilization. The payload of this vehicle should normally not exceed 5,000 pounds. Under combat emergency, and when the conditions are favorable or ideal, as indicated below, additional loads may be carried as stated. The vehicle, however, should never carry more than 10,000 pounds. Authorized payloads under various conditions are:

(1) DIFFICULT CONDITIONS. When operating under *difficult* conditions, payload should normally not exceed 5,000 pounds. The term *difficult* will apply to all operations involving use of untried landing sites, unless reconnaissance has definitely indicated conditions to be *favorable*. It also applies to surf at shore over 3 feet, wind over 15 miles per hour (white caps), and when the wave height at shipside is over 3 feet. In addition, it applies to operations involving coral, very soft sand, steep landing, mud, steep hills, and land distance to dump over 6 miles.

(2) FAVORABLE CONDITIONS. When operating under *favorable* conditions and combat emergency, payload may total 7,500 pounds. The term *favorable* will apply to operations involving use of reconnoitered landings where reasonably smooth and firm terrain is available, where surf at shore is less than 3 feet, wind is less than 15 miles per hour (no white caps), and waves at the shipside are less than 3 feet. The routes should be well marked. Landings on shore shall be definitely negotiable in low range second gear. In addition, land distance to dump must be less than 6 miles with only moderate hills.

(3) IDEAL CONDITIONS. When operating under *ideal* conditions and combat emergency, payload may total 10,000 pounds. The term *ideal* will apply to daylight operations over smooth, firm and gradually sloping landing, negotiable at a minimum of 30 pounds tire pressure. Surf at shore must be less than 2 feet, the wind less than 10 miles per hour and waves at shipside less than 1 foot. Land route to dump must

Description and Data

be reasonably level and smooth, and less than 3 miles long. Water hauls must be less than 1 mile long.

(4) TIRE PRESSURE. For payloads exceeding 5,000 pounds, tire pressures recommended on dash instruction plates and stencils should be increased 1 pound for each 1,000 pounds overload. Minimum pressure for very soft sand with 5,000 pounds payload shall be 12 pounds.

4. TABULATED DATA.

a. Shipping Data Plate. Shipping data plate, mounted on dash panel (fig. 5), lists the first ten items in subparagraph *b.* below.

b. General.

Maximum over-all length (fig. 6)	31 ft
Maximum over-all height—with ring mount (fig. 6)	9 ft 2¼ in.
Maximum over-all height—without ring mount (fig. 6)	8 ft 10 in.
Lowest operable height—with ring mount	8 ft 8¾ in.
Lowest operable height—without ring mount	7 ft 6 in.
Maximum over-all width (fig. 6)	98 in.
Shipping cubic—with ring mount	2,325 cu ft
Shipping cubic—without ring mount	2,236 cu ft
Shipping tonnage—with ring mount	58
Shipping tonnage—without ring mount	56
Nominal wheel base (fig. 6)	164 in.
Ground clearance—hull (fig. 6)	18 in.
Ground clearance—axle (fig. 6)	11½ in.
Tread—front (fig. 6)	63⅝ in.
Tread—rear (fig. 6)	63⅞ in.
Loaded water line length (fig. 6)	344 in.
Loaded free board—to deck—front (fig. 6)	24 in.
Loaded free board—to deck—rear (fig. 6)	16 in.
Loaded free board—to coaming—front	28 in.
Loaded free board—to coaming—rear	28 in.
Loaded draft—to front wheels	42 in.
Loaded draft—to rear wheels	51 in.
Cargo space—to top of coaming	196 cu ft
Cargo space—under tarpaulin bows	385 cu ft
Center of bows above floor—front	54 in.
Center of bows above floor—rear	49 in.
Crew (operating)	1
Tire size	11:00/18-10 ply

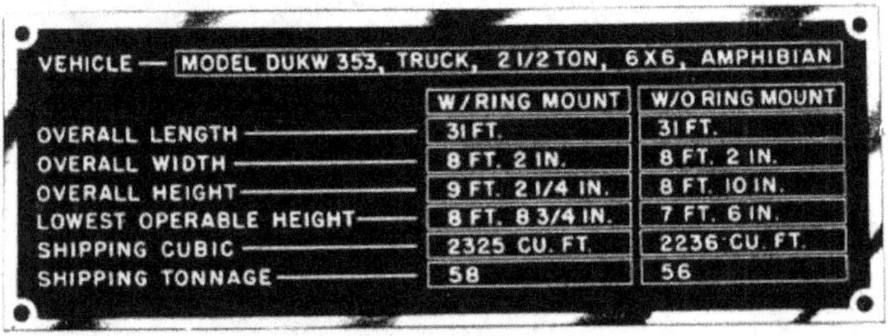

VEHICLE — MODEL DUKW 353, TRUCK, 2 1/2 TON, 6 X 6, AMPHIBIAN		
	W/RING MOUNT	W/O RING MOUNT
OVERALL LENGTH	31 FT.	31 FT.
OVERALL WIDTH	8 FT. 2 IN.	8 FT. 2 IN.
OVERALL HEIGHT	9 FT. 2 1/4 IN.	8 FT. 10 IN.
LOWEST OPERABLE HEIGHT	8 FT. 8 3/4 IN.	7 FT. 6 IN.
SHIPPING CUBIC	2325 CU. FT.	2236 CU. FT.
SHIPPING TONNAGE	58	56

RA PD 333181

Figure 5—Shipping Data Plate

Introduction

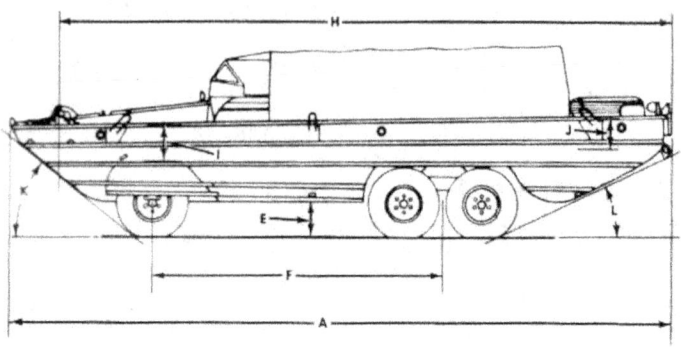

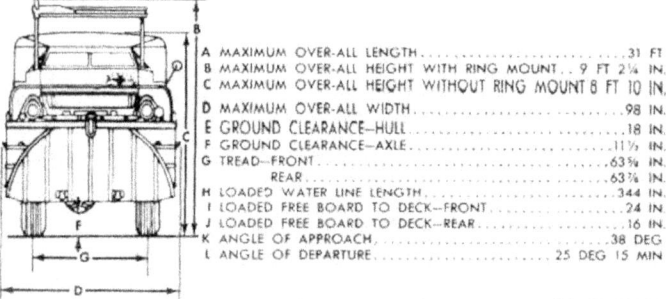

```
A  MAXIMUM OVER-ALL LENGTH..................................31 FT
B  MAXIMUM OVER-ALL HEIGHT WITH RING MOUNT..9 FT 2¼ IN.
C  MAXIMUM OVER-ALL HEIGHT WITHOUT RING MOUNT 8 FT 10 IN.
D  MAXIMUM OVER-ALL WIDTH..................................98 IN.
E  GROUND CLEARANCE—HULL...................................18 IN.
F  GROUND CLEARANCE—AXLE...................................11½ IN.
G  TREAD—FRONT.............................................63¾ IN.
   REAR....................................................63¾ IN.
H  LOADED WATER LINE LENGTH.................................344 IN.
I  LOADED FREE BOARD TO DECK—FRONT..........................24 IN.
J  LOADED FREE BOARD TO DECK—REAR...........................16 IN.
K  ANGLE OF APPROACH........................................38 DEG
L  ANGLE OF DEPARTURE.......................................25 DEG 15 MIN
```

RA PD 337226

Figure 6—Vehicle Dimensional Views

c. Weights (approx.) (without ring mount).

	Prior to Chassis Serial No. 2006	Chassis Serial No. 2005 to 2506	After Chassis Serial No. 2505
Chassis, hull, fuel, oil, and water (lb)	13,610	13,950	14,320
Equipment (lb)	560	560	560
Total weight fully equipped (lb)	14,170	14,510	14,880
Driver (lb)	175	175	175
Payload (lb)	5,000	5,000	5,000
Gross weight (lb)	19,315	19,655	20,055

d. Engine Data.

Type	Valve-in-head
Number of cylinders	6
Bore	$3\frac{25}{32}$ in.
Stroke	4 in.
Piston displacement (cu in.)	269.5
Weight (without accessories)	572 lb

TM 9-802
4-6

Tools, Parts, and Accessories

e. Maneuverability.

Minimum turning circle (land—outside wheel track)	
Left turn	72 ft
Right turn	70 ft
Minimum turning circle diameter (water)	
Left turn	40 ft
Right turn	40 ft
Angle of approach (fig. 6)	38 deg
Angle of departure (fig. 6)	25 deg 15 min.
Vertical object—at hull	17¼ in.
Vertical object—at front axle	11½ in.
Maximum grade descending ability	60 percent
Maximum grade ascending ability	60 percent

f. Performance.

	High	*Low*
Maximum land speed @ 2,750 maximum engine rpm (See Maximum Permissible Road Speed Plate on Dash) (fig. 17)		
Fifth (overdrive)	50 mph	22 mph
Fourth (direct)	40 mph	18 mph
Third	22 mph	10 mph
Second	11 mph	5 mph
First	7 mph	3 mph
Reverse	7 mph	3 mph

Maximum water speed (5,000 lb load, full throttle, smooth water-land miles indicated, NOT nautical miles)

	Speed
Reverse (prior to chassis serial No. 2506)	1.7 mph
Reverse (after chassis serial No. 2505)	2.5 mph
Second	See instruction plate on dash
Third	See instruction plate on dash

The economy range (miles per gallon) of third speed is approximately twice that of second speed.

Fourth and fifth (overdrive) speeds are not used when operating water propeller.

Section III

Tools, Parts, and Accessories

5. PURPOSE.

a. The lists in this section are for information only and must not be used as a basis for requisition.

6. ON-VEHICLE TOOLS.

a. Pioneer.

Quantity per Vehicle	Item Name	Stowage Location
1	AXE, chopping	Left side forward deck (fig. 7)
1	SHOVEL, D-handle	Left side forward deck (fig. 7)

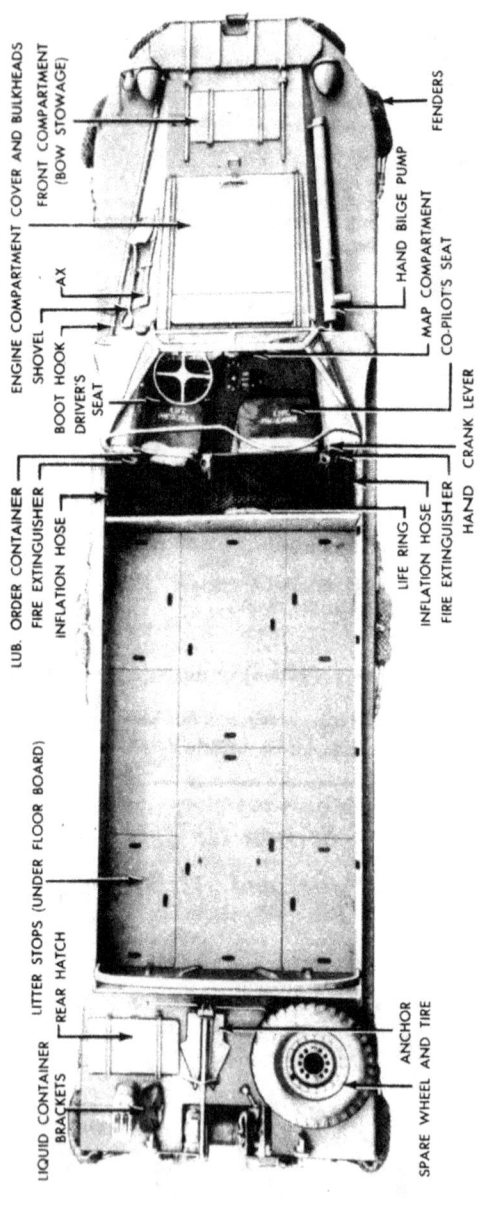

Figure 7 — On-Vehicle Stowage Points

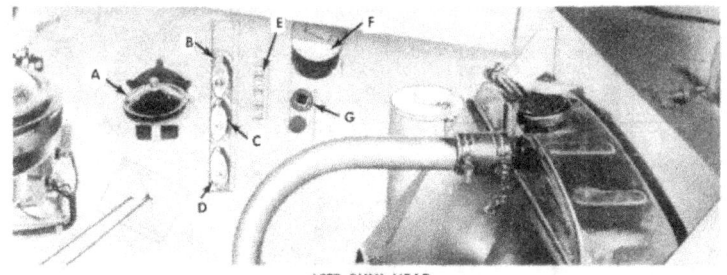
LEFT BULK HEAD

FRONT BULK HEAD

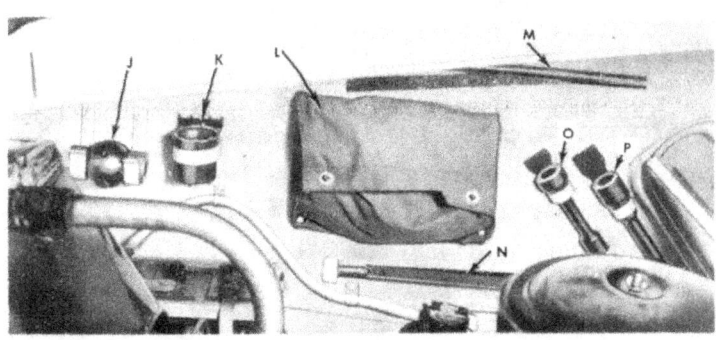
RIGHT BULK HEAD

A B.O. DRIVING LAMP-UNIT
B SERVICE TAIL AND STOP LAMP-UNIT
C B.O. TAIL LAMP-UNIT
D B.O. STOP LAMP-UNIT
E HULL DRAIN VALVE EMERGENCY PLUGS
F PROPELLER SHAFT HOUSING PLUG
G HULL BOTTOM PLUG
H JACK
I TIRE INFLATION TOOL
J STRUT JOURNAL
K WHEEL BEARING ADJUSTING NUT WRENCH
L SPARE PARTS BAG
M WRENCH HANDLE
N JACK HANDLE
O SIDE RING NUT WRENCH
P NUT WRENCH WHEEL

RA PD 337228

Figure 8—Engine Compartment Bulkhead Stowage

TM 9-802

Introduction

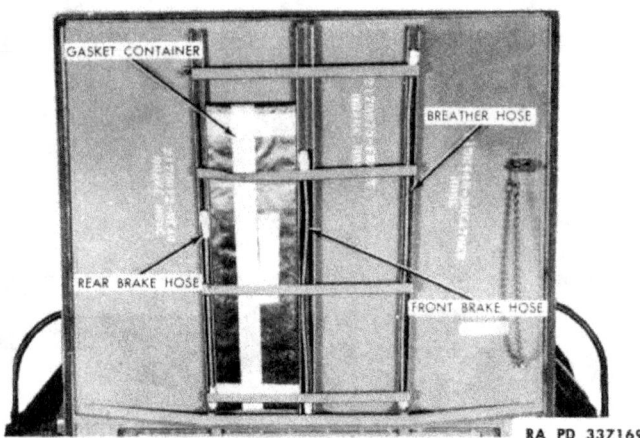

Figure 9—Stowage on Underside of Engine Compartment Cover

b. Vehicular.

Qty. per Vehicle	Item Name	Stowage Location
1	HAMMER, machinists, ball peen, (41-H-523)	Tool box (fig. 10)
1	HANDLE, wheel bearing adjusting and wheel stud nut wrench (41-H-1541-10)	Mounted, right wall engine compartment (fig. 8)
1	HANDLE, jack (41-H-1248-75)	Engine compartment (fig. 8)
1	JACK, hydraulic (41-J-72)	Tool box (fig. 10)
1	PLIERS, comb., 6 in. (41-P-1650)	Engine compartment (fig. 8)
1	SCREWDRIVER, common, H.D. 6 in. (41-S-1076)	Tool box (fig. 10)
1	SCREWDRIVER, carburetor adjusting (41-S-1101)	Tool box (fig. 10)
1	SCREWDRIVER, cross-recess head, No. 1 (41-S-1636)	Tool box (fig. 10)
1	SCREWDRIVER, cross recess head, No. 2 (41-S-1638)	Tool box (fig. 10)
1	SCREWDRIVER, cross-recess head, No. 3 (41-S-1640)	Tool box (fig. 10)
1	SCREWDRIVER, cross-recess head, No. 4 (41-S-1642)	Tool box (fig. 10)
1	TOOL, tire inflating device (41-I-3369-100)	Front engine compartment (fig. 8)
1	WRENCH, adjustable, crescent 12 in. (41-W-488)	Tool box (fig. 10)
1	WRENCH, adjustable, auto, 15 in. (41-W-450)	Tool box (fig. 10)
1	WRENCH, set or cap screw hollow head hexagon $1/4$ in. (41-W-2452)	Tool box (fig. 10)
1	WRENCH, set or cap screw, hollow head hexagon $5/16$ in. (41-W-2451)	Tool box (fig. 10)
1	WRENCH, set or cap screw, hollow head hexagon $1/2$ in. (41-W-2454)	Tool box (fig. 10)
1	WRENCH, set or cap screw, hollow head hexagon No. 8-32 (41-W-2450)	Tool box (fig. 10)

TM 9-802
6

Tools, Parts, and Accessories

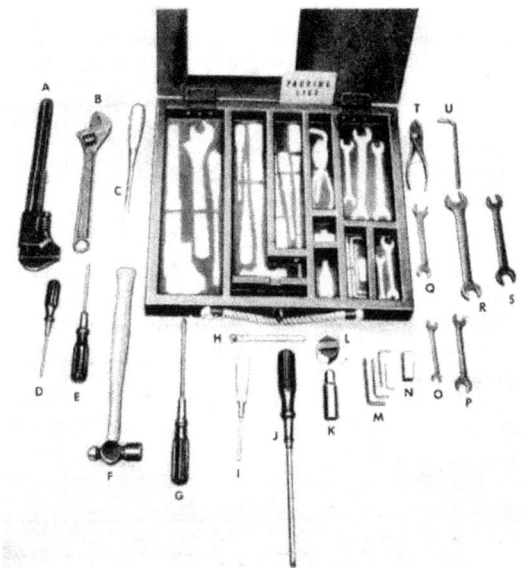

A ADJUSTABLE AUTO WRENCH
B ADJUSTABLE CRESCENT WRENCH
C SCREWDRIVER, COMMON, 6 in.
D CROSS-RECESS SCREWDRIVER NO. 1
E CROSS-RECESS SCREWDRIVER NO. 2
F MACHINIST'S HAMMER
G CROSS-RECESS SCREWDRIVER NO. 3
H TIRE GAGE
I CARBURETER ADJUSTING SCREWDRIVER
J CROSS-RECESS SCREWDRIVER NO. 4
K SPARK PLUG WRENCH
L HULL PLUG WRENCH ADAPTER
M SOCKET HEAD SET SCREW WRENCHES
N PROP. SHAFT HOUSING PLUG ADAPTER
O DOUBLE END WRENCH (3/8 & 7/16)
P DOUBLE END WRENCH (9/16 & 11/16)
Q DOUBLE END WRENCH (5/8 & 25/32)
R DOUBLE END WRENCH (1/2 & 19/32)
S DOUBLE END WRENCH (3/4 & 7/8)
T PLIERS
U SPARK PLUG WRENCH HANDLE

RA PD 337200

Figure 10—Tool Box and Contents

Quantity per Vehicle	Item Name	Stowage Location
1	WRENCH, set or cap screw, hollow head hexagon (plug type) 5/8 in.	Tool box (fig. 10)
1	WRENCH, engr's., dble. hd. 3/8 in. and 7/16 in. (41-W-991)	Tool box (fig. 10)
1	WRENCH, engr's., dble. hd. 9/16 in. and 11/16 in. (41-W-1005-5)	Tool box (fig. 10)
1	WRENCH, engr's., dble. hd. 5/8 in. and 25/32 in. (41-W-1008-10)	Tool box (fig. 10)
1	WRENCH, engr's., dble. hd. 3/4 in. and 7/8 in. (41-W-1012-5)	Tool box (fig. 10)
1	WRENCH, engr's., dble. hd. 1/2 in. and 19/32 in. (41-W-1003)	Tool box (fig. 10)
1	WRENCH, rear axle bearing (41-W-1493-30)	Mounted—Rt. side engine compartment (fig. 8)
1	WRENCH, spark plug w/handle (41-W-3335-50)	Tool box (fig. 10)

TM 9-802
6-7

Introduction

DAILY MAINTENANCE PLATE

WEEKLY MAINTENANCE PLATE

P.M. AND L.O. CONTAINER

RA PD 337229

Figure 11—Lubrication Order Container

Quantity per Vehicle	Item Name	Stowage Location
1	WRENCH, wheel hub nut	Mounted—Rt. side engine compartment (fig. 8)
1	WRENCH, wheel rim nut	Mounted—Rt. side engine compartment (fig. 8)
1	WRENCH, hull drain plug (41-W-876-50)	Mounted—R.H. air duct panel

7. ON-VEHICLE EQUIPMENT.

1	ADAPTER, lubr., gun (AD 6344)	Spare parts bag (fig. 8)
1	ADAPTER and hose, lubr., gun	Spare parts bag (fig. 8)
1	ANCHOR, including shackle and screw type pin	Rear deck (fig. 7)
2	BATTERY, flashlight	Glove compartment
1	BLOCK, snatch, ½ in. wire rope	Stern compartment (fig. 7)

22

TM 9-802

Tools, Parts, and Accessories

Quantity per Vehicle	Item Name	Stowage Location
1	BOW, fly top	In brackets behind driver's compartment
5	BOW, tarpaulin	Bow compartment—front hull
1	BOX, tool	Under Co-pilot's seat (fig. 10)
2	BUCKET, canvas	Under driver's seat
1	CATALOG, Ordnance, Std. Nom. List G501	Glove compartment
1	CHAIN, tow, utility	Stern compartment (fig. 7)
1	COMPASS, (Sherrill AFG-1)	Instrument panel
2	CONTAINER, 5 gal. liquid	Two brackets, rear deck (fig. 7)
1	COVER, Canvas, air intake grille	Stern compartment
1	CURTAIN, rear end	Stern compartment
2	EXTINGUISHER, fire, 2 lb CO_2	1—Rt. aisleway; 1—Left aisleway (fig. 7)
6	FENDERS, rope	Stern compartment
2	FENDERS, rope	Stern compartment
1	FLASHLIGHT case	Glove compartment
1	*FRAME, "A"	Brackets—rear deck
1	GAGE, tire pressure	Tool box (fig. 10)
2	ORDER, Lubrication, War Dept. No. 9-802	In bag mounted on driver's seat back (fig. 11)
2	GUIDE, Preventive Maintenance, 48 PM	In bag mounted on driver's seat back (fig. 11)
1	GUN, lubricating, hand type	Front underside of Co-pilot's seat
1	HOOK, boat, 9 ft	Left side forward deck (fig. 7)
1	HOOK, dirigo	Stern compartment
2	HOSE, tire inflation (W/chuck washer and spring yoke)	1—Rt. Aisleway; 1—Left aisleway (fig. 7)
1	KIT, first aid	Bracket—Rt. side panel under windshield (fig. 12)
1	LAMP, signal W/pistol grip wire and connector	Rt. side driver's compartment (fig. 12)
1	LEVER, hand crank	Right rear gun mount support (fig. 12)
1	LINK, tow chain	Chained to stern near pintle (fig. 23)
1	MANUAL, Technical TM 9-802 (in envelope)	Glove compartment
1	MIRROR, rear view	Left air exhaust duct (fig. 3)
1	OILER	Bracket on toeboard in driver's compartment (fig. 12)
2	PLATE, steel, No. 16 GA. 10 in. x 28 in.	Below cargo floor left side
3	PRESERVER, life, jacket type	Stern compartment
1	PRESERVER, life, ring type W/100 ft sash cord	Right aisleway (fig. 7)
1	PUMP, bilge, hand	Right side—forward deck (fig. 7)
1	RAGS, one pound, in bag	Stern compartment
2	ROPE, 1 in. dia., 50 ft length	Stern compartment
6	SANDPAPER, 2 sheets ea. No. 50, 36	Spare parts bag (fig. 8)
2	SHEATH, assy., containing	Glove compartment
1	KNIFE, hunting	
1	PLIERS, combination, 6 in.	
1	†SLING, cargo	Cargo body

*1 per 5 Vehicles
†2 per 25 Vehicles

Introduction

Quantity per Vehicle	Item Name	Stowage Location
1	*SLING, 105MM howitzer	Cargo body
1	SPONGE	Under driver's seat
4	STOP, litter, assembly	Under cargo compartment floor board (fig. 38)
1	TAPE, friction—roll	Spare parts bag (fig. 8)
1	TARPAULIN	Stern compartment
1	TOP, fly	Over driver's compartment
1	WHEEL, spare W/tire and tube 11:00-18	Rear deck (fig. 7)
1	WIPER, windshield—air operated	Windshield (fig. 12)
1	WIRE, iron—coil	Spart parts bag (fig. 8)

8. ON-VEHICLE SPARE PARTS.

1	BAG, spare parts	Engine compartment right side wall (fig. 8)
2	BEARING, tire pump con. rod	Spare parts bag
1	BELT, fan	Mounted on fan shroud (fig. 8)
1	CABLE, auxiliary 75 ft. ½ in. wire rope	Stern compartment
10	CAP, tire valve	Spare parts bag
1	COMPOUND, sealing—can	Stern compartment
1	CONDENSER, distributor	Spare parts bag
1	CONTAINER, gasket	Mounted underside engine hatch cover (fig. 9)
10	CORE, tire valve	Spare parts bag
3	DIAPHRAGM, tire inflating device	Spare parts bag
1	GASKET, air cleaner cover	Gasket container
1	GASKET, air cleaner to carbureter	Gasket container
1	GASKET, carbureter	Gasket container
1	GASKET, tire pump	Spare parts bag
1	GASKET, cylinder head to block	Gasket container
1	GASKET, exhaust pipe flange	Gasket container
1	GASKET, fuel pump to cylinder block	Gasket container
2	GASKET, governor to insulator	Gasket container
1	GASKET, inlet to exhaust manifold	Gasket container
1	GASKET, manifold, center	Gasket container
2	GASKET, manifold, front and rear	Gasket container
1	GASKET, oil pan plug	Spare parts bag
6	GASKET, spark plug	Spare parts bag
1	GASKET, thermostat housing	Gasket container
1	GASKET, valve push rod cover	Gasket container
1	GASKET, valve rocker arm cover	Gasket container
1	GASKET, vent housing	Gasket container
1	GASKET, water outlet	Gasket container
1	GASKET, water pump	Gasket container
1	HOSE, axle breather	Mounted underside engine hatch cover (fig. 9)
2	HOSE, central tire inflation	Spare parts bag
1	HOSE, front brake	Mounted underside engine hatch cover (fig. 9)
1	HOSE, rear brake	Mounted underside engine hatch cover (fig. 9)

*1 per 5 Vehicles

TM 9-802

Tools, Parts, and Accessories

Quantity per Vehicle	Item Name	Stowage Location
1	JOURNAL, water prop shaft strut	Bracket in engine compartment (fig. 8)
1	KEY, straight 1/8 in. sq x 1 3/8 in.	Spare parts bag
1	KEY, straight, 5/16 in. sq x 3 in.	Spare parts bag
1	KEY, straight 3/16 in. sq x 1 1/2 in.	Spare parts bag
1	KEY, Woodruff, 3/16 in. x 1 in.	Spare parts bag
1	KEY, Woodruff, 3/16 in. x 3/4 in.	Spare parts bag
1	KEY, Woodruff, 5/16 in. x 1 1/4 in.	Spare parts bag
1	KEY, Woodruff, 5/16 in. x 1 1/8 in.	Spare parts bag
1	KEY, Woodruff, 5/16 in. x 1 in.	Spare parts bag
2	KEY, Woodruff, 3/16 in. x 1 1/8 in.	Spare parts bag
3	KIT, chain connecting link	Spare parts bag
1	LAMP, auto miniature (MZ1269)	Mounted left side wall engine compartment (fig. 8)
1	LAMP, sealed-unit B.O. stop	Mounted left side wall engine compartment (fig. 8)
1	LAMP, sealed-unit B.O. tail	Mounted left side wall engine compartment (fig. 8)
1	LAMP, sealed-unit driving	Mounted left side wall engine compartment (fig. 8)
1	LAMP, sealed-unit comb. stop and tail	Mounted left side wall engine compartment (fig. 8)
1	LEVER, breaker, distributor	Spare parts bag
2	LINK, roller drive chain	Spare parts bag
6	PIN, cotter, stainless steel, 3/64 in. x 5/16 in.	Spare parts bag
1	PIN, cotter—kit	Spare parts bag
1	PIN, steering shaft spool	Spare parts bag
30	PIN, shear, winch drive shaft W/cotter pins	Container under stern deck
1	PLUG, drive shaft housing drain	Mounted left side wall engine compartment (fig. 8)
6	PLUG, hull air hose connection	Spare parts bag
1	PLUG, hull bottom drain	Mounted left side wall engine compartment (fig. 8)
4	PLUG, hull drain valve emergency	Mounted left side engine compartment (fig. 8)
1	PLUG, spark	Spare parts bag
1	ROTOR, distributor	Spare parts bag
10	SCREW, socket head set, 1/4 in. x 28 x 3/4 in.	Spare parts bag
3	SCREW, socket head set, No. 8 x 32 x 7/16 in.	Spare parts bag
1	SCREW, socket head set, 5/16 in. x 18 x 3/8 in.	Spare parts bag
2	SCREW, socket head set, 1/2 in. x 13 x 1/2 in.	Spare parts bag
4	SPRING, return, service brake	Spare parts bag
1	SUPPORT, breaker lever	Spare parts bag
6	WASHER, hull air hose connection plug	Spare parts bag
3	WASHER, tire inflation cap	Spare parts bag
3	WASHER, tire inflation nut	Spare parts bag

TM 9-802

Operating Instructions

PART TWO
OPERATING INSTRUCTIONS

Section IV
General

9. SCOPE.

a. Part two contains information for guidance of personnel responsible for operation of this equipment. It contains information on operation of equipment with description and location of controls and instruments.

Section V

Service Upon Receipt of Equipment

10. PURPOSE.

a. When a new or reconditioned vehicle is first received by the using organization, it is necessary for second echelon personnel to determine whether the vehicle has been properly prepared for service by the supplying organization, and to be sure it is in condition to perform any mission to which it may be assigned when placed in service. For this purpose, inspect all assemblies, subassemblies, and accessories to be sure they are properly assembled, secure, clean and correctly adjusted and/or lubricated. Check all tools and equipment against Section III (Tools, Parts, and Accessories), to be sure that every item is present, in good condition, clean, and properly mounted or stowed.

b. In addition, the using organization will perform a run-in test on all vehicles of at least 50 miles as directed in AR 850-15, according to procedures in paragraph 13 which follows.

c. Whenever practicable, the first echelon personnel (driver) will assist in the performance of these procedures.

11. CORRECTION OF DEFICIENCIES.

a. Deficiencies disclosed during the course of these services will be treated as follows:

(1) Correct any deficiencies within the scope of the maintenance echelons of the using organization before the vehicle is placed in service.

(2) Refer deficiencies beyond the scope of the maintenance echelons of the using organization to a higher echelon for correction.

Service Upon Receipt of Equipment

(3) Bring deficiencies of a serious nature to the attention of the supplying organization through proper channels.

12. SPECIFIC PROCEDURES.

a. Preliminary Service. Before the vehicle is moved to make the actual land and water run-in test, certain inspection and services will be performed as follows.

(1) FIRE EXTINGUISHERS. See that the portable fire extinguishers are present, fully charged, and in good condition. Shake liquid type to determine contents. Carbon dioxide type must be weighed. Test liquid type momentarily for proper operation, and mount all units securely.

(2) FUEL, OIL, AND WATER. Fill the fuel tank. Check engine crankcase and tire pump crankcase oil levels, and radiator coolant supply, and add as necessary to bring to correct levels. Allow room for expansion in fuel tank and radiator. During freezing weather, check value of antifreeze and add as necessary to protect cooling system against freezing. CAUTION: *If there is a tag attached to the filler cap, or steering wheel, concerning the oil in the engine crankcase or tire pump crankcase, follow instructions on the tag before driving the vehicle.*

(3) FUEL FILTER. Remove sediment bowl and screen from fuel pump (if so equipped), wash cleaner bowl in dry-cleaning solvent, remove accumulated dirt and water, and reinstall securely. Drain accumulated sediment and water from main fuel filter by removing drain plug. If any appreciable amount of sediment or water is present, remove the filter body and clean body and element. Drain water and sediment from bottom of fuel tank. CAUTION: *Do not allow drainage to drop into hull. Be sure hull drain plug is replaced securely.*

(4) BATTERIES. Make hydrometer test of the battery [par. 130*b*.(1)] and add clean water as necessary to bring electrolyte to $\frac{3}{8}$ inch above cell plates.

(5) AIR CLEANERS AND VENTILATORS. Inspect the carburetor, tire pump, and hydrovac cylinder air cleaners, and the engine and tire pump crankcase breathers (ventilators) to see that they are in good condition, secure, and not leaking excessively. Check the level of the oil in oil bath type cleaners and clean and service as necessary. Check the condition of the filters and the mesh type breathers and clean and service as necessary. See Lubrication Order No. 9-802 (par. 52). Be sure waterproofing tape has been removed from all units.

(6) ACCESSORIES AND DRIVES. Inspect accessible accessories such as carburetor, generator, regulator, starting motor, tire pump, bilge pumps, and winch for looseness and damage. Be sure that fan and generator drive belt adjustments are satisfactory (par. 118). See that tire pump drive chain (or drive shaft on front mounted tire pump) is in good condition and that drive chain is properly adjusted to have not more than $\frac{1}{2}$ inch deflection. See that bilge pump drive chain or belts has $\frac{1}{2}$ to $\frac{3}{4}$ inch deflection. Be sure all adjustments are properly secured.

(7) ELECTRICAL WIRING. Examine all accessible wiring and conduits. See that they are in good condition, securely connected, and properly supported.

(8) TIRES AND INFLATION SYSTEM. Inspect all tires (including spare) for damage. Tires should be properly inflated to the correct pressure for the existing terrain. (See caution plates in driver's compartment.) Remove all objects lodged in the treads and carcasses. See that valve stems are in correct position and that valve caps (if in use) are present and finger-tight. Check the operation of the tire inflation system (if so equipped) to be sure it functions properly, and that all components are secure. NOTE: *When tire inflation system is in use, valve cores should be removed from valve stems and stowed with spare parts kit.*

(9) WHEEL NUTS AND FLANGE BOLTS. Check all wheel assembly and mounting nuts to see if they are present and secure. If vehicle is equipped with tire inflation system, hub unit should be removed and the axle flange bolts checked for presence and security.

(10) HULL AND ATTACHMENTS. Inspect entire hull for damage, particularly for dents or punctures that might result in leakage. See that bulkheads, braces and any reinforcements are secure. Be sure all hull attachments, windshield, and hardware have been properly installed. Inspect the driver's compartment soft top and cargo space tarpaulin for damage to see that they are dry and properly installed, and securely lashed, or if not in use, that they are properly stowed. All rust spots or bare spots in finish should be cleaned with a wire brush and painted (par. 238).

(11) AMPHIBIAN SERVICES.

(a) V-Strut Bearing. Inspect bearing for looseness or damage and lubricate according to Lubrication Order No. 9-802.

(b) Rudder. Inspect rudder for looseness or damage, and test controls to be sure they operate properly and that cables are not excessively loose or binding.

(c) Propeller. Inspect propeller for looseness or damage. Test controls to be sure they operate properly and see that propeller is in proper alinement. CAUTION: *Only operate propeller momentarily out of the water.*

(d) Hull Plugs and Drain Valves. See that all hull drain plugs are present and properly installed in hull; that all drain valves are closed, and that drain valve emergency plugs are removed from hull bottom and placed in their racks. NOTE: *These emergency plugs are for use only when drain valves are inoperative.*

(e) Shaft Housing Seals. Inspect propeller shaft housing seals and interhousing drain to see if they are in good condition and that clamp rings and drain plugs are secure.

(f) Surf Boards. Inspect all surf boards for looseness or damage. See that they are properly secured, either in raised or lowered position.

(g) Hatches. Inspect all hatches to be sure they are in good condition. See that they are closed and properly secured against seals.

Service Upon Receipt of Equipment

(12) LUBRICATION. Perform a complete lubrication of the vehicle covering all intervals according to the instructions on the Lubrication Order No. 9-802 (par. 52), except gear cases. Omit only units covered in the preceding procedures. Check all gear case oil levels and add oil as necessary to bring to correct level. Change only if condition of oil indicates the necessity or if the oil is not of proper grade for existing atmospheric temperatures. NOTE: *Perform operations (13) to (16) inclusive during lubrication.*

(13) SPRINGS AND SUSPENSIONS. Inspect front springs and shock absorbers, rear springs, seats, and torque rods, and all spring brackets, shackles, U-bolts, bumper pads, and rebound clips for looseness or damage. Look particularly for shifted or broken spring leaves and excessive spring sag.

(14) STEERING LINKAGE. Inspect steering arms, rods, joints, and connections for looseness or damage. See that gear box, column, and wheel are secure, and check gear box for excessive lubricant leakage.

(15) VENTS (BREATHER TUBES). Inspect front and rear axle and pillow block breather vents and tubes for damage and see that they are secure. Be sure all waterproofing tape has been removed.

(16) PROPELLER SHAFTS AND PILLOW BLOCK. Inspect the accessible propeller shafts, U-joints, and pillow block for indications of looseness, damage, or excessive lubricant leakage.

(17) CHOKE. Examine the choke to be sure it opens and closes fully in response to operating choke button.

(18) ENGINE WARM-UP. Start engine, observing all starting precautions in paragraph 19, and noting if the starting motor is satisfactory and any tendency toward hard starting. Set hand throttle to run engine at fast idle during warm-up period. Reset choke button as necessary during warm-up so engine will run smoothly and to prevent overchoking and oil dilution.

(19) INSTRUMENTS.

(a) Oil Pressure Gage. Gage must register in normal range (engine hot) at idling speed.

(b) Ammeter. Ammeter may show high charging rate for first few minutes after starting engine until generator has restored to battery the current used, then indicate slight charge or zero with lights and accessories turned off. High charging rate for extended period may indicate a dangerously low battery or faulty regulator.

(c) Temperature Gage. Reading should increase gradually during warm-up to normal operating range, 160°F to 180°F. Maximum safe operating temperature, 220°F. CAUTION: *Do not move vehicle until engine temperature has reached at least 160°F.*

(d) Fuel Gage. Gage should indicate the approximate amount of fuel in tank. Ordinarily, tank will have been filled and gage should indicate "FULL."

(e) Tachometer. Tachometer should indicate engine speed in revolutions per minute. (Maximum 2750 RPM.) The red needle will register and remain at the maximum revolutions per minute reached.

TM 9-802
12-13

Operating Instructions

(f) Tank Pressure Air Gage. Tank pressure gage must read between 50 and 75 pounds.

(g) Tire Pressure Air Gage. With air control lever in neutral position and all tire line valves open, the gage should register existing tire pressure.

(h) Compass. Check and adjust compass as necessary according to instructions in paragraph 283.

(20) ENGINE CONTROLS. Observe if engine responds properly to all controls and if the controls operate without excessive looseness or binding. Be sure manifold heating valve is turned to "OFF" position.

(21) HORN AND WINDSHIELD WIPERS. See that these items are in good condition and secure. If tactical situation permits, test horn for proper operation and tone. Test operation of wipers and observe if blades operate through their full stroke and see that they contact glass evenly and firmly.

(22) GLASS AND REAR VIEW MIRRORS. Examine all body glass and mirrors. Inspect for looseness and damage. Adjust rear view mirrors for correct vision.

(23) LAMPS (LIGHTS) AND REFLECTORS. Clean all light lenses and reflectors and inspect the units for looseness and damage. If tactical situation permits, open and close all light switches and observe if lamps respond properly. Be sure all tape and paint are removed from blackout and blackout marker lights or any other lamp or reflector openings where tape has been used to prevent corrosion.

(24) LEAKS—GENERAL. Look on ground under vehicle and in engine compartment for indications of fuel, oil, coolant, and shock absorber or brake fluid leaks, and around gear cases for grease leaks. Trace all leaks found to their source and correct or report them.

(25) TOOLS, PARTS, AND ACCESSORIES. Be sure that all items are serviceable and that they are properly mounted or stowed. Be sure all wire lashings, tape, and cloth are removed from winch cables and hook. Test operation of winch jaw clutch, drag and automatic brakes (see paragraph 273).

13. RUN-IN TEST.

a. General Instructions. Perform the following procedures **b.**(1) to **c.**(7) inclusive during the road test (land and water) of the vehicle. On vehicles which have been driven 50 miles or more in the course of delivery, confine the run-in test to the least mileage (on land) or time (in water) necessary to make the proper observations, otherwise perform a land test run of approximately 40 miles, and a water test run of not less than 30 minutes. CAUTION: *During the land and water test run of the vehicle, continuous operation of the vehicle or engine at speeds beyond those specified on the caution plates must be avoided.*

b. Land Run.

(1) INSTRUMENTS AND GAGES. Do not move the vehicle until engine temperature registers 160°F. Maximum safe operating tempera-

TM 9-802
13

Service Upon Receipt of Equipment

ture is 220°F. Observe the readings of all pertinent instruments frequently during the test run to be sure they are indicating the proper function of the units to which they apply. When the vehicle is in motion (on land) the speedometer should register the vehicle speed in miles per hour and the odometer should record the accumulating mileage.

(2) BRAKES (SERVICE AND PARKING). When vehicle is first moved during land operation, and before gaining any appreciable speed, observe if there is any excessive pull to one side, chatter, grab, or squealing. Pedal should have $1/4$ to $1/2$ inch free-travel before moving master cylinder push rod, and at least 2 inches clearance from floor board when fully applied. Stop on a reasonable incline, and observe if parking brake will hold vehicle effectively; that locking device holds lever in applied position, and that lever has about $1/3$ ratchet travel in reserve.

(3) CLUTCH. Clutch pedal free-travel should be $2 1/2$ inches and never less than 1 inch. Clutch should engage without drag, noise, chatter, or grabbing and should not slip when fully engaged under load.

(4) TRANSMISSION AND POWER TAKE-OFF. Controls should shift easily and smoothly. Gears should operate without unusual noise or vibration and should not slip out of mesh during operation.

(5) TRANSFER CASES. The main and water propeller transfer case controls should shift easily and smoothly. The gears should operate without unusual noise and not slip out of mesh during operation.

(6) STEERING. Test the steering action for excessive binding or looseness and note any excessive pull to one side, wander, shimmy, or wheel tramp. See that column bracket and wheel are secure.

(7) ENGINE. Be on the alert for any unusual noise or abnormal operating characteristics such as lack of power and acceleration, backfiring, misfiring, stalling, overheating, or excessive exhaust smoke. Observe whether engine responds properly to all controls.

(8) UNUSUAL NOISES. Be on the alert throughout the test run for any unusual noise from the hull and attachments, frame, running gear, suspension, or wheels that might indicate looseness, damage, excessive wear, or inadequate lubrication. NOTE: *Halt the vehicle at 10-mile intervals or less, for services (9) to (11) following.*

(9) BRAKE BOOSTER OPERATION (HYDROVAC). While an assistant operates the brake pedal, listen at the hydrovac air cleaner for the sound of air movement as the pedal is applied and released. No air movement indicates the system is not operating properly.

(10) TEMPERATURES. Cautiously hand-feel each brake drum and wheel hub for abnormal temperatures. Examine all gear cases for indications of overheating, and note any excessive lubricant leakage at seals, gaskets, or connections.

(11) LEAKS (FUEL, OIL, AND COOLANT). With the engine running and the fuel, oil, and cooling systems under pressure, check all accessible components on these systems for leakage. Trace any leaks found to their source and correct or report them.

TM 9-802

Operating Instructions

c. Water Run.

(1) RUDDER AND CONTROLS. During water operation, observe at all times if the rudder controls function properly and if the rudder responds to control the vehicle headway. Be alert for excessive leakage at the rudder stuffing box.

(2) PROPELLER AND CONTROLS. As the propeller controls are operated, note any excessive looseness or binding. Be on the alert for any unusual noise or vibration of the propeller or shafting that might indicate damage, excessive wear, or inadequate lubrication.

(3) HULL LEAKS. Check the inside of the hull thoroughly for indications of water leakage.

(4) BILGE PUMPS. Be sure all waterproofing tape is removed from both bilge pump discharge holes. Check the operation of the power driven and hand bilge pumps to be sure they are in good condition. Observe whether water manifold control linkage is properly connected and that the valves function properly. Note any indication of restriction in the pump intakes or strainers. CAUTION: *The bilges must be kept free of dirt or refuse at all times.*

(5) HATCHES, SEALS, AND LATCHES. Be sure all waterproofing tape is removed from hatch and grille openings. Be on the alert for any indication of water leakage around the hatch seals. Be sure the edges of the hatches and the seals are in good condition and that the latches function properly to hold the hatch tight against the seals. The exhaust grille covers should be folded back and secured, except in sub-freezing weather. The cab heating doors at the lower front end of the cab should be closed. The exhaust recirculation ducts should be in closed position.

(6) ENGINE SPEED AND TEMPERATURES. During the water test run, operate the engine at full speed, and observe if it will turn up 2350 revolutions per minute at 180°F maximum temperature.

(7) UNUSUAL NOISES OR VIBRATION. Be on the alert during the entire test run for any unusual noise or vibration that would indicate looseness, damage, excessive wear, or inadequate lubrication in any of the moving parts or accessories.

d. Vehicle Publications and Reports.

(1) PUBLICATIONS. See that the vehicle Technical Manuals, Lubrication Orders, Form No. 48 (Driver's Trip Ticket and Preventive Maintenance Service Record), Form No. 26 (Accident Report), Form No. 478 (MWO and Major Unit Assembly Replacement Record) are in the vehicle, legible, and properly stowed. NOTE: *U.S.A. registration number and vehicle nomenclature must be filled in on Form No. 478 for new vehicles.*

(2) REPORTS. Upon completion of the run-in test, correct or report any deficiencies noted. Report the general condition of the vehicle to the designated individual in authority.

TM 9-802

Controls and Instruments

Section VI
Controls and Instruments

14. DRIVING CONTROLS.

a. Transmission. The transmission gearshift lever (fig. 12) is used to manually select the various gear ratios or speeds (five forward and one reverse) provided in the transmission. Power is transmitted directly through transmission in fourth speed, providing a 1 to 1 gear ratio. In fifth speed (overdrive), and all other speeds including reverse, the power is transmitted through gears of various sizes to provide the desired gear ratios. All gear ratios are selectively used in connection with axle transfer case to operate front and rear axles (par. 21f.). Reverse, first, and second speeds and, in some instances, third speed, are used in connection with water propeller transfer case to operate water propeller (par. 24).

b. Axle Transfer Case. Two levers are used to control operation of front and rear driving axles—transfer case shift lever and front axle declutching control lever (fig. 12). The transfer case provides two gear ratios or ranges which are used with transmission gears to obtain necessary speed and power to meet various road conditions. This transfer case is not used in connection with water propeller.

(1) TRANSFER CASE SHIFT LEVER. Used to select "HIGH" or "LOW" range as required to operate front and rear axles. Axles are disengaged when lever is placed into "N" (neutral) position (par. 21g.).

(2) FRONT AXLE DECLUTCHING CONTROL LEVER. Used to engage and disengage the front driving axle (par. 21h.). Lever can be placed in one of two positions—"IN" (engaged) or "OUT" (disengaged). Arrangement of the levers is such that transfer case cannot be placed into low range until front axle is engaged.

c. Water Propeller Transfer Case. Two types of water propeller transfer cases have been used—single-speed and two-speed. When placed into engaged position with transmission in reverse or forward speed, transfer case operates water propeller.

(1) SINGLE-SPEED (PRIOR TO CHASSIS SERIAL NO. 2506). Lever is pulled up to engage propeller, and pushed down to disengage (par. 24c.).

(2) TWO-SPEED (AFTER CHASSIS SERIAL NO. 2505). [Refer to note *(a)* below.] Two gear ratios are provided in this transfer case. The lever is placed into "STD" or "FWD" position for forward operation of water propeller with transmission normally in second forward gear ratio. The lever is placed into "OVERDRIVE" or "REV" position for reverse operation with transmission in reverse gear ratio. For close forward maneuvering, steep landings, ramp landings, and coral, the transfer case may be used in "OVERDRIVE" or "REV" position with transmission in first (par. 26e.).

Figure 12 — Driver's Compartment (After Chassis Serial No. 2005)

TM 9-802
14

Controls and Instruments

(a) *Note:* The water propeller transfer case instruction plate and floor board markings at the lever on early vehicles show transfer case lever positions as "FWD" and "REV" as shown in upper portion of figure 19. Later vehicles are equipped with modified plate and floor board markings as shown in lower portion of figure 19. To avoid confusion, plate and floor board markings should be changed to conform to those shown in lower position of figure 19.

d. Clutch. When clutch pedal, accessible to driver's left foot (fig. 12) is depressed, clutch is disengaged from engine flywheel, permitting the shifting of transmission, transfer cases, and power take-off. Clutch is engaged when pedal is released.

e. Steering. Vehicle is steered on land by conventional steering wheel (fig. 12) which controls movement of front wheels through a steering gear assembly and linkage. On water, movement of same steering wheel correspondingly controls movement of rear-mounted rudder which is linked to the steering gear column (par. 26b.).

f. Brakes. Two independently controlled vehicle brake systems are used—hand and service.

(1) HAND BRAKE. Hand brake lever, located to right of driver (fig. 12), is used to control application of a brake band assembly mounted on transfer case. This band operates directly on transfer case output shaft, transmitting braking effort to wheels through propeller shafts. Primary purpose of this brake is to hold vehicle in stationary position or to assist in bringing it to an emergency stop—not to brake vehicle during normal road operation. Lever is *pulled back* to apply brakes. A pawl in lower end of lever engages notches in sector at base of lever to hold it in various applied positions. Spring loaded release lever at the handle releases pawl from sector notches to permit release of brake by pushing lever forward.

A BILGE PUMP CONTROL LEVERS
B PUMP HEATING CONTROL LEVER
C WINCH POWER TAKE-OFF SHIFTING LEVER AND LOCK
D HORN BUTTON
E DIMMER SWITCH
F DRIVER'S COMPT. HEATER PANELS
G REAR VIEW MIRROR
H HULL DRAIN VALVE HANDLE (FRONT)
I HOUSING PLUG RETAINER
J INSTRUMENT PANEL
K WINDSHIELD WIPERS
L TACHOMETER AND GAGE PANEL
M COMPASS (PIONEER)
N MAP COMPARTMENT
O OILER
P FIRST AID KIT
Q HULL PLUG RETAINER
R FRONT AXLE DECLUTCHING CONTROL LEVER
S TRANSFER CASE SHIFT LEVER
T LOCATION OF FRONT BRAKE SHUT-OFF COCK
U HAND CRANK LEVER
V DUCT INSPECTION HOLE COVERS
W RADIO TERMINAL BOX
X FIRE EXTINGUISHERS
Y RING MOUNT SUPPORTS
Z TOOL BOX
AA CO-PILOT'S SEAT
AB CENTER INTAKE GRILLE
AC TIRE PRESSURE LINE VALVES
AD WATER PROPELLER SHIFT LEVER
AE FORWARD BILGE PUMP LUBRICATION FITTING
AF DRIVER'S SEAT
AG HULL DRAIN VALVE HANDLE (CENTER)
AH LASHING INSTRUCTIONS
AI TRANSMISSION GEARSHIFT LEVER
AJ STARTER PEDAL BUTTON
AK HAND BRAKE LEVER
AL ACCELERATOR PEDAL
AM BRAKE PEDAL
AN CLUTCH PEDAL
AO INTAKE STRAINER

RA PD 337230B

Legend for Figure 12

TM 9-802

Operating Instructions

(2) SERVICE BRAKES. Service brake pedal, accessible to driver's right foot (fig. 12), controls application and release of vacuum-hydraulic operated brake shoes at each wheel. Pressure applied to pedal in various degrees applies brakes correspondingly. Release of brakes is correspondingly as rapid as pressure on foot pedal is released.

g. Fuel.

(1) ACCELERATOR. Accelerator pedal, accessible to driver's right foot (fig. 12), is linked to carburetor and is used to accelerate or decelerate engine as desired. When pedal is completely released, engine will operate at set idling speed (par. 106*b*.). Acceleration from idling to any desired speed up to governed speed is obtained by depressing the pedal in various degrees.

(2) THROTTLE CONTROL. The throttle control button (marked "THROTTLE"), located on instrument panel (fig. 13), is interconnected to carburetor and may be used instead of accelerator pedal to accelerate engine; to set throttle to desired starting and warming-up speed (par. 19); or to hold sustained vehicle or auxiliary unit speed. The control button is pulled out in varying degrees to accelerate engine, and must be pushed in to decelerate.

(3) CHOKE CONTROL. The choke control button (marked "CHOKE"), located on instrument panel (fig. 13), is interconnected to carburetor choke valve. When control is pulled out, carburetor choke valve closes. Return spring on choke linkage returns choke valve to open position when control button is released.

(4) FUEL PUMP PRIMING LEVER. Lever, located on fuel pump in engine compartment (fig. 78 or 79), is used to prime carburetor if vehicle has been idle for long periods, or after fuel has been drained from system, then refilled. As a general rule, several up and down movements (approximately fifteen) of the lever will pump sufficient gas to carburetor for starting.

15. MISCELLANEOUS CONTROLS.

a. Winch. The power take-off, mounted on transmission case and meshed with transmission reverse idler gear, operates winch through a drive shaft when take-off shifting lever (fig. 12) is placed into correct positions. Lever has three positions—"L" (low), "R" (reverse), and "H" (high) with neutral ("N") positions in between. Uses of shifting lever, as well as controls at winch, are explained in paragraph 29.

b. Tire Pump (Prior to Chassis Serial No. 2006). Power tire pump on these vehicles is operated by chain from sprocket mounted on power take-off auxiliary drive shaft. The control shift rod, located near right rear corner of driver's seat, is pulled up to engage auxiliary drive shaft with power take-off idler shaft, and pushed down to disengage. Clutch must be disengaged before rod is moved to engaged or disengaged position (par. 30*b*.).

Controls and Instruments

c. Central Tire Pressure Control System (After Chassis Serial No. 2005). No control is necessary to operate power time pump on these vehicles, as it operates continuously when engine is running. Refer to paragraph 31 for operation of the system.

(1) INFLATION AND DEFLATION CONTROL LEVER. Lever, located on tachometer and gage panel (fig. 13), is used to inflate and deflate tires to various pressures. This lever has three positions: "INFLATE," "OFF," and "DEFLATE" (marked on panel adjacent to lever slot).

(2) LINE VALVES. Six line valves, located to the right of driver and mounted in left-hand riser of co-pilot's seat (fig. 12), permits inflation, deflation, or isolation of each individual tire. Each valve is closed by turning hand-wheel in clockwise direction. Correct positioning of these valves under various conditions is explained in paragraph 31.

d. Bilge Pumps. Both forward and rear bilge pumps operate constantly when water propeller is engaged. The pumping of the various compartments by the forward pump is controlled by manually operated rods or levers located directly in front of driver's seat (fig. 12). The rear bilge pump automatically serves the main (or center) compartment when water is approximately five inches deep in the bilge.

(1) FORWARD BILGE PUMP CONTROL RODS (PRIOR TO CHASSIS SERIAL NO. 4202). Five control rods extend from a manifold through floor board directly in front of driver's seat. Four of the rods selectively control the pumping of the main (center), front, left rear, and right rear compartments. Only *one compartment* can be pumped at one time (par 36*b.*). The fifth rod controls the draining of the manifold after water operation. Pull up each individual rod to open valves.

(2) FORWARD BILGE PUMP CONTROL LEVERS (AFTER CHASSIS SERIAL NO. 4201). Three levers located directly in front of driver's seat (fig. 12), selectively control the pumping of left rear, center (main), and right rear compartments. Compartments must be pumped *one at a time* by pulling up on correct lever (par. 36*b.*).

e. Hull Drainage. On vehicles prior to chassis serial No. 2006, after-water operation hull drainage is accomplished by removing hull bottom and propeller shaft housing plugs. In addition to bottom and housing plugs on vehicles after chassis serial No. 2005, each of the four hull compartments are provided with a drain valve equipped with an operating handle (par. 37).

f. Heat and Air Circulation. Control of bilge pump, cargo compartment, and driver's compartment heat and air circulation system is explained in paragraph 35.

g. Windshield Wipers.

(1) VACUUM OPERATED (PRIOR TO CHASSIS SERIAL NO. 2006). Control for left-hand windshield wiper is located on wiper body. Right-hand wiper is manually operated.

TM 9-802
15-16

Operating Instructions

(2) AIR OPERATED (AFTER CHASSIS SERIAL NO. 2005). Control for operation of both windshield wipers is located on gage panel (fig. 13).

16. INSTRUMENTS AND GAGES.

a. General. All instruments and gages, with the exception of the compass, are located on instrument, and tachometer and gage panels (fig. 13). Vehicles prior to chassis serial No. 2006 are equipped with instrument panel only, while later vehicles are equipped with both instrument, and tachometer and gage panels.

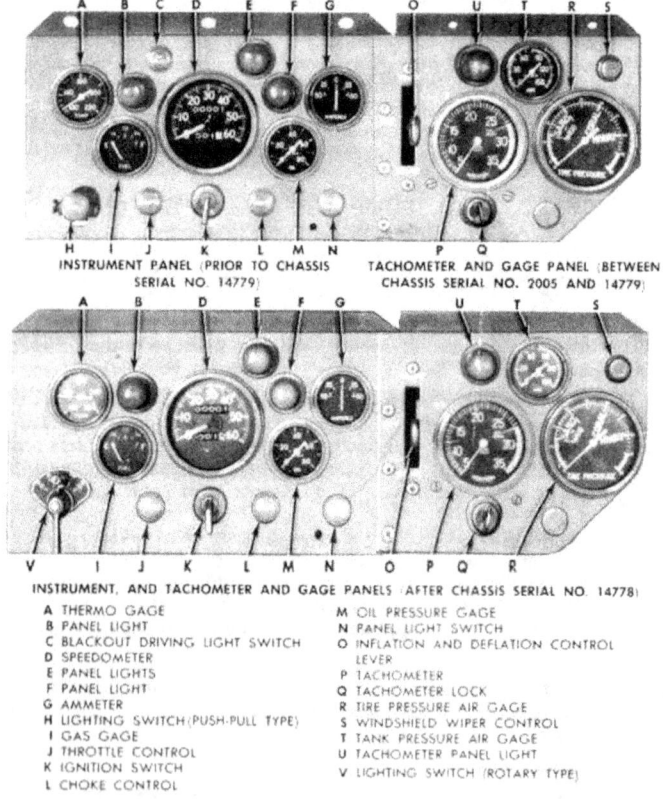

A THERMO GAGE
B PANEL LIGHT
C BLACKOUT DRIVING LIGHT SWITCH
D SPEEDOMETER
E PANEL LIGHTS
F PANEL LIGHT
G AMMETER
H LIGHTING SWITCH (PUSH-PULL TYPE)
I GAS GAGE
J THROTTLE CONTROL
K IGNITION SWITCH
L CHOKE CONTROL
M OIL PRESSURE GAGE
N PANEL LIGHT SWITCH
O INFLATION AND DEFLATION CONTROL LEVER
P TACHOMETER
Q TACHOMETER LOCK
R TIRE PRESSURE AIR GAGE
S WINDSHIELD WIPER CONTROL
T TANK PRESSURE AIR GAGE
U TACHOMETER PANEL LIGHT
V LIGHTING SWITCH (ROTARY TYPE)

RA PD 333242

Figure 13—Instrument Panel, and Tachometer and Gage Panel

Controls and Instruments

b. Gages.

(1) GAS (MARKED "FUEL"). This electrically operated gage, located on instrument panel (fig. 13), is interconnected with a fuel tank unit and indicates level of gasoline in fuel tank after ignition switch is turned "ON." The gage face is graduated from "E" (empty), "1/4," "1/2," "3/4," to "F" (full).

(2) OIL PRESSURE (MARKED "OIL"). Gage, located on instrument panel (fig. 13), indicates pressure of lubricant in engine crankcase, however, it does not indicate *quantity* of oil in crankcase. Face of gage is graduated from 0 to 80 pounds. When engine first starts, oil consistency may cause a sharp rise in pressure reading. As oil warms up, pressure should recede slowly to normal. Pressure readings may fluctuate as engine speed increases or decreases (par. 20c.). A sudden drop or an erratic fluctuation of pressure indicates trouble.

(3) THERMO (MARKED "TEMP"). Gage, located on instrument panel (fig. 13), is operated through a capillary tube connected to a thermal unit at the engine. It indicates temperature of water in cooling system—not *quantity* of water in system. Face of gage is graduated from 100°F to 220°F. Operating temperatures between 160°F and 220°F (205°F at high altitudes) are satisfactory for efficient engine operation. Temperatures above 220°F (250°F at high altitudes) or below 160°F, after engine warms up (par. 20b.), indicate improper cooling system operation.

(4) TANK PRESSURE AIR (MARKED "AIR"). Air gage, located on tachometer and gage panel (fig. 13), indicates air pressure in air storage tank. Face of gage is graduated from 0 to 150 pounds in multiples of 15 pounds. Normal operating pressure is between 50 and 75 pounds. Gage is used in connection with central tire pressure control system (par. 31) on vehicles after chassis serial No. 2005.

(5) TIRE PRESSURE (MARKED "TIRE PRESSURE"). Tire gage, located on tachometer and gage panel (fig. 13), indicates total tire pressure in all tires. Face of gage is graduated from 0 to 50 pounds. In addition, gage face is marked at correct operating pressures for "SAND or MUD," "CORAL," and "HI-WAY" operation. This gage is used in connection with central tire pressure control system (par. 31) on vehicles after chassis serial No. 2005.

c. Instruments.

(1) SPEEDOMETER (ON INSTRUMENT PANEL, FIG. 13). Speedometer indicates road speeds of vehicle in miles per hour, and records accumulated miles operated as well as "trip" miles. The trip recorder can be cleared by turning knurled knob located on under side of speedometer head. Instrument is operated through cable interconnected to axle transfer case, therefore will not record mileage or speed when vehicle is operating in water.

(2) TACHOMETER (ON TACHOMETER AND GAGE PANEL, FIG. 13). Tachometer indicates revolutions per minute of the engine. Two indicating needles are used; one indicates the engine operating revolutions, the other (red) registers the maximum revolutions reached

during a run. The red needle stays stationary at the highest reading, returning to zero after the key directly under head is turned. This instrument does not register accumulated revolutions.

(3) AMMETER. Located on instrument panel (fig. 13), indicates charging activity of generating circuit. Ammeter generally shows charge or plus (+) reading when engine is first started. Ammeter will generally show additional charge reading as engine speed is increased, depending upon the amount starter has drained the battery.

(4) COMPASS. Instrument is mounted in center of dash panel (fig. 12). Refer to paragraph 41.

(5) SIGNAL LIGHT. A signal light, on later vehicles, is mounted on a bracket to right of co-pilot's seat (fig. 117). This light, equipped with trigger switch, is used only for signal purposes.

17. SWITCHES.

a. Ignition. Ignition switch, located on instrument panel (fig. 13), is lever type. Lever handle must be turned to "ON" position before engine can be started or gas gage registers. Switch is shut off by returning lever to vertical position.

b. Starter. Starter switch, mounted on body of starter (fig. 89), is actuated by a foot operated pedal button (fig. 12), located to the right of accelerator pedal. Initial movement of pedal, through linkage, engages starter pinion with flywheel. Further movement of the linkage closes switch on starter.

c. Lighting (Main). Main lighting switch, located on instrument panel (fig. 13), is a four-position, push-pull type switch on vehicles prior to chassis serial No. 14479, and rotary type on vehicles after chassis serial No. 14478. This switch controls both service headlights and blackout marker lights, and service and blackout stop light and taillights. Switch is equipped with a circuit breaker which automatically opens circuit when a short circuit occurs, and closes circuit when thermostatic element in circuit breaker cools off. Operation is as follows (fig. 14):

(1) PUSH-PULL TYPE (FIG. 14).

(a) Off Position. Push knob completely in. All lights, both service and blackout, are then turned off. Blackout and service stop lights cannot be operated with switch in this position.

(b) Blackout Position. Pull to first stage. Blackout marker lights and blackout stop and taillights are then energized. Knob is locked in place with automatic plunger type lock when pulled to this position.

(c) Service Position. Switch locking button at left of switch body must be depressed before knob can be pulled to second stage or service position. Service headlights, service stop lights and taillights, and instrument panel lights are then energized.

(d) Service Stop Light Position. Pull knob completely out. Service stop lights may then be operated for daylight driving.

TM 9-802
17

Controls and Instruments

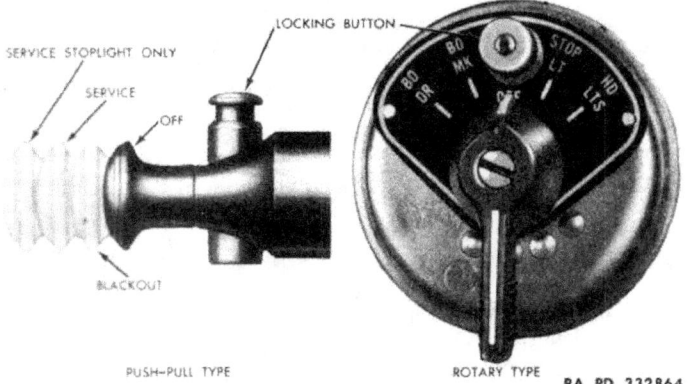

Figure 14—Lighting Switch Operating Positions

(2) ROTARY TYPE (FIG. 14). Switch is a five-position lever type. This switch is also equipped with a circuit breaker.

(a) Off Position. When lever is placed in "OFF" position, all lights, both service and blackout, are turned off.

(b) Blackout Position. When lever handle is turned to right to "BO MK" position, blackout front marker lights, and blackout stop and taillights are energized.

(c) Blackout Driving Light. Before lever can be turned to "BO DR" position, depress button. Left blackout driving light, as well as blackout marker, taillight, and stop light are energized.

(d) Service Stop Light Position. Before lever can be placed in "STOP LT" position from "OFF" position, lock plunger must be held in depressed position. When switch is in "STOP LT" position, service stop lights can be operated for daylight conditions.

(e) Service Position. Before switch can be placed in "HD LTS" position from "OFF," lock plunger must be depressed. With switch in this position, service headlights, taillights, and stop light are energized. Plunger need not be depressed when turning switch from "STOP LT" to "HD LTS" position.

d. Blackout Driving Light. Switch (marked "BO DRIVE"), is located on instrument panel (fig. 13) and when pulled out, energizes a blackout driving light which is installed adjacent to left-hand service headlight. The shielded driving light is used in addition to the standard blackout marker light when additional illumination is necessary during blackout conditions. Blackout driving light cannot be operated until the push-pull type main light switch is in blackout position (subpar. **c.**(1) above).

e. Panel Lights (Marked "PANEL LIGHTS"). Switch is located on instrument panel (fig. 13), and controls panel lights on instrument, and

41

TM 9-802
17-18

Operating Instructions

tachometer and gage panels, after main lighting switch is placed into service position [subpar. **c.**(1) or (2) above].

f. Dimmer. This is a foot-operated switch, accessible to driver's left foot (fig. 12), and is used to control upper and lower headlight beams. Switch is not operative until main lighting switch is in service position [subpar **c.**(1) or (2) above].

g. Stop Light. Stop light switch, which is connected to hydraulic master cylinder, is not directly actuated by driver. When brake pedal is depressed, hydraulic fluid pressure actuates the switch to light the stop lights when main lighting switch is in proper position (subpar. **c.** above).

h. Horn. Horn button is located in center of steering wheel on early vehicles and on side wall to left of driver (fig. 12) on late vehicles. Button must be depressed to sound the electric horn.

Section VII

Operation Under Ordinary Conditions

18. GENERAL.

a. The amphibian truck, on land, has the uses and characteristics of a conventional GMC 2½-Ton, 6x6 Truck, and is operated as such. However, additional experience in the use of marine controls and accessory equipment is necessary to operate the vehicle under ordinary amphibious conditions. Controls in driver's compartment are illustrated in figure 12. Tactical information and specialized operations such as navigation, mooring, loading, and winching problems are not included in this manual. Such information will be found in applicable field manuals, i.e., FM 55-150. Refer to paragraphs 14 through 17 of this manual for location and purpose of controls and instruments.

b. Service Upon Receipt of Equipment. Before a new or reconditioned vehicle is placed in service, be sure that services described in paragraphs 10 through 13 have been performed.

c. Before-operation Service. Perform services in items 1 through 5 in paragraph 56**b.** before attempting to start the engine. Start and warm up engine (par. 20), then complete the Before-operation services.

d. Instruction Plates and Stencils. There are a number of instruction plates and signs placed about the vehicle at points visible to the operator. These plates, which are in most part fastened to dash panel, give brief instructions on the use of various controls. Stenciled signs bearing precautionary and instructional messages are also placed at pertinent points on the vehicle. During process of vehicle production, various design changes necessitated instruction plate changes. *The instructions on the plates of the vehicle to be operated should be followed with exceptions as noted in succeeding paragraphs.*

TM 9-802
18-19

Operation Under Ordinary Conditions

e. CAUTION: *If any fuel has been spilled into the compartments of the hull, these compartments must be thoroughly cleaned and all fumes evacuated before attempting to start the engine. As a precaution, smoking or open flames should not be permitted in or near the compartments. All bow and stern compartments must be opened and thoroughly ventilated before and after engine operation. If fuel is known to have leaked into the bilge, the cargo compartment floor boards must be removed, and bilges cleaned and ventilated. Heed all Fire caution plates.*

19. STARTING AND STOPPING ENGINE.

a. Preliminary. If operating in cold temperatures, make certain that necessary preparations for cold weather operation are made (pars. 42 through 46).

b. Setting Controls.

(1) Place all controls into neutral or disengaged positions. Pull hand brake lever full back.

(2) Hold choke control (marked "CHOKE") out about halfway if engine is cold, or out all the way in extremely cold weather. If vehicle has been standing any length of time, fuel pump priming lever (fig. 78 or 79) should be worked up and down several times (approximately fifteen).

(3) Turn ignition switch lever to the left to "ON" position. Push clutch pedal down and hold down until engine is started.

c. Use of Starter.

(1) Push starter lever down and at same time depress accelerator pedal. Remove foot from starter lever after engine fires. Do not accelerate in short fast "spurts," but press evenly on accelerator pedal to obtain a

RA PD 337153

Figure 15—Use of Hand Crank Lever

43

fast idling until engine runs evenly, then use choke control as necessary to obtain even idling speed.

(2) Starter should not be engaged for periods longer than thirty seconds. After starter has been engaged without results, a period of ten to fifteen seconds should elapse before using it again. If engine will not start after a reasonable time, do not continue to use starter until reason for failure to start is determined and corrected (par. 62*a*.).

d. Hand Cranking. If starter fails to crank, and other causes for failure to start are corrected, engine can be started on land or water by hand cranking method. Towing method, on land only, will also start engine (par. 28*b*.). A cranking wheel is mounted on propeller shaft at rear of water propeller transfer case (fig. 15). This wheel is accessible after center air intake grille has been removed, and hinged wheel guard raised.

(1) Place transmission gearshift lever in second ("2") position. Place transfer case shift lever into "NEUT" position. *Engage water propeller* (pull up on lever on early vehicles; place lever into "STD" or "FWD" position on later vehicles). If on land, check at rear of vehicle to make sure water propeller is clear.

(2) Insert flat end of hand crank lever into a cog of wheel. Standing in cargo space (to rear of bulkhead) with back to right side of vehicle, pull sharply on crank lever. Turn engine over two or three times. Disengage crank lever from wheel.

(3) Pull hand throttle control ("THROTTLE") out about ½ inch. Hold or block choke control ("CHOKE") out about ½ inch unless choke has been used during repeated efforts to start engine with starter. Turn ignition switch to "ON" position.

(4) Reinsert crank lever into wheel. *Pull sharply on lever. Do not push on lever.* Several complete cranking strokes may be necessary before engine fires.

(5) When engine starts, immediately step on clutch pedal, disengage water propeller, and place transmission gearshift lever into "NEUT" (neutral) position. If engine does not start after several cranking strokes, determine cause of failure to start (par. 62*a*.).

e. Stopping Engine. Allow engine to idle for a few minutes, then turn ignition switch to "OFF" position.

20. ENGINE WARM-UP.

a. General. Engine should be permitted to operate through a short warm-up period whenever conditions permit. This warm-up pediod offers an opportunity for driver to check performance of the engine and to observe action of the various gages. Under no condition should the vehicle be placed into the water if the engine is not operating efficiently.

b. Operating Temperature. The thermostat in the radiator outlet starts to open at 160°F and is fully open at 185°F. Engine temperature at the thermo gage may be slightly higher than at the thermostat until the thermostat is fully open. As an example, thermo gage may register

Operation Under Ordinary Conditions

190°F to 195°F during the warm-up and then drop back to 180°F after thermostat is completely opened. The following precautions should be observed when checking temperature during warm-up or during operation.

(1) Temperature at which the engine should operate should not be below 160°F in any climate. This temperature should be attained as soon as possible during the warm-up period.

(2) Operating temperatures between 160°F and 220°F (205°F at high altitudes) are satisfactory for engine operation. Operating temperature of 180°F is generally used as average. Temperatures above 220°F (205°F at high altitudes) and below 160°F indicate improper cooling system operation.

(3) If temperature rises sharply and quickly to 220°F during warm-up period or during operation, engine should be stopped and cause of rapid increase in temperature determined and corrected.

c. Oil Pressure. When engine is first started, the consistency of the oil may cause a sharp rise in the pressure reading on the oil pressure gage. After the engine warms up, pressure should recede slowly to a normal reading. Definite oil pressure readings cannot be established, since many factors are involved such as oil viscosity, oil temperatures, bearing clearances, oil gage accuracy, etc. The following, however, should serve as a guide for minimum oil pressure readings.

(1) NEW VEHICLE OR WITH NEW OR REBUILT ENGINE. With engine operating at idling speed (510 rpm) and engine hot, minimum oil pressure reading should be 5 pounds. At governed speed (2750 rpm) with engine hot, minimum pressure should be 40 pounds.

(2) ENGINE WORN. At idling speed with engine hot, the oil gage needle should move off of the "peg." At governed speed, oil pressure reading should be 25 pounds minimum.

d. Ammeter. Ammeter may show charge or plus (+) reading during warm-up period. However, as general rule, the ammeter will not show a charge reading at slow idling speed. Ammeter should not show an excessive discharge during warm-up period.

e. Tank Pressure Air Gage (When Equipped With Central Tire Pressure Control). Tank pressure air gage should show steady increase of air pressure during warm-up period until the cut-out pressure of approximately 75 pounds is reached.

21. SHIFTING TRANSMISSION AND AXLE TRANSFER CASE.

a. General. The vehicle cannot be moved on land until the axle transfer case shift lever is placed into operating position ("HIGH" or "LOW"), with transmission gearshift lever in reverse or first forward speed. The axle transfer case is a medium by which the power is transferred from the transmission to the driving axles. Transmission gearshift positions do not in any way affect the selection of or shifting into the high and low ranges in the transfer case.

TM 9-802
19-20

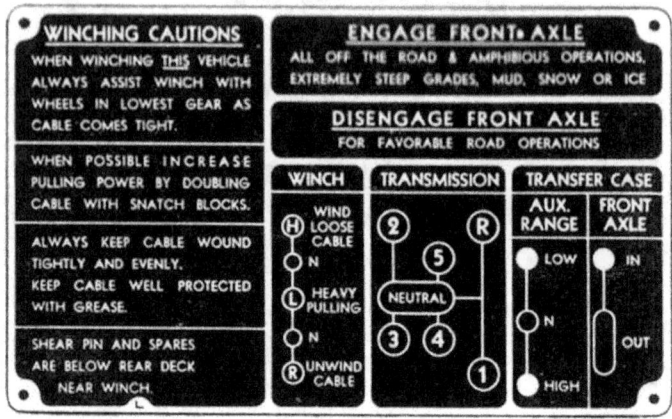

SHIFTING INSTRUCTION PLATE

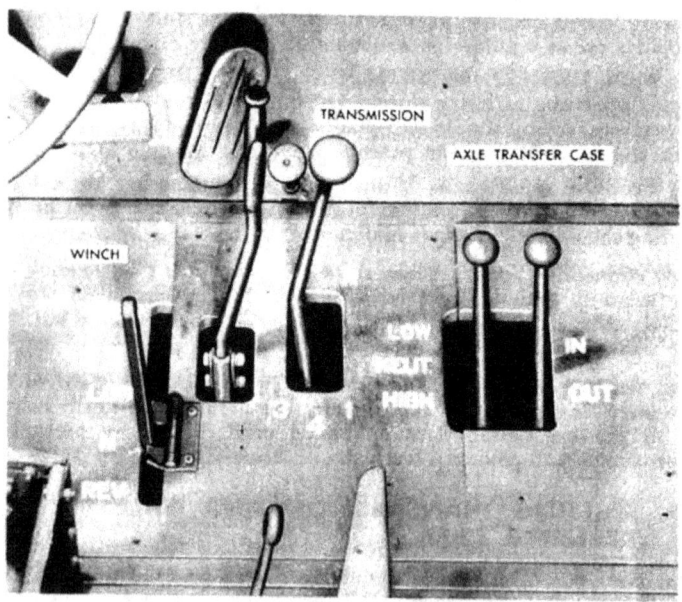

FLOOR BOARD SHIFTING MARKS

RA PD 333230

Figure 16—Shifting Instruction Plate and Floor Board Shifting Marks

TM 9-802

Operation Under Ordinary Conditions

b. Shifting Arrangements (fig. 16). The shifting instruction plate, mounted on dash panel in front of driver, illustrates the shifting patterns of winch power take-off shifting lever, transmission gearshift lever, and axle transfer case shift lever. The floor boards adjacent to the levers are also stenciled with the various shift positions.

c. Maximum Permissible Road Speeds. Maximum permissible road speeds, in miles per hour (land miles only) in the various transmission gear positions and transfer case gear ranges, are listed on a plate (fig. 17) attached to the dash panel. These speeds must not be exceeded.

d. Double-clutching. Double-clutching method should be used when shifting transmission and axle transfer case to minimize clashing of gears and the use of excessive force on the shift levers. When this method is used, the gears are synchronized before they are engaged, thus permitting smooth engagement with a minimum amount of effort.

(1) SHIFT FROM HIGH TO LOWER GEARS OR RANGE.

(a) Depress clutch pedal fully and at same time release accelerator pedal; *then* move shift lever into neutral ("N") position.

(b) Release clutch pedal; *then* accelerate engine momentarily.

(c) Depress clutch pedal again and release accelerator pedal; *then* shift from neutral to *next* lower gear or range.

(d) Release clutch pedal and at same time accelerate engine.

(2) SHIFT FROM LOW TO HIGHER GEAR OR RANGE. Follow steps *(a)* through *(d)* above except *do not accelerate engine between the shifts*.

e. Axle Transfer Case Power Ranges. Two power ranges are provided in the axle transfer case to be used with the various transmission gear positions when using driving axles. Various conditions

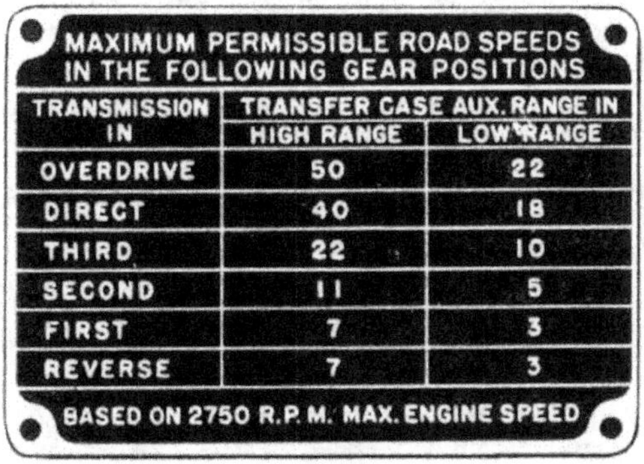

MAXIMUM PERMISSIBLE ROAD SPEEDS IN THE FOLLOWING GEAR POSITIONS		
TRANSMISSION IN	TRANSFER CASE AUX. RANGE IN	
	HIGH RANGE	LOW RANGE
OVERDRIVE	50	22
DIRECT	40	18
THIRD	22	10
SECOND	11	5
FIRST	7	3
REVERSE	7	3
BASED ON 2750 R.P.M. MAX. ENGINE SPEED		

RA PD 333225

Figure 17—Maximum Permissible Road Speed Plate

such as terrain, grade, and load must be taken into consideration before choice of transfer case high or low range can be determined.

(1) HIGH RANGE. As a general rule, high range is used when operating on a road where traction is not difficult and the load is light. This range may be used with front and rear axles driving, but generally with only rear axles driving.

(2) LOW RANGE. Transfer case cannot be operated in low range until front axle is engaged [subpar. *h.*(1) below]. With transfer case in low range, the greatest reduction is provided throughout all transmission gears. This range is used during off-the-road operations where maximum traction and power are required.

***f.* Driving Axle Combinations.** Vehicles may be driven by rear axles *only* or by front *and* rear axles. Front axle cannot be driven independently.

(1) REAR AXLES ONLY. Transfer case must be operated in high range only. Front axle declutching control lever must be in "OUT" position. Transfer case cannot be operated in low range with only rear axles driving.

(2) FRONT AND REAR AXLES. Front axle declutching control lever must be placed into "IN" position before transfer case is placed into low range. *After* front axle has been engaged, transfer case can be operated in either low or high range.

***g.* Shifting Transfer Case.**

(1) HIGH TO LOW RANGE. This shift should be made while vehicle is on hard ground before difficult terrain is encountered. *The speed of the vehicle must be reduced to below the maximum permissible speed of the transmission gear into which shift is made.* As an example, if transmission is in third speed and shift must be made from high to low transfer case range, speed of vehicle should be below 9 miles per hour as shown on plate (fig. 17). Shift as follows:

(*a*) Place front axle declutching control lever into "IN" position [subpar. *h.*(1) below].

(*b*) Place transfer case shift lever into "LOW" position, using double-clutching method [subpar. *d.*(1) above].

(2) LOW TO HIGH RANGE. This shift may be accomplished regardless of vehicle speed. However, while in low range, accelerate up to maximum permissible speed (fig. 17) for gear in which transmission is operating; then shift into high range as quickly as possible. Place transfer case shift lever into "HIGH" position, using double-clutching method [subpar. *d.*(2) above]. Front axle declutching control lever may then be placed in "OUT" position if desired.

***h.* Front Axle Engagement.** Front axle should be engaged only in off-the-road operations, slippery roads, on steep grades, or during hard pulling. In most cases, hard road operations require only the pulling ability of the two rear axles. However, if steep grades are encountered or if the vehicle must move an additional load, the front axle should be

Operation Under Ordinary Conditions

engaged to utilize the pulling ability of the three axles. The front axle should be used in getting vehicle under way, after which it may be disengaged providing the rear axles can pull the load without stalling the engine. Engage and disengage the front axle in following manner:

(1) ENGAGING. Front axle may be engaged at any vehicle speed without declutching. However, if transfer case is in high range, and it is desired to engage front axle, place front axle declutching control lever into "IN" position first, then make transfer case shift into low range as previously explained in subparagraph *g.*(1) above. Push declutching control lever forward quickly and all the way. If normal pressure on lever will not engage axle, "zig-zag" the front wheels while in motion until engagement is completed.

(2) DISENGAGING. Front axle may be disengaged at any vehicle speed.

(a) Transfer Case in High Range. Pull declutching control lever into "OUT" position without use of clutch.

(b) Transfer Case in Low Range. Place transfer case shift lever into "HIGH" position, using double-clutching method [subpar. *d.*(2) above]; *then* place front axle declutching control lever into "OUT" position.

(c) IMPORTANT: *If difficulty is encountered in disengaging front axle after exerting a normal pressure on the lever, push accelerator to the floor rapidly, then release instantly.* If difficulty is still encountered, "zig-zag" the front wheels, run over bumps in road, or run right front wheel over soft shoulder of road. If axle cannot be disengaged readily after trying above methods, stop the vehicle, shift into reverse, and back up slowly a few feet. While backing up, maintain pressure on lever until it releases and shifts into "OUT" position. Difficulty experienced when shifting front axle is not an indication of faulty shifting mechanism.

i. Shifting Transmission.

(1) LOW TO HIGH SPEEDS. Using double-clutching method [subpar. *d.*(2) above], shift lever from neutral into first speed. After necessary road speed has been obtained [see maximum permissible road speed plate (fig. 17)], shift into each higher speed successively in the same manner. *Do not exceed road speeds for each gear as indicated on plate. Do not skip speeds.*

(2) HIGH TO LOW SPEEDS. Transmission should always be shifted into next lower speed before engine starts to labor or before vehicle speed is appreciably decreased. The need for down-shifting is generally apparent when ascending a steep grade or when more power is needed to pull on rough terrain or in muck or sand. As a precautionary measure, the same ratio used to ascend a grade should be used when descending. When shifting to a lower gear at any rate of vehicle speed, make sure that engine speed is "synchronized" with vehicle speed before clutch is engaged. If clutch is engaged when engine is operating at lower than relative vehicle speed, the drive line may be damaged. Use double-clutching method [subpar. *d.*(1) above] and shift successively into lower speeds.

(3) REVERSING. Vehicles must be brought to a dead stop on land, or wheels stopped in water before transmission can be placed into reverse. Depress clutch pedal, shift lever through neutral into reverse ("R") position, then release clutch pedal and accelerate engine to necessary speed.

22. DRIVING ON LAND.

a. General. The methods employed to drive this vehicle on highways and rough terrain are the same as used to drive a conventional 6x6 truck. Sand, muck, swamps, mud, and coral, generally encountered when operating vehicle as an amphibian, require the tires to be deflated to specific pressures in addition to the correct use of the driving axles.

b. Steering. Rudder linkage (for water steering) is permanently linked to steering gear column; however, rudder action does not interfere with steering on land in the conventional automotive manner. Consideration must be taken of the vehicle width, and bow and stern overhang when making a turn.

c. Braking Vehicle. Application and release of service brakes (foot brakes) are accomplished in the conventional automotive manner. The driver applies pressure to foot pedal in varying degrees to brake vehicle as desired. Service brakes apply to all six wheels; therefore, only a normal amount of pedal pressure is required to actuate brakes, providing power system is functioning properly.

(1) CHECKING VEHICLE SPEED. Release accelerator pedal. Depress brake pedal slowly and evenly until vehicle is checked to desired speed. Do not "fan" pedal, but apply even pressure. This will permit the engine to assist in checking speed.

(2) NORMAL VEHICLE STOP. At the approach of a normal stop, release accelerator pedal, then check vehicle speed by even pressure on brake pedal. After vehicle speed is checked, depress clutch pedal, and increase pressure on brake pedal until vehicle is stopped.

(3) EMERGENCY STOP. Release accelerator, step sharply and hard on brake pedal, and at same time pull back on hand brake lever. Depress clutch pedal. This action should be used only in emergencies.

(4) HAND BRAKE LEVER. This lever should not be used to brake vehicle during normal driving. Primary purpose of hand brake is to hold vehicle in stationary position.

(5) FRONT BRAKE SHUT-OFF COCK. Always shut off the front brake shut-off cock when operating through wire or obstacles which might damage front brake hose. Lift up right floor board in driver's compartment to gain access to shut-off cock.

d. Use of Lights. Refer to paragraph 17c. for operation of light switches.

(1) SERVICE HEADLIGHTS. The driver must depend upon the service headlights for night visibility. These headlights, when aimed correctly and kept in good order, will provide adequate lighting for all conditions.

TM 9-802

Operation Under Ordinary Conditions

(a) High Beam. The high and low beams are controlled by foot-operated dimmer switch after main light switch is in service position. The high beam is generally used when there are no approaching vehicles, or when operating on unlighted roadways.

(b) Low Beam. The low or depressed beam should be used when approaching and passing another vehicle. The low beam may not throw light far enough ahead for clear road driving; however, when another vehicle is approaching, objects between the two vehicles show up in silhouette against the road. The visibility under this condition is somewhat greater than the clear road visibility with the high beam.

(2) BLACKOUT DRIVING LIGHT. This light is used only under blackout conditions and is controlled by a separate switch on instrument panel after push-pull type main light switch is placed into blackout position.

(3) BLACKOUT TAILLIGHTS AND MARKER LIGHTS. In convoy driving at night under blackout conditions, the blackout taillights and front marker lights will assist in estimating distances between vehicles.

(a) Blackout Taillights. The lens of each blackout taillight is divided into four parts, producing four distinct beams. This makes a total of eight distinct beams at the rear. When the vehicle ahead is less than 60 feet away, eight beams are visible; between 60 and 180 feet, four beams are visible; between 180 and 800 feet, two beams are visible; beyond 800 feet, no lights are visible.

(b) Front Marker Lights. Each marker light produces two beams, making a total of four beams visible at the front which are visible up to 60 feet. Between 60 and 800 feet, only two beams are visible; beyond 800 feet, the beams are not visible.

(4) SIGNAL LIGHTS. On late vehicles, a signal light is mounted on a bracket to right front of co-pilot seat. The light is equipped with a trigger handle and is used as a blinker signal.

e. Maximum Permissible Road Speeds. Use of driving axles and method of shifting transmission and transfer case are outlined in paragraph 21. The maximum permissible road speeds are outlined on instruction plate (fig. 17), mounted on dash. *These speeds must not be exceeded.*

f. Operating on Grades.

(1) ASCENDING GRADES. Front axle should be engaged when ascending steep grades. Always shift into lower transmission speeds before engine begins to labor. This can be accomplished most successfully when vehicle still has sufficient momentum to permit changing gears without bringing vehicle to a stop. Speed of the vehicle should be reduced below the maximum speed of gear into which shift should be made. See maximum permissible road speed plate on dash (fig. 17).

(2) DESCENDING GRADES. Always shift into lower transmission speed when descending steep grades. This will permit engine to act as

a brake to assist in controlling vehicle speed. Do not permit the vehicle to exceed maximum road speeds in any gear when driving down grades. Excessive engine speeds developed under such conditions are harmful to the engine.

(3) CAUTION: *When shifting to a lower gear at any rate of vehicle speed, make sure that engine speed is synchronized with vehicle speed before clutch is engaged. If clutch is engaged at the time engine is operating at lower than relative road speed, drive line parts may be damaged.*

23. OPERATION ON SAND, MUD, AND CORAL.

a. General. Sand, mud, and coral are generally encountered when operating in amphibious service. The succeeding subparagraphs briefly cover general precautions when operating over such terrain. Detailed information will be found in FM 55-150.

b. Sand. The most common type of terrain which must necessarily be crossed during amphibious operations is sand. It is therefore necessary that methods peculiar to sandy terrain must be used. Definite precautions must be taken or the winch must be used to pull the vehicle out.

(1) TIRE DEFLATION. Necessary tire deflation on sand depends upon the consistency of the sand. Deflation should be made according to the information shown in paragraph 32. If the vehicle is not equipped with central tire pressure control, it will be necessary to manually deflate the tires before operation. When in doubt about sand conditions or consistency, deflate to 12 pounds.

(2) DRIVING AXLES. Always engage the front axle, with transfer case in "LOW" range and transmission in second, for difficult sand and heavy loads. The maximum power of transmission first gear should be used if sand or mud is extremely soft and vehicle is heavily loaded.

(3) LAYING THE TRACK. One of the most important phases of traveling over sand is to "lay" the tracks over the sand, not "dig" them. With the tires properly deflated, travel over sand with full power and speed.

(4) DIGGING IN. If the drive wheels are permitted to spin, the action of the wheels will immediately dig in. The instant progress stops, release the clutch. Do not wait until the wheels spin before the power is cut off. When the vehicle cannot progress over the sand with sufficient speed, release the clutch immediately, back up far enough to permit a good forward run. Go forward again, *faster*. This procedure may be necessary several times. If the vehicle cannot go forward or backward without digging in, stop using the wheels and winch out.

(5) ANGLES. Always go up difficult sand grades *straight* and *square* never at an angle.

(6) TURNING. When the front wheels are turned sharply, much of their forward driving action is lost. There is also the added resistance of all wheels making separate tracks. Pick the best spots for necessary

Operation Under Ordinary Conditions

turns, then make the turns as wide as possible. Go at the tough places *straight* and *fast*. When traveling over sharply rising sand dunes where there is a possibility of bottoming, keep the vehicle moving fast. Do not get straddled on the crest.

(7) FOLLOWING. If more than one vehicle is operating to and from the water or over sandy beach, the leading driver should pick the best available path. The vehicles at the rear should follow in the leader's tracks whenever possible. No attempt should be made to pull out or make another track unless those vehicles ahead have made the roadway impassable. *Do not attempt to follow too close, as the vehicle ahead may have to back up to make another attempt forward.*

c. Soft Mud and Marshes. Avoid soft, sticky mud, marshes, and swamps. The vehicle can pull out of any mud ordinarily traveled over by a truck; however, under-water mud has a gripping characteristic which generally mires down any wheeled vehicle. Pick out another spot to land or enter the water. Avoid traveling close to banks which have a mucky appearance. Test depth and consistency with boat hook. Use all driving axles in low transfer case range with transmission in first or second speed.

d. Coral and Rocks. Deflate tires to 30 pounds. Drive over such terrain at a very *low* speed. Engage front axle, using low range and transmission speed, or first speed if there is a possibility of hidden coral heads.

24. WATER OPERATION.

a. General. The operation of the vehicle in water covers three important phases—entering the water, operating in the water, and leaving the water. Each phase of operation is equally important. The succeeding subparagraphs briefly outline the necessary important operations.

b. Preliminary Operations. Before entering into the water, before-operation services (par. 56) must be accomplished. The most important preparations are:

(1) Warm up engine (par. 20).

(2) Check operation of bilge pumps (par. 36e.).

(3) Close bilge drain valves and install plugs (par. 37).

(4) Deflate tires for operation on anticipated terrain (par. 32).

(5) Be sure all hatches are tightly clamped shut (par. 34c.).

(6) If vehicle is equipped with windshield surf board, set it up if surf is over five feet. Rig cab and cargo tarpaulins securely (par. 33). If surf is over 10 feet, remove cab cover and rig tarpaulin over cargo without bows. Set up rear surf board if used (par. 34f.) or rear end curtains (par. 34f.). Unless water is smooth, always set up bow surf board (par. 34e.).

(7) Load vehicle correctly. Refer to load markings at rear of vehicle (fig. 203).

TM 9-802
24

Operating Instructions

c. Operating Water Propeller. Water propeller should be engaged only when operating in water, for the purpose of testing bilge pumps before entering the water, or when hand-cranking engine. The vehicle must be stopped on land or the wheels momentarily stopped if wheels are operating in the water prior to making water propeller engagement.

(1) PRIOR TO CHASSIS SERIAL NO. 2506 (FIG. 30). The shifting lever on these vehicles has two positions, namely "IN" and "OUT."

(a) Engaging. Depress clutch pedal and decelerate engine. Place transmission shift lever into second speed for forward operation or reverse for reverse operation. "Pull up" water propeller shift lever to engage, then release clutch pedal and accelerate engine.

(b) Disengaging. To disengage water propeller while operating in water, it is necessary to depress clutch pedal. "Press down" on shift lever, then release clutch pedal. When leaving the water (when water propeller is clear of the water), it is not necessary to depress clutch pedal, merely "press down" on shift lever.

(2) AFTER CHASSIS SERIAL NO. 2505 (FIG. 19). [Refer to par. 14c.(2)(a) regarding change in plate and floor board markings.] Water propeller shift lever on these vehicles has three operating positions, two of which are marked on floor of vehicle, namely, "OVERDRIVE" or "REV," neutral (center position), and "STD" or "FWD." When the water propeller shift lever is placed in "OVERDRIVE" or "REV" position, *the direction of the propeller is not reversed* but furnishes an overdrive ratio which provides more speed when reversing with transmission shift lever placed in reverse position. The forward ("STD" or "FWD") position of the shift lever is generally used in combination with transmission second speed in forward drive; however, "OVERDRIVE" or "REV" position can be used in combination with transmission first speed in the case of close maneuvering, or when it will be necessary to quickly place the transmission into reverse.

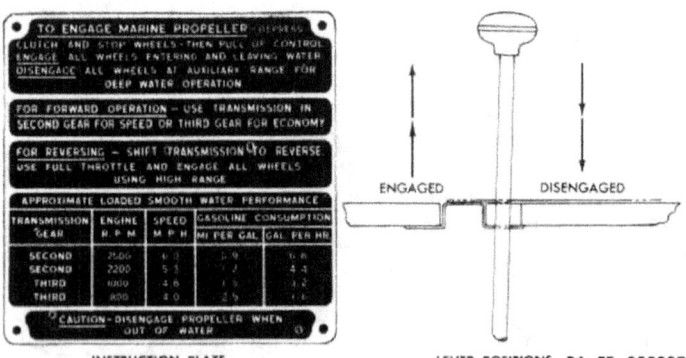

Figure 18—Water Propeller Instruction Plate and Lever Positions (Prior to Chassis Serial No. 2506)

TM 9-802
24

Operation Under Ordinary Conditions

(a) Engaging. Vehicle must be stopped on land, or wheels momentarily stopped if wheels are operating in the water, prior to engaging the water propeller. Depress clutch pedal, move water propeller shift lever from neutral position (center) into either "STD" or "FWD," or "OVERDRIVE" or "REV" position as necessary. Place transmission shift lever into second speed or reverse speed as necessary, release clutch pedal, then accelerate engine.

(b) Disengaging. Depress clutch pedal before propeller shift lever is moved into neutral position if vehicle is in the water. If the vehicle is leaving water and the propeller is clear of water, it is not necessary to depress the clutch pedal when disengaging.

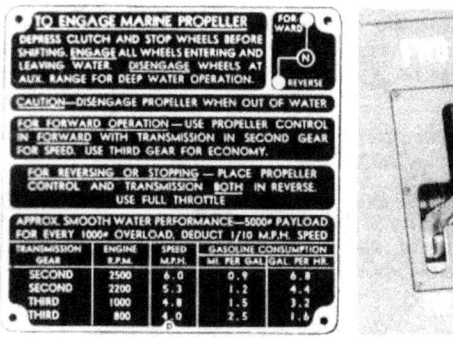 

INSTRUCTION PLATE AND FLOOR BOARD MARKINGS ON SOME VEHICLES

INSTRUCTION PLATE AND FLOOR BOARD MARKINGS ON LATER VEHICLES

RA PD 333219

Figure 19—Water Propeller Instruction Plate and Lever Positions (After Chassis Serial No. 2505)

25. ENTERING WATER.

a. Deflating Tires. Before entering water, deflate tires according to terrain conditions (par. 32).

b. Entering Over Coral or Sharp Rocks. Operate the vehicle at very low speed (second transmission speed, low range). Unless there is a heavy surf or strong current, do not engage propeller until fully afloat. This will prevent damage to propeller. If a heavy surf or strong current exists, stop momentarily before reaching the edge of water, engage propeller, then proceed at full throttle.

c. Entering Over Sand. If approach is made over sand, soft or hard, and no projecting rocks, enter at full throttle and keep full throttle until well in the clear. Use full throttle for momentum to carry through that period when the vehicle is neither wholly afloat nor wholly aground. Low range second is best when going out through shallows. High range second is best when entering directly into deep water.

d. Current. To offset the current's unavoidable turning effect, entry must be made at an angle *toward* the current.

e. Leaks. Just as soon as the vehicle enters the water, look down through the air intake grilles. If there is excessive leaking as indicated by an abnormal quantity of water in the bilge, *get back on land as quickly as possible*. If leaks are only normal, operate bilge pump valve levers (par. 36**b**.).

26. DRIVING IN THE WATER.

a. Disengaging Wheels. When vehicle is well out into deep water and there seems to be no necessity for the driving wheels, decelerate momentarily, then shift transfer case into neutral. This can generally be accomplished without using the clutch. *Do not disengage front axle as it will be needed when landing.*

b. Steering. Rudder of vehicle is mounted at stern. This rudder is operated and turned by cables attached to conventional steering gear column. As rudder is attached near stern, normal forward steering is obtained by forcing stern the opposite way from the desired forward turn. *The driver, however, turns steering wheel in the conventional automotive manner and direction.*

(1) Water steering requires more turning of steering wheel than is generally used when operating on land. The wheel not only requires more turning, but it must be turned *in time*. There is considerable lag at both start and finish of a turn while operating in water. It is therefore necessary to anticipate any turns, particularly in rough water. *Swing wheel ahead of time and swing it hard.*

(2) Rudder response will be less at reduced speed, however, at even very low speed, the rudder will answer if occasional short spurts of power are made.

Operation Under Ordinary Conditions

(3) Bear in mind that under extremely adverse sea conditions, reduction of speed will reduce trouble from waves. When landing before a heavy surf, steer absolutely in front of waves and maintain full throttle to assure maximum steering control.

(4) When steering close to an object in water, remember that the stern has a tendency to swerve *toward* the object when vehicle is steered *away* from it.

(5) Reverse steering in water under average conditions requires approximately the same technique as used in reversing a land vehicle. However, when operating in strong winds and rough water, reverse steering will be uncertain. The most satisfactory reverse steering can be secured by forcing stern in desired direction while still driving ahead. This starts stern of vehicle turning, and as water propeller is placed into reverse, this turn will generally be maintained.

c. Emergency Steering.

(1) If rudder is knocked off or any part of linkage is broken or disconnected, engage all wheels, high range, in addition to water propeller. Some control should be retained due to the action of the front wheels. If unable to turn as desired, manually disengage water propeller, shift transmission to third speed, in which combination full throttle should give better steering with wheels alone. Engage water propeller and shift back to second speed transmission when on desired course.

(2) If steering cable is cause of failure, disconnect at stern and steer by hand in rear compartment to assist front wheel steering. Additional steering can be secured by using floor boards or shovel held at an angle against the bow or stern of the vehicle.

d. Forward Driving.
Under normal conditions, water propeller should be operated with transmission in second speed, full throttle. Third speed can be used to decrease fuel consumption as indicated on dash instruction plate (fig. 19). The indicated loss of speed becomes greater in rough water, also the engine temperature will increase. If fuel must be conserved in extremely hot weather, shift back to second speed every few minutes to keep the temperature down. Bear in mind that the temperature of the engine will decrease when lower transmission speeds are used.

e. Reversing.
There are two methods of reversing, depending upon the type of shift lever on the vehicle. Reversing the water propeller is also the only method of stopping the vehicle in water.

(1) PRIOR TO CHASSIS SERIAL NO. 2506. With water propeller in engaged position depress clutch pedal, place transmission into reverse, then release clutch pedal and accelerate engine full throttle. Engaging all wheels in high range will assist in reversing.

(2) AFTER CHASSIS SERIAL NO. 2505. Prior to the point where reversing is necessary, the water propeller shift lever may be placed into "OVERDRIVE" or "REV" position (fig. 19) and transmission into first speed for any forward maneuvering. When necessary to reverse the water propeller, it is then necessary to depress clutch pedal and pull transmission gearshift lever straight back into reverse ("R").

Release clutch pedal and use full throttle of engine. If it is necessary to maneuver forward, it is only necessary to depress clutch pedal and place transmission gearshift lever into first ("1") position. As previously explained, placing water propeller shift lever into "OVERDRIVE" or "REV" position does not reverse the direction of the water propeller. This can only be accomplished when the transmission is placed into reverse.

f. Water Propeller Failure. If water propeller is rendered inoperative, some progress can be made by using all wheels in transfer case high range, third transmission speed, and full throttle. Water propeller should be disengaged. Under extremely favorable conditions, speed will approximate two miles per hour (land miles). If engine fails with vehicle near shore, shovels, tarpaulin bows, floor boards, etc., will make useful paddles. If impossible to paddle against adverse winds or current, anchor vehicle until assistance arrives.

27. LANDING.

a. General. Prepare for the most difficult conditions. Pick out the most favorable spot for landing. Avoid extremely steep beaches, soft sticky mud, swamps, mashes, stumps, fallen logs, sharp rocks, boulders, and heavy weed patches. In rough water, set up bow and rear surf plates and rig cargo tarpaulin if surf looks heavy.

b. Approach. Observe the effect of the current. Start approach far enough up stream so that current will not carry the vehicle below the landing point. Engage all driving wheels while still clear of shallow water. Come in square with the waves and stay that way until out of the water. Front wheels should be in a straight-ahead position when touching land.

c. Landing Over Sand.

(1) Use main transfer case, *low range*, with transmission in second gear for most landings. Transfer case high range is advantageous only for unloaded vehicle on a well known hard and flat beach. *The maximum power of transmission in first gear with low range transfer case should be used with heavily loaded vehicle in extreme conditions (extremely steep or soft landings).* If landing has been attempted with a wrong gear combination, causing vehicle to stop momentarily, do not attempt to re-start ahead from this point. Back out and make a new attempt forward with the correct gear combination.

(2) When the wheels ground, continue to operate at full throttle until up on the beach. If the vehicle is coming in with the waves at an angle to the beach, square around slowly to drive straight up the beach.

(3) If progress stops, cut power immediately. Do not allow wheels to dig in. If stopped with vehicle mostly in the water, back up, full throttle, using propeller with all wheels in high range until well clear, then try a better spot. If stopped with the vehicle mostly clear of water, winch forward. If stuck in the surf, rig rear closure and tarpaulins immediately and keep bilge pumps operating.

Operation Under Ordinary Conditions

(4) Deflated tires can be operated for limited distances at reduced speeds. Wait until the vehicle is clear of the sand and in a safe position to inflate on vehicles not equipped with central tire pressure control system.

d. Landing Over Coral or Sharp Rocks. *Use low range, second, and when wheels ground, cut speed to three to four miles per hour.* Stay at that speed until out of water and over all coral or sharp rocks. *Disengage propeller for its protection just as soon as wheels ground and there is no longer possibility of surf action causing vehicle to momentarily float.*

28. TOWING THE VEHICLE.

a. General. Instructions in succeeding subparagraphs cover the methods of towing vehicle on land only. Methods required to tow vehicle in water are covered in FM 55-150.

b. Towing to Start Engine. Engine may be started in following manner:

(1) Tow chain or line should be of sufficient length to permit maneuverability of both vehicles. Do not hook line on *winch chock;* use tow chain shackles or pintle hook.

(2) Place transmission in fourth (fifth, if traction is difficult). Place transfer case in high range with front axle disengaged.

(3) Turn on ignition switch. Disengage clutch for the first 100 feet. When towed vehicle reaches approximately 10 miles per hour, slowly engage clutch. Disengage clutch immediately after engine starts.

c. Towing Disabled Vehicles. Particular care must be exercised when towing damaged vehicles to repair bases to make certain that no additional damage occurs while vehicle is being towed. *Do not hook on front cable guide.* Use front shackles or pintle hook.

(1) TOWING VEHICLES WITH ALL WHEELS ON GROUND.

(a) If transfer case on vehicle to be towed is not damaged, shift transmission and transfer case into neutral. In these positions, gears in transmission are not in motion; however, driving gears are revolving in transfer case, and gears will cause enough lubricant splash to provide lubrication for pocket bearings and main shaft bushings.

(b) If transfer case is damaged, propeller shafts should be disconnected at front axle pinion, forward rear axle pinion, and pillow block. Secure shafts. Place bolts, nuts, and bearings in driver's compartment.

(2) TOWING VEHICLE WITH FRONT WHEELS OFF GROUND. Whenever vehicle is to be towed with front wheels off ground, vehicle must be supported in such a manner that wheels of forward rear axle contact ground. Disconnect propeller shafts at forward rear axle and pillow block. Secure ends of shafts.

(3) TOWING VEHICLE WITH REAR WHEELS OFF GROUND. Vehicle should be towed backwards only after other methods have proven unsatisfactory. When towing vehicle backwards, make certain

Operating Instructions

CLOSED   OPENED

RA PD 337197

Figure 20—Use of Pintle Hook

that front axle declutching lever is placed in "OUT" or disengaged position.

d. Use of Pintle Hook (fig. 20). To open, remove pin, then lift up latch and pull up lock with hand. To close, push down lock. Latch will then be placed. Insert pin.

Section VIII

Operation of Auxiliary Equipment

29. WINCH.

a. General. The winch assembly, which is mounted on rear deck of vehicle, can be used for pulling either to the front or back. This assembly is basically the same as used on the conventional GMC 6x6, 2½-Ton Truck. The winch is operated by power take-off on the left side of the transmission through drive shafts which extend from the power take-off to the winch assembly.

b. Use of Winch. The winch can be used to assist the vehicle in extracting itself from sand or mud, to assist another vehicle, or with an A-frame for loading and unloading. When the winch is used forward, the cable must be led through the guides in rear bulkhead and

TM 9-802
29

Operation of Auxiliary Equipment

directly under windshield, then through chock on front of vehicle. When winching astern, the cable leads directly from the winch drum. The winch cable must not be used for land towing, as this will kink the cable on the drum. Refer to paragraph 28 for land towing instructions.

c. Use of Cable. The winch will be more powerful with all cable, down to last layer, off of drum before the pull is started. Pay out as much cable as possible from the drum before starting the pull. Cable guides in the hull permit winch cable to be pulled straight onto winch drum when winching from the front. When winching from the rear, this straight pull cannot always be obtained. If necessary to pull at an angle from the rear, cable must be guided evenly onto the drum, using hand crank lever as shown in figure 23.

d. Winch Shear Pin. The cable is protected by a shear pin in the winch drive mechanism. This pin will break when the load on cable exceeds approximately 10,000 pounds. The shear pin is located below the rear deck at the coupling where the winch drive shaft goes through the stern. Spare shear pins are kept in a rack close to this position. After winching, shear pin should always be removed (par. 274) and replaced with a new pin if the old pin is marked.

e. Rigging. Use of snatch blocks, sand anchor, and methods of rigging winch tackle under various conditions are covered in FM 55-150. When using snatch block in connection with pintle hook, use as illustrated in figure 23.

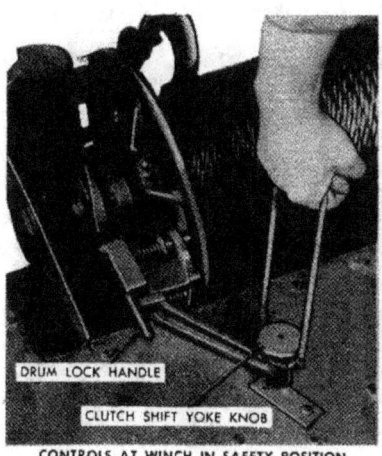

CONTROLS AT WINCH IN SAFETY POSITION POWER TAKE-OFF CONTROL LEVER

RA PD 337142

Figure 21—Controls at Winch and Driver's Compartment

Operating Instructions

f. Controls.

(1) POWER TAKE-OFF CONTROL LEVER. The control lever, which extends from the power take-off through the driver's compartment floor, has three operating positions—"HIGH," "LOW," and "REV" (reverse), with "N" (neutral) positions in between. Lever lock, attached to the floor board beside the lever, holds the lever in neutral ("N") position between "REV" and "LOW" (fig. 21). This lock prevents accidental engagement of the power take-off. An automatic safety brake on the worm shaft of the winch mechanism will support a load on the winch cable when the control lever is being shifted into various operating positions.

(2) CLUTCH SHIFT YOKE KNOB. The clutch shift yoke knob (fig. 21) operates a jaw clutch which engages and disengages the winch drum. The jaw clutch must be engaged for the winch power drive to have effect. When in the disengaged position (knob moved toward the left side of the vehicle), the winch drum will rotate freely on its shaft.

(3) DRUM LOCK HANDLE. The drum lock handle, which is spring loaded, engages one of several holes in the winch drum flange when the clutch shift yoke knob is in disengaged position. When the shift yoke knob is engaged, lock handle will be released from the drum.

g. Safety or Under-way Control Positions. When vehicle is under-way or when winch is not operating, the clutch shift yoke knob must be placed in disengaged position with drum lock handle engaged, handle down (fig. 22). The power take-off control lever must be in "N" (neutral) position between "REV" and "LOW," with lever lock over the lever (fig. 22). With the controls in these positions, the cable will not unwind from drum when under-way nor can the winch be operated by accidental shifting of power take-off control lever.

HAND WINDING POSITION

OPERATING POSITION

RA PD 337165

Figure 22—Winch Operating and Hand Winding Positions

TM 9-802
29

Operation of Auxiliary Equipment

h. Hand Winding or Hook-up. When necessary to hand wind or unwind cable from drum by hand to make a hook-up, place clutch shift yoke knob in disengaged position with drum lock handle pulled up (fig. 22). Drum can then be revolved in either direction to permit hand winding or to unwind cable to make the desired hook-up.

i. Pulling or Winding In. After making the desired hook-up, either at the front or rear, check effectiveness of winch brake, then position the controls in following manner:

(1) At the winch, place clutch shift yoke knob into engaged position with drum lock handle down (fig. 22). Depress clutch pedal, place power take-off control lever into "LOW" if load is heavy, or into "HIGH" to take up slack or if load is light. Before starting to wind in the cable, cable already on the drum must be tightly and evenly wound. This will provide a smooth surface for additional cable to wind on. If necessary, the hand crank lever may be used to guide the cable as shown in figure 23.

(2) ENGINE OPERATING SPEEDS. Winch pulling speeds are based on a maximum engine speed of 1,000 revolutions per minute which must not be exceeded. This is approximately one-third full throttle. Do not race engine when using the winch.

j. Paying Out. Whenever cable is under load, the winch power take-off control lever must be shifted into reverse ("REV"). At winch,

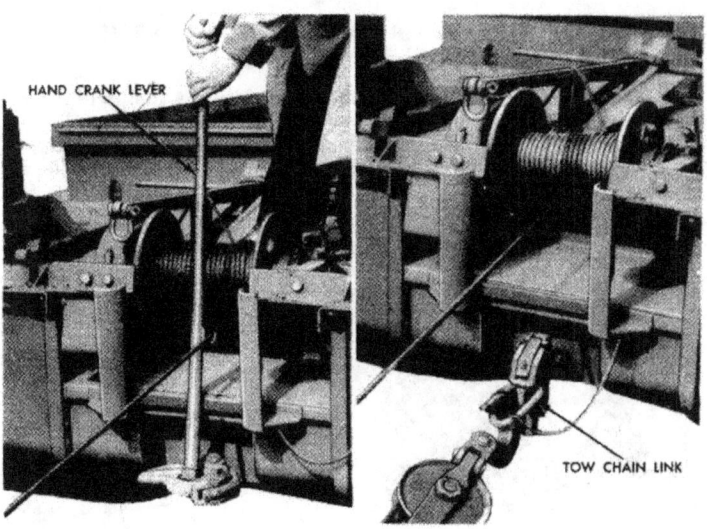

RA PD 337157

Figure 23—Use of Hand Crank Lever and Tow Chain Link

TM 9-802
29-30

Operating Instructions

place shift yoke knob into engaged position (fig. 22). Depress clutch pedal, then shift power take-off control lever into reverse. Release clutch pedal and accelerate engine as necessary to pay-out cable. When cable becomes slack, and there is more than 10 feet of additional cable to be payed out, the shift yoke knob should be placed into disengaged position (fig. 22) and the cable pulled out by hand. The paying out of the cable should be stopped when at least 5 turns remain on the drum, otherwise the cable load will fall directly on the cable end attachment. This is particularly important when afloat.

k. Use of Driving Wheels with Winch. If vehicle is assisting itself with its own winch, front and rear axles must be used. Power take-off control lever must be in "LOW," transmission gear shift in first, and transfer case in "LOW" range. Always start the wheels operating the instant winch cable starts to take the load. Do not start wheels until all slack in cable is taken up.

l. Winding Cable. Cable should be wound on the drum with some load on the cable. Cable can be attached to an anchor or tree and the vehicle pulled forward by the winch with controls placed in pull-in position (subpar. *j.* above). Winding on the first layer of cable is the most important. Coils of cable must be tight against each other to prevent coils on next layer compressing down between them. Use the hand crank lever in manner shown in figure 23 to guide the cable evenly on the drum.

30. USE OF TIRE PUMP (PRIOR TO CHASSIS SERIAL No. 2006).

a. General. The tire pump, located under driver's compartment, is chain driven from transmission power take-off. This pump supplies air to a storage tank mounted inside hull below right-hand air exhaust grille. Air lines from tank deliver air to hose at each end of aisle at

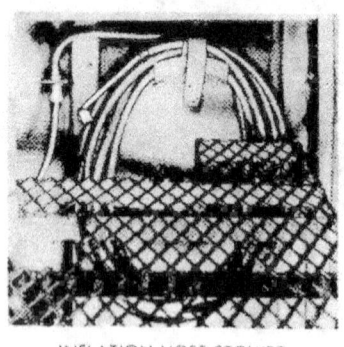
INFLATION HOSE STOWED

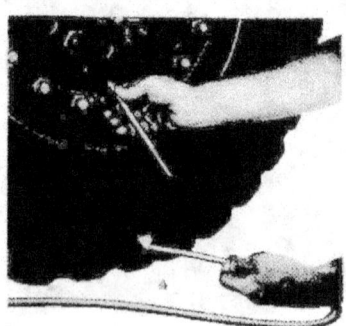
INFLATING TIRE

RA PD 307384

Figure 24—Method of Manually Inflating Tires

TM 9-802
30-31

Operation of Auxiliary Equipment

rear of driver's compartment (fig. 12). Each air hose is equipped with a conventional chuck.

b. Operation. Tire pump should generally be operated only during tire inflation; however, tire pump may be operated a few minutes prior to inflation to build up pressure in tank.

(1) Place transmission and transfer case into neutral.

(2) Depress clutch pedal, pull up control shift rod at right side of driver's seat.

(3) Release clutch pedal, then accelerate engine to about one-half engine speed on earlier vehicles (with air-cooled tire pumps), or approximately 2500 revolutions per minute on later vehicles (with water cooled tire pumps).

(4) Inflate individual tires with air hose and chuck (fig. 24) to proper pressures (par. 32).

(5) After inflation, stop pump operation by depressing clutch pedal, then pushing control shift rod down.

31. CENTRAL TIRE PRESSURE CONTROL (AFTER CHASSIS SERIAL No. 2005).

a. General. The central tire pressure control system enables the driver to inflate or deflate tires on all wheels at the same time, with the vehicle standing or moving on land or in the water. The driver can operate the controls while in driving position.

b. Operation. The power tire pump, mounted in front compartment and driven by engine, operates constantly while engine is run-

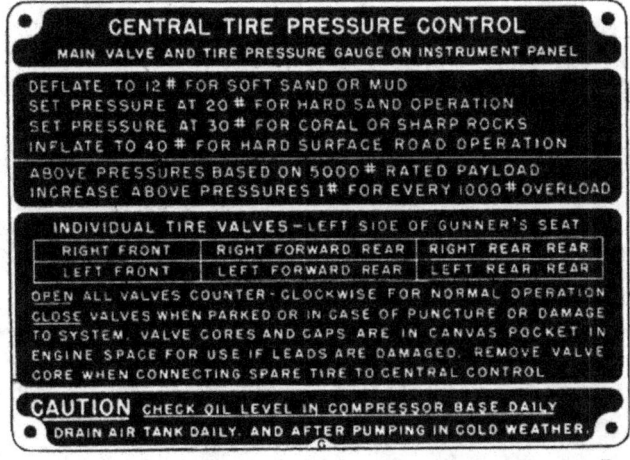

RA PD 333226

Figure 25—Central Tire Pressure Control Instruction Plate

TM 9-802
31

Operating Instructions

A INFLATION AND DEFLATION CONTROL LEVER
B TANK PRESSURE GAGE
C TIRE PRESSURE GAGE
D LINE VALVE FOR RIGHT FRONT TIRE
E LINE VALVE FOR RIGHT FORWARD REAR TIRE
F LINE VALVE FOR RIGHT REAR REAR TIRE
G LINE VALVE FOR LEFT FRONT TIRE
H LINE VALVE FOR LEFT FORWARD REAR TIRE
I LINE VALVE FOR LEFT REAR REAR TIRE

RA PD 333238

Figure 26—Central Tire Pressure Controls

ning; however, governor on tire pump cuts out (stops compression) when pressure reaches approximately 75 pounds and cuts in (starts compression) when pressure is depleted to 50 pounds. Air lines from storage tank deliver the air through manually controlled inflation and deflation valves, then through six line valves, which are individually connected to inflating devices at each wheel hub. The tire pressure gage on gage panel indicates pressure of all tires. This gage is also marked showing proper pressures for sand, coral, or highway operation (par. 32).

c. Instruction Plate. The instruction plate (fig. 25) mounted on dash panel, indicates operating tire pressures, line valve positions, and brief operating instructions. Reference should be made to paragraph 32 for proper tire pressures and instructions on earlier plates must be changed.

d. Inflating Tires. With all line valves open, tire pressure gage will show existing pressure in all tires. Engine must be started before tire pump will operate. Vehicles may be under way or parking during inflation or deflation. Air pressure gage (fig. 26) on gage panel should register at least 50 pounds before attempting to inflate tires in following manner:

(1) OPEN ALL LINE VALVES (FIG. 26). Open each line valve (mounted to the right of driver on side of co-pilot's seat). Turn each valve handwheel counterclockwise until stem bottoms.

(2) POSITION LEVER (FIG. 26). Place control lever (on gage panel) in "INFLATE" position (up). Notch in lever slot will hold lever in position.

(3) CHECK PRESSURE. During inflation, intermittently place control lever into "OFF" position to check tire pressure on tire pressure gage (fig. 26). Gage will not show an accurate reading while lever is

Operation of Auxiliary Equipment

in "INFLATE" position. After correct tire pressures are attained (par. 32), place lever into "OFF" position.

e. Deflating Tires. Tires can be deflated while vehicle is under way or standing in following manner:

(1) OPEN ALL LINE VALVES. All line valves must be open to deflate all tires {subpar. *d.*(1) above}.

(2) POSITION LEVER. Place control lever into "DEFLATE" position. The control lever slot on some vehicles is equipped with a notch to lock lever into deflate position; however, on later vehicles, it is necessary to *hold* lever in this position.

(3) CHECK PRESSURE. To check pressure, place control lever momentarily into "OFF" position several times during deflation. Tire pressure gage will not accurately register pressure reading with lever in "DEFLATE" position. After correct pressure is reached (par. 32), place lever into "OFF" position.

f. Parking Vehicle. All line valves should be closed when vehicle is parked for any length of time. This will minimize any leaks which may have developed in the system. Turn each valve handwheel clockwise until stem bottoms.

g. Localizing and Isolating Leaks. If a small leak occurs in one of the tires, or in line leading to a tire, localize the leak by closing all line valves, then reopening one at a time, watching tire pressure gage to determine which tire is leaking. After leak has been localized, one of two methods may be used to maintain pressure in other tires.

(1) Isolate the defective tire by closing correct line valve (fig. 26). Open valves to other tires, then inflate these tires to correct pressure. Close valves to good tires, then open valve to leaky tire. Place control lever into "INFLATE" position at intermittent intervals to maintain pressure in defective tire. If it is impossible to maintain pressure in defective tire because of a large leak, close valve and open valves to other tires. Change the defective tire as soon as possible.

h. Total Failure of System. If system fails (except tire pump), remove inflating devices, hoses, and struts and install valve cores in valve stems of each tire. A hose and chuck are mounted on right and left sides of vehicle behind seats. Shut-off cock on air tank must be opened. It is not necessary to use tire inflating control lever. Tires may also be inflated from an outside source under these conditions. Install valve caps on valve stems after inflating tires.

i. Changing Tires. Whenever a tire is to be changed, close the line valve leading to that tire. After change is made (par. 213), open line valve.

32. TIRE PRESSURES.

a. General. The most important preparation for operation over various terrain is inflating or deflating the tires to correct operating pressures. Necessarily, tire inflation depends upon the consistency of the ground. The tires are designed to operate at low pressures if neces-

EARLY TYPE LATE TYPE RA PD 333248

Figure 27—Early and Late Type Tire Pressure Gages

sary. The dash instruction plate (fig. 25) and stencils on the vehicle designate proper pressures under various conditions. In addition, the tire pressure gage (fig. 27) is also marked with correct pressures.

b. Changes in Tire Pressures. Actual experience has necessitated changes in tire pressure for sand and soft ground operation. Instruction plates, stencils, and tire pressure gages on some vehicles indicate that tires must be deflated to 10 pounds when operating in sand or soft ground. *This figure should be changed on all plates, signs, and gages (fig. 27) to 12 pounds* on each vehicle. The correct operating pressures are as follows:

(1) Soft Sand or Mud—12 lb

(2) Hard Sand—20 lb

(3) Coral or Sharp Rocks—30 lb

(4) Hard Surface Roads—40 lb

(5) *NOTE: Above pressures are based on maximum pay load of 5,000 lb*

33. CURTAINS, TARPAULINS, AND LASHINGS.

a. Driver's Compartment Top Cover and Side Doors (Prior to Chassis Serial No. 2006).

(1) TOP COVER (FIG. 28). A tubular metal bow, mounted on a support clamp at each side behind the driver's compartment, serves as a rear support for driver's compartment top cover. The bow can be lifted out after loosening the bow clamps. Top cover is fitted with a bead which slides into channel on windshield upper frame. Rear edge of cover is pulled over rear bow and lashed down with ropes.

(2) SIDE DOORS (FIG. 28). The side doors or curtains are equipped with metal frames and composition windows. Doors are equipped with catches which hold them in closed position against rear bow. To re-

TM 9-802
33

Operation of Auxiliary Equipment

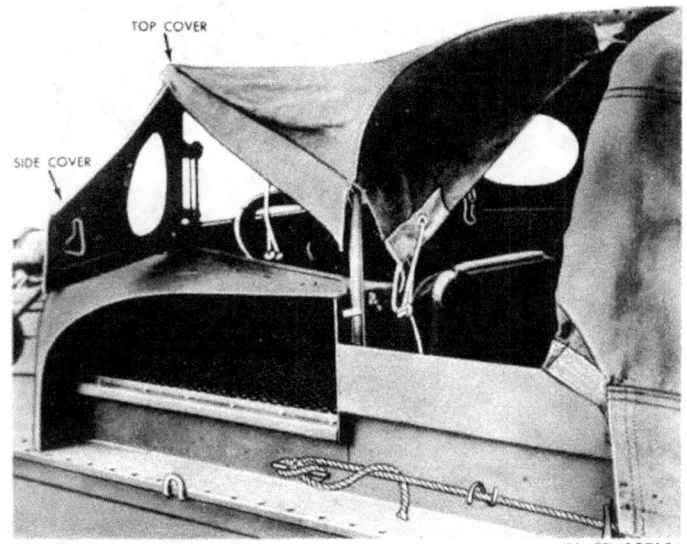

Figure 28—Driver's Compartment Top Cover and Side Doors (Prior to Chassis Serial No. 2006)

move, open doors wide, then raise to disengage the hinge rod ends from the brackets.

b. Driver's Compartment Top Cover (After Chassis Serial No. 2005) (fig. 29). A metal bow, clamped to rear of driver's compartment, serves as a rear support for top cover. Bow can be removed by loosening wing nuts at each leg of bow. The top cover is fitted with a bead which slides into a channel on front of windshield upper frame. Zippers on sides connect top cover with top of windshield side wings. Straps, buckles, and two tie-down ropes hold rear corners in proper position.

c. Cargo Space Tarpaulin. Five bows (four on early vehicles) fit into pockets in side coaming, and can be removed by raising bows straight up. A one-piece tarpaulin fits over bows, covering entire cargo space. An integral extension or additional tarpaulin at front end can be pulled forward and lashed over air intake grille aisle. Figures 30 and 31 illustrate progressive operations necessary to install and lash tarpaulin. Early vehicles are equipped with a folding surf board at rear end of cargo space (par. 34f.); however, later vehicles are equipped with rear end curtain lashed to rear bow.

d. Tarpaulin Stowage. When tarpaulins are not in use, stow as directed in paragraph 7. Do not stow wet tarpaulins for any length of time.

CAB COVER INSTALLED ON WINDSHIELD

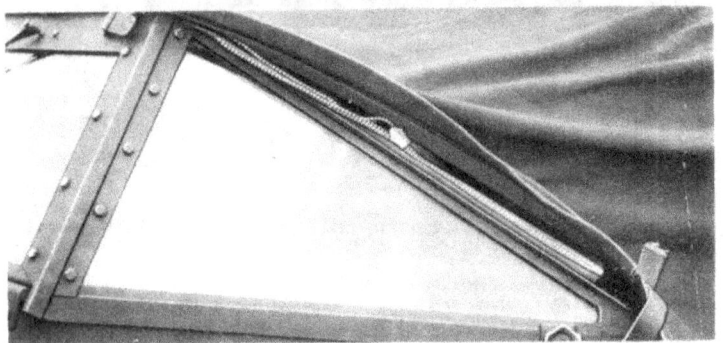
CAB COVER READY TO INSTALL AT WINDSHIELD WING

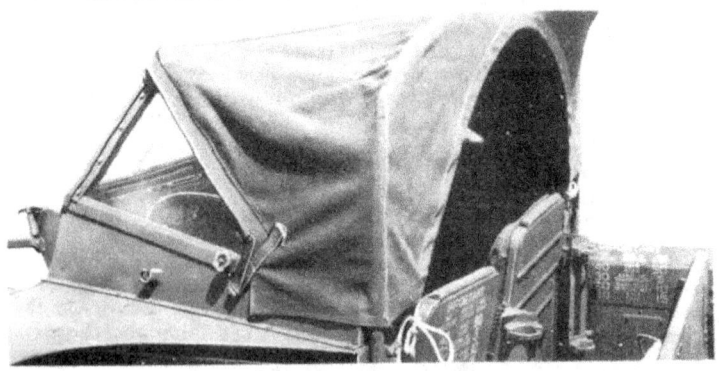
CAB COVER INSTALLED

RA PD 307340

Figure 29—Driver's Compartment Top Cover (After Chassis Serial No. 2005)

Operation of Auxiliary Equipment

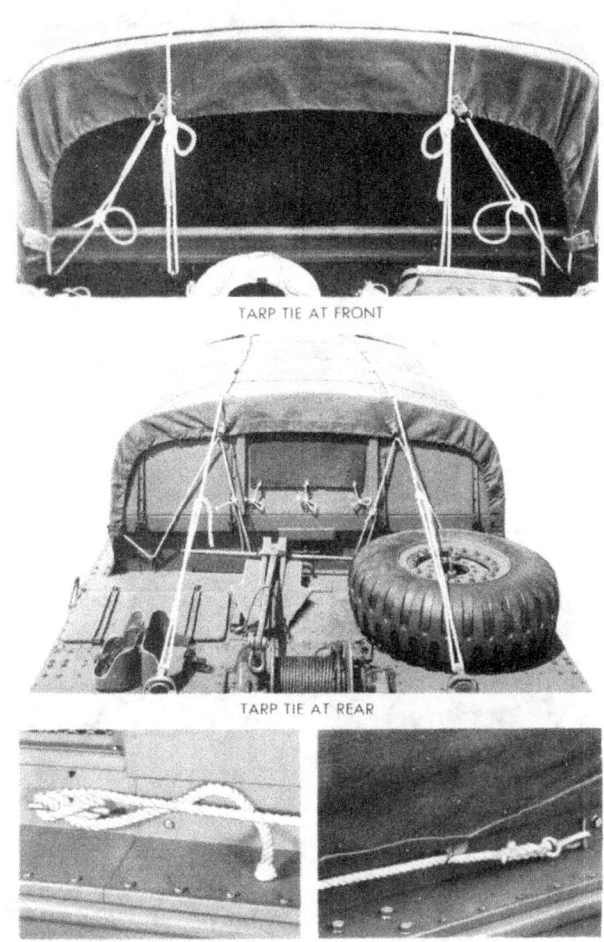

TARP TIE AT FRONT

TARP TIE AT REAR

LASHING AT SIDE FRONT   LASHING AT SIDE REAR

RA PD 307339

Figure 30—Cargo Compartment Tarpaulin Lashing

CARGO COMPARTMENT BOWS

CARGO TARP PREPARATORY TO MOUNTING

TARP MOUNTED—NOT LASHED

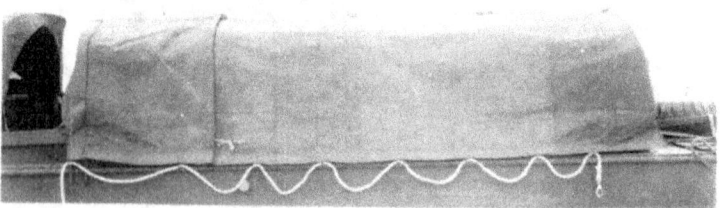
TARP LASHING AT SIDES

RA PD 307357

Figure 31—Cargo Compartment Tarpaulin Lashing

TM 9-802

Operation of Auxiliary Equipment

e. Lashing Instructions. There are several types of lashing, lifting and mooring eyes, and shackles placed about the vehicle (fig. 32). These must be used as directed on the lashing instruction sheet placed behind driver's compartment at left-hand side on later vehicles. Use the eyes and shackles only as directed in subparagraphs (1) through (7) below. Key letters refer to figure 32:

(1) MOORING EYES (A). These eyes must not be used for sideways pulls. Use for hold-down lashing but keep the lashings close to a vertical plane.

(2) LIFTING EYES (B). These eyes are suitable for lifting loaded vehicle with use of a sling. These eyes can be used, if necessary, for hold-down lashings providing lashings are kept close to a vertical plane of the sides.

(3) LIFTING EYES (C AND D). The two davit eyes can be used when lifting fully loaded vehicle; however, they must be only used for vertical loads. These eyes must not be used for lashings.

(4) LASHING EYES (E). These eyes are suitable for any type lashing.

(5) TOW CHAIN LINK (F). The pear-shaped link is used to supplement pintle hook (I), giving increased lashing space. This link is suitable for any type lashing.

(6) WINCH CHOCK (G). This chock must not be used for any type lashing. It is only to be used as a winch cable guide when winching at the front.

(7) TOW HOOK SHACKLES (H). These shackles are suitable for any type lashing.

f. Lashing Fenders. Fenders must be correctly installed, otherwise the vulnerable points on the vehicle will not be protected. Eight fenders are furnished with the vehicle. An additional one may be used if available. For purpose of explanation in the following steps, fenders shown on figure 32 are numbered from 1 through 8. Fender lashing lines must be passed back and forth through the fender eyes as many times as the length of line will permit. With the end of the line, make a "rolling hitch" (approximately 18 inches of line required). All fenders are identical with a lashing line at each end and one in the middle except "1" and "3" (fig. 32), which have lines only at one end.

(1) LASH NO. "1" AND "2" FENDERS TOGETHER (FIG. 32). Lay "1" and "2" fenders on the ground. Join "1" to "2" at the end which has no lashing. Join by overlapping the loops, and lash together so that there is a space of 10 inches between the fenders.

(2) INSTALL NO. "1" AND "2" FENDERS. Hold up the pair of fenders so that No. "2" is centered under its lashing eye. Lead the line at the end of No. "2" through the forward lifting eye, then back through the loop of the fender, lashing line with a "rolling hitch." Lead the line at end of No. "1" fender through the eye near bow shackle, pulling line as tight as possible before lashing. Lead the middle line of fender No. "2" through the eye at edge of deck just above the fender. Bring the line down over the outside of fender, through the

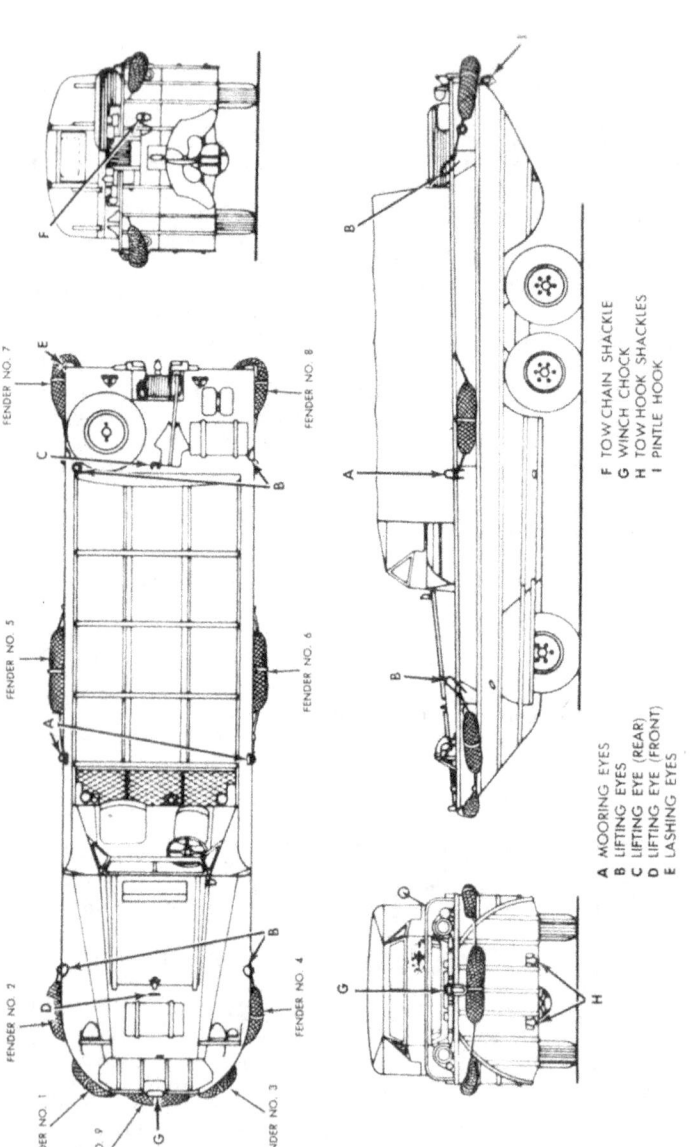

Figure 32—Lashing Instructions

Operation of Auxiliary Equipment

lower eye, then lash line, taking as many turns as possible. Lash the middle of fender No. 1 in the same manner.

(3) INSTALL NO. "3" AND "4" FENDERS (FIG. 32). Install No. "3" and "4" fenders in same manner as described in steps (1) and (2) above.

(4) INSTALL NO. "5" AND "6" FENDERS (FIG. 32). Hold up fender No. "5" so that it is centered between the upper and lower fender eyes. Lash the rear of fender to rear fender eye. Lash the front of fender to mooring eye. It is important that line be lashed around the forward end of mooring eye. Install fender No. "6" in the same manner.

(5) INSTALL NO. "7" AND NO. "8" FENDERS (FIG. 32). About three-fourths of each rear fender must be along the side of vehicle. Hold the fender up in that position, then lash the forward end to the lifting eye. Pound rear end of fender until it conforms to rear corner. Lash rear end of fender to fender eye in rear.

(6) INSTALL EXTRA FENDER (IF AVAILABLE) (FIG. 32). An additional fender in the center of bow (No. "9", fig. 32) can be used if available. The top center fender eyes for fenders No. "1" and "3" may be used to lash the ends. The middle lashing can be passed around in back of winch chock, then outside the fender and down to the fender eyes near the bow tow shackle.

34. WINDSHIELD, HATCHES, AND SURF BOARDS.

a. Windshield (Prior to Chassis Serial No. 2006). Windshield can be placed in two positions—tilted or completely lowered (fig. 205). Loosen adjusting arm clamp knob on each side to tilt windshield frame forward at the bottom. Tighten knobs to hold in position. Loosen clamp knob on each side at bottom of frame. Lower frame forward to rest on two deck rest stanchions. Tighten the knobs to hold firmly in lowered position.

b. Windshield (After Chassis Serial No. 2005). The windshield and wing assembly (fig. 207) can be lowered forward by loosening wing clamp knob on each wing. After windshield and wings are lowered forward, spring type hold-down catch on each side must be pulled up to hold assembly rigidly in place. Latches on wings are used to hold wings to main assembly.

c. Hatches. The hatch covers on the engine compartment and on front and rear hatches are held in closed position with lock bolts and wing nuts. Each hatch cover is equipped with seals which prevent entry of water when covers are locked down in place. The engine compartment cover can be held in open position when lock chain on cover is engaged with a lock notch on left side of windshield.

d. Windshield Surf Board (Prior to Chassis Serial No. 2006). This surf board (fig. 197), when in raised position, protects windshield from heavy surf. The board is latched in raised position against windshield bracket on both sides. In lowered position it is secured with latches on engine hatch cover.

e. Front Surf Board (All Vehicles). The front surf board (fig. 196) is hinged to bow and can be raised and lowered on two support braces. Upper ends of braces are hinged to surf board. Lower ends of braces are clamped to brackets on front deck with either spring load or screw type catches. This surf board must always be in raised position when entering the surf.

f. Rear Surf Board. The rear surf board and wing assembly (fig. 198) hinges at the rear of cargo compartment. In raised position, the wings are latched to the right- and left-hand cargo compartment coaming. In lowered position, the wings are folded inward, then entire assembly is folded to rear and supported by brackets on the rear deck. This surf board is replaced by rear end curtain on later vehicles.

35. AIR CIRCULATION.

a. Cooling and Heating Air Circulation System Intake. Cooling air enters the engine compartment through air intake grilles located in aisle to rear of driver's compartment. The air is drawn forward under the driver's compartment into engine compartment by action of engine fan.

(1) NOTE: *Many of the vehicles are equipped with an auxiliary air scoop located directly in front of windshield on front deck. It has been found through experience that this auxiliary air intake is not necessary providing other air circulation controls are properly positioned. These scoops should be permanently fastened down and sealed as described in paragraph 228f.*

b. Exhaust. The warm air is exhausted into front compartment, then through an air duct on each side of the engine compartment. The warm air is then exhausted through an air exhaust grille located at each side of driver's compartment above deck level. Warm air can be bypassed from exhaust ducts through driver's compartment, cargo compartment, or bilge pump system.

c. Air Circulation Control. Air circulation must be controlled properly to obtain efficient engine temperature as well as adequate heating in cold weather. Instructions as outlined in subparagraphs (1) through (4) below, as well as the proper maintenance of the engine cooling system must be accomplished.

(1) AIR INTAKE GRILLES. The grilles must be unobstructed and uncovered during moderate and hot weather. A special cover (with the vehicle) can be spread partially or completely over grille during cold weather. Whenever the cover is used, a frequent check of the engine temperature must be made, and cover removed if thermo gage reads over 180°F. If operating in rough water, intake grilles can be partially shielded with tarpaulin to prevent entry of water.

(2) AIR EXHAUST GRILLES. Adjustable closure doors are used at each exhaust grille. When doors are closed, hot air normally exhausted

Operation of Auxiliary Equipment

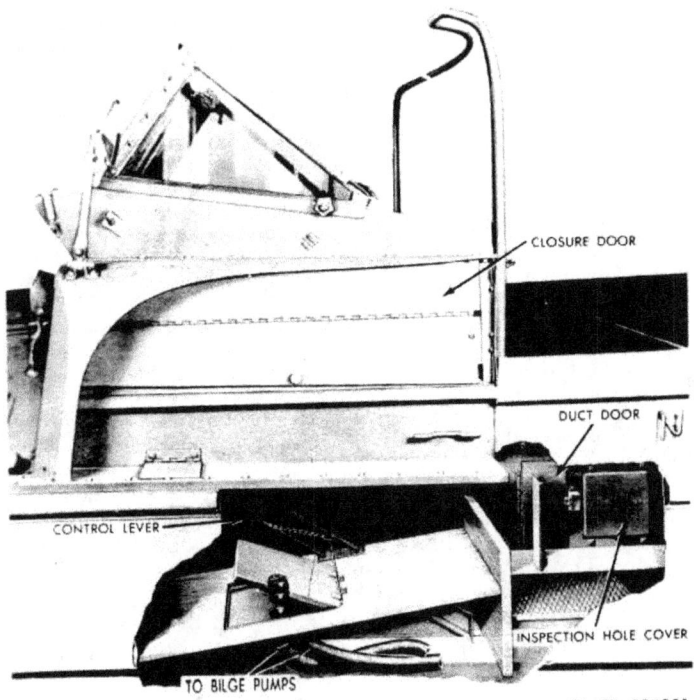

Figure 33—Air Exhaust Grille Cover and Circulation Duct Door

through the grilles is forced into the bilge pump heating system and recirculation ducts. The closure doors fold inward and are held in open position by holdup hooks. Pull down to close (fig. 33). In warm or hot weather, *these doors must be in open position*. During cold weather, the doors can partially or completely cover the grilles, depending upon severity of the weather. Whenever the doors are partially or completely closed, bilge heating and recirculating duct dampers should be opened [subpars. (3) and (4) below]. NOTE: *Closure doors should remain open under most conditions. These doors are not intended to prevent entry of water. There are a very few instances when complete covering of the exhaust grilles is necessary. Then constant check of engine operating temperature should be made.*

(3) BILGE PUMP HEATING SYSTEM. Hot air is directed to the front and rear bilge pumps through three flexible tubes connected between the bottom of air exhaust duct and the bilge pumps. Control lever at the left of the driver controls a deflector or damper. During cold weather, the lever must be raised to open position to direct hot air

to bilge pumps. The exhaust grilles [subpar. (2) above] should be partially or completely covered with the closure doors when deflecting hot air to the pumps.

(4) HEATER DUCTS. A heater duct extends between the rear panels of the right- and left-hand air exhaust ducts and the cargo compartment rear bulkhead. When the air exhaust grilles are covered, hot air is forced through these ducts and exhausted through outlets into the rear compartment. Hot air is then drawn forward under cargo compartment floor by action of engine fan. The ducts to the rear compartments can be opened or closed by removing inspection hole cover (fig. 33), located at each end of air intake grille aisle, then pulling door forward to open, or inward to close. The duct doors are held in open or closed positions with spring latches.

(5) HEATING DRIVER'S COMPARTMENT. The driver's compartment is heated by opening panel located in each right- and left-hand compartment wall at each end of toeboard (fig. 12). Maximum heat will be obtained when air exhaust closure doors are in closed position; however, driver's compartment will receive some heat when sliding panels are opened regardless of position of other air circulation controls.

d. Moderate and Hot Weather. During moderate and hot weather operation, set air circulation controls in following manner:

(1) AIR INTAKE [SUBPAR. c.(1) ABOVE]. Keep unobstructed and clear. If necessary to shield from heavy surf, watch temperature. If necessary, remove shield temporarily to bring temperature down.

(2) AIR EXHAUST [SUBPAR. c.(2) ABOVE]. Keep open.

(3) BILGE PUMP HEATING [SUBPAR. c.(3) ABOVE]. Keep lever in closed position.

(4) HEATER DUCTS [SUBPAR. c.(4) ABOVE]. Keep both duct doors closed.

(5) DRIVER'S COMPARTMENT [SUBPAR. c.(4) ABOVE]. Keep both panel doors closed.

e. Cold Weather. During moderate or severe cold weather, set air circulation controls in following manner:

(1) AIR INTAKE [SUBPAR. c.(1) ABOVE]. During moderately cold weather intake grille can be partially covered; however, watch temperature of engine, and remove cover if temperature becomes excessive. In extremely cold weather, grilles can be completely covered if necessary to obtain proper temperature.

(2) AIR EXHAUST [SUBPAR. c.(2) ABOVE]. Partially or completely close as necessary to maintain proper bilge pump or compartment heating.

(3) BILGE PUMP HEATING [SUBPAR. c.(4) ABOVE]. Place lever in open position.

(4) HEATER DUCTS [SUBPAR. c.(4) ABOVE]. Open both doors.

(5) DRIVER'S COMPARTMENT [SUBPAR. c.(5) ABOVE]. Open both panels as necessary to maintain crew comfort.

TM 9-802
36

Operation of Auxiliary Equipment

36. BILGE PUMP OPERATION.

a. General. The pumping of the bilge, while operating in the water, is accomplished by two bilge pumps located in the bilge. Pumps are operated by chain or belt from the water propeller drive shaft when water propeller is engaged. *Correct positioning of the forward pump manifold levers, maintenance of the piping and strainers of both pump systems, and the cleaning of the bilges are essential and important operations when the vehicle is operating in the water.* Reference should be made to paragraph 35**e.** for the proper heating of the bilge pumps, and to paragraphs 42 through 46 for proper operation and precautions during cold weather.

b. Forward Bilge Pump System. The forward bilge pump system serves the right and left rear, center, and front compartments.

(1) CONTROL RODS OR LEVERS. The pumping of the various compartments depends upon the position of the valve rods or levers located on driver's seat front riser (fig. 12).

(2) PUMPING COMPARTMENTS (PRIOR TO CHASSIS SERIAL NO. 4202). Four control rods are used on these vehicles to pump the various compartments. The fifth rod is used only to drain the manifold after water operation during cold weather. *Only one compartment at a time can be pumped; therefore all rods except the one controlling the compartment to be pumped must be pushed down.* All of the rods must not be closed at one time. One rod must be in open position (generally the center compartment rod) even when there is no leakage to be handled. Alternate opening rods every few minutes during operation in still water.

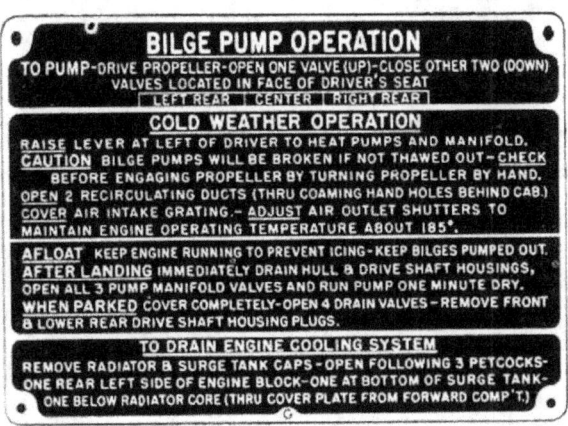

RA PD 333228

Figure 34—Bilge Pump Operation Instruction Plate (After Chassis Serial No. 4201)

(a) Rod Positions. From left to right—1st, left rear compartment; 2nd, main compartment; 3rd, manifold drain; 4th, front compartment; 5th, right rear compartment.

(3) PUMPING COMPARTMENTS (AFTER CHASSIS SERIAL NO. 4201). Three control levers are used to selectively pump the left rear, center, and right rear compartments (fig. 34). *Compartments must be pumped one at a time, with the other two levers in off position (lever down).* Alternately pump the compartments and *always keep one lever in pumping (up) position.* See instruction plate (fig. 34).

(4) STRAINERS. Each bilge pump is equipped with a strainer which must be kept clean (pars. 243 and 249). On vehicles prior to chassis serial No. 4202, the intake strainers to rear of driver's seat must also be cleaned as directed in paragraph 243**c**.

(5) OUTLET. The forward bilge pump outlet is located to the left of driver on the deck, just forward of the air intake grille. The driver can check action of pump by observing discharge.

c. Rear Bilge Pump System. This pump serves the center compartment and does not start pumping until water is approximately five inches deep in the bilge. The outlet is located to left of driver on deck just to the rear of the mooring eye. Refer to paragraphs 250 through 253 for maintenance operations.

d. Hand Bilge Pump Operation. The hand bilge pump, which is stowed on right front deck, can be used if necessary. Prime this pump by holding it overboard so that water will be forced up through bottom of unit.

e. Testing Bilge Pumps. Bilge pump systems may be checked on land by operating water propeller. Several buckets full of water should be placed in each compartment for this check. Run water propeller only long enough to make the test.

37. HULL DRAINAGE.

a. General. During water operation, the bilge pumps will keep the bilges clear of water except that which may become trapped in the propeller shaft housings or in the hull bottom below the pump strainers. On early vehicles, the only method by which the trapped water can be drained while on land is the removal of the hull bottom and propeller shaft housing drain plugs. On later vehicles, the hull is also equipped with four manually operated drain valves which drain four compartments of the hull.

b. Plugs. All vehicles are equipped with three bottom and three propeller shaft housing plugs. The hull bottom plugs are primarily access plugs, the removal of which permit the drainage of the transmission, transfer case, and engine crankcase. The three propeller shaft housing plugs provide access to universal joint lubrication fittings. Later vehicles are equipped with retainers mounted in drivers' compartment (fig. 35) where plugs can be stowed when not in use. The

TM 9-802

Operation of Auxiliary Equipment

HULL BOTTOM PLUG RETAINER

HOUSING PLUG RETAINER

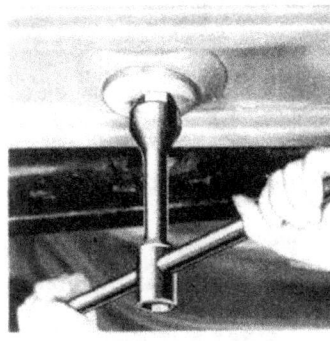
REMOVING BOTTOM PLUG

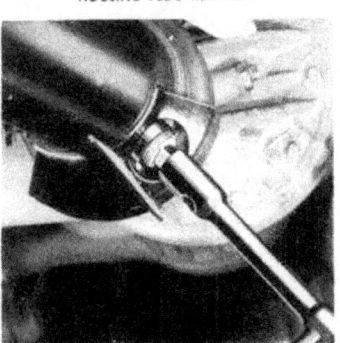
REMOVING HOUSING PLUG

RA PD 333240

Figure 35—Hull and Housing Plug Retainers and Method of Removal

retainers can be fabricated and mounted on early vehicles if desired. Housing and hull bottom spare plugs are stowed in engine compartment.

c. Draining Hull and Housings (Prior to Chassis Serial No. 2006). On these vehicles it is necessary to remove all hull bottom plugs and propeller shaft housing plugs to completely drain the hull and housings. Use the plug adapter tool issued with the vehicle, using the wheel nut wrench in manner illustrated in figure 35. After draining hull and housings, reinstall plugs *before entering water*, or place them in retainers (subpar. **b.** above) if remaining on land. Hull bottom plugs on these vehicles are *not* interchangeable. Identification can be made in following manner:

(1) ENGINE CRANKCASE HULL BOTTOM PLUG. The numeral "1" is stamped on forward ring and on plug.

(2) TRANSMISSION HULL BOTTOM PLUG. The numeral "2" is stamped on the center ring and on plug.

(3) TRANSFER CASE HULL BOTTOM PLUG. The numeral "3" is stamped on the rear ring and on plug.

Operating Instructions

d. Draining Hull and Housings (After Chassis Serial No. 2005).

(1) HULL DRAINAGE. Hull bottom plugs may be removed (fig. 35) to complete drainage on these vehicles; however, the four manually operated drain valves located in four compartments will generally drain the hull sufficiently. Operating handles for drain valves are located as follows:

(a) Left and Right Rear Compartments. Located in right and left rear corners of cargo compartment. Handles extend above floor boards. Left handle must point to rear in closed position. Right handle must point to front in closed position.

(b) Main or Center Compartment. Located directly behind the driver's seat. Handle extends above intake grille. Handle must point to left in closed position.

(c) Front Compartment. On vehicles between chassis serial No. 2005 and 4201, handle is located directly behind the generator in engine compartment, and is accessible after raising compartment hatch cover. On later vehicles, an extension handle extends through toeboard into left front corner of driver's compartment. Handle must point to left in closed position.

(d) IMPORTANT: *Four emergency drain valve plugs are provided in vehicle and stowed in a retainer on left-hand bulkhead of engine compartment (fig. 8). These plugs may be screwed into valve seat from underneath hull in the event drain valves become inoperative.*

(2) PROPELLER SHAFT HOUSING DRAINAGE (FIG. 35). On these vehicles, it is only necessary to remove the plug from the lower rear housings to drain the two rear housings. Drain tube extends from the upper rear housing to the lower. Remove the plug in front to drain front shaft housing.

38. A-FRAME.

a. General. An A-frame assembly is furnished with some vehicles (approximately one in five). This assembly is mounted at rear of vehicle and is used in connection with the winch for loading and unloading. Connecting brackets are mounted on all vehicles. Installation and removal instructions are covered in paragraphs 279 through 281.

b. Operation. Raising and lowering of cargo with A-frame is accomplished by operating winch (par. 29). The maximum capacity of A-frame is 5,000 pounds. Ballast of 1,000 pounds on forward d.ck is required with maximum load on land. Use of A-frame on land and method of stabilizing vehicle when afloat are explained in FM 55-150.

39. FIRE EXTINGUISHERS.

a. General. Two carbon tetrachloride or carbon dioxide fire extinguishers are furnished with each vehicle (fig. 12). Extinguishers are mounted immediately to rear of driver's compartment at right- and left-hand side of air intake grille aisle (fig. 36).

TM 9-802
39

Operation of Auxiliary Equipment

b. Carbon Tetrachloride Extinguisher (fig. 36).

(1) OPERATION. Remove extinguisher from bracket. Turn handle to left to unlock, then pump handle in and out. Direct spray at hottest part of flame—preferably against a hot, solid surface. Put out one section of fire completely before attempting to extinguish another. *Action of carbon tetrachloride on flame produces a toxic gas; avoid exposure to fumes. Refill extinguisher immediately after use.*

(2) REFILLING. Check quantity of extinguisher liquid by locking handle, and then shaking. Extinguisher must be completely full at all times. Remove plug and gasket from top of extinguisher. Using funnel, fill extinguisher completely with fire extinguisher liquid (K002-01-00440), then install gasket and plug. Do not use water or liquids other than fire extinguisher liquid. Container and funnel must be clean and free from moisture, since extinguisher liquid and water combine into a liquid highly corrosive to interior mechanism of extinguisher.

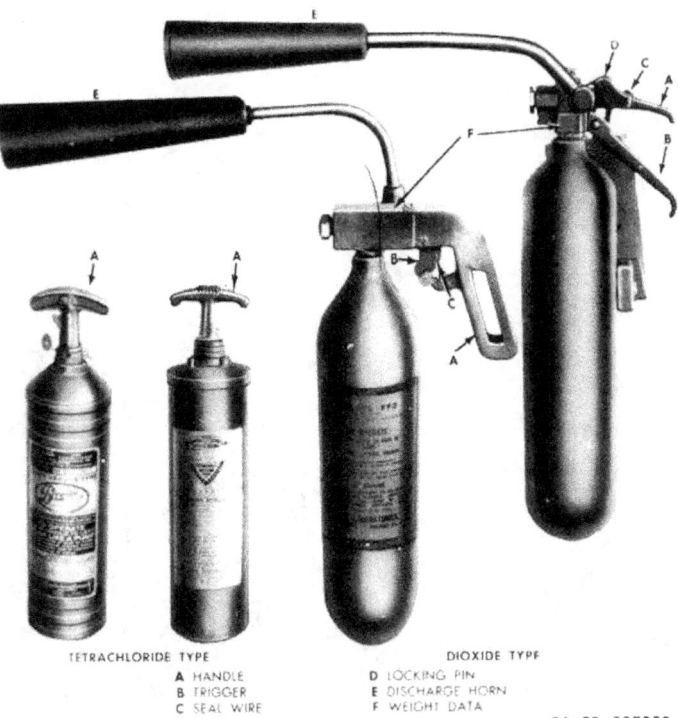

TETRACHLORIDE TYPE
A HANDLE
B TRIGGER
C SEAL WIRE

DIOXIDE TYPE
D LOCKING PIN
E DISCHARGE HORN
F WEIGHT DATA

RA PD 337232

Figure 36—Fire Extinguisher Types

TM 9-802
39-40

Operating Instructions

c. Carbon Dioxide Extinguisher (fig. 36).

(1) OPERATION. Yank extinguisher from bracket, then swing discharge horn up into position. Pull locking pin out of trigger, (carbon dioxide type only) then squeeze trigger. Direct spray at base of flame, or at nearest part of flame. Discharge spray in short bursts, moving to new flame area as soon as first section is extinguished. *Do not touch carbon dioxide "snow"—intense cold of ejected material will cause painful injury.*

(2) RECHARGING. Necessity for recharging can be determined only by weighing extinguisher. Follow instructions on extinguisher label or attached tag for location of weight stamp, and whether or not weight includes discharge horn. Exchange extinguisher for recharged extinguisher, at higher echelon, if weight is more than 4 ounces under fully charged weight. If weight exceeds fully charged weight, exchange extinguisher, since excessive internal pressure will rupture safety seal, discharging contents and rendering extinguisher useless until recharged.

40. LITTER STOPS.

a. General. Four litter stop assemblies are included in late vehicles. The litter stop assemblies, two on each side of vehicle are mounted on hull coaming. The stops prevent litter sliding off sides of vehicle (fig. 37).

RA PD 337144

Figure 37—Litter Stops Installed

Operation Under Unusual Conditions

Figure 38—Litter Stop Stowage

b. Installation. The stops are interchangeable and can be used on either side of the vehicle. Each assembly is equipped with three braces which extend over the coaming, and are held securely by a wing nut and clamp (fig. 37). Install one side only, then place litters in position. After litters are in position, install other side. Remove stops after use.

c. Stowage (fig. 38). Lift up the left front cargo compartment floor board. Insert litter stops through opening, and move stops forward until rear braces are hooked to rear bilge pump discharge tube. The front ends of the stops must rest on hull bottom.

41. COMPASS.

a. General. Four types of magnetic compasses, Hull, Pioneer, Sherrill AEG or AEG-1, and Sherrill M6 are used in vehicles which are equipped with such instruments. Detailed instructions covering initial adjustment, compensations, and daily check are included with each instrument. Installation and removal instructions are covered in paragraphs 282 through 284. Use of the compass is covered in FM 55-150.

Section IX
Operation Under Unusual Conditions

42. GENERAL.

a. This section includes instructions on the operation, preparation, and maintenance of vehicle under cold weather and extreme hot weather

Operating Instructions

conditions. The instructions augment the normal maintenance, operation, and lubrication sections in this manual.

43. SPECIAL AMPHIBIAN COLD WEATHER PRECAUTIONS.

a. In addition to the maintenance instructions outlined in paragraphs 44, 45, and 46, special cold weather precautions must be taken when operating an amphibian during freezing temperatures.

b. Bilge Pump System. Both bilge pumps are driven from the water propeller drive shaft. If vehicle stands in freezing temperatures, any accumulation of water or moisture in the pump system will quickly freeze. If the pumps are not thawed prior to operating the water propeller, considerable dam to pumps will occur.

(1) TESTING PUMPS PRIOR TO OPERATION. Place all shifting levers (transmission, power take-off, and transfer cases) into "OUT" or "NEUTRAL" positions. Lift up a cargo space floor board. Turn the water propeller shaft several times *by hand—not with hand crank lever.* If the shaft cannot be turned easily by hand, the pumps are frozen and must be thawed out [step (2) below] *before operating water propeller.*

(2) THAWING BILGE PUMP SYSTEM. Start engine and warm up thoroughly (par. 20). Set air circulation and heating controls to direct the hot air into the cargo compartment and around bilge pumps (refer to par. 35). Test pump action [step (1) above] after several minutes of engine operation. *Do not engage water propeller* until certain that pumps are thawed. Make certain that all bilge pump intake and outlet screens are free and clean. Check action of forward bilge pump manifold valve rods or levers (par. 36*b.*).

c. After-operation Precautions. After water operation, immediately pump bilges as dry as possible with the bilge pumps. Disengage water propeller and permit engine to operate. Quickly perform following operations:

(1) Set air controls to permit hot air to circulate in bilges (par. 35).

(2) Drain hull by removing all hull bottom plugs, and opening all drain valve handles (par. 37). Reinstall all plugs. Wipe bilge dry with sponge or rags.

(3) On early vehicles, lift forward bilge pump manifold drain cock rod up (par. 36*b.*) to drain the valves completely. Check condition of pump system bleeder, intake, and outlet screens, and clean if necessary. On early vehicles, clean the intake strainers at rear of driver's seat. Do not shut engine off until assured that all portions of the bilge are free from ice.

(4) Drain moisture from air tank by opening drain cock.

(5) Rig tarpaulins over cargo space and air intake grilles to prevent entry of water, ice, or snow.

Operation Under Unusual Conditions

d. Before-operation Precautions. *Do not attempt to move vehicle by its own power or by towing until following operators are accomplished:*

(1) Test bilge pump for ice formation (subpar. **b.** above).

(2) Make certain that all ice formations in bilge and propeller shaft housings have thawed. Use heat circulation (par. 35) to thaw out the bilge. Remove all hull botom and housing plugs, and examine for ice. Propeller shafts must be free of ice before vehicle is moved. Inspect the rear propeller shaft housing inter drain (if so equipped) for frozen condition.

(3) Make certain that all drain valves operate freely.

e. During-operation Precautions. Position hot air circulation controls to maintain heat in bilge, and to obtain proper engine temperature (par. 35). When operating on land, open hull drain valves. Keep hull bottom and housing plugs in place. Protect the cargo compartment and air intake grille with tarpaulins.

44. COLD WEATHER FUEL AND LUBRICANTS.

a. Fuels for Low Temperatures.

(1) TYPES. Winter grade of gasoline is designed to reduce cold weather starting difficulties; therefore, the winter grade of motor fuels procured under U.S. Army Specifications 2-103, grade C, latest revision, will be used in vehicles. Within the continental limits of the United States, the winter grade of gasoline meeting U.S. Army Specifications 2-114, grade C, will be used, if available.

(2) STORAGE AND HANDLING. Due to condensation of moisture from the air, water will accumulate in tanks, drums, and containers. At low temperatures, this water will form ice crystals that will clog fuel lines and carbureter jets unless the following precautions are taken:

(a) Be sure that all containers are thoroughly clean and free from rust before storing fuel in them.

(b) If possible, after filling or moving a container, allow the fuel to settle 24 hours before filling vehicle tank from it.

(c) Keep all closures of containers tight to prevent snow, ice, dirt, and other foreign matter from entering.

(d) Wipe all snow or ice from dispensing equipment and from around fuel tank filler cap before removing cap to refuel vehicle. After filling tank, replace cap securely.

(e) Add one quart of denatured alcohol, grade 3, to the fuel tank at start of winter season, and $1/2$ pint at each refueling. This will reduce the hazard of ice formation in the fuel.

(f) Strain the fuel through any type of strainer that will prevent the passage of water. CAUTION: *Gasoline flowing over a surface generates static electricity that will result in a spark unless means are provided to ground the electricity. A metallic contact between the container and the tank must be made to insure an effective ground.*

Operating Instructions

(g) Keep tank full, if possible. The more fuel there is in the tank, the smaller will be the volume of air from which moisture can be condensed.

b. Lubricants. Reference must be made to Lubrication Order No. 9-802 (pars. 52 and 53) for type of lubricant specified for cold weather operations. Following subparagraphs augment the Lubrication Order.

(1) TRANSMISSION, TRANSFER CASES, DIFFERENTIALS, AND WINCH WORM HOUSINGS.

(a) SAE 80 universal gear lubricant where prescribed on Lubrication Order No. 9-802 is suitable for use at temperatures as low as −20°F; however, if consistent temperature below 0°F is anticipated, drain the gear cases while warm and refill with grade 75 universal gear lubricant which is suitable for operation at all temperatures below +32°F without dilution.

(b) After accomplishing operations itemized in paragraph 43, warm up engine thoroughly, place transmission in first gear, and drive vehicle about 100 yards, being careful not to stall the engine. This will heat gears to the point where normal operation can be expected.

(2) OTHER LUBRICATION POINTS.

(a) If vehicle has been operated at least 1,000 miles using No. 0 general purpose grease for lubrication, no special precautions are necessary for the rear spring seat bearings. If quantities of No. 1 general purpose grease are in these bearings, it will be necessary to disassemble and wash in dry-cleaning solvent, dry, and then relubricate with No. 0 general purpose grease for satisfactory operation.

(b) Wheel bearings, and grease cups using No. 2 general purpose grease, shall be lubricated with the same lubricant at all times. If repacking must be performed at sufficiently low temperature that thorough hand-packing cannot be accomplished, No. 0 general purpose grease may be used until temperature returns to above 0°F.

(c) All other places where No. 0 general purpose grease is specified above 0°F will be lubricated with the same grease below 0°F.

(d) When extreme low temperatures are encountered and No. 0 general purpose grease is not satisfactory where specified above, GREASE, O.D. No. 00 Ordnance Department Specification AXS-1169 may be used.

(e) *Hydrovac Cylinders.* Lubricate with shock absorber fluid, light, at all temperatures. Do not use shock absorber fluid in hydraulic brake systems.

(f) Drain steering gear housing if possible, or use suction gun to remove as much lubricant as possible. Refill with grade 75 universal gear lubricant.

(g) For oilcan points where engine oil is prescribed for above 0°F, use special preservative lubricating oil.

c. Keeping Crankcase Oil Fluid.

(1) Several methods for keeping crankcase oil sufficiently fluid for proper lubrication are listed below. Preference should be given to the different methods in the order listed, according to the facilities available.

TM 9-802

Operation Under Unusual Conditions

(a) Keep the vehicle in a heated enclosure when it is not being operated.

(b) When the engine is stopped, drain the crankcase oil while it is still hot and store in a warm place until the vehicle is to be operated again. If warm storage is not available, heat the oil before reinstalling. NOTE: *Do not get the oil too hot; heat only to the point where the bare hand can be inserted without burning. Tag the vehicle in a conspicious place in the driver's compartment to warn personnel that the crankcase is empty.*

(c) Dilute the crankcase oil. Crankcase oils may be diluted with gasoline or Diesel fuel according to their availability, with preference given to gasoline. One of the two following procedures will be used to provide the engine with properly diluted engine oil for cold starting:

(2) USING GASOLINE AS A DILUENT.

(a) Fill engine crankcase to the "FULL" mark with the grade of engine oil prescribed for use at temperatures from +32°F to 0°F. Add 1½ quarts of gasoline for each 5 quarts of crankcase oil capacity. EXAMPLE: *Crankcase with capacity of 10 quarts will require 3 quarts of gasoline as an oil diluent.*

(b) Run the engine 5 to 10 minutes to mix the lubricant and diluent thoroughly.

(c) Stop the engine and note that the level of the diluted oil is above the normal "FULL" mark on the indicator. This level should be marked on indicator for future reference.

(d) The presence of a large percentage of light diluent will increase oil consumption and, for that reason, the oil level should be checked frequently. Use the grade of engine oil prescribed for use between +32°F and 0°F to maintain the oil level to "FULL" mark on indicator during operation.

(e) If vehicle is operated 4 hours or more at operating temperature, redilution will be necessary if it is anticipated that the vehicle will be left standing unprotected for 5 hours or more. This can be accomplished by adding engine oil prescribed for use between +32°F and 0°F to the "FULL" mark; then adding gasoline to the dilution mark on indicator described in step (c) above.

(3) USING DIESEL FUEL OIL AS A DILUENT.

(a) If Diesel fuel is used as diluent, drain the crankcase while the engine is still warm and refill, using engine oil prescribed for temperatures between +32°F to 0°F diluted with grade X Diesel fuel oil in the proportion of 1½ quarts of Diesel fuel to 5 quarts of engine oil. The presence of a large percentage of diluent will increase oil consumption and therefore, the oil level will be checked frequently during operation and maintained to "FULL" mark on indicator with engine oil diluted with Diesel fuel as described above. CAUTION: *When Diesel fuel is used as a diluent, the quantity of diluent necessary for starting is added when the crankcase is refilled and maintained by the addition of diluted make up oil. Further additions of diluent prior to overnight shut-down are unnecessary.*

Operating Instructions

d. If the vehicle is to be kept outdoors, and if the crankcase cannot be drained or diluted, shelter the engine compartment with a tarpaulin. About 3 hours before engine is to be started, outside heat must be applied to crankcase.

45. PROTECTION OF COOLING SYSTEM.

a. Cooling systems must be protected with antifreeze compound for operation below +32°F. The following instructions apply to use of new antifreeze compound. For use of reclaimed antifreeze solutions, refer to Ordnance Field Service Technical Bulletin 700-20 dated 13 October 1942.

b. Before adding antifreeze compound, it is necessary that the cooling system be clean (par. 117**c.**) and completely free from rust. If the cooling system has been cleaned recently, it may be necessary only to drain, refill with clean water, and again drain. Otherwise, the system must be cleaned as described in paragraph 117.

c. Heaters, water-cooled tire pumps, and other units in the cooling system must be cleaned in addition to the radiator and engine water jacket. When the system is drained, follow procedures described in paragraph 117**b.** for complete drainage.

d. All hoses must be inspected and replaced if deteriorated. Hose clamps, plugs, and petcocks are to be inspected and tightened if necessary. Radiator leaks must be repaired before adding antifreeze compound. Exhaust gas or air leakage into the cooling system must be corrected. If there are indications of a coolant leakage at the cylinder head, it must be corrected by tightening the cylinder head bolts (par. 88). Replace the cylinder head gasket if necessary.

e. Inspect thermostat to see that it closes completely. Look for evidence of sticking in open or closed position. Operation of the thermostat can be checked by heating in a pail of water to make certain that it will open in hot water. If thermostat does not open or close completely (par. 120**c.**), does not function freely, or is badly rusted, it must be replaced.

f. When the cooling system is clean and tight, fill the system with water to about one-third capacity; then add antifreeze compound, using the proportion of antifreeze compound to the cooling system capacity indicated below. The system must be protected to at least 10°F below the lowest expected temperature to be experienced during the winter season.

ANTIFREEZE TABLE

Lowest Expected Temperature	Pints of Antifreeze Compound Per Gallon of Cooling System Capacity
+10°F	2
0°F	2½
−10°F	3
−20°F	3½
−30°F	4
−40°F	4½
−50°F	5

Operation Under Unusual Conditions

g. After adding antifreeze compound, fill with water to the prescribed level; then start and warm up the engine to normal operating temperature.

h. The engine must then be stopped and the solution checked with a hydrometer, adding antifreeze compound if required.

i. In service, the coolant must be inspected weekly for strength and color. Rusty solution should be drained, the cooling system thoroughly cleaned, and new solution of the required strength added.

j. Cautions.

(1) Antifreeze compound (51-C-1554-15) is the only antifreeze authorized for Ordnance materiel.

(2) It is essential that antifreeze solutions be kept clean. Use only containers and water that are free from dirt, rust, and oil.

(3) Use an accurate hydrometer. To test a hydrometer, use 1 part antifreeze compound to 2 parts water. This solution should produce a hydrometer reading of 0°F.

46. MAINTENANCE OF VEHICLES DURING COLD WEATHER.

a. General. In preparing a vehicle for operation at subzero temperatures, special attention to details of electrical and mechanical maintenance will reduce difficulties encountered. Special attention to these details should be continued in scheduled maintenance throughout the period of subzero operation.

b. Electrical Systems.

(1) GENERATOR AND STARTER. Check brushes for wear and springs for tension and see that brushes and commutator are clean. Oil or grease on the brushes or commutator will affect operation of the generator and will prevent the electrical contact required for the large surges of current in the starter required for good starting. Wash the throw-out mechanism and gear in dry-cleaning solvent to remove grease and dirt. Heavy grease or dirt may keep the gears from being meshed or cause them to remain in mesh after the engine starts running. The latter will ruin the starter and necessitate repairs. Clean and wash the splined shaft and oil lightly with special preservative lubricating oil.

(2) WIRING. Check, clean, and tighten all connections, especially the battery terminals. Care should be taken that no short circuits are present.

(3) COIL. Clean and see that connections are tight.

(4) DISTRIBUTOR. Clean thoroughly and clean or replace points (par. 99). Check the points frequently. Slightly pitted points may prevent the engine from starting.

(5) SPARK PLUGS. Clean and adjust or replace if necessary. If it is

Operating Instructions

difficult to make the engine fire, reduce the gap to 0.005 inch less than that recommended for normal use (par. 101**b**.). This will make ignition effective at the reduced voltage likely to prevail.

(6) IGNITION TIMING. Check carefully (par 97).

(7) BATTERIES.

(a) The efficiency of batteries decreases sharply with decreasing temperatures, and becomes practically nil at –40°F. When the battery has been chilled to a temperature below –30°F, it should preferably be heated before attempting an engine start unless a warm slave battery is available. See that the battery is always fully charged, with the hydrometer reading between 1.275 and 1.300. A fully charged battery will not freeze at temperatures likely to be encountered even in arctic climates, but a fully discharged battery will freeze and rupture at –5°F.

(b) Do not add water to a battery when it has been exposed to subzero temperatures unless the battery is to be charged immediately. If water is added and the battery is not put on charge, the layer of water will stay at the top and freeze before it has a chance to mix with the acid.

(c) Following table lists freezing temperature of electrolyte at various specific gravities:

Specific Gravity at 60°F	Freezing Temperature Degrees F	Specific Gravity at 60°F	Freezing Temperature Degrees F
1.100	+18	1.220	–31
1.120	+14	1.240	–51
1.140	+ 8	1.260	–75
1.160	+ 2	1.280	–92
1.180	– 6	1.300	–95
1.200	–17		

c. Other Chassis Points.

(1) OIL PRESSURE GAGE. Oil pressure gage depends on oil pressure transmitted through a small tube. The gage may fail to register pressure due to congealed oil in the tube. Where this condition is experienced, the gage may be prepared for subzero operation. Disconnect the gage tube at the gage and at the opposite end while the oil is hot and see that the tube is clear. Plug the lower end of the tube with special lubricating grease, then fill the gage tube with denatured alcohol, grade 3, and reconnect.

(2) CHOKE. A full choke may be necessary to secure the rich air-fuel mixture required for cold weather starting. Check the butterfly valve to see that it will close all the way, and otherwise function properly.

(3) WATER PUMPS. Prior to the advent of cold weather, inspect water pumps and service if required.

(4) FUEL SYSTEM. Drain fuel pump, and drain and clean filters weekly, or more often according to experience, to remove water and dirt.

(5) CHASSIS.

(a) Freezing has a tendency to cause brakes to stick or bind when vehicles are parked at subzero temperatures. A blow torch may be used

Operation Under Unusual Conditions

to warm up these parts if they bind when attempting to move the vehicle. Parking the vehicle with the brake released will eliminate most of the binding. Precaution must be taken, under these circumstances, to block the wheels or otherwise prevent movement of the vehicle.

(b) Inspect the vehicle frequently. Shock resistance of metals, or resistance against breaking, is greatly reduced at extremely low temperatures. Operation of vehicles on hard, frozen ground causes strain and jolting which will result in screws breaking or nuts jarring loose.

(c) Disconnect oil-lubricated speedometer cables at the drive end when operating vehicles at temperatures consistently below −20°F. These cables often fail to work properly at these temperatures, and sometimes break due to the excessive drag caused by the high viscosity of the oil with which they are lubricated. Grease-lubricated cables should operate satisfactorily at all temperatures providing they are coated with No. 0 general purpose grease and there is no excess grease in the housing. When extreme low temperatures are encountered and No. 0 general purpose grease is not satisfactory, grease, O.D., No. 00 Ordnance Department Tentative Specifications AXS-1169, may be used.

47. HOT WEATHER OPERATION.

a. General. Operation of these vehicles during high temperatures requires regular maintenance, at prescribed intervals, of cooling system units, filtering devices, air cleaners, electrical units, and air circulation ducts.

b. Cooling System Maintenance.

(1) COOLING LIQUID. Formation of scale and rust in cooling system occurs more often during operation in extremely high temperatures; therefore, rust preventives should always be added to the cooling liquids (par. 117*a.*). Use only clean water. Avoid the use of water that contains alkali or other substances which may cause scale and rust formation.

(2) CLEANING COOLING SYSTEM Cooling system should be thoroughly cleaned and flushed at frequent intervals when operating in extremely high temperatures (par. 117*c.*).

(3) FAN BELT AND WATER PUMP. Fan belt should be inspected at regular intervals and adjusted if necessary (par. 118*a.*). Water pump must be kept in good operating condition.

(4) THERMOSTAT. Check operation of thermostat (par. 120*c.*). Thermostat must open at calibrated temperature to prevent overheating of cooling liquid.

(5) HOSE CONNECTIONS. Check connections frequently for leaks.

c. Oil Filters. Oil filter elements must be checked and replaced at more frequent intervals if vehicle is operating in hot, sandy regions. Crankcase vent air cleaner must be serviced at frequent intervals.

d. Air Cleaners. If vehicle is operating extensively in sandy or dusty regions, carbureter air cleaner should be cleaned daily. If vehicle operates in dust storm areas, cleaner should be cleaned immediately after such storms occur.

Operating Instructions

e. Battery.

(1) WATER LEVEL. In torrid zones, cell water level should be checked daily and replenished if necessary with pure distilled water. If this is not available, any water fit to drink may be used. However, continuous use of water with high mineral content will eventually cause damage to battery and should be avoided.

(2) SPECIFIC GRAVITY. Batteries operating in torrid climates should have a weaker electrolyte than for temperate climates. Instead of 1.300 gravity, the electrolyte should be adjusted to around 1.230 for a fully charged battery. This will prolong the life of the negative plates and separators. Under this condition, battery should be recharged at about 1.160. Where freezing conditions do not prevail, there is no danger with gravities from 1.230 to 1.075

(3) SELF-DISCHARGE. A battery will "self-discharge" at a greater rate at high temperatures if standing for long periods. This must be taken into consideration when operating in torrid zones. If necessary to park for several days, battery should be removed and stored in a cool place.

f. Air Circulation. The efficiency of the air circulation system depends on the proper setting of the controls (par. 35), the regular cleaning of the air ducts and passages, and the maintenance of the seals around radiator core and between engine compartment and front compartment.

(1) AIR CIRCULATION CONTROLS. Position air circulation controls for hot weather operation as described in paragraph 35**d**.

(2) AIR CIRCULATION PASSAGES. Do not cover air intake grilles or stow any material in hold under grilles. Keep all passages and ducts thoroughly clean so that hot air can quickly exhaust. Inspect radiator core frequently, and *keep clear of paper, leaves, etc.* A small restriction of radiator core will increase temperature. *Maintain the seals around core and between engine compartment and front compartment to prevent recirculation of hot air in the engine compartment.*

Section X

Demolition To Prevent Enemy Use

48. DESTRUCTION OF MATERIEL IN EVENT OF IMMINENT CAPTURE.

a. Tactical situations may arise when, owing to limitations of time or transportation, it will become impossible to evacuate all equipment. In such situations it is imperative that all materiel which cannot be evacuated is destroyed to prevent its capture and use by the enemy.

b. The destruction of materiel, subject to capture or abandonment in the combat zone, will be undertaken only when, in the judgment of the military commander concerned, such action is necessary.

Demolition To Prevent Enemy Use

c. If possible, all machine guns mounted in vehicles prior to their destruction will be detached and salvaged.

d. All echelons will be trained in effective destruction of materiel issued to them.

49. METHODS OF DESTRUCTION.

a. General. Destruction will be as complete as available time, equipment, and personnel will permit. If thorough destruction of all parts cannot be completed, the most important features of the materiel will be destroyed. Parts essential to the operation or use of the materiel and those which cannot be easily duplicated will be destroyed or removed. The same essential parts will be destroyed on all like units to prevent construction by the enemy of one complete unit from several damaged ones by "cannibalization."

b. Choice of Methods. The destruction methods outlined below are arranged in order of effectiveness. Destruction should be by the first method suggested if possible. If this cannot be used, one of the other methods will be followed in the priority shown. Whichever method is used, the sequence outlined will be followed to assure uniformity of destruction.

c. Command Decisions. Certain of the methods outlined require special tools and materials, such as TNT and incendiary grenades, which may not be items of normal issue. The issue of such special tools and material, the vehicles for which issued, and the conditions under which destruction will take place are command decisions in each case according to the tactical situation.

d. Destruction of Vehicles.

(1) BY SINKING. Where deep water is available close to shore, the simplest method of destroying the vehicle is to run it off-shore and sink it, keeping a boat or vehicle to get the crews back to shore. In no case, however, will a vehicle be destroyed by sinking in water less than 50 feet deep because of the ease of salvage. The sinking may be done in one of two ways:

(a) The four drain valves on vehicles equipped with them (after chassis serial No. 2005) should be opened at sea. The vehicle will sink in five to ten minutes after the engine has stopped running.

(b) Vehicles not having drain valves (prior to chassis serial No. 2006) should be run out into the water with one of the large hull plugs removed. This may be done only if the vehicle does not have to go too far to reach the necessary deep water. Otherwise, one of the methods outlined below must be used.

(2) BY TNT CHARGE. Portable fire extinguishers are first removed and emptied and the fuel tank punctured. A two-pound charge of TNT is placed on top of the clutch housing and, if time permits, two pounds placed as low as possible on the left side of the engine. Tetryl nonelectric caps, with at least five feet of safety fuse, are inserted in each charge. The fuses should be ignited from outside the vehicle while per-

sonnel should take cover quickly, since gasoline fumes may be exploded prematurely by burning fuses. Elapsed time will be one to two minutes if charges are prepared beforehand and carried in vehicle.

(3) BY GUNFIRE. Portable fire extinguishers are first removed and emptied, the fuel tank punctured and, if time is available, all doors and hatches opened. The vehicle is then fired on, using tank, antitank or other artillery, or antitank rockets or grenades, and aiming at the engine. If a good fire is started, the vehicle may be considered destroyed. Elapsed time: About five minutes per vehicle.

(4) BY SMASHING UNITS. Portable fire extinguishers are removed and emptied and the fuel tanks punctured. All vital parts (such as distributor, carbureter, radiator, engine block, air and oil cleaners, generator, control levers, crankcase, and transmission) should be smashed with a heavy ax, pick, or sledge. Spare gasoline, oil or other inflammable material is poured over entire unit and ignited.

e. Destruction of Tires.

(1) GENERAL. Rubber is such a critical item that, whenever materiel is subject to capture or abandonment, an attempt to destroy pneumatic tires, including the spare, must always be made even if time will not permit destruction of any other part of the vehicle. With adequate planning and training, however, the destruction of tires may be accomplished in conjunction with destruction of the vehicle without increasing the time necessary.

(2) BY INCENDIARY GRENADES. An M14 incendiary grenade is ignited under each tire. When this method is combined with the destruction of vehicles by TNT, the incendiary fires must be well started before the TNT is detonated.

(3) BY DAMAGING AND BURNING. Tires may be damaged with an ax, pick, or by heavy machine-gun fire, deflating them first, if possible. Spare gasoline may be poured on tires, dousing each one, and ignited.

PART THREE
MAINTENANCE INSTRUCTIONS

Section XI
General

50. SCOPE.

a. Part three contains information for the guidance of the personnel of the using organizations responsible for the maintenance (first and second echelon) of this equipment. It contains information for the performance of the scheduled lubrication and preventive maintenance of the major systems and units and their functions in relation to other components of the equipment.

Section XII
Special Organizational Tools and Equipment

51. PURPOSE.

a. This special tool list is for information only, and is not to be used as a basis for requisition. Tools listed (except oiler) are illustrated in figure 39.

Name	Federal Stock No.	Mfr. Tool No.
ADAPTER, puller, steering wheel	41-A-18-251	TEC-50-35
OILER, engineers' 1 qt, 22-in. spout, shock absorber refill	13-0-710	EAG-400
PULLER, pitman arm	41-P-2951-35	KM-J-2288
PULLER, propeller	41-P-2951-48	KM-J-2326
PULLER, spring shackle pin	41-P-2951-85	KM-J-2310
WRENCH, socket, cylinder head bolt	41-W-2964-700	KM-J-187-1
WRENCHES, governor, in sets, consisting of:	41-W-1496-695	
WRENCH, set or cap screw, hex, ⅛-in.	41-W-2410-10	KS-A-25264
WRENCH, governor adjusting	41-W-1496-725	KS-A-24283

Maintenance Instructions

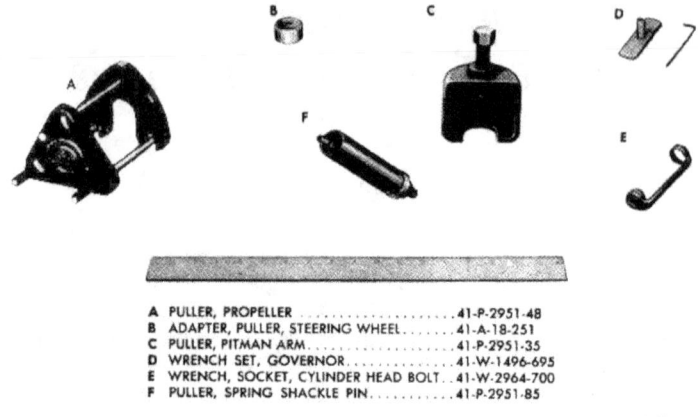

A PULLER, PROPELLER 41-P-2951-48
B ADAPTER, PULLER, STEERING WHEEL 41-A-18-251
C PULLER, PITMAN ARM 41-P-2951-35
D WRENCH SET, GOVERNOR 41-W-1496-695
E WRENCH, SOCKET, CYLINDER HEAD BOLT .. 41-W-2964-700
F PULLER, SPRING SHACKLE PIN 41-P-2951-85

RA PD 337233

Figure 39—Organizational Special Tools

Section XIII
Lubrication

52. LUBRICATION ORDER.

a. Reproductions of War Department Lubrication Order 9-802 (figs. 40 and 41) prescribe first and second echelon lubrication maintenance.

b. A lubrication order is placed on or is issued with each item of materiel and is to remain with it at all times. In the event the materiel is received without a copy, the using arm shall immediately requisition a replacement in conformance with instructions in FM 21-6.

c. Instructions on the lubrication order are binding on all echelons of maintenance and there shall be no deviations.

d. Hourly, daily, weekly, monthly and 6-months intervals, when prescribed, in each case, indicate minimum service to be performed. Daily intervals marked with asterisk on the lubrication order will be serviced daily after water operation and, when possible, every 8 hours during water operation.

e. Lubricants are prescribed in the "Key" in accordance with three temperature ranges, above $+32°F$, $+32°F$ to $0°F$, and below $0°F$. The time to change grades of lubricants is determined by maintaining a close check on operation of the materiel during the approach to changeover periods. Sluggish starting is an indication that lubricants are thickening and is a signal to change to grades prescribed for the next lower temperature range. Ordinarily it will be necessary to change grades of lubricants *only when air temperatures are consistently in the next higher or lower range.*

Lubrication

53. DETAILED LUBRICATION INSTRUCTIONS.

a. Lubrication Equipment. Each piece of materiel is supplied with lubrication equipment adequate to maintain the materiel. Be sure to clean this equipment both before and after use. Operate lubricating guns carefully and in such manner as to insure a proper distribution of the lubricant.

b. Points of Application.

(1) Lubrication fittings, grease cups, oilers and oil holes are readily located by reference to the lubrication order. Wipe these devices and the surrounding surfaces clean before applying lubricant.

(2) Where relief valves are provided, apply new lubricant until the old lubricant is forced from the vents.

c. Cleaning. Use dry-cleaning solvent, or Diesel fuel oil to clean or wash all parts. Use of gasoline for this purpose is prohibited. After washing, dry all parts thoroughly before applying lubricant.

d. Lubrication Notes on Individual Units and Parts. The following instructions supplement the notes on the lubrication order.

(1) WHEEL BEARINGS. Remove bearing cone assemblies from hub. Wash bearings, cones, spindle and inside of hub and dry thoroughly. Do not use compressed air. Inspect bearing cup and cones and replace if damaged. Coat the spindle and inside of hub and hub cap with No. 2, general purpose grease to a maximum thickness of $1/16$ inch only to retard rust. Lubricate bearings with No. 2, general purpose grease with a packer, or by hand, kneading lubricant into all spaces in the bearing. Use extreme care to protect the bearings from dirt, and immediately reassemble and replace wheel. Do not fill hub or hub cap. The lubricant in the bearing is sufficient to provide lubrication until the next service period. Any excess might result in leakage into the drum. Adjust bearings in accordance with instructions in paragraph 214*b*. and 215*b*. When truck has been operated in water, and will be out of service one week or more, remove bearings and clean and pack regardless of period since the service was last performed.

(2) UNIVERSAL JOINTS AND SLIP JOINTS. Use general purpose grease No. 1 for temperatures above $+32°F$ or general purpose grease No. 0 below $+32°F$. Apply grease to universal joints on propeller shafts until it overflows at the relief valves, and apply to the slip joints until lubricant is forced from the vents at the universal joint end of the splines. Universal and slip joints on winch drive shaft are not provided with vents. Lubricate until grease appears around journals and splines. The forward rear axle and front of propeller shaft pillow block universal joints are encased in large watertight tubes and are covered by bellows. Remove plugs to lubricate joints. Replace plugs after lubricating.

(3) HYDROVAC CYLINDER. Every 6 months, remove pipe plugs and add $1/2$ ounce of light shock absorber fluid, through each opening. Replace plugs. To insure proper spread of lubricant in hydrovac cylinder, start engine and make three or four severe brake applications.

WAR DEPARTMENT LUBRICATION ORDER LO 9-802

20 JANUARY 1945 (Supersedes WDLO No. 505, 3 June 1944)

TRUCK, AMPHIBIAN, 2½ TON, 6X6 (GMC "DUKW 353")

References: ORD 7 SNL G-501; TM 9-802

Clean fittings before lubricating. Lubricate after washing. Clean parts with SOLVENT, dry cleaning or OIL, fuel, Diesel. Dry before lubricating. Lubricate dotted arrow points on both sides. Opposite points are shown by short arrows.

Hourly intervals apply to actual time in water and/or land operation and will be used when occurring before equivalent intervals.

Serviced From Under Hull

Lubricant • Interval

C, fig. 43	Front Axle Differential	GO	W
	Fill and Level Check level		
C, fig. 43	Front Axle Differential Drain	M	
	Drain and refill. Cap. 6½ qt. (See Gear Case Note)		
C, fig. 44	Spring Shackle	CG	D*
F, fig. 49	Shock Absorber	SAL	M
D, fig. 49	Universal Joint and Steering Knuckle Brgs. (See Note)	CG	W
A and B, fig. 49	Front Wheel Bearings	WB	M
	Remove, clean and repack		
B, fig. 44	Tire Inflating Mechanism	CG	D*
	Sparingly (Some models) Set air pressure at 40 lbs. before lubricating		
E, fig. 44	Tie Rod	CG	D*
F, fig. 44	Drag Link	CG	D*
B, fig. 42	Crankcase Drain Drain and refill Cap. 11½ qt. (See Note)		M
A, fig. 46	Universal Joint	CG	D*
D, fig. 44	Spring Bolt	CG	M
B, fig. 43	Transmission Drain Drain and refill Cap. 5½ qt. (See Gear Case Note)	CG	6M
	Speedometer Cable Remove care and coat lightly with No. 0 (Reached from inside hull)		

Serviced From Inside Hull

Interval • Lubricant

M	OE	Tire Pump Crankcase Breather (See Note)	E, fig. 49
M	OE	Tire Pump Air Cleaner (Some models) (See Note)	
W	OE	Tire Pump Governor Plungers (Some models)	
M		Tire Pump Crankcase Drain Drain and refill. Cap. 1 pt. (See Note)	
D	OE	Tire Pump Crankcase Fill and Level Check level	
6M	WB	Tire Pump Drive Shaft Universal Joint (Some models) Remove, clean and repack	
W		Differential Vent (Reached from inside hull) (See Note)	C, fig. 43

Serviced Through Engine Compartment Hatch

M		Oil Filter Drain (See Note)	C, fig. 42
M	OE	Generator (Some models)	A, fig. 50
D	OE	Crankcase Fill	A, fig. 42
D	OE	Crankcase Ventilator Air Cleaner Check level (See Note)	E, fig. 42
D		Crankcase Level Check level	A, fig. 42
D	OE	Carburetor Air Cleaner Check level (See Note)	D, fig. 42
M	WB	Distributor Shaft Turn cap down 1 full turn. refill as required	F, fig. 42
M	OE	Starter 6 to 8 drops	B, fig. 50
W	PM	Starter Drive and Linkage Manipulate engaging lever while oiling	

RA PD 337234

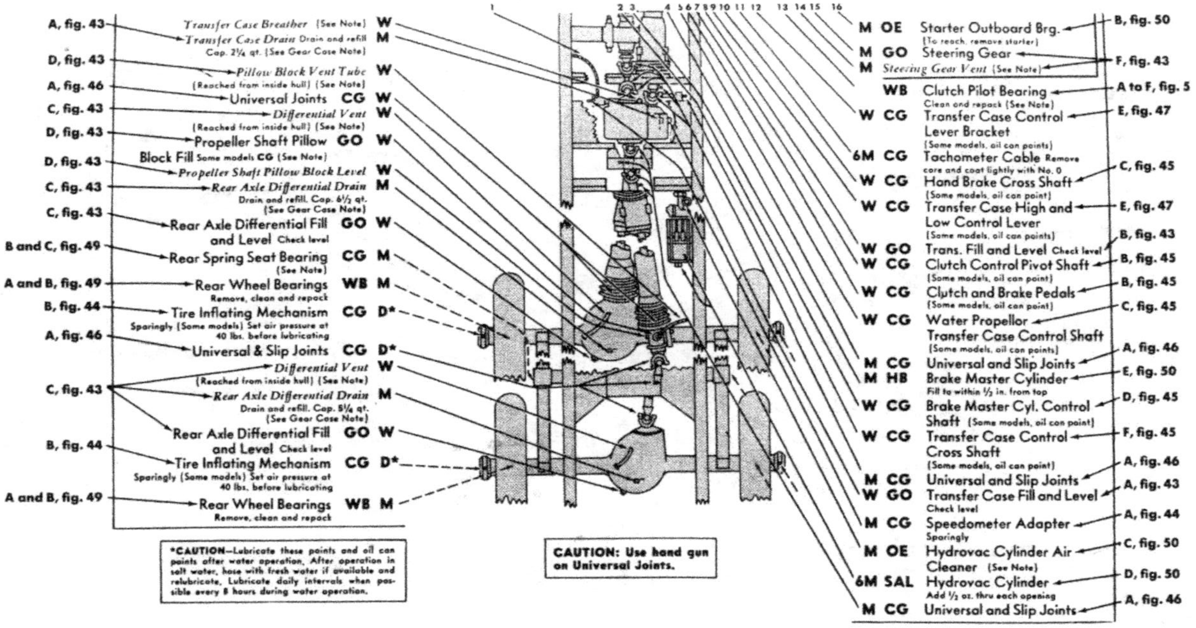

A, fig. 43 Transfer Case Breather (See Note) W
Transfer Case Drain Drain and refill Cap. 2¾ qt. (See Gear Case Note) M
D, fig. 43 Pillow Block Vent Tube (Reached from inside hull) (See Note) W
A, fig. 46 Universal Joints CG W
C, fig. 43 Differential Vent (Reached from inside hull) (See Note) W
D, fig. 43 Propeller Shaft Pillow Block Fill Some models CG (See Note) GO W
D, fig. 43 Propeller Shaft Pillow Block Level W
C, fig. 43 Rear Axle Differential Drain Drain and refill. Cap. 6½ qt. (See Gear Case Note) M
C, fig. 43 Rear Axle Differential Fill and Level Check level GO W
B and C, fig. 49 Rear Spring Seat Bearing (See Note) CG M
A and B, fig. 49 Rear Wheel Bearings Remove, clean and repack WB M
B, fig. 44 Tire Inflating Mechanism Sparingly (Some models) Set air pressure at 40 lbs. before lubricating CG D*
A, fig. 46 Universal & Slip Joints CG D*
C, fig. 43 Differential Vent (Reached from inside hull) (See Note) W
Rear Axle Differential Drain Drain and refill. Cap. 5¼ qt. (See Gear Case Note) M
Rear Axle Differential Fill and Level Check level GO W
B, fig. 44 Tire Inflating Mechanism Sparingly (Some models) Set air pressure at 40 lbs. before lubricating CG D*
A and B, fig. 49 Rear Wheel Bearings Remove, clean and repack WB M
*CAUTION—Lubricate these points and oil can points after water operation. After operation in salt water, hose with fresh water if available and relubricate. Lubricate daily intervals when possible every 8 hours during water operation.
CAUTION: Use hand gun on Universal Joints.
1 2 3 4 5 6 7 8 9 10 11 12 13 14 15 16
M OE Starter Outboard Brg. (To reach, remove starter) B, fig. 50
M GO Steering Gear F, fig. 43
M Steering Gear Vent (See Note)
WB Clutch Pilot Bearing Clean and repack (See Note) A to F, fig. 5
W CG Transfer Case Control Lever Bracket (Some models, oil can points) E, fig. 47
6M CG Tachometer Cable Remove core and coat lightly with No. 0
W CG Hand Brake Cross Shaft (Some models, oil can point) C, fig. 45
W CG Transfer Case High and Low Control Lever (Some models, oil can points) E, fig. 47
W GO Trans. Fill and Level Check level B, fig. 43
W CG Clutch Control Pivot Shaft (Some models, oil can point) B, fig. 45
W CG Clutch and Brake Pedals (Some models, oil can point) B, fig. 45
W CG Water Propellor C, fig. 45
Transfer Case Control Shaft (Some models, oil can points)
M CG Universal and Slip Joints A, fig. 46
M HB Brake Master Cylinder Fill to within ½ in. from top E, fig. 50
W CG Brake Master Cyl. Control Shaft (Some models, oil can point) D, fig. 45
W CG Transfer Case Control Cross Shaft (Some models, oil can point) F, fig. 45
M CG Universal and Slip Joints A, fig. 46
W GO Transfer Case Fill and Level Check level A, fig. 43
M CG Speedometer Adapter Sparingly A, fig. 44
M OE Hydrovac Cylinder Air Cleaner (See Note) C, fig. 50
6M SAL Hydrovac Cylinder Add ½ oz. thru each opening D, fig. 50
M CG Universal and Slip Joints A, fig. 46

RA PD 337234

Figure 40—Lubrication Order 9-802 (Chassis)

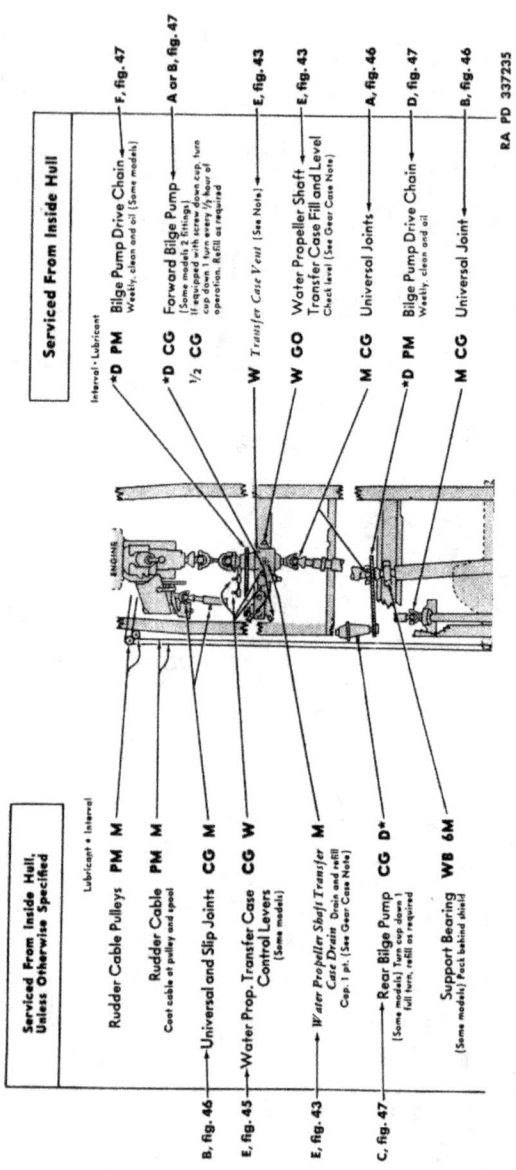

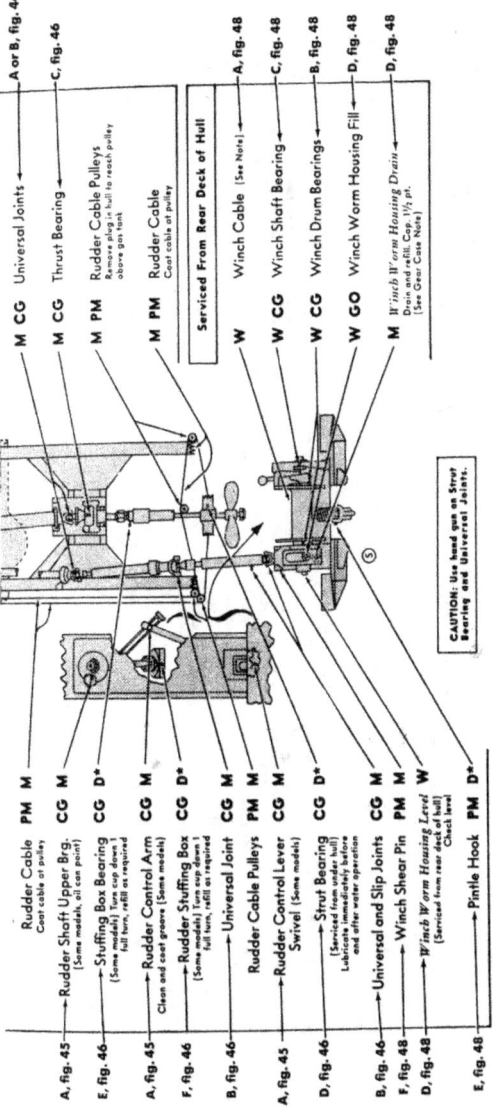

Figure 41—Lubrication Order 9-802 (Water Propeller)

NOTES

AIR CLEANERS—(Oil bath type) Fill oil reservoir to bead level. Every month or 192 hours disassemble, wash all parts and refill. (Mesh type) Every month or 192 hours wash filter element and recoil. Drain excess oil and replace filter. Used crankcase oil or OE (SAE 10) above 0°F., or OE (SAE 10) will be used in both types.

BREATHERS AND VENTS—Weekly, inspect axle and pillow block vent tubes, make certain they are not clogged. Remove breathers from steering gear and main and water propeller transfer cases, clean and re-install.

CRANKCASE—Drain only when engine is hot. After refilling, run engine a few minutes; recheck level.

CRANKCASE BELOW 0°F.—If heated storage, winterization kit or heater are available or oil can be drained after operation, use OE (SAE 10) undiluted. Otherwise, dilute as follows: Add OE (SAE 10) to FULL mark. Then add 3½ qt. gasoline. Run engine 5 to 10 minutes. Mark new higher level on dipstick with file. CAUTION: Check level every 4 hours of operation, add OE (SAE 10) to regular FULL mark as required. After operation, check level. If level is below regular FULL mark, add OE (SAE 10) to regular FULL mark. Then add gasoline to new higher level mark. If level is at or above regular FULL mark, add gasoline to new higher level mark. Run engine 5 to 10 minutes to mix oil and diluent.

knuckle support, use only plug in steering knuckle support. Monthly or every 192 hours, remove, wash all parts, dry, reassemble and repack with CG. Do not fill above plug level. Daily, after water operation, dry exterior surfaces of ball joints and coat with PM.

OIL FILTER—Every 6 months, while crankcase is being drained, remove element, clean inside of case and install new element.

PROPELLER SHAFT PILLOW BLOCK—On models provided with fitting and drain tube at bottom, remove bushing with fitting and drain water. Replace and apply CG until it is visible at level plug in side of housing. On models not provided with drain, apply GO through top filler hole until level with side plug hole. Replace level and filler plugs.

DISTRIBUTOR—Monthly, when distributor is cleaned, wipe breaker cam lightly with CG and lubricate breaker arm pivot and wick under rotor with 1 or 2 drops of OE.

CLUTCH PILOT BEARING—When engine or clutch is removed, clean and repack bearing with WB. After cleaning, fill cavity in crankshaft behind pilot bearing, fill release bearing inside recess, and coat shaft spline and release fork socket and stud with WB.

oil drain valves with PM. One drain valve located under left front of engine; one each at rear corners of cargo compartment under floor plate and one at rear of driver's seat.

WINCH CABLE—Coat outer coils with COMPOUND, rust preventive, thin film. Monthly, unwind cable, clean and recoat.

STEERING COLUMN UPPER BEARING—When steering gear is disassembled, clean and repack steering column upper bearing with WB. Also coat steering column horn contacts lightly, to prevent rusting.

OIL CAN POINTS—Daily, after water operation, lubricate Throttle Control Rod Ends, sliding surface of Winch Jaw Clutch, Tire Inflation Joints and Clevises, Tire Inflation Control Valve Plungers and Linkage, Rudder Control Rod Ends (some models), Pintle Hook, Transfer Case Control Lever Bushings and Rods, Hand and Foot Brake Control Linkage (some models), Tire Pump Shift Control (some models), Clutch Control Linkage (some models), Yokes, Clevises, Hinges, Latches, etc., with PM.

DO NOT LUBRICATE—Fan, Water Pump, Generator (some models), Clutch Release Bearing, Winch Drive Shaft Support Bearings, Shock Absorber Links, Chassis Springs.

RA PD 337235 B

GEAR CASES—Fill gear cases to plug levels before operation and after draining. Drain only after operation. Clean magnetic drain plugs in transfer case and water propeller transfer case before replacing. If water is present in front or rear differential gear cases at weekly check, drain and refill.

FRONT WHEEL UNIVERSAL JOINT AND STEERING KNUCKLE BEARINGS—Remove inspection plug. Remove lubricating fitting underneath joint, drain any water present and replace fitting. Apply lubricant through fitting until lubricant is visible at plug opening. Where two plugs are provided, one on top of joint, the other at front of steering

REAR SPRING SEAT BEARINGS—Apply CG through fittings until lubricant appears around seal at inside of seat. Every 6 months, remove spring seat, clean and repack with CG.

TIRE PUMP—Drain only after operation. Refill to level of filler plug hole. Use OE (SAE 10) undiluted below 0°F. Drain after operation, when engine will not be run for 4 hours or more. Tire pump on some models located on left of transmission below driver's seat. Monthly on these models, clean and lubricate drive chain with PM.

HULL DRAIN PLUGS AND DRAIN VALVES—After water operation remove and coat hull plug threads with CG and

Copy of this Lubrication Order will remain with the equipment at all times; instructions contained therein are mandatory and supersede all conflicting lubrication instructions dated prior to 20 January 1945.
[A.G. 300.8 (20 January 1945)].

By Order of the Secretary of War:
G. C. MARSHALL,
Chief of Staff

Official:
J. A. ULIO,
Major General,
The Adjutant General.

KEY

LUBRICANTS	LOWEST ANTICIPATED AIR TEMPERATURE		
	above + 32°F.	+ 32°F. to 0°F.	below 0°F.
OE—OIL, engine			
Crankcase	SAE 30	SAE 10	See Note
Other Points	SAE 30	SAE 10	PS
GO—LUBRICANT, gear, universal	Grade 90	Grade 90	Grade 75
CG—GREASE, general purpose	No. 1	No. 0	No. 0
PM—OIL, lubricating, preservative, medium	PM	PM	PS
WB—GREASE, general purpose, No. 2			
PS—OIL, lubricating, preservative, special			
HB—FLUID, hydraulic brake			
SAL—FLUID, shock-absorber, light			

INTERVALS
½—½ Hour
D—Daily or 8 Hours
W—Weekly or 48 Hours
M—Monthly or 192 Hours
6M—6 Months

LO 9-802

Requisition additional Lubrication Orders in conformance with instructions and list in FM 21-6.

Notes for Figures 40 and 41

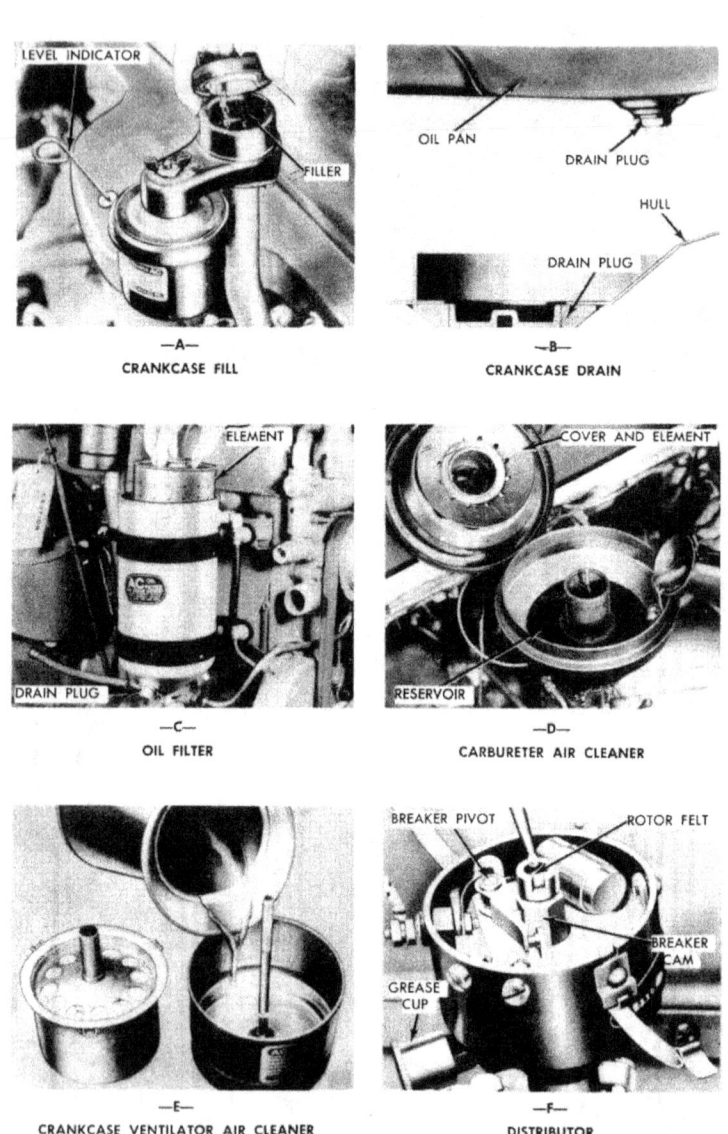

Figure 42—Localized Lubrication Views

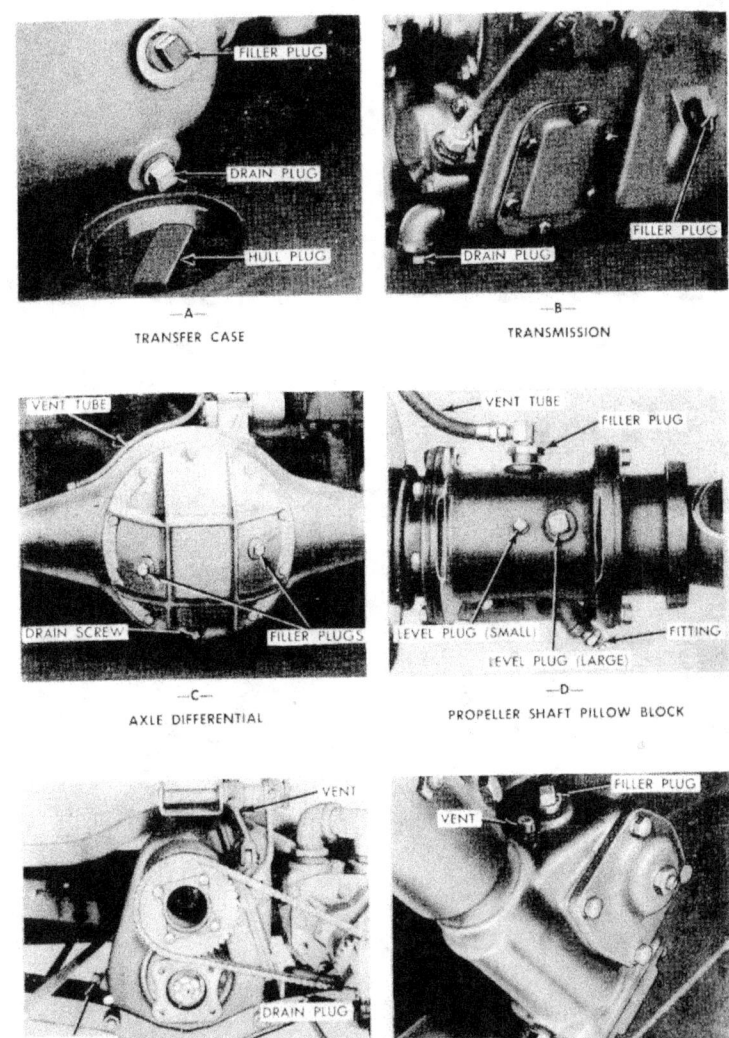

Figure 43—Localized Lubrication Views

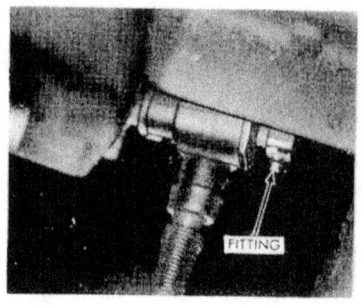
—A—
SPEEDOMETER ADAPTER

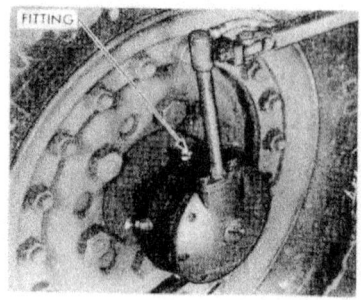
—B—
TIRE INFLATING MECHANISM

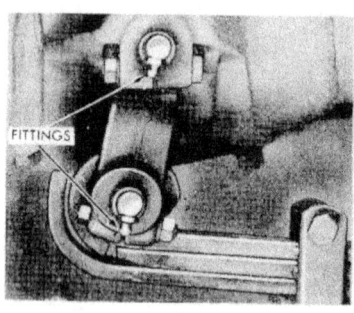
—C—
SPRING SHACKLES

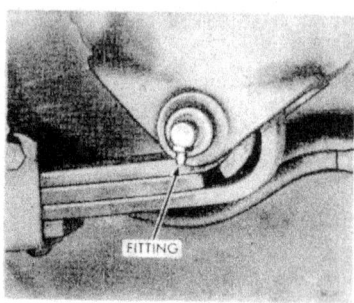
—D—
SPRING BOLTS

—E—
TIE ROD ENDS

—F—
DRAG LINK

RA PD 337238

Figure 44—Localized Lubrication Views

—A—
RUDDER LINKAGE

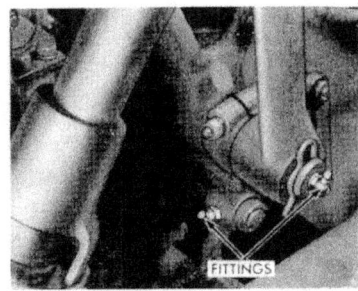
—B—
CLUTCH AND BRAKE PEDAL LINKAGE

—C—
HAND BRAKE AND TRANSFER CASE
CONTROL CROSS SHAFTS

—D—
BRAKE MASTER CYLINDER CONTROL SHAFT

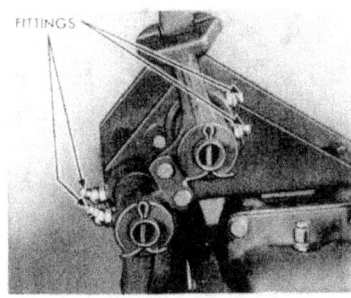
—E—
WATER PROPELLER TRANSFER CASE
CONTROL LEVERS

—F—
TRANSFER CASE CONTROL CROSS SHAFT

RA PD 337239

Figure 45—Localized Lubrication Views

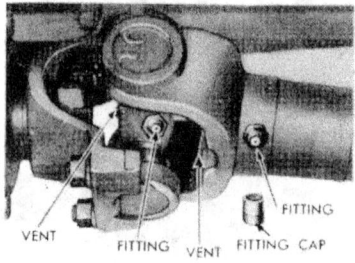

—A—
AXLE AND WATER PROPELLER SHAFT
UNIVERSAL AND SLIP JOINTS

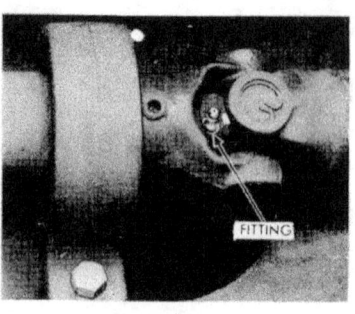

—B—
WINCH PROPELLER SHAFT UNIVERSAL
AND SLIP JOINTS

—C—
MIDSHIP SHAFT BEARING

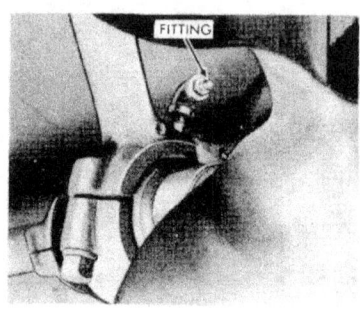

—D—
STRUT BEARING

—E—
STUFFING BOX BEARING

—F—
RUDDER STUFFING BOX

RA PD 337240

Figure 46—Localized Lubrication Views

—A—
FORWARD BILGE PUMP (EARLY MODELS)

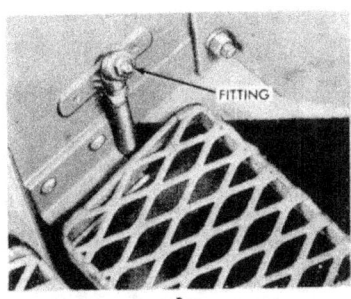
—B—
FORWARD BILGE PUMP (LATE MODELS)

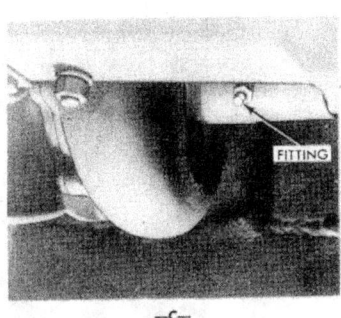
—C—
REAR BILGE PUMP

—D—
REAR BILGE PUMP DRIVE CHAIN

—E—
TRANSFER CASE HIGH AND LOW SPEED LEVER AND BRACKET

—F—
FORWARD BILGE PUMP DRIVE CHAIN (LATE MODELS)

RA PD 337241

Figure 47—Localized Lubrication Views

—A—
WINCH CABLE

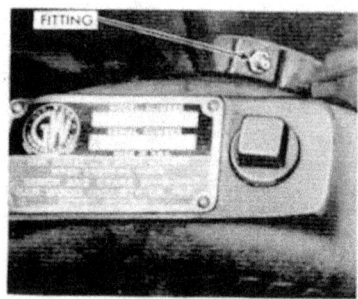
—B—
WINCH DRUM BEARINGS

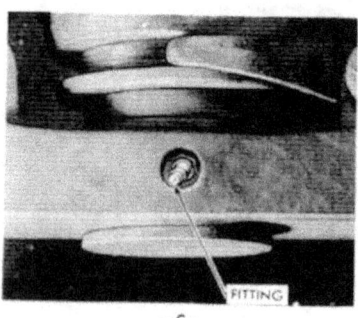
—C—
WINCH SHAFT BEARING

—D—
WINCH WORM HOUSING

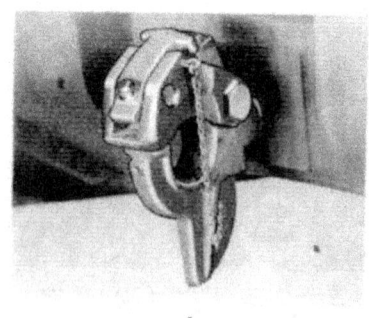
—E—
PINTLE HOOK

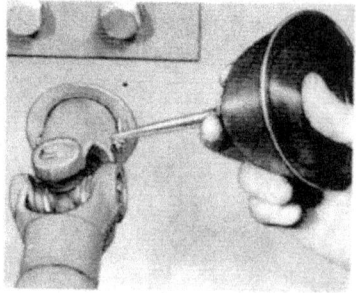
—F—
WINCH SHEAR PIN

RA PD 337242

Figure 48—Localized Lubrication Views

—A—
WHEEL HUBS

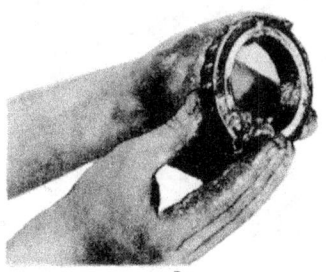
—B—
BEARINGS

—C—
REAR SPRING SEAT BEARINGS

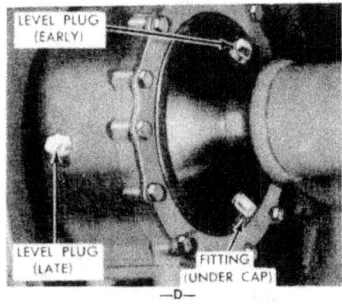
—D—
UNIVERSAL JOINT AND STEERING
KNUCKLE BEARINGS

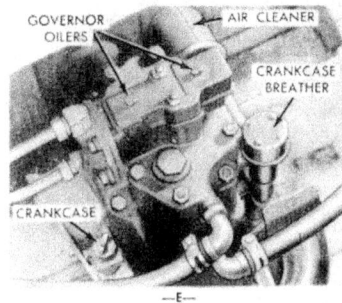
—E—
TIRE PUMP

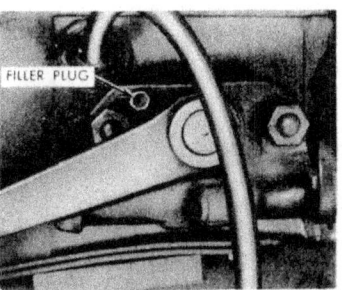
—F—
SHOCK ABSORBERS

RA PD 337243

Figure 49—Localized Lubrication Views

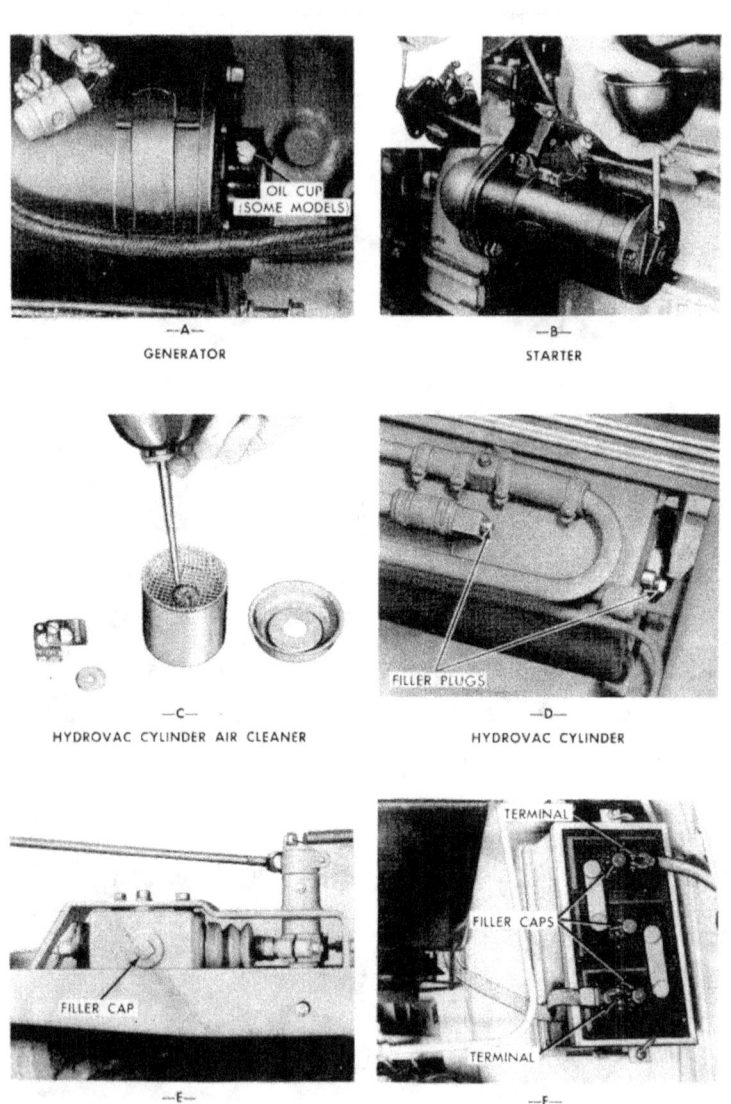

Figure 50—Localized Lubrication Views

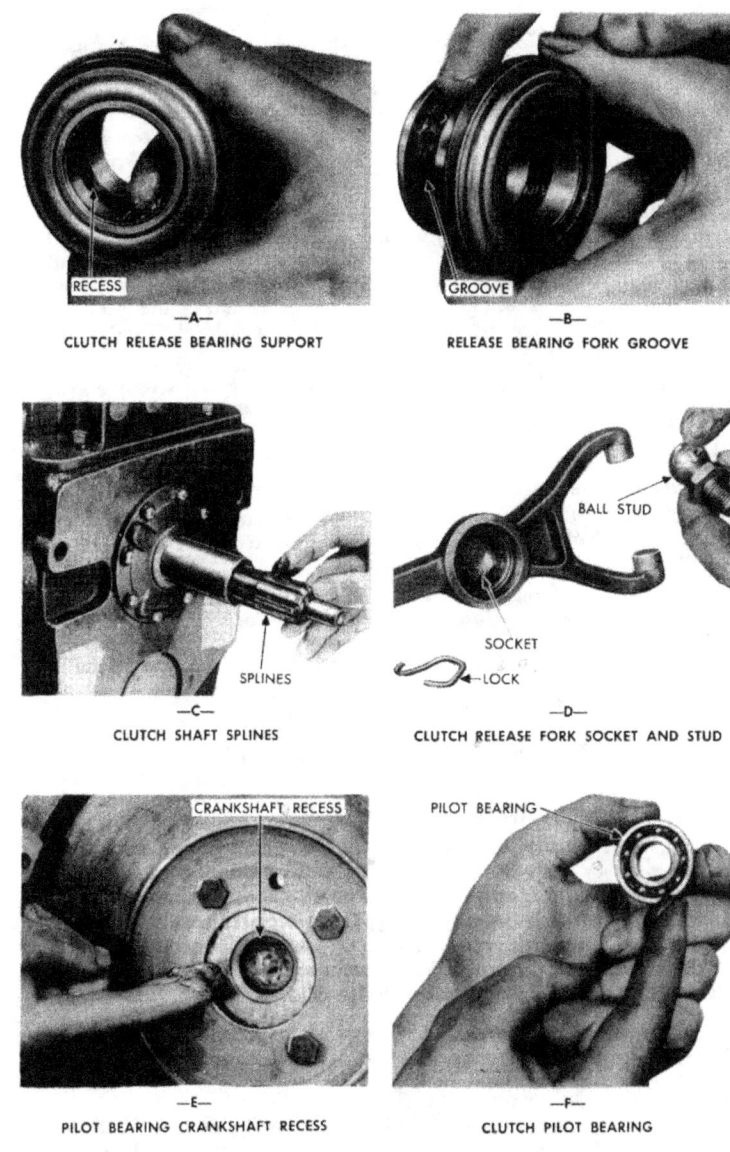

Figure 51—Localized Lubrication Views

(4) WINCH PROPELLER SHAFT SHEAR PIN. Monthly, lubricate both ends of pin with medium lubricating preservative oil above 0°F, or special lubricating preservative oil below 0°F. Every 6 months, disconnect universal joint from winch worm shaft. Clean shaft, shear pin and inside of yoke. Coat yoke and winch worm shaft with general purpose grease, No. 1, above +32°F or No. 0 for below +32°F and reinstall. Keep spare shear pins coated with medium preservative oil to prevent rusting.

(5) SHOCK ABSORBERS. Monthly, remove plug and check fluid level. If fluid is below plug level, disconnect link between arm and axle. Fill to plug level with light shock absorber fluid. Pump arm slowly to expel air from shock absorber. Repeat filling and pumping operations until all air is removed and fluid is at fill hole level. Install filler plug. Reconnect link between arm and axle.

(6) STEERING COLUMN UPPER BEARING. When steering gear is removed for inspection or repair, clean and repack steering column upper bearing with No. 2 general purpose grease. Also coat steering column horn contacts lightly, to prevent rusting.

e. Reports and Records.

(1) REPORTS. Unsatisfactory performance of materiel will be reported to the Ordnance Officer responsible for maintenance in accordance with TM 37-250.

(2) RECORDS. A record of lubrication may be maintained in the Preventive Maintenance Roster (W.D., A.G.O. Form No. 460).

Section XIV

Preventive Maintenance Services

54. GENERAL INFORMATION.

a. Responsibility and Intervals.
Preventive maintenance services as prescribed by AR 850-15 are a function of using organization echelons of maintenance, and their performance is the responsibility of the commanders of such organizations. These services consist generally of before, during, at-halt, after operation, and weekly services performed by the driver, and the scheduled services to be performed at designated intervals by organizational maintenance personnel.

b. Definition of Terms.
The general inspection of each item applies also to any supporting member or connection, and is generally a check to see whether the item is in good condition, correctly assembled, secure, or excessively worn.

(1) The inspection for "good condition" is usually an external visual inspection to determine whether the unit is damaged beyond safe or serviceable limits. The term "good condition" is explained further by the following: Not bent or twisted, not chafed or burned, not broken

Preventive Maintenance Services

JOE DOPE

Overloading a DUKW's plumb cockeyed.
In ideal* seas 5 tons barely ride.
Despite what you think,
More weight makes it sink.
Ask Joe Dope—the darn fool has just tried!

Don't be a dope! **HANDLE EQUIPMENT RIGHT!**

* SEE PARAGRAPH 3r FOR LOADING INSTRUCTIONS UNDER IDEAL, FAVORABLE, AND DIFFICULT CONDITIONS.

or cracked, not bare or frayed, not dented or collapsed, not torn or cut, not deteriorated.

(2) The inspection of a unit to see that it is "correctly assembled" is usually an external visual inspection to see whether it is in its normal assembled position in the vehicle.

(3) The inspection of a unit to determine if it is "secure" is usually an external visual inspection; a wrench, hand-feel, or a pry-bar check for looseness. Such an inspection must include any brackets, lock washers, lock nuts, locking wires, or cotter pins used in assembly.

(4) "Excessively worn" will be understood to mean worn beyond serviceable limits, or to a point likely to result in failure if the unit is not replaced before the next scheduled inspection.

55. DRIVER MAINTENANCE (FIRST ECHELON).

a. Purpose. To insure mechanical efficiency it is necessary that the vehicle be systematically inspected at intervals each day it is operated, and weekly so defects may be discovered and corrected before they result in serious damage or failure. Certain scheduled maintenance services will be performed at these designated intervals. Any defects or unsatisfactory operating characteristics beyond the scope of first echelon to correct must be reported at the earliest opportunity to the designated individual in authority. The services set forth in paragraphs 56, 57, 58, and 59 are the maximum services to be performed by the driver before-operation, during-operation, at-halt, and after-operation and weekly.

Maintenance Instructions

Minimum Driver Daily and Weekly Maintenance is covered by the plates attached to the instrument panel of the vehicle (fig. 11). On vehicles not equipped with plates, a reproduction of the items may be made and mounted on the right-hand side of the driver's compartment. Spray sheet with ignition insulation compound (52-C-3099-20) or clear shellac to protect.

b. Use of Form No. 48, Driver's Trip Ticket and Preventive Maintenance Service Record. Driver preventive maintenance services are listed on Form No. 48, Driver's Trip Ticket and Preventive Maintenance Service Record, which is designed to cover the maximum inspections and services necessary for the proper maintenance of the 2½-Ton, 6x6 Amphibian Truck, Model DUKW-353, popularly known as "The Duck." Every organization must thoroughly school each driver in performing the maintenance procedures set forth in this manual. The items listed on Form No. 48 (mounted as shown in fig. 11) are expanded in the manual to provide specific procedures for accomplishment of the inspections and services. The services are arranged to facilitate inspection and conserve the time of the driver. The item numbers are, with minor exceptions, identical with those shown on W.D., Form No. 48, "Driver's Trip Ticket and Preventive Maintenance Service Record."

56. BEFORE-OPERATION SERVICE.

a. Purpose. This inspection schedule is designed primarily as a check to see that the vehicle has not been damaged, tampered with, or sabotaged since the "After-operation Service" was performed. Various combat conditions may have rendered the vehicle unsafe for operation and it is the duty of the driver to determine whether the vehicle is in condition to carry out any mission to which it is assigned. This operation will not be entirely omitted, even in extreme tactical situations.

b. Procedures. Before-operation Service consists of inspecting items listed below according to the procedure described, and correcting or reporting any deficiencies. Upon completion of the service, results will be reported promptly to the designated individual in authority.

(1) ITEM 1, TAMPERING AND DAMAGE. Inspect the vehicle generally for any injury that may have occurred from tampering, sabotage, falling debris, shellfire, or collision since parking.

(2) ITEM 2, FIRE EXTINGUISHERS. Examine the fire extinguishers to be sure they are in good condition, fully charged and securely mounted. Shake liquid type to determine contents (par. 39**b.**). Carbon dioxide type must be weighed (par. 39**c.**). Be sure nozzles are not clogged.

(3) ITEM 3, FUEL, OIL, AND WATER. Check the supply of fuel, engine oil, and coolant and add as necessary. Investigate or report any unusual losses. Do not fill fuel tanks or radiator to overflowing, leave room for normal expansion. NOTE: *During weather when antifreeze is in use, if it becomes necessary to add any considerable amount of coolant, have value of antifreeze checked and add sufficient to protect*

Preventive Maintenance Services

cooling system against freezing. Check level of oil in tire pump (compressor) crankcase, and add as necessary to bring to correct level. See that spare cans are filled and securely mounted

(4) ITEM 4, ACCESSORIES AND DRIVES. Inspect units such as carbureter, generator, starting motor, air cleaners, fuel and oil filters, tire pump (compressor) and bilge pumps for looseness and damage. Be sure fan and generator drive belt adjustment provides $1/2$ inch finger pressure deflection (fig. 86). See that tire pump drive chain (or drive shaft on front mounted tire pump) is in good condition, and that drive chain is properly adjusted to have not more than $1/2$ inch deflection (fig. 232). See that bilge pump drive chain (pars. 246 and 251) or belts (par. 240) has $1/2$ to $3/4$ inch deflection. Be sure all adjustments are properly secured.

(5) ITEM 6, LEAKS: FUEL, OIL, AND COOLANT. Look under the vehicle and in engine compartment for indications of fuel, oil, or coolant leaks. Trace any leaks found to their source and correct or report them.

(6) ITEM 7, ENGINE WARM-UP. Start engine, taking all necessary starting precautions outlined in paragraph 20. Observe if starting motor action is satisfactory, particularly if it has adequate cranking speed and if it engages and disengages properly without excessive noise. Set hand throttle so engine will run at fast idle during warm-up period, and reset choke as necessary for engine to run smoothly and to prevent overchoking and oil dilution. CAUTION: *If satisfactory oil pressure for safe operation of the engine is not indicated in 30 seconds, stop engine and investigate or report condition.*

(7) ITEM 9, INSTRUMENTS.

(a) Oil Pressure Gage. Gage must register at normal reading with engine hot at idling speed (par. 20c.).

(b) Ammeter. Ammeter may show high charging rate for first few minutes after starting engine until generator has restored to battery the current used, then indicate slight charge or zero with lights and accessories turned off. High charging rate for extended period may indicate a dangerously low battery or faulty regulator.

(c) Temperature Gage. Reading should increase gradually during warm-up to normal operating range, 160°F to 180°F. Maximum safe operating temperature, 220°F. CAUTION: *Do not move vehicle until engine temperature has reached at least 160°F.*

(d) Fuel Gage. Gage should indicate the approximate amount of fuel in tank. Ordinarily, tank will have been filled and gage should indicate "FULL."

(e) Tachometer. Tachometer should indicate engine speed in revolutions per minute. (Maximum 2750 RPM.) The red needle will register and remain at the maximum revolutions per minute reached. Tachometer does not indicate under 500 revolutions per minute.

(f) Tank Pressure Air Gage. Tank pressure gage must read between 50 and 75 pounds.

Maintenance Instructions

(g) Tire Pressure Air Gage. With air control lever in neutral position and all tire line valves open, the gage should register existing tire pressure (par. 32).

(h) Compass. Check compass and adjust as required according to instructions in paragraph 283.

(8) ITEM 24, AMPHIBIAN SERVICES.

(a) V-Strut Bearing. Inspect bearing for looseness or damage and lubricate according to Lubrication Order No. 9-802.

(b) Rudder. Inspect rudder for looseness or damage, and test controls to be sure they operate properly.

(c) Propeller. Inspect propeller for looseness or damage. Test controls to be sure they operate properly and see that propeller is in proper alinement. CAUTION: *Only operate propeller momentarily out of the water.*

(d) Hull Drain Plugs and Valves. See that all hull drain plugs are present and properly installed in hull, and that all drain valves are closed (par. 37).

(e) Shaft Housing Seals. Inspect propeller shaft housing seals to see if they are in good condition and that clamp rings and drain plugs are secure.

(f) Surf Boards. Inspect all surf boards (figs. 196, 197, and 198) for looseness or damage. See that they are properly secured either in raised or lowered position.

(g) Hatches. Inspect all hatches to be sure they are in good condition. See that they are closed and properly secured against seals.

(9) ITEM 19, HULL, LOAD, AND TARPAULIN. Inspect hull generally for damage that might make the vehicle unsafe for water operation. See that bilges under cargo space are clean. Any cargo must be properly distributed and secure. See that tarpaulin and driver's compartment top cover assembly are in good condition and properly installed and lashed, or if not in use, properly stowed (fig. 7).

(10) ITEM 13, WHEEL NUTS AND FLANGE BOLTS. See that all wheel mounting and assembly nuts and hub flange bolts are present and secure. On those vehicles equipped with the central tire inflation device, see that the unit is properly and securely assembled to the wheel hub (figs. 243 and 244).

(11) ITEM 14, TIRES. Inspect all tires (including spare) for damage. Remove all objects lodged in treads or carcasses. Be sure valve stems are in correct position and that all valve caps (where used), are present and finger-tight. Check operation of tire inflation system (if so equipped) to be sure it functions properly (par. 31).

(12) ITEM 15, SPRINGS AND SUSPENSIONS. Inspect front springs and shock absorbers, rear springs, seats and torque rods, and all spring brackets, shackles, U-bolts, and rebound clips for looseness or damage. Look particularly for shifted or broken spring leaves and excessive spring sag.

TM 9-802
56-57

Preventive Maintenance Services

(13) ITEM 16, STEERING LINKAGE. Inspect steering arms, rods, joints, and connections for looseness or damage. See that gear box, column, and wheel are secure, and check gear box for excessive lubricant leakage.

(14) ITEM 10, HORN AND WINDSHIELD WIPERS. If tactical situation permits, test horn for proper operation and tone. Test action of windshield wipers. Examine wiper motors, blades, and arms for looseness and damage and see that blades contact glass evenly and firmly and operate through their full stroke.

(15) ITEM 11, GLASS AND REAR VIEW MIRRORS. Clean all vehicle glass and inspect it for looseness and damage. Adjust rear view mirrors for correct vision.

(16) ITEM 12, LAMPS (LIGHTS) AND REFLECTORS. Clean off light and safety reflector lenses and inspect units for looseness and damage. If tactical situation permits, open and close all light switches (fig. 14) and observe if lamps respond properly.

(17) ITEM 18, PINTLE HOOK AND BOW SHACKLES. Inspect these items for looseness or damage. See that pintle hook operates properly and latches securely (fig. 20).

(18) ITEM 20, DECONTAMINATOR. Examine cylinder for damage and full charge. Shake to determine contents. Be sure unit is securely mounted.

(19) ITEM 21, TOOLS AND EQUIPMENT. Check all vehicle and pioneer tools and standard or special equipment against Section III, (Tools, Parts, and Accessories), to be sure all items are present, and see that they are serviceable and properly mounted or stowed.

(20) ITEM 22, ENGINE OPERATION. After normal operating temperature has been reached, engine should idle smoothly with choke fully opened and throttle closed. Accelerate and decelerate a few times and observe any unsatisfactory operating characteristics or unusual noise, vibration, or exhaust smoke.

(21) ITEM 23, DRIVER'S PERMIT AND VEHICLE PUBLICATIONS. The driver must have his operator's permit on his person. Vehicle and equipment manuals, Lubrication Order, W.D. Form No. 48 (Driver's Trip Ticket and Preventive Maintenance Service Record) (fig. 11), Form No. 26 (Driver's Report—Accident, Motor Transportation), and Form No. 478 (MWO and Major Unit Assembly Replacement Record), must be present, legible, and properly stowed.

57. DURING-OPERATION SERVICE.

a. Observations. While vehicle is in motion, listen for any sounds such as rattles, knocks, squeals, or hums that may indicate trouble. Look for indications of trouble in cooling system and smoke from any part of the vehicle. Be alert for odors indicating overheated components or units (such as generator, brakes, or clutch), leaks in fuel system or exhaust system, or other trouble. When brakes are used, water propeller

Maintenance Instructions

operated, gears shifted, or the vehicle turned, consider this a test and note any unsatisfactory or unusual performance. Watch the instruments constantly for unusual behavior indicating possible trouble in systems to which they apply.

b. Procedures. During-operation Services consist of observing items listed below according to the procedures following each item, and investigating any indications of serious trouble. Note minor deficiencies to be corrected or reported at earliest opportunity, usually the next scheduled halt.

(1) ITEM 37, AMPHIBIAN SERVICES.

(a) Leaks—Bilge Compartments. Immediately upon entering the water, inspect the interior of the hull for indications of leakage. See that bilge compartments are kept clean at all times.

(b) Hull Valves. Test all hull valves to see that they open and close properly. Allow sufficient water to enter bilges to perform *(c)* following.

(c) Check Operation of Pumps—Pump Intakes and Strainers. Test both power driven bilge pumps to be sure they are operating properly (par. 36). Observe if the water manifold control linkage is properly connected, and if the valves function properly, noting any indication of restriction in the pump intakes or strainers. Turn down grease cups $1/2$ turn on forward bilge pump (early models) every $1/2$ hour during water operation.

(d) Propeller Stuffing Box. Be on the alert during water operations, for any indication of overheating or leakage at propeller stuffing box (fig. 230).

(e) Rudder. During water operation, observe at all times if rudder controls function properly and if vehicle responds to rudder action effectively.

(f) Rope Fenders. Be sure fenders are all present, and properly and securely lashed to hull (fig. 32).

(2) ITEM 27, FOOT AND HAND BRAKES. When vehicle is first moved during land operation and before gaining any appreciable speed, test service foot brakes to be sure they stop the vehicle effectively, and observe if there is any excessive pull to one side, chatter, grab, or squealing. Pedal should have $1/4$ to $1/2$ inch free-travel before moving master cylinder push rod, and at least 2 inches clearance from floor board when fully applied. Stop on a reasonable incline, and observe if hand (parking) brake will hold vehicle effectively; that locking device holds lever in applied position, and that lever has about $1/3$ ratchet travel in reserve.

(3) ITEM 28, CLUTCH. Clutch pedal free-travel should be $2\frac{1}{2}$ inches and never less than 1 inch. Clutch should engage without drag, noise, chatter or grabbing and should not slip when fully engaged under load.

(4) ITEM 29, TRANSMISSION AND WINCH POWER TAKE-OFF. Controls should shift easily and smoothly. Gears should operate without unusual noise or vibration, and not slip out of mesh during operation.

(5) ITEM 30, TRANSFER CASES. The main and water propeller

Preventive Maintenance Services

transfer case controls should shift easily and smoothly. The gears should operate without unusual noise and not slip out of mesh during operation.

(6) ITEM 31, ENGINE AND CONTROLS. Driver should be on the alert for deficiencies in engine performance such as lack of power and acceleration, misfiring, backfiring, unusual noise, or indications of overheating or excessive smoke. Observe whether or not engine accelerates satisfactorily and controls operate without excessive looseness or binding. During water operation at full speed, check for 2,350 minimum revolutions per minute and 180°F maximum temperature. If radio noise, during operation of vehicle, is reported, driver will cooperate with radio operator in locating the interference, Section XXVI.

(7) ITEM 32, INSTRUMENTS. Observe all instruments frequently during operation of the vehicle to be sure they indicate or record the proper function of the units to which they apply. Speedometer should register vehicle speed in miles per hour and odometer should record total accumulating mileage. There should be no unusual noise in instrument or cable or any pointer fluctuation.

(8) ITEM 33, STEERING GEAR. Be on the alert for any unusual steering characteristics such as excessive looseness or binding, pull to one side, shimmy, wander, or wheel tramp. Be sure column bracket and steering wheel are secure.

(9) ITEM 34, RUNNING GEAR. Be on the alert during land operation of the vehicle for any unusual noise or operating characteristics from wheels, axles, propeller shafts, U-joints, springs, or suspension units that might indicate looseness, damage, excessive wear, or inadequate lubrication.

(10) ITEM 35, CARGO COMPARTMENT. During operation of the vehicle, be on the alert for indications of loosened body assembly or mounting nuts or screws, attachments or hardware, or shifting of load.

(11) ITEM 36, GUNS—MOUNTINGS. On vehicles equipped with mounted guns, inspect the elevating, traversing, and locking mechanisms to be sure they operate properly. See that all mountings are in good condition and secure.

58. AT-HALT SERVICE.

a. Importance. At-halt Service may be regarded as minimum maintenance procedures, and should be performed under all tactical conditions even though more extensive maintenance services must be slighted or omitted altogether.

b. Procedures. At-halt Services consist of investigating any deficiencies noted during land or water operation, inspecting items listed below according to the procedures following the items, and correcting any deficiencies found. Deficiencies not corrected should be reported promptly to the designated individual in authority.

(1) ITEM 53, AMPHIBIAN SERVICES.

(a) V-Strut Bearing. Inspect the bearing for indications of looseness

and for damage, and lubricate the bearing according to Lubrication Order No. 9-802.

(b) Rudder. Inspect the rudder for indications of looseness or damage, and remove any objects wound around rudder assembly. Investigate and correct any unsatisfactory steering condition noticed during water operation.

(c) Propeller. Inspect water propeller for looseness, damage, and proper alinement. Remove any objects wound around propeller or shaft. Lubricate propeller stuffing box (see Lubrication Order No. 9-802, figs. 40 and 41).

(d) Hull Drain Plugs and Valves. Examine hull drain plugs for looseness and damage. Open hull drain valves and drain bilges, observing if valves and controls operate properly.

(e) Surf Boards. Inspect all surf boards for looseness or damage (figs. 196, 197, and 198).

(f) Hatches. Examine hatch covers, seals and latches for damage, and investigate and correct or report any indication of leakage noticed.

(g) Bilge Compartments. After draining bilges, inspect compartments for indications of leakage or damage. Clean out dirt and refuse from bilges and from around drain valves and pump intake screens (fig. 211). Close drain valves.

(2) ITEM 38, FUEL, OIL, AND WATER SUPPLY. Check to see that there is adequate fuel, oil, and coolant to operate vehicle to next scheduled halt. Replenish as supply and tactical situation permits. CAUTION: *If engine is hot, add water slowly with engine at fast idle.*

(3) ITEM 39, TEMPERATURES: HUBS, BRAKE DRUMS, TRANSFER CASES, TRANSMISSION, AND AXLES. Hand-feel all wheel hubs and brake drums for overheating. Check power train gear cases for indications of excessive temperatures and note any excessive lubricant leakage at seals or gaskets.

(4) ITEM 40, VENTS (BREATHER TUBES—4). Inspect all axle and pillow block vents and tubes to see that they are in good condition, secure, and not clogged.

(5) ITEM 41, PROPELLER SHAFT HOUSING SEALS. Inspect all housing seals for damage and be sure all ring clamps and drain plugs are secure.

(6) ITEM 42, SPRINGS AND SUSPENSIONS. Inspect and service in same manner as in Before-operation, item 15.

(7) ITEM 45, TIRES AND INFLATION SYSTEM. Examine all tires for damage, and remove any objects lodged in treads or carcasses. Inspect tire inflation system components, outside of hull, for indications of looseness or damage.

(8) ITEM 46, LEAKS: FUEL, OIL, AND COOLANT. Look in engine compartment for indications of fuel, oil, or coolant leaks. Trace any leaks found to their source, and investigate and correct or report them.

(9) ITEM 47, ACCESSORIES AND BELTS. Inspect and service in same manner as in Before-operation, item 4.

Preventive Maintenance Services

(10) ITEM 50, TOWING CONNECTIONS. Inspect pintle hook and bow shackles for looseness and damage. See that pintle hook operates properly and latches securely.

59. AFTER-OPERATION AND WEEKLY SERVICE.

a. Purpose. After-operation servicing is particularly important because at this time the driver inspects the vehicle to detect any deficiencies that may have developed, and to correct those he is permitted to handle. He should report results of the inspection to the designated individual in authority. If this schedule is performed thoroughly, the vehicle should be ready to roll again on a moment's notice. The Before-operation Service, with a few exceptions, is then necessary only to ascertain whether the vehicle is in the same condition in which it was left upon completion of the After-operation Service. The After-operation Service should never be entirely omitted, even in extreme tactical situations, but may be reduced to the bare fundamental services outlined for the At-halt Service, if necessary.

b. Procedures. When performing the After-operation Service the driver must remember and consider any irregularities noticed in the Before-operation, During-operation, and At-halt Services. The After-operation Service consists of inspecting and servicing the following items. Those items of the After-operation Service that are marked by an asterisk (*) require additional Weekly Services, the procedures for which are indicated in subparagraph *(b)* of each applicable item.

(1) ITEM 55, ENGINE OPERATION. Before stopping the engine, accelerate and decelerate a few times and note any excessive or unusual noise or vibration or exhaust smoke. Investigate any unsatisfactory condition observed during operation.

(2) ITEM 56, INSTRUMENTS. Observe if all pertinent instruments continue to indicate or record the proper function of the units to which they apply.

(3) ITEM 57, HORN AND WINDSHIELD WIPERS. Investigate and correct or report any unsatisfactory operation of these items noted during operation. Stop engine.

(4) ITEM 54, FUEL, OIL, AND WATER. Fill the fuel tank. Check engine and tire pump (compressor) oil levels, and add as necessary to bring to correct level. Check radiator coolant for proper level and contamination (par. 117). CAUTION: *Loosen pressure cap cautiously. Do not fully remove until properly vented and steam has escaped.* Add coolant as needed. In freezing weather if any appreciable amount is added, have value of antifreeze checked, and added as necessary to protect the cooling system against freezing (par. 45). See that any fuel or water used from spare cans is replenished.

(5) ITEM 74, *GEAR CASES (WEEKLY ONLY). Check level and condition of lubricant in front and rear axles, transmission, transfer cases, and steering gear case, and report if low or contaminated. Proper level (except steering gear case) is from lower edge of filler hole when hot, to ½ inch below when cool. Refer to Lubrication Order No. 9-802.

TM 9-802

Maintenance Instructions

(6) ITEM 86, AMPHIBIAN SERVICES.

(a) V-Strut Bearing. Remove any foreign material wound around strut, propeller, or rudder. Inspect bearing for looseness and damage.

(b) Rudder. Inspect rudder for looseness and damage. Investigate and correct or report any unsatisfactory steering condition noticed during water operation.

(c) Propeller. Inspect the propeller for looseness and damage.

(d) Hull Drain Plugs and Valves. Remove all hull drain plugs (par. 37) and open hull drain valves and drain the bilge compartments.

(e) Clean Bilge Compartments. Clean out all dirt and refuse from bilges.

(f) Clean Pump Intake and Strainers. Remove all dirt and refuse from in and around pump intakes and strainers. If possible, flush the bilges with clean water. Coat hull drain plugs with general purpose grease and replace them securely. Close hull drain valves (except in freezing weather).

(g) Shaft Housing Seals. Inspect propeller shaft housings and seals for damage. See that housing seal clamp rings are secure. Remove housing drain plugs and drain off any accumulation of water. Replace drain plugs securely.

(h) Surf Boards. Examine all surf boards for damage and see that they are properly attached and secured.

(i) Hatches. Inspect all hatches and their seals and latches to see that they are in good condition. Investigate and correct or report any leakage noted.

(j) Clean Hull. Wipe off all excess dirt and grease from hull sides and decks, and inspect the painted surfaces for rust spots or polished spots that might result in leaks or cause glare or reflections. Correct any unsatisfactory condition found, or report for attention by higher echelon.

(7) ITEM 84, *CLEAN ENGINE (WEEKLY). Remove all dirt and refuse from engine compartment. If washing is not possible, wipe off excess dirt and grease. Clean out radiator core air passages and remove any obstructions from grilles. If possible, wash exterior of engine and inside of engine compartment with dry-cleaning solvent and wipe thoroughly dry. CAUTION: *Do not get solvent on electrical wiring or equipment.*

(8) ITEM 65, AIR CLEANERS AND BREATHERS. Inspect the carburetor, tire pump, and hydrovac cylinder air cleaners, and the engine and tire pump crankcase breathers to see if they are in good condition and secure. Check level of oil in oil bath type cleaners and add oil to proper level. If vehicle has been operated under severe conditions of dust or sand, clean and service all units as often as necessary, according to Lubrication Order No. 9-802.

(9) ITEM 62, *BATTERY.

(a) Inspect battery for damage, loose hold-downs or connections and for leaks. Be sure cell caps are present and finger-tight.

Preventive Maintenance Services

(b) Weekly. Clean battery and carrier. Examine terminals for corrosion. If necessary, clean connections, grease them lightly and tighten them securely. If electrolyte is low, add clean water to bring level to 3/8 inch above plates. CAUTION: *In freezing weather do not add water until just before vehicle is to be operated.*

(10) ITEM 66, *FUEL FILTERS.

(a) Inspect main fuel filter (fig. 80) and fuel pump filter (fig. 78) for looseness, damage, or leaks. Drain sediment and water from main filter by removing drain plug. CAUTION: *Do not allow drainings to run down into hull.*

(b) Weekly. Remove main filter bowl and element and fuel pump sediment bowl and screen. Clean in dry-cleaning solvent and reassemble securely (par. 110). Drain water and sediment from bottom of fuel tank. Drain only until fuel runs clean, using every precaution against fire.

(11) ITEM 68, *TIRES.

(a) See that tires are inflated to the correct pressure for the existing terrain condition (par. 32). Inspect all tires for damage. Remove any objects lodged in treads or carcasses. Inspect components of tire inflation device (if so equipped) for looseness or damage.

(b) Weekly. Report badly worn or otherwise unserviceable tires for repair or replacement. Mechanical defects that might contribute to such wear should be investigated and corrected or reported. Rotate unevenly worn but still serviceable tries to other wheel positions to even up wear (fig. 175).

(12) ITEM 71, *PROPELLER SHAFTS AND PILLOW BLOCK.

(a) Inspect accessible propeller shafts, U-joints, and pillow block for indications of looseness, damage, or excessive lubricant leakage.

(b) Weekly. Drain off accumulated water and lubricate U-joints and pillow block according to instructions on Lubrication Order No. 9-802.

(13) ITEM 73, LEAKS: FUEL, OIL AND COOLANT. Check within engine compartment for indications of fuel, oil and coolant leaks. Trace any leaks found to source and correct or report them.

(14) ITEM 72, VENTS (BREATHER TUBES—4). Inspect front and rear axle and pillow block breather vents and tubes for damage. See that they are secure and not clogged.

(15) ITEM 59, LAMPS (LIGHTS) AND REFLECTORS. Clean all light and safety reflector lenses and inspect these units for looseness and damage. If any unsatisfactory condition was observed during operation of the lights or switches, investigate and correct or report the condition.

(16) ITEM 60, FIRE EXTINGUISHERS. Inspect units for damage and full charge. Shake liquid type to check contents (par. 39**b**.). Carbon dioxide type must be weighed (par. 39**c**.). If extinguishers were used or damaged, report for refill or exchange. Be sure nozzles are not clogged. Mount units securely.

Maintenance Instructions

(17) ITEM 61, DECONTAMINATOR. Inspect unit for damage and full charge. Shake to check contents. Mount unit securely.

(18) ITEM 63, FAN BELT AND PUMP CHAINS. Inspect fan and generator drive belt, tire pump chain, and bilge pump belt and/or chains to see if they are in good condition. See that fan and generator drive belt adjustment and bilge pump drive belt or chain are adjusted to provide $\frac{1}{2}$ to $\frac{3}{4}$ inch finger pressure deflection. Tire pump chain should have $\frac{1}{2}$ inch deflection.

(19) ITEM 64, ELECTRICAL WIRING. Examine contents and wiring for looseness or damage. Tighten all loose connections and clean all accessible wiring. If vehicle is radio noise suppressed, be sure all radio noise suppression bond clips, straps, filters, condensers, and suppressors on all units are securely connected or mounted. Tighten all conduit coupling ring nuts (where used).

(20) ITEM 67, ENGINE CONTROLS. Examine engine and accessory controls for loose, worn, or binding linkage.

(21) ITEM 69, SPRINGS AND SUSPENSIONS. Inspect in same manner as in Before-operation, item 15.

(22) ITEM 70, STEERING LINKAGE. Inspect in same manner as in Before-operation, item 16.

(23) ITEM 75, AIR TANKS. Inspect tire inflation system air tank for looseness or damage. See that all connections are secure. Drain off water and close drain cock.

(24) ITEM 77, TOWING CONNECTIONS. Inspect all tow shackles and pintle hook for looseness and damage. Be sure pintle hook operates properly and latches securely.

(25) ITEM 78, HULL, LOAD, AND TARPAULIN. Inspect entire hull for damage. Look particularly for dents or punctures that might result in leaks. See that bulkheads, braces, and any reinforcements are secure. Close all hatches. Make sure they fit evenly and tightly against the seals and lock them securely. See that any cargo carried is properly distributed and secured. Inspect the driver's compartment top cover and cargo space tarpaulins for damage, and see that they are properly installed and securely lashed or, if not in use, that they are properly stowed.

(26) ITEM 79, *WINCH.

(a) Inspect the winch assembly and mountings for looseness or damage. Investigate and correct or report any unsatisfactory condition noticed during operation, particularly of the jaw clutch and winch brakes (par. 273).

(b) Weekly. Unwind the winch cable, clean it thoroughly with light engine oil or a mixture of oil and kerosene. Inspect the cable for broken strands, rust, flat spots or other damage. As the cable is rewound evenly and tightly on the winch drum (fig. 23) apply a coating of thin film rust preventive compound. Be sure the cable end is properly secured.

(27) ITEM 81, GUN MOUNTINGS. On vehicles so equipped, inspect

Preventive Maintenance Services

any gun mountings for damage. See that they operate properly and are correctly and securely assembled and mounted.

(28) ITEM 82, *TIGHTENING.

(a) Tighten all vehicle assembly or mounting nuts or screws which this inspection has indicated as necessary.

(b) Weekly. Tighten all wheel mounting and assembly nuts or screws, gear case mountings, manifold nuts, accessories and hull attachments, spring clips and U-bolts, or any other points where inspection or experience has indicated the necessity on a weekly or mileage basis.

(29) ITEM 85, *TOOLS AND EQUIPMENT.

(a) Check all vehicle and pioneer tools and items of equipment against section III, (Tools, Parts, and Accessories), to see that all items are present, and see that they are serviceable and properly mounted or stowed.

(b) Weekly. Clean all tools and items of equipment. Apply paint or preservative where necessary to protect against rust or corrosion. Mount or stow all items securely.

(30) ITEM 83, LUBRICATION—W. D. LUBRICATION ORDER NO. 9-802.

(a) Lubricate all points of the vehicle indicated on the Lubrication Order No. 9-802 as requiring daily attention. See notes (par. 53).

(b) Weekly. Lubricate all points of the vehicle requiring attention on a weekly basis or where this inspection or experience has indicated the necessity.

60. ORGANIZATIONAL MAINTENANCE (SECOND ECHELON).

a. Frequency. The frequency of preventive maintenance services outlined herein is considered a minimum requirement for normal operation of vehicles. Under unusual operating conditions such as extreme temperatures, severe dust, sandy or extremely wet terrain, or amphibious operations, it may be necessary to perform certain maintenance services more frequently.

b. First Echelon Participation. The drivers should accompany their vehicles and assist the mechanics while periodic second echelon preventive maintenance services are performed. Ordinarily the vehicle should be presented for a scheduled preventive maintenance service in a reasonably clean condition; that is, it should be dry, and not caked with mud or grease to such an extent that inspection and servicing will be seriously hampered. However, the vehicle should not be washed or wiped thoroughly clean, because certain types of defects such as cracks, leaks, and loose or shifted parts or assemblies are more evident if the surfaces are slightly soiled or dusty.

c. Sources of Additional Information. If instructions other than those contained in the general procedures in paragraph **d.,** or the specific procedures in paragraph **l.,** which follow, are required for

Maintenance Instructions

proper performance of a preventive maintenance or for correction of a deficiency, they may be secured from other sections of this manual or from the designated individual in authority.

d. General Procedures. These general procedures are basic instructions which are to be followed when performing the services on the items listed in the specific procedures. NOTE: *The second echelon personnel must be thoroughly trained in these procedures so that they will apply them automatically.*

(1) When new or overhauled subassemblies are installed to correct deficiencies, care must be taken to see that they are clean, correctly installed, and properly lubricated and adjusted.

(2) When installing new lubricant retainer seals, and the new seal is a leather seal, it should be soaked in SAE No. 10 engine oil for not more than 30 minutes. The oil should be warm, not hot, if practicable. Then, the leather lip should be worked carefully by hand before installing the seal. The lip must not be scratched or marred.

e. Definition of Terms. Refer to paragraph 54b.

f. Special Services. These are indicated by repeating the item numbers in the columns which show the interval at which the services are to be performed and show that the parts or assemblies are to receive certain mandatory services. For example, an item number in one or both columns opposite a TIGHTEN procedure, means that the actual tightening of the object must be performed. The special services include:

(1) ADJUST. Make all necessary adjustments in accordance with the pertinent section of this manual, special bulletins, or other current directives.

(2) CLEAN. Clean units of the vehicle with dry-cleaning solvent to remove excess lubricant, dirt, and other foreign material. After the parts are cleaned, rinse them in clean solvent and dry them thoroughly. Take care to keep the parts clean until reassembled and be certain to keep cleaning solvent away from rubber or other material which it will damage. Clean the protective grease coating from new parts since this material is usually not a good lubricant.

(3) SPECIAL LUBRICATION. This applies both to lubrication operations that do not appear on the vehicle Lubrication Order and to items that do appear on the Order but should be performed in connection with the maintenance operations if parts have to be disassembled for inspection or service.

(4) SERVE. This usually consists of performing special operations, such as replenishing battery water, draining and refilling units with oil, and changing or cleaning the oil filter, air cleaner, or cartridges.

(5) TIGHTEN. All tightening operations should be performed with sufficient wrench torque (force on the wrench handle) to tighten the unit according to good mechanical practice. Use a torque-indicating wrench where specified. Do not overtighten, as this may strip threads or cause distortion. Tightening will always be understood to include the correct installation of lock washers, lock nuts, lock wire, or cotter pins provided to secure the tightening.

TM 9-802
Preventive Maintenance Services

g. Special Conditions. When conditions make it difficult to perform all preventive maintenance procedures at one time, they can sometimes be handled in sections, planning to complete all operations within the week if possible. All available time at halts and in bivouac areas must be utilized, if necessary, to assure that maintenance operations are completed. When time is limited by the tactical situation, items with Special Services in the columns should be given first consideration.

h. Work Sheet. The numbers of the preventive maintenance procedures that follow are identical with those outlined on W.D., A.G.O. Form No. 461 which is the "Preventive Maintenance Service Work Sheet for Wheeled and Half-track Vehicles." Certain items on the work sheet that do not apply to this vehicle are not included in the procedures in the manual. In general, the numerical sequence of items on the work sheet is followed in the manual procedures, but in some instances there is deviation for conservation of the mechanic's time and effort.

i. Specific Procedures. The procedures for performing each item in the 1000-mile (monthly) and 6000-mile (6-month) maintenance procedures, whichever shall occur first, are described in the following chart. Each page of the chart has two columns at its left edge corresponding to the 6000-mile and the 1000-mile maintenance respectively. Very often it will be found that a particular procedure does not apply to both scheduled maintenances. In order to determine which procedure to follow, look down the column corresponding to the maintenance due, and wherever an item number appears perform the operations indicated opposite the number. NOTE: *If the item number is suffixed with a dagger sign (†), only the services indicated opposite the item number are to be performed at this time. This symbol means additional attention to the item at another time during this maintenance service is necessary, and the item number will again be repeated.*

6,000 Mile (Six-Month) Maint.	1,000 Mile (Monthly) Maint.	
		BLOCK VEHICLE SECURELY
62		Front Propeller Shafts (Joints, Seals, and Flanges). Remove housing and seals (par. 182), disassemble (TM 9-1802B), and clean propeller shaft and universal joints, and examine all parts thoroughly to see if they are in good condition and not excessively worn. Lubricate joints and sleeves at assembly, (par. 53) and be sure that the joints are properly alined with each other.
73		Rear Propeller Shafts (Joints, Seals, and Flanges). Inspect and service in the same manner as for item 62.
74		Center Bearing "Pillow Block" (Seals, Vent, Lubricant Level, and Mounting). Remove (par. 184*b.*) and disassemble (TM 9-1802B) pillow block, and examine bearings and seals to see if they are in good condition and not excessively worn. Be sure vent opening is not clogged and that tube is not damaged. Reassemble and mount securely.
74	74	Special Lubrication. Bring lubricant to proper level. See Lubrication Order No. 9-802 (pars. 52 and 53).

131

Maintenance Instructions

6,000 Mile (Six-Month) Maint.	1,000 Mile (Monthly) Maint.	
61		**Front Axle (Differential, Bearings, Seals, and Vent).** Remove differential cover. Clean parts and examine them to see if they are in good condition and not excessively worn. Examine pinion seal for indications of leakage. Adjust bearings and gears as necessary, (TM 9-1802B).
61	61	Inspect housing to see if it is in good condition and securely assembled and mounted. Clean vent tube. **Special Lubrication.** Bring lubricant to correct level (par. 53).
75		**Rear Axles (Differentials, Bearings, Seals, and Vents).** Inspect and service in same manner as for item 61.
75	75	Inspect housing to see if it is in good condition and securely assembled and mounted. Clean vent tube. **Special Lubrication.** Bring lubricant to correct level (par. 53).
117		**Propeller Shaft Housings (Seals, Boots, Plugs, and Drain).** Thoroughly examine removed propeller shaft housings, seals, and boots for good condition. Clean, prime, and repaint all painted surfaces of housings, including the inside (par. 238). Assemble propeller shafts and housings and connect interhousing drain, (par. 183*b*.).
47	47	†**Tires and Rims.** Examine tires for cuts, bruises, and blisters. Look for irregular tread wear such as flat spots, cupping, feather edges, and one-sided wear. Remove embedded glass, nails, and stones from treads.
47		†Dismount all tires (par. 213), clean and paint rims and bead locks, and examine tubes to see if they are in good condition. NOTE: *Do not reinstall wheels and tires until items 52 and 60 have been performed.*
53	53	**Front Brakes.** Remove front wheels, hubs, and drums. Inspect as follows. **Drums.** Examine drums to see if they are distorted or scored, and if drum to hub mountings are secure. Clean and paint outside and non-working inside surfaces of drums (par. 198). **Wheel Cylinders.** Examine cylinders to see if they are in good condition, securely mounted and connected, and look for indications of fluid leaks. Be sure cylinder caps are not rusted or corroded (par. 198*a*.).
54	54	**Front Brake Shoes (Lining, Links, Guides, and Anchors)** (fig. 161). Inspect these items to see if they are in good condition, correctly assembled, and secure. Look for rusted or binding linkage, weak or rusted return springs, and be sure guides and anchors are free. If linings are worn to a thickness of ⅛ inch or less, or are oil soaked, replace, (par. 196, or TM 9-1802B). **Adjust.** Adjust front brake shoes to compensate for wear if linings have been replaced (par. 188).
48	48	**Rear Brakes.** Inspect and service in same manner as for item 53, (fig. 162).
49	49	**Rear Brake Shoes (Linings, Links, Guides, and Anchors)** Inspect and service in same manner as for item 54, (par. 197) †NOTE: *Items marked with a dagger* (†) *are given additional services later in these procedures. Perform only the services designated after the item.*

Preventive Maintenance Services

6,000 Mile (Six-Month) Maint.	1,000 Mile (Monthly) Maint.	
60	60	**Front Wheels (Bearings, Seals, Flanges, and Nuts).** **Clean.** Disassemble wheel bearings (par. 214), and examine for excessive wear and damage. Replace bearings and cups as necessary. Examine seals to see if they are in good condition. Clean rust and corrosion from wheels, and repaint if necessary. **Lubricate.** Repack, (Lubrication Order No. 9-802), assemble, and adjust wheel bearings (par. 214). **Drive Flanges and Bolts.** Make certain that drive flange and bolts and special studs are installed correctly (fig. 172) and securely tightened (par. 173*d*.) (85-95 foot-pounds).
	55	**Steering Knuckle (Front Axle U-joints, Bearings, and Seals).** Remove front axle shaft and U-joint assemblies (par. 173*b*.), clean thoroughly, and without disassembly of U-joints, inspect all parts for damage or excessive wear. **Special Lubrication.** Repack constant velocity universal joints with fresh lubricant (par. 173*e*.), and install axle shafts into housings.
58	58	**Front Shock Absorbers and Links.** Inspect shock absorber bodies for leaks. See that bodies are secured to the hull and that links which connect arms to axle are in good condition and secure. Test action of shock absorbers (par. 206*b*.), and add fluid if necessary (Lubrication Order No. 9-802).
56		**Front Springs (Clips, Leaves, U-bolts, Hangers, and Shackles).** Inspect front springs to see if they are in good condition, correctly assembled, and securely mounted. Look particularly for excessive sag and for shifted leaves. Tighten all U-bolts, clips, eye-bolts, and shackles (par. 205). Inspect rubber bumpers for deterioration, looseness, and damage.
77		**Rear Springs.** Inspect and service applicable items in same manner as in item 56, (par. 207).
52	52	**Rear Wheels (Bearings, Seals, Flanges, and Nuts).** Inspect and service in the same manner as for item 60 except use 70-80 foot-pounds on axle flange bolts (par. 215).
51	51	**Rear Spring Seats and Bearings.** Inspect rear spring seat assemblies externally to see if they are in good condition and secure. Lubricate, (see paragraphs 52 and 53).
51		Remove rear spring seat and outer bearing only, (par. 208), clean inner and outer bearings, and housing, and inspect all parts for excessive wear and damage, and replace if necessary. Before assembling parts, make sure that hub is properly packed with lubricant and bearings thoroughly lubricated (pars. 52 and 53).
47	47	†**Tires and Rims.** Reinstall wheel and tire assemblies, first making sure valve stems are in good condition and in correct position, and that valve caps (if not equipped with central tire pressure control systems) are present and finger-tight.
83	83	**Brake Lines (Fittings, Hose).** Inspect to see that these units (fig. 157) are in good condition, securely connected or supported, and not leaking.
118	118	†**Hull (Drain Valves and Plugs).** Examine all hull bottom plugs to see that they are in good condition and secure. Oil, adjust (if necessary), and close the four hull drain valves. Clean and repaint all bare or rusted spots as necessary.
		†NOTE: *Items marked with a dagger (†) are given additional services later in these procedures. Perform only the services designated after the item.*

133

TM 9-802
60

Maintenance Instructions

6,000 Mile (Six-Month) Maint.	1,000 Mile (Monthly) Maint.	
64		**Hand Brake (Drum and Lining).** Examine drum for scoring and lining for worn or oil-soaked condition. Clean up or replace drum if necessary (par. 202). Replace linings if worn to 1/8 inch or less, or if lining is oil-soaked, (par. 201, or TM 9-1802B). **Adjust.** Adjust clearance between lining and drum (par. 200).
119		†**Bilge Pumps (Valves, Controls, and Lines and Strainers).** Disassemble bilge pumps (TM 9-1802C), and pump manifold valve mechanism, clean all parts and inspect them to see if they are in good condition, and not excessively worn. Repaint all pipes, (pars. 238 and 244).
119	119	See that manifold valve controls operate properly. Clean and inspect screens, strainers, pump system piping (pars. 243, 249, and 253), hose, and clamps.
29	29	**Drive Chains (Bilge Pumps and Tire Pump).** Clean drive chains and inspect chains and sprockets to see if they are in good condition and not excessively worn. Lubricate chains (pars. 52 and 53), and adjust for proper alinement and correct deflection (pars. 240, 246, 251, and 260).
67	67	**Brake Master Cylinder (Vent, Fluid Level, Leaks, and Switch).** Inspect master cylinder to see if it is in good condition, secure, and not leaking. Fill reservoir to proper level (pars. 52 and 53). Be sure filler plug vent is not clogged; that stop light switch is securely installed and connected.
68	68	**Hydrovac (Air Cleaner, Hose, Cylinder, and Vacuum Check Valve).** Examine hydrovac unit and connections to see if they are in good condition and secure. **Serve.** Clean and service air cleaner element and parts (par. 189*b*.). Oil element with engine oil (Refer to Lubrication Order No. 9-802).
68		**Special Lubrication.** Remove 2 plugs and lubricate cylinder (Refer to Lubrication Order No. 9-802).
68		**Vacuum Check Valve.** Remove, disassemble, and clean vacuum check valve (par. 190). Check vacuum lines and connections for looseness and damage. Tighten or replace as necessary.
82	82	**Fuel Tank (Fittings and Lines).** Inspect tank, lines, and fittings to see if they are in good condition, securely mounted and connected, and not leaking. Drain accumulated water and sediment from fuel tank (par. 111*c*.). Drain only until fuel runs clear. Refill tank. Examine cap, vent, and gasket to see that they are in good condition. Be sure cap pressure valve mechanism is clean and free (par. 111*b*.).
36	36	†**Carbureter (Choke, Throttle and Linkage).** Inspect carbureter to see if it is in good condition, securely mounted and connected, and not leaking. See if choke and throttle operate properly in response to controls (par. 107), and if linkage is excessively worn. Remove cover and clean float chamber (par. 106*c*.). †NOTE: *Items marked with a dagger (†) are given additional services later in these procedures. Perform only the services designated after the item.*

134

Preventive Maintenance Services

6,000 Mile (Six-Month) Maint.	1,000 Mile (Monthly) Maint.	
37	37	**Fuel Filter.** Inspect filter to see that it is in good condition and securely mounted and connected. Clean filter element and sediment bowl (par 110*b*.).
30		**Tachometer and Speedometer Drive.** Clean and inspect drive cables to see if they are in good condition. Lubricate according to Lubrication Order No. 9-802.
38	38	†**Fuel Pump (Strainer Bowl, Screen, and Lines).** Remove fuel pump strainer bowl (on two-valve pump, fig. 78, par. 109*b*.), and inspect all accessible pump parts to see if they are in good condition. Clean bowl and strainer screen, reassemble, hand prime system and check all connections and lines between tank, filter, pump, and carburetor for leaks.
34	34	**Air Cleaners (Carburetor and Tire Pump).** Remove carburetor air cleaner, tire pump air cleaner, and tire pump breather, clean thoroughly, inspect parts to see if they are in good condition, and service with proper oil as designated in Lubrication Order No. 9-802.
35	35	**Crankcase Breather and Ventilator.** Clean and refill crankcase breather air cleaner (Lubrication Order No. 9-802). Disassemble and clean crankcase ventilator valve (par. 92). Check ventilator system, lines, and connections to see if they are in good condition and tighten as necessary.
21		**Compression Test.** Test compression of all cylinders (par. 85*c*.) and record readings on back of form No. 461. Correct or report deficiencies.
20	20	**Spark Plugs.** Clean and inspect all spark plugs to see if they are in good condition. Regap to 0.025 inch on Type 44 plugs, and 0.030 inch on Type 44 Com. plugs, and reinstall, using new gaskets. Inspect radio noise resistor-suppressors for scorching, cracks, and secure mountings and connections (par. 139). When installing shielding after item 31, be sure mountings are secure.
32		**Coil and Wiring.** Examine the coil to see that it is in good condition, clean, and securely mounted. All high voltage ignition wiring should be in good condition, clean, and securely fastened. Be sure radio noise suppression condenser is in good condition and secure (fig. 113).
31	31	**Distributor.** Observe whether the distributor body and external attachments are in good condition and secure (fig. 66). Examine other parts of the distributor as follows: **Cap, Rotor, and Points.** Examine rotor and cap for cracks and burned contacts. Replace if necessary. Clean and adjust points (0.018 to 0.024 inch gap). Replace points if excessively burned or pitted (par. 99), also replace condenser if excessive burned condition exists at points. **Clean.** Remove the distributor body and shaft assembly (par. 98); wash the distributor thoroughly in dry-cleaning solvent, dry with compressed air, and reinstall in correct position for timing. NOTE: *In cleaning the distributor, remove the wick and lubrication cup, clean and dry them while removed, and reinstall them after the distributor has been cleaned and thoroughly dried.* †NOTE: *Items marked with a dagger (†) are given additional services later in these procedures. Perform only the services designated after the item.*

Maintenance Instructions

6,000 Mile (Six-Month) Maint.	1,000 Mile (Monthly) Maint.	
		Special Lubrication. Lubricate the cam surfaces, movable breaker arm pin, wick, and drive shaft according to Lubrication Order No. 9-802.
31		**Centrifugal Advance.** Install rotor on upper end of distributor camshaft and note whether camshaft can be rotated by finger force through the normal range of movement which is permitted by the centrifugal advance mechanism. Turn in direction of drive shaft rotation and release to test for binding.
22	22	**Battery (Cables, Hold-downs, Carrier, and Record Gravity and Voltage).** Inspect battery case for cracks and leaks. Clean top of battery. Inspect cables, terminals, bolts, posts, straps, and hold-downs for good condition. Test specific gravity and voltage (par. 130), and record on W.D., A.G.O. Form No. 461. Specific gravity readings below 1.225 indicate battery should be recharged or replaced. For extremely hot weather (95°F and above) see instructions in paragraph 47. For cold weather instructions, see paragraph 46. Electrolyte level should be ⅜ inch above top of plates. Perform high-rate discharge test, according to instructions for "condition" test which accompany instrument, and record voltage on W.D., A.G.O. Form No. 461. Cell variation should not be more than 30 percent. NOTE: *Specific gravity must be above 1.225 to make this test.* Bring electrolyte to proper level by adding distilled or clean water (par. 130). Clean entire battery and carrier. Repaint carrier if corroded, (par. 129). Clean battery cable terminals, terminal bolts and nuts, and battery post and grease lightly. Inspect bolts for serviceability. Tighten terminals and hold-downs carefully to avoid damage to battery.
26	26	**Water Pump and Fan (Belt and Shroud).** Inspect applicable items to see if they are in good condition, correctly assembled, securely mounted, and not leaking. Be sure fan blades revolve without interfering with shroud or radiator core. **Adjust.** Adjust fan belt according to paragraph 118a.
25	25	**Radiator (Hose, Core, Mounting, Cap, Gasket, and Overflow Tank).** Inspect the above components to see if they are in good condition; that mountings and connections are secure; that cap fits filler neck and cap vent is open and free. Inspect entire system for leaks, and examine coolant for contamination (par. 117). If condition of coolant warrants cleaning, clean cooling system only according to paragraph 117, and correct directives regarding proper procedure, cleaner, neutralizer, and inhibitor. During freezing weather, check antifreeze value and record on back of form No. 461. Remove all dirt, insects, and refuse from core air passages and straighten bent cooling fins. Inspect and clean air ducts. Check shroud side of core seals for proper air circulation.
71	71	**Transmission.** Inspect housing to see if it is in good condition and see that all external assembly nuts or screws and all mountings are secure.
72	72	**Transfer Cases (Axle and Water Propeller).** Inspect both transfer case housings to see if they are in good condition, and see that all external assembly nuts and screws and all mountings are secure.

Preventive Maintenance Services

6,000 Mile (Six-Month) Maint.	1,000 Mile (Monthly) Maint.	
65	65	**Clutch Pedal (Free-travel, Linkage, and Return Spring).** Inspect pedal and all operating linkage to see if they are in good condition, correctly assembled, and securely mounted. Be sure return spring has sufficient tension to bring pedal to correct released position. **Adjust.** Adjust pedal free-travel (should be 2½ inches and never less than 1 inch), see paragraph 153.
66	66	**Brake Pedal (Free-travel, Linkage, and Return Spring).** Inspect in same manner as for item 65. **Adjust.** Adjust pedal free-travel and toeboard clearance. Pedal should have ½ inch free-travel before meeting resistance and sufficient reserve travel and pedal clearance to under side of toe board, see paragraph 191.
81	81	**Wiring and Conduits.** Inspect all accessible low voltage wiring and conduits to see that they are in good condition, and securely connected and supported. Wipe off accumulated dirt, oil, or moisture.
81		**Clean.** Clean and tighten all connections and coat wiring connections with gray insulating enamel (52-E-5210).
104	104	**Radio Bonding (Suppressors, Filters, Condensers, and Shielding).** See that all units not covered in the foregoing or following specific procedures are in good condition and securely mounted and connected. Be sure all additional noise suppression bond straps and internal-external toothed lock washers listed in paragraphs 138 through 142 are inspected for looseness or damage, and see that contact surfaces are clean. NOTE: *If cleaning and tightening of mounting and connections, and replacement of defective radio noise suppression units does not eliminate the trouble, the radio operator will report the condition to the designated individual in authority.*
57	57	**Steering (Arms, Tie Rod, Drag Link, Pitman Arm, and Housing).** Inspect all above components to see if they are in good condition, correctly assembled, and secure.
57		Drain steering gear housing and if lubricant is contaminated, remove and disassemble steering gear assembly (TM 9-1802C). Thoroughly clean and inspect parts, replace steering housing oil and water seals. **Adjust.** Adjust worm bearings and sector gear (par. 217) before reinstalling steering gear assembly. Lubricate (pars. 52 and 53).
63		**Engine Mountings, Braces, and Ground Straps.** Examine all engine mountings and ground straps to see if they are in good condition and secure. Adjust engine stabilizer (strut) rod (par. 95) and tighten mountings as necessary (par. 95).
33	33	**Manifolds and Heat Control.** Examine all manifolds and gaskets to see if they are in good condition and not leaking and see that all mounting and connections are secure (par. 87). Be sure heat control valve is in "OFF" position.
27	27	**Generator, Starting Motor, and Switch.** Examine these units to see if they are in good condition and securely connected and mounted. Remove inspection covers and inspect brushes to see if they are in good condition, free in brush holders, properly spring loaded, and connected. If necessary, clean commutator end of generator and starting motor (pars. 124 and 127). Check starting motor switch retracting spring for proper tension and tighten all mountings securely. Be sure radio noise condensers and filters on starting motor and generator are in good condition and secure.

Maintenance Instructions

6,000 Mile (Six-Month) Maint.	1,000 Mile (Monthly) Maint.	
39	39	**Starting Motor Action, Noise, and Speed.** Start engine, observing action of starting motor, particularly if it engages and disengages properly without unusual noise and has adequate cranking speed. While starting engine, note if action of hand throttle and choke is satisfactory, and if pertinent instruments indicate the proper function of units to which they apply.
18	18	**Cylinder Head and Gaskets.** Inspect head and gaskets to see if they are in good condition and look for indication of oil, coolant, and compression leaks. After engine has warm-up to 160-180°F, test tightness of cylinder head bolts with a torque wrench (70-80 foot-pounds). See paragraph 86.
19	19	**Valve Mechanism (Clearance, Lubrication, and Cover Gasket).** Inspect all valve mechanism components to see if they are in good condition, correctly and securely assembled, and that oil is being delivered properly. Adjust valve clearances (intake 0.012 inch and exhaust 0.016 inch) with engine temperature at 160-180°F (par. 86). Be sure valve cover gasket is in good condition when reinstalling cover. NOTE: *Valve clearance must always be adjusted after tightening of cylinder head bolts.*
42	42	**Engine Idle and Vacuum Test.** Adjust carburetor so engine idles smoothly at 510 revolutions per minute (par. 106).
42		Make a vacuum test according to instructions (par. 85*b*.).
43	43	**Regulator Unit (Connections, Voltage, Current, and Cut-out).** Inspect regulator assembly and radio noise filter unit to see if they are in good condition and securely connected and mounted.
43		After regulator has reached normal operating temperature, connect a low voltage tester and test to see if voltage and current regulators and cut-out properly control generator output (TM 9-1802A). When reinstalling regulator cover, be sure it is thoroughly sealed against leakage (par. 128).
38		†**Fuel Pump Pressure.** Attach test gage and check fuel pump pressure (par. 109). Pressure should be 3½ pounds for 2-valve pump or 5 pounds for 6-valve pump.
36		†**Carburetor and Governor.** Inspect these units to see if they are in good condition, secure, and not leaking. Test operation of both units to be sure they function properly. If necessary, adjust carburetor and/or governor according to instructions, paragraphs 106 and/or 108.
28	28	**Tire Pump (Governor and Front Mounted Tire Pump Drive).** Inspect tire pump units (all types) to see if they are in good condition, securely mounted, and that all connections, (air and/or water) are tight. Look for water leaks (water-cooled type), and oil leaks on all types. Check action of governor and adjust as necessary to cut in at 50 pounds and out at 75 pounds (par. 265). On front mounted tire pump, inspect drive shaft and U-joint assembly to see that all components are in good condition and secure.
28		Remove and inspect front drive shaft and U-joint (par. 267), and reinstall securely.
		Special Lubrication. Lubricate compressor drive assembly, see Lubrication Order No. 9-802.
		†NOTE: *Items marked with a dagger (†) are given additional services later in these procedures. Perform only the services designated after the item.*

Preventive Maintenance Services

6,000 Mile (Six-Month) Maint.	1,000 Mile (Monthly) Maint.	
44	44	**Power Tire Inflation System (Hose, Lines, Fittings, and Tank).** Inspect hose, lines, control valves, inflation devices on wheel hubs, and struts to see if they are in good condition, correctly assembled, and securely mounted or connected. Be sure valves and hub devices operate properly. Drain condensation from air tank and check tank safety valve for proper operation (see pars. 263 and 271). Be sure all hose, tank, and lines are properly supported.
123	123	**Hand Bilge Pump.** Straighten body of pump as necessary. Lubricate foot valve and plunger with light engine oil.

85	85	†**Vehicle Lubrication.**
		 Lubrication Fittings. Lubricate the following points according to Lubrication Order No. 9-802.
		   Axle Propeller Shafts—Accessible Inside of Hull (12)
		   Winch Drive Shaft (7)
		   Water Propeller Shaft—Accessible Inside of Hull (3)
		   Water Propeller Shaft Thrust Bearing (1)
		   Transfer Case Controls (4)
		   Water Propeller Control Rods (4)
		   Master Cylinder Shaft (2)
		   Clutch Mechanism (2)
		   Hand Brake Linkage (2)
		   Speedometer Adapter (1)
		   Rudder Control Linkage (2)
		   Winch, Drum, and Shaft Bearings (3)
		   Rear Spring Seats (2)
		 Oilcan Points. Oil the following points according to Lubrication Order No. 9-802.
		   Steering Cable Pulleys (6)
		   Starting Motor Linkage
		   Starting Motor Internal Drive Mechanism and Oil Cup
		   Hand and Foot Accelerator Linkage
		   Carbureter Acceleration Pump
		   Hand Choke
		   Tire Pump Governor (2)
		   Rear Generator Bearing (Late Models Only)

16	16	†**Gear Oil Levels.**
		 Special Lubrication. Drain and refill following according to Lubrication Order No. 9-802.
		   Transfer Cases and Transmission.
		   Thoroughly clean all vents.
		   Add lubricant as needed in steering gear housing.

91	91	**Lamps (Lights, Head, Tail, Stop, Black-out, and Instrument Panel).** Inspect all light units to see if they are in good condition and securely mounted and connected. Test all switches and observe if lamps respond properly. Be sure to include stop light and see that foot switch controls the head lamp-unit beams properly.
86	86	**Toe-in and Turning Stops.** Use gage to check and adjust front wheel toe-in (par. 170). Be sure turning stops are in place and adjusted to properly control turning angle.

†NOTE: *Items marked with a dagger* (†) *are given additional services later in these procedures. Perform only the services designated after the item.*

Maintenance Instructions

6,000 Mile (Six-Month) Maint.	1,000 Mile (Monthly) Maint.	
122	122	**Rudder (Adjustment, Cables, Linkage).** Inspect all rudder control mechanism (figs. 191 and 192), to see if above components are in good condition, correctly and securely assembled and mounted. Replace cables if any signs of rust exist. **Adjust.** Set wheels straight and adjust rudder to straight-ahead position. Set indicator marks at top of steering wheel. Turn wheels full left and check for proper clearance in end of rudder control arm groove. Adjust as necessary. See paragraph 223. **Special Lubrication.** Lubricate rudder cable for full travel of cable at each of 6 pulleys and steering column spool as steering wheel is turned full to right and left. Lubricate rudder control arm groove and ball.
120		†**Water Propeller (Shafts and Bearings).** Inspect propeller and drive shafts to see if they are in good condition, securely mounted and assembled, and see if shafts and propeller run true. Be sure forward and thrust bearings are in good condition, secure, and not excessively worn (par. 256). Repack shields on forward support bearing (par. 257).

LAND TEST

1	1	**Before-operation Inspection.** Perform those items of the Before-operation Services not already covered in the foregoing specific procedures. See paragraph 56.
3	3	**Dash Instruments and Gages.** **Oil Pressure Gage.** Gage must register a normal reading (engine hot) at low idling speed (see paragraph 20c.). **Ammeter.** Ammeter should indicate zero or slight positive (+) reading with engine at fast idle, accessories and lights off. **Temperature Gage.** Normal temperature reading is at least 160°F. **Fuel Gage.** Fuel gage must indicate approximate level of fuel in tank. **Tachometer.** Tachometer indicates engine speed in revolutions per minute. Red pointer will remain at maximum revolutions per minute attained. **Tank Pressure Air Gage.** Tank pressure gage must read between 50 and 75 pounds. **Tire Pressure Air Gage.** With air control lever in neutral position and all tire line valves open, gage should register existing tire pressure. **Speedometer and Odometer.** Speedometer must indicate vehicle land speed without unusual fluctuation or grind; odometer must record accumulated land mileage.
4	4	**Horn and Windshield Wipers.** If tactical situation permits, test horn for proper operation and tone. Test wipers to see if they function properly; if blades and arms are in good condition, and contact glass evenly and firmly through full stroke.
		†NOTE: *Items marked with a dagger (†) are given additional services later in these procedures. Perform only the services designated after the item.*

Preventive Maintenance Services

6,000 Mile (Six-Month) Maint.	1,000 Mile (Monthly) Maint.	
5	5	**Brakes (Foot and Hand, Action, and Braking Effect).** Test brakes for smoothness and effective braking. Pedal reserve clearance must be at least 2 inches to toeboard when applied. Hand brake reserve travel must be one-third of the ratchet range (par. 200).
6	6	**Clutch (Free-travel, Drag, Noise, Chatter, Grab, and Slip).** Clutch pedal free-travel should be 2½ inches and never less than 1 inch (par. 153). Clutch should engage without drag, noise, chatter, or grabbing and operate without slippage when fully engaged under load.
7	7	**Transmission, Power Take-off, and Transfer Cases (Lever Action, Declutching, Vibration, and Noise).** Controls should shift easily and smoothly. Gears should operate without unusual noise or vibration and not slip out of mesh during operation.
8	8	**†Steering.** During road test, observe if steering mechanism operates without excessive looseness or binding, side pull, wander, or shimmy. Note any looseness of column bracket or steering wheel.
9	9	**Engine Performance.** **Idle.** Engine should idle smoothly without stalling when decelerated to shift gears. **Acceleration, Power, and Noise.** Be on the alert for deficiencies in engine performance such as lack of usual power and acceleration and note any unusual noise that might indicate loose, excessively worn, or inadequately lubricated parts or accessories, or ping indicating excessive carbon or improper timing. **Governed Speed.** Test for governor surge at full throttle in low range second gear. If necessary, adjust governor (par. 108), and seal after completion of road test.

WATER TEST RUN

118	118	**†Hull Leaks.** Remove all floor boards, clean all bilges thoroughly, and inspect inside of hull for indications of leaks. Look for bare or rusted spots on painted surfaces. Examine hull including bulkheads, frame, and braces for broken assembly welds and loose or missing assembly bolts.
119	119	**Bilge Pumps.** Test both power driven bilge pumps (par. 36), to see if they are properly operating. Observe if valve control linkage is properly connected and if valves function properly. Examine bilge pump shaft packing to see if it is in good condition, and clean drain hole in centrifugal pump (Higgins). Test operation of hand bilge pump.
8	8	**Steering (In Water).** During water test run, observe if vehicle responds to action of rudder effectively.
9	9	**Engine (Speed and Temperature).** Run at full throttle in water and observe if engine turns up 2350 minimum revolutions per minute with engine temperature not over 180°F.
		†NOTE: *Items marked with a dagger (†) are given additional services later in these procedures. Perform only the services designated after the item.*

Maintenance Instructions

6,000 Mile (Six-Month) Maint.	1,000 Mile (Month-ly) Maint.	
120	120	†**Water Propeller Stuffing Box.** Examine stuffing box to see that it does not run hot and if it is in good condition, securely connected, and not leaking.
118	118	†**Hull Bilges.** At completion of water test run, remove (3) hull bottom plugs, drain bilges thoroughly, and reinstall plugs securely. NOTE: *Correct or report any deficiency found or noted during test.*
24	24	**Oil Filter.** Inspect filter to see if it is in good condition, securely mounted and connected, and not leaking.
	24	**Clean.** Drain oil filter sediment bowl.
24		**Serve.** Replace oil filter element (par. 91). See Lubrication Order No. 9-802.
23	23	**Crankcases (Engine and Tire Pump).** Drain and refill engine crankcase and tire pump base. Run engine for 2 minutes, then stop engine, recheck oil level and fill to "FULL" mark on oil stick. Inspect for leaks. See Lubrication Order No. 9-802.
85	85	†**Special Lubrication (Axle Propeller Shaft Universal Joints).** Lubricate (3) shaft universal joints through housing drain holes. Replace all housing plugs securely, and lubricate the following units, according to Lubrication Order No. 9-802. Propeller Strut. Inter-Axle Points (3) Tire Inflation Hubs (6) Front Spring Shackles and Brackets (6) Tie Rod Ends (2) Drag Links Ends (2) Propeller and Rudder Stuffing Boxes (2) Bilge Pumps (2)
87	87	**Winch (Clutch, Brakes, Drive, Shear Pin, Cable, Oil Condition and Level).** Inspect winch assembly, drive shaft and U-joints to see if they are in good condition and correctly and securely assembled and mounted. Test jaw clutch to see if it operates properly and latches securely. Test operation of drag and automatic brakes, see paragraph 273. Remove and examine shear pin to see if it is in good condition, and U-joint is free on shaft. Clean and lubricate shaft and pin and install pin securely. **Clean and Serve.** Inspect winch cable and auxiliary cable for kinks, broken strands, or rust. Clean, and as cable is rewound evenly and tightly, apply a coating of thin film rust preventive compound.
87	87	**Special Lubrication.** Examine winch worm housing for water. If necessary, drain worm housing thoroughly and refill with new lubricant (Lubrication Order No. 9-802). †NOTE: *Items marked with a dagger (†) are given additional services later in these procedures. Perform only the services designated after the item.*

Preventive Maintenance Services

6,000 Mile (Six-Month) Maint.	1,000 Mile (Monthly) Maint.	
16	16	†**Gear Lubricant Levels.** Check axle differentials (3) and refill to correct level. Check lubricant in front axle universal joints and pillow block and refill to correct level. **Leaks.** Inspect for lubricant leaks at following points: Wheels (6) Front Axle U-joints (2) Axle Differentials (3) Pillow Block Winch Worm Housing Steering Gear Housing Propeller and Main Transfer Cases
85	85	†**Special Lubrication.** Clean, oil, and free up all items such as joints, pivots, bolts, hinges, clamps, wing nuts, shackles, pintle hook, switch, and controls—inside and outside of hull. Clean and oil outside of front axle U-joints. See Lubrication Order No. 9-802.
103	103	**Paint and Markings (Hull).** Remove hull fenders, thoroughly clean and dry hull—inside and out. Clean all rusted spots thoroughly and inspect carefully for weakened spots in hull, repair and paint as necessary including numbers, markings, and stencils (par. 238). Install hull fenders (par. 33).
100	100	**Tarpaulins, Fenders, and Lashings.** Inspect top tarpaulin and bows, and hull fenders (par. 33) to see that they are in proper place and in good condition. If in use, be sure all lashings are in place and secure, otherwise see that all items are properly stowed (pars. 6, 7, and 8).
TOOLS AND EQUIPMENT		
131	131	**Tools (Vehicle and Pioneer).** Check tools against paragraphs 6 and 7 to see that all items are present. See that they are in good condition and properly mounted or stowed. Tools with cutting edges should be sharpened and properly protected. Items mounted on outside of vehicle having bright surfaces should be painted or otherwise treated to prevent rust and glare or reflection.
132	132	**Fire Extinguishers.** Inspect all units to be sure they are in good condition. Be sure nozzles are not clogged, and that they are fully charged (par. 39). Mount them securely.
133	133	**Decontaminator.** Inspect units to be sure they are in good condition, fully charged, and mounted securely. NOTE: *Solution deteriorates and must be renewed every 90 days.*
134	134	**First-aid Kit.** Inspect kit to be sure the contents and case are in good condition, that all items are intact and properly packed. Stow kit securely.
135	135	**Publication and Form No. 26.** Be sure all vehicle manuals, Form 48 (Driver's Trip Ticket and Preventive Maintenance Service Record), Lubrication Orders, Form No. 26 (Driver's Report—Accident, Motor Transportation), and Form No. 478 (MWO and Major Unit Assembly Replacement Record) are present, legible, and safely stowed.
		†NOTE: *Items marked with a dagger (†) are given additional services later in these procedures. Perform only the services designated after the item.*

Maintenance Instructions

6,000 Mile (Six-Month) Maint.	1,000 Mile (Monthly) Maint.	
138	138	Spare Shearpins. Be sure spare supply of shearpins are present, in good condition, well lubricated, and properly stowed.
139	139	Fuel and Water Cans and Brackets. Inspect spare liquid cans to be sure they are in good condition and full. See that brackets are securely mounted and install cans securely.
141	141	Modifications (MWO's Completed). Inspect vehicle thoroughly to determine if all modification work orders have been completed and entered on Form No. 478. Enter all modifications and Major Unit Assembly Replacements made at time of this service.

Section XV
Trouble Shooting

61. GENERAL.

a. Scope. The information contained in this section includes a compilation of trouble symptoms which might be encountered in the operation of the vehicle, together with the possible causes and possible remedies. Only those difficulties which can be detected by the using arm are included. Whenever practical, the trouble shooting procedures are classified according to each section of the manual. In some instances, a symptom indicating trouble in one unit may be caused by difficulty in another unit; therefore, cross references to the related units are made whenever this condition exists.

b. Diagnosing Causes. The causes of trouble symptoms or faults in a vehicle of this type may be varied; therefore, a hit-and-miss search would result in a tedious guessing contest. The diagnosis of symptoms is an orderly process of eliminating causes of the symptom. An orderly process means to check the most probable or common cause first.

62. ENGINE.

a. Engine Fails to Start. When engine fails to start, a deficiency in one of two systems is most commonly the cause. The most probable cause is ignition system trouble, with fuel system as the next. One of the quickest methods to determine whether starting trouble is caused by the ignition system or the fuel system is the spark test.

(1) SPARK TEST. Disconnect one wire from spark plug. With ignition switch "ON" and starter cranking engine, hold free end of wire about 3/8 inch away from engine block. Note the spark. If there is no spark, the trouble lies in the ignition system. If there is a spark, the trouble will be most commonly found in the fuel system.

Trouble Shooting

(2) NO SPARK. The action of the ammeter will further aid in the diagnosis of this condition. Normally the ammeter will show a slight discharge with needle oscillating between two and four amperes. Definite procedures are necessary if engine does not start when ammeter action is normal or abnormal. These procedures follow:

(a) Ammeter Shows No Discharge (Zero). A zero reading on the ammeter, with ignition turned "ON" and starter cranking engine, indicates that no current is flowing in the ignition primary circuit; therefore, the following checks should be made on the units of the primary circuit:

1. First make sure that the ignition switch is fully turned "ON" and that wiring connections at switch are clean and tight.
2. Turn on headlights to ascertain that current is flowing through ammeter. If ammeter does not show discharge, turn off headlight switch; then use jumper lead or test lamp at battery side of ammeter and make flash test to determine if current is flowing to the ammeter. Clean and tighten connections in circuit between starter and ignition switch.
3. Remove distributor cap and check condition of points and point opening. Adjust, clean, or replace points as necessary.
4. Check continuity of circuit through primary wire from ignition switch terminal screw to coil, then from coil to distributor, using a jumper lead or test lamp. If current flows through primary wire from switch to coil, and not from coil to distributor, replace the coil. If current flows through primary wire to distributor, the trouble is in the distributor.
5. Check continuity of circuit from ammeter to ignition switch, then through ignition switch with switch turned "ON." Replace wiring or switch as necessary.

(b) Ammeter Shows Normal Discharge (Oscillating Between Two and Four Amperes). If the ammeter oscillates between two and four amperes discharge with switch turned "ON" and starter cranking engine, the primary circuit is functioning correctly; trace the secondary circuit in the following manner:

1. Remove coil to distributor high tension wire from distributor cap. Hold end of wire about $\frac{3}{8}$ inch from a ground. With starter cranking engine or "rocking" points, note spark. If a hot, snappy spark results, reinsert wire in distributor cap and continue with test. If a weak spark results, replace the condenser in the distributor (par. 100). If a weak spark persists, replace the coil (par. 102). If no spark results, check high tension wire from coil to distributor for continuity of circuit. Replace with wire known to be good.
2. With high tension wire from coil to distributor inserted in distributor cap, remove cap. With starter cranking engine, observe inside of cap for visible current leaks.

Maintenance Instructions

   3. Check condition of distributor cap center electrode by holding one end of a high tension wire on electrode and the other end about ⅜ inch from a ground. Crank engine with starter. Spark should jump gap from high tension wire to ground. If no spark is produced, replace the cap.

   4. Remove high tension wire from coil to distributor at distributor cap. Hold end of high tension wire about ⅜ inch from the rotor. Crank engine and watch for spark. If spark is seen, the rotor is defective and must be replaced.

   5. After determining that secondary current arrives at spark plug wires, test each spark plug wire for continuity of circuit. Replace wires which do not test correctly.

(c) Ammeter Shows Constant Normal Discharge (Does Not Oscillate). A constant normal discharge at the ammeter (two to four amperes) indicates that the primary circuit is not being interrupted. Check in the following sequence:

   1. Disconnect primary wire from coil to distributor at distributor. If ammeter drops to zero, check as explained in 2. through 4. below. If ammeter does not drop to zero, reconnect wire to distributor and disconnect at coil. If ammeter does not drop to zero, the coil is defective and must be replaced (par. 102).

   2. Check distributor points and clean, adjust, or replace if necessary (par. 99).

   3. Check insulation on movable point and on distributor primary terminal. Replace points or distributor as necessary (par. 99 or 98).

   4. Disconnect condenser pigtail. Make flash test between pigtail terminal and distributor primary wire terminal. If flash occurs, replace condenser (par. 100).

(d) Ammeter Shows Abnormal Discharge (Over Four Amperes) with Ignition Switch "ON," Zero with Switch "OFF." If the ammeter shows abnormal discharge with ignition switch "ON" and zero with switch "OFF," the trouble lies beyond the ignition switch and ahead of the primary exit at the coil. Make tests in the following sequence:

   1. With ignition switch "ON," disconnect wire at dead side of switch. If ammeter returns to zero, the switch is correct. If ammeter does not return to zero, the switch is defective. Replace with one known to be good (par. 144j.). Reconnect wire to switch.

   2. With switch known to be functioning properly, disconnect wire at primary entrance of coil. If ammeter returns to zero, check terminal of coil for grounded condition. If the terminal is not grounded, replace the coil (par. 102). If terminal is grounded, correct grounded condition or replace coil (par. 102).

Trouble Shooting

3. If the ammeter still shows abnormal discharge after disconnecting primary wire at coil, replace wire from switch to coil.

(e) Ammeter Shows Abnormal Discharge with Ignition Switch Either "ON" or "OFF." If abnormal discharge exists with ignition switch either "ON" or "OFF," the trouble is between the ammeter and ignition switch. Shorts may also exist in lighting circuit (between ammeter and light switch) and in generator circuit. Test in following sequence:

1. Remove wires from discharge side of ammeter. Ammeter should then return to zero. Touch terminal of light circuit wire to ammeter terminal. If ammeter shows discharge, trace short in wire from ammeter to light switch. If no short is present, generator circuit should be checked. If generator circuit does not cause discharge, the trouble lies either in the ignition switch or in the ammeter to ignition switch wire.

2. With ammeter to switch wire disconnected at both ends, connect a jumper lead to ammeter terminal and to ignition switch terminal. If discharge still shows, replace ignition switch (par. 144*j*.). If ammeter returns to zero, replace ammeter to ignition switch wire.

(3) WEAK SPARK AT PLUGS.

(a) This condition may be caused by a weak battery. Check battery and charge or replace as necessary (par. 130***b***.).

(b) Remove distributor cap and check condition of points. Clean up and adjust, or replace if necessary (par. 99).

(c) Check condition of rotor and cap. Replace cap if electrodes are burned, or rotor if segment is burned. Make sure wires are fully seated in sockets in distributor cap.

(d) Check condenser for short and replace if necessary (par. 100).

(e) Check all connections in circuit from starter to distributor. Clean and tighten as necessary.

(f) Check condition of high tension wires. Replace if wet or swollen.

(g) If items *(a)* through *(f)* do not eliminate trouble, replace ignition coil (par. 102).

(4) GOOD SPARK AT PLUGS. When engine will not start with good spark at plugs, first determine that the fuel tank is not empty, then proceed as follows:

(a) Remove float level sight plug from carbureter bowl (on engine side).

(b) If no fuel can be seen, remove drain plug from bottom of bowl. If no fuel flows out, make check as itemized in *(f)* below.

(c) If fuel is level with sight plug hole, failure to start may be caused by flooded combustion chambers due to excessive use of choke, or by fuel not reaching the cylinder due to a dirty carbureter. Check choke mechanism, or clean fuel bowl(par. 106***c***.).

TM 9-802

Maintenance Instructions

(d) If fuel flows out of sight plug hole, carbureter float needs adjustment (TM 9-1802A), or fuel pump pressure is excessive (par. 109c.).

(e) If fuel does not flow out of sight plug hole, but does flow out of drain plug hole, check fuel pump for operation (par. 109c.). If fuel pump is operating properly, carbureter float level requires adjustment (TM 9-1802A).

(f) If fuel is not reaching carbureter as in *(b)*, check fuel pump operation; check line between fuel pump and fuel filter; clean fuel filter; check lines between fuel filter and fuel tank.

b. Engine Runs But Operates Improperly.

(1) CONTINUOUS MISFIRING.

(a) The most common cause of this condition is dirty spark plugs. First determine that current is flowing to each plug, then remove plugs and check for dirty electrodes. Clean up and adjust spark gap, or replace plugs as necessary (par. 101). Dirty plugs are an indication of faulty valve operation, or worn piston rings allowing oil to enter combustion chamber.

(b) Inspect high tension wires. Replace if wet or if insulation is swollen or deteriorated.

(c) Remove distributor cap and check for burned electrodes or cracks. Replace cap if defective.

(d) Conditions contributing to low compression will also cause misfiring in one or more cylinders. If remedies given in *(a)*, *(b)*, and *(c)* do not correct the trouble, check compression of all cylinders (par. 85c.) and make necessary repairs or notify higher authority.

(2) ERRATIC MISFIRING AT IDLING SPEEDS.

(a) One of the most common causes of misfiring at idling speed is incorrect carbureter idling adjustment or incorrect float level adjustment. Make carbureter idling adjustment (par. 106b.) or float level adjustment (TM 9-1802A), then check operation of choke mechanism. Free up and adjust as necessary (par. 107b.).

(b) Check ignition system units, starting with spark plugs, until all ignition causes are corrected or eliminated.

(c) Check for vacuum leaks at intake manifold gasket, vacuum lines, and carbureter. Check possibility of water entering cylinder due to a leaking cylinder head gasket.

(d) If the condition still exists after making corrections *(a)*, *(b)*, and *(c)*, check valve clearance and valve mechanism operation, perform engine compression test, and make necessary adjustments and repairs or notify higher authority.

(3) MISFIRING AT HIGH SPEEDS OR UNDER FULL LOAD. Misfiring at high speeds or under full load is commonly caused by a weak secondary current in the ignition circuit. Weak valve springs, however, will also cause misfiring at high speeds.

(a) Remove spark plugs and make sure they are the correct type. Clean up and adjust gap. Make sure that gap is same on all plugs (par. 101).

Trouble Shooting

(b) Remove distributor cap and check point opening and test spring tension (par. 99). Adjust point opening and spring tension or replace points as necessary.

(c) A weakened coil caused by shorting out of secondary winding will cause misfiring. Replace coil with one known to be good (par. 102). Leaks throughout the high tension wires will also weaken the current and cause misfiring. Check condition of all high tension wires and replace if necessary. Make sure that sockets in distributor cap are thoroughly cleaned of corrosion and that wires are fully seated.

(d) Check operation of valve springs and replace any that are weak.

(4) BACKFIRING.

(a) As a general rule, backfiring into the muffler indicates too rich a fuel mixture. Backfiring into the carburetor indicates too lean a mixture. Make necessary adjustments at carburetor (par. 106b.).

(b) Check all fuel lines for restrictions and clean air cleaner (par. 105). Clean carburetor fuel bowl if necessary (par. 106c.).

(c) Sticking valves or weak valve springs will also cause backfiring. Check for and correct these conditions. Make sure cylinder head gasket is in good condition.

(d) Extremely late ignition timing will cause backfiring. Check timing and make necessary adjustments (par. 97).

c. Engine Miscellaneous Operating Faults.

(1) EXCESSIVE FUEL CONSUMPTION. For a diagnosis of causes of excessive fuel consumption, refer to paragraph 64b.

(2) EXCESSIVE OIL CONSUMPTION.

(a) The first step to be taken when an engine uses an excessive amount of oil is to make a thorough inspection for leaks. Check all oil lines and tighten connections or replace as necessary.

(b) Overspeeding the engine will result in excessive oil consumption. Poor driving practices should be corrected.

(c) Worn pistons or piston rings are a common cause of excessive oil consumption. Perform engine compression test and make necessary repairs or notify higher authority.

(d) Overheating will cause excessive oil consumption. Refer to paragraph 66b.

(e) Remove crankcase ventilator valve and clean thoroughly to prevent sticking (par. 92).

(f) Report loosened connecting rod or main bearings to higher authority.

(3) LACK OF POWER.

(a) The primary cause of lack of power is poor compression. Perform engine compression test and make necessary correction or notify higher authority.

(b) Conditions in the fuel system which contribute to lack of power are covered in paragraph 64g.

(c) Improper ignition timing will result in a lack of power. Refer to paragraph 63e.

(d) Overheating also results in a lack of power. Refer to paragraph 66b.

(e) A clogged exhaust system or bent exhaust pipe or tail pipe will result in a lack of power. Check for these conditions and clean out or replace pipes as necessary (pars. 114 and 115).

(f) Dragging brakes or improperly inflated tires simulate a lack of power. Check for these conditions and make necessary corrections.

(4) ENGINE FAILS TO DEVELOP MAXIMUM PERMISSIBLE RPM. This condition is usually an indication that the governor is dirty and must be replaced (par. 108).

(5) OPERATING KNOCKS. Noises in an engine generally termed as "operating knocks" may be caused by (a) overloading the engine, (b) carbon in the combustion chamber, (c) incorrect ignition timing, (d) low octane fuel, and (e) pre-ignition.

(a) Overloading the Engine. This noise occurs when an engine is placed under extreme load. Generally the noise is reduced after shifting to a lower transmission gear. This knock may be due to a combination of causes, all of which may be generally remedied by using correct transmission speeds.

(b) Carbon Knocks. This knocking is caused by accumulation of carbon in combustion chambers and is most noticeable when engine is hot and when engine is accelerated. The remedy is cleaning carbon from cylinder head.

(c) Timing Knock. Too early ignition timing may cause a knock that may be mistaken for a carbon knock. The engine may also kick back when starting. Check the ignition timing and make necessary corrections (par. 97).

(d) Fuel Knock. A poor grade of gasoline may cause a knock or "ping" similar to a carbon knock. Use a better grade of gasoline or readjust ignition timing (manual advance) to accomplish smooth running with grade of fuel used.

(e) Pre-ignition. One of the causes of pre-ignition (auto-ignition) is the use of wrong type spark plugs. Make certain that correct plugs are used. Also idle engine for 30 seconds before turning off ignition switch.

(6) MECHANICAL KNOCKS. Mechanical knocks are noises that result from wear or improper adjustments. These knocks are not always easy to locate accurately, as no two engines have exactly the same sound with the same faulty condition. In many instances, causes of mechanical knocks will evidence themselves by other symptoms. Correct diagnosis of mechanical knocks requires experience and practice on the particular type of engine to be serviced.

(a) Diagnosis of Mechanical Knocks. The first step in analyzing a mechanical knock is to be sure that the noise is in the engine. If the noise can be heard with the vehicle stopped and clutch disengaged, the fault is generally in the engine. The engine should be warmed up to

Trouble Shooting

operating temperature. Check to see that all cylinders are firing, then try engine under load to bring out the knock. Eliminate the possible causes such as carbon and valves, then proceed as follows to localize the knocks so that corrections may be made or a proper report made to a higher authority.

1. *Crankshaft and Bearing Knocks.* Loose bearings are usually indicated by heavy dull knock, more noticeable on acceleration of engine when under load. This knock can generally be located by shorting out cylinders on both sides of loose bearing. End play is usually indicated by intermittent knock which may disappear when slight pressure is put on clutch pedal.
2. *Piston and Connecting Rod Knocks.* Knock caused by loose connecting rod bearing can be shorted out. Loose piston pin noise generally doubles when cylinder is shorted out. Loose piston or piston "slap" is more noticeable when engine is cold and can be generally shorted out. Broken piston pin or ring noise usually has a sharp clicking sound and cannot be shorted out.
3. *Camshaft Knocks.* These knocks generally occur at half engine speed. Gear cover should be removed and play in gears and shaft checked by higher echelon.
4. *Timing Gear Noises.* A "humming" noise may indicate tight gears. Loose gears and other timing gear faults may be indicated by a rattle or knock.
5. *Valve Mechanism Knocks.* If valve mechanism knocks cannot be eliminated by valve clearance adjustment, notify higher authority.
6. *Water Pump Knocks.* If knocks definitely point to water pump, remove assembly and replace (par. 119).
7. *Other Engine Noises.* Check possible sources of other noises, such as loose fan blades, engine mounting, and muffler parts.

d. Engine Lubrication System.

(1) GENERAL. The most common trouble experienced with engine lubrication systems is the result of neglecting to use proper grade of oil or to keep oil to proper level. The use of oil of incorrect viscosity will contribute to several engine troubles, while neglecting to keep crankcase oil to proper level will finally result in a damaged engine. Use the correct grade of oil, keep it to proper level, and change it at regular intervals.

(2) LOW OIL PRESSURE. Low or no oil pressure is commonly caused by a clogged oil pump screen, broken oil lines, or worn main bearings. If the gage is known to be correct, and proper grade of oil is used, remove oil pan, clean screen, and examine oil pump for worn gears. Check oil lines for breaks or leaks, and make necessary corrections.

(3) EXCESSIVE OIL CONSUMPTION. Refer to subparagraph c.(2) above.

63. IGNITION SYSTEM.

a. General. The diagnosis of trouble symptoms in this paragraph is of those which pertain only to the ignition system. Reference should be made to paragraph 62 for a diagnosis of like symptoms. When diagnosing any ignition system trouble, the mechanic should visualize the ignition wiring diagram (fig. 68) and keep in mind the fundamental action of the two ignition circuits, *primary* and *secondary*.

b. Engine Misfires.

(1) Remove spark plugs and clean and adjust point gap. Replace with new plugs if porcelain is cracked (par. 101).

(2) Remove distributor cap and check condition of points. Adjust point opening or replace points as necessary (par. 99).

(3) Check condition of high tension cables. Replace cables if frayed, wet, or swollen.

(4) Check for other causes such as valves, valve springs, or poor compression and make necessary corrections.

(5) If trouble is still present, check ignition coil and condenser and replace if necessary (par. 100 or 102).

c. Engine Backfires.

(1) Backfiring may be caused by crossed spark plug wires or a cracked distributor cap. Check wires and attach in correct firing order (1-5-3-6-2-4). Inspect distributor cap and replace if damaged.

(2) A faulty condenser will cause backfiring. Check condenser and replace if necessary (par. 100).

d. Excessive "Ping" (Detonation) Under Load or at High Speed.

(1) This condition can be caused by improper ignition timing or by using an inferior grade of fuel. Make sure a good grade of fuel is used and make necessary manual advance adjustment (par. 97c.).

(2) "Ping" or knock caused by pre-ignition cannot be corrected by retarding the spark. Pre-ignition is caused by an overheated spot such as exhaust valve head, carbon deposit, or center electrode of spark plug igniting the fuel charge before the regularly timed spark at the plug. This condition can be corrected by using spark plugs of proper heat range, correcting exhaust valve clearance, or removing cylinder head and cleaning carbon deposits from top of pistons and cylinder head.

e. Engine Overheating or Lack of Power.

(1) This condition is sometimes caused by improper ignition timing. Check timing adjustment and make necessary corrections (par. 97).

(2) If this does not eliminate the trouble, check for other causes such as defective cooling system, poor compression, wrong type oil, etc.

64. FUEL AND AIR INTAKE SYSTEM.

a. General. Many symptoms which might indicate fuel system trouble are in reality due to faulty ignition or valves. Before making any extensive adjustments or repairs on the fuel system, the ignition system and valve operation should be thoroughly checked.

b. Excessive Fuel Consumption. The causes of excessive fuel consumption are listed below in logical sequence.

(1) FUEL LEAKS.

(a) Fuel Lines. Inspect all fuel lines for leaks, and check and tighten all connections.

(b) Carbureter. Fuel leaks at carbureter will be evidenced by the presence of fuel on the outside of the carbureter. Leak could be caused by loose drain plugs or improperly installed channel plugs. Tighten drain plugs or replace carbureter as necessary.

(c) Fuel Pump. Check for leaks around fuel pump bowl. Tighten thumb nut at top of bowl. If leak continues, replace gasket between bowl and pump.

(d) Fuel Filter. Leakage may occur at fuel filter bowl. Tighten cover screw at top of filter and tighten drain plug. If leak is still present, replace bowl to cover gasket.

(2) IMPROPER CARBURETER ADJUSTMENT OR CARBURETER CONTROLS STICKING.

(a) Adjust idling mixture and choke controls (pars. 106*b.* and 107*b.*).

(b) Air shutter (choke) not returning to fully open position will cause excessive fuel consumption. Soak carbureter air intake in kerosene to cut corrosion, then free up and lubricate shutter shaft.

(c) Adjust accelerator pump stroke for seasonal operation (TM 9-1802A).

(3) VALVE IN FUEL TANK CAP STUCK CLOSED. In extremely hot weather, this condition will cause excessive pressure in the fuel tank, which will result in excessive fuel consumption. Clean or replace cap (par. 111*b.*).

(4) CARBURETER PARTS WORN. If excessive fuel consumption is still evident after making corrections as directed in steps (1), (2), and (3) above, carbureter parts are worn, necessitating an overhaul of the unit. Replace carbureter with a new or rebuilt unit (par. 106).

c. Engine Idles Too Fast.

(1) Improper throttle adjustment, preventing the throttle plate from returning to closed position will cause engine to idle too fast. Properly adjust hand throttle (par. 107).

(2) Check return spring and replace with new spring if damage is apparent.

(3) Soak carbureter throttle body in kerosene to cut corrosion, then free up and lubricate throttle shaft.

d. Engine Dies When Idling.

(1) This condition is usually caused by improper carbureter idling speed or idling mixture adjustment. Make necessary adjustments (par. 106*b.*).

(2) Sticking choke control or crankcase ventilator valve will also cause engine to die. Free up and lubricate choke cable shaft and service crankcase ventilator valve.

(3) If trouble is still present, the idling circuit in the carbureter is clogged. Replace carbureter with a new or rebuilt unit (par. 106).

e. Low Fuel Pressure.

(1) Low fuel pressure is usually indicated when engine falters at high speeds. This condition may be caused by air leaking into the fuel lines. Tighten all fuel line connections and tighten fuel pump and fuel filter covers.

(2) Plugged fuel lines or clogged intake valve in fuel tank cap will cause low or no fuel pressure. Clean out or replace lines or cap as necessary.

(3) Test fuel pressure (par. 109c.).

(4) If low pressure is still evident, the fuel pump diaphragm is broken or the fuel pump valves are leaking. Replace diaphragm or valves as necessary.

(5) If the fuel pump linkage is worn excessively, replace pump (par. 109).

f. Engine Falters on Acceleration.

(1) This condition is usually caused by faulty operation of the carbureter accelerator pump or by dirt in the metering jets. In either case, the carbureter must be replaced with a new or rebuilt unit (par. 106).

(2) Air in the fuel lines will also contribute to this condition. Carefully check all lines for leaks.

g. Overheating or Lack of Power.

(1) Too lean a fuel mixture will cause the engine to overheat. Adjust carbureter (par. 106b.).

(2) Use of a low octane rating fuel will result in a lack of power. In this case, the ignition timing must be adjusted to compensate for the fuel used. This means that the lower the octane rating of the fuel, the more the spark must be retarded (par. 97).

65. EXHAUST SYSTEM.

a. The operator can readily detect any trouble in the exhaust system by unusually loud combustion noises in hull front compartment or engine compartment, or by the odor of exhaust fumes.

b. Odor of Exhaust Fumes.

(1) Check for blown out muffler and replace if necessary.

(2) Tighten all exhaust pipe connections.

(3) Check for leaking manifold gasket or cracked manifold. Replace gasket or manifold as necessary (par. 87).

c. Excessive Combustion Noises.
This condition is caused by a blown out muffler, loose manifold, or a blown manifold gasket. Tighten manifold or replace gasket or muffler as necessary (par. 87).

Trouble Shooting

d. Excessive Rattling. This condition is caused by muffler mountings loose. Tighten all mountings firmly.

66. COOLING SYSTEM.

a. General. Since the function of the cooling system is to control operating temperature of the engine, it is logical to assume that the cause of an overheated engine lies in the cooling system; however, late ignition timing or improper or insufficient lubricating oil in the engine crankcase will cause the engine to overheat, even though the cooling system is functioning properly. Check these items before making any extensive tests or repairs on the cooling system.

b. Overheating.

(1) Check for broken or loose fan belt. Replace belt or adjust to proper tension (par. 118).

(2) Check all radiator hose connections; water pump mounting bolts, seal, and gasket; thermostat housing bolts and gasket, cylinder head bolts and gasket, and make necessary repairs to correct leakage.

(3) Check radiator core for leakage and replace with new radiator assembly if such a condition is found (par. 121). Check for clogged air passages through radiator core and clean out if necessary.

(4) Cooling liquid may be escaping through an internal leak such as an internally cracked cylinder head or block, or a defective cylinder head gasket. Such leakage would be evidenced by bubbles or foam on the oil dip stick, or by a raised oil level in the crankcase. In this case, notify higher authority.

(5) An inoperative thermostat will cause engine to overheat. Remove thermostat and test, or replace with one known to be good (par. 120).

(6) Air suction or exhaust gas leakage into the system will cause rapid rusting and corrosion of engine parts, and this rust and corrosion will eventually clog the small water passages in the radiator core. In the event the cooling system is clogged, perform flushing operations (par. 117); in the event this does not clean out the system, notify higher authority.

(7) An improperly operating water pump will cause engine to overheat. To determine if the water pump is functioning properly, remove radiator filler cap, run engine at medium speed, and notice the action of the water. Do not confuse action caused by vibration with circulation; there will be a distinct noticeable current if the water pump is operating properly.

c. Overcooling. Overcooling is caused by the thermostat being stuck open. This is evidenced by the fact that the engine does not warm up to proper operating temperature. If such a condition exists, remove the thermostat and test, or replace with one known to be good (par. 120).

67. STARTING SYSTEM.

a. General. If the engine fails to start after repeated and satisfactory operations of the starter, cause of failure cannot be attributed to the starting system, but to other functioning systems of the engine such as the ignition system or fuel system.

b. Starter Fails to Operate.

(1) The first item to check when the starter fails to operate is the battery. If the battery is run down, recharge or replace (par. 130).

(2) Loose or broken battery or ground cable will cause starter failure. Thoroughly clean terminals and tighten or replace cables as necessary.

(3) Starter switch contact terminal sometimes becomes corroded or burned, preventing a good contact. Check for this condition and replace switch if necessary (par. 124c.).

(4) If, after making the above corrections, the starter still fails to operate, it is in need of an overhaul and must be replaced with a new or rebuilt unit (par. 124d.).

c. Starter Noisy.

(1) Starter noise may be due to loose mounting. Tighten bolt and stud nut attaching starter to clutch housing.

(2) Lubricate starter (Lubrication Order No. 9-802).

(3) If still noisy, the starter requires an overhaul and must be replaced with a new or rebuilt unit (par. 124d.).

d. Slow Cranking Speed.

(1) This condition may be caused by a weak battery or loose cable connections. Check for and correct these conditions.

(2) Perform line voltage tests to determine if there is excessive resistance in circuit and make necessary corrections (par. 124b.).

(3) If the starter still operates slowly after making the above corrections, it is in need of overhaul and must be replaced with a new or rebuilt unit (par. 124d.).

68. GENERATING SYSTEM.

a. General. Since the generator and regulator functions are directly related, both units must be considered when checking symptoms of failure in the generator circuit. When the ammeter shows an unsatisfactory reading, make sure the ammeter is correct before making any repairs on the generating system.

b. High Charging Rate with Fully Charged Battery.

(1) Check generator to regulator ground wire for damage or loose connections.

(2) Clean and tighten all terminals and connections in generator circuit.

(3) If condition still exists, either the voltage regulator is in need of adjustment, or the generator is in need of an overhaul. In either case, replace with a new or rebuilt unit (par. 127 or 128).

Trouble Shooting

c. Low Battery and Low or No Charging Rate.

(1) Check all wires between generator and regulator for signs of worn insulation or other damage. Clean and tighten all connections.

(2) If this does not correct the trouble, either the generator or regulator, or both, must be replaced with new or rebuilt units (par. 127 or 128).

d. Noisy Generator.

(1) Check and tighten all generator mounting bolts. Check drive belt tension and adjust if necessary (par. 118).

(2) If noise still is present, generator is in need of overhaul and must be replaced with a new or rebuilt unit (par. 127).

69. BATTERY AND LIGHTING SYSTEM.

a. General. Reference to wiring diagram (fig. 99 or 100) will show that a single circuit from battery to main light switch is common to all lamps on the vehicle. At main light switch this single circuit is divided into multiple circuits, each of which is common to two or more lamps (except service stop lamp). These circuits are then taken to various junction points where they are divided into individual circuits, each of which is taken to a single lamp. The return path of each circuit is through ground to battery. Dividing the circuits in this manner provides a convenient and logical method of locating the source of trouble. The use of a voltmeter or trouble lamp, and adhering to the following principles will aid in locating trouble in the lighting system.

(1) Source of trouble common to all lamps will be located in that part of the circuit common to all lamps.

(2) Source of trouble common to two or more—but not all—lamps will be located in that part of the circuit common only to the lamps affected.

(3) Source of trouble at a single lamp will be confined to the individual circuit of the lamp affected.

b. One Lamp Will Not Light. This condition is the result of an open circuit or grounded wire between the lamp ground and the feed wire junction. Open circuit or grounded wire may be caused by a burned out or broken filament; poor ground at lamp; corroded contacts or terminals; broken wire; frayed insulation, grounded or shorted terminals; defective main light switch or stop light switch (stop light only).

c. Two or More Lamps Will Not Light. The cause of this condition will be located between the main light switch and the individual lamp junction. Cause may be defective main light switch; defective individual light switch; loose or corroded terminals; broken wire.

d. All Lamps Will Not Light. The cause of this condition will be located between the point where the battery ground strap attaches to the frame and the main light switch.

(1) The cause may be a discharged battery; corroded battery terminals; corroded or broken battery cable or ground strap. These points can be checked by cranking engine with starter. If cranking speed is normal, trouble lies between the starter and main light switch.

(2) Other causes are loose or corroded terminals; defective main light switch; defective circuit breaker; defective ammeter; short circuit or ground at some point in system which causes the circuit breaker to operate. The only remedy is to methodically check the system until the fault is located and corrected.

(3) A vehicle not in use for some time may possibly have all lamp contacts corroded to the point where lamps are inoperative. A remote possibility of failure is that all filaments may have been broken by shock.

e. Lamps Give Insufficient Light. This condition may be caused by excessive resistance in circuit or by a discharged battery. Check condition of battery, then look for loose or corroded terminals and contacts, and frayed insulation on wires.

f. Frequent Lamp Failure. Frequent burning out of lamps is the result of high voltage at lamps. This is caused by a defective or improperly adjusted voltage regulator.

g. Discharged Battery. A discharged battery may be caused by loose or corroded terminals in any of the electrical circuits. Check for and correct such conditions. Shorted or dry battery cells will also result in a discharged battery. Replenish water or replace battery as necessary (par. 130). Check generator charging rate and replace generator if necessary (par. 127).

h. Overheated Battery. This condition is caused by a defective or improperly adjusted voltage regulator. Replace regulator (par. 128).

70. RADIO NOISE SUPPRESSION SYSTEM.

a. Locate Source of Noise. To locate the source of radio interference emanating from the vehicle, the use of a radio receiver in the vehicle or in an adjacent vehicle will be required. Noting the type of interference present in the receiver will help determine the cause of the trouble. To determine if the noise is coming from the vehicle itself or from an outside source, drive the vehicle at least 100 feet from other vehicles. Turn engine off and turn radio on. Any noise heard will be from an outside source. Start engine. Any noise heard will come from the vehicle itself.

(1) ENGINE. Operate engine with vehicle not in motion and listen for noises in the receiver. If a crackling or clicking noise is present, accelerate the engine and turn ignition switch off with engine running at high speed. If noise stops immediately, the interference is being caused by the ignition circuit (subpar. *b.* below). If an irregular clicking or chattering continues a few seconds after the ignition is shut off, interference is being caused by the generating circuit (subpar. *c.* below).

Trouble Shooting

If the interference is in the form of a whining or whirring noise which varies with engine speed, turn the ignition off. If the tone of the sound lowers in pitch but continues for a few seconds after the ignition is turned off, it is caused by the generator (subpar. *d.* below).

(2) VEHICLE. Operate the vehicle and note whether there is any interference present in the receiver. If clicking or scratching noise is present, stop the vehicle, but leave the engine running. If noise continues when motion of vehicle stops, it may be attributed to faulty ignition shield and cover mounting (subpar. *e.* below). If noise stops when motion of vehicle stops, it may be attributed to loose connections in vehicle wiring (subpar. *f.* below).

b. Ignition Circuit. Make sure ignition circuit is functioning properly (par. 63). Improper spark plug gaps, improper ignition system adjustments, or worn parts will affect the suppression system. Clean and tighten all wiring connections. Tighten engine mountings. With engine running, remove and replace spark plug wires from spark plugs one at a time, listening for a lessening of the frequency of clicks in the receiver. If removal of one of the wires reduces or eliminates the interference, the spark plug suppressor is defective and must be replaced. Test condenser on ignition shield and replace if defective.

c. Generating Circuit. Check regulator mounting bolts and tighten if necessary. Internal-external toothed lock washers must be in place between regulator base and mounting bracket to ground regulator. Test filters and replace if faulty. Test condenser on generator and replace if faulty.

d. Generator. Check and tighten all generator connections and mounting bolts. If noise still is present, replace generator assembly (par. 127).

e. Ignition Shield and Cover. Inspect ignition shield and cover mounting. Make sure all mounting bolts and nuts are tight and that all toothed washers are in place.

f. Wiring. Inspect all wiring for worn, frayed, or otherwise damaged insulation. Replace if defective. Clean and tighten all connections.

71. CLUTCH.

a. General. The clutch is designed for maximum efficiency and long life and, with reasonable care, no operating difficulty should be encountered. Natural wear will occur, however, and must be compensated for.

b. Clutch Slipping.

(1) Improper adjustment (no pedal free-travel) will cause the clutch to slip. Adjust pedal free-travel (par. 153).

(2) If this does not eliminate the condition, it may be due to worn facings, grease on facings, clutch disc hub binding on transmission main drive gear, or insufficient spring tension. Any of these causes necessitate replacing the clutch assembly (pars. 155 and 156).

Maintenance Instructions

c. Clutch Grabbing and Chattering.

(1) This condition may be caused by improperly operating the clutch. If this is the cause, the condition may be eliminated by correcting poor driving practices.

(2) Check and tighten engine mounting bolts. Also inspect and tighten all transmission mounting bolts. See that engine stabilizer rod is properly connected.

(3) If grabbing and chattering condition persists, it may be caused by grease on facings, worn splines on clutch shaft or in disc hub, facing loose on disc, or pressure plate scored or rough. Any of these conditions require replacing the clutch assembly (pars. 155 and 156). When making replacement, inspect for worn splines on transmission main drive gear, and replace transmission if this condition is found (pars. 158 and 159).

d. Rattling.

(1) A rattling sound, appearing to originate in the clutch, may be heard if the clutch pedal pull back spring is disconnected. Connect spring and check for continued rattling.

(2) If rattling continues, it is due to weak pressure plate retracting springs or excessive clearance between driving lugs and cover. In either case, the clutch assembly must be replaced (pars. 155 and 156).

72. TRANSMISSION AND POWER TAKE-OFF.

a. Excessive Noise.

(1) Noise which seemingly comes from the transmission may be caused by another assembly such as axle, transfer case, propeller shaft universal joint, or clutch; therefore, before replacing the transmission because of noise, make sure that difficulty does not exist elsewhere.

(2) Improper or insufficient lubricant may cause transmission noise. Change or add lubricant as directed on Lubrication Order No. 9-802.

(3) Transmission noise may be caused by gears or bearings being worn, broken, or loose on shafts. These causes require replacing the transmission. Check power take-off mounting nuts and tighten as necessary. Incorrect number of gaskets between the power take-off and transmission will cause noise. Install correct number of gaskets (par. 168). Excessively worn power take-off gears necessitate replacing the power take-off assembly (pars. 167 and 168).

b. Hard Shifting.

(1) Hard shifting may be caused by too heavy lubricant in transmission. Service transmission as directed on Lubrication Order No. 9-802.

(2) Check for loose transmission to clutch housing bolts. Tighten all bolts firmly.

(3) Hard shifting may be due to improper clutch pedal adjustment, causing the clutch to fail to release. Adjust clutch pedal free-travel (par. 153).

Trouble Shooting

(4) If remedies prescribed in steps (1), (2), and (3) above do not eliminate the condition, it is due to scored shift rods, burred gear teeth, or binding in the control cover assembly. Replace transmission or power take-off assembly.

c. Transmission Slipping Out of Gear.

(1) Transmission may slip out of gear if, when shifting, the engaging teeth are only partially engaged. Always move gearshift lever sufficiently to move gear to complete engagement before releasing the clutch pedal.

(2) If, after considerable use of the transmission, end play develops in mainshaft and gears due to wear, the transmission may slip out of gear. Likewise, end play in main drive gear may contribute to difficulty in keeping transmission in 4th speed.

(3) Engine stabilizer rod not properly adjusted will increase the tendency for transmission to slip out of gear. Adjust as directed in paragraph 95a.(11).

(4) Broken or weak poppet springs or worn notches in shift rails will allow transmission to slip out of gear. Replace transmission assembly (pars. 158 and 159).

(5) Bent shift forks, causing only partial engagement of gears when gearshift lever has been placed in position, will tend to allow gears to become disengaged. This condition also necessitates replacing the transmission (pars. 158 and 159).

d. Loss of Lubricant.
Lubricant loss may be due to damaged gaskets or worn oil seals at power take-off or transmission assembly. Loose power take-off to transmission stud nuts, gear case cover retaining bolts, or bearing retaining cap attaching bolts may also permit lubricant to escape. Tighten bolts or replace gaskets or oil seals as necessary.

73. AXLE TRANSFER CASE.

a. Hard Shifting.

(1) Hard shifting may not be due to any difficulty in the transfer case, but due to improper driving practices. Follow driving and shifting procedures as directed in paragraph 21.

(2) Tightness in control linkage due to rust, corrosion, dirt, or need of lubrication will cause hard shifting. Inspect, clean, and lubricate linkage.

b. Slips Out of Gear.

(1) Transfer case will slip out of gear if gears do not fully engage due to improperly adjusted control linkage. Adjust control linkage (par. 161).

(2) A weak or broken shift shaft poppet ball spring will cause transfer case to jump out of gear. This condition requires replacement of transfer case assembly (pars. 162 and 163).

c. Loss of Lubricant.
This condition is caused by worn or damaged flange hubs, oil seals, or damaged gaskets. Replace oil seals (TM 9-1802B) or replace transfer case (pars. 162 and 163).

74. FRONT AND REAR AXLES.

a. General. An unusual noise is usually the first indication of improper functioning of axle driving parts. Noises which seem to come from the axles may be caused by some other unit such as transmission, transfer case, wheels loose, or damaged tire inflating devices or struts. Some conditions in the front axle directly affect the steering of the vehicle, and are listed in paragraph 79.

b. Continuous Axle Noise.

(1) This condition may be caused by some difficulty in the axle or by improperly or unevenly worn tires.

(2) To determine if noise is caused by axle or by tires, drive vehicle on soft terrain. If this stops the noise, it is being caused by the tires and not by the axle. Inflate tires to proper pressure or replace as necessary.

(3) If noise continues on soft terrain, it is caused by worn or improperly adjusted wheel bearings, worn or improperly adjusted differential gears or bearings, insufficient lubricant in the differentials and steering knuckles, or by loose or damaged tire inflating devices or struts. Add lubricant, adjust wheel bearings (pars. 214 and 215), replace axle assembly (pars. 175 and 176, or 179 and 180), or tighten inflating device lock bolts or replace device or strut (par. 270).

c. Axle Noise on Drive Only or on Coast Only. This condition is an indication that the differential pinion and ring gear are out of adjustment or worn excessively. To correct this condition, replace complete axle assembly (pars. 175 and 176, or 179 and 180).

d. Excessive Backlash in Axle Driving Parts.

(1) This condition may be caused by loose axle shaft or drive flange bolts, worn holes in flanges, or by worn splines on axle shafts. Tighten bolts or replace axle shafts as necessary (par. 173 or 178).

(2) If excessive backlash still exists, replace axle assembly (pars. 175 and 176, or 179 and 180).

75. PROPELLER SHAFTS.

a. Excessive Noise or Vibration.

(1) Need of lubrication in the universal joints will result in excessive propeller shaft noise. Lubricate all universal joints (Lubrication Order No. 9-802).

(2) If propeller shafts are not assembled with universal joints in the same plane, vibration will result. Check for this condition and if found, disconnect propeller shafts and place universal joints in same plane.

(3) Check for loose pillow block mounting bolts and tighten if necessary.

(4) Worn universal joint bearings or journals, or sprung propeller shaft will cause vibration and noise. Check for these conditions and replace propeller shaft assembly if necessary (par. 183).

(5) Loose transfer case mounting bolts will cause a noise or vibration

76. BRAKE SYSTEM.

a. Excessive Pedal Pressure and Poor Stop.

(1) This condition is most commonly caused by normal wear of the brake linings. Correct by adjusting brake shoes (par. 188).

(2) Tighten all connections in vacuum system, and clean or replace Hydrovac air cleaner (par. 189). Inspect vacuum check valve at manifold and replace if not operating properly (par. 190).

(3) Inspect brake shoes and linings. If linings are grease soaked or worn excessively or, if the brake shoes are twisted or sprung, replace brake shoe and lining assemblies (pars. 196 and 197).

(4) Check for obstructed brake lines, and clean or replace lines as necessary.

(5) Check brake pedal and linkage for bent or broken condition, and replace damaged parts (par. 191).

(6) If the condition still exists after making the above corrections, the trouble lies in the Hydrovac. Replace the Hydrovac assembly (par. 189).

(7) In extremely cold weather, with the wrong type fluid in the system, the fluid will thicken and will not flow freely through the lines and openings. This will cause extreme pedal pressure. Drain and flush system and refill with proper fluid (par. 187).

b. Pedal Goes to Floor Board.

(1) If this condition comes about gradually, it is due to normal wear of the brake linings. Check linings and adjust (par. 188), or replace brake shoe and lining assemblies as necessary (pars. 196 and 197).

(2) If the pedal goes to the floor suddenly, it may be due to a leak in the hydraulic system, or the pedal linkage has become broken or disconnected. Check for broken or leaking lines or connections, especially in the flexible hoses. If a leak occurs in the front wheel brake lines, rear brakes can be used by shutting off the shut-off cock inside right-hand frame side rail. Replace lines or tighten connections as necessary, and bleed brake system (par. 187). Check for disconnected or broken pedal linkage; make necessary connections, replacements, and adjustments.

(3) Air trapped in the hydraulic system will sometimes permit the pedal to go to the floor. Bleed the entire brake system (par. 187).

c. Noisy Brakes.
This condition is caused by dirty brake linings, excessively worn linings, loose lining rivets, twisted or sprung brake shoes, distorted drums, or broken brake shoe return springs. Replace

brake shoe and lining assemblies (pars. 196 and 197), or brake drums (par. 195).

d. Springy, Spongy Pedal Action. Brake shoes needing adjustment due to normal wear, or air in the hydraulic system will cause a springy, spongy pedal action. Check brake shoe adjustment and make necessary corrections (par. 188). If pedal action is still soft, bleed brake system (par. 187).

e. One Brake Drags.

(1) This condition may be caused by an improperly adjusted brake shoe. Check adjustment and make necessary correction (par. 188).

(2) Check brake mechanism for corrosion or binding, or for a weak or broken brake shoe return spring, and treat or replace parts as necessary (par. 198).

(3) Check wheel bearing adjustment and correct if necessary (pars. 214 and 215).

(4) Defective wheel cylinder cups or corroded end covers on cylinder will sometimes prevent brake shoes from returning to released position. Check for these conditions and replace wheel cylinder if necessary (par. 194).

f. All Brakes Drag.

(1) Dirt and corrosion in the brake shoe linkage or wheel cylinders is the most common cause of dragging brakes. Clean and lubricate linkage, or replace wheel cylinders as necessary (par. 194).

(2) Brakes will drag if the by-pass port in the master cylinder is restricted. This port may be closed by dirt, by a swollen piston cup, or by the piston not fully returning to the rear of the cylinder due to bent or broken linkage. Make necessary adjustments or replace master cylinder (par. 192).

(3) A defective check valve in the Hydrovac slave cylinder will also cause the brakes to drag. This condition necessitates replacing the Hydrovac (par. 189).

(4) Weak or broken brake shoe return springs will cause brakes to drag, although this condition would rarely occur at all wheels at the same time.

g. Locked Brakes. There are several conditions which may contribute to brakes locking. When one or more of the brakes lock, the following symptoms, causes, and remedies should be studied.

(1) WHEEL CYLINDER STICKING. Locking of brakes may be caused by sticking of the wheel cylinder piston, or rusting of the end covers on wheel cylinder, preventing the return of the brake shoes after a brake application. This is generally caused by old gummy fluid or corrosion. This usually occurs on one or two brakes at a time, but never on all six brakes unless the vehicle has been stored for some time near salt water. To remedy piston sticking condition, drain all fluid and flush the entire hydraulic system with fresh fluid. Wheel cylinder assemblies which are in rusted condition must be replaced (par. 194).

Trouble Shooting

(2) DIRT IN BRAKE FLUID. Dirt in the fluid may enter when refilling the master cylinder during bleeding operations. Extreme cleanliness of the fluid containers during this operation is necessary. This symptom may be diagnosed by removing the vacuum hose from the Hydrovac unit. Brakes should then release as all vacuum will then be depleted. To correct such conditions, replace the Hydrovac unit (par. 189), drain and flush the system, and fill with clean fluid (par. 187).

(3) DIRTY HYDROVAC AIR CLEANER. The valve in the Hydrovac relay valve may be stuck in open position due to sand or dust drawn in through the air cleaner. Such symptoms can also be diagnosed by removing the vacuum hose from the Hydrovac unit. To correct such conditions, it is necessary to replace the Hydrovac unit (par. 189). To avoid repeated failures, the Hydrovac air cleaner should be cleaned more often, particularly when the vehicle is operating in dusty areas.

(4) BRAKE LINKAGE OUT OF ADJUSTMENT. Locked brakes may be caused by the brake pedal linkage being out of adjustment or the brake pedal return spring weak or broken. In either case, slight pedal movement when driving over rough roads will build up the fluid pressure and apply the brakes. This condition may be diagnosed by opening the bleed screw slightly on one wheel cylinder to release the fluid pressure. Brakes should then return to the released position. If this condition exists, the pedal and linkage adjustments should be made as described in paragraph 191.

77. SPRING SUSPENSION.

a. Hard Riding.

(1) This condition is usually present when the vehicle is overloaded. Refer to nomenclature plate for correct load.

(2) Hard riding will also result from insufficient lubrication or frozen shackles. Lubricate shackles, remove and clean, or replace as necessary (par. 205).

b. Over Flexible.

(1) The most probable cause of this condition is insufficient fluid in the shock absorbers. Refill shock absorbers to proper level (par. 206).

(2) Examine springs and replace if leaves are broken (par. 205 or 207).

(3) If over flexibility still exists, the shock absorbers are not operating properly and must be replaced (par. 206).

c. Spring Leaf Failure.

(1) Breakage of spring leaves is most commonly caused by overloading the vehicle or by driving at excess speed over rough terrain. Refer to nomenclature plate for correct load, and reduce speed over rough terrain when possible.

(2) Loose rebound clips will cause spring breakage. To prevent this, keep rebound clips tight.

(3) Excessively tightened front spring rear bracket bolts will also

cause spring breakage. Check installation of bracket bolts and, if bolts are tightened sufficiently to cause spring to bind in bracket, adjust the installation of bolts (par. 205).

(4) Frozen shackles due to lack of lubrication will also cause springs to break. Remove shackles and clean or replace as necessary. Lubricate as directed on Lubrication Order No. 9-802.

(5) Dragging brakes will sometimes cause springs to break. Refer to paragraph 76 for causes and remedies of this condition.

d. Excessive Noise.

(1) Excessive spring noise may be caused by worn shackle bolts or spring eye bolts, or by worn shackle or spring eye bushings. Check for these conditions and replace bolts or springs as necessary (par. 205).

(2) Check for loose spring mounting bolts and tighten as necessary.

(3) Loose or damaged rear spring seat bearings will result in excessive noise. Examine bearings and adjust or replace if necessary (par. 208).

78. WHEELS, TIRES, AND HUBS.

a. General. When localizing wheel and tire trouble symptoms, consideration must also be taken of various related systems such as brakes, wheel alinement, and steering gear system. Deficiencies in these systems or units will affect performance of wheels, tires, and wheel bearings.

b. Excessive or Uneven Tire Wear.

(1) Unequal pressures in the tires will cause uneven tire wear. Inflate all tires to correct pressure.

(2) Front wheel misalinement will cause excessive tire wear. Check front wheel alinement and make necessary corrections (par. 170).

(3) Bent wheels or damaged wheel bearings will result in uneven tire wear. Replace wheels or bearings as necessary.

(4) Operating vehicle on a dry, hard surfaced road with front axle engaged will result in excessive wear on the front tires.

c. Hard Steering. This condition may be caused by underinflated tires, steering gear in need of adjustment or lubrication, front wheels out of alinement, or wheel bearings in need of adjustment. Check these items in the sequence given and make necessary corrections.

d. Wheels Pounding. Wheel bearings that are damaged or in need of adjustment will produce a pounding at the wheels. A bent wheel will also cause this condition. Replace or adjust wheel bearings (par. 214 or 215), or replace wheel (par. 212), as necessary.

e. Shimmy.

(1) Unevenly worn or unevenly inflated front tires will cause front wheels to shimmy. Replace tires or inflate to correct pressure as necessary.

(2) Loose or damaged front wheel bearings will also cause this condition. Adjust or replace bearings as necessary (par. 214 or 215).

Trouble Shooting

(3) Any condition contributing to improper front wheel and axle alinement may cause front wheel shimmy. Front axle alinement is affected by loose steering knuckle bearings, front spring leaves broken, spring bolts, shackles, or bushings worn, spring center bolt broken, and a bent axle housing or chassis frame. Check front wheel and axle alinement and make necessary corrections (par. 170). Also check for faulty shock absorbers and replace if necessary (par. 206).

79. STEERING SYSTEM.

a. General. Proper operation of the steering system is closely related to other units in the vehicle. Hence, whenever diagnosing steering difficulties, other allied factors must also be checked. A symptom indicating possible trouble in the steering system may also be evidence of deficiency in other units, that is, front axle alinement, front spring suspension, tire inflation, wheel and tire mounting, wheel bearing adjusment, and brakes.

b. Hard Steering (Land Operation).

(1) If this condition exists on a vehicle just out of the repair shop, the worm bearings, sector gear lash, or drag link ends may be adjusted too tight. Check these adjustments and correct if necessary (par. 217). Other causes listed below will result in this condition after vehicle has been in service for some time.

(2) Lack of lubrication in the steering gear or in the steering knuckle bearings will also cause hard steering. Lubricate as directed on Lubrication Order No. 9-802.

(3) Inspect drag link and replace if bent (par. 222).

(4) Front wheel and axle misalinement will cause hard steering. Check alinement and make necessary corrections (par. 170).

c. Wander or Lack of Steering Control (Land Operation).

(1) This condition may be caused by loose steering gear mountings, Pitman arm loose on sector shaft, or too much sector gear lash. Check these items and make necessary corrections (par. 217 or 218).

(2) Check for loose drag link ends and adjust or replace drag link as necessary (par. 222).

(3) Check front wheel and axle alinement and make necessary corrections (par. 170).

(4) If the condition still exists, the steering gear parts are worn, necessitating replacement of the steering gear assembly (par. 219).

d. Road Shock Transmitted to Steering Wheel (Land Operation).

(1) This condition may develop after vehicle has been in service some time. Cause may be found in one of the following: loose wheel bearings, worn tie rod ends, or loose steering gear mounting bolts.

Maintenance Instructions

e. Unequal Turning Radius to Right and Left (Land Operation).

(1) On a vehicle just out of the repair shop, this condition would be caused by improperly adjusted steering knuckle stop screws.

(2) This condition may come about by the drag link being bent, or front axle shifting on spring. A slight difference in turning radius may be caused by unequal adjustment of stops at steering knuckles.

f. Vehicle Pulls to One Side (Land Operation).

(1) On early vehicles, this may be caused by unequal tire pressures. Carry same pressure in all tires.

(2) If brakes are out of adjustment so that brake shoes drag at one side of vehicle, the vehicle will tend to pull toward the side on which the brakes are dragging. Adjust brakes (par. 188).

(3) Check for damaged or loose wheel bearings, and replace or adjust as necessary (par. 214).

g. Vehicle Fails to Respond to Steering Controls (Water Operation).

(1) Cable spool shear pin may have failed or cable may be broken. Install new shear pin or employ emergency means of steering.

(2) Improper driving practices will sometimes cause this condition. Consult paragraph 26 for proper driving practices.

80. BILGE PUMP SYSTEMS.

a. General. Information given in subparagraph ***b.*** below applies to both types of front bilge pump systems (Oberdorfer and Gould) unless otherwise stated in text. When references are made to other paragraphs for adjustments, replacements, etc., the first reference applies to the Oberdorfer system and the second applies to the Gould system. Information in subparagraph ***c.*** applies only to the rear bilge pump system (Higgins).

b. Front Bilge Pump Systems (Oberdorfer and Gould).

(1) PUMP FAILS TO DISCHARGE WATER.

(a) Bilge pump will not discharge water if all valves are closed. One valve must be open at all times. If valve will not remain open, adjust packing (par. 241***b.*** or 247***b.***).

(b) Plugged bleeder screen and intake strainer screens will prevent pump from discharging water. Clean screens, and clean out bilges to prevent a repetition of the trouble. Make sure cover gaskets on strainer box (Oberdorfer system) are in good condition and properly seated (par. 243***c.***).

(c) In the Oberdorfer system, pump may not be operating due to a slipping or broken drive belt. If belt is slipping, odor of burning rubber will be noticed. Adjust or replace belt as necessary (par. 240). In the Gould system, check for broken drive chain, chain off sprockets, or sheared sprocket key. Replace chain and adjust, or replace key as necessary (par. 246).

Trouble Shooting

(d) Check possibility of pump being locked by attempting to turn pump by hand. If locked, replace pump (par. 241 or 247). In cold weather, pump may be frozen. Refer to paragraph 43.

(e) Air leaks in intake lines will prevent pump from pumping water. Tighten all hose clamps, replace deteriorated hoses and clamps, and tighten or replace pump packing (par. 242 or 248).

(f) Make sure that all valves close properly. Inspect and clean valves, or replace if necessary (par. 242 or 248).

(2) NOISY PUMP ACTION.

(a) Oberdorfer bilge bump action will be noisy (howl) if operating with all valves closed. Refer to (1)(a) above.

(b) Lack of lubrication will result in noisy pump action. Lubricate pump as directed on Lubrication Order No. 9-802.

(c) Check intake strainer screens and clean out if plugged. If screens are plugged with rust and scale, clean and paint inside of tubes (par. 244 or 249).

(3) DRIVE BELT WEARS RAPIDLY (OBERDORFER SYSTEM). Rapid wearing of drive belt is caused by misalinement of pulleys. Aline pulleys (par. 240).

(4) DRIVE CHAIN WEARS RAPIDLY (GOULD SYSTEM). Rapid wearing of drive chain may be due to insufficient lubrication, improper adjustment, or misalinement. Lubricate chain (Lubrication Order No. 9-802), adjust chain, or aline sprockets as necessary (par. 246).

c. Rear Bilge Pump System (Higgins).

(1) PUMP FAILS TO DISCHARGE WATER.

(a) Pump will not discharge water if intake screen is plugged. Clean screen thoroughly.

(b) Check for broken drive chain or chain off sprockets. Install chain, using new part if broken or excessively worn, and aline sprockets (par. 251).

(2) PUMP ACTION NOISY.

(a) Noisy pump action may be due to lack of lubricant, or pump may be loose on mountings. Lubricate pump (Lubrication Order No. 9-802), or tighten pump mounting as necessary.

(b) Noisy pump action may also be caused by worn bearings, end play in impeller shaft, or impeller loose on shaft. Any of these conditions necessitate replacing the pump (par. 252).

(3) DRIVE CHAIN WEARS RAPIDLY. Rapid wearing of drive chain may be due to insufficient lubrication, improper adjustment, or misalinement. Lubricate chain (Lubrication Order No. 9-802). Adjust chain, or aline sprockets (par. 251).

81. WATER DRIVE SYSTEM.

a. General. Since the main transmission is always operating in conjunction with the water propeller transfer case, it is well to check condition of the former unit in order to eliminate the possibility of difficulty existing there. When trouble is definitely located in the water propeller transfer case, a replacement of the unit will in most intances be necessary. Trouble in the propeller drive shafts, universal joints, and bearings will be generally indicated by symptoms similar to those described in paragraph 75.

b. Excessive Vibration.

(1) A propeller which is bent or loose will cause vibration. Check condition of propeller and retaining nut.

(2) If bolts which attach strut to hull are loose, or if spherical journal is not clamped firmly to strut, vibration will result.

(3) Rough bearings at water propeller transfer case universal joints, or at thrust bearing assembly will cause noise and vibration in drive line. A check should be made to see if bearings are properly lubricated, as lack of lubrication could be mistaken for a failed bearing.

(4) A bent or sprung condition in propeller drive shafts will cause vibration. If shafts are found to be bent or sprung, they must be replaced (par. 257).

c. Hard Shifting of Transfer Case.

(1) Due to the fact that with axle transfer case in gear the main shaft in water propeller transfer case is always turning when vehicle is in motion, it is necessary to stop vehicle completely before the water propeller transfer case can be shifted *into* gear. Apparent hard shifting may actually be due to poor driving practice, that is, not bringing vehicle to complete stop before attempting to shift.

(2) Binding at linkage pivot points caused by insufficient lubrication will cause hard shifting. Lubricate as directed on Lubrication Order No. 9-802.

82. TIRE INFLATION SYSTEMS.

a. Tire Pump Governor Fails to Operate Properly.

(1) Failure of tire pump governor to cut in or out at correct pressure indicates need of adjustment. Adjust governor setting (par. 265).

(2) Governor may be sticking due to need of lubrication. Lubricate as directed on Lubrication Order No. 9-802.

(3) Improper governor operation may be caused by leakage in tank to governor air lines. Check lines for leaks and make necessary corrections.

b. Loss of Air Pressure.

(1) Loss of air pressure may be due to leakage in tire inflating devices. Slight leaks in new inflating devices, or after installing new diaphragms, may occur. After unit has been in operation for a short time, diaphragm will seat and leakage should stop. If leakage continues, check shim thickness or replace diaphragm as necessary (par. 270*d*.).

(2) Leakage may occur at inflating device to valve stem hose connection if connection is improperly tightened. Tighten connection *finger-tight only*. Tightening with pliers will damage fitting.

Trouble Shooting

(3) Check all air lines and connections for leaks. Replace lines or tighten connections as necessary.

(4) Test each tire individually for loss of air pressure and replace tire in which leakage is evident (par. 213).

c. Tire Pressure Build-up.

(1) A slight tire pressure build-up is to be experienced due to road friction and heat. Deflate tires if in excess of proper pressure (par. 32).

(2) Tire pressure build-up may be caused by a leaking tire inflating control valve. Replace inflation and deflation control valves assembly (par. 268).

d. Slow Pressure Build-up in System.

(1) Slow pressure build-up may be caused by a dirty tire pump air cleaner or by leaking air lines. Service air cleaner (par. 266) and check all air lines for leaks.

(2) If the above remedies do not increase rate of pressure build-up, tire pump is in need of repairs and must be replaced (par. 266).

e. Tire Pump Noisy.

(1) Loose tire pump mounting bolts, loose drive shaft to tire pump or engine bolts, or worn drive shaft universal joint will cause noise. Tighten bolts or replace drive shaft (par. 267).

(2) Check level of lubricant in tire pump and bring up to correct level (Lubrication Order No. 9-802).

(3) If tire pump noise persists after making the above corrections, tire pump is in need of repairs and must be replaced (par. 266).

(4) On vehicles prior to chassis serial No. 2006, an improperly adjusted drive chain will cause noise. Adjust chain (par. 262).

f. Oil Leaks at Tire Pump.

(1) Oil leaks at tire pump may be caused by too high an oil level or by a clogged crankcase breather. Correct oil level and service crankcase breather (Lubrication Order No. 9-802).

(2) Leakage may occur at crankshaft bearing cap oil seal or at tire pump crankcase cover plate. Replace crankshaft oil seal (par. 266c.), or replace cover plate gasket.

g. Water in Air System. Water will accumulate in air system due to condensation if air tank is not drained often enough. Condensation must be drained from air tank daily.

h. Safety Valve Does Not Blow Off. If safety valve fails to blow off, or blows off at wrong pressure, it is stuck due to rust and corrosion or is improperly adjusted. Adjust safety valve or replace as necessary (par. 271b.).

i. Rapid Wear of Tire Pump Drive Chain (Prior to Chassis Serial No. 2006 Only). Rapid wear of drive chain is due to lack of lubrication or to improper chain alinement. Lubricate chain (Lubrication Order No. 9-802), and adjust chain alinement if necessary (par. 262).

83. WINCH.

a. Winch Fails to Operate When Winch Power Take-off Lever Is Shifted Into Gear.

(1) Winch will not operate unless sliding clutch is engaged. Engage as directed in paragraph 29.

(2) If the winch still fails to operate with sliding clutch handle in engaged position and power take-off in gear, check winch drive shaft. If shaft revolves, the shear pin is sheared and must be replaced (par. 274).

b. Winch Drum Overruns Cable as Cable Is Pulled Out by Hand. Drag brake should be adjusted to prevent drum from overrunning cable as cable is pulled from drum. Adjust brake if necessary (par. 273).

c. Winch Fails to Hold Load. This condition is caused by the winch brake being out of adjustment. Adjust brake as directed in paragraph 273.

d. Excessive Heat at Winch Brake Cover. If this condition is present, the automatic brake is adjusted too tight, or the wrong type lining has been installed. Adjust brake (par. 273), or replace brake band assembly (par. 273**d**.).

e. Noisy Operation. Noisy operation is usually caused by insufficient lubrication. Add lubricant as directed on Lubrication Order No. 9-802.

Section XVI
Engine Description, Data, Maintenance, and Adjustment On Vehicle

84. DESCRIPTION AND DATA.

a. Description. The engine is a six-cylinder, in-line, valve-in-head type, three-point mounted in front of chassis. Engine and accessories are accessible for service after engine hatch cover is raised.

b. Data.

(1) GENERAL.

```
Engine type ............................................... 6 cyl. valve-in-head
Bore and stroke ................................................. 3-25/32 x 4 in.
Oil pan capacity ............................. See Lubrication Order No. 9-802
```

(2) ADJUSTMENT DATA.

Valve Clearance (hot)
```
  Intake ................................................................. 0.012 in.
  Exhaust ............................................................... 0.016 in.
Spark plug gap ........................... (44) 0.025 in.—(44 com.) 0.030 in.
Distributor point opening ................................. 0.018 to 0.024 in.
```

Engine Description, Data, Maintenance, and Adjustment On Vehicle

Cylinder Head Bolt Tightening Torque
Preliminary (par. 88b.) .... 35 ft-lb
Final (par. 88b.) .... 70-80 ft-lb

c. Repair. Repair procedures for the components of the engine will be found in TM 9-1802A

85. TUNE-UP.

a. General. An engine tune-up is an orderly process of checking engine and accessory equipment to determine if they are within original specifications, and to accomplish such adjustments and repairs so that new engine performance is restored. This tune-up procedure can be accomplished at regular intervals or whenever performance of engine indicates need of such operations. The gage readings given below apply to sea level—there will be approximately a 1-inch drop for each 1,000 feet of altitude.

b. Vacuum Reading. Remove manifold fitting and attach a vacuum gage to intake manifold. Make carbureter idling adjustments (par. 106b.). With the engine running at normal idling speed, the vacuum gage reading should be about 18 to 21 inches, and indicator should be steady. Diagnosis of engine condition can be made by observing action of gage as follows:

(1) GAGE ACTION WITH ENGINE AT IDLING SPEED.

(a) If indicator drops several inches at regular intervals, the cause is generally valve sticking or defective spark plug.

(b) If the indicator drops occasionally, a spark plug is not firing or the gap in a plug is set too close.

(c) If the reading is low with a steady indicator, the causes may be late ignition timing, leaky manifold gaskets, or valves adjusted too tight.

(d) If the reading is high with indicator varying from 6 to 12 inches every revolution, the cause is generally late valve timing.

(2) GAGE ACTION ON ACCELERATION AND DECELERATION. With engine idling, open throttle quickly. Vacuum should fall to 2 inches. Close throttle. Gage should then read at least 24 inches. If reading is low on deceleration, diluted oil or defective piston rings generally exists.

c. Compression Test. A compression test may also be made, in order to determine the need of internal repairs before tune-up procedures are accomplished. This test will indicate condition of pistons, rings, and valve mechanism. Compression pressure depends upon cranking speeds, engine temperature, oil viscosity, compression ratio, and the condition of the engine. Make test in following manner:

(1) REMOVE ALL SPARK PLUGS. Turn ignition switch off and pull hand throttle button all the way out. Insert a compression gage in one spark plug hole. Crank engine 10 to 12 turns with starter. Note highest gage reading while engine is being cranked. Take a reading at each cylinder in the same manner.

(2) ANALYZE THE READINGS. While readings on some engines may be higher than on others due to conditions mentioned in subparagraph **b.** above, the readings in any one engine should be reasonably high (100 lb or more), and all cylinders should show uniform readings within approximately 10 pounds.

(*a*) Pour a liberal amount of light engine oil through spark plug hole in cylinder having low reading. Allow sufficient time for oil to spread around rings. Take another reading. If compression is appreciably increased in cylinder so treated, piston or rings require replacement. If no change in compression reading is noted, check the valve mechanism.

(*b*) An extremely low reading in two adjacent cylinders may indicate a cylinder head gasket leak.

(*c*) If compression cannot be corrected with operations allocated to echelon making test, notify higher authority for proper correction.

d. Tune-up Sequence. Drain and refill crankcase, then service oil filter and crankcase vent cleaner (Refer to lubrication Order No. 9-802). Proceed with following operations in sequence shown.

(1) Service and adjust spark plugs (par. 101).

(2) Clean and tighten battery and ignition cables.

(3) Test and service battery (par. 130).

(4) Service distributor cap, rotor, and points (pars. 98 and 99).

(5) Check ignition timing (par. 97).

(6) Check and adjust valve clearance (par. 86).

(7) Service carbureter (par. 106**c.**), fuel filter (par. 110**b.**), air cleaner (par. 105), fuel pump (par. 109), and fuel tubes.

86. VALVE CLEARANCE AND ADJUSTMENT.

a. Warm Up Engine. Warm up engine to operating temperature (at least 160°F). Allow engine to run at idling speed while adjustments are being made.

b. Remove Cylinder Head Rocker Arm Cover. Disconnect crankcase ventilator tube from fitting at the rocker arm cover. Remove two cover retaining stud nuts, then remove cover.

c. Check Cylinder Head Bolts. Tighten cylinder head bolts, using a torque wrench (41-W-3630) and special wrench (41-W-2964-700), to a maximum of 70-80 foot-pounds. Use tightening sequence shown in figure 56.

d. Adjust Valve Clearance. Insert feeler gage (0.012-inch for intake and 0.016-inch for exhaust) between rocker arm and valve stem at each valve. Using a wrench and screwdriver, loosen rocker arm ball stud nut, and tighten or loosen stud until proper clearance is obtained. Tighten nut, then recheck clearance.

e. Install Cylinder Head Rocker Arm Cover. Check cover mating surface for distortion. Install cover over gasket (G085-01-00777), then install and tighten stud nuts snugly. Only a very light pressure is required to prevent leakage if cover and gasket are in good condition. If a leak occurs, do not attempt to correct by excessively tightening nuts. Check gasket for particles of dirt, breaks, or mislocation, and replace if necessary. After cover has been installed, connect ventilator tube to fitting on cover.

87. INTAKE AND EXHAUST MANIFOLDS.

a. Description. Intake and exhaust manifolds are each one-piece type, bolted together to form a complete unit. Unit is mounted to cylinder head, with gaskets and pilot rings between cylinder head and manifolds. Manifold heat control is set and must be kept at "OFF" position at all times inasmuch as engine operates under full load during amphibious operations.

b. Removal.

(1) REMOVE CARBURETER. Remove air cleaner, carbureter, and governor (pars. 105c., 106d., and 108b.).

(2) DISCONNECT VENTILATOR AND VACUUM TUBES. Disconnect crankcase ventilator tube at ventilator valve. Disconnect Hydrovac line at check valve, then unscrew tee with check valve and ventilator valve from manifold. On early models, disconnect windshield wiper line from tee.

(3) DISCONNECT EXHAUST PIPE. Remove three bolts connecting exhaust pipe to manifold. Separate exhaust pipe from manifold and remove gasket.

(4) REMOVE MANIFOLDS FROM CYLINDER HEAD. In the event manifold to cylinder head studs are rusted or corroded, clean the threads extending through the nut thoroughly using a wire brush, then remove nuts, washers, and clamps. Pull manifold unit from cylinder head and remove gaskets and pilots rings.

(5) SEPARATE MANIFOLDS. Remove two exhaust to intake manifold bolts and lock washers. Remove two nuts and lock-washers from exhaust to intake manifold studs, then separate manifolds.

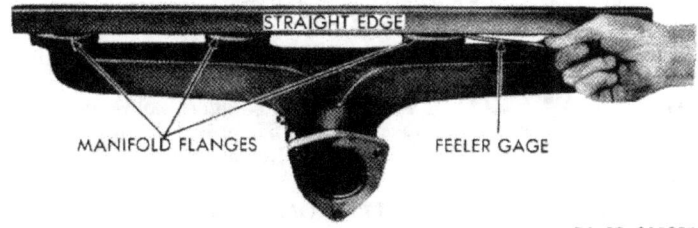

Figure 52—Checking Exhaust Manifold Flange Alinement

Figure 53—Exhaust Manifold Clearance Points

c. Installation.

(1) INSPECT MANIFOLDS. Inspect manifolds for warpage by placing on a surface plate with a straight edge (fig. 52). Variation of flanges must not exceed $\frac{1}{32}$ inch. Grind as necessary on a surface grinder or with similar equipment. Check clearance between end studs and exhaust manifold stud holes (fig. 53). If clearance of approximately $\frac{1}{16}$ inch does not exist, file stud holes to provide necessary clearance. Also, clamping surfaces for washers and clamps (fig. 53) must be smooth for at least $\frac{1}{16}$ inch beyond edge of washers and clamps. Grind manifold as necessary. Remove rust, scale, carbon deposits, and any gasket material from face of cylinder head ports. Clean out pilot ring seats.

(2) ASSEMBLE MANIFOLDS. Considerable care must be exercised when assembling and installing manifolds. Position exhaust manifold gasket and assemble intake to exhaust manifold, tightening bolts and stud nuts only finger-tight.

(3) INSTALL MANIFOLD ASSEMBLY. Position pilots in cylinder head intake ports solidly and not cocked. Install front, center, and rear gaskets over cylinder head studs (fig. 54). Position manifold assembly over studs and pilot rings, maintaining clearances given in step (1) above. Install washers and clamps over studs, then install stud nuts, tightening them alternately. After manifolds are secured to cylinder head, tighten intake to exhaust manifold bolts and stud nuts firmly.

(4) CONNECT EXHAUST PIPE. Insert three bolts up through exhaust pipe flange and manifold. Make sure that flange seal and gasket are in place. Install nuts on bolts and tighten alternately and firmly. Install lock nuts.

(5) COMPLETE THE INSTALLATION. Screw tee, with Hydrovac vacuum check valve and ventilator valve, into manifold. Connect Hydrovac vacuum line at check valve. Connect crankcase ventilator tube at

Engine Description, Data, Maintenance, and Adjustment On Vehicle

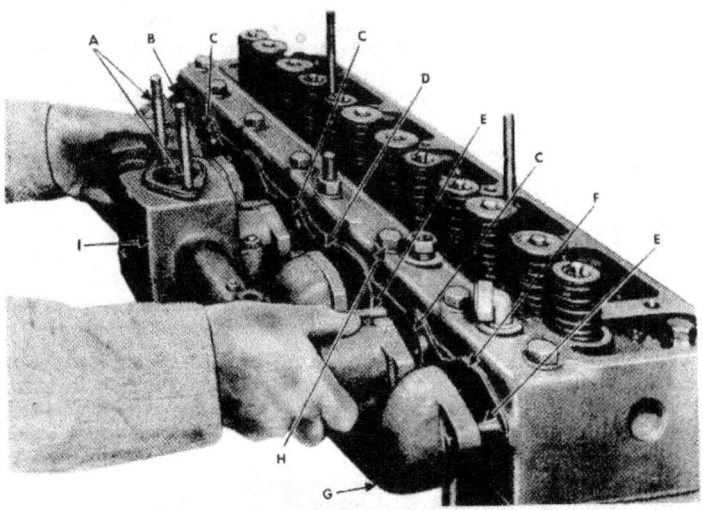

A CARBURETOR TO MANIFOLD STUD
B MANIFOLD GASKET—FRONT (2185907 SET)
C PILOT
D MANIFOLD GASKET—CENTER (2185907 SET)
E MANIFOLD TO CYLINDER HEAD STUD
F MANIFOLD GASKET—REAR (2185907 SET)
G EXHAUST MANIFOLD (G501-7002112)
H CYLINDER HEAD BOLT (G058-30-00620)
I INTAKE MANIFOLD (G501-02-87316)

RA PD 333198

Figure 54—Installing Manifold Assembly

ventilator valve. Install gasket and insulator over intake manifold studs, then install governor, carbureter, and air cleaner (pars. 108, 106, and 105). On early models, connect windshield wiper line to tee.

(6) RETIGHTEN. Run engine through warm-up period, then check tightness of manifold stud nuts.

88. CYLINDER HEAD AND GASKET.

a. Removal.

(1) REMOVE MANIFOLD. Remove air cleaner (par. 105*b*.). Disconnect ventilator line at rocker arm cover and at ventilator valve and remove line. Disconnect windshield wiper line at manifold (on early models). Disconnect Hydrovac vacuum line at check valve. Disconnect fuel tube at carbureter, also throttle and choke controls. Disconnect exhaust pipe from manifold by removing three bolts. Remove manifold to cylinder head stud nuts, washers, and clamps, then pull manifold with governor and carbureter from head.

(2) REMOVE WATER BY-PASS TUBE. Partially drain cooling system (par. 117*b*.), then disconnect water by-pass tube at by-pass tee and at rear of cylinder head. Remove by-pass tube clip nut and bolt, then bend clip so tube can be removed.

Maintenance Instructions

(3) DISCONNECT THERMO GAGE, OIL LINE, AND THERMOSTAT HOUSING. Unscrew thermo bulb retaining nut and pull bulb from cylinder head adapter. Disconnect oil line at front of cylinder head. Remove two bolts which attach thermostat housing to cylinder head and remove the gasket.

(4) REMOVE IGNITION SHIELD AND OIL FILTER. Remove ignition shield and coil (par. 139**b**.). Remove oil filter (par. 91**c**.).

(5) REMOVE VALVE PUSH ROD AND ROCKER ARM COVERS. Remove two oil filter tube clamp to bracket bolts and remove clamp. Remove bolt attaching dip stick tube bracket to filler tube bracket. Remove remaining bolts attaching push rod cover to cylinder head and block and remove oil filter bracket, oil filler tube bracket, and push rod cover. Remove two stud nuts and lift rocker arm cover off head.

(6) REMOVE VALVE ROCKER ARM ASSEMBLY. Remove ten bolts and lock washers which attach rocker arm shaft brackets to cylinder head. Remove nuts from two rocker arm cover studs. Lift oil overflow tube and gasket from rear bracket. Lift rocker arms, shaft, and brackets as an assembly from head.

(7) REMOVE CYLINDER HEAD. Lift push rods out of engine. Remove 15 cylinder head bolts, then lift head up from block.

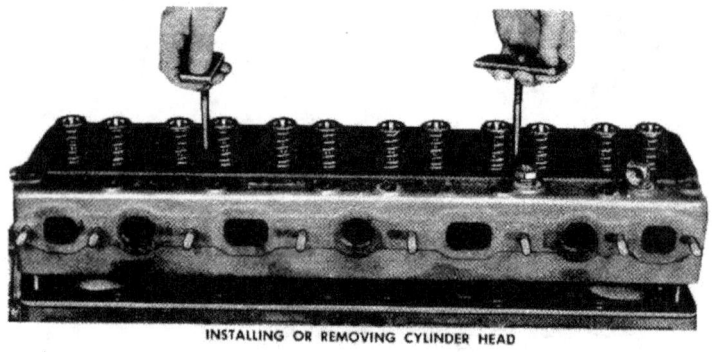

RA PD 332988

Figure 55—Installing Cylinder Head

Engine Description, Data, Maintenance, and Adjustment On Vehicle

PRELIMINARY TIGHTENING WITH TORQUE WRENCH

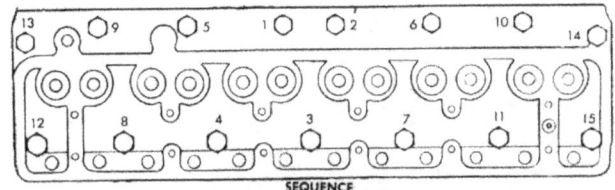

SEQUENCE

FINAL TIGHTENING WITH TORQUE WRENCH AND SPECIAL SOCKET

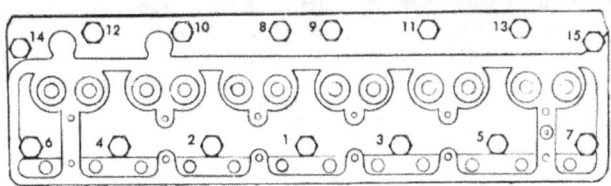

SEQUENCE

RA PD 333207

Figure 56—Cylinder Head Tightening Sequence—Preliminary Tightening to 35 Foot-Pounds—Final Tightening to 70-80 Foot-Pounds

Maintenance Instructions

b. Installation.

(1) CLEAN CYLINDER HEAD AND BLOCK. Thoroughly clean gasket surface of cylinder head and block. Remove all dirt and carbon from top of pistons, cylinder bores, and head. Make certain that bolt holes in block are clean, as dirt or water will prevent tightening bolts.

(2) POSITION GASKET AND CYLINDER HEAD. It is important to maintain alinement of head and gasket with block. This is simplified by use of four guide pins made from cylinder head bolts (fig. 55). Install guide pins in the corner bolt holes of the block. Place gasket over guide pins carefully, with side of gasket marked "TOP" toward cylinder head. This is essential to aline water passage holes in gasket with those in block and head. Place cylinder head over guide pins, then lower carefully onto block. Insert all cylinder head bolts, except where guide pins are, and tighten finger-tight. Use a screwdriver and remove four guide pins, then install four bolts finger-tight.

(3) TIGHTEN BOLTS (PRELIMINARY). Cylinder head bolts must be tightened evenly and in a definite manner to prevent distortion of head. Two sequences are required; preliminary and final. For sequence to be used during preliminary tightening, refer to upper portion of figure 56. Start at No. 1 bolt and tighten all bolts with torque wrench (41-W-3630) to 35 foot-pounds.

(4) INSTALL VALVE ROCKER ARM ASSEMBLY. Install push rods in place with "cup" end towards top. Position rocker arm shaft front bracket copper gasket in recess in cylinder head, then carefully locate rocker arm assembly over cover studs as shown in figure 56. Make certain that rocker arms are positioned over push rods correctly. Install 10 bolts in the following manner:

(a) Install three 3¼-inch bolts with lock washers in left side of front and intermediate brackets and tighten finger-tight; then place oil overflow tube, with cork gasket in position, on rear bracket and install a 3¼-inch bolt with lock washer; tighten bolt finger-tight. Install two cover stud nuts with lock washers and tighten finger-tight. NOTE: *It may be necessary to tap brackets either to front or rear to allow bolts to enter threads freely.*

(b) Install six 1⅛-inch bolts in right side of brackets and tighten finger-tight. Finally, tighten all bracket bolts and cover stud nuts firmly. NOTE: *On early vehicles bearing cylinder head casting or part number 6107412, thoroughly coat threads of the six 1⅛-inch bolts with joint and thread compound (52-C-3115) before installing them. Also after they are finally tightened, apply a small amount of compound to under side of each tapped hole, accessible in spark plug recesses. On late vehicles bearing cylinder head number 2136477, tapped holes do not extend through the spark plug recesses, therefore, compound is not required.*

(5) FINAL TIGHTEN CYLINDER BOLTS. Using sequence as shown in lower portion of figure 56, tighten all head bolts to 70-80 foot-pounds. Use special wrench (41-W-2964-700) with torque wrench (41-W-3630).

Engine Description, Data, Maintenance, and Adjustment On Vehicle

(6) INSTALL PUSH ROD COVER. Position gasket and cover to block and secure in following manner:

(a) Install nine 1/4-20 x 1/2 hex-head cross-recess bolt and lock washer assemblies in front and rear end holes, No. 5 hole (from front) in top row, and in No. 3, 4, 6, 8, 9, and 10 holes (from front) in bottom row.

(b) Place oil filter bracket in position and secure with 1/4-20 x 5/8 bolts in two bottom holes and in top front hole.

(c) Place oil filler tube bracket in position and secure with 1/4-20 x 3/4 bolt and lock washer assemblies in front hole where it overlaps oil filter bracket. Place 1/4-inch flat washer between oil filler tube bracket and cover (at rear hole) and install 1/4-20 x 5/8 bolt and lock washer.

(d) Install ignition shield and coil (par. 139b.).

(e) Position oil filler tube clamp to bracket and install two bolts, lock washers, and nuts. Attach dip stick tube bracket to filler tube bracket with bolt, lock washer, and nut.

(7) COMPLETE THE INSTALLATION.

(a) Install oil filter (par. 91e.).

(b) Connect oil line at front of head.

(c) Position gasket and connect thermostat housing to head with two bolts and lock washers.

(d) Place thermo gage bulb in position in head adapter and secure with retaining nut. Tighten firmly.

(e) Coat threads of water by-pass tube flange nuts at each end of tube with mica base antiseize compound (52-C-3081) and install tube in position. Screw flange nuts into their respective fittings until tight. Place clip around tube (be sure insulation is in place under clip) and install clip bolt, lock washer, and nut.

(f) Fill cooling system (par. 117a.).

(g) Install manifolds [par. 87c., steps (3), (4), (5), and (6)].

(h) Warm up engine, check tightness of cylinder head bolts, adjust valve clearance, and install rocker arm cover (par. 86c., d., and e.).

89. OIL PAN.

a. Removal.

(1) REMOVE ENGINE. Before oil pan can be removed, it is necessary to remove engine from the vehicle (par. 94).

(2) REMOVE OIL PAN. Unscrew drain plug (G133-03-40618) and allow to drain from engine. Loosen oil pan attaching screws alternately, then remove screws in the same manner while supporting pan. Carefully lower pan from engine.

b. Installation (fig. 57).

Before attempting to install oil pan, remove flywheel underpan and underpan extension to provide clearance to position pan over gaskets. Remove all particles of old gaskets from oil pan and cylinder block, also from front and rear main bearing caps. Clean oil pan with dry-cleaning solvent.

TM 9-802
89-90

Maintenance Instructions

A OIL PAN ASSEMBLY
B OIL PUMP SCREEN
C OIL PUMP
D REAR OIL PAN SEAL (G501-700 1948-SET)
E OIL PAN GASKET (G501-700 1948-SET)
F FRONT OIL PAN SEAL (G501-700 1948-SET)
G OIL PAN GASKET (G501-700 1948-SET)
H OIL PUMP TO CYLINDER BLOCK PIPE

RA PD 333199

Figure 57—Installing Oil Pan

(1) INSTALL GASKETS AND SEALS. Install new right and left side oil pan gaskets on block with gasket cement. Carefully position front and rear seals (gaskets) in grooves of main bearing caps.

(2) INSTALL OIL PAN. Carefully position oil pan, making certain that front and rear seals in bearing caps are not tilted or pushed out of place. Hold oil pan in position with two cross-recessed bolts installed finger-tight at center of each side of oil pan; then install four hex bolts and lock washers, one at each side of front and rear bearing caps, tightening these finger-tight also. Install balance of cross-recessed bolts, tightening finger-tight, or at least start them into threads. Tighten four hex-head bolts firmly, then tighten 18 cross-recessed bolts.

(3) INSTALL FLYWHEEL UNDERPAN AND EXTENSION. Position and install underpan extension on flywheel housing with two cross-recessed screws and lock washers, tightening screws firmly. Position and install flywheel underpan to flywheel housing with four cross-recessed screws and lock washers, tightening screws firmly.

(4) INSTALL OIL. Install drain plug with gasket and tighten snugly. Refill crankcase with proper lubricant (Lubrication Order No. 9-802).

90. OIL PUMP.

a. Removal. Remove oil pan (par. 89a.). Unscrew oil pump to cylinder block tube nut at cylinder block connector. Loosen pump to block bracket set screw lock nut, then remove set screw (fig. 58). Pull pump and tube from block evenly.

Engine Description, Data, Maintenance, and Adjustment On Vehicle

A SET SCREW D SCREEN G DISTRIBUTOR SHAFT
B NUT E OIL PUMP H TUBE
C RETAINER F ELBOW I CONNECTOR

RA PD 337246

Figure 58—Removing and Installing Oil Pump

b. Installation.

(1) POSITION PUMP. Position pump in block bracket and tube in connector at the same time. Make certain that pump seats solidly in bracket and that tube is alined in connector, also that distributor shaft rotates freely. If not, tap tube lightly with a rawhide hammer as necessary to free up shaft and aline tube.

(2) SECURE PUMP. Thread coupling nut into connector and tighten securely, then install set screw with lock nut in bracket, tightening set screw just enough to secure pump. Over-tightening set screw will cause distributor shaft to bind. Tighten lock nut firmly and install oil pan (par. 89**b**.).

91. OIL FILTER AND LINES.

a. Description. The replaceable element type oil filter is mounted on right-hand side of engine. A portion of the oil passing through the valve rocker arm oil tube is directed through the oil filter where foreign elements are absorbed. Filtered oil is then returned directly to the engine oil pan through the fuel pump mounting

b. Filter Element Replacement (fig. 59).

(1) REMOVE ELEMENT. Remove cover stud nut and lock washer, then remove cover with gasket and spring. Remove drain plug and allow oil to drain. Remove filter element. Clean filter shell and cover with clean rag dipped in dry-cleaning solvent. Wipe all parts dry with a clean rag.

(2) INSTALL ELEMENT. Screw drain plug into bottom of filter shell and tighten firmly. Place new filter element into filter shell. With a new cover gasket in place, install spring, cover, nut gasket, and nut. Tighten nut snugly.

TM 9-802
91-92

Maintenance Instructions

- A COVER STUD NUT
- B NUT GASKET (G501-01-94055)
- C FILTER COVER
- D COVER GASKET (G085-30-02400)
- E COVER SPRING
- F ELEMENT (G104-15-69147)
- G INLET TUBE CONNECTOR
- H SHELL AND STUD
- I DRAIN PLUG
- J OUTLET TUBE CONNECTOR
- K CLAMP BOLT
- L FILTER CLAMP
- M OIL LEVEL INDICATOR (G501-02-32469)

RA PD 337203

Figure 59—Oil Filter Installed and Disassembled

    c. Filter Assembly Replacement. Disconnect inlet and outlet tubes at filter. Remove four filter clamp to bracket bolts. Withdraw filter and clamps as an assembly. Loosen upper and lower clamp screws to remove clamps from filter. Reinstall in reverse manner.

    d. Oil Lines and Connections. Oil lines and their connections are securely fastened in position with clips and may be readily removed or installed. Lines and connections are accessible from engine compartment.

92. CRANKCASE VENTILATION SYSTEM.

    a. Operation. The ventilation of the crankcase, and the removal of fuel and water vapors from within the engine are accomplished by the circulation of air actuated by manifold vacuum. Air is drawn into crankcase through an oil bath breather (at oil filler tube) and, after circulating through the engine, is drawn upward and out of the engine through the

Engine Description, Data, Maintenance, and Adjustment On Vehicle

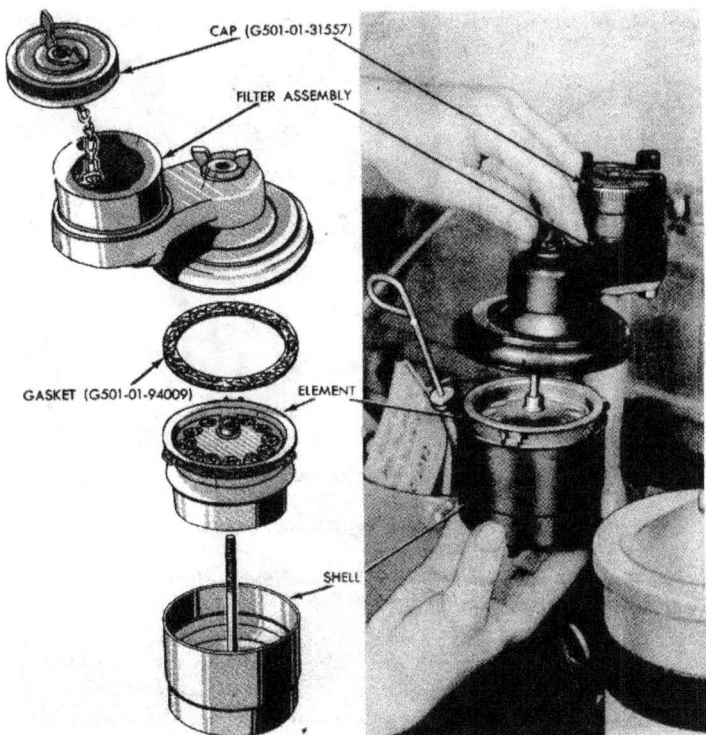

RA PD 337147

Figure 60—Engine Crankcase Breather

valve rocker arm cover, entering combustion chamber of the engine through the intake manifold. The ventilator line is connected to an elbow at the center of the valve rocker arm cover. The opposite end of the line is connected to a tee installed at the center of the intake manifold, and contains a spring loaded plunger type valve which acts as a restriction for vapor flow.

b. Cleaning Crankcase Breather (fig. 60). Loosen wing nut, then withdraw shell and element. Clean as directed on Lubrication Order No. 9-802. Check condition of breather shell gasket and replace if cracked or deteriorated in any way. Insert element into shell and install to filler assembly. Tighten wing nut firmly. Replace oil filler cap if not in good condition.

c. Ventilator Line and Valve Removal (fig. 61). Disconnect tube at rocker arm cover elbow and at valve elbow. Remove valve from

TM 9-802
92-93

Maintenance Instructions

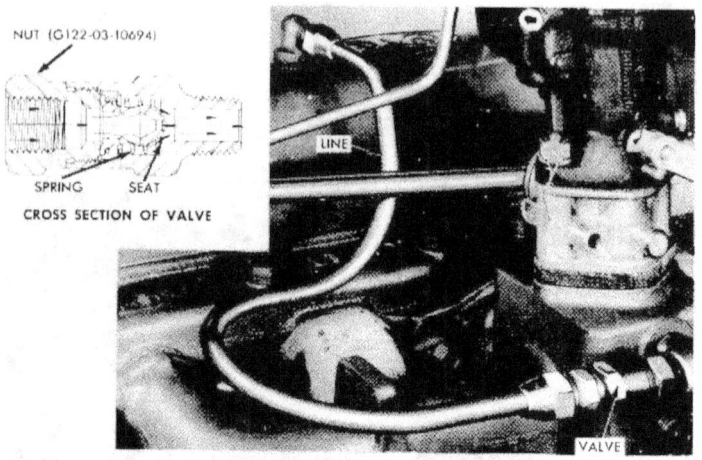

Figure 61—Crankcase Ventilator Line and Valve

intake manifold tee. Remove nut from valve body which permits removal of restrictor valve and spring from body.

d. Cleaning Valve. Wash all valve parts in dry-cleaning solvent to loosen accumulated foreign matter. Blow parts clean and dry with compressed air.

e. Ventilator Line and Valve Installation. Install spring and restrictor valve inside valve body and thread nut into body. Tighten nut firmly. Apply mica-base antiseize compound (52-C-3081) to male threads of valve. Screw valve into intake manifold tee. Install line connection on valve elbow finger-tight, then install opposite end of line on valve rocker arm elbow, making certain that tube is alined properly. Tighten both connections firmly.

Section XVII
Engine Removal and Installation

93. COORDINATION WITH HIGHER ECHELON.

a. Replacement of this major assembly with a new or rebuilt unit is normally a third echelon operation, but may be performed in an emergency by second echelon, provided authority for performing this replacement is obtained from the appropriate commander. Tools needed for

TM 9-802
93-94

Engine Removal and Installation

the operation which are not carried in second echelon may be obtained from a higher echelon of maintenance.

94. REMOVAL.

a. General. In an emergency, the engine may be removed by two mechanics by performing the operations in the sequence given. However, the operations are greatly facilitated and time required is reduced to a minimum by using four mechanics. Mechanics will be termed "A," "B," "C," and "D," stationed in the vehicle as follows:

"A"—Left side of engine in engine compartment
"B"—Right side of engine in engine compartment
"C"—Left side of transmission under driver's compartment
"D"—Right side of transmission under driver's compartment

Each mechanic will perform operations designated to him by the letter preceding the title of the operation. Example, step (3) below: "A" and "C"—*Remove Gear Bilge Pump Front Intake Tube and Control Valve.* The letters "A" and "C" preceding the title means that this operation is performed by mechanic "A," stationed in engine compartment at left side of engine, and mechanic "C," stationed under driver's compartment at left side of transmission.

RA PD 337218

Figure 62—Engine Removal—Left-hand Side

187

TM 9-802
94

Maintenance Instructions

b. Special Tools and Equipment. A hoist of at least a 1,000-pound capacity is needed to remove engine unit from the hull. An A-frame mounted on another vehicle (par. 280) may be used. A special engine lifting sling (41-S-3832-7) is also required.

c. Procedure (figs. 62 and 63). The design of the vehicle necessitates removing the engine and transmission as a unit. After engine and transmission assembly is removed from the vehicle, transmission may be removed from the engine if necessary.

(1) "A," "B," "C," and "D"—REMOVE ENGINE HATCH COVER AND FLOOR BOARDS. Unfasten lock bolts, remove hinge pins, and remove engine hatch cover. Remove driver's compartment floor boards and three front sections of cargo compartment floor boards. Lift out center air intake grille (behind driver's compartment). Shift power take-off shift shaft into high speed (so shift shaft clears left side engine mounting bracket while engine is being removed). Shift transmission into second speed and water propeller transfer case into forward position.

RA PD 337224

Figure 63—Engine Removal—Right-hand Side

Engine Removal and Installation

(2) "B" AND "D"—REMOVE BATTERY AND CLOSE FUEL VALVE. Disconnect battery cables at battery. Remove two wing nuts and tray from top of battery. Then lift out battery with a suitable lifting strap, being careful not to spill electrolyte. Shut off fuel valve underneath right side of driver's compartment.

(3) "A" AND "C"—REMOVE GEAR BILGE PUMP FRONT INTAKE TUBE AND CONTROL VALVE (PRIOR TO CHASSIS SERIAL NO. 4202). Disconnect two hose connections, one in engine compartment at left side of engine and one near bilge pump valves under driver's floor board. Loosen intake pipe clamp at frame side rail in engine compartment and remove rear section of pipe. Remove front compartment bilge pump valve for access to transmission brackets and drive shaft.

(4) "A"—REMOVE CARBURETER CLEANER. Refer to paragraph 105c.

(5) "A" AND "B"—DRAIN COOLING SYSTEM. Refer to paragraph 117b.

(6) "A"—DISCONNECT EXHAUST PIPE. Disconnect exhaust pipe at exhaust manifold by removing three flange to manifold bolts, nuts, and lock nuts. Remove gasket and flange seal.

(7) "A"—DISCONNECT CHOKE AND THROTTLE CONTROLS AT CARBURETER. Loosen choke control swivel and control clip screws and pull choke control free from choke lever. Loosen hand throttle stop collar and throttle clip screws and pull throttle control free from throttle lever.

(8) "A"—DISCONNECT VACUUM WINDSHIELD WIPER TUBE AT MANIFOLD (PRIOR TO CHASSIS SERIAL NO. 2006). Pull windshield wiper tube off from manifold fitting.

(9) "A"—DISCONNECT GENERATOR TO REGULATOR WIRING HARNESS. Disconnect wires at armature filter, armature, field, and ground terminals at generator.

(10) "A"—DISCONNECT TEMPERATURE GAGE THERMAL UNIT. Unscrew thermo gage bulb retaining nut and pull bulb from cylinder head adapter.

(11) "A"—DISCONNECT ACCELERATOR LINKAGE. At underside of toeboard, disconnect idler lever to bell crank rod from idler lever and allow rod to fall forward.

(12) "A"—REMOVE CLUTCH AND BRAKE PEDALS. At underside of toeboard, remove nut from each pedal rod. Loosen pedal rod by tapping pedal lever at top center to free rod from lever.

(13) "A"—REMOVE STARTER PEDAL ROD. At underside of toeboard, remove clevis pin and disconnect starter pedal rod from cross shaft. Unscrew starter button and remove starter pedal rod.

(14) "A"—DISCONNECT OIL GAGE TUBE. Disconnect oil gage flexible tube at toeboard. Use two wrenches to prevent twisting tube.

(15) "C"—REMOVE VALVE COVER, IGNITION SHIELD COVER, AND COVER BRACKET. It may be necessary to remove the valve cover, ignition shield cover, and shield cover support bracket, depending upon the type of sling, chains, or ropes used for the engine unit removal. Lift off parts after removing attaching bolts, cap screws, or nuts.

(16) REMOVE TIRE PUMP WATER TUBES.

(a) "D"—Prior to Chassis Serial No. 2006. Disconnect water tubes at top left rear of engine, at drain cock in the left lower rear of the cylinder block, and tire pump connections under air intake grilles. Remove tubing.

(b) "A" and "B"—After Chassis Serial No. 2005. Disconnect tire pump water tubes at engine thermostat housing and at left lower rear of cylinder block. Push tubes to side of compartment.

(17) "B"—REMOVE FAN BLADE ASSEMBLY.

(a) Prior to Chassis Serial No. 606. Remove four bolts attaching fan blade assembly and spacer to water pump pulley. Lift out fan blade assembly and spacer.

(b) After Chassis Serial No. 605. Remove water pump shaft nut and four bolts attaching fan blade assembly to pulley. Lift out fan blade assembly.

(18) "B"—REMOVE RADIATOR UPPER HOSE CONNECTION AND INLET PIPE. Loosen hose clamp at radiator and cylinder head water outlet, and disconnect and remove hoses and pipe. Loosen hose clamp and disconnect overflow hose at radiator.

(19) "B"—REMOVE TIRE PUMP DRIVE SHAFT (AFTER CHASSIS SERIAL NO. 2005). Refer to paragraph 267*b.*

(20) "A" AND "B"—REMOVE RADIATOR SHROUD ASSEMBLY. Remove bolts on each side of shroud and remove upper and lower shroud as an assembly.

(21) "B"—REMOVE RADIATOR LOWER HOSE AND OUTLET PIPE. Loosen hose clamps and disconnect hose at radiator and water pump. Remove radiator outlet hoses and pipe.

(22) "A" AND "B"—REMOVE RADIATOR. Remove top seal plate with felt, and lower seal retainer with felt from inside front compartment. Remove the three bolts at each side which secure the radiator to support. Remove radiator carefully.

(23) "B"—DISCONNECT WIRING AT STARTER. Disconnect ammeter, battery, and condenser wires at starter switch terminal. Disconnect primary wire from ignition coil post at ignition shield. After chassis serial No. 1499, disconnect radio junction box wire at starter switch terminal.

(24) "B"—REMOVE TIMING COVER PLATE TO CROSSMEMBER BOLT NUTS. Remove cotter pins (if used) from two timing cover plate to crossmember bolts and remove nuts.

(25) "C" AND "D"—REMOVE HAND BRAKE SECTOR AND CROSS SHAFT BRACKETS ASSEMBLY. Remove clevis pin and dis-

Engine Removal and Installation

connect hand brake pull rod at forward end. Remove three bolts securing hand brake sector bracket to left side of transmission, and two bolts and one nut attaching cross shaft bracket to right side of transmission. Disconnect water propeller transfer case control spring. To remove assembly, move left side rearward so bracket will clear lower stud at right side.

(26) "C"—REMOVE POWER TAKE-OFF SUPPORT BRACKET. Remove bolts attaching bracket to top of transmission and to power take-off. Remove bracket.

(27) "C"—REMOVE WINCH POWER TAKE-OFF LEVER. At left of transmission, remove clevis pin to disconnect winch power take-off shift shaft. Remove lever from transmission stud by removing cotter pin and retaining washer.

(28) "C"—DISCONNECT WINCH DRIVE SHAFT. Remove hex head set screw which holds yoke of drive shaft universal joint to power take-off shaft. Push drive shaft rearward from power take-off.

(29) "C"—REMOVE CLUTCH AND BRAKE PEDAL AND BRACKET ASSEMBLY. Disconnect clutch adjusting link at left of clutch housing, unhook pull back spring, and remove lock and adjusting nuts. Remove cotter pin and clevis pin to disconnect brake pedal to master cylinder rod at forward end. Remove two bolts attaching bracket to clutch housing and remove bracket assembly, including levers and shaft.

(30) "D" — REMOVE TRANSFER CASE AND FRONT AXLE SHIFT LEVERS. Refer to paragraph 161e.

(31) "C"—DISCONNECT ENGINE STABILIZER ROD.

(a) Prior to Chassis Serial No. 2506. At left rear of transmission, remove cotter pin and clevis pin to disconnect stabilizer rod from water propeller transfer case control cross shaft left-hand bracket.

(b) After Chassis Serial No. 2505. At left rear of transmission, remove cotter pin, washer, and winch power take-off lever from pivot stud. Remove retaining nut and washer from pivot stud and remove stabilizer rod from pivot stud. (To relieve strain of stabilizer rod on stud, insert pry bar between front side of left rear engine mounting bracket and inside of frame bracket and pry engine towards rear.)

(32) "C"—DISCONNECT TIRE PUMP CHAIN AND CONTROL ROD (PRIOR TO CHASSIS SERIAL NO. 2006). Loosen adjusting bolt nuts above and below front end of tire pump support to loosen chain. Disassemble connecting link and remove drive chain. Disconnect tire pump control rod at power take-off shifter shaft by removing cotter and clevis pins.

(33) "C" AND "D"—REMOVE WATER PROPELLER TRANSFER CASE CROSS SHAFT AND BRACKETS (PRIOR TO CHASSIS SERIAL NO. 2506). At left rear of transmission, disconnect shift rod and control rod at cross shaft lever by removing cotter pin and clevis pin. Remove stud nut attaching right-hand cross shaft bracket to transmission. Remove power take-off bracket, cross shaft, and lever as an

assembly. Prior to Chassis Serial No. 2006, remove mounting stud nut and pull left-hand cross shaft bracket clear from mounting stud and tire pump support.

(34) "D"—DISCONNECT PROPELLER SHAFT AT TRANSMISSION. Disconnect universal joint flange from transmission companion flange by removing four nuts, washers, and bolts.

(35) "D"—DISCONNECT HYDROVAC VACUUM LINE. Loosen hose clamp and disconnect hose from vacuum line at the right side of clutch housing.

(36) "D"—UNFASTEN TACHOMETER CABLE. At right side of transmission case, disconnect tachometer cable by unscrewing swivel nut from transmission fitting.

(37) "C" AND "D"—REMOVE ENGINE REAR SUPPORT BOLTS. Remove one insulator to engine bracket bolt from each rear mounting.

(38) "B"—DISCONNECT FUEL TUBES AND REMOVE FUEL FILTER. Refer to paragraph 110c.

(39) "C" AND "D"—REMOVE TRANSMISSION COVER. Remove the seven remaining cap screws on the top of the transmission and remove transmission cover and shift lever assembly for clearance. Cover the transmission opening with a clean cloth.

(40) "A," "B," "C," AND "D"—REMOVE ENGINE. Swing hoist, chain fall, or A-frame in position to lift engine out of hatch. Engine may be removed using engine removal sling (41-S-3832-7) (figs. 62 and 63). If sling is not available, heavy rope which is part of the DUKW equipment may be used. Raise engine assembly sufficiently to allow forward movement until clear of rear mounting brackets. Move rear end of engine towards right side of engine compartment so that the power take-off will clear the steering gear housing. At the same time, raise front of engine upward out of compartment opening, holding the rear down until it clears toeboards. Lift engine until clear of engine compartment opening. If necessary to remove transmission, refer to paragraph 158.

95. INSTALLATION.

a. Engine Unit Installation (figs. 62 and 63). It should be understood that prior to installation, all engine unit parts (for example, engine support insulator) must be inspected, and if necessary, replaced. If transmission was removed, it must be installed on engine as directed in paragraph 159. Refer to paragraph 94a. for explanation of letters preceding operation titles.

(1) "A," "B," "C," AND "D"—PLACE ENGINE UNIT IN ENGINE COMPARTMENT. Supported by hoist or A-frame with suitable ropes, chains, or sling (41-S-3832-7), lower engine into engine compartment, guiding rear of engine assembly down under toeboards. Then, with unit supported on a level to clear front support bolts, move engine rearward to aline bolts with front support. Line up rear supports (fig. 64) then lower engine into position.

TM 9-802

Engine Removal and Installation

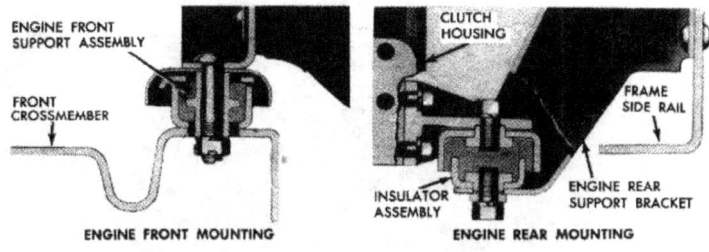

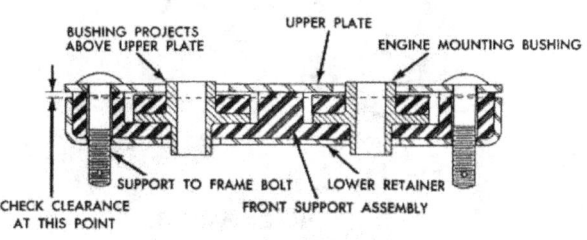

Figure 64—Engine Front and Rear Mounting

(2) "B"—INSTALL TIMING COVER PLATE TO CROSSMEMBER BOLT NUTS. Replace engine timing cover plate to crossmember bolt nuts with $7/16$-inch Marsden self-locking nuts; also replace engine front support bolt nuts with $3/8$-inch Marsden self-locking nuts if not already in use.

(3) "C" AND "D"—INSTALL TRANSMISSION COVER (FIG. 65). Place transmission gears in neutral and fit cover on transmission, making sure shift forks engage grooves in gears. Install cover cap screws except second from rear on left side. Check shift lever operation.

(4) "C" AND "D"—INSTALL ENGINE REAR SUPPORT BOLTS (FIG. 64). Install one bolt in rear support at each side of engine.

(5) "C"—CONNECT WINCH DRIVE SHAFT. Place key in keyway and drive universal joint yoke onto power take-off shaft. Check to be sure front and rear joints are assembled in same plane. Tighten hex head set screw securely.

(6) "D"—CONNECT PROPELLER SHAFT AT REAR OF TRANSMISSION. Install four bolts, lock washers, and nuts to connect universal joint flange to transmission companion flange. Be sure front and rear joints are assembled in same plane.

(7) "C"—INSTALL CLUTCH AND BRAKE PEDALS AND BRACKET ASSEMBLY. Attach bracket assembly to left side of clutch housing with two lock washers and bolts. Do not draw bolts tight until

TM 9-802

Maintenance Instructions

RA PD 56163

Figure 65—Transmission Cover Installation

after hand brake assembly has been installed. Connect brake pedal to master cylinder rod. Connect clutch adjusting link to release fork, using adjusting and lock nuts. Hook clutch pedal pull-back spring to release fork.

(8) "C" — INSTALL POWER TAKE-OFF SUPPORT BRACKET. Place bracket in position and install cover screw and lock washer at top of transmission case and two bolts and lock washers at power take-off. Do not draw bolts tight until hand brake bracket has been installed.

(9) "C" AND "D"—INSTALL WATER PROPELLER TRANSFER CASE CROSS SHAFT AND BRACKETS (PRIOR TO CHASSIS SERIAL NO. 2506). On vehicles prior to chassis serial No. 2006, place left-hand cross shaft bracket on left side of transmission, with holes in bracket fitted over two studs and adjusting bolt inserted through front end of tire pump support. Install rear stud washer and nut. Place right-hand cross shaft bracket, cross shaft, and lever as an assembly on right side of transmission. Left end of cross shaft must be inserted in bushing in left bracket; then install washer and nut on stud to attach right bracket. Connect shift rod and control rod to lever on cross shaft using clevis pins and cotter pins.

(10) "C"—INSTALL AND ADJUST TIRE PUMP CHAIN AND CONNECT CONTROL ROD (PRIOR TO CHASSIS SERIAL NO. 2006 ONLY). Place drive chain around sprockets and install connecting link. Tighten adjusting and lock nuts at front end of tire pump support

Engine Removal and Installation

to tighten and adjust chain. Install clevis pin and cotter pin to connect tire pump bell crank control rod and power take-off shift shaft.

(11) "C"—CONNECT ENGINE STABILIZER ROD.

(a) Prior to Chassis Serial No. 2506. At left rear of transmission, install clevis pin and cotter pin to connect stabilizer rod to water propeller transfer case control cross shaft left-hand bracket.

(b) After Chassis Serial No. 2505. Fit end of stabilizer rod over pivot stud, after checking stabilizer rod for length. Stabilizer rod should be lined up with stud hole at transmission case.

(12) "C"—INSTALL WINCH POWER TAKE-OFF LEVER. At left side of transmission, place winch power take-off lever on pivot stud and install flat washer and cotter pin. Connect lower end of lever to power take-off shaft link with clevis pin.

(13) "D"—CONNECT TACHOMETER CABLE. Connect tachometer cable to fitting at right rear of transmission. Tighten swivel nut.

(14) "D"—CONNECT HYDROVAC LINE. At right side of clutch housing, connect Hydrovac vacuum line with connecting hose. Tighten hose clamp.

(15) "D"—INSTALL TRANSFER CASE AND FRONT AXLE SHIFT LEVERS. Refer to paragraph 161f.

(16) "C" AND "D"—INSTALL HAND BRAKE SECTOR AND CROSS SHAFT BRACKETS ASSEMBLY. Place assembly over transmission with left bracket to rear so that right bracket can fit over transmission stud. Secure right bracket with lock washers, nut, and bolts. Install ground strap and flat washer under front bolt. In left bracket, install short bolt at bottom, medium bolt at top rear, and long bolt in front. Place spacer between bracket and transmission at front and rear bolts. Tighten clutch and brake pedal bracket assembly bolts and power take-off bracket bolts. Connect hand brake pull rod with clevis pin. On vehicles prior to chassis serial No. 2506, connect water propeller transfer case control return spring. Spring hooks into clevis pin at shift rod and extension hooks over hand brake cross shaft.

(17) "A"—CONNECT STARTER CONTROL. Insert starter pedal rod up through toeboard and connect to cross shaft with clevis pin. Screw starter button on top of pedal rod.

(18) "A"—CONNECT OIL GAGE TUBE. At underside of toeboard, connect flexible tube to oil line. Use two wrenches to prevent twisting tube.

(19) "A"—CONNECT CLUTCH AND BRAKE PEDALS. At underside of toeboard, insert brake and clutch pedal rod ends in pedal levers and install nuts and cotter pins. Adjust clutch pedal free-travel to $2\frac{1}{2}$ inches (par. 153). Connect and adjust brake pedal to master cylinder rod (par. 191c.).

(20) "A"—INSTALL CARBURETER AIR CLEANER. Refer to paragraph 105e.

Maintenance Instructions

(21) "A"—CONNECT EXHAUST PIPE. Install exhaust pipe to manifold gasket and flange seal, then install and tighten firmly three flange to manifold bolts, nuts, and lock nuts.

(22) "A"—CONNECT REGULATOR WIRING HARNESS TO GENERATOR. Refer to figure 99 or 100.

(23) "A"—CONNECT VACUUM WINDSHIELD WIPER TUBE AT MANIFOLD (PRIOR TO CHASSIS SERIAL NO. 2005). Connect windshield wiper tube at manifold by sliding tube over manifold fitting.

(24) "A"—CONNECT CHOKE CONTROL AND HAND THROTTLE AT CARBURETER. Refer to paragraph 107**b**. and **c**.

(25) "A"—CONNECT TEMPERATURE GAGE THERMAL UNIT. Place thermo gage bulb in position in cylinder head adapter and secure with retaining nut. Tighten firmly.

(26) "A"—CONNECT ACCELERATOR LINKAGE. At underside of toeboard, connect idler lever to bell crank rod with washer and cotter pin.

(27) "A" AND "C"—INSTALL GEAR BILGE PUMP FRONT INTAKE TUBE AND CONTROL VALVE (PRIOR TO CHASSIS SERIAL NO. 4202). At left of transmission, screw the control valve into manifold and connect control rod with cotter pin. Install front intake tube and connect hose at bilge pump valve and to front tube section in engine compartment. Tighten tube to frame clamp bolts.

(28) "A" AND "B"—INSTALL RADIATOR. Place radiator between supports. Install three bolts, lock washers, and nuts at each side. Be sure felt air seals at top and bottom of radiator are in place.

(29) "B"—CONNECT RADIATOR LOWER HOSE AND OUTLET PIPE. Install radiator outlet pipe and connect hose at radiator and water pump. Install extra drive belt on shroud brackets on vehicles after chassis serial No. 2005.

(30) "A"—INSTALL RADIATOR SHROUD. Attach shroud to radiator support with four bolts, nuts, and lock washers on each side.

(31) "B"—INSTALL TIRE PUMP DRIVE SHAFT (AFTER CHASSIS SERIAL NO. 2005). Refer to paragraph 267**d**.

(32) "B"—CONNECT RADIATOR UPPER HOSE AND INLET PIPE. Install radiator inlet pipe and hose at radiator and cylinder head water outlet. Connect overflow hose at radiator with hose clamp.

(33) "B"—INSTALL FAN ASSEMBLY.

(a) Prior to Chassis Serial No. 606. Place spacer and fan blade assembly in position over end of water pump shaft and attach with four bolts and new lock washers.

(b) After Chassis Serial No. 605. Attach fan blade assembly to water pump pulley with four bolts, new lock washers, and water pump shaft nut.

(34) INSTALL TIRE PUMP WATER TUBES.

(a) "D"—Prior to Chassis Serial No. 2006. Place water tubes over left side of transmission and connect hoses at tire pump under air intake

Ignition System

grilles, in engine compartment at left rear of engine, and at drain cock at left lower rear of cylinder block.

(b) "A" and "B"—After Chassis Serial No. 2005. Connect water tubes at thermostat housing and at left-hand lower rear of cylinder block.

(35) "B"—INSTALL FUEL FILTER AND LINES. Refer to paragraph 110d.

(36) "B"—CONNECT WIRING AT STARTER. Place ammeter, battery, and condenser wire terminals on starter switch terminal and install lock washer and nut. Attach primary wire to ignition coil post at ignition shield. After chassis serial No. 1499, install radio junction box wire on starter switch terminal.

(37) "B"—INSTALL BATTERY. Lower battery into place on tray at front right side of engine compartment, with positive (+) terminal towards the front. Locate upper tray over battery. Install wing nuts and tighten. Attach battery cables and coat with grease to prevent corrosion.

(38) "A" AND "B"—FILL COOLING SYSTEM. Refer to paragraph 117a.

(39) "A," "B," "C," AND "D"—INSTALL ENGINE HATCH COVER AND FLOOR BOARDS. Place hatch cover in position on front deck. Install hinge pins and fasten cover down with lock bolts. Install driver's compartment floor boards and three front sections of cargo compartment floor boards. Close front compartment hatch cover and fasten lock bolts. Fasten guard over crank wheel on propeller shaft. Replace center air intake grille. Place water propeller transfer case and transmission shift levers in neutral position.

(40) "A," "B," "C," AND "D"—TEST AFTER INSTALLATION. Check oil level before starting engine. Start engine, keeping hand on ignition switch to shut off engine if trouble develops. Note operation of ammeter, oil gage, and heat indicator while engine is allowed to run a few minutes, until assured that operation is satisfactory.

(41) RECORD OF REPLACEMENT. Record the replacement on W.D., A.G.O. Form No. 478, MWO and Major Unit Assembly Replacement Record.

Section XVIII

Ignition System

96. GENERAL.

a. Description. The ignition system consists of the source of power (battery or generator), ignition switch, ignition coil, distributor, condenser, spark plugs, and high and low tension wiring. The coil, distrib-

TM 9-802

Maintenance Instructions

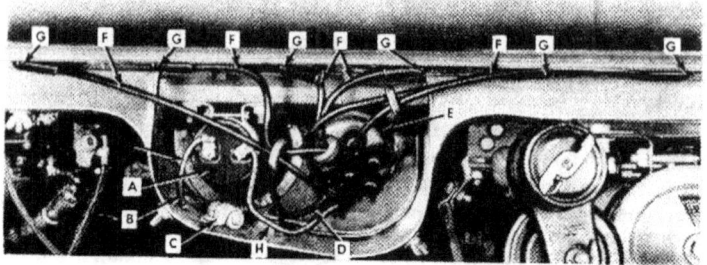

A IGNITION COIL
B INSULATED PRIMARY TERMINAL
C PRIMARY CIRCUIT CONDENSER
D HIGH TENSION WIRE
E DISTRIBUTOR

F IGNITION CABLE
G SPARK PLUGS
H LOW TENSION WIRE
I COIL TO SHIELD WIRE

RA PD 333244

*Figure 66—Ignition System Units Installed
(Prior to Chassis Serial No. 14779)*

utor, spark plugs, and high tension cables are shielded by an ignition shield (figs. 66 and 67) and cover to suppress radio interference noise and protect the units from moisture.

b. Repair Operations. Repair operations on distributor assembly are described in TM 9-1802A.

c. Circuit Description. There are two distinct electrical circuits in the ignition system, the PRIMARY and the SECONDARY (fig. 68). When these circuits are kept in mind, as well as the functions of the

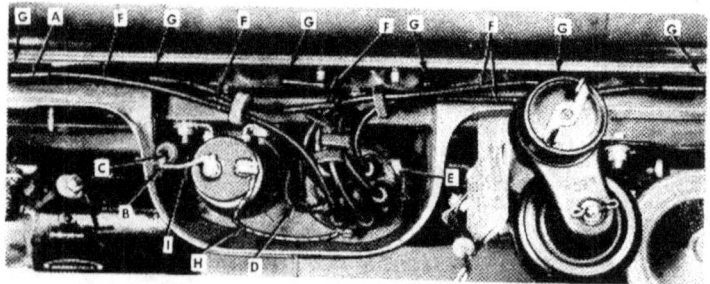

A IGNITION COIL
B INSULATED PRIMARY TERMINAL
C PRIMARY CIRCUIT CONDENSER
D HIGH TENSION WIRE
E DISTRIBUTOR

F IGNITION CABLE
G SPARK PLUGS
H LOW TENSION WIRE
I COIL TO SHIELD WIRE

RA PD 337253

*Figure 67—Ignition System Units Installed
(After Chassis Serial No. 14778)*

Ignition System

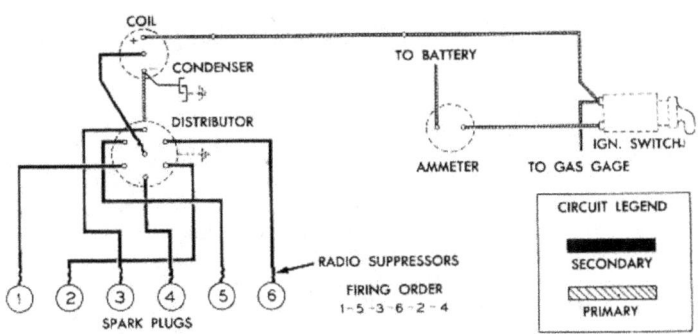

Figure 68—Ignition System Circuits

various units in the system to accomplish these circuits, a better understanding may be had of the operation of the entire system.

(1) PRIMARY CIRCUIT. The primary, or low tension circuit, includes the source of electrical energy (battery or generator), distributor contact points and circuit-breaker mechanism, primary circuit of the ignition coil, and condenser.

(2) SECONDARY CIRCUIT. The secondary, or high tension circuit, includes the secondary circuit of the coil, distributor rotor and cap, high tension cables, and spark plugs.

d. Data.

(1) DISTRIBUTOR.

```
Make ............................................. Delco Remy
Model (Prior to Chassis Serial No. 14779) ............. 1110135
Model (After Chassis Serial No. 14778) ................ 1110182
Breaker point gap ........................... 0.018 to 0.024 in.
Breaker arm tension ................................. 17 to 21 oz
Firing order ........................................ 1-5-3-6-2-4
Initial ignition timing ...... 5 degrees before upper dead center (Steel Ball)
```

(2) SPARK PLUGS.

```
Make ..................................................... AC
Type ............................................. 44 or 44 Com.
Size .................................................... 14MM
Point gap (44) ........................................ 0.025 in.
Point gap (44 Com.) ................................... 0.030 in.
```

(3) IGNITION COIL.

```
Make .............................................. Delco Remy
Model .................................................. 1115149
```

97. IGNITION TIMING.

a. General. Timing the ignition system includes the initial timing, or setting of the distributor mechanism to permit opening of the points

TM 9-802

Maintenance Instructions

at correct firing intervals, and manual advance, or retarding or advancing the point opening to compensate for the various grades of fuel which may be used.

b. Initial Timing.

(1) REMOVE IGNITION SHIELD COVER (FIG. 113). Loosen crankcase ventilator tube nut at manifold. Loosen two stud nuts at top of rocker arm cover. Lift rocker arm cover sufficiently to clear flange on ignition shield cover. Loosen four wing nuts on some models or three stud nuts on other models, attaching cover to shield. Lift cover up to remove from shield.

(2) LOCATE NO. 1 CYLINDER FIRING POSITION. Locate No. 1 cylinder spark plug cable on distributor cap, then place a mark on distributor body opposite No. 1 cable in cap. Remove distributor cap. On latest models also remove rotor and housing cover. Clean and adjust point opening if necessary (par. 99**b.**).

(3) SET MANUAL ADVANCE. Set manual advance at zero, halfway between "R" and "A" (fig. 69).

(4) CHECK TIMING. Do not turn ignition switch on. Crank engine slowly, using hand crank lever (par. 19**d.**), until flywheel mark is alined with pointer on flywheel housing (fig. 70). With ignition timing mark alined with pointer, rotor should point toward mark placed on distributor body. Timing should be checked by methods described in steps *(a)*, *(b)*, and *(c)* below.

(a) NOTE: *Before check is made as described in step (c) below, bear in mind that the engine is normally set to idle at 510 revolutions per minute (par. 106b.). A check of the ignition timing, however, can-*

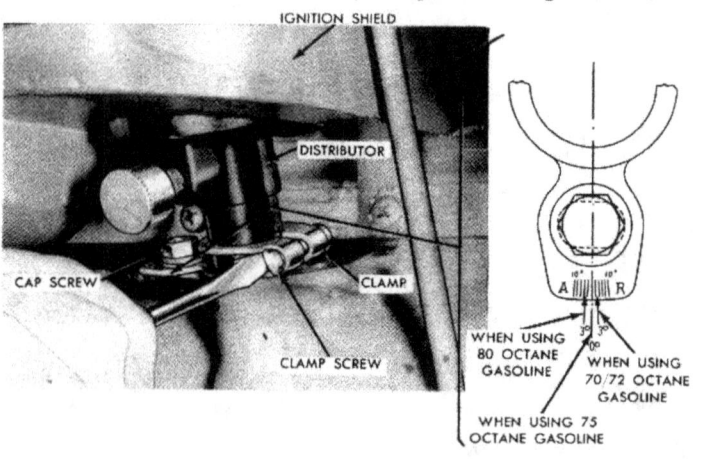

Figure 69—Timing Adjustments

Ignition System

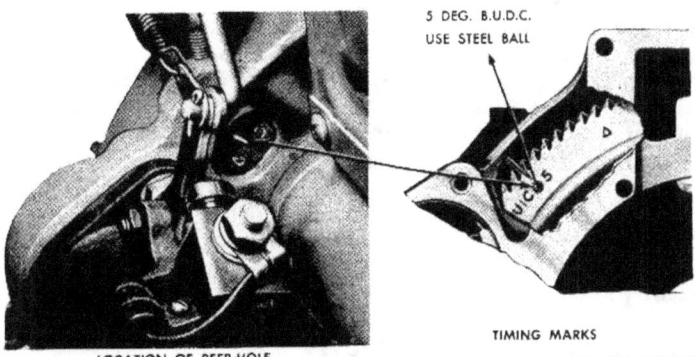

Figure 70—Flywheel Timing Marks

not be made at that speed, as the distributor centrifugal advance cuts in at approximately 400 revolutions per minute. It is therefore necessary that idling speed be reduced to 350 revolutions per minute when ignition timing check is made. After check is made, readjust idling speed as described in paragraph 106**b**.

(b) With Engine Not Running. With ignition timing mark alined with pointer on flywheel housing and distributor rotor at No. 1 spark plug cable position, points should just begin to open. Loosen clamp screw (fig. 69) and turn distributor housing clockwise until points close. Disconnect high tension coil cable at distributor cap, turn on ignition switch and, while holding end of high tension cable ¼ inch from ground, turn distributor housing counterclockwise until spark occurs. When spark occurs, points are open. While holding distributor in this position, tighten clamp screw firmly. Turn ignition switch off.

(c) With Engine Running. Attach one lead of timing light (41-L-1440) to No. 1 spark plug terminal and other lead to ground. Start engine and run at idling speed of 350 revolutions per minute [refer to step *(a)* above]. Direct beam of timing light toward flywheel housing peephole. Timing light flashes make ignition timing mark on flywheel appear stationary. Loosen clamp screw (fig. 69) and move distributor body clockwise or counterclockwise as necessary to synchronize flashes with flywheel mark when it is alined with pointer on flywheel housing. Tighten clamp screw.

(5) INSTALL IGNITION SHIELD COVER (FIG. 113). Lift rocker arm cover sufficiently to clear flange on ignition shield cover. Locate ignition shield cover firmly in place on shield. Tighten four wing nuts on some models or three stud nuts on other models which attach cover to shield. Locate rocker arm cover on rocker arm cover gasket and tighten rocker arm cover stud nuts. Tighten crankcase ventilator tube nut at manifold.

Maintenance Instructions

c. Manual Adjustment (fig. 69).

(1) DRIVE VEHICLE. After engine has been thoroughly warmed up, drive vehicle, using grade of fuel expected to be used in service. Engine should not "ping" or "clatter" excessively under load and full throttle.

(2) ADJUST MANUAL ADVANCE. A slight amount of "ping" is not objectionable. If excessive amount of knock exists, loosen clamp screw (fig. 69) and turn distributor body toward "R" on distributor clamp until knock is minimized. Tighten clamp screw. With manual advance set at "zero," engine should perform satisfactorily when 75 octane fuel is used. It will be necessary to retard manual advance approximately three degrees when using 70-72 octane fuel, and advance three degrees with 80 octane fuel. Several trials and adjustments may be necessary to obtain good performance with grade of gasoline used.

98. DISTRIBUTOR ASSEMBLY.

a. General. The distributor is mounted on the right-hand side of the engine and is driven from the camshaft by spiral cut gears. The lower end of the distributor shaft is tongued and engages a slot in the upper end of the oil pump shaft to drive the oil pump. The distributor is a mechanical unit designed to distribute the secondary (high) voltage in correct sequence to the spark plugs, and to vary the spark automatically to provide efficient operation of the engine. The distributor is equipped with two types of spark control, centrifugal advance and manual advance.

b. Corrosion Prevention and Waterproofing Procedure. Remove terminals from distributor cap and thoroughly clean contacting surfaces. Apply a thin coating of petrolatum to terminals and install. Clean distributor cap, rotor, and primary terminal connection. Paint exterior of distributor and wiring with red synthetic paint (glyptal, 52-P-8057-710). If not available, use ignition insulating compound (52-C-3099-20). Let compound dry before attempting to start engine.

c. Removal.

(1) SET DISTRIBUTOR AT NO. 1 PISTON FIRING POSITION. Remove ignition shield cover [par. 97*b*.(1)]. Make certain that flywheel housing pointer is alined with ignition timing mark on flywheel and that No. 1 piston is in firing position [subpar. *d*.(2) below]. Remove spark plug and secondary cables from distributor cap. Loosen terminal nut at side of distributor housing and remove primary wire.

(2) REMOVE GREASE CUP. Remove distributor shaft grease cup from housing. Grease cup is located under ignition shield.

(3) REMOVE DISTRIBUTOR. Loosen clamp bolt (fig. 69) and lift distributor (G501-01-52015) straight up from engine. Do not crank engine while distributor is removed.

d. Installation.

(1) PLACE ROTOR AT NO. 1 FIRING POSITION. Remove distributor cap and turn distributor assembly shaft until rotor points approximately to No. 1 spark plug cable position.

Ignition System

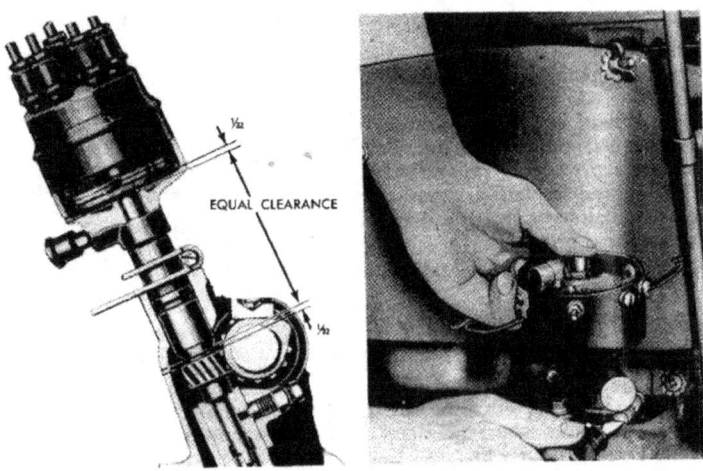

Figure 71—Distributor Operating Position

(2) PLACE ENGINE IN NO. 1 FIRING POSITION. If engine has been cranked since the removal of distributor, it will be necessary to again place engine with No. 1 piston in firing position. Remove valve rocker arm cover. Hand crank engine and observe movement of No. 1 intake valve (second valve from the front). When it is noticed that intake valve is closing (raising up), continue to crank slowly and at same time watch flywheel timing mark peephole. Crank slowly until flywheel housing pointer is on the ignition timing mark (fig. 70). Engine is then in No. 1 firing position.

(3) INSTALL DISTRIBUTOR. Before installing distributor assembly, again check position of flywheel marking. Turn rotor to mark on housing indicating No. 1 spark plug terminal, then turn rotor slightly clockwise. As distributor is inserted into place, the spiral gear will cause rotor to turn back (counterclockwise). It may be necessary to insert the assembly several times to finally bring rotor to No. 1 firing position. The grease cup opening in distributor housing should be at right-angles to the engine when distributor is in correct position.

(4) CHECK OPERATING CLEARANCE. It is important that a slight clearance be maintained between upper and lower end of distributor housing at points shown in figure 71. When distributor is first placed in operating position, lower end of housing will contact drive gear. Before tightening clamp screw, place fingers under housing and thumb on rotor. While holding rotor down, raise housing approximately $\frac{1}{32}$ inch. Be sure to equalize clearance at top and bottom. Tighten clamp screw while distributor is held in this position.

TM 9-802
98-99

Maintenance Instructions

(5) CHECK POINT OPENING. Check and adjust point opening (par. 99**b**.).

(6) INSTALL CABLES. Install spark plug cables to distributor cap (fig. 66 or 67) in correct sequence (1-5-3-6-2-4). Install secondary cable in distributor cap. Install primary wire connection to distributor housing terminal and tighten nut. Paint all high tension cables from distributor cap to spark plugs, and from ignition coil to distributor cap with ignition insulating compound (52-C-3099-20), taking care not to paint rubber ferrules.

(7) CHECK TIMING. Check initial timing as described in paragraph 97, then install ignition shield cover [par. 97**b**.(5)].

99. DISTRIBUTOR POINTS.

a. General. Distributor points consist of a breaker lever and a contact point and support assembly (fig. 72). Distributor points should be inspected at regular intervals and cleaned, adjusted, or replaced as necessary. Points may be cleaned with a fine contact file. Do not use emery cloth or a dirty file.

b. Point Adjustment.

(1) CLEAN POINTS AND CAP. Remove ignition shield cover [par. 97**b**.(1)]. Remove distributor cap (G102-04-00420) and rotor (G102-01-03121), also housing cover on latest models. Examine rotor, cap, and cover (when used) for signs of cracks and burns. Clean cap inside

A POINT OPENING
B CLAMP SCREW
C ADJUSTING SCREW
D BREAKER LEVER SUPPORT
E BREAKER LEVER
F PRIMARY TERMINAL
G CAM
H CONDENSER
I BREAKER PLATE

RA PD 337164

Figure 72—Distributor Point Installation and Adjustment

Ignition System

and out. Clean sockets with a wire brush. Clean points thoroughly, using a fine magneto-type file.

(2) CHECK BREAKER ARM SPRING TENSION. Hand crank engine slowly until breaker lever pad rests on a high point of distributor cam. With contact spring scale, check tension of arm spring in manner illustrated in figure 73. If tension falls below 17 ounces, replace points as described in subparagraphs *c*. and *d*. below.

(3) GAGE AND ADJUST POINTS (FIG. 72). With a feeler gage, measure point opening. If not within 0.018 to 0.024 inch, loosen clamp screw and turn eccentric screw until opening is correct. Tighten clamp screw after adjustment is made. Reinstall rotor and cap. Install ignition shield cover [par. 97*b*.(5)].

c. Point Removal (fig. 72).

(1) REMOVE BREAKER LEVER. Remove ignition shield cover [par. 97*b*.(1)]. Remove cap and rotor. Loosen primary terminal nut, then remove condenser pigtail connection from terminal. Pull up on breaker lever and remove from pivot, at the same time removing end of lever spring from primary terminal.

(2) REMOVE CONTACT POINT AND SUPPORT. Remove clamp screw, then lift off contact point and support (G085-33-02520) over eccentric screw.

d. Point Installation.

(1) INSTALL CONTACT POINT AND SUPPORT. Place contact point and support assembly in position in distributor over eccentric screw. Install clamp screw and tighten securely.

(2) INSTALL BREAKER LEVER. Place breaker lever over pivot and at the same time, install end of lever spring over terminal. Install condenser pigtail connection over terminal. Tighten terminal nut securely.

(3) CHECK BREAKER LEVER SPRING TENSION. New breaker lever springs are generally stronger than required in operation. Check the tension (17 to 21 oz) in manner illustrated in figure 73. If necessary to decrease pressure, *slightly* bend spring in manner shown in figure 73. To increase point pressure, lever arm must be removed and spring bent away from lever. Avoid excessive distortion of the spring, as only a small change in spring tension is normally required.

(4) ADJUST POINT OPENING. Adjust opening as described in subparagraph *b*. above. Check timing (par. 97).

100. DISTRIBUTOR CONDENSER.

a. General. The condenser is mounted in body of distributor and is connected across distributor points. The purpose of condenser is to reduce distributor point arc by its ability or capacity to store up electrical energy.

b. Removal. Remove ignition shield cover [par. 97*b*.(1)]. Remove distributor cap and rotor, also housing cover on late models. Remove

TM 9-802
100-101

Maintenance Instructions

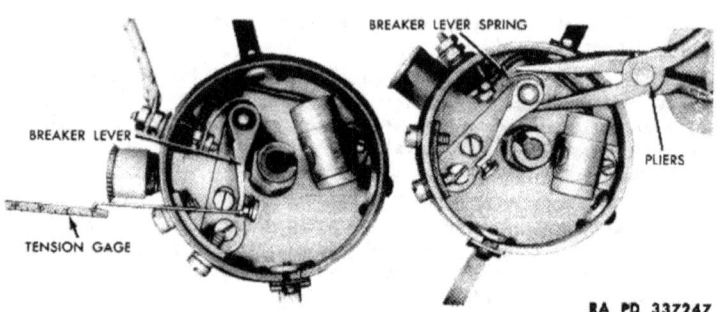

Figure 73—Testing and Adjusting Breaker Lever Spring Tension

screw and lock washer attaching condenser to breaker plate. Remove nut and washer from primary terminal and remove condenser lead from terminal. Lift condenser (G102-15-39899) out of distributor.

c. Installation. Position condenser on breaker plate and attach with screw and lock washer. Place condenser lead on primary terminal and attach with nut and washer. Install rotor housing cover (late models) and distributor cap. Install ignition shield cover [par. 97*b*.(5)].

101. SPARK PLUGS.

a. Removal. Remove ignition shield cover [par. 97*b*.(1)]. Disconnect spark plug cables and suppressors from spark plugs by pulling suppressor off spark plug terminal. Use spark plug wrench furnished with vehicle and unscrew spark plugs (0040-1557987) from cylinder head. Ordinary wrenches may crack or damage porcelain.

b. Cleaning and Adjusting.

(1) CLEAN SPARK PLUGS. Spark plugs should be cleaned with standard sand blast cleaning equipment or with the use of dry-cleaning solvent. If points and porcelain are excessively burned, new spark plugs should be installed.

(2) ADJUST POINT GAP. Setting gap in a spark plug is a precision operation and should be treated as such. Proper gap for model 44 provides 0.025 inch between side electrode and center electrode, 0.030 for model 44 Com. Use either model plug in sets of six only. When regapping is necessary, bend side electrode only, not center electrode. It is not only necessary to set gap properly, but all plugs should have same gap opening. Use a standard round feeler gage.

c. Installation. Use new gasket (G122-0193970) and thread plug into cylinder head with fingers. Use standard spark plug wrench and tighten plug until it bottoms, then turn one-quarter to one-half turn until firm. Do not use force in tightening the plug. It is not necessary to "crush" the gasket. Examine spark plug cables carefully and make certain that the suppressors at the plugs are tight and each cable thor-

Fuel and Air Intake System

oughly seated in distributor cap in the correct firing order (1-5-3-6-2-4). Install ignition shield cover [par. 97**b**.(5)].

d. Corrosion Prevention and Waterproofing Procedure. Remove and clean terminals. Install and tighten firmly. Paint plugs and suppressors with red synthetic paint (glyptol, 52-P-8057-710) and allow to dry.

102. IGNITION COIL.

a. Description. Ignition coil is oil-filled and hermetically sealed to prevent entrance of moisture. High tension terminal is protected by porcelain insulator which has high resistance to leakage across its surface and is not damaged by any leakage which might occur.

b. Corrosion Prevention and Waterproofing Procedure. Remove and thoroughly clean terminals and contacting surfaces. Install bolted terminals and tighten. Apply a thin coat of petrolatum on high tension terminal, and install terminal in cap all the way. Paint coil and terminals with red synthetic paint (glyptal, 52-P-8057-710). If not available, use ignition insulating compound (52-C-3099-20). CAUTION: *Do not paint rubber ferrules.*

c. Removal. Remove ignition shield cover [par. 97**b**.(1)] Remove nuts and lock washers at terminals and remove wires. Remove two nuts and internal-external toothed lock washers attaching coil bracket to cylinder head. Lift coil (G085-83-00861) up and remove secondary cable from terminal at bottom of coil.

d. Installation. Install secondary cable on terminal at bottom of coil. Position coil and install coil bracket over mounting studs and install nuts and internal-external toothed lock washers. Tighten nuts securely. Attach distributor terminal wire (No. 14 tan with red and black cross-tracer) to negative (−) terminal and (No. 14 black) to positive (+) terminal. Tighten terminal nuts securely. Install ignition shield cover [par. 97**b**.(5)].

Section XIX

Fuel and Air Intake System

103. GENERAL.

a. Operation. Fuel is drawn from rear mounted fuel tank through a filter by action of the fuel pump which is mounted on and operated by the engine. The pump forces the fuel, as required, into the carbureter where it is properly mixed with air drawn through an oil bath air cleaner mounted directly on carbureter. Acceleration and deceleration is accomplished by a foot-operated accelerator pedal or hand throttle control linked to the carbureter. A hand-operated choke control pro-

Maintenance Instructions

vides a richer mixture if necessary when starting or operating a cold engine. A velocity type governor mounted between the intake manifold and carbureter prevents overspeeding the engine. An electrical gage system provides means of determining level of fuel in tank.

b. Data.

```
Governor—make and model .................... King Seeley—KS V5-146
Carbureter—make ............................................. Zenith
    Type and model—early vehicles—die cast .................... 28AV11
                    late vehicles—cast iron ................. 30BW11GM
    Identification plate stamped—early vehicles ............. 2135998-9778B
                                    late vehicles .............. 2137474-10046
Fuel pump—make ................................................... AC
    Model (2-valve pump) ......................................... AF
    Model (6-valve pump) ......................................... BF
Fuel filter—make and type ..................................... AC—T2
Air cleaner—make and type ................................ AC—Oil bath
Fuel tank capacity .......................................... 40 gal
```

c. Repair. Instructions for repair operation on various units of the fuel and air intake system are covered in other manuals as follows:

(1) Carbureter—Die Cast—TM 9-1826C or TM 9-1802A. Cast Iron—TM 9-1826C.

(2) Governor—TM 9-1802A. NOTE: *TM 9-1802A states that there are 12 active coils in operating spring. This should read "11 active coils."*

(3) Fuel Pump—Two valve (Type AF) TM 9-1802A; six valve (Type BF) TM 9-1828A.

d. Important. *Fuel tank, lines, filter, fuel pump, and carbureter are located in the enclosed compartments in the hull. All compartments which contain fuel units must be thoroughly ventilated before and after operation. If fuel fumes are detected at any time, all hatch covers and floor boards must be raised and complete ventilation of the compartment immediately made. Maintenance of all fuel connections to prevent fuel leaks is extremely important. Do not carry an open flame into any compartment at any time.*

104. MANIFOLD HEAT CONTROL.

a. Important. A manually controlled manifold heat control valve is installed in the exhaust manifold to permit the bypassing of hot exhaust gas around intake manifold. This control valve can be placed in three operating positions—on, medium, and off. As the engine is enclosed in a compartment, efficient vaporization of the fuel does not require the bypassing of exhaust gas around the intake manifold. *Always keep the manifold heat control valve in "OFF" position.*

105. AIR CLEANER.

a. Description. The air cleaner is an oil-bath type mounted directly on carbureter. Two types of cleaner mountings have been used, depending upon the type of carbureter. The air cleaner used on the die-cast

Fuel and Air Intake System

carbureter is termed "clamp-on" type, being secured to carbureter by means of a clamp. The cleaner used with the cast-iron type is termed "flange mounted" type, being secured to carbureter by a mating flange and bolts.

b. Operation. Air entering the cleaner passes into the cleaner oil chamber. Due to impact and sudden reversal of air flow, most all of the dirt in the air is thrown into the oil and settles to the bottom of the reservoir. Partially cleaned air passes through a dense oil-saturated mesh where the remaining dust is trapped.

c. Removal.

(1) CLAMP-ON TYPE (FIG. 74). Loosen bolt nut which attaches air cleaner brace to air cleaner. Loosen clamp bolt which clamps air cleaner to carbureter, then lift cleaner from top of carbureter.

(2) FLANGE MOUNTED TYPE (FIG. 74). Unscrew wing nut at center of cleaner cover, then lift cleaner shell with element and cover as an assembly from cleaner center tube.

d. Cleaning (Both Types). Dust and dirt in the air entering air cleaner is loaded with minute particles of abrasive which, if permitted to enter the engine, will cause rapid wear of moving parts. Importance of keeping the air cleaner in proper condition should be impressed upon those responsible for the mechanical upkeep of the engine. Maintenance instructions printed on carbureter air cleaner and crankcase air cleaner are contrary to approved maintenance instructions outlined. To prevent misunderstanding of maintenance instructions, paint decalcomanias with black paint. Remove air cleaner and clean as directed on Lubrication Order No. 9-802.

e. Installation.

(1) CLAMP-ON TYPE (FIG. 74). Inspect cleaner to carbureter gasket and cleaner clamp seal. Air cleaner cover gasket (G104-15-93762) must be checked for condition and replaced if necessary. Position cleaner on top of carbureter, directing cleaner brace bolt into notch at top of brace. Hold air cleaner down firmly while tightening clamp bolt. Tighten air cleaner to brace bolt nut firmly.

(2) FLANGE MOUNTED TYPE (FIG. 74). Inspect air cleaner element gasket (G104-15-69171) and air cleaner to carbureter gasket (G113-01-93812). Gasket must be in good condition to form a good seal. Replace with new parts if necessary. Install cleaner shell over cleaner tube, and turn as necessary to engage bracket with flat of carbureter flange. Position cover and element (G508-7000692) on shell, then thread wing nut onto stud and tighten firmly.

106. CARBURETER.

a. Description. The carbureter is Zenith down-draft type of double venturi design, and is a balanced unit, maintaining the proper ratio between carbureter air intake and fuel bowl. Two carbureter constructions have been used, differing in type of material. The die-cast carbu-

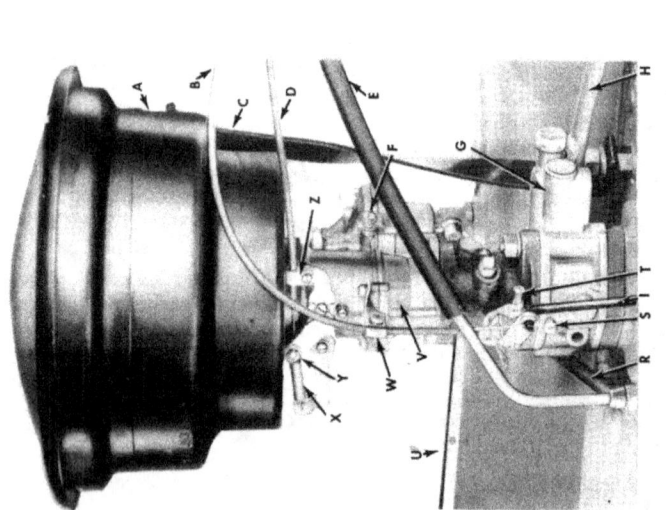

DIE CAST TYPE

Figure 74—Air Cleaner, Carbureter, and Controls Installed

RA PD 3372:

CONTROL LEVERS

Legend for Figure 74

A AIR CLEANER
B HAND THROTTLE (G501-01-39940)
C AIR CLEANER BRACE
D CHOKE CONTROL (GM-1990648)
E WINDSHIELD WIPER TUBE
F IDLING MIXTURE ADJUSTING SCREW
G GOVERNOR (G508-7000444)
H CYLINDER HEAD WATER BY-PASS TUBE
I CARBURETER CONTROL ROD
J CONTROL LEVER SPRING—INNER (G501-7002106)
K ACCELERATOR PEDAL TO CARBURETER CONTROL LEVER ROD
L CARBURETER INNER CONTROL LEVER ADJUSTING SCREW
M CARBURETER OUTER CONTROL LEVER
N CARBURETER INNER CONTROL LEVER
O CARBURETER INNER CONTROL LEVER STOP
P CONTROL LEVER SPRING—OUTER (G085-01-02160)
Q BRAKE VACUUM LINE CONNECTION
R CRANKCASE VENTILATOR TUBE
S HAND THROTTLE STOP COLLAR
T IDLING SPEED ADJUSTING SCREW
U CARBURETER FUEL TUBE
V CARBURETER (DIE CAST) (G501-01-31595) (CAST-IRON) (G508-7000445)
W HAND THROTTLE CLIP
X CHOKE RETURN SPRING
Y CHOKE CONTROL SWIVEL
Z CHOKE CONTROL CLIP
AA THROTTLE LEVER RETURN SPRING

RA PD 3372:

TM 9-802
106

Maintenance Instructions

RA PD 6461/

Figure 75—Positioning Carbureter to Governor Gasket

reter is used prior to chassis serial No. 5899, and between 6602 and 7230. The cast-iron carbureter is used on later vehicles. All fuel mixture adjustments, except idling, are determined by calibration of the various jets and cannot be changed without disassembling the carbureter and changing the jets.

b. Idling Speed and Idling Mixture Adjustment (fig. 74). Warm-up engine to normal operating temperature (at least 160°F) and allow to run long enough to completely normalize engine (approximately 15 or 20 minutes). On vehicles not equipped with tachometer, attach an electric tachometer (18-T-230) to distributor. Remove manifold fitting and attach a vacuum gage (41-G-500) to intake manifold.

(1) IDLING SPEED. Adjust engine idling speed by turning stop screw on carbureter throttle lever until engine reaches idling speed of at least 510 revolutions per minute.

(2) IDLING MIXTURE. Set idling adjusting screw to give highest reading on vacuum gage by turning screw gradually to the right, then to the left. If engine idles too fast after this adjustment, check tachometer reading and readjust until engine reaches proper idling speed [step (1) above]. Regulation of idling mixture in no way affects function of carbureter at higher speeds.

c. Cleaning Fuel Bowl. Carbureter fuel bowl may be cleaned without removing carbureter from engine as follows:

(1) Remove air cleaner (par. 105c.).

(2) Drain fuel bowl, then remove fuel pump inlet tube at carbureter.

(3) Remove screws and lock washers which attach air intake body to fuel bowl.

(4) Remove air intake body. CAUTION: *Raise the air intake assembly slightly and loosen gasket from fuel bowl assembly. Lift the air intake with gasket clear of the bowl to avoid damaging the float.*

(5) Clean fuel bowl thoroughly with a clean dry cloth. Reassemble in the following manner:

(*a*) Position gasket on carbureter fuel bowl.

Fuel and Air Intake System

(b) Position air intake assembly on fuel bowl.

(c) Install screws and lock washers, then tighten assembly screws evenly and firmly.

(d) Connect fuel pump inlet tube at carburetor.

(e) Install air cleaner (par. 105**e.**).

d. Carbureter Assembly Removal (fig. 74).

(1) Remove air cleaner (par. 105**c.**).

(2) Disconnect choke control (par. 107**b.**) and hand throttle control (par. 107**c.**).

(3) Place a suitable container below carbureter to catch fuel drainage, then disconnect fuel pump inlet tube at carbureter. Break carbureter seal (G501-03-82821), then remove two carbureter to manifold nuts and lock washers. Remove carbureter from manifold.

e. Carbureter Assembly Installation (fig. 74).

(1) Install gasket (G133-01-93852) between carbureter and governor (fig. 74).

(2) Install carbureter in position over manifold studs. Install two stud lock washers and nuts, then install governor to carbureter seal. Place fuel pump inlet tube in position in carbureter fitting, then tighten flange nut.

(3) Connect choke control (par. 107**b.**) and hand throttle control (par. 107**c.**).

(4) Install air cleaner (par. 105**e.**). Make idling speed and mixture adjustments (subpar. **b.** above).

107. CARBURETER CONTROLS.

a. Description. Carbureter controls consist of a hand choke control, hand throttle control, and accelerator pedal and linkage. These units are accessible in driver's compartment and engine compartment.

b. Choke Control. All key letters in steps (1) and (2) below refer to figure 76.

(1) REMOVAL.

(a) Remove Control Assembly at Carbureter. Remove air cleaner (par. 105**c.**). After loosening set screw at control wire swivel (W), remove swivel from end of wire. Loosen screw which attaches control assembly to clip on carbureter, then remove wire from clip.

(b) Remove Control Assembly. Remove nut and lock washer which attaches control wire at back of panel. Pull control assembly (A) from panel at front.

(2) INSTALLATION.

(a) Install Control Assembly at Panel. Thread control assembly (A) through opening in instrument panel, sliding lock washer and nut over wire. Tighten nut securely.

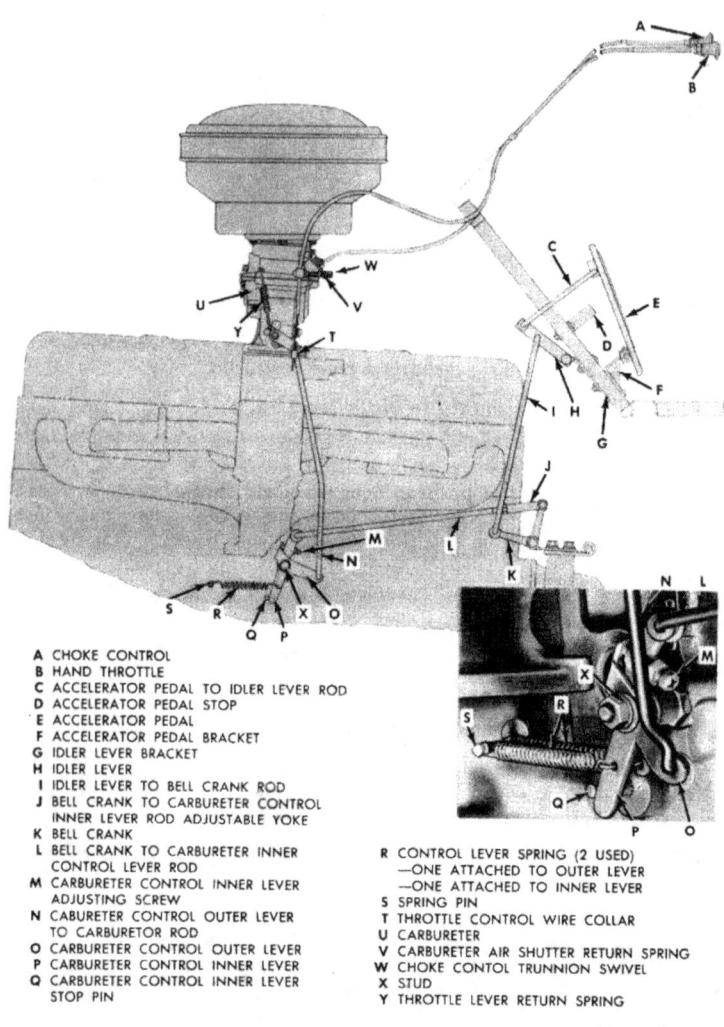

- A CHOKE CONTROL
- B HAND THROTTLE
- C ACCELERATOR PEDAL TO IDLER LEVER ROD
- D ACCELERATOR PEDAL STOP
- E ACCELERATOR PEDAL
- F ACCELERATOR PEDAL BRACKET
- G IDLER LEVER BRACKET
- H IDLER LEVER
- I IDLER LEVER TO BELL CRANK ROD
- J BELL CRANK TO CARBURETER CONTROL INNER LEVER ROD ADJUSTABLE YOKE
- K BELL CRANK
- L BELL CRANK TO CARBURETER INNER CONTROL LEVER ROD
- M CARBURETER CONTROL INNER LEVER ADJUSTING SCREW
- N CABURETER CONTROL OUTER LEVER TO CARBURETOR ROD
- O CARBURETER CONTROL OUTER LEVER
- P CARBURETER CONTROL INNER LEVER
- Q CARBURETER CONTROL INNER LEVER STOP PIN
- R CONTROL LEVER SPRING (2 USED)
  —ONE ATTACHED TO OUTER LEVER
  —ONE ATTACHED TO INNER LEVER
- S SPRING PIN
- T THROTTLE CONTROL WIRE COLLAR
- U CARBURETER
- V CARBURETER AIR SHUTTER RETURN SPRING
- W CHOKE CONTOL TRUNNION SWIVEL
- X STUD
- Y THROTTLE LEVER RETURN SPRING

RA PD 337250

Figure 76—Control Linkage

(b) Install Control Assembly at Carbureter. Insert control assembly (A) through clip on carbureter and tighten clip screw firmly. The flexible loom on the control assembly must be flush with inside edge of clip. Pass flexible wire through choke lever swivel.

Fuel and Air Intake System

(3) ADJUST. Pull out choke button until $1/16$ inch clearance exists between button and instrument panel, then firmly tighten swivel set screw. Pull out choke button, then check position of carbureter choke valve.

c. Throttle Control. All key letters in steps (1) through (3) below refer to figure 76.

(1) REMOVAL.

(a) Disconnect Control Assembly at Carbureter. Loosen control assembly clip screw at carbureter. Loosen wire collar (T) set screw, then slide collar off wire.

(b) Remove Control Assembly. Remove nut and lock washer at back of instrument panel. Pull throttle control assembly (B) out through front of panel.

(2) INSTALLATION.

(a) Install Control Assembly at Panel. Insert control assembly (B) through opening in instrument panel, sliding lock washer and nut over wire. Tighten nut firmly.

(b) Install Control at Carbureter. Insert wire loom through clip at carbureter then tighten clip screw firmly. Pass wire through hole in carbureter rod (N), and install wire collar (T) over wire.

(3) ADJUST. With carbureter throttle in closed position, that is, idling speed adjusting screw tight against its stop, adjust wire collar (T) so there is $1/4$ inch clearance between carbureter control rod (N) and wire collar (T). Tighten collar set screw firmly. Test throttle opening with foot accelerator. Throttle lever should not contact control loom when in full throttle position. If necessary, readjust loom in clip.

d. Accelerator Pedal and Linkage. All key letters in steps (1) through (3) below refer to figure 76.

(1) REMOVAL. Instructions given here are for removing accelerator and linkage progressively, beginning with accelerator pedal. However, these parts may be replaced individually if so desired.

(a) Remove Pedal and Pedal to Idler Lever Rod. In driver's compartment, remove cotter pin and clevis pin from pedal to toeboard bracket (F). In engine compartment, remove rod cotter pin and washer at idler lever (H). Pedal (E) and rod (C) can now be removed as a unit from driver's compartment.

(b) Remove Idler Lever and Lever to Bell Crank Rod. Remove cotter pin and washer which retain idler lever (H) to lever bracket (G). Remove cotter pin and washer which retain rod (I) to bell crank (K), and remove lever (H) and rod (I) as a unit.

(c) Remove Bell Crank to Control Lever Rod. Remove bell crank (K) to bracket cotter pin, washer, and clevis pin. Remove cotter pin and washer from rod (L) at carbureter control lever (P), then remove bell crank (K) and control rod (L) as a unit.

(d) Remove Carbureter Control Levers (at Cylinder Block). Unhook inner and outer control lever springs (R) from return spring pin

Maintenance Instructions

(S) and levers (O) and (P). Remove cotter pin and washer from lower end of control lever to carbureter rod (N), and remove rod from lever (O). Remove nut and washer from control lever stud, then remove both control levers.

(e) Remove Carbureter Control Lever to Carbureter Rod. Loosen set screw in hand throttle control wire collar, and remove collar. Withdraw wire from end of rod (N), then remove rod from carbureter lever.

(2) INSPECT THROTTLE LEVER STUD (FIG. 76). Before any linkage is installed, the throttle lever stud must be inspected and cleaned if necessary. If the stud is loose in the cylinder block or if a leak has developed, remove stud and clean. Apply a coat of joint and thread compound (52-C-3115) to the stud threads. Firmly install stud into cylinder block. Be sure all rods are installed so they will work freely.

(3) INSTALLATION.

(a) Install Carbureter Control Levers (at Cylinder Block). Place inner control lever (P) in position in outer control lever (O) with extension pointing downward. Assemble both levers to stud and install plain washer, lock washer, and nut. Hook springs (R) over spring pin (S) with heavier spring on inside; then hook heavy spring into outer control lever (O), and lighter spring into inner control lever (P).

(b) Install Carbureter Control Lever to Carbureter Rod. Insert rod (N) into carbureter lever from engine side, then insert throttle control wire through end of rod (N). Install lower end of rod (N) through outer control lever (O) on engine and install washer and cotter pin. Adjust inner control lever (P) adjusting screw to provide approximately $1/8$ inch clearance between end of screw and outer lever (O), then tighten lock nut. Install control wire collar (T) [subpar. c.(2) and (3) above].

(c) Install Bell Crank to Carbureter Control Lever Rod. Insert bent end of rod (L) through upper end of inner control lever (P) and secure with washer and cotter pin.

(d) Install Bell Crank. Install bell crank (K) to left-hand side of bell crank bracket with clevis pin, washer, and cotter pin. Do not attach rod (L) to bell crank at this time.

(e) Install Idler Lever. Assemble idler lever (H) to left-hand side of idler bracket (G) and secure with washer and cotter pin.

(f) Install Idler Lever to Bell Crank Rod. Position ends of rod (I) in center hole of idler lever (H) and in opening of lower arm of bell crank (K). End of rod to which washer is welded must be at bell crank (K).

(g) Install Accelerator Pedal and Idler Lever Rod. Attach pedal (E) to bracket (F) with pin, washer, and cotter pin. Attach rod (C) to pedal (E) and idler lever (H) and secure with washer and cotter pin. Rod must travel through floor board freely.

(h) Adjust Bell Crank to Carbureter Control Lever Rod Yoke. With accelerator pedal (E) depressed completely on stop (D), open carbureter throttle to full throttle position by forcing lower end of carbu-

Fuel and Air Intake System

reter inner control lever (P) toward rear of vehicle, overruling the return spring (R). With inner control lever (P) in this position, adjust rod (L) adjustable yoke so clevis pin holes in yoke line up with opening in end of upper arm of bell crank (K). Install clevis pin and cotter pin and tighten yoke lock nut.

108. GOVERNOR.

a. Description. A velocity type governor, mounted between the intake manifold and carbureter, is employed to protect the engine from being operated beyond a predetermined safe and economical speed. Governor is sealed at time of adjustment. Seal should not be broken unless authorized by higher authority.

b. Assembly Removal. Remove carbureter (par. 106**d**.), then lift governor from carbureter to manifold studs.

c. Cleaning Governor Air Filter (fig. 77). Accumulation of dirt in governor can be controlled considerably by frequent and regular cleaning of governor stabilizer cylinder and piston air filter element, located in governor body beneath a perforated metal cover. After governor is removed, clean as follows:

(1) Pry out metal cover carefully with a sharp pointed punch. Do not damage cast projections on governor body.

(2) Pick out filter felt and inner metal cover.

(3) Wash filter felt in dry-cleaning solvent and allow to dry. Do not use air on felt.

(4) Blow out stabilizer cylinder and piston, directing air in quick bursts through atmospheric hole in governor air cleaner chamber.

(5) Install inner cover, then moisten filter felt slightly with clean oil before installing felt in governor body.

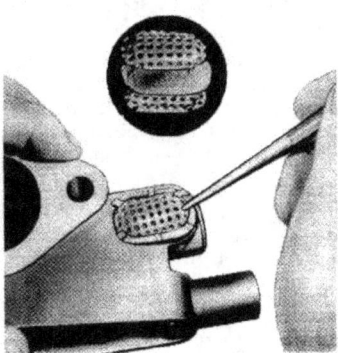
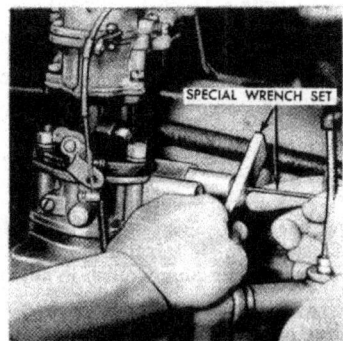

PRY OUT AIR FILTER COVER   USE OF SPECIAL WRENCH SET (41-W-1496-695)

RA PD 337161

Figure 77—Servicing Governor

TM 9-802

Maintenance Instructions

(6) Install outer cover and secure in governor body. It may be necessary to bend cover to install; however, it can be flattened again by tapping with a hammer after it is positioned in governor body.

d. Assembly Installation. Governor is marked with an arrow indicating carbureter side. Place a new governor to manifold insulator gasket (G501-01-94026) over carbureter to manifold studs, then place governor over studs so that arrow on governor points upward (toward carbureter). Install carbureter to governor gasket between carbureter and governor. This gasket incorporates two slots which allow vacuum to bypass through governor housing for operation of the carbureter power system. Gasket must be in good condition. Install carbureter (par. 106e.).

e. Governor Adjustment. The correct governed speed of engine is 2750 revolutions per minute, road load, transmission in direct drive, and engine warmed up to normal operating temperature. Use a reliable tachometer (18-T-230) for vehicles not equipped with panel tachometer. If a tachometer is not available, check governed vehicle speed while driving on a level road with transfer case in high range and transmission in direct drive (4th speed). Set governor to maintain 40 miles per hour, plus or minus one mile per hour. This will give maximum engine speed of 2750 revolutions per minute. If road space, local speed limits, or other conditions prevent checking governor at 40 miles per hour, the next lower gear position may be used by referring to "Maximum Permissible Road Speed Plate" (fig. 17) for correct speeds. The governor setting, however, will be more accurate at 40 miles per hour.

(1) SPEED ADJUSTMENT. Break governor seal (G501-03-82816), then turn adjusting cap as necessary to obtain 2750 revolutions per minute maximum engine speed. One complete turn will alter vehicle speed from four to five miles per hour. Check governed speed by road test and when satisfactory, reseal governor.

(2) CORRECTION OF SURGE (FIG. 76). Surge is the intermittent deceleration or acceleration of engine speed with the throttle held wide open. Adjustment for surge must be made only to the point of removing the surge. Over adjustment will result in slow governor opening. Wrench set (41-W-1496-695), comprising a hollow wrench and a hex plug wrench, is required as follows:

(a) Break governor seal and remove adjusting cap. Insert hollow wrench into adjusting screw housing and engage lugs in adjusting screw bushing. Insert hex plug wrench into hole in hollow wrench, engaging hex plug wrench in adjusting screw.

(b) Turn hex plug wrench clockwise one complete turn, then hold hex plug wrench from turning and turn hollow wrench clockwise one-quarter turn or until surge is eliminated and engine runs steadily at 2750 revolutions per minute.

(c) Road test vehicle to check surge. When satisfactory adjustment has been made, reseal governor.

Fuel and Air Intake System

(3) CORRECTION OF SLOW GOVERNOR OPENING (FIG. 76). Slow governor opening is a decided loss in speed, when load is applied, while operating with wide open throttle. Correction is made in same manner as correction for surge [step (2) above], except turn wrenches in counterclockwise direction. Make adjustment for slow governor opening very carefully, as over adjustment will cause surge.

109. FUEL PUMP.

a. Description. The fuel pump, mounted on the right-hand side of the engine (figs. 78 and 79), is a diaphragm type, mechanically operated from the camshaft. Pump is also equipped with a hand priming lever which may be used to pump an initial supply of fuel into the carburetor in case the vehicle has run out of fuel, or the carburetor bowl has been emptied for any reason. Two types of pumps are used; two-valve pump (fig. 78) used prior to engine serial No. 270-523270, and the six-valve pump (fig. 79) after engine serial No. 270-523269.

b. Cleaning—Two-valve Pump Only. When pump fuel bowl and strainer screen are removed for cleaning, parts that are damaged or will not clean up must be replaced. Unscrew bail clamp thumb nut, located at top of bowl, and move bail so bowl can be removed. Lift bowl and strainer screen (fig. 78) from pump and thoroughly clean them with dry-cleaning solvent. Strainer screen and bowl gasket must be in good condition. Replace if necessary. Install strainer screen and bowl. Position bowl bail over bowl and tighten thumb nut snugly.

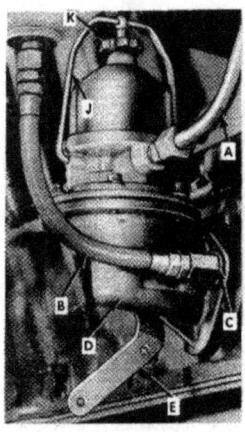 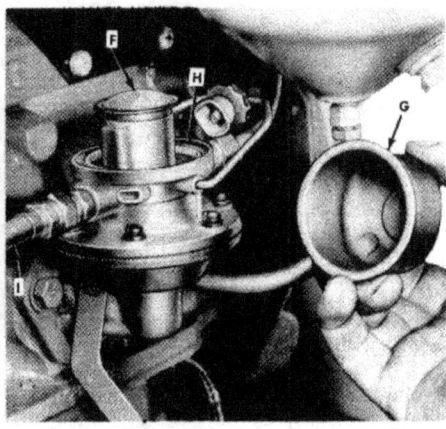

A FUEL PUMP TO CARBURETOR FUEL TUBE
B OIL FILTER RETURN LINE
C FUEL PUMP MOUNTING STUD
D FUEL PUMP (G085-30-04460)
E HAND PRIMER
F STRAINER SCREEN
G STRAINER BOWL
H STRAINER BOWL GASKET (G085-30-02240)
I FUEL FILTER TO FUEL PUMP HOSE (G501-02-17831)
J BOWL BAIL
K BAIL THUMB NUT

RA PD 333218

Figure 78—Two-valve Fuel Pump Installed

TM 9-802
109

Maintenance Instructions

A FUEL PUMP TO CARBURETER FUEL TUBE
B OIL FILTER RETURN LINE
C FUEL PUMP MOUNTING STUD
D FUEL PUMP (GM 1537927)
E HAND PRIMER
F FUEL FILTER TO FUEL PUMP HOSE

RA PD 337286

Figure 79—Six-valve Fuel Pump Installed

c. Fuel Pump Tests. Two tests are required on fuel pump to determine if pump is operating satisfactorily. The first test [subpar. (1) below], is to determine if pump is creating an overpressure. The second test [subpar. (2) below], is to determine whether or not pump is giving enough yield to insure sufficient flow of fuel to carbureter at all times. Tests must be made with pump mounted on engine.

(1) STATIC PRESSURE TEST.

(a) Disconnect fuel pump to carbureter tube and install necessary adapter and tee fitting in pump outlet, then attach pressure gage (41-G-500) with rubber tubing.

(b) Plug remaining tee opening and run engine at 2000 to 2500 revolutions per minute on fuel remaining in carbureter. Less than one minute operation of engine should be sufficient for this test. Reading on gage is the static pressure of fuel pump and should be 3½ pounds maximum for the two-valve fuel pump, and 5 pounds maximum for six-valve fuel pump. A pump creating an overpressure requires replacement.

(2) CAPACITY BLEED TEST. NOTE: *This test need only be made if the static pressure test is within limits listed in step* (1) *above. Test is made as follows:*

220

TM 9-802
109-110

Fuel and Air Intake System

(*a*) Insert a tee fitting in carbureter inlet, then attach fuel pump to carbureter tube to tee and note time necessary to fill a pint measure with fuel from remaining outlet of tee with engine running at idling speed. Time required is 45 seconds.

(3) ANALYSIS OF TESTS. If tests do not show a pressure over the maximum, and shows at least minimum flow in capacity, fuel pump can be considered efficient.

d. Pump Removal (figs. 78 and 79). Disconnect fuel inlet and outlet tube at fuel pump, also oil return line at pump forward mounting stud. Remove forward mounting stud, also rearward mounting bolt, then remove pump from vehicle. Remove pump inlet and outlet fuel line connectors for installation in replacement pump.

e. Pump Installation. Install inlet and outlet fuel line connectors in pump. Place pump in position on engine, using a new mounting gasket (G085-30-02240), and install special hollow mounting stud with copper washer in forward position (figs. 78 and 79), and mounting bolt with copper washer in rearward position. Connect pump inlet and outlet tubes, also oil return line to special hollow stud. Test pump for efficient operation (subpar. *c*. above).

110. FUEL FILTER.

a. Description. The fuel filter (fig. 80) comprises a disk type (laminated) strainer and is mounted on the right-hand frame side rail. The filter is accessible for service through the engine compartment.

FILTER INSTALLED

DISASSEMBLING FILTER

A FUEL FILTER TO FUEL PUMP HOSE (G501-02-17B31)
B FUEL FILTER COVER
C COVER SCREW
D FUEL TANK TO FUEL FILTER LINE
E FUEL FILTER MOUNTING BRACKET
F FILTER STRAINER GASKET
G FILTER STRAINER
H FILTER STRAINER SPRING
I BOWL GASKET
J BOWL
K FILTER MOUNTING BRACKET BOLTS

RA PD 337179

Figure 80—Servicing Fuel Filter

TM 9-802

Maintenance Instructions

b. Cleaning Strainer.

(1) DRAIN FILTER. Close fuel line shut-off cock, located at fuel filter prior to chassis serial No. 2006, and underneath co-pilot's seat after chassis serial No. 2005. Remove drain plug and drain fuel from filter. Catch fuel in a container, do not allow to drain into hull.

(2) REMOVE FILTER BOWL AND STRAINER. Unscrew cover screw and remove filter bowl with strainer. Do not lose bowl gasket. Remove strainer from filter bowl and wash it thoroughly in dry-cleaning solvent. Be sure all particles are removed from between disk and strainer. Do not use air. Allow strainer to dry, then wash filter bowl with dry-cleaning solvent and wipe dry with clean cloth.

(3) INSTALL FILTER BOWL AND STRAINER. Inspect filter bowl gasket, strainer gasket, and cover screw gasket and replace if found not to be in good condition. Place spring and strainer over stem in bowl. NOTE: *Two types of elements are used (paper and copper), also two different springs. Springs must not be interchanged.* With gaskets in position, assemble bowl to cover. Be sure bowl seats properly on gasket. Install drain plug.

c. Assembly Removal.

(1) DRAIN FILTER. Remove drain plug and allow fuel to drain from filter. *Catch fuel in a container. Do not allow to drain into hull.*

(2) REMOVE FILTER. Disconnect inlet and outlet hoses at filter. Remove two filter to mounting bracket bolts and remove filter from vehicle (fig. 80).

(3) REMOVE CONNECTIONS. Unscrew shut-off cock or fuel line connector from removed fuel filter for installation in replacement filter. Note relative position of shut-off cock or fuel line connector so that they may be assembled properly in replacement filter (fig. 80).

d. Assembly Installation.

(1) INSTALL CONNECTIONS. On vehicles prior to chassis serial No. 2006, install shut-off cock in opening marked "IN" and connector in opening marked "OUT." On vehicles after chassis serial No. 2005, install a connector in both openings.

(2) INSTALL FILTER. Position filter on mounting bracket and install two mounting bolts, lock washers, and nuts. Connect inlet and outlet fuel hoses and tighten flange nuts securely. Be sure drain plug and cover screw are tight to prevent leaks and that shut-off cock is in open position.

111. FUEL TANK.

a. Description. The fuel tank (fig. 81) is rectangular in shape and is mounted in the rear compartment approximately underneath the spare wheel and tire. Prior to chassis serial No. 2006, fuel tank, spare wheel, and tire are mounted on left-hand side of vehicle. After chassis serial No. 2005 these parts are mounted on right-hand side. The tank is held securely in place with two mounting straps.

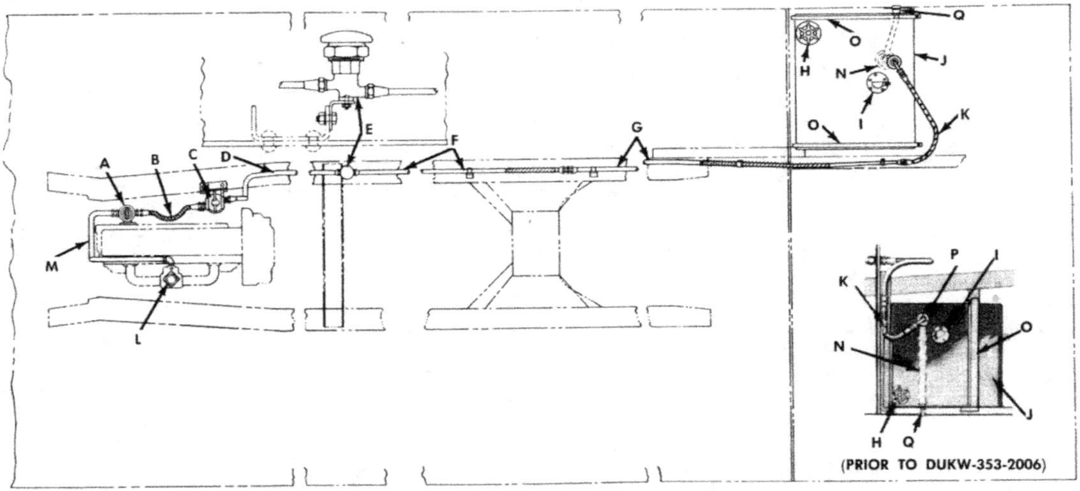

(PRIOR TO DUKW-353-2006)

A FUEL PUMP
B FUEL FILTER TO FUEL PUMP HOSE
C FUEL FILTER
D SHUT-OFF VALVE TO FUEL FILTER FUEL TUBE
E FUEL SHUT-OFF VALVE
F TRUNNION CROSSMEMBER TO SHUT-OFF VALVE FUEL LINE
G BULKHEAD TO TRUNNION CROSSMEMBER FUEL LINE
H FUEL TANK FILLER CAP (G501-01-31572)
I FUEL GAGE TANK UNIT
J FUEL TANK
K FUEL HOSE AT TANK
  (G501-02-17839) (DUKW-353-006 THRU 2005)
  (G501-02-17832) (DUKW-353-2006 AND AFTER)
L CARBURETER
M FUEL PUMP TO CARBURETER FUEL TUBE
N FUEL TANK DRAIN (UNDERNEATH TANK)
O FUEL TANK SUPPORT STRAP
P FUEL TANK DRAIN COCK (UNDERNEATH TANK)
Q DRAIN TUBE HULL OPENING PLUG

Figure 81—Fuel Tank and Tubes

RA PD 3

b. Fuel Filler Cap and Filler Tube Screen.

(1) FUEL FILLER CAP.

(a) Removal and Cleaning. Remove cap by turning to left as far as possible. After cap is removed, cap chain and chain retainer can be removed from filler tube. Clean cap and valve mechanism by slushing in dry-cleaning solvent.

(b) Installation. Before installing filler cap, make sure valve mechanism is not stuck or corroded by checking movement of valves with a blunt piece of wood or pencil. If fuel tank cap is found to be loose after installation and gasket is in good condition, bend and rework tongs with pliers, bending tong toward tank cap. This will permit the cap to fit tightly on fuel tank filler tube. If valves or cap gasket are not in good condition, replace with new cap (G501-01-31572). Install retainer with chain attached in filler tube, then install cap on filler tube and secure by turning to right as far as possible.

(2) FILLER TUBE SCREEN.

(a) Removal and Cleaning. Remove filler cap, chain, and retainer, then remove screen retainer and screen. Clean screen by slushing in dry-cleaning solvent.

(b) Installation. Install screen in filler tube, pointed end down, then install screen retainer, filler cap chain, and chain retainer. Tighten cap firmly.

c. Draining Tank.
Remove filler cap and open drain cock in bottom of fuel tank. Remove drain hose end plug at outside of hull. Fuel may be caught in a suitable container. Close drain cock and replace plug. CAUTION: *Drain cock at bottom of fuel tank must be kept closed and the end plug at hull installed at all times except when draining tank.*

d. Fuel Tank Removal.

(1) REMOVE SPARE WHEEL AND REAR DECK FRONT PLATE. Drain tank (subpar. **c.** above). Remove spare wheel and rear deck front plate as directed in paragraph 229**d**. On vehicles after chassis serial No. 2005, remove two nuts, washers, and bolts from front and rear ends of support channel located above fuel tank and remove channel from vehicle. This provides room to remove tank from vehicle.

(2) REMOVE RUDDER CABLE RIGHT-HAND PULLEY (AFTER CHASSIS SERIAL NO. 2005). Using a C-clamp, clamp two small wooden blocks to rudder cables immediately to the rear of the rear compartment bulkhead. This will keep cables taut and prevent them fouling at the steering gear spool, and also eliminate necessity of adjusting rudder alinement. Remove two nuts and lock washers that hold right-hand cable pulley brackets to hull. Remove pulley and pulley bracket from hull.

(3) REMOVE TANK. Disconnect wire at fuel tank gage terminal unit. Disconnect fuel line hose at top of tank. Loosen drain hose from tank connection. Remove nuts from two fuel tank mounting strap T-

Exhaust System

bolts, and position straps to permit removal of tank. Tank may then be removed from vehicle.

e. Fuel Tank Installation.

(1) INSTALL TANK. Make certain that antisqueak strips on fuel tank support and mounting straps are in good condition. Place fuel tank on tank support. Secure by placing the two mounting straps in position and installing two T-bolt nuts and lock nuts. Install drain hose on tank connection and tighten hose clamp bolt. Close drain cock, then install drain hose coupling plug. Connect fuel hose to top of fuel tank. Tighten connections securely. Connect electrical wire to tank gage unit terminal.

(2) INSTALL RUDDER CABLE RIGHT-HAND PULLEY (AFTER CHASSIS SERIAL NO. 2005). Position pulley bracket over mounting studs and install two lock washers and nuts. CAUTION: *Do not pry against pulley to move it into position.* Remove C-clamp and wooden blocks from rudder cables.

(3) INSTALL REAR DECK FRONT PLATE SUPPORT CHANNEL (AFTER CHASSIS SERIAL NO. 2005). Place support channel in position and install two bolts, lock washers, and nuts at front and rear ends.

(4) INSTALL REAR DECK FRONT PLATE AND SPARE WHEEL. Install as directed in paragraph 229d.

112. FUEL TUBES.

a. Description. Special metal fuel tubes (fig. 81), covered with protective looms wherever necessary, extend between the fuel tank and carbureter. Flexible hose is provided at the fuel tank and between the fuel filter and the fuel pump to eliminate the possibility of fuel line breakage. A shut-off cock is provided in the fuel lines, located at the fuel filter prior to chassis serial No. 2006, and underneath the co-pilot's seat after chassis serial No. 2005, for convenience when performing service operations on the system. A drain hose extends between the fuel tank and hull side opening for draining the tank.

b. Replacement. The fuel lines are securely fastened in position with clips and may be readily removed or installed. Refer to figure 81 for relative position and accessibility of the various lines.

c. Cleaning. Whenever fuel tubes show corrosion, clean tubes thoroughly; then apply two coats of zinc chromate primer (52-P-20624) or one coat of thin film rust preventive compound (14-C-507).

Section XX

Exhaust System

113. GENERAL.

a. Description. The exhaust system (fig. 82) consists of an exhaust pipe, muffler, tail pipe, and attaching parts. The function of the ex-

Maintenance Instructions

haust system is to carry away engine exhaust gases and to muffle engine combustion noises. The exhaust pipe is attached to the engine exhaust manifold with three bolts, a gasket, seal, and flange, and extends through the bulkhead seal into the muffler, which is mounted in the front compartment. The muffler tail pipe extends from the muffler through the right-hand air exhaust duct tunnel. A steering gear shield is mounted on exhaust pipe to protect steering gear from excessive heat.

b. Replacement of Component Parts. The component parts of the exhaust system generally can be replaced in sections. If necessary to replace all component parts, operations in succeeding paragraphs 114 and 115 should be accomplished. However, if only necessary to replace certain sections of the system, accomplish operations described in respective paragraphs covering the particular parts to be replaced.

c. CAUTION: *Before performing any operations on the exhaust system, both the front and engine compartment hatch covers should be raised and sufficient time allowed to permit thorough ventilation of both compartments.*

114. EXHAUST PIPES.

a. Engine to Bulkhead Exhaust Pipe. Key letters in steps (2) and (3) below refer to figure 82.

(1) EXHAUST PIPE EXTENSION (EARLY VEHICLES). If difficulty is experienced in maintaining a tight seal at the bulkhead, condition may be corrected by adding a $\frac{3}{4}$-inch extension to the pipe at bulkhead end. Modify pipe as shown in figure 83. Exhaust pipes on later vehicles are longer and do not require this extension.

(2) REMOVAL.

(a) Loosen Front Exhaust Pipe to Bulkhead Clamp Bolt. In front compartment, loosen exhaust pipe flange clamp bolt (W) and nut.

(b) Disconnect Exhaust Pipe at Manifold. Remove three flange to manifold bolts, nuts, and lock nuts (fig. 84). Pull exhaust pipe down from manifold and out of bulkhead seal (V). Loosen upper and lower exhaust pipe shield clamp bolt (N) and nuts. Remove steering gear housing shield (J).

(3) INSTALLATION.

(a) Position Exhaust Pipe at Bulkhead and Manifold. Insert end of exhaust pipe (Q) into bulkhead seal flange (U), then position other end of exhaust pipe at exhaust manifold (G). Install exhaust pipe to manifold gasket (L) and flange seal (M), then install and tighten firmly three flange to manifold bolts, nuts, and lock nuts (fig. 84).

(b) Install Steering Gear Shield. Position steering gear shield (J) to upper and lower clamps (N), then firmly tighten upper and lower clamp nuts and bolts. Tighten front exhaust pipe flange clamp bolt (W) and nut in front compartment.

b. Front Exhaust Pipe and Bulkhead Seal. Key letters in steps (1) and (2) below refer to figure 82.

TM 9-802

Exhaust System

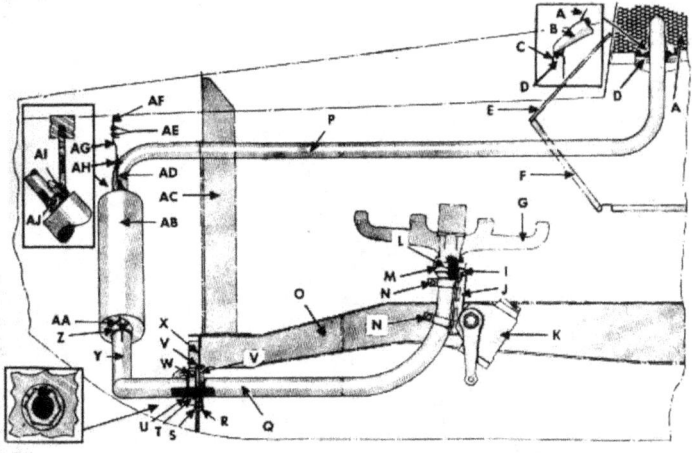

- A RIGHT-HAND AIR DUCT SCREEN
- B MUFFLER TAIL PIPE ASSEMBLY
- C COAMING
- D MUFFLER TAIL PIPE TO COAMING BOLT
- E UPPER TOEBOARD
- F LOWER TOEBOARD
- G EXHAUST MANIFOLD
- I EXHAUST PIPE TO MANIFOLD FLANGE
- J SHIELD
- K STEERING GEAR HOUSING
- L FLANGE GASKET (G085-01-00778)
- M FLANGE SEAL (G133-03-82851)
- N EXHAUST PIPE TO SHIELD CLAMP
- O FRAME SIDE RAIL (LH)
- P MUFFLER TAIL PIPE ASSEMBLY
- Q ENGINE TO BULK HEAD EXHAUST PIPE ASSEMBLY
- R SEAL RETAINING RING (G501-03-69907)
- S FLANGE ASSEMBLY TO RETAINING RING BOLT
- T EXHAUST PIPE TO SEAL FLANGE CLAMP
- U EXHAUST PIPE TO BULK HEAD SEAL FLANGE ASSEMBLY
- V EXHAUST PIPE TO BULK HEAD SEAL (G501-03-82804)
- W CLAMP BOLT
- X BULK HEAD
- Y BULK HEAD TO MUFFLER EXHAUST PIPE ASSEMBLY
- Z MUFFLER TO EXHAUST PIPE CLAMP
- AA CLAMP BOLT
- AB MUFFLER ASSEMBLY
- AC RADIATOR SUPPORT
- AD MUFFLER LOWER SUPPORT STRAP
- AE STRAP TO DECK SUPPORT CHANNEL BOLT
- AF DECK SUPPORT CHANNEL
- AG MUFFLER UPPER SUPPORT STRAP
- AI CLAMP BOLT
- AJ TAIL PIPE TO MUFFLER CLAMP

RA PD 333195

Figure 82—Exhaust System

(1) REMOVAL.

(a) Remove Front Exhaust Pipe Assembly. Remove exhaust pipe to seal flange clamp bolt (W), nut, and washer. Remove muffler to exhaust pipe clamp bolt (AA), nut, and washer. Remove upper to lower support strap bolt and nut (AH). Push muffler assembly (AB) toward front until exhaust pipe end (Y) can be removed from muffler (AB). Withdraw front exhaust pipe assembly (Y).

(b) Remove Bulkhead Seal. Remove exhaust pipe to seal flange clamp (Y). Remove six seal flange assembly to retaining ring bolts (S). The exhaust pipe to bulkhead seal flange assembly (U) and one exhaust pipe to bulkhead seal (V) must be removed while in front compartment. On engine side of bulkhead, loosen rear exhaust pipe assembly

227

TM 9-802
114-115

Maintenance Instructions

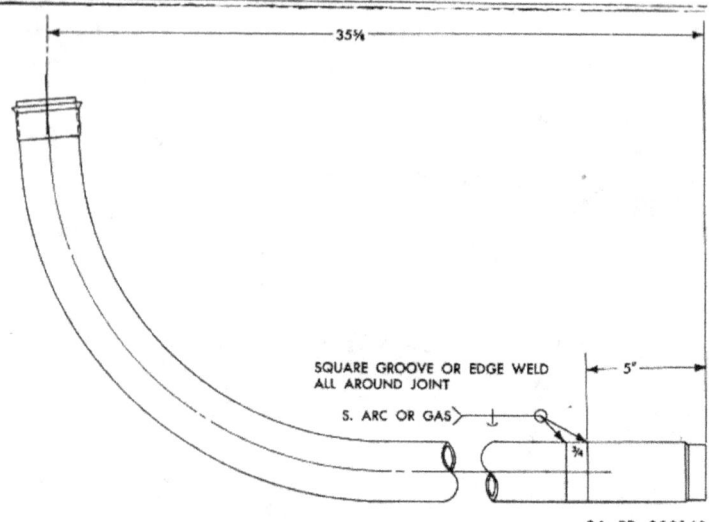

Figure 83—Exhaust Pipe Extension

(Q) at the exhaust manifold (C) to remove the seal retaining ring (R) and the other exhaust pipe to bulkhead seal (V).

(2) INSTALLATION.

(a) Install Exhaust Pipe to Bulkhead Seal. Retaining ring and bulkhead seal are accessible when radiator drain hole cover is removed in front compartment. Install bulkhead seal and flange assembly (U) with six flange assembly to retaining ring bolts (S). Tighten bolts (S) firmly. Working in front compartment, hold seal retaining ring (R) and one bulkhead seal (V) in place in engine compartment.

(b) Connect Front Exhaust Pipe to Bulkhead Seal Flange. Install exhaust pipe to seal flange clamp (T) over bulkhead seal flange (U), then insert end of exhaust pipe (Y) into flange (U). Install flange clamp bolt, washer, and nut (W) and tighten firmly.

(c) Attach Exhaust Pipe to Muffler. Install exhaust pipe to muffler clamp bolt (AA), washer, and nut and tighten firmly. Install upper to lower support strap bolt and nut (AH). Position straps to hold muffler assembly (AB) rigidly, then tighten support strap bolt and nut (AH).

115. EXHAUST MUFFLER AND TAIL PIPE.

a. Muffler Assembly. Muffler assembly used on early vehicles is smaller than the one used on later vehicles. Mufflers are not interchangeable as an assembly; however, larger muffler can be installed by making necessary modifications. Removal and installation procedures are the

TM 9-802
115

Exhaust System

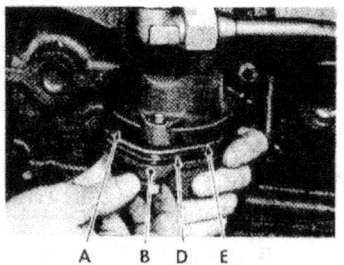 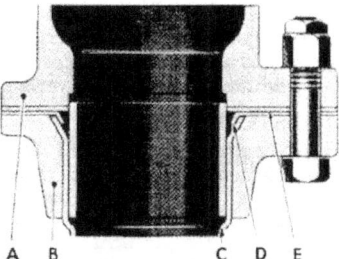

A MANIFOLD
B EXHAUST PIPE FLANGE
C EXHAUST PIPE

D EXHAUST PIPE FLANGE SEAL
E EXHAUST PIPE FLANGE GASKET

RA PD 64621

Figure 84—Exhaust Pipe to Manifold Connections

same for both mufflers. Key letters in steps (1) and (2) below refer to figure 82.

(1) REMOVAL.

(a) Disconnect Tail Pipe from Muffler. Remove tail pipe to muffler clamp bolt (AJ), nut, and washer. Pull tail pipe (P) from muffler assembly.

(b) Disconnect Front Exhaust Pipe from Muffler. Remove one muffler to exhaust pipe clamp bolt (AA), nut, and washer. Pull muffler assembly (AB) from front exhaust pipe (Y). Muffler assembly (AB) may then be withdrawn.

(2) INSTALLATION.

(a) Attach Muffler to Front Exhaust Pipe. Insert end of the front exhaust pipe (Y) into muffler assembly (AB). Install muffler to exhaust pipe clamp bolt (AA), washer, and nut. Do not tighten at this time.

(b) Attach Muffler to Tail Pipe. Insert end of tail pipe (P) into muffler (AB) and install muffler to tail pipe clamp bolt (AJ), washer, and nut. Tighten clamp bolt and nut at tail pipe (P) and front exhaust pipe (Y) ends firmly. Muffler assembly (AB) should be held rigidly; however, upper and lower support strap (AD) and (AG) must be positioned to support assembly without strain at the front exhaust pipe (Y) and at tail pipe (P).

b. Muffler Tail Pipe. Key letters in steps (1) and (2) below refer to figure 82.

(1) REMOVAL.

(a) Disconnect Tail Pipe from Coaming. Working on the outside of vehicle at the right-hand air exhaust screen (A), remove two exhaust tail pipe to coaming bolts (D), washers, and nuts.

(b) Disconnect Tail Pipe at Muffler. Working inside of front compartment, remove tail pipe to muffler clamp bolt (AJ), nut, and washer.

TM 9-802
115-116

Maintenance Instructions

If necessary to remove upper and lower support straps (AD) and (AG), remove two upper straps to deck support channel bolts (AE), nuts, and washers. Pull muffler tail pipe (P) away from muffler (AB), then withdraw tail pipe (P) through front compartment.

(2) INSTALLATION.

(a) Position Muffler Tail Pipe. Insert tail pipe (P), outer end first, through front compartment, then position outer end of tail pipe (B) at coaming. Install and tighten two tail pipe to coaming bolts (D), washers, and nuts.

(b) Attach Tail Pipe to Muffler. Insert tail pipe (P) in muffler flange and install tail pipe to muffler clamp bolt (AJ), washer, and nut. Upper and lower straps are attached together with one bolt (AH) and nut, with bolt hole elongated. Position upper and lower straps (AD) and (AG) so there is no strain at the muffler and tail pipe clamp (AJ). After muffler and tail pipe have been positioned, tighten upper to lower support strap bolt (AH) and nut.

Section XXI
Cooling System

116. GENERAL.

a. Description. The cooling system is sealed type comprising the following units: radiator, overflow tank, water pump, fan blades, drive belt, thermostat, temperature gage, cylinder head water by-pass tube, filler cap, overflow tank pressure cap, and tubes and fittings connecting the radiator to the engine and the water pump (fig. 85). The water, drawn from the radiator by the action of the water pump, is force-circulated through the radiator core and water passages of the engine. The water is returned through the upper connections to the radiator where it is cooled by the action of the fan. A pressure cap on overflow tank maintains a pressure of approximately four pounds in the cooling system when the engine warms up to normal operating temperatures. The fan, which draws the air through the intake grille located just to rear of the driver's compartment, forces air through shrouded radiator, then through exhaust ducts. Hot air exhausts through two exhaust grilles or is bypassed into the compartments for heating purposes.

b. Data.

Cooling system capacity
    Water-cooled tire pump .... 21 qt
    Air-cooled tire pump .... 20 qt
    Water pump type .... Packless
    Radiator type .... Fin and tube

Thermostat
    Starts to open .... 156°F to 165°F
    Fully open .... 185°F

Cooling System

c. Repair. Repair procedures for the cooling components will be found in TM 9-1802A.

117. SERVICING COOLING SYSTEM.

a. Filling System.

(1) CAUTION: *Do not pour cold water into cooling system when engine temperature is above 200°F. Also, cold water poured into the cooling system regardless of engine temperature, will close the thermostat and not allow the engine water passages to completely fill. After filling system with cold water, always run engine until normal operating temperature is reached (theromstat opens), then add water as necessary until liquid appears and will remain in radiator filler neck. Do not use salt water except in extreme emergencies. When fresh water is not available and emergency necessitates the use of sea water for coolant, add 1½ ounces of corrosion inhibitor compound (51-C-1588-775) to each gallon used. As soon as possible, drain system of sea water, flush, and refill with fresh water.*

(2) FILL SYSTEM. Close radiator cylinder block and overflow tank drain cocks (if necessary). If above +32°F, partially fill the system with clean fresh water, add a corrosion inhibitor compound (51-C-1588-775), then add water until liquid level is visible through filler neck. In extremely hot weather, also half-fill radiator overflow tank. If there is a possibility that temperatures below +32°F will be encountered, fill system about one-quarter full, add sufficient antifreeze for the lowest expected temperature (par. 45), then fill until liquid level is visible through filler neck. Install radiator cap, then start engine and run it at a fast idle until temperature gage shows normal operating temperature. Stop engine and check coolant level, adding water if necessary.

b. Draining System. Run engine at fast idle until normal engine operating temperature is reached (at least 165°F) to stir up any loose rust, scale, etc. Remove radiator filler cap (painted black). It is not necessary to remove overflow tank pressure cap (painted white). From inside front compartment, remove metal snap plug or plate, as case may be, located below radiator in upper right-hand corner of front compartment bulkhead. Radiator drain cock (G501-01-39660) can then be opened. Open drain cocks at bottom of overflow tank and at left side of cylinder block. Hull may be drained as described in paragraph 37.

c. Preventive Cleaning. To clean the cooling system of rust, scale, or sludge, use a cleaning compound followed by a neutralizer to stop the action of the cleaner. One package of cleaning compound (51-C-1568-500) provides enough cleaner and neutralizer to clean a cooling system of a four-gallon capacity. Neutralizing and flushing after cleaning is very important, as the cleaner contains a strong acid which, if not completely removed, will attack the parts of the cooling system. Also, precautions should be taken not to spill any cleaning compound on the skin, clothing, or vehicle paint.

A OVERFLOW TANK
B OVERFLOW TANK OVERFLOW TUBE
C OVERFLOW TANK CAP (G501-7001952)
D RADIATOR OVERFLOW TUBE (GM-2201945)
E RADIATOR CAP (G501-7001953)
F RADIATOR
G FAN SHROUD—UPPER
H FAN SHROUD—LOWER
I SPARE DRIVE BELT
J RADIATOR OUTLET PIPE
K TIRE PUMP WATER RETURN TUBE
L RADIATOR OUTLET PIPE HOSE (3500-083429)
M WATER BY-PASS TUBE TEE
N WATER PUMP
O DRIVE BELT
P CYLINDER HEAD WATER OUTLET
Q WATER BY-PASS TUBE
R FUEL TUBE
S GENERATOR ADJUSTING ARM
T RADIATOR INLET PIPE HOSE
U WATER PUMP PULLEY
V TIRE PUMP WATER TUBE
W FAN GUARD
X FAN BLADE ASSEMBLY
Y RADIATOR INLET PIPE

RA PD 333229

Figure 85—Cooling System Units

Cooling System

(1) CLEAN SYSTEM. Drain system (subpar. **b.** above), then close radiator and cylinder block drain cocks. Disconnect overflow tank and place a clean container under overflow tube to catch any overflow which may be needed to maintain proper liquid level in the radiator. Be sure temperature of engine is below 200°F. Pour cleaning compound (one container to every four gallons of cooling system capacity) into radiator, then fill system with water. Temporarily install a pressure type cap (same as used on overflow tank) on radiator. Start engine and run at a fast idle to heat solution to at least 180°F. Continue to run engine for at least 30 minutes. Stop engine, remove radiator cap, open radiator and cylinder block drain cocks, and allow system to drain completely.

(2) NEUTRALIZE SYSTEM. Close radiator and cylinder block drain cocks. Pour neutralizer (one container to every four gallons of cooling system capacity) into radiator, then fill system with water and install pressure cap. Start engine and run it at a fast idle to heat solution to at least 180°F. Continue to run engine for at least 10 minutes. Drain system (subpar. **b.** above).

(3) FLUSH SYSTEM.

(a) CAUTION: Do not flush system by inserting a hose in the radiator with the engine running and drain cocks open. This procedure will close the thermostat and stop circulation of the water through the engine.

(b) Close Radiator and Cylinder Block Drain Cocks. Fill system with clean fresh water, then install a pressure type cap on radiator. Start engine and run it at a fast idle to bring engine operating temperature to at least 180°F. Continue to run engine for at least 5 minutes. Remove the pressure type cap, then drain system (subpar. **b.** above). If water is discolored to any extent, repeat this flushing operation. Replace the temporary pressure cap with the regulator radiator cap.

(4) CLEAN RADIATOR, OVERFLOW TANK CAP, OVERFLOW TUBE, TANK, AND DRAIN TUBE. Clean pressure cap (on overflow tank) by spraying a stream of water, preferably hot, through the holes in the valve cage while moving the pressure valve up and down with blunt instrument or pencil. Cap gasket (G103-15-93621) must be in good condition. Clean out overflow pipe with a stream of water. Rinse out overflow tank, then connect overflow tank pipe. Clean out dirt, trash, and insects embedded in the air passages of the radiator core, using compressed air or a stream of water; but do not use steam. CAUTION: *Do not hold air or water hose too close to the radiator or use excessive air pressure, as damage to radiator may result. Clean out any obstruction in drain hose with a soft wire.*

d. Air Suction and Exhaust Gas Leakage Tests. Air circulating through the cooling system, as well as exhaust gas leaking into the system, causes rapid corrosion and rust formation which will eventually clog the system and cause overheating and loss of cooling liquid. The air may be drawn into the system due to low liquid level in the radiator, leaky water pump, or loose fitting connections. Exhaust gas may be blown into the cooling system past the cylinder head gasket or through cracks in the cylinder head and block.

(1) AIR SUCTION TEST. Remove radiator cap. Adjust level of cooling liquid in radiator, allowing room for expansion so as to avoid any overflow loss during test. Replace radiator cap. Cap must form an airtight seal. Attach a length of rubber tube to lower end of overflow tube; this connection must be airtight. Run engine with transmission in neutral gear at a safe speed until temperature gage stops rising and remains stationary. Without changing engine speed, place end of rubber tube in a bottle of water, avoiding kinks and sharp bends that might block flow of air. Watch for bubbles in bottle of water. The continuous appearance of bubbles indicates that air is being sucked into the cooling system. Correct condition by tightening cylinder head bolts, water pump mounting bolts, hose clamps, and fitting connections. Also examine all hoses carefully and if cracked, swollen, or deteriorated, replace with new parts.

(2) EXHAUST GAS LEAKAGE TEST. Start test with engine cold. Remove drive belt (par. 118*b*.) to prevent pump operation. Drain cooling system until cooling liquid level is at top of thermostat housing, but no lower. This can be determined by loosening up cylinder head outlet from thermostat housing to check level of liquid. If liquid leaks from this connection, continue to drain system until liquid no longer leaks. Remove thermostat (par. 120*b*.). Make sure thermostat housing is full of liquid (add if necessary), then with transmission in neutral gear, start engine and accelerate it several times. Watch for bubbles in water in thermostat housing while accelerating engine, also when engine speed drops back to normal. The appearance of bubbles or sudden rise of cooling liquid indicates exhaust gas leakage into cooling system. Make test quickly before boiling starts, as steam bubbles will give misleading results. If exhaust gas leakage is evident, replace cylinder head gasket (par. 88), then test again. If leaks are still evident, it indicates cylinder head or block is cracked. Notify higher authority. If no leak is apparent, install thermostat (par. 120*d*.), install and adjust drive belt (par. 118), then fill radiator.

118. DRIVE BELT.

a. Adjustment. Fan, water pump, and generator are driven from engine crankshaft by a V-type belt. Belt is accessible through the engine compartment hatch cover opening, and is adjusted in the following manner:

(1) Loosen two generator to mounting bracket bolt nuts or through-bolt nut, as the case may be, then loosen generator to adjusting arm bolt.

(2) Move generator toward engine to decrease tension, or away from engine to increase tension. A light pressure (approximately 10 to 15 lb) on belt at a point midway between generator and water pump pulley must cause a $1/2$-inch deflection (fig. 86).

(3) Tighten generator to adjusting arm bolt, then tighten two generator to mounting bracket bolt nuts or through-bolt nut, as the case may be.

TM 9-802
118

Cooling System

RA PD 333233

Figure 86—Drive Belt Adjustment

b. Removal.

(1) PRIOR TO FRONT MOUNTED TIRE PUMP. Loosen adjusting arm to generator bolt and generator to bracket bolt nuts, or through-bolt nut, as the case may be, then move generator toward engine as far as possible. Remove drive belt from generator, water pump, and crankshaft pulley, then remove drive belt over fan assembly.

(2) WITH FRONT MOUNTED TIRE PUMP. Removal procedure for drive belt is the same as step (1) above, except that tire pump drive shaft must be disconnected from engine crankshaft to completely remove belt. For drive shaft removal, refer to paragraph 267*b*.

c. Installation.

(1) PRIOR TO FRONT MOUNTED TIRE PUMP. Thread drive belt over fan blades, then position drive belt over water pump, generator, and crankshaft pulleys. Adjust drive belt (subpar. *a*. above).

(2) WITH FRONT MOUNTED TIRE PUMP.

(a) NOTE: *A spare drive belt is provided for emergencies, and is mounted over tire pump drive shaft and secured to fan guard by two*

TM 9-802
118-119

Maintenance Instructions

clips. If spare belt is used, tire pump drive shaft need not be removed for drive belt installation. Spare drive belt should, however, be replaced as soon as possible.

(*b*) When necessary to install a belt, disconnect tire pump drive shaft (par. 267**b**.), then thread drive belt over fan blades and position over water pump, generator, and crankshaft pulleys. Install another spare belt in place, then connect tire pump drive shaft (par. 267**d**.). Adjust drive belt (subpar. **a**. above).

119. FAN AND WATER PUMP.

a. Description. A four-blade fan assembly is attached to the water pump pulley. The water pump is a belt driven, packless type, equipped with sealed type ball bearings which require no lubrication.

b. Design Change. Water pump design was changed after chassis serial No. 605. This change altered the mounting of fan blades. On vehicles prior to chassis serial No. 606, a spacer was used between fan blades and pulley. Refer to figure 87 for distinguishing external differences between the two water pumps. On all vehicles from chassis serial No. 605 through 11978, a spare fan spacer is placed on bulkhead in engine compartment just in front of overflow tank on left side. A stencil on bulkhead reads: "Fan spacer used with water pump 2103002." This means that if a 6x6 GMC truck water pump is used on an amphibian after chassis serial No. 605, the spacer must be used when mounting fan blades.

c. Fan and Water Pump Removal.

(1) REMOVE FAN BLADE ASSEMBLY.

(*a*) *Prior to Chassis Serial No. 606.* Remove four bolts attaching fan

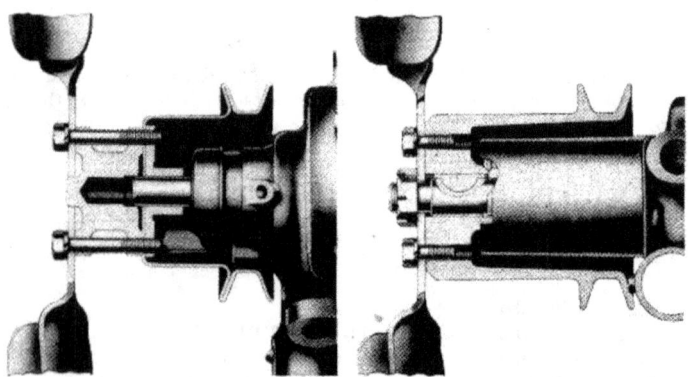

PRIOR TO DUKW 353-606　　　　　AFTER DUKW 353-605

RA PD 307317

Figure 87—Water Pump Design Differences

Cooling System

blade assembly to pulley, then remove fan blade assembly. Spacer used between fan and pulley will remove with fan blade assembly.

(b) After Chassis Serial No. 605. Remove lock nut from water pump shaft at forward side of fan hub. Remove four bolts which attach fan blade assembly to pulley, then remove fan blade assembly.

(2) REMOVE PUMP CONNECTIONS. Drain system (par. 117*b.*). Remove drive belt from water pump pulley. Loosen radiator outlet pipe to water pump hose clamp screws at water pump and remove hose from water pump. Loosen water by-pass elbow hose clamp screws and remove hose from by-pass tee.

(3) REMOVE WATER PUMP. Remove four water pump to cylinder block bolts, then remove pump from cylinder block. Unscrew water by-pass elbow from water pump for installation in replacement pump.

d. Fan and Water Pump Installation.

(1) INSTALL BY-PASS ELBOW. Coat elbow threads with mica base anti-seize compound (52-C-3081). Screw water by-pass elbow firmly into water pump.

(2) INSTALL PUMP ON ENGINE. Place a new water pump to cylinder block gasket (G085-1100960) in position on pump, then place water pump in position on engine. Install one $\frac{7}{8}$-inch bolt with lock washer in water pump bolt hole just above water inlet and tighten finger-tight, then install remaining three bolts with lock washers, assembling fuel and oil lines clip and generator adjusting arm. Tighten all four bolts evenly and firmly.

(3) INSTALL PUMP CONNECTIONS. Install water by-pass elbow hose to tee and tighten clamp screws. Install radiator outlet pipe to water pump inlet and tighten hose clamp screws.

(4) INSTALL DRIVE BELT. Install drive belt and adjust (par. 118).

(5) INSTALL FAN (PRIOR TO CHASSIS SERIAL NO. 606). Position fan blade assembly over pilot on spacer, then position spacer and fan blade assembly over end of water pump shaft and against forward end of pulley. Concave side of blade must be toward radiator. Install four fan blade assembly to water pump pulley bolts with lock washers and tighten firmly. Fill system (par. 117*a.*).

(6) INSTALL FAN (AFTER CHASSIS SERIAL NO. 605). Position fan blade assembly over end of water pump shaft and against forward side of pulley with holes alined for installation of bolts. Concave side of blade must be toward radiator. Install four fan blade assembly to water pump pulley bolts with lock washers and tighten firmly. Install lock nut on water pump shaft and tighten firmly. Fill system (par. 117*a.*).

120. THERMOSTAT.

a. Description. Thermostat is bellows type, mounted in housing at cylinder head water outlet. Thermostat comprises a restriction valve which is thermostatically operated, and is calibrated to open gradually

TM 9-802
120

Maintenance Instructions

- A BY-PASS TEE
- B INSULATION
- C BY-PASS TUBE CLIP
- D CYLINDER HEAD WATER BY-PASS TUBE
- E FUEL PUMP TO CARBURETOR FUEL LINE
- F THERMOSTAT HOUSING
- G THERMOSTAT (G122-04-0200)
- H WATER PUMP BY-PASS INLET ELBOW
- I HOSE (G501-0217805)
- J GASKET (G085-31-06280)
- K WATER PUMP (G501-03-45883)
- L GASKET
- M DRIVE BELT (G508-01-18253)

RA PD 333197

Figure 88—Thermostat Removal

as engine temperatures increase. Valve in thermostat starts to open at approximately 156°F to 165°F and is fully opened at approximately 185°F. When the temperature of the cooling liquid in the engine is below the calibration of the thermostat, the valve in the thermostat remains closed, restricting the flow of the cooling liquid through the radiator. However, a by-pass around the thermostat permits circulation of the cooling liquid through the engine water passages until normal operating temperature is reached. The thermostat then is open and permits full circulation of the cooling liquid.

b. Removal. Drain radiator (par. 177**b.**). Remove hose from radiator inlet pipe at cylinder head water outlet. Remove two water outlet to thermostat housing bolts and lock washers and lift outlet off of thermostat housing. Raise and remove thermostat from housing.

c. Testing. Remove all accumulation of rust or other foreign material from assembly. Make visual inspection of valve. Seepage hole should not be clogged. Make visual inspection of thermostat assembly for bent or dislocated frame. Test in the following manner:

(1) CHECK FULL OPEN TEMPERATURE. Heat a pan of water to 185°F. Check temperature with a thermometer. Submerge thermostat in water. Valve should raise to the fully open position.

(2) CHECK CLOSING TEMPERATURE. Submerge thermostat in a pan of water at a temperature of 150°F. Under these conditions, valve should be at closed position.

(3) CHECK FOR "START-TO-OPEN" TEMPERATURE. Submerge thermostat in a pan of water 10°F above the rated start-to-open temperature (marked on thermostat body). Valve should move to partially open position. NOTE: *Do not attempt to repair thermostat. Units which fail to function properly as indicated by above tests must be discarded and replaced with new units.*

d. Installation. Position thermostat in housing. Place a new water outlet gasket (G085-31-06300) in position and assemble outlet to thermostat housing. Install two water outlet to thermostat housing bolts with lock washers, assembling cylinder head water by-pass tube clip to left-hand cap screw. Tighten bolts firmly. Install hose to radiator inlet pipe and cylinder head water outlet and tighten hose clamps firmly. Refill radiator to proper level (par. 117a.).

121. RADIATOR.

a. Description. Radiator assembly consists of a fin and tube type core with upper and lower tanks. Radiator is mounted in a vertical position at forward end of engine. Air blown by action of fan cools cooling liquid as it flows through radiator. A conventional sealing type filler cap is used on radiator.

b. Removal.

(1) DRAIN SYSTEM. Drain cooling system (par. 117b.).

(2) REMOVE TIRE PUMP DRIVE SHAFT AND COUPLING ASSEMBLY (AFTER CHASSIS SERIAL NO. 2005 ONLY). Refer to paragraph 267b.

(3) REMOVE UPPER AND LOWER RADIATOR SEALS. From front compartment, remove three radiator top seal plate to deck reinforcement screws and remove plate and felt seal. Remove four screws attaching radiator lower seal retainer to front bulkhead and remove retainer and felt seal.

(4) REMOVE CORE TO SUPPORT BOLT NUTS. In front compartment, remove six (three each side) radiator to support bolt nuts and lock washers.

(5) REMOVE RADIATOR INLET PIPE. In engine compartment, loosen four radiator inlet hose clamp screws and remove inlet pipe with hose.

(6) DISCONNECT OVERFLOW TUBE HOSE. Loosen radiator overflow tube hose clamps and remove hose from overflow tube.

(7) REMOVE FAN BLADES AND SHROUD. Remove fan blades [par. 119c.(1)]. Remove eight nuts (four each side), lock washers, and bolts (shroud to radiator supports) and remove upper and lower shroud as an assembly.

(8) REMOVE RADIATOR OUTLET PIPE. Loosen four radiator outlet pipe hose clamp screws and remove pipe with hose.

Maintenance Instructions

(9) REMOVE RADIATOR. Remove six (three each side) radiator to side support bolts, then raise radiator straight up to remove from vehicle.

c. Installation.

(1) POSITION RADIATOR. Place radiator in position and insert six (three each side) radiator to side support bolts.

(2) INSTALL RADIATOR TO SIDE SUPPORT BOLT NUTS. From front compartment, install radiator to side support bolt lock washers and nuts. Tighten firmly.

(3) INSTALL UPPER AND LOWER RADIATOR SEALS. With felt strip in place on radiator top seal plate, install plate to deck reinforcement with three new screws. Then with felt strip in place on radiator lower seal retainer, install retainer to front bulkhead with four new screws. *Be sure felt strips are in good condition and will form a good seal.*

(4) INSTALL RADIATOR OUTLET PIPE. Install radiator outlet pipe, using new hose if any signs of deterioration are present. Tighten hose clamps firmly.

(5) INSTALL FAN SHROUD AND BLADES. Position upper and lower fan shroud assembly and secure with eight bolts (four each side), lock washers, and nuts. Be sure felt clipped to upper and lower shrouds is in good condition. Replace if necessary. Install fan blades [par. 119*d*. (5) or (6)].

(6) INSTALL RADIATOR INLET PIPE. Install radiator inlet pipe, using new hose if any signs of deterioration are present. Tighten hose clamp firmly.

(7) CONNECT OVERFLOW TUBE. Install hose over radiator overflow tube and tighten hose clamp firmly.

(8) INSTALL TIRE PUMP DRIVE SHAFT AND COUPLING. Follow procedure given in paragraph 267*d*. Fill cooling system (par. 117*a*.).

122. OVERFLOW TANK.

a. Description. Overflow tank is mounted on left-hand radiator support (fig. 85). Overflow from radiator, caused by expansion or surging of steam vapor within cooling system, passes through a tube to overflow tank. Overflow tank is equipped with a pressure cap which controls pressure within cooling system. When cooling liquid cools and contracts, resulting vacuum draws condensed liquid from overflow tank into radiator.

b. Removal. Remove pressure cap and open drain cock to drain tank. Disconnect radiator overflow tube at overflow tank. Remove four nuts, lock washers, and bolts (overflow tank to side support), then remove tank.

Starting System

c. Installation.

(1) INSTALL TANK. Place overflow tank in position and install four tank to side support bolts, lock washers, and nuts.

(2) CONNECT OVERFLOW TUBE. Connect radiator overflow tube to tank drain cock tee.

(3) FILL COOLING SYSTEM. Replace overflow tank pressure cap and refill radiator as necessary to bring cooling liquid to proper level (par. 117a.).

Section XXII
Starting System

123. GENERAL.

a. Description. The starter, attached to the right-hand side of the clutch housing, is equipped with an over-running clutch drive which is manually shifted into engagement with the flywheel. The starter switch, mounted on starter, completes the electrical circuit between the battery and the starter. The upper end of the shift lever engages the switch button after the pinion has fully engaged the flywheel gear, or when the spring is sufficiently compressed to force the pinion into mesh as soon as armature rotates. When engine has started, action of the over-running clutch allows the pinion to rotate at flywheel speed.

b. Data.

```
Starting Motor
  Make ................................................ Delco Remy
  Model.........(Not waterproofed) ........................ 1107418
  Model.........(Waterproofed) ............................ 1107453
  Voltage ............................................... 6
  Rotation ........(Viewed from driving end)............... Clockwise
```

c. Corrosion Prevention and Waterproofing Procedure. Remove battery cable at starter. Clean the terminal and contact. Install cable, tighten securely, and paint terminal and switch with red synthetic paint (glyptal). Make certain that paint does not interfere with operation of starter shift lever. Spray exterior cleaned surfaces of starter with red synthetic paint (glyptal, 52-P-8057-710). If not available use ignition insulating compound (52-C-3099-20).

d. Repair. Starter repair operations are given in TM 9-1802A.

124. STARTER.

a. Cleaning Commutator. Remove cover band and inspect commutator for dirty condition, roughness, burned spots, and high mica. If commutator is dirty, it can sometimes be cleaned with a strip of 2/0 flint paper. Never use emery cloth to clean commutator. All dust must

TM 9-802
124

Maintenance Instructions

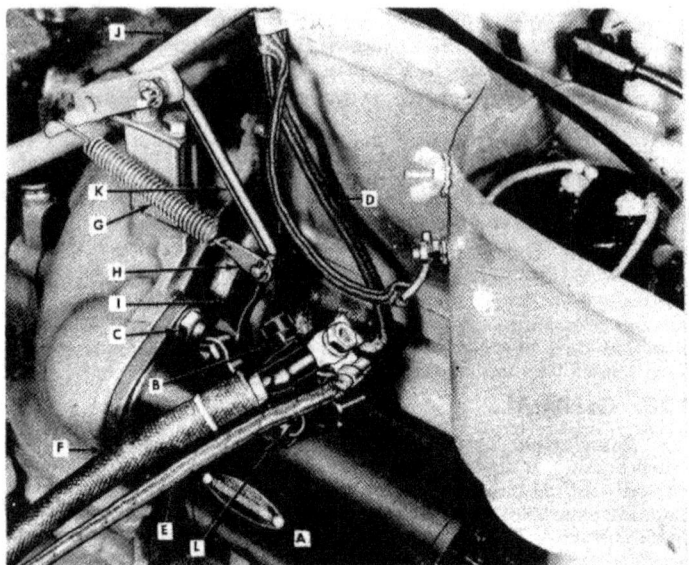

A STARTER
B STARTER SWITCH
C MOUNTING STUD NUT
D JUNCTION BLOCK TO STARTER SWITCH AND COIL WIRING HARNESS
E RADIO TERMINAL BOX WIRING HARNESS
F BATTERY CABLE
G PULL BACK SPRING
H PULL BACK SPRING CLIP
I STARTER SHIFT LEVER
J STARTER PEDAL ROD ASSEMBLY
K STARTER TO ROD LINK
L STARTER SWITCH CONDENSER

RA PD 337191

Figure 89—Starter Installed

be blown from starter after commutator has been cleaned. If commutator is rough, burned, or has high mica, starter should be replaced. Inspect condition of brushes (G085-34-00180) and pigtail connections. If pigtail connections are loose they should be tightened. If appreciable brush wear is evident or brushes are sticking in holders, brushes should be replaced.

b. Line Voltage Tests. Check cable leads and connections to determine if they are in good condition and tight, and without excessive resistance. Excessive resistance produces abnormal voltage drop which may lower voltage at starter to such a low value that normal operation of starter will not be obtained. Abnormal voltage drop can be detected with a low reading voltmeter.

(1) TESTING PROCEDURE.

(a) Check voltage drop between grounded battery terminal (negative) and vehicle frame. Place one prod of voltmeter (17-T-5575) on negative (−) battery terminal and other on vehicle frame. With starter

Starting System

cranking engine while ignition switch is off, voltage reading must be less than 1/10 volt. If more than this, there is excessive resistance in this circuit.

(b) Check voltage drop between ungrounded battery terminal and starter terminal stud with voltmeter while starter is operated. If reading is more than 1/10 volt, there is excessive resistance in circuit.

(c) Check voltage drop between starter housing and vehicle frame, using voltmeter. This must be less than 1/10 volt.

(d) If excessive resistance is found in any of the three circuits, disconnect cables and clean the connections. If cables appear frayed, replace with new ones of correct size. Check condition of ground strap and replace if necessary.

c. Switch Replacement (fig. 89).

(1) REMOVAL. Disconnect ground strap from negative (-) battery terminal. Remove starter switch terminal nut, two cables, and condenser wire. Remove two screws and lock washers which attach switch to starter housing. Remove condenser and starter switch (G085-33-03560) from starter.

(2) INSTALLATION. Position switch and condenser on starter housing and install two attaching screws and lock washers. Tighten screws firmly. Connect ammeter cable, starter cable, and condenser wire to switch terminal. Install lock washer and nut, tightening firmly. Connect ground strap to negative (-) battery terminal.

d. Starter Assembly Replacement (fig. 89).

(1) REMOVAL. Remove ground strap from negative (-) battery terminal. Remove fuel filter as described in paragraph 110c. Remove battery cable, ammeter cable, and condenser wire from starter switch terminal. Unhook starter pedal pull back spring. Remove cotter pin from lever. Remove pull back spring clip from link, then remove link from lever. Remove nut and lock washer from stud, then remove bolt and lock washer which attach starter to clutch housing. Pull starter assembly (G085-11-01-540) or (3500-1107453, waterproofed) straight from housing.

(2) INSTALLATION.

(a) Position Starter. Position starter on clutch housing with switch at top. Install stud nut at top, and bolt at bottom, using internal-toothed lock washer under nut and bolt head. Tighten nut and bolt alternately until starter is seated firmly in place.

(b) Connect Linkage. Connect lever link to shift lever, install spring clip on link, and secure with cotter pin. Hook pedal pull back spring to spring clip.

(c) Connect Cables. Clean switch terminal post and cable terminals thoroughly. Install condenser wire, battery cable, and ammeter cable to switch terminal post. Install lock washer and nut on terminal. Tighten nut firmly. Connect ground strap to negative (-) battery terminal. Install fuel filter (par. 110**d**.). Test action of starter.

125. STARTER CONTROLS.

a. General. Control linkage comprises a lever and shaft assembly bolted with brackets to clutch housing, with a link connecting the starter shift lever and bracket lever.

b. Removal (fig. 89). Remove starter pedal button. Remove toeboard. Disconnect linkage and spring at starter lever. Remove two bolts which attach brackets on each side of clutch housing. Remove lever and shaft assembly from clutch housing.

c. Installation (fig. 89). Position lever and shaft assembly on clutch housing with brackets and spacers in place. Install and tighten bolts. Connect link and spring clip to starter shift lever. Install pull back spring. Anti-rattle springs are used at link connection to bracket, and at pedal shaft bracket to shaft. Install toeboard, then install starter pedal button.

Section XXIII

Generating System

126. DESCRIPTION AND DATA

a. Description. Generating system comprises generator, three-unit regulator, and connecting wires. System functions to keep battery charged and to furnish, when engine speeds permit, current for ignition, lighting, and other electrical accessories. Generating circuit is shown in figure 90. Only generator and regulator are covered in this section; refer to other electrical sections for information covering other electrical units.

b. Data.

(1) GENERATOR.

Make .... Delco Remy

Four models, all of which are interchangeable, have been used in the following order: 1105864, 1105870, 1105873, and 1105874.

Voltage 6
Rotation—Viewed from driving end .... Clockwise

(2) REGULATOR.

Make .... Delco Remy
Model 1118468

c. Repair. Generator inspection, test, and repair procedures are listed in TM 9-1802A. Generator regulator adjustment and repair procedures are also listed in TM 9-1802A.

TM 9-802

Generating System

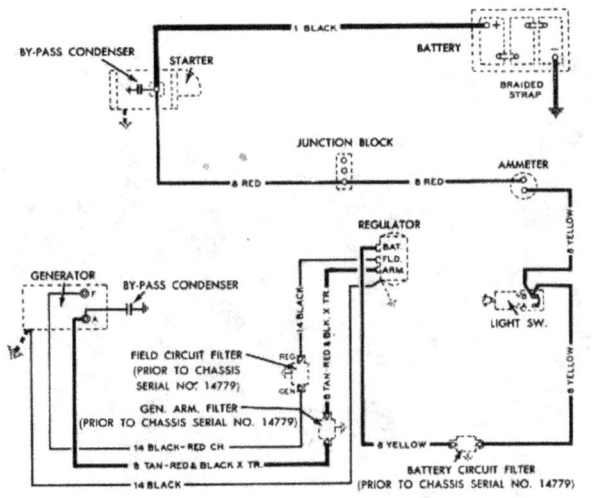

Figure 90—Generating Circuit

127. GENERATOR.

a. Description. Generator (fig. 91) is a shunt wound, two-brush type, mounted on left side of engine and driven by belt from the crankshaft pulley in conjunction with the water pump. Generator is cooled by air drawn through openings in rear of generator by fan mounted behind drive pulley.

(1) The air scoop mounted on rear end of generator on early vehicles has been eliminated. The removal of this scoop is recommended so that the possibility of water entering generator through the scoop will be eliminated. Removal of this part also provides better access to the bilge below engine.

b. Removal.

(1) DISCONNECT WIRES. Remove ground strap at battery terminal. Remove two nuts and lock washers which attach harness wires and condenser pigtail to generator terminals. Remove screw and two internal-external toothed lock washers attaching condenser and ground wire to generator housing and lay condenser aside. Remove cross recessed screw, lock washer, flat washer, and clip attaching wiring harness to generator housing.

(2) LOOSEN DRIVE BELT. Remove cap screw, lock washer, and flat washer attaching generator to adjusting arm.

(3) REMOVE GENERATOR. Remove generator to bracket through-bolt, nut, and internal-external toothed lock washer, then lift belt from generator pulley; generator (3500-1105874) can now be removed.

245

TM 9-802
127

Maintenance Instructions

A GENERATOR
B GENERATOR BRACKET
C GENERATOR TO BRACKET BOLT
D GENERATOR ADJUSTING ARM
E ADJUSTING ARM BOLT
F LOCK WASHER
G PLAIN WASHER
H GENERATOR TO REGULATOR WIRING HARNESS
I HARNESS CLIP
J GENERATOR-BY-PASS CONDENSER
K GROUND SCREW
L ARMATURE TERMINAL
M FIELD TERMINAL
N DRIVE BELT

RA PD 333217

Figure 91—Generator Installed

c. Installation.

(1) INSTALL GENERATOR. Lower generator into place and install generator to bracket through-bolt, nut, and internal-external toothed lock washer. Tighten finger-tight.

(2) INSTALL DRIVE BELT. Place belt in recess in generator pulley. Attach generator to adjusting arm, using flat washer, lock washer, and cap screw. Adjust belt tension (par. 118a.), then tighten generator to bracket through-bolt.

(3) CONNECT WIRES. Install condenser and ground wire (No. 14 black) on generator housing, using screw and two internal-external toothed lock washers. Be certain two internal-external toothed lock washers are used, one next to generator housing and one under head of screw. Attach condenser pigtail and armature wire (No. 8 tan-red and black cross tracer) to "ARM" terminal on generator with nut and lock washer. Attach field wire (No. 14 black-red check) to "FLD" terminal on generator with nut and lock washers. Tighten nuts securely. Install ground strap at battery.

Generating System

d. Polarizing Generator. When generator or regulator wires have been disconnected, especially when new unit is being installed, generator must be polarized after units are installed, *before engine is started*. Failure to polarize generator will cause regulator points to vibrate excessively and burn. Remove wire (No. 14 black-red check) from "FLD" terminal at generator. Use jumper wire to *momentarily* connect "FLD" terminal on generator and "BATTERY" terminal on regulator. This allows a momentary surge of battery current to reach generator field, which automatically gives generator the correct polarity with respect to battery it is to charge. Attach wire to generator "FLD" terminal [subpar. c.(3) above].

e. Corrosion Prevention and Waterproofing Procedure. Clean generator terminals and contacting surfaces. Tighten securely and paint with red synthetic paint (glyptal, 52-P-8057-710). If not available, use ignition insulating compound (52-C-3099-20). CAUTION: *Do not paint "V" in pulley.*

128. GENERATOR REGULATOR.

a. Description. The generator regulator is a three-unit type, mounted in engine compartment on left air duct panel above and to the left of the engine. The regulator unit contains a cut-out relay which automatically opens and closes the circuit between generator and battery as needs require; voltage regulator which controls generator voltage; and a current regulator which controls generator amperage out-put.

b. Removal (fig. 92).

(1) DISCONNECT WIRES. Remove ground strap from battery terminal. Remove nuts and lock washers from "ARMATURE," "FIELD," and "BATTERY" terminals on regulator and remove wires. Remove screw and lock washer attaching ground wire to regulator.

(2) REMOVE REGULATOR. Remove four nuts and lock washers from bolts attaching regulator to left air duct panel and remove regulator (G85-33-02250). Notice that internal-external toothed lock washers are used between regulator legs and panel.

c. Installation (fig. 92).

(1) INSTALL REGULATOR. Install regulator on left air duct panel with terminals down and attach with four bolts, nuts, and lock washers. Be sure internal-external toothed lock washers are installed between regulator legs and panel. Tighten nuts securely.

(2) CONNECT WIRES. Install wires on terminals as follows, and attach with nuts and lock washers:

"BATTERY" terminal—No. 8-yellow
"ARMATURE" terminal—No. 8-tan—red and black cross tracer
"FIELD" terminal—No. 14-black—red check
"GROUND" terminal—No. 14-black

(3) POLARIZE GENERATOR. Correct polarization as described in paragraph 127d.

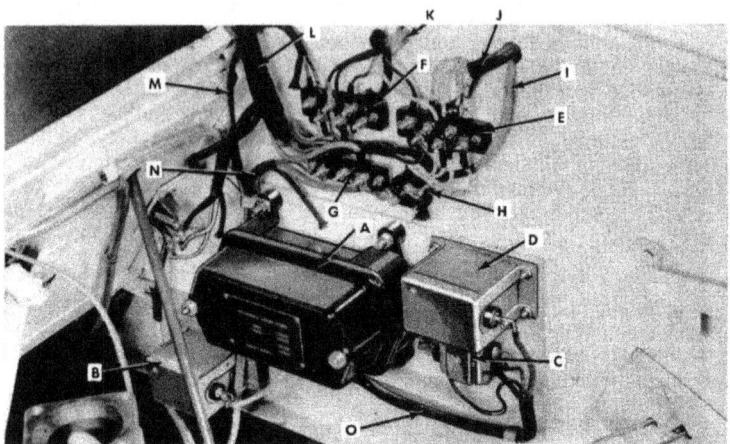

PRIOR TO CHASSIS SERIAL NO. 14779

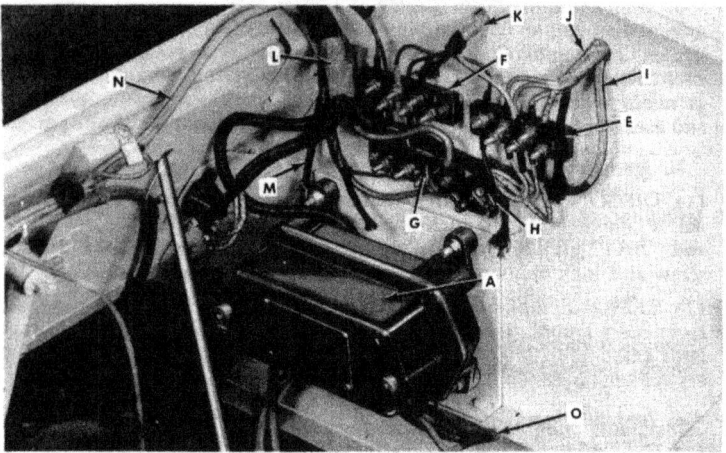

AFTER CHASSIS SERIAL NO. 14778

A GENERATOR REGULATOR
B BATTERY CIRCUIT FILTER
C FIELD CIRCUIT FILTER
D ARMATURE CIRCUIT FILTER
E JUNCTION BLOCK—FRONT
F JUNCTION BLOCK—REAR
G JUNCTION BLOCK—3 POST
H HORN CIRCUIT BREAKER
I HORN WIRING HARNESS
J HEADLIGHT WIRING HARNESS
K STOP AND TAILLIGHT WIRING HARNESS
L INSTRUMENT PANEL WIRING HARNESS
M JUNCTION BLOCK TO STOP LIGHT SWITCH WIRING HARNESS
N JUNCTION BLOCK TO STARTER AND COIL WIRING HARNESS
O GENERATOR TO GENERATOR REGULATOR AND JUNCTION BLOCK WIRING HARNESS

RA PD 333250

Figure 92—Generator Regulator and Filters Installation

Battery and Lighting System

d. Regulator Cover. Voltage regulators may become inoperative in service due to dust and moisture collecting inside regulator cover. A check of this condition discloses that improper sealing of gasket between regulator cover and base is a major contributing factor. Improper tightening of knurled nut on stud that secures cover against gasket and base may permit dust and moisture to enter around gasket. Nut will not tighten properly against cover if stud threads are heavily plated or stud shoulder is too high. To check for and correct this condition, proceed as follows:

(1) Clean interior surface of regulator cover. Paint interior of cover with red synthetic paint (glyptal, 52-P-8057-710) and allow to dry.

(2) Seal regulator cover and regulator stud plate with caulking compound (52-C-3086-200).

(3) Press firmly on each end of assembled regulator cover after tightening knurled nut securely. If cover can be moved at all, it is evident that nut is bottomed without compressing cover gasket.

(4) Remove knurled nut and check stud threads for heavy plating or other accumulated material which might prevent proper tightening. Clean threads if necessary, using a $1/4$-28 threading die.

(5) Install stud. Check condition of cover gasket and replace if damaged. Position cover on regulator, thread knurled nut on stud, tightening firmly by hand. Finally, press firmly on ends of cover to see that it seats properly.

(6) Paint terminals and regulator with red synthetic paint (glyptal, 52-P-8057-710). If not available, use ignition insulating compound (52-C-3099-20).

Section XXIV
Battery and Lighting System

129. GENERAL.

a. Description. Six-volt battery is mounted at right side of engine in engine compartment. Ground strap connects negative (−) post of battery to frame side rail. Battery to starter cable connects positive (+) post of battery to starter switch terminal. Engine ground strap is connected to hand brake cross shaft bracket and engine rear support bracket. Lighting system comprises headlights, blackout driving light, blackout marker lights, service stop and taillight, and blackout stop and taillight. Proper functioning of lighting system is dependent upon keeping battery properly charged, terminals and connections tight and free from corrosion, and lenses clean. Blackened lamps also reduce the efficiency of the lighting system. The entire lighting system is controlled by lighting switch on the instrument panel. System is protected by a thermal-type circuit breaker mounted on back of lighting switch.

Maintenance Instructions

b. Corrosion Prevention and Waterproofing.

(1) BATTERY AND CABLES. Whenever battery, battery cable, or ground strap is removed, or in the event of corrosion at terminals, clean battery posts and terminals thoroughly. Clean cable terminals by immersing in solution of ammonia and water. Scrape battery posts lightly to remove loose corrosion, then apply solution of ammonia and water. After connecting cables to battery, tighten firmly, then paint with red synthetic paint (glyptal, 52-P-8057-710).

(2) BATTERY TRAYS. Whenever battery is removed, examine battery trays, supports, adjacent air lines, and hull under battery for corrosion. Vehicles after chassis serial No. 4402 have parts in proximity to battery painted with acid-resisting paint. Earlier vehicles should be so treated at earliest opportunity. Remove all corrosion, then treat battery trays, supports, adjacent air lines, and hull under battery with acid-resisting black paint (52-P-100). If acid-resisting paint is not available, use synthetic red paint (glyptal, 52-P-8057-710).

(3) JUNCTION BLOCKS. Whenever wiring at lighting junction blocks is disconnected, or if corrosion is evident, thoroughly clean connecting parts. After connecting terminals to junction block, paint block and terminals with red synthetic paint (glyptal, 52-P-8057-710) or, if not available, use ignition insulating compound (52-C-3099-20).

(4) LIGHTS (EXTERIOR). Before installing lights, remove old caulking compound from mounting and wiring holes in deck. Apply a liberal quantity of caulking compound (52-C-3086) around hole, then install light. After pressing wiring grommet into place, build up a bead of caulking compound around grommet and wire. Junction of doors, lens, and body of lights may be sealed with nonhygroscopic adhesive tape (27-T-185-212) or (27-T-185-224), which can also be used for sealing exterior wiring to lamps. Paint tape with ignition insulating compound (52-C-3099-20), avoiding painting glass. Metal surfaces inside lights can be painted with red synthetic paint (glyptal, 52-P-8057-710) or with ignition insulating compound (52-C-3099-20), providing paint is not permitted to touch lamp base, contact, or glass. Terminals inside lights should be cleaned and coated with a thin film of petrolatum before installation.

130. BATTERY AND CABLES.

a. Description. Battery is an electrochemical device for converting electrical energy into chemical energy. Battery governs voltage of electrical system, provides energy for starter and ignition system while engine is being started, and supplies energy, under limited conditions, to lights and other electrical accessories. Battery and cables are accessible in engine compartment, after lifting engine compartment hatch cover.

b. Testing, Charging, and Filling.

(1) TEST SPECIFIC GRAVITY OF ELECTROLYTE. Using an accurate hydrometer, check each battery cell for specific gravity of electro-

Battery and Lighting System

lyte. Fully charged battery should test between 1.275 and 1.300 under normal operating conditions. If reading is below 1.225, charge battery or replace with a fully charged battery.

(2) TEST CELL CONDITION. All cells of battery must have specific gravity reading of 1.225 or more to make this test. Test high-rate discharge condition of each cell, using universal battery tester according to instructions accompanying instrument. If condition of any two cells varies more than 30 percent, battery is faulty and must be replaced. Refer to paragraph 46*b*. (cold weather) and 47*e*. (hot weather) for maintenance of battery during unusual operating conditions.

(3) FILLING BATTERY. Remove caps from battery cells and inspect level of electrolyte at intervals specified in Preventive Maintenance Services section. Electrolyte must cover top of plates, but not exceed a level of $3/8$ inch above plates. Add pure distilled water as necessary. If distilled water is not available, use clean rain water or melted snow—or any water fit to drink. However, continuous use of water with high mineral content will eventually cause damage to battery, and should be avoided.

(4) CHARGING. When tests indicate necessity for charging battery, use a charging rate of 1.0 ampere per positive plate per cell—a rate of 9.0 amperes for 19 plate battery, or 12.0 amperes for 23 plate battery. Continue charging for 2 hours after specific gravity and terminal voltage shows no further rise. Do not permit temperature of electrolyte to rise above 110°F.

c. Battery Removal (fig. 93). Loosen cable terminal bolt nuts. Spread terminals slightly and lift from battery posts. Remove two hold-down rod nuts from rods, then remove hold-down tray from top of battery. Using battery lifter strap, raise battery straight up. Avoid tilting battery and spilling electrolyte during lifting.

d. Battery Installation (fig. 93.) Test each cell of battery as described in subparagraph **b.** above. Clean terminals and contacting surfaces of battery and cables, making sure all corrosion is removed. Cable terminals may be cleaned by immersing in a solution of ammonia and water. Position battery on tray, using battery lifter strap to lower into position. Positive (+) post (large diameter post) must be to front of vehicle. Position hold-down tray over battery with hold-down rods projecting through tray. Install hold-down rod nut on each rod and tighten firmly. Connect cables to battery, tightening terminal clamp bolt nuts firmly.

e. Cables. To determine if cables are satisfactory, test as described in paragraph 124*b*. Clean cable terminals of corrosion by immersing in a solution of ammonia and water. Battery posts and other parts to which cables connect must also be clean and free from corrosion. Use ammonia and water to clean battery posts. Scrape or wire-brush steel parts to which cables attach. After cables are connected, paint terminals as described in paragraph 129*b*.(1) above.

TM 9-802
130

Maintenance Instructions

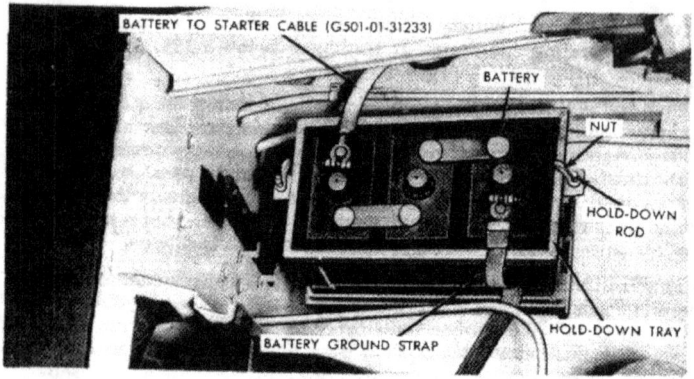

Figure 93—Battery Installed

(1) BATTERY GROUND STRAP.

(a) Removal. Loosen clamp bolt nut on ground strap terminal at battery, then lift terminal from battery post. Remove nut, washers, and bolt which attach strap to frame, then remove strap.

(b) Installation. Position ground strap to battery post and frame, threading strap through battery tray. Connect strap to frame with bolt, washers, and nut, making sure bolting surfaces are clean. Connect cable terminal to battery post, tightening clamp bolt nut firmly.

(2) BATTERY TO STARTER CABLE (FIG. 93).

(a) Removal. Loosen clamp bolt nut on terminal at battery and lift terminal off battery post. Remove nut and washer attaching cable terminal to starter switch stud, then remove cable from switch. Remove screws which attach cable clips to air duct panels, remove clips, and remove cable from vehicle.

(b) Installation. Position cable terminal on starter switch stud, install washer and nut, and tighten nut firmly. Position cable terminal on battery post, then tighten terminal clamp bolt nut firmly. Install cable clips and attaching screws.

(3) ENGINE GROUND STRAP.

(a) Removal. Remove bolt and lock washer which attach strap to hand brake cross shaft bracket. Remove bolt, washers, and nut which connect strap to engine rear support bracket, then remove strap.

(b) Installation. Make sure all contact surfaces are clean, connect engine ground strap to engine rear support bracket with bolt, washers, and nut. Connect strap to hand brake cross shaft bracket with bolt, lock washer, and flat washer, tightening bolt firmly.

252

Battery and Lighting System

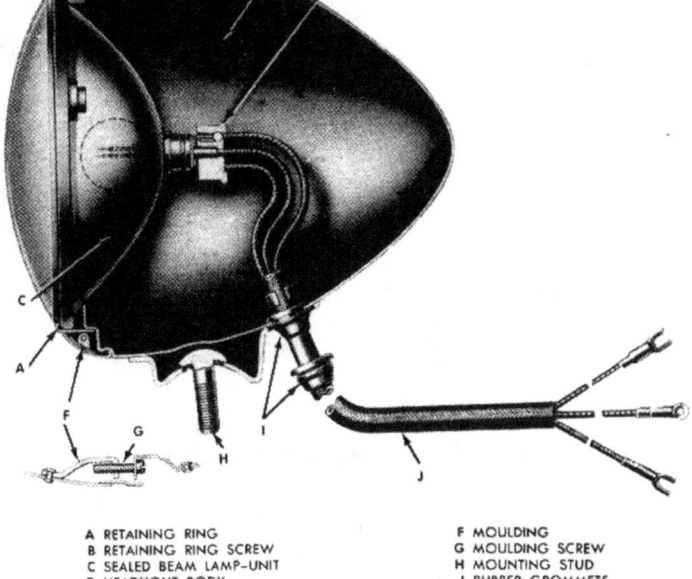

A RETAINING RING
B RETAINING RING SCREW
C SEALED BEAM LAMP-UNIT
D HEADLIGHT BODY
E WIRING PLUG

F MOULDING
G MOULDING SCREW
H MOUNTING STUD
I RUBBER GROMMETS
J WIRING ASSEMBLY

RA PD 333189

Figure 94—Headlight Assembly (G501-70-01932)

131. HEADLIGHTS.

a. Description. Headlights mounted on front corners of front deck are double filament sealed beam type (fig. 94). Headlights are controlled by lighting switch and foot-operated dimmer switch. Dimmer switch, which selects high or low headlight beam, is operative only when lighting switch is in service position. Headlights must be accurately aimed to insure effective headlight beams.

b. Aiming Adjustment (figs. 95 and 96).

(1) POSITION VEHICLE. Position vehicle on level ground, 25 feet from a vertical surface, such as a wall, with vehicle centerline perpendicular to surface. Measure height of headlight center from ground, then draw a horizontal line on surface at this height. Project centerline of vehicle and draw a vertical centerline on surface. Measure distance between light centers, divide this distance equally on both sides of center mark, and draw two vertical lines at these points, representing headlight centers.

TM 9-802
131

Maintenance Instructions

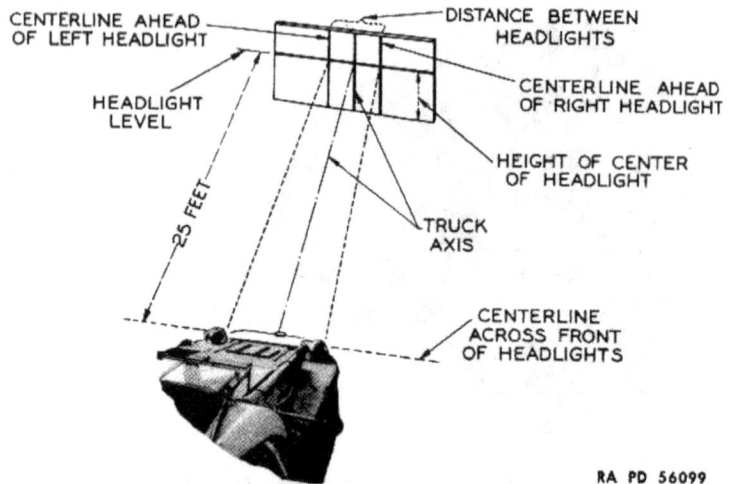

Figure 95—Headlight Aiming Chart

(2) ADJUST PATTERN. Turn on headlight high beam. Cover one light while adjusting other. From inside front compartment, loosen headlight nut and aim light so that beam pattern registers with horizontal and vertical lines as shown in figure 96. Tighten headlight nut firmly, making sure adjustment is not disturbed while tightening nut. Adjust other headlight in same manner.

c. Lamp-unit Removal (fig. 94). When lamp-unit burns out, entire unit must be replaced, since lamp, lens, and reflector are sealed as a unit. Remove moulding screw at bottom of light and remove moulding. Remove three screws which attach retaining ring to headlight body, then remove retaining ring. Pull sealed beam lamp-unit from light body, disconnecting wiring plug from unit as unit is removed.

d. Lamp-unit Installation (fig. 94). Connect wiring plug to sealed beam lamp-unit, then position unit in headlight body. Position retaining ring to unit, then attach ring to light body with three screws. Install moulding with clip engaging slot at top of light body. Install moulding screw at bottom, and tighten firmly.

e. Headlight Removal. From inside front compartment, disconnect headlight wiring from junction block, then remove nut and washers from light mounting stud. Loosen rubber grommet from deck panel, then pull wiring through as headlight is lifted from deck and removed.

f. Headlight Installation. Position headlight on vehicle with mounting stud inserted in hole in mounting plate. Position wiring through hole in deck panel, then press rubber grommet into place in deck panel. From inside front compartment, connect headlight wiring

Battery and Lighting System

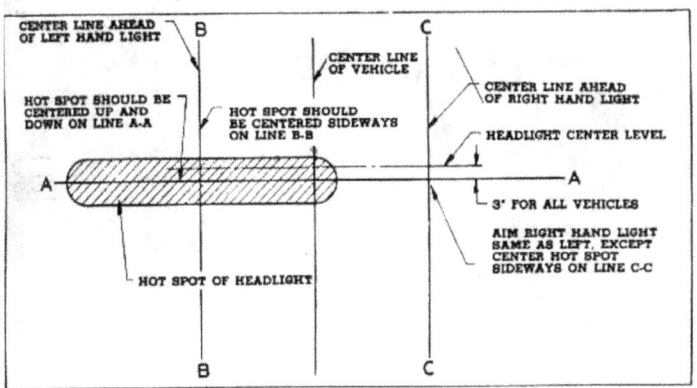

Figure 96—Headlight Aiming Pattern

to junction block, making sure that wires are connected to wires of same color in harness. Install washers and nut on mounting stud, then adjust beam pattern (subpar. *b.* above).

132. BLACKOUT DRIVING LIGHT.

a. Description. Blackout driving light (fig. 97) is mounted on left front corner of front deck, to the left of left headlight. Light is controlled by "BO DRIVE" switch on instrument panel, which is operative only when lighting switch is in blackout position. Light is equipped with a lamp-unit consisting of lens, reflector, lamp, and beam visor, sealed as a unit.

b. Lamp-unit Removal (fig. 97). Remove door screw from bottom of light door, pull door out at bottom, and raise lamp-unit upward to free clip at top of light body. Loosen two screws and disconnect two wires at back of lamp-unit. Using a screwdriver, loosen three springs attaching ring and lamp-unit in door to separate ring, door, and lamp-unit.

c. Lamp-unit Installation (fig. 97). Position light door to lamp-unit with split in door at bottom of lens. Position ring to back of lamp-unit and force three springs under flange of door. Connect wire to lamp-unit, then connect ground wire to retaining ring, tightening screws firmly. Install lamp-unit in light body with clip engaged in slot in top of light. Install door screw at bottom of light.

d. Driving Light Removal. Disconnect wire at junction block inside front compartment. Remove nut and washers from light mounting stud at bracket. Pull wire up through deck panel, after loosening rubber grommet.

Maintenance Instructions

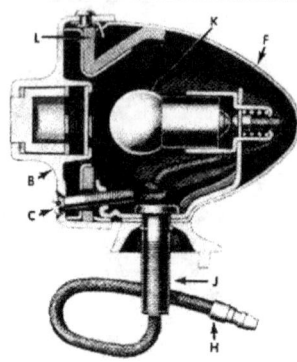
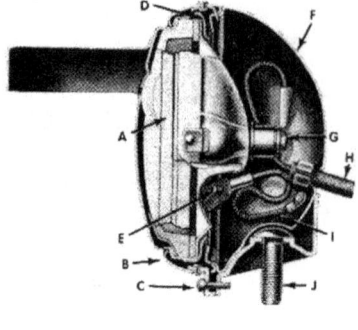

BLACKOUT MARKER LIGHT
(M001-02-14509)

A BLACKOUT DRIVING SEALED LAMP–UNIT
 (M001-01-07347)
B DOOR ASSEMBLY
C DOOR SCREW
D RING ASSEMBLY
E GROUND WIRE SCREW
F BODY ASSEMBLY

BLACKOUT DRIVING LIGHT
(G121-03-67632)

G TERMINAL SCREW
H WIRE ASSEMBLY
I GROUND WIRE
J MOUNTING STUD
K LAMP
L DOOR GASKET (G150-01-94148)

RA PD 333190

Figure 97—Blackout Marker and Driving Lights

e. Driving Light Installation. Position light on deck with mounting stud in mounting bracket, then install washers and nut. Insert wire through hole in deck, then press rubber grommet into place in deck panel. From inside front compartment, connect wire at junction block. Position beam visor in a horizontal position, pointing straight ahead of vehicle, then hold lamp while tightening nut firmly.

133. BLACKOUT MARKER LIGHTS.

a. Description. Blackout marker lights (fig. 97), mounted on front deck at side of each headlight, are illuminated only when lighting switch is in blackout position. Blackout marker lights incorporate a specially designed lens and a colored filter which diffuses the light beam.

b. Door, Gasket, and Lamp Removal (fig. 97). Remove screw at bottom of light door. Pull door out at bottom, then lift up to disengage door clip from light body. Remove gasket from inside door. Push lamp inward and turn counterclockwise to remove lamp from socket.

c. Door, Gasket, and Lamp Installation (fig. 97). Push lamp into socket and turn clockwise, then test lamp by turning on lighting switch. Install gasket in door. Install door on light body, with clip on door engaging slot in top of body. Install door screw at bottom of door, tightening screw firmly.

TM 9-802
133-134

Battery and Lighting System

d. Marker Light Removal. From inside front compartment, disconnect wire at connector. Remove nut and lock washer from mounting stud. Remove blackout marker light by lifting straight up from deck.

e. Marker Light Installation. Position marker light on vehicle with wire and mounting stud in hole in deck, and with locating dowel on bracket in dowel hole in deck. From inside front compartment, install lock washer and nut on mounting stud, tightening firmly. Connect wire at connector.

134. STOP AND TAILLIGHT.

a. Description. Stop and taillights, mounted on rear deck, consist of two units. The left-hand light incorporates a combination service stop and tail lamp-unit in the upper portion and a blackout tail lamp-unit in the lower portion (fig. 98). Right-hand light contains a blackout stop lamp-unit in the upper portion and a blackout tail lamp-unit in the lower portion. The beams of stop and taillights are diffused in such a manner as to be invisible from above.

b. Lamp-unit Removal (fig. 98). Remove two screws which attach door to light body and remove door. Remove each lamp unit by pulling outward from body of light.

c. Lamp-unit Installation (fig. 98). Install lamp-unit into body in correct position. Lower units on both sides are marked "BLACKOUT TAIL SIGNAL," upper right-hand unit is marked "BLACKOUT STOP SIGNAL," while upper left-hand unit is unidentified. Position door

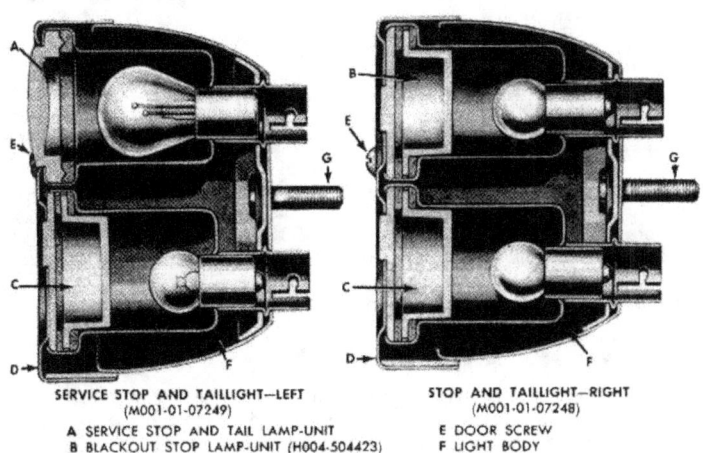

SERVICE STOP AND TAILLIGHT—LEFT
(M001-01-07249)
  A SERVICE STOP AND TAIL LAMP-UNIT
  B BLACKOUT STOP LAMP-UNIT (H004-504423)
  C BLACKOUT TAIL LAMP-UNIT (G085-33-00220)
  D LIGHT DOOR

STOP AND TAILLIGHT—RIGHT
(M001-01-07248)
  E DOOR SCREW
  F LIGHT BODY
  G MOUNTING STUD

RA PD 333191

Figure 98—Blackout and Service Stop and Taillight Assemblies

TM 9-802
134-136

Maintenance Instructions

over lamp-unit and body and install two screws. Tighten screws sufficiently to hold door to body.

d. Light Removal (fig. 98). Remove wiring connectors from sockets at back of light by pressing inward on connector, turning counterclockwise, and withdrawing from socket. Remove two nuts and lock washers from mounting studs, then pull light from bracket.

e. Light Installation (fig. 98). Position light to bracket with studs in bracket holes. Install lock washers and nuts, tightening nuts firmly. Insert wiring connectors in sockets, press inward, and turn clockwise to lock in position. Connect wires in correct position; left-hand light—double contact plug in upper socket, single contact plug in lower socket; right-hand light—No. 16 black-red tracer in upper socket, No. 16 white in lower socket. Slide connector sleeve back over loom to determine color of wire. Check operation of lights to make sure lights are properly connected.

Section XXV
Wiring, Harnesses, and Circuits

135. GENERAL.

a. The electrical system of these vehicles is six-volt type. Units used in various electrical systems are described in other sections of this manual as follows:

```
Ignition system .................................Pars.  96 through 102
Starting system ................................Pars. 123 through 125
Generating system .............................Pars. 126 through 128
Battery and lighting system ...................Pars. 129 through 134
Radio noise suppression system ...............Pars. 138 through 142
Instruments, gages, and switches..............Pars. 143 through 151
```

b. Circuits. Electrical system of these vehicles is divided into the following circuits: Ignition, starting, generating, lighting, fuel gage, and horn. Circuit diagrams (figs. 99 and 100) illustrate in a schematic manner the various electrical circuits throughout the vehicle. Each circuit can be readily traced with a conventional test light or buzzer equipment to establish continuity of circuit.

136. WIRING AND HARNESSES.

a. Location. General arrangement of various wiring harnesses and electrical units is illustrated in figures 99 and 100. Each harness is located to provide maximum accessibility for replacement or other service.

b. Splices. Whenever it is necessary to splice a wire, or repair one that is broken, always use solder to bond the splices. Use insulating tape profusely to cover all bare wires.

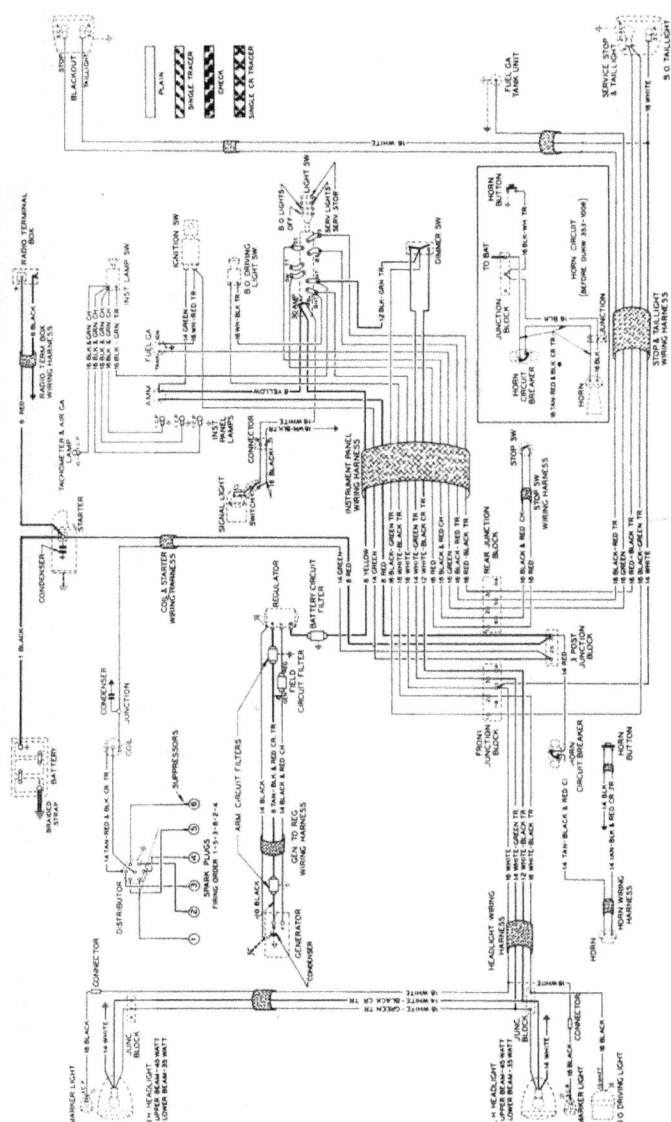

Figure 99—General Electrical Circuit Diagram (Prior to Chassis Serial No. 14779)

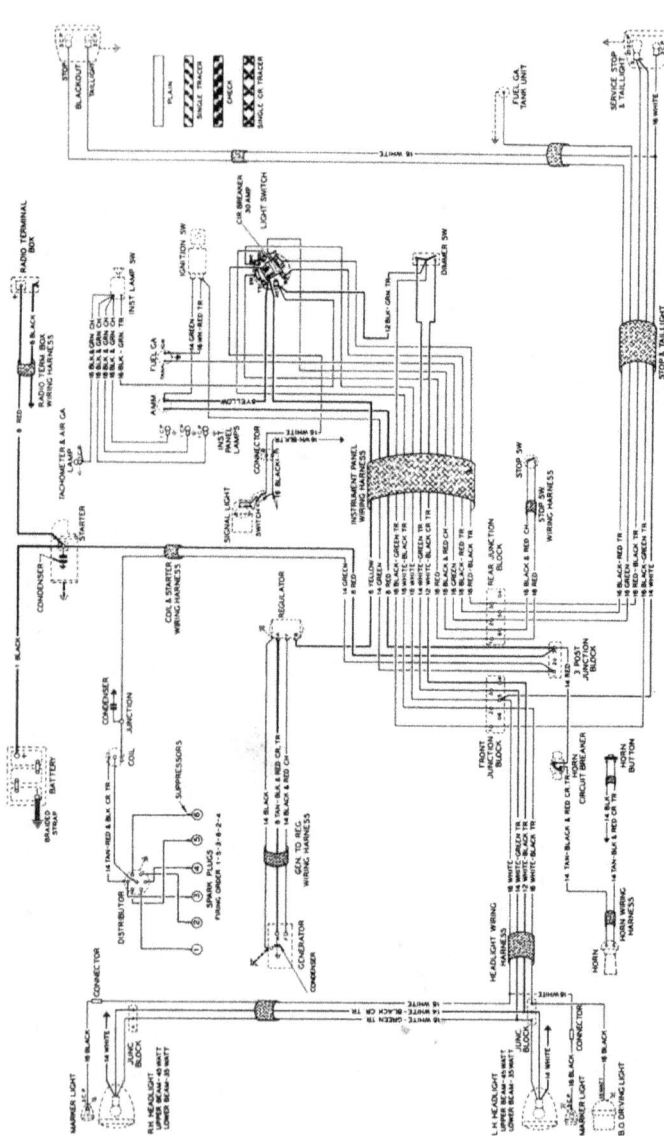

Figure 100—General Electrical Circuit Diagram (After Chassis Serial No. 14778) RA PD 337251

TM 9-802
136

Wiring, Harnesses, and Circuits

c. Identification. Each wire can readily be identified by its size, color, and pattern. Each wire size and color, also pattern design, is shown in figures 99 and 100. Whenever practical, a group of wires are arranged into harnesses. Wires which are included in a harness are indicated by showing them as passing through a loom (figs. 99 and 100). In several instances it has not been possible or practical to show several short wires at instrument panel within the cab wiring harness loom.

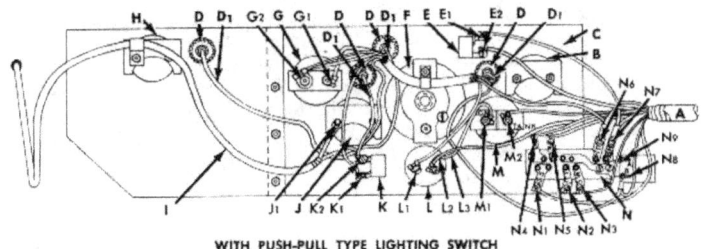

WITH PUSH-PULL TYPE LIGHTING SWITCH

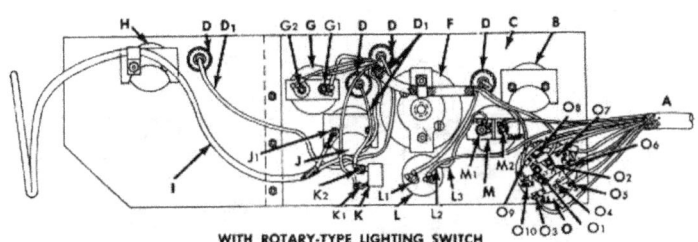

WITH ROTARY-TYPE LIGHTING SWITCH

- **A** INSTRUMENT PANEL WIRING HARNESS
- **B** THERMO GAGE
- **C** INSTRUMENT PANEL
- **D** INSTRUMENT PANEL LIGHT
  - D_1 NO. 16 BLACK—GREEN CH.
- **E** BLACKOUT DRIVING LIGHT SWITCH (PRIOR TO CHASSIS SERIAL NO. 14779)
  - E_1 NO. 16 WHITE—BLACK TR.
  - E_2 NO. 16 WHITE—BLACK TR.
- **F** SPEEDOMETER
- **G** AMMETER
  - G_1 NO. 8 RED
  - G_2 NO. 8 YELLOW AND NO. 14 GREEN
- **H** TANK PRESSURE AIR GAGE
- **I** COMPASS WIRING HARNESS
- **J** OIL GAGE
  - J_1 NO. 16 BLACK (COMPASS GROUND)
- **K** INSTRUMENT LIGHT SWITCH
  - K_1 NO. 16 BLACK—GREEN TR.
  - K_2 NO. 16 BLACK—GREEN CH.
- **L** IGNITION SWITCH
  - L_1 NO. 14 GREEN
  - L_2 NO. 14 GREEN
  - L_3 NO. 16 WHITE—RED TR.
- **M** GAS GAGE
  - M_1 NO. 16 WHITE—RED TR.
  - M_2 NO. 16 GREEN
- **N** LIGHTING SWITCH (PRIOR TO CHASSIS SERIAL NO. 14779)
  - N_1 "S S" NO. 16 BLACK—RED CH.
  - N_2 "T T" VACANT
  - N_3 "S W" NO. 16 RED
  - N_4 "S" NO. 16 RED—BLACK TR.
  - N_5 "B S" NO. 16 BLACK—RED TR.
  - N_6 "H T" NO. 12 AND 16 BLACK—GREEN TR.
  - N_7 "B H T" NO. 16 WHITE WITH NO 16 WHITE—BLACK TR.
  - N_8 "B" NO. 8 YELLOW
  - N_9 "A" NO. 16 WHITE
- **O** LIGHTING SWITCH (AFTER CHASSIS SERIAL NO. 14778)
  - O_1 "B A T" NO. 8 YELLOW
  - O_2 "A" NO. 16 WHITE
  - O_3 "B S" NO. 16 BLACK—RED TR.
  - O_4 "S S" NO. 16 BLACK—RED CH.
  - O_5 "S" NO. 16 RED—BLACK TR.
  - O_6 "B O D" NO. 16 WHITE—BLACK TR.
  - O_7 "B H T" NO. 16 WHITE
  - O_8 "S W" NO. 16 RED
  - O_9 "T T" VACANT
  - O_{10} "H T" NO. 12 AND 16 BLACK—GREEN TR.

RA PD 337156

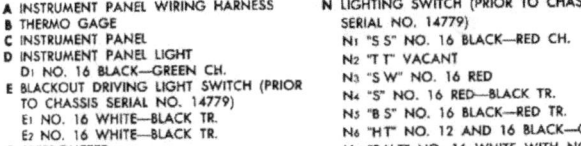

Figure 101—Instrument Panel Wiring Connections

Maintenance Instructions

(1) METHOD OF IDENTIFICATION. Any individual wire within a harness can be determined by referring to figures 102 through 111. As an example: If wire is identified as being E-1 at one end, the opposite end will be E-2. Whenever one or more wires are spliced into "E" circuit, outlet ends of these wires would then be identified as E-3 or E-4. Wire size, color, circuit, and terminal connection of each wire is listed below each wiring harness illustration.

d. Waterproofing. Whenever it is necessary to disconnect any wiring at junction blocks or other electrical unit, it is important that necessary precautions be taken to prevent corrosion formation after reinstallation. At time of installation, tighten terminal securely. *Bear in mind that a clean and tight connection is a good connection.* After tightening, apply a coat of gray insulating enamel (52-E-5210) or, if not available, use red synthetic paint (glyptal, 52-P-8057-710) or ignition insulating compound (52-C-3099-20). Waterproofing as described will effectively retard corrosion and prevent moisture formation.

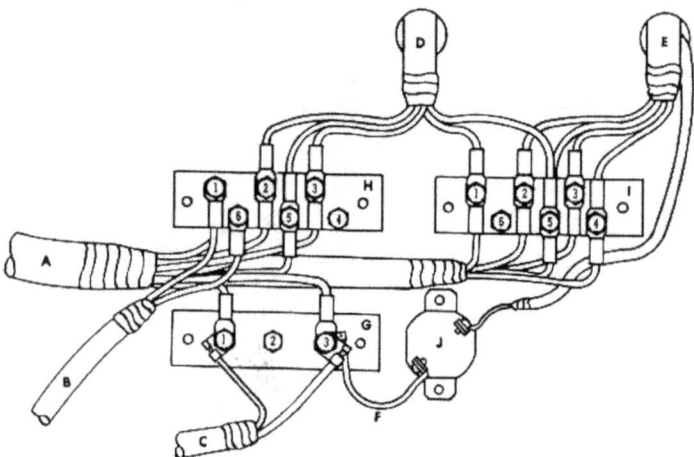

- **A** INSTRUMENT PANEL WIRING HARNESS
- **B** JUNCTION BLOCK TO STOP LIGHT SWITCH WIRING HARNESS
- **C** JUNCTION BLOCK TO STARTER AND COIL WIRING HARNESS
- **D** STOP AND TAILLIGHT WIRING HARNESS
- **E** HEADLIGHT WIRING HARNESS
- **F** HORN CIRCUIT BREAKER TO JUNCTION BLOCK WIRE (NO. 14 RED)
- **G** JUNCTION BLOCK—3 POST
  - 1—NO. 14 GREEN
  - 2—VACANT
  - 3—NO. 8 RED
- **H** JUNCTION BLOCK—REAR
  - 1—NO. 16 RED
  - 2—NO. 16 GREEN
  - 3—NO. 16 RED—BLACK TR.
  - 4—VACANT
  - 5—NO. 16 BLACK—RED. TR.
  - 6—NO. 16 BLACK—RED CH.
- **I** JUNCTION BLOCK—FRONT
  - 1—NO. 16 BLACK—GREEN TR.
  - 2—NO. 16 WHITE—BLACK TR.
  - 3—NO. 14 WHITE—GREEN TR.
  - 4—NO. 12 WHITE—BLACK CR. TR.
  - 5—NOS. 14 AND 16 WHITE
  - 6— VACANT
- **J** HORN CIRCUIT BREAKER
  - J1 NO. 14 RED
  - J2 NO. 14 TAN-RED AND BLACK CR. TR.

RA PD 333254

Figure 102—Wiring Harness Connections at Junction Blocks and Horn Circuit Breaker

TM 9-802
136

Wiring, Harnesses, and Circuits

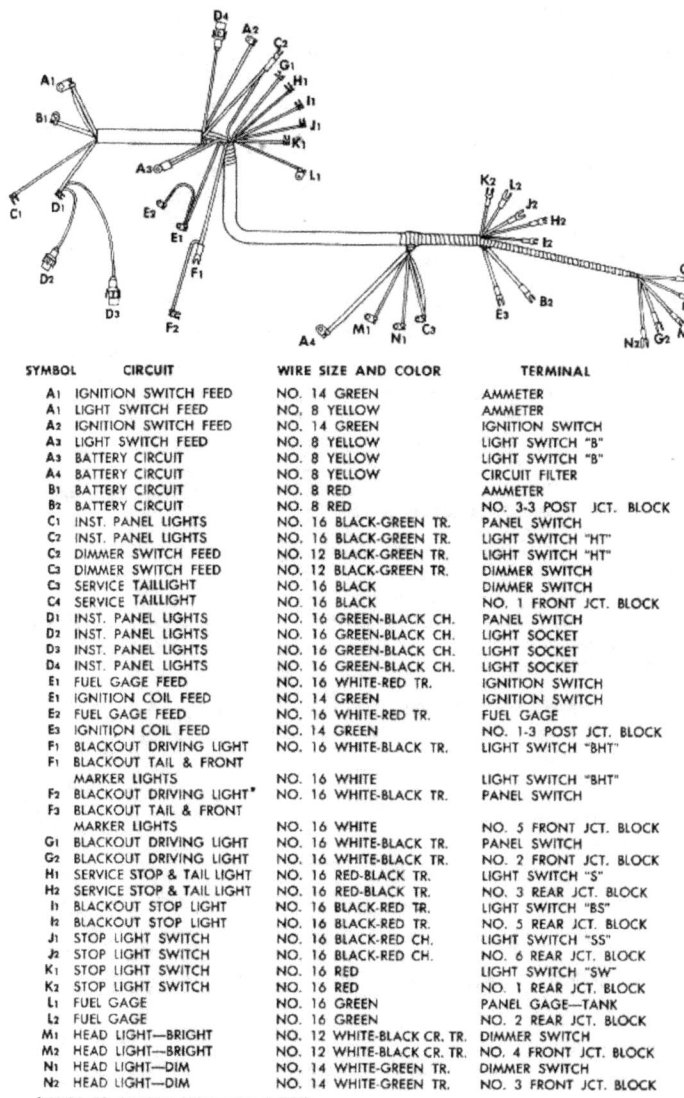

SYMBOL	CIRCUIT	WIRE SIZE AND COLOR	TERMINAL
A1	IGNITION SWITCH FEED	NO. 14 GREEN	AMMETER
A1	LIGHT SWITCH FEED	NO. 8 YELLOW	AMMETER
A2	IGNITION SWITCH FEED	NO. 14 GREEN	IGNITION SWITCH
A3	LIGHT SWITCH FEED	NO. 8 YELLOW	LIGHT SWITCH "B"
A3	BATTERY CIRCUIT	NO. 8 YELLOW	LIGHT SWITCH "B"
A4	BATTERY CIRCUIT	NO. 8 YELLOW	CIRCUIT FILTER
B1	BATTERY CIRCUIT	NO. 8 RED	AMMETER
B2	BATTERY CIRCUIT	NO. 8 RED	NO. 3-3 POST JCT. BLOCK
C1	INST. PANEL LIGHTS	NO. 16 BLACK-GREEN TR.	PANEL SWITCH
C2	INST. PANEL LIGHTS	NO. 16 BLACK-GREEN TR.	LIGHT SWITCH "HT"
C2	DIMMER SWITCH FEED	NO. 12 BLACK-GREEN TR.	LIGHT SWITCH "HT"
C3	DIMMER SWITCH FEED	NO. 12 BLACK-GREEN TR.	DIMMER SWITCH
C3	SERVICE TAILLIGHT	NO. 16 BLACK	DIMMER SWITCH
C4	SERVICE TAILLIGHT	NO. 16 BLACK	NO. 1 FRONT JCT. BLOCK
D1	INST. PANEL LIGHTS	NO. 16 GREEN-BLACK CH.	PANEL SWITCH
D2	INST. PANEL LIGHTS	NO. 16 GREEN-BLACK CH.	LIGHT SOCKET
D3	INST. PANEL LIGHTS	NO. 16 GREEN-BLACK CH.	LIGHT SOCKET
D4	INST. PANEL LIGHTS	NO. 16 GREEN-BLACK CH.	LIGHT SOCKET
E1	FUEL GAGE FEED	NO. 16 WHITE-RED TR.	IGNITION SWITCH
E1	IGNITION COIL FEED	NO. 14 GREEN	IGNITION SWITCH
E2	FUEL GAGE FEED	NO. 16 WHITE-RED TR.	FUEL GAGE
E3	IGNITION COIL FEED	NO. 14 GREEN	NO. 1-3 POST JCT. BLOCK
F1	BLACKOUT DRIVING LIGHT	NO. 16 WHITE-BLACK TR.	LIGHT SWITCH "BHT"
F1	BLACKOUT TAIL & FRONT MARKER LIGHTS	NO. 16 WHITE	LIGHT SWITCH "BHT"
F2	BLACKOUT DRIVING LIGHT*	NO. 16 WHITE-BLACK TR.	PANEL SWITCH
F3	BLACKOUT TAIL & FRONT MARKER LIGHTS	NO. 16 WHITE	NO. 5 FRONT JCT. BLOCK
G1	BLACKOUT DRIVING LIGHT	NO. 16 WHITE-BLACK TR.	PANEL SWITCH
G2	BLACKOUT DRIVING LIGHT	NO. 16 WHITE-BLACK TR.	NO. 2 FRONT JCT. BLOCK
H1	SERVICE STOP & TAIL LIGHT	NO. 16 RED-BLACK TR.	LIGHT SWITCH "S"
H2	SERVICE STOP & TAIL LIGHT	NO. 16 RED-BLACK TR.	NO. 3 REAR JCT. BLOCK
I1	BLACKOUT STOP LIGHT	NO. 16 BLACK-RED TR.	LIGHT SWITCH "BS"
I2	BLACKOUT STOP LIGHT	NO. 16 BLACK-RED TR.	NO. 5 REAR JCT. BLOCK
J1	STOP LIGHT SWITCH	NO. 16 BLACK-RED CH.	LIGHT SWITCH "SS"
J2	STOP LIGHT SWITCH	NO. 16 BLACK-RED CH.	NO. 6 REAR JCT. BLOCK
K1	STOP LIGHT SWITCH	NO. 16 RED	LIGHT SWITCH "SW"
K2	STOP LIGHT SWITCH	NO. 16 RED	NO. 1 REAR JCT. BLOCK
L1	FUEL GAGE	NO. 16 GREEN	PANEL GAGE—TANK
L2	FUEL GAGE	NO. 16 GREEN	NO. 2 REAR JCT. BLOCK
M1	HEAD LIGHT—BRIGHT	NO. 12 WHITE-BLACK CR. TR.	DIMMER SWITCH
M2	HEAD LIGHT—BRIGHT	NO. 12 WHITE-BLACK CR. TR.	NO. 4 FRONT JCT. BLOCK
N1	HEAD LIGHT—DIM	NO. 14 WHITE-GREEN TR.	DIMMER SWITCH
N2	HEAD LIGHT—DIM	NO. 14 WHITE-GREEN TR.	NO. 3 FRONT JCT. BLOCK

*(PRIOR TO CHASSIS SERIAL NO. 14779)

RA PD 337287

Figure 103—Instrument Panel Wiring Harness

TM 9-802
137

Maintenance Instructions

137. WIRING AND HARNESS REPLACEMENT.

a. General. Each individual wire or various harness assemblies can be removed by disconnecting at junction blocks, switches, gages, or other electrical units. Remove clips and grommets necessary to accomplish removal. When wires have been disconnected and clips or grommets removed, the wire or harness can then be completely removed. When installing, locate the wire or harness in its correct position, being sure that clips and grommets are installed. Attach individual wires to the respective unit or junction block terminal. Tighten connections. Apply waterproofing material as directed (par. 136**d**.). *Bear in mind, a clean and tight electrical connection is a good connection.*

b. Instrument Panel Wiring Harness (fig. 103). This harness, identified by a red tracer in the loom, extends from the rear of the instrument panel (fig. 101) through toeboard to the junction blocks on the engine compartment panel (fig. 102), also to the foot-operated dimmer switch. Wiring harness used prior to chassis serial No. 2006 also incorporated two wires which connected to fuel gage circuit breaker; however, the circuit breaker has been eliminated. Wiring at rear of the instrument panel is accessible from the driver's compartment. Raise the engine hatch cover to gain access to the junction blocks (fig. 102) and dimmer switch when replacing harness.

c. Horn to Junction Block Harness (fig. 104). This harness is used prior to chassis serial No. 1006. These vehicles have the horn on the right forward deck. Harness connects horn with junction block under forward deck. Raise the front deck center panel hatch cover and the engine hatch cover to gain access to the harness and junction block connections when replacing harness.

d. Horn and Horn Button Harness (fig. 105). This harness is used after chassis serial No. 1005. These vehicles have the horn located

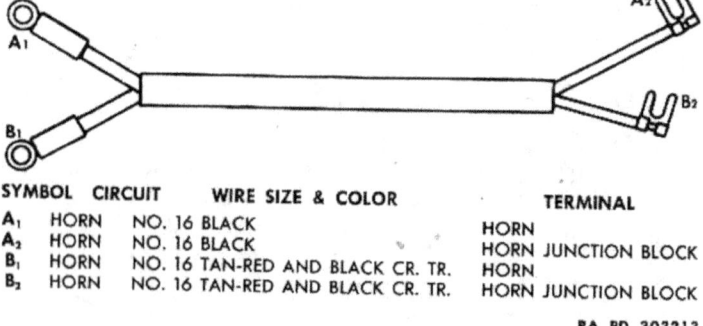

SYMBOL	CIRCUIT	WIRE SIZE & COLOR	TERMINAL
A_1	HORN	NO. 16 BLACK	HORN
A_2	HORN	NO. 16 BLACK	HORN JUNCTION BLOCK
B_1	HORN	NO. 16 TAN-RED AND BLACK CR. TR.	HORN
B_2	HORN	NO. 16 TAN-RED AND BLACK CR. TR.	HORN JUNCTION BLOCK

RA PD 303213

Figure 104—Horn to Junction Block Wiring Harness (Prior to Chassis Serial No. 1006)

Wiring, Harnesses, and Circuits

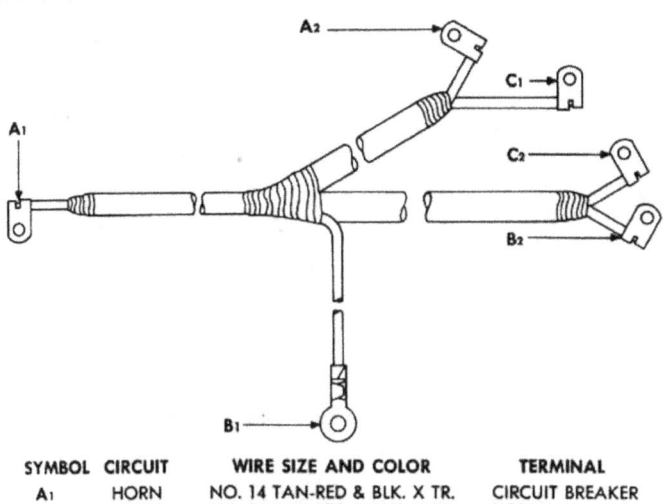

SYMBOL	CIRCUIT	WIRE SIZE AND COLOR	TERMINAL
A_1	HORN	NO. 14 TAN-RED & BLK. X TR.	CIRCUIT BREAKER
A_2	HORN	NO. 14 TAN-RED & BLK. X TR.	HORN
B_2	HORN	NO. 14 BLACK	GROUND
B_2	HORN	NO. 14 BLACK	HORN BUTTON
C_1	HORN	NO. 14 TAN-RED & BLK. X TR.	HORN
C_2	HORN	NO. 14 TAN-RED & BLK. X TR.	HORN BUTTON

RA PD 303166

Figure 105—Horn to Horn Button Wiring Harness (After Chassis Serial No. 1005)

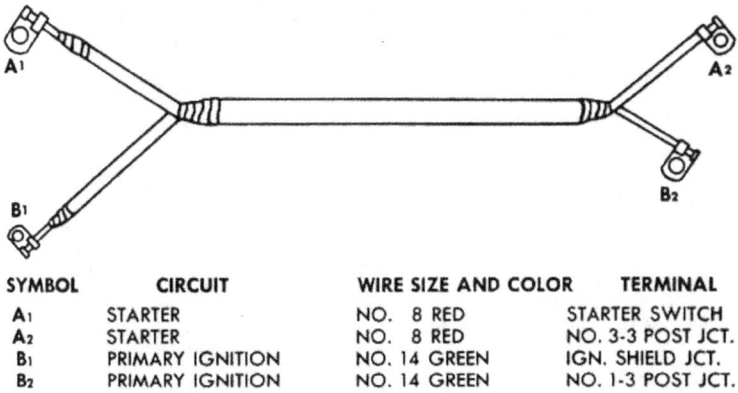

SYMBOL	CIRCUIT	WIRE SIZE AND COLOR	TERMINAL
A_1	STARTER	NO. 8 RED	STARTER SWITCH
A_2	STARTER	NO. 8 RED	NO. 3-3 POST JCT.
B_1	PRIMARY IGNITION	NO. 14 GREEN	IGN. SHIELD JCT.
B_2	PRIMARY IGNITION	NO. 14 GREEN	NO. 1-3 POST JCT.

RA PD 303214

Figure 106—Junction Block to Coil and Starter Wiring Harness

Maintenance Instructions

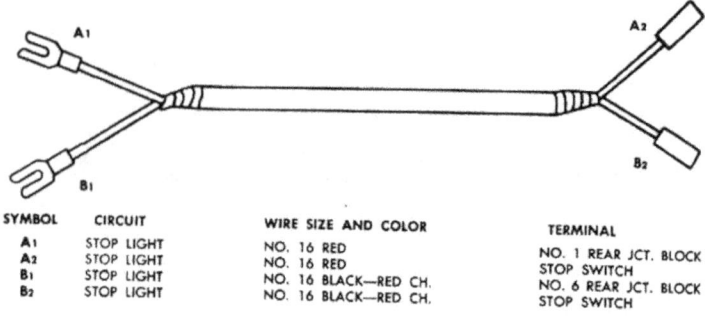

SYMBOL	CIRCUIT	WIRE SIZE AND COLOR	TERMINAL
A₁	STOP LIGHT	NO. 16 RED	NO. 1 REAR JCT. BLOCK
A₂	STOP LIGHT	NO. 16 RED	STOP SWITCH
B₁	STOP LIGHT	NO. 16 BLACK—RED CH.	NO. 6 REAR JCT. BLOCK
B₂	STOP LIGHT	NO. 16 BLACK—RED CH.	STOP SWITCH

RA PD 333184

Figure 107—Junction Block to Stop Light Switch Wiring Harness

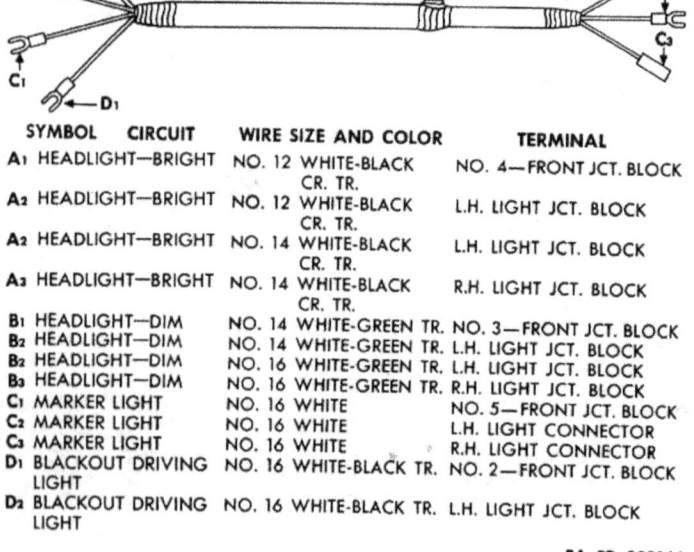

SYMBOL	CIRCUIT	WIRE SIZE AND COLOR	TERMINAL
A₁	HEADLIGHT—BRIGHT	NO. 12 WHITE-BLACK CR. TR.	NO. 4—FRONT JCT. BLOCK
A₂	HEADLIGHT—BRIGHT	NO. 12 WHITE-BLACK CR. TR.	L.H. LIGHT JCT. BLOCK
A₂	HEADLIGHT—BRIGHT	NO. 14 WHITE-BLACK CR. TR.	L.H. LIGHT JCT. BLOCK
A₃	HEADLIGHT—BRIGHT	NO. 14 WHITE-BLACK CR. TR.	R.H. LIGHT JCT. BLOCK
B₁	HEADLIGHT—DIM	NO. 14 WHITE-GREEN TR.	NO. 3—FRONT JCT. BLOCK
B₂	HEADLIGHT—DIM	NO. 14 WHITE-GREEN TR.	L.H. LIGHT JCT. BLOCK
B₂	HEADLIGHT—DIM	NO. 16 WHITE-GREEN TR.	L.H. LIGHT JCT. BLOCK
B₃	HEADLIGHT—DIM	NO. 16 WHITE-GREEN TR.	R.H. LIGHT JCT. BLOCK
C₁	MARKER LIGHT	NO. 16 WHITE	NO. 5—FRONT JCT. BLOCK
C₂	MARKER LIGHT	NO. 16 WHITE	L.H. LIGHT CONNECTOR
C₃	MARKER LIGHT	NO. 16 WHITE	R.H. LIGHT CONNECTOR
D₁	BLACKOUT DRIVING LIGHT	NO. 16 WHITE-BLACK TR.	NO. 2—FRONT JCT. BLOCK
D₂	BLACKOUT DRIVING LIGHT	NO. 16 WHITE-BLACK TR.	L.H. LIGHT JCT. BLOCK

RA PD 303164

Figure 108—Headlight Wiring Harness

Wiring, Harnesses, and Circuits

at front left side of the windshield, and the horn button is mounted on air duct panel at left of driver. Raise the engine hatch cover to gain access to the horn circuit breaker (fig. 102) and harness when replacing harness.

e. Junction Block to Ignition Coil and Starter Harness (fig. 106). This harness extends along the under side of the toeboard to connect the ignition coil and starter switch to the junction blocks on the engine compartment panel (fig. 102). Raise the engine hatch cover to gain access to the harness and connections when replacing harness.

f. Junction Block to Stop Light Switch Harness (fig. 107). This harness extends from the junction blocks (fig. 102) on the engine compartment panel over the top of the left-hand wheelhouse and along the left-hand frame side rail to the stop light switch. Raise the engine hatch cover to gain access to the junction blocks on the engine compartment panel when replacing harness.

g. Headlight Harness (fig. 108). This harness extends from the junction blocks (fig. 102) through the engine compartment panel, and along the top of the floor channel to headlight junction blocks on the under side of forward deck. Raise the front deck center panel hatch cover and the engine hatch cover to gain access to the harness and connections when replacing harness. Headlight wiring used prior to chassis serial No. 1006 also incorporated two wires which extended between horn and horn junction block.

h. Generator to Generator Regulator and Filters Harness (fig. 109). This harness connects the generator, at the left-hand side of the engine, to the regulator and filters, when used, mounted on the

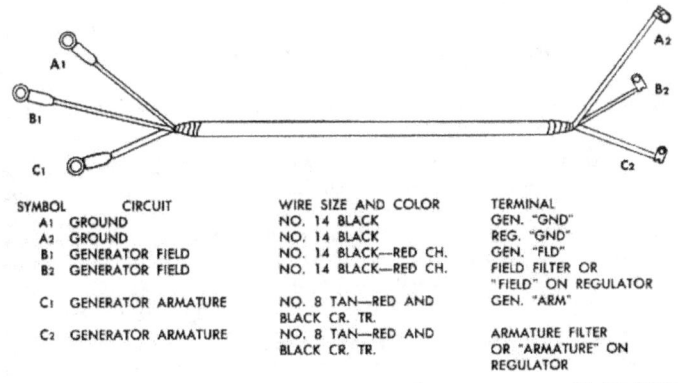

SYMBOL	CIRCUIT	WIRE SIZE AND COLOR	TERMINAL
A1	GROUND	NO. 14 BLACK	GEN. "GND"
A2	GROUND	NO. 14 BLACK	REG. "GND"
B1	GENERATOR FIELD	NO. 14 BLACK—RED CH.	GEN. "FLD"
B2	GENERATOR FIELD	NO. 14 BLACK—RED CH.	FIELD FILTER OR "FIELD" ON REGULATOR
C1	GENERATOR ARMATURE	NO. 8 TAN—RED AND BLACK CR. TR.	GEN. "ARM"
C2	GENERATOR ARMATURE	NO. 8 TAN—RED AND BLACK CR. TR.	ARMATURE FILTER OR "ARMATURE" ON REGULATOR

RA PD 333192

Figure 109—Generator to Generator Regulator and Filters Wiring Harness

TM 9-802
137

Maintenance Instructions

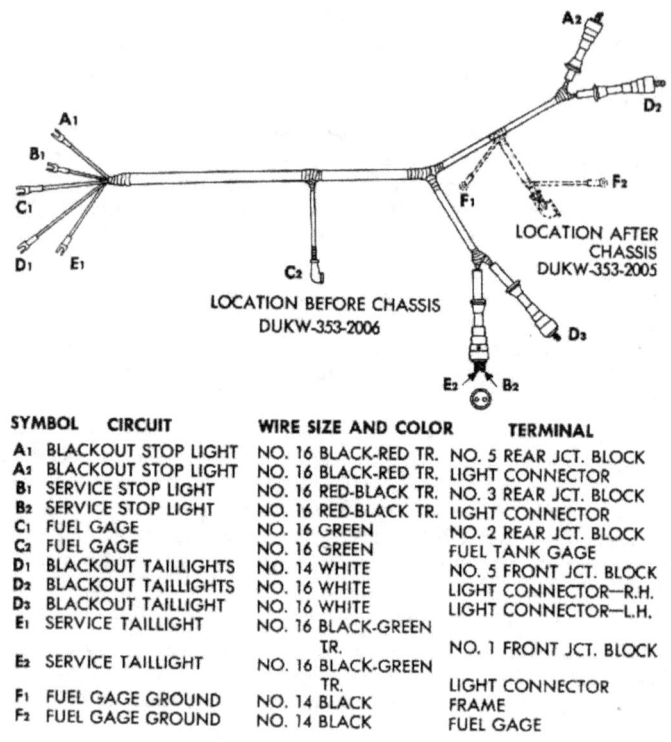

SYMBOL	CIRCUIT	WIRE SIZE AND COLOR	TERMINAL
A_1	BLACKOUT STOP LIGHT	NO. 16 BLACK-RED TR.	NO. 5 REAR JCT. BLOCK
A_2	BLACKOUT STOP LIGHT	NO. 16 BLACK-RED TR.	LIGHT CONNECTOR
B_1	SERVICE STOP LIGHT	NO. 16 RED-BLACK TR.	NO. 3 REAR JCT. BLOCK
B_2	SERVICE STOP LIGHT	NO. 16 RED-BLACK TR.	LIGHT CONNECTOR
C_1	FUEL GAGE	NO. 16 GREEN	NO. 2 REAR JCT. BLOCK
C_2	FUEL GAGE	NO. 16 GREEN	FUEL TANK GAGE
D_1	BLACKOUT TAILLIGHTS	NO. 14 WHITE	NO. 5 FRONT JCT. BLOCK
D_2	BLACKOUT TAILLIGHTS	NO. 16 WHITE	LIGHT CONNECTOR—R.H.
D_3	BLACKOUT TAILLIGHT	NO. 16 WHITE	LIGHT CONNECTOR—L.H.
E_1	SERVICE TAILLIGHT	NO. 16 BLACK-GREEN TR.	NO. 1 FRONT JCT. BLOCK
E_2	SERVICE TAILLIGHT	NO. 16 BLACK-GREEN TR.	LIGHT CONNECTOR
F_1	FUEL GAGE GROUND	NO. 14 BLACK	FRAME
F_2	FUEL GAGE GROUND	NO. 14 BLACK	FUEL GAGE

RA PD 303217

Figure 110—Stop and Taillight Wiring Harness

engine compartment panel. Raise the engine hatch cover to gain access to connecting units when replacing harness.

i. Stop and Taillight Harness (fig. 110). This harness extends from the junction block, on the engine compartment panel, through the panel and rearward along the under side of the left-hand hull coaming and under the rear deck to the stop and taillights, also to fuel tank unit gage. Raise the engine hatch cover to gain access to the junction block on the engine compartment panel. Raise the hatch cover to gain access to the wiring under the rear deck when replacing harness.

j. Radio Terminal Box Wiring Harness (fig. 111). This harness is used after chassis serial No. 1499, and connects the starter switch with the radio junction box. The harness extends from the starter switch along the under side of the driver's compartment floor board to the radio junction box, located in the right front corner of the cargo compartment on early models and at right side of air intake grille on late

Radio Noise Suppression System

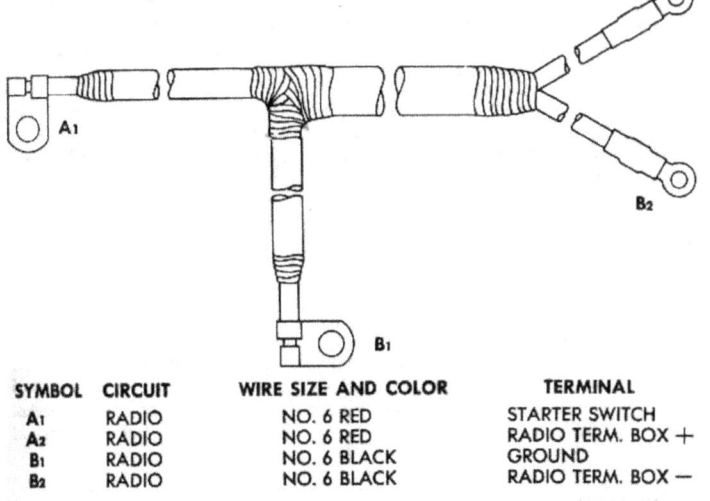

SYMBOL	CIRCUIT	WIRE SIZE AND COLOR	TERMINAL
A₁	RADIO	NO. 6 RED	STARTER SWITCH
A₂	RADIO	NO. 6 RED	RADIO TERM. BOX +
B₁	RADIO	NO. 6 BLACK	GROUND
B₂	RADIO	NO. 6 BLACK	RADIO TERM. BOX −

RA PD 303165

Figure 111—Radio Terminal Box Wiring Harness

models. Raise the engine hatch cover to gain access to the starter switch, and remove right-hand air intake grille for access to harness when replacing.

Section XXVI

Radio Noise Suppression System

138. GENERAL.

a. Radio noise suppression is the suppression of the noise disturbances from the electrical system of the vehicle which would interfere with the proper reception of radio signals, or permit detection of the vehicle location by highly sensitive receivers.

b. The sources of the electrical noise interference may be basically divided into four groups—Ignition Circuit, including coil, distributor, and spark plugs—Generating Circuit, including generator and regulator—Battery Circuit—and Starting Circuit.

c. Suppression is accomplished by the use of spark plug suppressors, ignition shield, and condensers. Prior to chassis serial No. 14779, radio suppression included a battery circuit filter, generator field circuit filter,

269

and a generator armature filter. After chassis serial No. 14778, this phase of suppression is taken care of by two condensers connected to "ARMATURE" and "BATTERY" terminals of the generator regulator, and the filters are no longer used.

d. Corrosion Prevention and Waterproofing Procedure. All filters, condensers, and suppressors must be painted with red synthetic paint (glyptal, 52-P-8057-710). If not available, use ignition insulating compound (52-C-3099-20).

139. IGNITION CIRCUIT.

a. General. Radio suppression of the ignition system comprises ignition shield and cover, ignition coil condenser, and the spark plug suppressors.

b. Ignition Shield and Cover (fig. 113). Ignition shield and cover encloses the distributor, ignition coil, spark plugs and cables, and is part of the radio suppression system. In addition to radio suppression, the shield also affords protection against water reaching these electrical units.

c. Shield Removal.

(1) REMOVE IGNITION SHIELD COVER (FIG. 113). Loosen crankcase ventilator tube nut at manifold. Loosen two stud nuts at top of rocker arm cover. Lift rocker arm cover sufficiently to clear flange on ignition shield cover. Loosen four wing nuts on some models or three stud nuts on other models attaching cover to shield. Lift cover up to remove from shield.

(2) REMOVE SHIELD (FIG. 113).

(a) Prior to Chassis Serial No. 14779. Remove ignition shield cover [step (1) above]. Remove distributor (par. 98). Remove five cross-recessed head screws which attach ignition shield to valve push rod cover and cylinder block. Ignition shield can now be removed.

(b) After Chassis Serial No. 14778. Remove ignition shield cover [step (1) above]. Remove distributor cap and spark plug cables as an assembly and lay aside. Remove primary wire from negative (−) terminal of coil. Remove outer nut, lock washer, and wire from coil condenser terminal. Loosen five cap screws attaching top of shield to valve push rod cover and cylinder block. Remove two cap screws and internal-external toothed lock washers inside ignition shield and three cap screws, internal-external toothed lock washers, and flat washers below ignition shield. Remove cross-recessed head screw at lower outer edge of ignition shield and lay front and rear cover plates aside. Ignition shield can now be lifted up and removed.

d. Shield Installation.

(1) INSTALL SHIELD (FIG. 113).

(a) Prior to Chassis Serial No. 14779. Locate ignition shield in its correct position against valve push rod cover. Install five cross-recessed

Radio Noise Suppression System

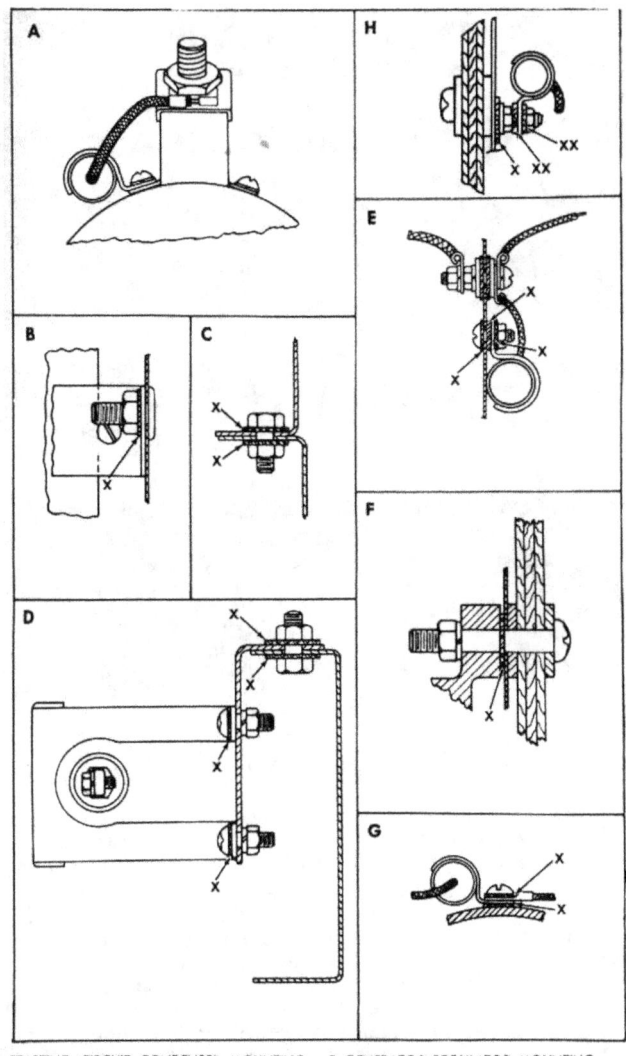

A STARTING CIRCUIT CONDENSER MOUNTING
B IGNITION COIL MOUNTING
C GENERATOR REGULATOR BRACKET MOUNTING
D BATTERY CIRCUIT FILTER AND BRACKET MOUNTING
E IGNITION COIL CONDENSER MOUNTING
F GENERATOR REGULATOR MOUNTING
G GENERATOR ARMATURE CONDENSER MOUNTING
H REGULATOR CONDENSER MOUNTING
X INTERNAL—EXTERNAL TOOTHED LOCK WASHER
XX EXTERNAL TOOTHED LOCK WASHER

RA PD 337252

Figure 112—Installation of Radio Suppression Units

TM 9-802
139

Maintenance Instructions

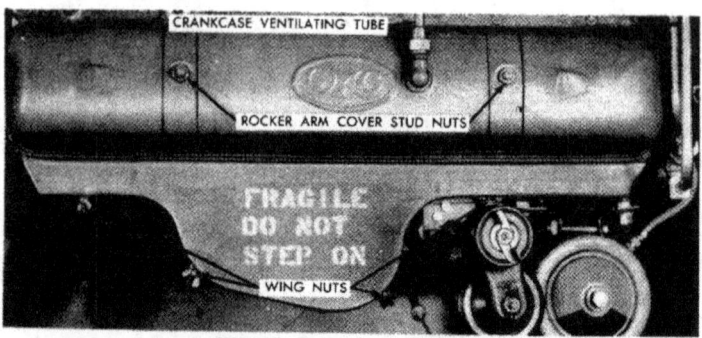

PRIOR TO CHASSIS SERIAL NO. 14779

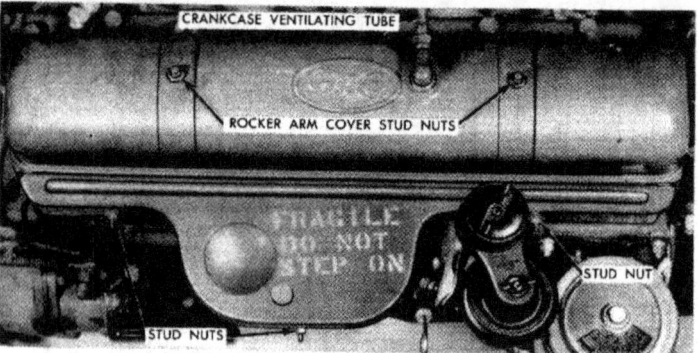

AFTER CHASSIS SERIAL NO. 14778

RA PD 337249

Figure 113—Ignition Shield Installed

head screws with internal-external toothed lock washers which attach shield to valve push rod cover. Install distributor (par. 98). Adjust ignition timing (par. 97). Install ignition shield cover [step (2) below].

(b) After Chassis Serial No. 14778. Locate ignition shield in its correct position against valve push rod cover. Tighten five cap screws which attach shield to valve push rod cover along upper edge. Install two cap screws and internal-external toothed lock washers inside shield at upper edge. Install distributor cap and spark plug cables, making certain cables are in correct firing sequence (1-5-3-6-2-4). Install cross-recessed head screw which attaches front and rear cover plates to ignition shield below distributor. Install three cap screws, flat washers, and internal-external toothed lock washers which attach bottom of ignition shield and two lower covers to valve push rod cover and cylinder block. Install primary coil wire (No. 14 green) to coil condenser terminal on outside of ignition shield with lock washer and nut. Attach distributor terminal wire (No. 14 tan-red and black cross tracer) to negative (−) terminal of coil.

TM 9-802
139-140

Radio Noise Suppression System

(*c*) If the primary ignition wire connection and terminal screw on ignition shield become dirty, moisture may easily short the ignition system. This wire terminal connection should be thoroughly cleaned, and painted with red synthetic paint (glyptal, 52-P-8057-710); if not available, use ignition insulating compound (52-C-3099-20).

(2) INSTALL IGNITION SHIELD COVER (FIG. 113). Lift rocker arm cover sufficiently to clear flange on ignition shield cover. Locate ignition shield cover firmly in place on shield. Tighten four wing nuts on some models or three stud nuts on other models which attach cover on rocker arm cover gasket and tighten rocker arm cover stud nuts. Tighten crankcase ventilator tube nut at manifold.

e. Ignition Coil Mounting (fig. 112). Ignition coil bracket is attached to ignition shield by two studs, nuts, and internal-external toothed lock washers. Nuts must be drawn up securely against lock washers.

f. Ignition Coil Condenser Mounting (fig. 112). Ignition coil condenser is mounted inside of ignition shield by a bolt, three internal-external toothed lock washers, and nut. Make certain internal-external toothed lock washers are used under head of bolt and under nut, also between shield and condenser bracket.

g. Spark Plug Suppressors. Seven suppressors are used, one at each spark plug and one at the distributor cap center electrode. Suppressors are screwed onto the end of the cables. Make certain threaded stud in suppressor screws firmly into the strands of cable wire.

140. GENERATING CIRCUIT.

a. Description. Radio noise suppression of the generating system on vehicles prior to chassis serial No. 14779 comprises the following units: Field circuit filter, armature filter, and generator armature condenser. On vehicles after chassis serial No. 14778, two condensers have been installed at "ARMATURE" and "BATTERY" terminals of generator regulator, and filters have been eliminated.

b. Field Circuit Filter and Armature Filter Mounting. Filters are mounted on generator regulator bracket. In mounting filters, make certain that internal-external toothed lock washers are used between head of screw and bracket, between bracket and nut, and between mounting hole in filter and nut. Nuts must be tightened firmly on lock washers to assure a good ground connection.

c. Generator Armature Condenser Mounting (fig. 112). Armature condenser is mounted on generator housing with two internal-external toothed lock washers and one screw. One internal-external toothed lock washer is used between head of mounting screw and condenser clip, and one between condenser clip and generator housing.

Maintenance Instructions

d. Generator Regulator Mounting (fig. 112). Generator regulator is mounted on generator regulator bracket and attached to left-hand air duct panel by four cross-recessed head screws. Make certain internal-external toothed lock washers are used between generator regulator and bracket. Use plain lock washers under nuts.

e. Generator Regulator Bracket Mounting (fig. 112). Regulator bracket is mounted on driver's compartment floor support channel by two bolts and nuts. Internal-external toothed lock washers are used between bolt heads and bracket and between support channel and nuts.

f. Regulator Condenser Mounting (After Chassis Serial No. 14778). Two condensers are mounted on regulator and condenser support bracket near base of regulator. One condenser pigtail attaches to "BATTERY" terminal of regulator with a split type lock washer and nut, other condenser pigtail attaches to "ARMATURE" terminal of regulator in same manner. Never attach condensers to "FIELD" terminal. Condensers are attached to mounting screw by external toothed lock washers and nuts. Make certain that an external toothed lock washer is used under condenser mounting clip and another external toothed lock washer is used between condenser mounting clip and nut. Loosen nut a few turns and slide condenser off mounting screw for removal.

141. BATTERY CIRCUIT.

a. General. Radio noise suppression of the battery circuit is accomplished by use of a battery circuit filter prior to chassis serial No. 14779. Battery circuit suppression after chassis serial No. 14778 is accomplished by condenser attached to "BATTERY" terminal of regulator.

b. Battery Circuit Filter Mounting (fig. 112). Battery circuit filter is mounted on filter support bracket by four cross-recessed head screws, four internal-external toothed lock washers, four lock washers (split type), and nuts. Internal-external toothed lock washers are used under screw heads and lock washers (split type) under nuts.

c. Battery Circuit Filter Support Bracket Mounting (fig. 112). Support bracket is mounted in same manner as generator regulator bracket (par. 140e.).

142. STARTING CIRCUIT.

a. General. Radio noise suppression of the starting circuit is accomplished by a condenser mounted on starter switch.

b. Starting Circuit Condenser Mounting (fig. 112). Starting circuit condenser is mounted on starter switch and is held in place by switch attaching screw. One lock washer (split type) is used under head of screw.

Section XXVII

Instruments, Gages, and Switches

143. INSTRUMENT AND GAGE PANELS.

a. Description. Instrument panel (figs. 114 and 115) is mounted directly in front of driver and includes instruments, gages, and switches as described in paragraphs 16 and 17. On vehicles after chassis serial No. 2005, an additional panel (tachometer and air gage panel) is mounted to right of, and attached to instrument panel. This panel includes tachometer, tachometer lock, air tank gage, tire air gage, tire inflating control lever, panel light, and valve for windshield wipers.

b. Corrosion Prevention and Waterproofing. Prior to installation of instrument panel or whenever correction is evident, treat as follows:

(1) If panel is mounted in vehicle, loosen panel from supports. Remove and clean all attaching terminals and contact surfaces. Connect terminals, tightening terminal screws and nuts firmly.

(2) Paint terminals with red synthetic paint (glyptal, 52-P-8057-710) or ignition insulating compound (52-C-3099-20). Mask face of each instrument on panel with masking tape, leaving a small margin of glass exposed around outer circumference of mask. Margin must be sufficiently large to permit sealing of glass with coating material, but small enough to leave markings on face legible after removal of tape. Spray all component parts of the instrument panel, front and back, with ignition insulating compound (52-C-3099-20). Red synthetic paint (glyptal, 52-P-8057-710) can be used, but only on back of panel.

c. Instrument Panel Removal (figs. 114 and 115).

(1) From inside engine compartment, loosen thermo gage plug in cylinder head. Drain engine coolant to below level of plug, then remove plug. Disconnect choke and throttle control at carbureter (par. 107**b.** and **c.**). Disconnect battery to starter cable from battery post.

(2) Unscrew nut and disconnect oil gage tube from oil gage at back of instrument panel. Unscrew nut at back of speedometer and disconnect speedometer cable from speedometer.

(3) Disconnect all wiring at back of instrument panel. Unscrew nut at speedometer clamp and remove wiring harness clip on early vehicles. On later vehicles, pry open clip to free harness. Remove instrument panel lights from panel.

(4) Remove nut, washer, and bolt which attaches panel to steering column brace. Remove three nuts, washers, and screws which attach panel to instrument panel support. Remove three flathead screws which attach panel to lower windshield panel. Remove three nuts, washers, and bolts which attach tachometer and air gage panel to instrument panel, if vehicle is so equipped. Remove instrument panel, withdrawing thermo gage tube, and throttle and choke conduits through opening in toeboard as panel is removed.

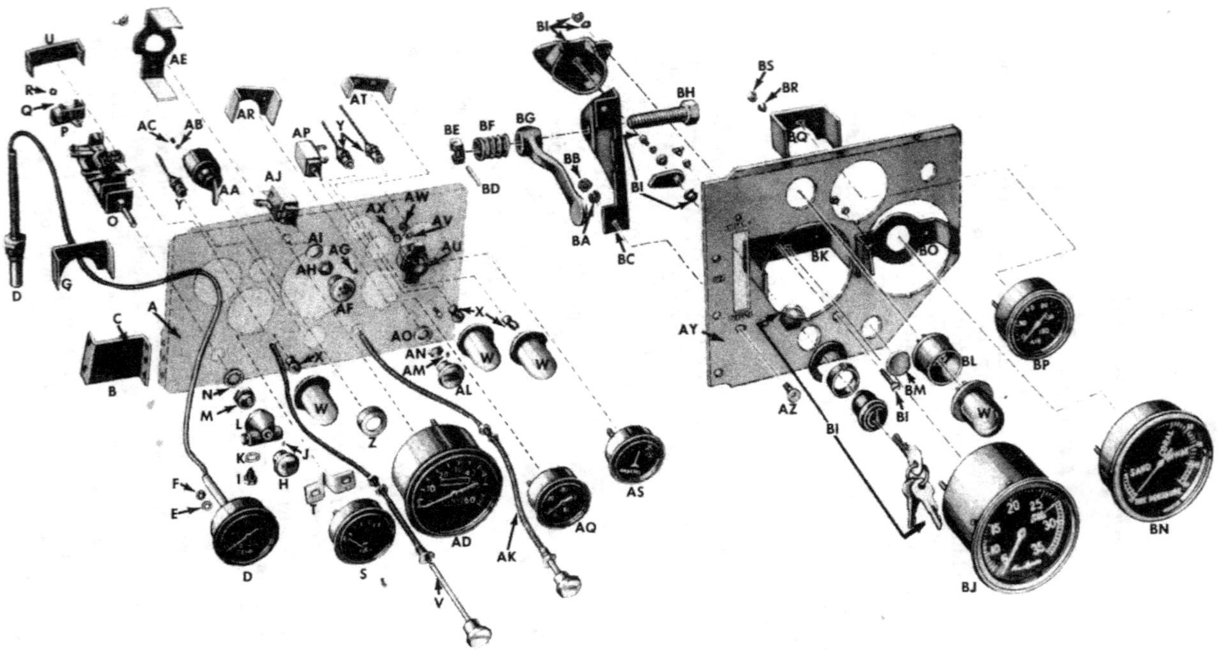

RA PD 337254

Figure 114—Disassembled View of Instrument and Tachometer Panels

A INSTRUMENT PANEL FACE PLATE
B INSTRUMENT PANEL SUPPORT
C SUPPORT TO PANEL SCREW
D THERMO GAGE (G501-01-94072)
E LOCK WASHER
F NUT
G MOUNTING CLAMP
H LIGHTING SWITCH KNOB
I SWITCH CONTROL STUD
J KNOB SET SCREW
K INTERNAL-TOOTHED LOCK WASHER
L LIGHTING SWITCH CONTROL
M SWITCH MOUNTING NUT
N INTERNAL-TOOTHED LOCK WASHER
O LIGHTING SWITCH (G501-03-93784)
P LIGHTING SWITCH CIRCUIT BREAKER (G508-7000418)
Q LOCK WASHER
R NUT
S GAS GAGE (G085-33-01460)
T TERMINAL SEPARATOR
U MOUNTING CLAMP
V THROTTLE CONTROL
W PANEL LIGHT SHIELD
X PANEL LAMP
Y PANEL LIGHT SOCKET
Z MOUNTING NUT
AA IGNITION SWITCH (G162-1690371)
AB LOCK WASHER
AC SCREW
AD SPEEDOMETER
AE MOUNTING CLAMP
AF BLACKOUT SWITCH KNOB
AG SET SCREW
AH NUT
AI WASHER
AJ BLACKOUT DRIVING LIGHT SWITCH
AK CHOKE CONTROL
AL INSTRUMENT LIGHT SWITCH KNOB
AM SET SCREW
AN NUT
AO WASHER
AP INSTRUMENT LIGHT SWITCH (2580-1995620)
AQ OIL GAGE (G501-01-94071)
AR MOUNTING CLAMP
AS AMMETER (G085-33-00030)
AT MOUNTING CLAMP
AU FUEL GAGE CIRCUIT BREAKER (PRIOR TO DUKW-353-2006)
AV LOCK WASHER
AW NUT
AX SCREW
AY TACHOMETER AND AIR GAGE PANEL
AZ BOLT
BA LOCK WASHER
BB NUT
BC CONTROL LEVER BRACKET
BD COTTER PIN
BE NUT
BF CONTROL LEVER SPRING
BG TIRE INFLATING CONTROL LEVER
BH BOLT
BI TACHOMETER LOCK
BJ TACHOMETER (G501-02-11415)
BK MOUNTING CLAMP
BL LAMP SHIELD EXTENSION
BM BUTTON PLUG
BN AIR TIRE GAGE (G501-70-02109)
BO MOUNTING CLAMP
BP AIR TANK GAGE (G501-70-02110)
BQ MOUNTING CLAMP
BR LOCK WASHER
BS NUT

RA PD 3372

Legend for Figure 114

Maintenance Instructions

d. Instrument Panel Installation (figs. 114 and 115).

(1) Position panel in vehicle, inserting thermo gage tube, and throttle and choke conduits through opening in toeboard as panel is positioned. Install three screws and washers attaching panel to lower windshield panel. Install three screws, washers, and nuts attaching panel to support. Install bolt, washer, and nut attaching panel to steering column brace. Install three bolts, washers, and nuts attaching instrument panel to tachometer panel, if vehicle is so equipped.

(2) Connect wiring at back of instrument panel. Refer to figures 101 and 103 for wire size, color, and terminal connection. Attach wiring harness to speedometer stud with clip and nut on early vehicles. On later vehicles, position harness in clip, then close clip. Insert instrument panel lamps and sockets into shields in panel, then push into place.

(3) Connect speedometer cable to speedometer, tightening cable nut firmly. Connect oil gage tube to gage and tighten nut firmly.

(4) From inside engine compartment, attach throttle and choke controls to carbureter (par. 107*b*. and *c*.). Install thermo gage plug in cylinder head, tightening plug firmly. Fill engine cooling system with coolant (par. 117*a*.). Connect battery starter cable to battery post, tightening clamp bolt nut firmly.

e. Tachometer and Air Gage Panel Removal (After Chassis Serial No. 2005) (figs. 114 and 115).

(1) Close six tire inflating line valves at side of co-pilot's seat. Open air tank drain cock and exhaust air from system. Disconnect air lines at tire air gage and air tank gage. Disconnect two air lines at windshield wiper valve.

(2) Remove clevis pin at back of panel which connects tire inflating control lever to linkage. Disconnect tachometer drive shaft from tachometer.

(3) Remove three nuts, washers, and bolts which attach tachometer panel to instrument panel. Remove two screws and washers which attach panel to lower windshield panel. Pull panel straight back, remove panel light socket from panel, then remove panel.

f. Tachometer and Air Gage Panel Installation (After Chassis Serial No. 2005) (figs. 114 and 115).

(1) Position panel in vehicle and hold in place. Install panel light in shield from back of panel.

(2) Connect tachometer drive shaft to tachometer. Connect air lines to windshield wiper valve and to air gages. Tighten air line tubing nuts firmly.

(3) Install two screws attaching panel to lower windshield panel. Install three bolts, washers, and nuts attaching tachometer panel to instrument panel. Connect tire inflating control lever to linkage with clevis pin, and secure with a new cotter pin. Close air tank drain cock and open six tire inflating line valves.

Instruments, Gages, and Switches

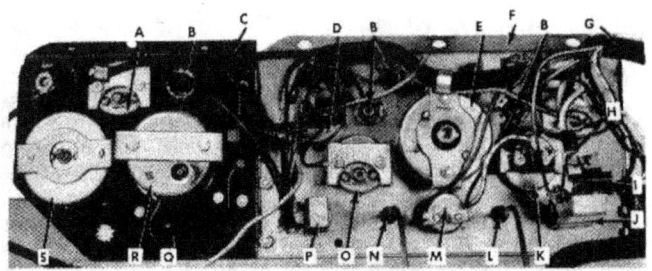

WITH PUSH-PULL TYPE LIGHTING SWITCH

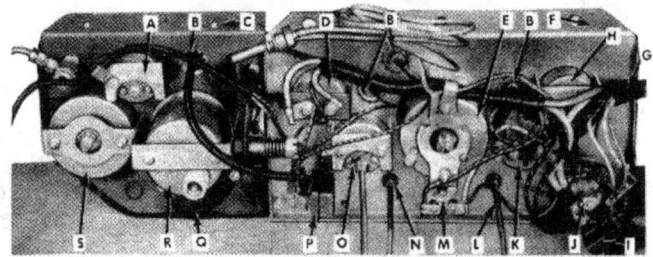

WITH ROTARY-TYPE LIGHTING SWITCH

- A AIR PRESSURE GAGE
- B PANEL LIGHT SOCKET
- C TACHOMETER AND AIR GAGE PANEL
- D AMMETER
- E SPEEDOMETER
- F INSTRUMENT PANEL FACE PLATE
- G INSTRUMENT PANEL WIRING HARNESS
- H THERMO GAGE
- I LIGHTING CIRCUIT BREAKER
- J LIGHTING SWITCH
- K GAS GAGE
- L THROTTLE CONTROL
- M IGNITION SWITCH
- N CHOKE CONTROL
- O OIL GAGE
- P INSTRUMENT LIGHT SWITCH
- Q TACHOMETER LOCK
- R TACHOMETER
- S TIRE PRESSURE GAGE

RA PD 337255

Figure 115—Rear View of Instrument and Tachometer Panels

144. INSTRUMENT PANEL UNIT REPLACEMENT.

a. General. Instruments, switches, and controls, mounted on instrument panel, can be replaced individually without necessity of removing instrument panel assembly.

b. Thermo Gage (figs. 114 and 115).

(1) REMOVAL. From inside engine compartment, drain engine coolant to below level of thermal plug, then remove plug from cylinder head. Remove two gage mounting nuts and washers, then remove clamp from back of gage. Push on back of gage and remove from front of instrument panel as thermal plug is withdrawn through hole in toeboard.

(2) INSTALLATION. Insert thermal plug through openings in instrument panel and toeboard as gage is positioned in panel. Install mounting clamp on back of gage, attaching with two lock washers and nuts.

Install thermal plug in cylinder head, then fill engine cooling system with coolant.

c. Gas Gage (figs. 114 and 115).

(1) REMOVAL. Remove two nuts and washers which attach wire terminals to gage. Remove two mounting clamp nuts and lock washers, then remove clamp. Press on back of gage to remove from front of panel.

(2) INSTALLATION. Position gage in instrument panel, install mounting clamp at back of gage, then install two washers and nuts. Connect wires to gage terminals, then install two lock washers and terminal nuts.

d. Oil Gage (figs. 114 and 115).

(1) REMOVAL. Disconnect oil gage tube from oil gage. Remove two gage mounting nuts and lock washers, then remove mounting clamp from gage. Remove gage from front of panel.

(2) INSTALLATION. Position gage in panel, install mounting clamp on back, and install two mounting nuts and washers. Connect oil gage tube to gage, tightening nut firmly.

e. Ammeter (figs. 114 and 115).

(1) REMOVAL. Remove two terminal nuts and washers, then disconnect wires from ammeter. Remove two mounting nuts and washers, remove mounting clamp, and remove ammeter from front of instrument panel.

(2) INSTALLATION. Position ammeter in instrument panel. Install mounting clamp and attach with two lock washers and nuts. Connect wires to terminals and install two lock washers and nuts. Ammeter must show charge with engine running at moderate speed. Reverse wiring to terminals if ammeter shows a discharge.

f. Speedometer (figs. 114 and 115).

(1) REMOVAL. Unscrew drive cable nut at back of speedometer, then disconnect cable. Remove two mounting nuts and washers, then remove wiring harness clip and mounting clamp. Press on back of speedometer and remove from front of instrument panel.

(2) INSTALLATION. Position speedometer in instrument panel. Install mounting clamp at back of speedometer, install wiring harness clip, then install two mounting lock washers and nuts. Connect drive cable to speedometer, making sure tongue on drive shaft is properly engaged in speedometer. Tighten drive cable nut firmly.

g. Instrument Light Switch (figs. 114 and 115).

(1) REMOVAL. Loosen set screw in knob, then unscrew knob from switch. Remove mounting nut and washer at face of instrument panel. Press on switch at front of panel to remove from back of panel. Remove two screws and washers attaching wires to switch, then remove switch.

Instruments, Gages, and Switches

(2) INSTALLATION. Attach wires to switch with two screws and lock washers, tightening screws firmly. Position switch in instrument panel from back of panel. Install washer and nut on switch. Screw knob on switch, then tighten set screw firmly.

h. Blackout Driving Light Switch (Prior to Chassis Serial No. 14779). Except or marking on knob, blackout driving light switch is identical with instrument light switch. Refer to subparagraph g. above; removal and installation operations are same for both switches.

i. Lighting Switches (figs. 114, 115, and 116). Two types of lighting switches are in use. Vehicles prior to chassis serial No. 14779 are equipped with push-pull type switch (fig. 116). Rotary type switch is used on vehicles after chassis serial No. 14778.

(1) PUSH-PULL TYPE SWITCH REMOVAL (PRIOR TO CHASSIS SERIAL NO. 14779). Loosen set screw in knob, then unscrew knob. Loosen hex head cap screw at bottom of switch bushing. Press switch locking plunger and pull switch bushing off end of switch. Remove nut and washer from switch at front of instrument panel. Push on front of switch to remove from back of panel. Disconnect wires from switch terminals, then remove switch. Remove two screws which attach lighting switch circuit breaker to switch to remove circuit breaker.

(2) PUSH-PULL TYPE SWITCH INSTALLATION (PRIOR TO CHASSIS SERIAL NO. 14779). Attach circuit breaker to switch with two nuts and washers. Connect wires to switch terminals. Terminal markings are shown in figure 116. Wire connections are shown in paragraphs 135 through 137. Position switch in instrument panel, then install washer and nut. Compress switch locking plunger, then position bushing on switch. Tighten hex head cap screw at bottom of bushing while pressing bushing firmly against panel. Screw knob onto switch, then tighten set screw firmly. Test operation of switch (par. 17c.).

(3) ROTARY TYPE SWITCH REMOVAL (AFTER CHASSIS SERIAL NO. 14778). Remove screw which attaches switch lever to switch, then remove lever. Remove switch mounting nut and washer, then remove escutcheon plate. Push on switch shaft and remove switch from back of instrument panel. Disconnect wiring at terminal screws. Remove circuit breaker from switch by removing two screws.

(4) ROTARY TYPE SWITCH INSTALLATION (AFTER CHASSIS SERIAL NO. 14778). Assemble circuit breaker to switch with two screws. Connect wires to switch terminals. Terminal markings are shown in figure 116. Wire connections are shown in paragraphs 135 through 137. Position switch in instrument panel then install escutcheon plate, lock washer, flat washer, and nut. Position switch lever on switch shaft then install lever screw.

j. Ignition Switch (figs. 114 and 115).

(1) REMOVAL. Unscrew round nut from switch at front of instrument panel. Use spanner wrench or punch in holes in nut to loosen nut. Push on switch to remove from rear of panel. Remove two screws and washers from terminals on switch and disconnect wires.

Maintenance Instructions

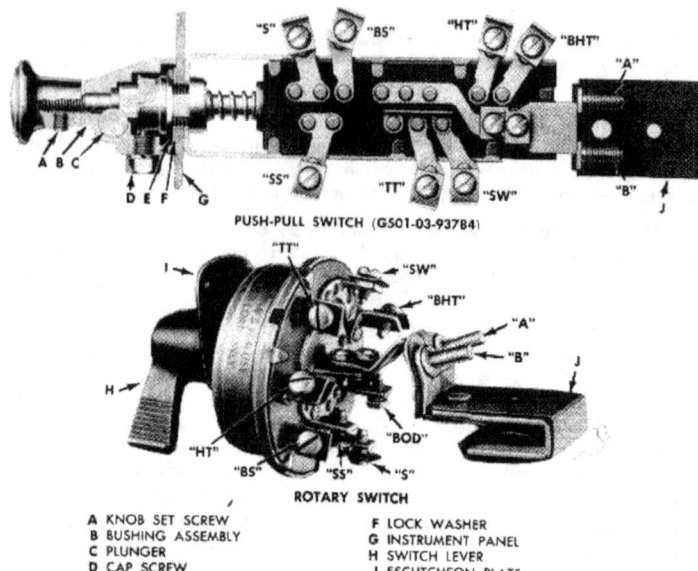

A KNOB SET SCREW
B BUSHING ASSEMBLY
C PLUNGER
D CAP SCREW
E SWITCH MOUNTING NUT
F LOCK WASHER
G INSTRUMENT PANEL
H SWITCH LEVER
I ESCUTCHEON PLATE
J CIRCUIT BREAKER (G508-7000418)

RA PD 337256

Figure 116—Lighting Switches and Terminal Markings

(2) INSTALLATION. Connect wires to switch terminals with two screws and lock washers. Position switch in instrument panel, and install round nut on switch. Tighten nut firmly, using spanner wrench or punch.

k. Instrument Panel Lights (figs. 114 and 115).

(1) REMOVAL. Insert screwdriver under panel light shield and pry shield, lamp, and socket free from instrument panel. Using screwdriver, pry center part of socket to side to dislodge from shield. Push in on top of lamp, then turn counterclockwise to remove lamp.

(2) INSTALLATION. Insert lamp into socket, then press on top of lamp with finger, at the same time turning clockwise. Press lamp and socket firmly into shield. Position shield, lamp, and socket in instrument panel, making sure slot in shield is in proper position for illumination of instruments. Press assembly of shield, lamp, and socket firmly into position.

l. Choke and Throttle Controls.
Replacement of choke and throttle controls is described in paragraph 107.

TM 9-802

Instruments, Gages, and Switches

145. GAGE PANEL UNIT REPLACEMENT (After Chassis Serial No. 2005).

a. General. Whenever removing any unit to which air lines attach, always close six tire inflating line valves at side of co-pilot's seat, then open air tank drain cock and exhaust air from system before disconnecting air lines.

b. Tachometer (figs. 114 and 115).

(1) REMOVAL. At back of panel, unscrew drive shaft nut, then pull drive shaft free from tachometer. Remove two mounting nuts and washers, remove mounting clamp from back of tachometer, then remove tachometer from front of panel.

(2) INSTALLATION. Position tachometer in gage panel, then install mounting clamp on back, attaching clamp with two lock washers and nuts. Connect drive shaft to tachometer, making sure drive shaft core is properly engaged with tachometer. Tighten drive shaft nut firmly.

c. Tachometer Lock (figs. 114 and 115).

(1) REMOVAL. Remove two screws, washers, and nuts which attach lock cover to back of panel, then remove cover. Remove screw and washers which attach trip lever to lock shaft, then remove lever from shaft. Remove nut from lock at back of panel, then remove lock cylinder from front of panel.

(2) INSTALLATION. Position lock cylinder in gage panel with keyway at top. Install nut on lock at back of panel. Position trip lever on lock shaft, then install attaching screw and washers. Position lock cover on back of panel, then install attaching screws, washers, and nuts.

d. Air Tank Gage (figs. 114 and 115).

(1) REMOVAL. Unscrew air line nut at back of gage and disconnect line from gage. Remove two mounting nuts and washers. Remove mounting clamp, then remove gage from front of panel.

(2) INSTALLATION. Position gage in panel, then install mounting clamp and attaching washers and nuts. Connect air line to gage, tightening air line nut firmly.

e. Tire Air Gage (figs. 114 and 115). Removal and installation operations are same as described for air tank gage (subpar. *d.* above).

f. Windshield Wiper Valve (figs. 114 and 115).

(1) REMOVAL. Disconnect air line tubes from back of valve. Remove mounting nut at face of panel. Push valve from front of panel, and remove from back.

(2) INSTALLATION. Position valve in gage panel from back, then install mounting nut at face of panel. Connect air line tubes to valve, tightening connections firmly.

g. Tire Inflating Control Lever (figs. 114 and 115).

(1) REMOVAL. Disconnect lever from linkage by removing cotter pin and clevis pin at back of gage panel. Remove two nuts, washers, and

bolts which attach bracket to panel. Remove lever and bracket assembly from back of panel.

(2) INSTALLATION. Position lever and bracket on back of panel and install two attaching bolts, washers, and nuts. Connect lever to linkage with clevis pin, then secure pin with cotter pin.

146. SPEEDOMETER AND TACHOMETER DRIVE.

a. Speedometer Drive Cable Removal. Disconnect cable from axle transfer case after unscrewing cable nut. Remove cable clips after removing attaching screws, bolts, and nuts. Disconnect cable from speedometer by unscrewing cable nut. Remove drive cable through engine compartment.

b. Speedometer Drive Cable Installation. Position drive cable in vehicle. Connect cable to axle transfer case, making sure that cable tongue is properly engaged in drive gear shaft. Install clips and attaching screws, bolts, and nuts. Connect drive cable to speedometer, making sure shaft is properly engaged with speedometer. Install an additional cable clip (H004-03-27721) on vehicles prior to chassis serial No. 7402 not so equipped, to prevent short circuiting headlight wiring by contact of cable with dimmer switch terminals. Attach clip to toeboard with wood screw, locating screw approximately 12 inches from top of board and 5 inches from outer end of board.

c. Speedometer Shaft Removal. Disconnect drive cable from speedometer and from axle transfer case. At transfer case end of cable, pull shaft from casing with pliers sufficiently to expose retaining (C-shaped) washer. Remove washer with fingers. Remove speedometer shaft (G501-03-84676) by pulling out of casing from speedometer end of shaft.

d. Speedometer Shaft Installation. Coat shaft lightly with general purpose grease, No. 0. Insert transfer case end of shaft into speedometer end of casing, then feed shaft completely into casing. With pliers, pull transfer case end of shaft out of casing sufficiently to expose retaining washer groove in shaft. Install retaining washer in groove. Then ease pull on cable to permit proper seating of washer in casing. Connect cable to axle transfer case, then connect cable to speedometer.

e. Tachometer Drive Shaft Removal (After Chassis Serial No. 2005). Unscrew drive shaft nut at back of tachometer and free shaft from tachometer. Remove screws which attach toeboard closure plate and remove plate. Disconnect shaft at transmission. Remove drive shaft clips by removing attaching screws. Withdraw drive shaft through engine compartment.

f. Tachometer Drive Shaft Installation (After Chassis Serial No. 2005). Position shaft in vehicle, then connect shaft to transmission. Install shaft clips and attaching screws. Install toeboard closure plate and attaching screws, making sure closure plate grommet is correctly positioned. Connect shaft to tachometer, making sure drive shaft core is properly engaged in tachometer.

Instruments, Gages, and Switches

g. Tachometer Drive Shaft Core Removal (After Chassis Serial No. 2005). Disconnect drive shaft at transmission, then disconnect drive shaft at tachometer. At tachometer end, withdraw core (G501-70-01947) from drive shaft casing. If core is broken, remove other part of core by withdrawing from transmission end of casing.

h. Tachometer Drive Shaft Core Installation (After Chassis Serial No. 2005). Coat core lightly with general purpose grease, No. 0. Insert transmission end of core in tachometer end of casing and feed core completely into casing. Connect drive shaft to transmission, then connect shaft to tachometer, making sure core is properly engaged.

147. DIMMER SWITCH.

a. Removal. From inside engine compartment, remove two screws and washers which attach switch to switch bracket. Pull switch from bracket, then remove three terminal screws to disconnect wiring.

b. Installation. Connect wires to switch terminals with three screws and lock washers. Double wires (black with green tracer) must be connected to terminal marked "BATT." Position switch in switch bracket and install screws and washers, tightening screws firmly. When installing a new switch on vehicles prior to chassis serial No. 3794, it may be necessary to increase size of holes in bracket and toeboard. If replacing original switch with late type waterproof switch, enlarge hole in bracket from 1 inch to $1\frac{1}{8}$ inch and in toeboard from $1\frac{1}{8}$ inch to $1\frac{5}{16}$ inch.

148. FUEL TANK GAGE UNIT.

a. Removal. Enter right rear compartment under fuel tank headfirst, and assume a position in extreme rear of compartment between tank and hull. Disconnect wire from gage terminal after removing nut. Remove five screws and gaskets which attach gage to tank. Lift gage and gasket from tank, tilting gage as necessary to remove.

b. Installation. Coat both sides of a new gasket with gasket cement (52-C-685). Assemble gasket to gage, then position gasket and gage in tank. Note that five screw holes are spaced to permit installation in tank in only one position. Aline holes, then install five screws, using either a copper annular gasket or lead washer on each screw. Also attach ground wire to one of the screws. Tighten screws evenly and firmly. Connect wire to gage terminal, then install nut.

149. STOP LIGHT SWITCH.

a. Removal. Before replacing switch, connect switch wires together and turn on lighting switch. If stop lights fail to illuminate, trouble is elsewhere than in switch. Disconnect wires at switch, then unscrew switch (G122-03-93660) from brake master cylinder. Install new switch immediately after removal of old switch to prevent loss of brake fluid. CAUTION: *Do not apply brakes while switch is removed, as brake fluid would be lost through opening; also it would be necessary to bleed the entire brake system due to admission of air into system.*

b. Installation. Screw switch into outlet fitting on brake master cylinder, tightening switch firmly. Connect wires to terminals on switch.

150. HORN AND BUTTON.

a. General. Electric vibrating-type horn is mounted on a bracket attached to front deck. Horn is controlled by a button mounted on air duct panel at left of driver; on vehicles prior to chassis serial No. 1151, horn button is mounted in center of steering wheel. Horn circuit is protected by a thermal-type circuit breaker (G104-15-26008) mounted on left-hand air exhaust duct panel inside engine compartment.

b. Horn Removal. Remove caulking compound at horn terminals, then disconnect horn wires at terminals. Remove two cap screws and washers attaching horn to mounting bracket, then remove horn.

c. Horn Installation. Position horn on mounting bracket, then install attaching cap screws and washers. Connect horn wires to horn terminals, making sure connections are clean and free from corrosion. Apply a thin coating of petrolatum to terminals. Build up a heavy coating of caulking compound (52-C-3086) over terminals and on wiring from terminals to deck. Shape compound with fingers, building up a fillet around grommet in deck.

d. Horn Button Removal (After Chassis Serial No. 1151). Remove nut and name plate from horn button at left side of driver's compartment, then push button into air exhaust duct. Enter left-hand air duct through front compartment. Disconnect horn wires from button and remove button.

e. Horn Button Installation (After Chassis Serial No. 1151). Station assistant in driver's compartment, then enter left-hand air exhaust duct. Connect wires to horn button. Position button in hole in air exhaust duct panel and hold while assistant installs horn button name plate and nut.

151. SIGNAL LIGHT
   (After Chassis Serial No. 14778).

a. Lamp-unit Removal (fig. 117). Pry up three light shield spring clips and remove shield. Remove door screw at bottom of light, then remove door by pulling out at bottom and disengaging clip at top. Disconnect two wires at back of sealed lamp-unit. With screwdriver, pry retaining springs out of engagement with door then remove retaining ring and sealed lamp-unit.

b. Lamp-unit Installation (fig. 117). Position lamp-unit and retaining ring in door. Engage springs in door flange, then attach two wires to terminals on back of lamp-unit. Position door to body of light, with door clip engaged in slot in body, and install door screw. Position

Clutch and Controls

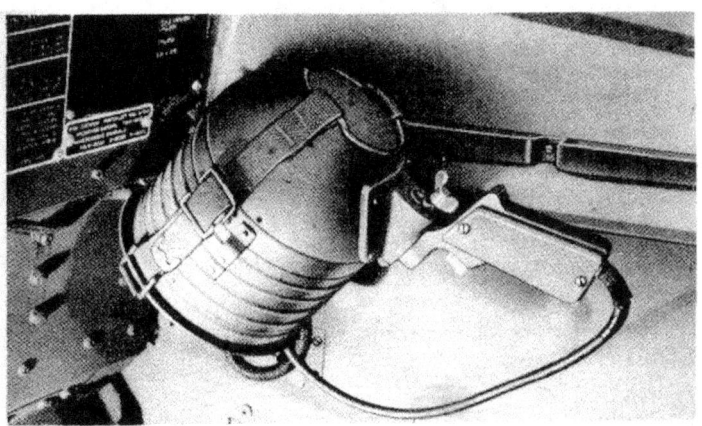

RA PD 337257

Figure 117—Signal Light Installed

light shield to light with sights at top. Engage three light shield spring clips with pegs in light body.

c. Light Removal (fig. 117). Unscrew connector plug coupling nut at socket under support bracket. Pull plug from socket. Unfasten hold-down strap buckle, then lift light from support bracket and remove from vehicle.

d. Light Installation (fig. 117). Connect plug to socket, then tighten plug coupling nut firmly. Position wire from plug in notch in bracket and block, then position wire from pistol grip in notch. Position signal light on bracket, then fasten hold-down straps on light. Push wires up through notch so that all excess wire is contained in light shield, between light and bracket.

Section XXVIII
Clutch and Controls

152. GENERAL.

a. Description. The clutch consists of two separate assemblies, clutch disc assembly, and clutch cover and pressure plate assembly. The driven disc transfers engine power from the flywheel to the transmission main drive gear shaft. The clutch cover and pressure plate provide attachment or release of the driven disc to the flywheel.

b. Data.

DRIVEN DISC AND FACINGS

Facings

Quantity	2
Outside diameter	11½ in.
Inside diameter	6¾ in.

Clutch Pressure Spring

Type	Diaphragm
Quantity	1
Number	753930
Outside diameter	9 in.

Clutch Release Bearing Support

Type	Sealed ball
Make	New Departure
Number (bearing and support assembly)	2140122

Clutch Pilot Bearing

Type	Shielded ball
Make	New Departure
Number	907109

c. Repair. Repair procedures for the clutch components are described in TM 9-1802A.

153. CLUTCH PEDAL FREE-TRAVEL ADJUSTMENT.

a. *Clutch pedal free-travel is the movement of the pedal before the clutch starts to disengage.* Pedal free-travel must be 2½ inches with new facings. As the facings wear, adjusting nuts on the adjusting link should be backed off to maintain a 2½-inch free-travel until the lock nut is at the end of the thread; then clutch may be operated until free-travel is reduced to 1 inch at which time clutch driven member assembly (with new facings) must be replaced.

b. Adjustment.

(1) CHECK PEDAL FREE-TRAVEL. Pedal free-travel must be checked with the *hand* and *not with foot,* as this check is very sensitive. If pedal free-travel of clutch is less than 2½ inches, and lock nut has not already been adjusted to the end of the adjusting link threads, adjust pedal [step (2) below].

(2) ADJUST PEDAL (FIG. 118). Loosen check nuts on adjusting link and turn adjusting nut in or out as may be required to obtain proper free-travel of foot pedal. With pedal free-travel definitely established, turn up check nut firmly against adjusting nut to prevent adjustment from coming loose, then recheck pedal free-travel. After limit of adjustment is reached, any free-travel in excess of 1 inch is satisfactory.

154. CLUTCH PEDAL AND LINKAGE.

a. Description. Clutch pedal is connected to release fork through linkage (fig. 118). Release fork is ball stud mounted in clutch housing. Inner end of fork engages groove in release bearing support for actuation of release bearing.

TM 9-802

Clutch and Controls

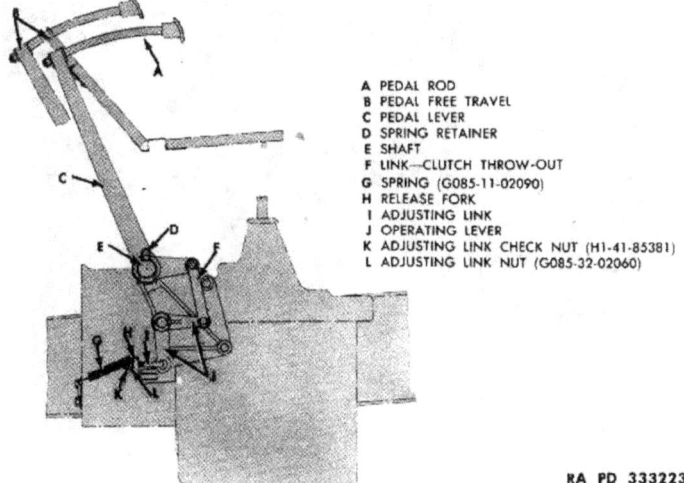

A PEDAL ROD
B PEDAL FREE TRAVEL
C PEDAL LEVER
D SPRING RETAINER
E SHAFT
F LINK—CLUTCH THROW-OUT
G SPRING (G085-11-02090)
H RELEASE FORK
I ADJUSTING LINK
J OPERATING LEVER
K ADJUSTING LINK CHECK NUT (H1-41-85381)
L ADJUSTING LINK NUT (G085-32-02060)

RA PD 333223

Figure 118—Pedal and Linkage Installed

b. Removal. Key letters in steps (1) and (2) below refer to figure 118.

(1) REMOVE PEDAL ROD AND PEDAL LEVER. Remove driver's compartment left-hand floor board. Remove cotter pin and nut retaining pedal rod (A) to pedal lever (C). Remove pedal rod from pedal lever. Disconnect clutch throw-out link (F) from pedal lever (C) by removing cotter pin and clevis pin. Remove lubrication fitting and retainer spring (D) from pedal lever shaft (E), then remove pedal lever.

(2) REMOVE THROW-OUT LINK, OPERATING LEVER, AND ADJUSTING LINK. Unhook pull back spring (G) from clutch pull back spring bracket. Remove check nut (K) and adjusting nut (L) from adjusting link (I); then remove link (I) from release fork (H). Drive out pin which retains washer and operating lever (J) to operating lever shaft. Remove throw-out link (F), operating link (J), and adjusting link (I) as a unit.

c. Installation. Key letters in steps (1) and (2) below refer to figure 118.

(1) INSTALL ADJUSTING LINK, OPERATING LEVER, AND THROW-OUT LINK. Position operating lever (J) over operating lever shaft and secure with washer and pin. Install adjusting link (I) to lower end of operating lever (J), then thread adjusting link (I) through release fork (H) and secure with adjusting nut (L) and check nut (K). Do not tighten these nuts at this time. Install throw-out link (F) to

Figure 119—Alining Clutch

upper arm of operating lever (J) and secure with clevis pin and cotter pin.

(2) INSTALL PEDAL LEVER AND PEDAL ROD. Position pedal lever (C) on shaft (E). Secure lever with spring retainer (D), then install lubrication fitting in end of shaft (E). Install upper end of throwout link (F) to pedal lever (C) and secure with clevis pin and cotter pin. Install pedal rod (A) to pedal lever (C) with nut and cotter pin. Tighten nut firmly. Install pull back spring (G) to pull back spring bracket and adjusting link (I).

(3) ADJUST. Adjust clutch pedal free-travel (par. 153).

155. CLUTCH REMOVAL.

a. Remove Power Plant. Remove power plant as described in paragraph 94.

b. Remove Transmission. Remove transmission (par. 158). Clutch release bearing assembly (H012-40-0021) is then accessible.

c. Remove Release Fork and Ball Stud Assembly. Disconnect pedal pull back spring. Remove check nut and adjusting nut, then remove adjusting link. With a 3/4-inch offset open end wrench, hold ball stud from inner side of clutch housing, then with a 7/8-inch wrench, remove ball stud support from outer side of clutch housing. Release fork with ball stud can then be removed.

d. Remove Clutch Assemblies. Insert clutch alining tool (41-T-3085) (fig. 119) through clutch assembly and driven disc hub. Loosen

Clutch and Controls

RA PD 337143

Figure 120—Removing Pilot Bearing

the nine clutch cover to flywheel bolts one turn at a time until diaphragm spring is fully released; then completely remove all bolts and withdraw clutch alining tool. Clutch pressure plate assembly and clutch driven member assembly (G501-02-89686) can then be lowered.

e. Remove Clutch Pilot Bearing (If Necessary). Adjust special puller (41-P-2900-15) or equivalent with thumb screw until fingers on puller are closed (fig. 120). Insert puller through bore of bearing as far as it will go, then tighten thumb screw to spread fingers of puller behind bearing. Slide weight sharply against stop nut on puller shaft several times to remove the bearing.

156. CLUTCH INSTALLATION.

a. Install Clutch Pilot Bearing. Before bearing is installed, lubricate as described on Lubrication Order No. 9-802. Use alining tool (41-T-3085) with three ⅝-inch washers over end of tool. Install pilot bearing in crankshaft recess. Install bearing squarely with shielded side toward transmission.

b. Position Driven Disc, and Cover and Plate Assembly. While holding driven disc in place against flywheel (long portion of hub toward flywheel), position cover and pressure plate assembly in place. Insert clutch alining tool (41-T-3085) through clutch housing, cover and pressure plate, and driven disc assembly (fig. 119).

TM 9-802
156

Maintenance Instructions

Figure 121 — Installing Clutch Assembly

c. Attach Cover Assembly to Flywheel. Rotate cover until "X" mark on cover is alined with "X" mark on flywheel (fig. 121). Install clutch cover to flywheel bolts and tighten alternately and gradually (one turn at a time). After cover is secured, withdraw alining tool.

d. Clean, Lubricate, and Install Ball Stud. Lift ball stud retainer spring out of fork and withdraw ball stud. Lubricate ball seat in fork as specified on Lubrication Order No. 9-802; then install ball stud and retainer spring. Be sure to place ends of ball retainer spring downward so that spring will be completely seated in grooves in fork.

e. Install Clutch Release Fork and Linkage. Install fork and ball stud assembly, with fingers at inner end of fork in groove of release bearing sleeve; then thread support into ball stud. Ball stud and support must be drawn up firmly. Attach adjusting link to clutch pedal and through fork arm, then install adjusting nut, check nut, and pull back spring.

f. Install Transmission and Power Plant. Install release bearing assembly and transmission assembly (par. 159), then install power plant (par. 95).

g. Adjust Pedal Free-travel. Adjust as described in paragraph 153.

Transmission

Section XXIX
Transmission

157. GENERAL.

a. Description. The transmission is a selective sliding gear type with five speeds forward and one reverse. Fourth speed is direct drive and fifth speed is overdrive. Gears are selected manually by a conventional gearshift lever. Engine, clutch, and transmission are mounted as a unit. Power take-off is attached to left-hand side of transmission. Gears for driving tachometer are located at rear end of transmission countershaft on vehicles after chassis serial No. 2005.

b. Make and Model. Clark Equipment Co. 204 VO-319.

c. Repair. Operations necessary to repair transmission components are described in TM 9-1802B.

158. TRANSMISSION REMOVAL.

a. Remove Power Plant. Whenever replacement of transmission assembly is necessary, the complete power plant unit should be removed from vehicle. This will save time, as the attaching parts are readily accessible with the power plant removed. Remove power plant unit as described in paragraph 94.

b. Drain Transmission. Remove drain plug and drain all lubricant from transmission and power take-off.

c. Remove Power Take-off. Remove stud nuts and washers which attach power take-off to transmission, then remove power take-off.

d. Remove Transmission Mounting Bolts. Remove engine flywheel underpan; then remove two transmission lower mounting bolts, accessible from inside clutch and flywheel housing. Support transmission assembly and remove transmission upper mounting bolts.

e. Remove Transmission. Pull transmission assembly straight away from clutch and flywheel housing. CAUTION: *Do not allow weight of transmission to rest on clutch disc hub.*

159. TRANSMISSION INSTALLATION.

a. Lubricate Release Bearing. Before installing transmission assembly, fill clutch release bearing inside recess and coat main drive gear splines with grease (Lubrication Order No. 9-802). Clutch release bearing must be positioned at clutch fork prior to transmission installation.

b. Position Transmission at Clutch and Flywheel Housing. Support transmission with main drive gear (clutch shaft) alined with clutch driven disc hub; then move transmission toward engine so that main drive gear passes through clutch release bearing and clutch disc and into pilot bearing in center of crankshaft.

c. Install Transmission Mounting Bolts. Install two transmission upper mounting bolts, then from inside clutch and flywheel housing, install two transmission lower mounting bolts and install lock wire through holes in bolt heads. Install engine flywheel underpan.

d. Install Power Take-off Assembly. Attach power take-off assembly to transmission as described in paragraph 168.

e. Install Lubricant in Transmission. Be sure drain plugs in power take-off and transmission are firmly tightened; then fill transmission case with lubricant as directed on Lubrication Order No. 9-802.

f. Install Power Plant. Install power plant as described in paragraph 95.

Section XXX
Axle Transfer Case and Controls

160. GENERAL.

a. Description. The axle transfer case is essentially a two-speed auxiliary transmission unit driven from the transmission. Power from transmission is transmitted to the three driving axles through propeller shafts. The hand brake drum and band are mounted at rear of transfer case and the speedometer is driven from mechanism assembled in the idler shaft front cap. Two manually operated levers are linked to transfer case shifting mechanism. One lever controls engagement and disengagement of transfer case in high or low range; the other controls engagement and disengagement of front axle.

b. Data.

```
Type ............................. Two-speed with front axle declutching
Make ..................................................... G.M.
```

Gear Ratios
```
High ........................................................ 1.16 to 1
Low ......................................................... 2.63 to 1
```

c. Repair. Operations necessary to repair transfer case and control linkage are described in TM 9-1802B.

161. CONTROLS AND LINKAGE.

a. General. The axle transfer case shift levers are supported on a cross shaft which is mounted in a bracket attached to frame right-hand side rail. Cross shaft and bracket are accessible after driver's compartment right-hand floor board is removed. Rearward end of control rods, cross shaft, levers, and bracket are accessible after air intake grille is removed.

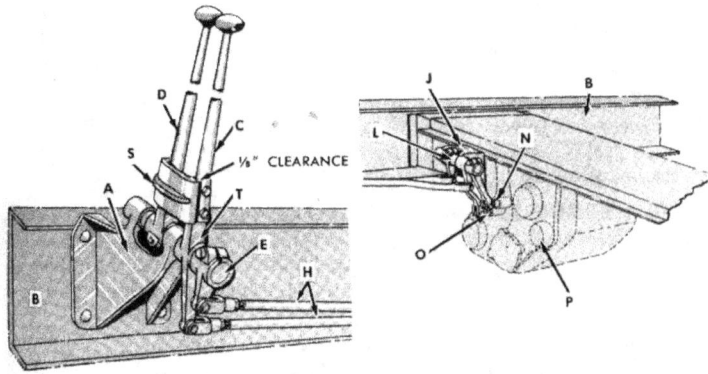

CONTROLS AND LINKAGE INSTALLATION

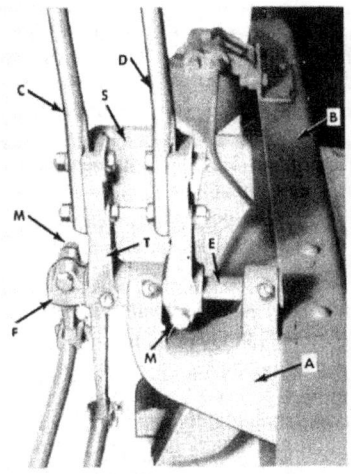

SHIFT LEVERS AND LINKAGE (FRONT)

LEVERS AND LINKAGE (REAR)

A CONTROL LEVER FRAME BRACKET
B FRAME SIDE RAIL
C TRANSFER CASE SHIFT LEVER
D DECLUTCHING CONTROL LEVER
E CROSS SHAFT
F DECLUTCHING CONTROL LOWER LEVER
G ADJUSTABLE YOKES
H CONTROL RODS
I OUTER LEVER
J REAR CROSS SHAFT BRACKET
K INNER LEVER
L REAR CROSS SHAFT
M CLAMP BOLT
N SHIFTER SHAFT (HIGH AND LOW)
O SHIFTER SHAFT (DECLUTCHING)
P AXLE TRANSFER CASE
Q TRANSFER CASE SUPPORT
R DECLUTCHING CONTROL LEVER (REAR)
S DECLUTCHING CONTROL LEVER (LOWER)
T TRANSFER CASE SHIFT LEVER (LOWER)

RA PD 337207

Figure 122—Axle Transfer Case Controls

TM 9-802

Maintenance Instructions

b. Control Linkage Adjustment. On early vehicles, the control rod adjustable yokes are at forward end, while on later vehicles, the adjustable yokes are at rear end. The control linkage requires adjustment whenever any one of the following conditions is present: (1) Levers contact floor board before levers are completely shifted; (2) no clearance, or clearance in excess of $1/8$ inch exists between declutching control lower lever and lower transfer case shift lever with declutching control lever in "OUT" position and transfer case shift lever in neutral. Key letters in following steps refer to figure 122.

(1) PLACE SHIFTER SHAFTS IN NEUTRAL ("NEUT") POSITION. Disconnect both control rods (H) at ends where adjustable yokes (G) are used. Move front axle declutching shifter shaft (O) to the disengaged (out) position and move transfer case high and low range shifter shaft (N) to neutral position.

(2) ADJUST DECLUTCHING CONTROL ROD. Place front axle declutching control lever (D) in a position slightly to rear of vertical; then with shifter shaft (O) remaining in disengaged position, turn adjustable yoke (G) on declutching control rod (H) to shorten or lengthen rod to permit insertion of clevis pin at adjustable yoke without moving control lever (D). With rod adjusted to correct length, tighten lock nut at yoke and connect rod, using clevis pin and cotter pin.

(3) ADJUST HIGH AND LOW CONTROL ROD. Adjust transfer case high and low control rod (H) length to obtain $1/8$ inch clearance (fig. 122) between lower declutching control lever and lower transfer case shift lever.

c. Rear Controls and Linkage Removal. Key letters in following steps refer to figure 122.

(1) REMOVE CONTROL RODS. Remove clevis pins from ends of each control rod (H); then push control rods under axle transfer case and remove through cargo floor center section opening.

(2) REMOVE AND DISASSEMBLE LINKAGE AT TRANSFER CASE. Remove clevis pins which connect levers (I and K) to shifter shafts (N and O). Remove three bracket to transfer case support bolts; then remove cross shaft (L), bracket (J), and levers (I and K) through air intake grille opening. Loosen lever clamp bolts (M); then move outer (right-hand) lever (I) to expose Woodruff key in cross shaft. Remove key and withdraw inner (left-hand) lever (K), and cross shaft (L) from bracket (J) and declutching lever (R). Remove inner (left-hand) lever (K) and Woodruff key from cross shaft (L).

d. Rear Controls and Linkage Installation. Key letters in following steps refer to figure 122.

(1) ASSEMBLE REAR CONTROLS. Install Woodruff key and inner (left-hand) lever (K) on cross shaft (L). Insert cross shaft (L) through declutching lever (R) and into support on bracket (J). Hold outer (right-hand) lever (I) with thrust face against support on bracket (J); then drive cross shaft (L) through lever (I) and into operating position.

Axle Transfer Case and Controls

Install Woodruff key in key slot and clamp levers in position on cross shaft, using clamp bolts (M).

(2) INSTALL LINKAGE AT TRANSFER CASE. Bolt cross shaft bracket (J) to transfer case support (Q), using new lock washers on bolts. Connect levers (K and I) to transfer case shifter shafts (N and O), using clevis pins secured with new cotter pins.

(3) INSTALL CONTROL RODS. Install control rods (H) between lower end of shift levers (C and D) and rear control levers (I and R). Be sure to adjust rod length (subpar. *b.* above) before installing clevis pins at end of rod where adjustable yokes are used. Lubricate linkage as directed on Lubrication Order No. 9-802.

e. Shift Lever Removal. Key letters in following steps refer to figure 122.

(1) DISCONNECT CONTROL RODS. Remove clevis pins attaching forward end of control rods (H) to shift levers (F and C).

(2) REMOVE UPPER LEVERS. Remove two bolts attaching upper shift levers to lower levers, then remove upper levers.

(3) REMOVE LOWER LEVERS AND CROSS SHAFT. Loosen clamp bolt in front axle declutching control lever (D), move lever (D) outward (to right) until Woodruff key in shaft (E) is exposed, then remove key. Loosen clamp bolt in declutching control lower lever (F) and remove lever from end of cross shaft (E). Remove Woodruff key from key slot, and slide transfer case shift lever (C) off from shaft (E). Drive cross shaft (E) toward outer side of frame, stripping declutching control lever (D) from cross shaft as it is removed from bracket.

f. Shift Lever Installation. Key letters in following steps refer to figure 122.

(1) INSTALL CROSS SHAFT. From outer side of frame side rail, enter cross shaft (E) through support bracket (A). Pass end of cross shaft (E) through declutching control lever (D) as the cross shaft is moved to operating position in bracket (A).

(2) INSTALL TRANSFER CASE SHIFT LEVER AND DECLUTCHING CONTROL LOWER LEVER. Install transfer case shift lever (C) on inner end of cross shaft (E); then with Woodruff key in key slot, install declutching control lower lever (F) on shaft (E). Place Woodruff key in key slot adjacent to declutching control lever, move lever to operating position, and install clamp bolts in both levers.

(3) INSTALL UPPER LEVERS AND ATTACH CONTROL RODS. Attach upper shift levers to lower levers, using bolts with new lock washers. Connect rods (H) to lower ends of levers, using clevis pins secured with new cotter pins. When connecting control rods, be sure linkage is adjusted as directed in subparagraph *b.* above. Lubricate as directed on Lubrication Order No. 9-802.

162. AXLE TRANSFER CASE REMOVAL.

a. Procedure. Key letters in following steps refer to figure 123.

(1) REMOVE FLOOR BOARDS AND CARGO COMPARTMENT FRONT BULKHEAD. Cargo compartment front bulkhead (par. 230*b*.), air intake grille sections, and driver's compartment and cargo compartment floor sections must be removed to permit access to disconnect points when removing axle transfer case.

(2) DISCONNECT CONTROL RODS. Remove clevis pins which attach control rods to rear linkage. Disconnect and remove cross shaft lever to hand brake rod (H).

(3) REMOVE WATER PROPELLER FRONT DRIVE SHAFT. Remove water propeller front drive shaft (F) as described in paragraph 257*b*.

(4) REMOVE HAND BRAKE DRUM AND BAND. Remove hand brake drum and band (L) as described in paragraphs 201 and 202.

(5) DISCONNECT PROPELLER SHAFTS AND SPEEDOMETER CABLE. Remove the U-joint to flange bolts at the three axle transfer case flanges (G). One propeller shaft will have been disconnected in step (4) above. Disconnect speedometer drive shaft from tube nut at transfer case idler shaft front cap by loosening knurled nut and lifting cable casing and adapter from transfer case.

(6) REMOVE TRANSFER CASE AND CROSSMEMBER FROM VEHICLE. Remove seven crossmember to frame bracket bolts (A) at each end of crossmember (B); then with suitable lifting equipment, lift transfer case and crossmember assembly from vehicle.

(7) SEPARATE TRANSFER CASE FROM CROSSMEMBER. Disconnect rear cross shaft levers from transfer case shifter shafts (J). Bend locks away from bolt heads, then remove four support to transfer case bolts at each side of case. Remove crossmember assembly (B) from transfer case (D).

163. AXLE TRANSFER CASE INSTALLATION.

a. Procedure. Key letters in following steps refer to figure 123.

(1) ATTACH TRANSFER CASE TO CROSSMEMBER ASSEMBLY. With rear controls and linkage attached to crossmember assembly (B), position crossmember and transfer case with mounting bolt holes alined. Install support to transfer case bolts (four at each side) with lock plate under heads of each pair of bolts. Connect rear cross shaft levers to transfer case shifter shafts.

(2) INSTALL TRANSFER CASE AND CROSSMEMBER IN VEHICLE. Lower transfer case and crossmember into place in vehicle and install fourteen bolts (A) with new lock washers which attach crossmember to frame brackets.

(3) CONNECT SPEEDOMETER CABLE. Connect speedometer drive shaft adapter to tube nut at transfer case idler shaft front cap. Tongue

TM 9-802
163

Axle Transfer Case and Controls

PHANTOM VIEW OF AXLE TRANSFER CASE AND PROPELLER SHAFTS INSTALLED

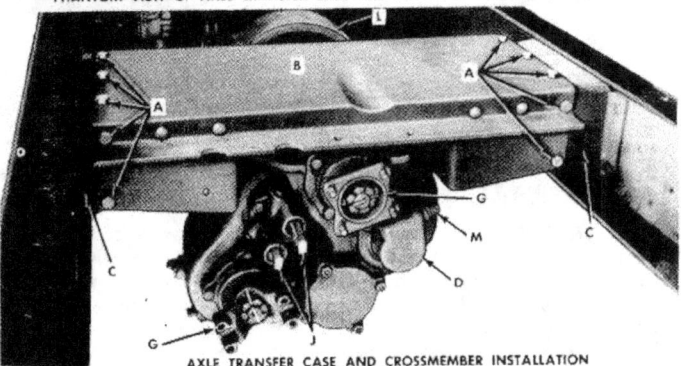

AXLE TRANSFER CASE AND CROSSMEMBER INSTALLATION

A MOUNTING BOLTS
B CROSSMEMBER
C FRAME BRACKETS
D AXLE TRANSFER CASE
E WATER PROPELLER TRANSFER CASE
F WATER PROPELLER FRONT DRIVE SHAFT
G AXLE TRANSFER CASE FLANGES
H HAND BRAKE ROD
I AXLE TRANSFER CASE CONTROL RODS
J SHIFTER SHAFTS
K BILGE PUMP DRIVE CHAIN AND SPROCKET
L HAND BRAKE BAND AND DRUM
M SPEEDOMETER DRIVE SHAFT TUBE NUT

RA PD 337258

Figure 123—Disconnect Points for Axle Transfer Case Replacement

on adapter must be inserted into driven gear shaft and knurled nut firmly tightened onto tube nut threads.

(4) CONNECT PROPELLER SHAFTS TO TRANSFER CASE. Position three propeller shafts at their respective flanges (G) on transfer case and install flange bolts. Do not connect transfer case to pillow shaft until hand brake drum has been installed [step (5) below].

(5) INSTALL HAND BRAKE DRUM AND BAND. Install hand brake drum and band (pars. 201 and 202), and adjust hand brake as described in paragraph 200*b*.

TM 9-802
163-165

Maintenance Instructions

(6) INSTALL WATER PROPELLER FRONT DRIVE SHAFT. Install water propeller front drive shaft (F) as described in paragraph 257*b*.

(7) CONNECT CONTROL RODS. Adjust transfer case control rods as necessary (par. 161*b*.) and connect rear ends of rods at rear cross shaft levers. Install cross shaft lever to hand brake rod. Length of this rod must be adjusted so that, with hand brake lever in released position, clevis pins may be readily inserted (par. 203*b*.).

(8) PREPARE TRANSFER CASE FOR SERVICE. When transfer case installation is completed, check lubricant level and service as required. Adjust control linkage as described in paragraph 161*b*.

(9) INSTALL CARGO COMPARTMENT FRONT BULKHEAD AND FLOOR BOARDS. Install cargo compartment front bulkhead as described in paragraph 230*b*. Install air intake grille sections and install driver's compartment and cargo compartment floor boards.

Section XXXI
Power Take-off and Controls

164. GENERAL.

a. Description. The power take-off is a dual two-speed and reverse type having two output shafts. The assembly is mounted on the left-hand side of the transmission assembly through the use of studs and nuts, and a support bracket connected between the power take-off and top of the transmission case. Shifting mechanism incorporated within the power take-off assembly provides for the use of the two output shafts simultaneously or separately. On vehicles prior to chassis serial No. 2006, the power take-off transmits power for driving the tire pump and winch, while the unit is used to drive only the winch on vehicles after chassis serial No. 2005. The power take-off is manually controlled through linkage connected with control levers extending into the driver's compartment.

b. Data.

Type	Dual two-speed and reverse
Make	Gar Wood
Model	67 Y 6000LDG-2
Drive	Transmission

c. Repair. Operations necessary for repair of power take-off are described in TM 9-1802B.

165. CONTROLS AND LINKAGE.

a. General. Power take-off control for winch operation consists of a lever which pivots on a special stud at left side of transmission. Lever is connected to power take-off shift shaft arm (E) through a short link

TM 9-802
165

Power Take-off and Controls

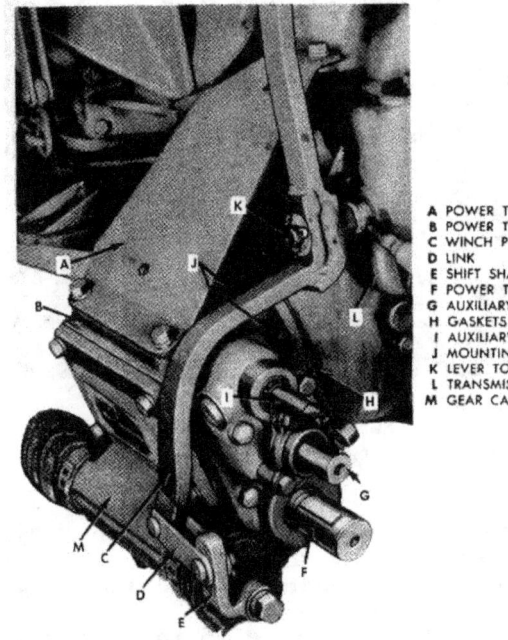

A POWER TAKE-OFF BRACKET
B POWER TAKE-OFF ASSEMBLY
C WINCH POWER TAKE-OFF LEVER
D LINK
E SHIFT SHAFT ARM
F POWER TAKE-OFF SHAFT (TO WINCH)
G AUXILIARY DRIVE SHAFT
H GASKETS
I AUXILIARY SHIFT SHAFT
J MOUNTING STUD NUTS
K LEVER TO TRANSMISSION STUD
L TRANSMISSION CASE
M GEAR CASE COVER

RA PD 337184

Figure 124—Power Take-off and Winch Control Installation

(D) at the lower end (fig. 124). A hinge type lever lock is attached to floor board to prevent accidental engagement of winch power take-off control lever. On vehicles prior to chassis serial No. 2006, on which the power take-off is used to drive the power tire pump, an additional control is used to shift the power take-off auxiliary drive mechanism.

b. Winch Controls and Linkage Removal. Key letters in following steps refer to figure 124.

(1) DISCONNECT LEVER LINK FROM POWER TAKE-OFF. Remove driver's compartment left-hand floor board and left-hand front section of cargo compartment floor board. Enter bilge and remove clevis pin which connects link (D) to power take-off shift shaft arm (E).

(2) REMOVE LEVER AND LINK FROM VEHICLE. Remove cotter pin and flat washer retaining winch power take-off lever on transmission stud (K). Remove lever (C) from stud and lift lever assembly from vehicle. Link (D) may be removed from lever by removing clevis pin.

(3) REMOVE LEVER LOCK (IF NECESSARY) (FIG. 125). Remove wood screws attaching winch power take-off lever lock to driver's compartment floor board, and remove lock.

TM 9-802
165

Maintenance Instructions

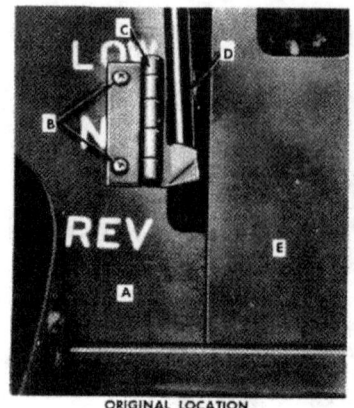 

ORIGINAL LOCATION — NEW LOCATION

A LEFT-HAND FLOOR BOARD
B WOOD SCREWS
C LEVER LOCK
D WINCH CONTROL LEVER
E CENTER FLOOR BOARD

RA PD 337180

Figure 125—Winch Control Lever Lock Locations

c. Winch Controls and Linkage Installation. Key letters in following steps refer to figure 124.

(1) INSTALL LINK ON LEVER. Attach lever link sections (D) to lower end of lever (C), using clevis pin.

(2) ATTACH WINCH CONTROL LEVER TO TRANSMISSION STUD. Position winch control lever (C) on special stud at transmission and install flat washer and cotter pin to hold lever in place.

(3) CONNECT LEVER LINK TO POWER TAKE-OFF. Enter bilge through cargo compartment floor section opening and connect lever link (D) to arm (E) on power take-off shift shaft.

(4) INSTALL WINCH CONTROL LEVER LOCK (IF REMOVED). Install winch control lever lock on center floor board in driver's compartment, relocating if necessary as described in subparagraph *d.* below.

d. Winch Control Lever Lock Relocation. Vehicles prior to chassis serial No. 5103 and between 6602 and 6901 were produced with winch control lever lock attached to left-hand floor board as shown in figure 125. However, when lever lock has been removed from any vehicle, it should be reworked and/or installed as directed in following operations.

(1) REWORK LEVER LOCK. Grip lock in vise and bend flat corner to correspond with bend at opposite end of lock.

(2) INSTALL LOCK ON FLOOR BOARD. Place winch control lever in neutral ("N") position, then place lever lock on center floor board (fig. 125) and install two wood screws to attach lock. Be sure lock does not bind on lever and that hinge action is free.

e. Tire Pump Control Linkage Replacement. Instructions for removal and installation of tire pump controls and linkage are given in paragraph 261.

166. OIL SEALS

a. General. Oil seals used in power take-off gear case cover at shift shaft and at auxiliary drive unit may be replaced after these respective parts have been removed from the power take-off assembly. Figure 126 shows views of various operations necessary to replace the power take-off oil seals. Oil seals are spring loaded type. Seals should be soaked in warm engine oil to make leather portion soft and pliable prior to installation.

b. Shift Shaft Oil Seal Replacement.

(1) DRAIN TRANSMISSION. Drain all lubricant from transmission assembly by removing hull bottom plug and transmission drain plug.

(2) DISCONNECT POWER TAKE-OFF LEVER (FIG. 124). Remove clevis pin which connects lever link with shift shaft arm.

(3) REMOVE POWER TAKE-OFF GEAR CASE COVER. Remove cover to gear case cap screws, then remove the power take-off gear case cover and shifting mechanism as an assembly.

(4) DISASSEMBLE SHIFTING MECHANISM.

(a) Loosen boot clamp screws, then remove cap screws from front end of shift shaft and remove forward boot.

(b) Remove poppets, springs, and balls from cover and remove yoke from shift shaft. Withdraw shift shaft with rearward boot and arm attached. Remove old oil seals from cover.

(c) Inspect surface of shift shaft for corroded or scored condition. If shift shaft surface is rough or scored it should be refinished or the shift shaft should be replaced, as surface must be perfectly smooth if oil seals are to function properly.

(5) INSTALL OIL SEALS. Coat oil seal recess in cover with cement (52-C-685); then drive or press new oil seals into place in cover with seal lips toward inside of cover. Refer to figure 126.

(6) ASSEMBLE SHIFTING MECHANISM.

(a) Carefully insert shift shaft through oil seals and into operating position. End of shaft with arm and boot attached must be at rear of cover assembly.

(b) Install shift yoke on shift shaft, using a new lock washer under yoke to shaft cap screw head. Be sure yoke fits firmly against shift shaft with dowel pin in place.

(c) Install balls, springs, and poppets in cover. Install shift shaft boot on forward end of shaft, position boots and clamps at cover, and tighten clamp screws.

(7) INSTALL GEAR CASE COVER AND CONNECT CONTROL LINKAGE. Coat a new cover to gear case gasket with gasket cement

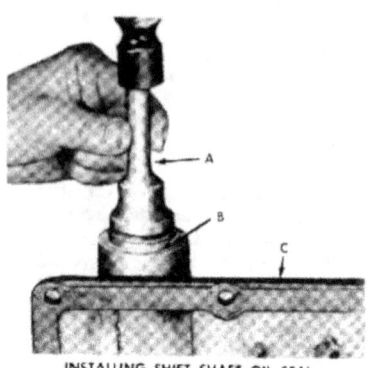
INSTALLING SHIFT SHAFT OIL SEAL

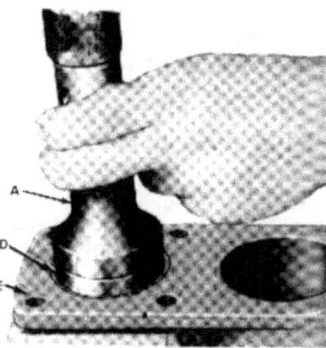
INSTALLING POWER TAKE-OFF SHAFT OIL SEAL

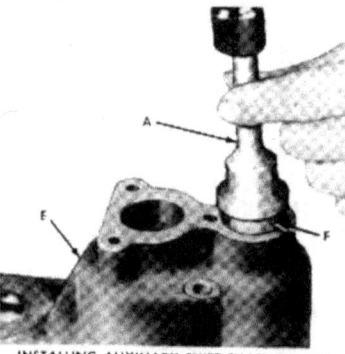
INSTALLING AUXILIARY SHIFT SHAFT OIL SEAL

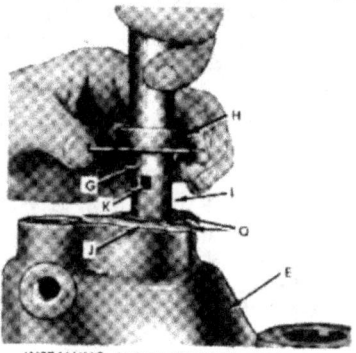
INSTALLING AUXILIARY DRIVE SHAFT CAP AND OIL SEAL ASSEMBLY

A OIL SEAL REPLACER
B SHIFT SHAFT OIL SEAL (H013-05-00023)
C GEAR CASE COVER
D POWER TAKE-OFF SHAFT OIL SEAL (H013-05-00050)
E AUXILIARY DRIVE SHAFT COVER
F AUXILIARY SHIFT SHAFT OIL SEAL (H013-05-00050)
G SHIM STOCK
H AUXILIARY DRIVE SHAFT CAP (INCLUDES OIL SEAL)
I AUXILIARY DRIVE SHAFT
J DRIVE SHAFT BUSHING LOCK PLATE
K KEY SLOT
L POWER TAKE-OFF SHAFT
M IDLER GEAR SHAFT
N AUXILIARY DRIVE SHIFT SHAFT
O POPPET
P AUXILIARY COVER TO GEAR CASE GASKET
Q LOCK PLATE GASKET

INSTALLING AUXILIARY DRIVE ASSEMBLY

RA PD 337212

Figure 126—Power Take-off Oil Seal Installation

Power Take-off and Controls

(52-C-685), then position gasket at power take-off gear case. Install gear case cover assembly, using care to engage shift yoke with groove in sliding gear. Connect control lever with shift shaft arm by installing clevis pin through link and arm. Before operating vehicle, fill transmission with lubricant as indicated on Lubrication Order No. 9-802.

c. Auxiliary Drive Oil Seal Replacement.

(1) DRAIN TRANSMISSION. Remove hull bottom plug and transmission drain plug and allow all lubricant to drain from transmission.

(2) DISCONNECT TIRE PUMP DRIVE AND LINKAGE (PRIOR TO CHASSIS SERIAL NO. 2006 ONLY) (FIG. 231). Remove clevis pin which attaches rod (V) to shift shaft. Remove tire pump drive chain (E) and sprocket (F) as described in paragraph 260.

(3) DISCONNECT WINCH DRIVE SHAFT FROM POWER TAKE-OFF. Loosen U-joint to power take-off shaft set screw and drive U-joint yoke off shaft. Remove Woodruff key from shaft.

(4) REMOVE AUXILIARY DRIVE SHAFT AND HOUSING ASSEMBLY (FIG. 126). Remove six cap screws which attach auxiliary drive shaft cover (C) to gear case; then remove the cover with auxiliary drive shaft (I) and shifting mechanism.

(5) DISASSEMBLE AUXILIARY DRIVE MECHANISM (FIG. 126). Remove shift shaft eye and lock nut from end of auxiliary shift shaft (N), then remove poppet. Withdraw shift shaft, yoke, and sliding clutch from cover (C). Remove three cap screws which attach auxiliary drive shaft cap and oil seal assembly (H) and bushing lock plate (J), then remove the cap and oil seal assembly. Auxiliary drive shaft and bushing may be removed from housing while replacing oil seals. Remove and discard power take-off shaft oil seal (D) and auxiliary shift shaft oil seal (F).

(6) INSTALL OIL SEALS (FIG. 126). Coat oil seal recesses in auxiliary drive housing with cement (52-C-685); then press or drive power take-off shaft oil seal and auxiliary shift shaft oil seal into place in auxiliary drive shaft cover (C). Oil seals must seat squarely and firmly in cover.

(7) ASSEMBLE AUXILIARY DRIVE MECHANISM (FIG. 126).

(a) With auxiliary drive shaft spacer and bushing in place on shaft (I) insert assembly into cover (E). Install bushing lock plate (J) over end of auxiliary drive shaft with a new gasket on each side of lock plate. Tangs on lock plate must engage notches in bushing. Use a roll of shim stock as illustrated to protect oil seal against damage as auxiliary drive shaft cap and oil seal assembly is installed over end of shaft (I) and key slot (K). Install cap screws to attach cap (H) and lock plate (J) to cover.

(b) Place sliding clutch in shift shaft yoke and insert end of shift shaft (N) through cover (E). Carefully guide end of shift shaft through oil seal (F) and at the same time turn sliding clutch as necessary to aline female splines with male splines on end of auxiliary drive shaft. Install poppet ball, spring, and screw in side of cover (C). Install auxiliary shift shaft eye in end of shaft and tighten lock nut.

(8) INSTALL AUXILIARY DRIVE ASSEMBLY ON POWER TAKE-OFF AND CONNECT LINKAGE (FIG. 126). Be sure all old gasket is removed from power take-off assembly; then, using gasket cement (52-C-685) on both sides of new cover to gear case gasket (P), position gasket at gear case. Insert a roll of thin shim stock through power take-off shaft oil seal (D); then position auxiliary drive assembly at power take-off, with shim stock over power take-off shaft (L) to protect seal leather as it passes over key slot and shoulder on shaft. Move auxiliary drive assembly against gasket (P) and install attaching cap screws. Vehicles prior to chassis serial No. 2006 have a chain driven tire pump. Connect rod (V, fig. 231), to auxiliary shift shaft by installing clevis pin through rod yoke and shift shaft eye.

(9) INSTALL TIRE PUMP DRIVE SPROCKET AND CHAIN (PRIOR TO CHASSIS SERIAL NO. 2006 ONLY) (FIG. 231). Install tire pump drive sprocket (F) and chain (E) as described in paragraph 260.

(10) FILL TRANSMISSION WITH LUBRICANT. Lubricate transmission as directed on Lubrication Order No. 9-802.

167. POWER TAKE-OFF REMOVAL.

a. The power take-off assembly is accessible after left-hand and center floor boards in driver's compartment, and cargo compartment left-hand front section have been removed.

b. Procedure.

(1) DRAIN TRANSMISSION. Remove hull bottom plug and transmission drain plug and allow all lubricant to drain from transmission.

(2) REMOVE TIRE PUMP CHAIN AND DRIVE SPROCKET (PRIOR TO CHASSIS SERIAL NO. 2006) (FIG. 231). Remove tire pump chain (E) and drive sprocket (F) as described in paragraph 260.

(3) DISCONNECT WINCH DRIVE SHAFT. Loosen set screw which holds winch drive shaft U-joint onto power take-off shaft and drive joint from shaft.

(4) DISCONNECT CONTROLS. Remove clevis pin attaching link at lower end of winch control lever to power take-off shift shaft arm (fig. 124). On vehicles prior to chassis serial No. 2006, disconnect rod (E, fig. 231) at auxiliary drive shift shaft.

(5) REMOVE POWER TAKE-OFF (FIG. 124). Remove bolts attaching support bracket to transmission and power take-off, then remove bracket. Remove six stud nuts which attach power take-off assembly to transmission. Power take-off may then be removed by pulling the assembly off studs at transmission. Remove gaskets used as spacers between power take-off and transmission.

168. POWER TAKE-OFF INSTALLATION.

a. Correct backlash between power take-off intermediate gear and transmission reverse idler gear is obtained by installing gaskets as necessary. Three gaskets will usually give correct backlash.

Front Axle

b. Procedure.

(1) INSTALL GASKETS. Coat three gaskets on both sides with gasket cement (52-C-685) and position gaskets at transmission case.

(2) MOUNT POWER TAKE-OFF ON TRANSMISSION (FIG. 124). Place power take-off assembly over studs and against transmission then install lock washers and stud nuts. Check backlash, which should be approximately 0.005 to 0.008 inch between power take-off intermediate gear and transmission reverse idler gear. Backlash can be checked by noting amount of movement while attempting to twist auxiliary drive shift back and forth with this unit engaged. If backlash is excessive (noise), remove one gasket from between power take-off and transmission. If movement is not sufficient (tight), add one gasket.

(3) INSTALL POWER TAKE-OFF SUPPORT BRACKET (FIG. 124). Install power take-off support bracket, attaching bracket to power take-off and transmission with bolts secured with lock washers.

(4) CONNECT WINCH DRIVE SHAFT. With Woodruff key in slot in shaft, install winch drive shaft front U-joint on power take-off shaft. Tighten set screw firmly to hold U-joint in position.

(5) INSTALL POWER TIRE PUMP DRIVE SPROCKET AND CHAIN (FIG. 231). Install tire pump drive sprocket and chain as described in paragraph 260.

(6) CONNECT CONTROLS (FIGS. 124 AND 231). Connect rod (V, fig. 231) at power take-off auxiliary drive shift shaft, using clevis pin secured with cotter pin. Attach link (D) at lower end of winch control lever to power take-off shift shaft arm (E), using clevis pin secured with cotter pin. Refer to figure 124.

(7) REFILL TRANSMISSION WITH LUBRICANT. Fill transmission with lubricant as indicated on Lubrication Order No. 9-802.

Section XXXII

Front Axle

169. GENERAL.

a. Description. The front axle is single-reduction with banjo type housing. The axle shafts are full-floating type with constant-velocity universal joints at the steering knuckles. Axle assembly is mounted on semi-elliptic springs, and is operated from transfer case through a propeller shaft.

b. Data.

```
Type ..................................................Single Reduction
Ratio ...........................................................6.66 to 1
Type of constant-velocity joints .........................Bendix-Weiss
```

Maintenance Instructions

c. Repair. Repair of front axle components, and the checking and correction of caster, camber, and turning angle are described in TM 9-1802B.

170. TOE-IN ADJUSTMENT.

a. Toe-in is the amount by which front wheels are closer together at the front than at the rear with wheels in straight-ahead position (A minus B, fig. 127). Various conditions will affect toe-in, such as loose wheel bearings, bent axle housing, bent steering knuckle, and an improperly adjusted or bent tie rod. Incorrect toe-in will cause excessive tire wear and difficult steering.

b. Checking Toe-in. Inflate tires to "Hi-way" pressure (40 lb); then place vehicle on smooth, level surface with wheels in *straight-ahead* position. Place gage (41-G-510) between the wheels ahead of the axle, with ends of gage bearing against tire side walls and both pendant chains just touching the ground. Adjust gage pointer to zero ("0"). Move vehicle *forward* until gage is brought in *back* of axle, with both pendant chains just touching the ground. The gage will indicate amount of toe-in or toe-out. The correct toe-in (A minus B, fig. 127) is $\frac{1}{16}$ to $\frac{3}{16}$ inch.

c. Adjustment.

(1) CHECK AXLE CONDITION. Check and correct all conditions which contribute to faulty toe-in, namely, loose wheel bearings, worn steering knuckle support (tie rod) bushings, bent steering knuckle, damaged wheel, bent tie rod, and bent axle housing.

(2) REMOVE TIE ROD. Remove cotter pin and nut from each tie rod yoke bolt. After driving each bolt out of yoke and steering knuckle support, tie rod assembly may be withdrawn. Remove left-hand yoke inner clamp bolt and lock. Loosen the other yoke clamp bolts on right- and left-hand sides.

(3) ADJUST. Using gage reading (subpar. *b.* above) as a guide, turn yokes in or out to obtain correct toe-in (fig. 128). Toe-in will be *increased* approximately $\frac{1}{8}$ inch when right-hand yoke (coarse threads) is turned one *full turn off* of tie rod (toward wheel). Left-hand yoke is turned onto rod only to bring adjustment within correct limits ($\frac{1}{16}$ to $\frac{3}{16}$ in.) and to aline both yokes on tie rod. Reversing this procedure reduces the amount of toe-in. Install tie rod temporarily and check with gage (subpar. *b.* above).

(4) INSTALL TIE ROD (FIG. 128). After adjustment is completed, install tie rod to steering knuckle supports with yoke bolts and nuts. Tighten nuts firmly, then back nut off one-quarter turn and aline cotter pin hole. Install new cotter pin. Insert lock in left-hand yoke, seating lock in tie rod keyway and alining it with yoke bolt hole. Install and tighten yoke clamp bolts, lock washers, and nuts. Lubricate tie rod ends (Lubrication Order No. 9-802).

Front Axle

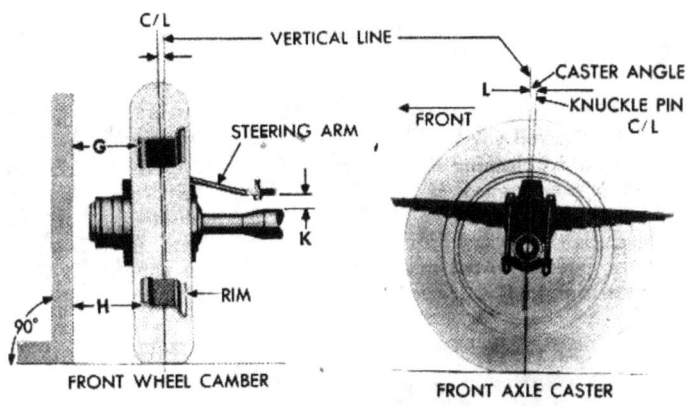

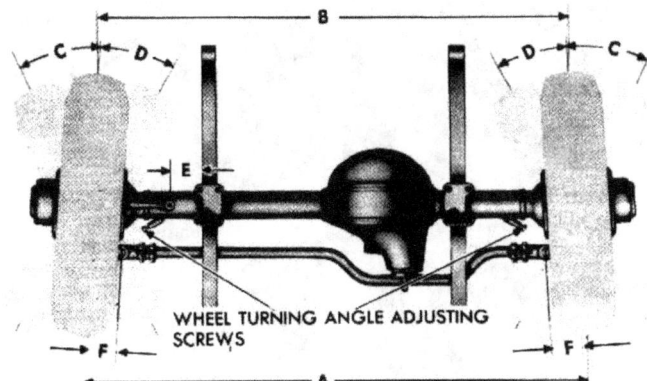

A MINUS B TOE-IN
C TURNING ANGLE (INSIDE)
D TURNING ANGLE (OUTSIDE)
E CENTER LINE OF STEERING ARM BALL TO OUTSIDE OF SPRING
F BACKING PLATE TO CENTERLINE OF TIE-ROD YOKE BOLT

H MINUS G WHEEL CAMBER (INCHES)
J WHEEL CAMBER (DEGREES)
K BOTTOM OF STEERING ARM TO TOP OF AXLE HOUSING
L CASTER ANGLE (DEGREES)

RA PD 303002

Figure 127—Front Wheel Alinement Chart

171. TIE ROD ASSEMBLY.

a. Description. Tie rod is solid type with a double offset to clear differential carrier, and is connected to steering knuckle supports by

TM 9-802
171

Maintenance Instructions

yokes, threaded onto each end of rod. The rod is held in correct position with a lock which is fitted into a keyway in rod, and held in place by inner clamp bolt of the left-hand yoke.

b. Removal and Installation. After removal [par. 170c.(2)], clean yoke bolts, tie rod yokes, and steering knuckle support bushings thoroughly with dry-cleaning solvent. Make certain that lubrication channel in bolts is not clogged. If bushings in supports are scored or worn, notify higher authority. Examine yokes and tie rod thoroughly for damage, such as distortion and cracked or bent condition. If these conditions are evident, install new parts. Install tie rod temporarily, then check toe-in and adjust if necessary (par. 170c.).

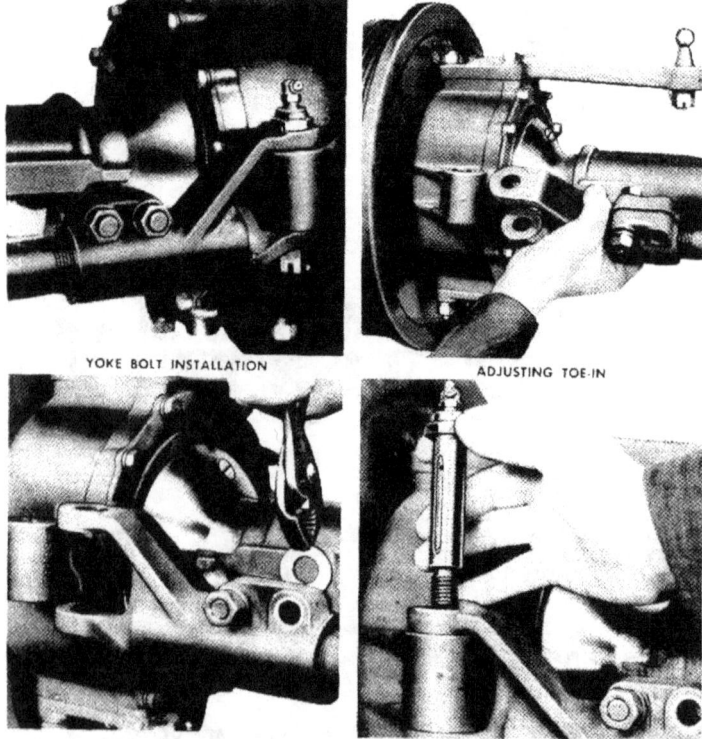

RA PD 337193

Figure 128—Adjusting and Installing Tie Rod

Front Axle

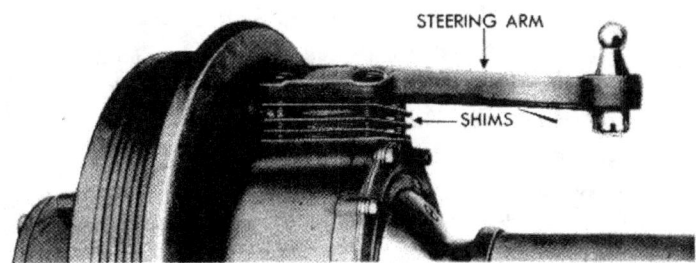

Figure 129—Steering Arm Installation

172. STEERING ARM.

a. Description. The steering arm is mounted on left-hand side of front axle housing (fig. 129), and is attached on top of steering knuckle support with studs, nuts, and lock washers. A ball stud is fitted in end of arm and held in place with a nut and cotter pin.

b. Removal.

(1) DISCONNECT BRAKE HOSE AND DRAG LINK. With vehicle placed on level surface and front wheels turned to extreme left, raise left-hand end of axle with jack. Close front brake shut-off cock. Unhook brake hose suspension spring, then disconnect brake hose from hull and wheel cylinder (par. 193*b*.). Disconnect drag link from steering arm ball stud.

(2) REMOVE BALL STUD AND STEERING ARM. Remove four nuts and lock washers which attach arm to steering knuckle support. Carefully lift steering arm with ball stud off studs. Be sure that shims are not disturbed when steering arm is removed. After removing cotter pin, loosen ball stud nut until nut extends beyond ball stud threads. Tap nut firmly with a hammer until ball is loose. Remove nut from ball stud, then remove stud from steering arm.

c. Installation.

(1) INSTALL STEERING ARM AND BALL STUD. Make certain that the nut fits freely on ball stud threads. Thoroughly clean and dry ball stud taper and tapered seat in steering arm. Insert ball stud in steering arm, then tap firmly with soft-faced hammer to seat stud. Tighten nut firmly and secure with new cotter pin. Clean shim face of steering arm, then apply a thin coating of light rust preventive compound (14-C-349-880) over face. With original shims in place, install arm on studs and secure with lock washers and nuts. Tighten nuts firmly.

(2) INSTALL BRAKE HOSE AND DRAG LINK. Install brake hose to wheel cylinder and hull (par. 193*b*.). Turn on front brake shut-off cock. Install drag link on ball stud. Bleed the two front wheel cylinders (par. 187). Remove jack.

Maintenance Instructions

173. AXLE SHAFT AND UNIVERSAL JOINT.

a. Description. Axle shafts are full-floating type with a Bendix-Weiss constant-velocity universal joint at each steering knuckle. Each axle shaft is splined at inner end in differential side gears, and outer end in drive flange which is attached to wheel hub.

b. Removal.

(1) REMOVE WHEELHOUSE SKIRT, TIRE INFLATING DEVICE, AND WHEEL. With vehicle placed on a level surface, remove wheelhouse skirt, tire inflating device, and wheel and tire (par. 212c.).

(2) REMOVE DRIVE FLANGE.

(a) Prior to Chassis Serial No. 2006. If lock plates are used, pry plate tangs away from cap screws. If not, remove eight cap screws and lock washers. Install two cap screws into tapped holes in drive flange. Tighten screws alternately until flange is free from hub. Remove drive flange and gasket (G085-31-05780).

(b) After Chassis Serial No. 2005. Remove five cap screws and lock washers. Before removing the three tire inflating device to hub locking bolts, note if hub and wheel bolts are marked as described in paragraph 211. Remove axle shaft drive flange as described in step *(a)* above.

(3) REMOVE HUB AND DRUM ASSEMBLY. Remove hub and drum assembly (par. 214).

(4) REMOVE BRAKE SHOE ASSEMBLY AND ANCHOR PLATE (FIG. 130). Install clamp on wheel cylinder to prevent brake fluid leakage. Remove brake shoe return spring. Remove six cap screws and lock washers which attach brake shoe anchor plate to anchor plate spacer, then remove anchor plate and brake shoe assembly.

(5) REMOVE BRAKE FLANGE PLATE AND STEERING KNUCKLE (FIG. 130). Remove 12 cap screws and lock washers which attach spacer, oil deflector, flange plate, and steering knuckle to knuckle support. Remove following parts in order named: anchor plate spacer, inner oil deflector, brake flange plate (with wheel cylinder attached), and knuckle. NOTE: *Brake flange plate must be supported with a wire after removing, to prevent strain on brake hose.*

(6) REMOVE AXLE SHAFT AND UNIVERSAL JOINT ASSEMBLY. Pull axle shaft and universal joint assembly out of housing.

c. Cleaning, Inspection, and Special Lubrication.

(1) CLEANING. Clean axle shaft and universal joint thoroughly with dry-cleaning solvent. *Do not disassemble universal joint.* Flex joint several times so that all parts can be thoroughly cleaned.

(2) INSPECTION. Examine balls and ball races for grooved, scratched, or pitted condition. To determine if excessive play or backlash exists in universal joint, refer to TM 9-1802B. Examine axle shaft oil seal (G085-31-12520), thrust washers (G085-31-15360) in steering knuckles, and axle housing for scoring or damage. Replace if necessary (TM 9-1802B). Inspect axle shaft splines for nicks, cracks, or distortion.

Front Axle

- A AXLE SHAFT
- B STEERING KNUCKLE SPINDLE
- C HUB
- D BRAKE ANCHOR PLATE SPACER
- E OIL DEFLECTOR
- F BRAKE FLANGE PLATE
- G THRUST WASHERS
- H AXLE HOUSING
- I SEALING POINTS—USE COMPOUND
- J SHIMS
- K JOINT SEAL ASSEMBLY
- L LOWER TRUNNION
- M STEERING ARM
- N FRONT AXLE SHAFT OIL SEAL (G085-31-12520)
- O THRUST WASHER
- P FRONT BEARING INNER OIL SEAL ASSEMBLY

RA PD 337260

Figure 130—Steering Knuckle and Universal Joint Assembly

(3) SPECIAL LUBRICATION. Pack new lubricant (Lubrication Order No. 9-802) well into universal joint until it fills all space between balls and universal joint yokes. Also spread lubricant liberally on surfaces which contact thrust washers and bushing in steering knuckle.

d. Installation.

(1) INSERT AXLE SHAFT (FIG. 131). Insert shaft assembly into axle housing and guide splined end into differential side gear splines. Use care not to damage axle shaft oil seal.

(2) INSTALL STEERING KNUCKLE AND BRAKE FLANGE PLATE. Position steering knuckle support gasket, coated with a thin film of chassis grease, on face of knuckle support. Install steering knuckle, with drain slot toward bottom, over end of axle shaft on gasket (fig. 131). Install the following parts, in the order named, on steering knuckle: brake flange plate, inner oil deflector, and anchor plate spacer. Coat threads of cap screws which attach parts to knuckle support with cement (52-C-644) or compound (52-C-3115). Tighten cap screws alternately and firmly. Use new lock washers.

(3) INSTALL ANCHOR PLATE AND BRAKE SHOE ASSEMBLY. Place anchor plate and brake shoe assembly in position, then attach with six cap screws, using new lock washers. Tighten cap screws firmly. Install brake shoe return spring, then remove clamp from wheel cylinder.

Maintenance Instructions

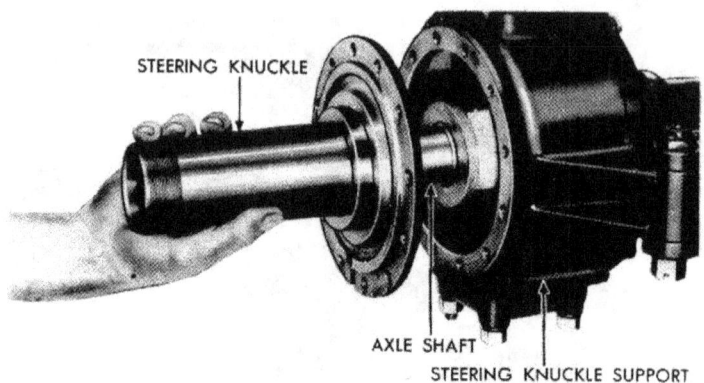

Figure 131—Axle Shaft and Steering Knuckle Spindle Installation

(4) INSTALL HUB AND DRUM ASSEMBLY. Install hub and drum and adjust wheel bearings (par. 214).

(5) INSTALL DRIVE FLANGE.

(a) Prior to Chassis Serial No. 2006. Clean axle drive flange and hub face thoroughly. Place new gasket, coated with grease, on drive flange face. Install drive flange over splined end of axle shaft, pressing firmly until gasket and drive flange seat against hub. Install eight cap screws and new lock washers (discard lock plates if used), then tighten cap screws using torque wrench (85 to 95 ft-lb torque).

Front Axle

(*b*) *After Chassis Serial No. 2005*. Install drive flange as directed in step (*a*) above. Tire inflating device to hub locking bolts must be located and installed as directed in paragraph 211.

(6) INSTALL WHEEL, INFLATING DEVICE, AND WHEEL-HOUSE SKIRT. Install wheel and tire inflating device, then install wheelhouse skirt (par. 212*d*.). Lubricate steering knuckle (Lubrication Order No. 9-802).

174. HOUSING OUTER END SEALS.

a. Description (figs. 132 and 133). Axle housing outer end seals are installed on inner side of each steering knuckle support around spherical surface of joint housing. Each seal assembly consists of a gasket, outer retainer, oil seal, gasket, spring retainer, dust seal, seal retainer, and inner retainer. The oil seal is composed of felt and neoprene to prevent leakage of lubricant. The composition dust seal is spring loaded and bears tightly against spherical surface of joint housing. When seals are in good condition and properly installed, dust and water will not enter housing, providing hub inner seal is also in good condition.

b. Test for Leaks. When inspection indicates that water has entered knuckle support housing, the following test must be made to determine cause of leaks before any attempt is made to correct the condition.

RA PD 333138

Figure 132—Air Hose Installed for U-Joint Leakage Test

Maintenance Instructions

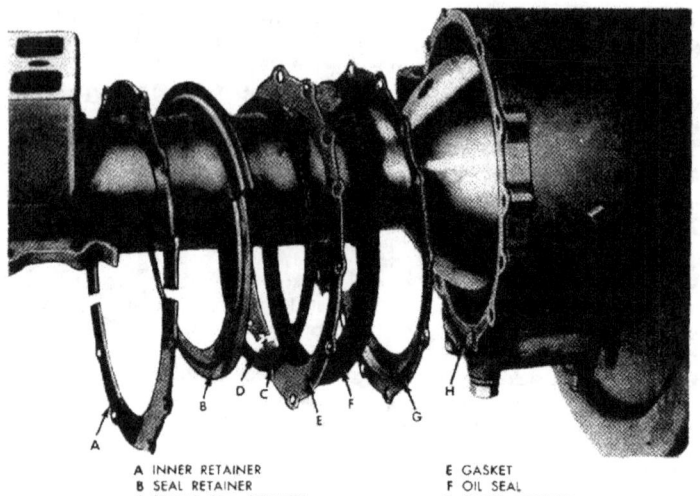

A INNER RETAINER
B SEAL RETAINER
C SPRING SEAL RETAINER
D DUST SEAL
E GASKET
F OIL SEAL
G OUTER RETAINER
H GASKET

RA PD 333211

Figure 133—Housing Outer End Seal Components

(1) INSTALL AIR HOSE. Remove level plug (fig. 132) and install ⅜-inch pipe reducing bushing. Exhaust air pressure from air storage tank. Remove chuck from emergency inflation hose and connect hose to bushing in level plug hole.

(2) APPLY AIR PRESSURE TO STEERING KNUCKLE SUPPORT. Charge air storage tank to 15 pounds air pressure. Open valve at tank and apply pressure to steering knuckle housing assembly. Apply light engine oil at all joints and seals around assembly. Check for leaks and escaping air.

(3) LOCALIZE LEAKS. If leaks are evident at seals and joints (fig. 130), and air pressure in tank drops to zero quickly, leakage may exist at wheel bearing oil seal. Check bearing oil seal by removing axle drive flange and applying enough wheel bearing grease evenly in splines of axle flange to temporarily seal and prevent air from leaking past wheel bearing seal. Reinstall axle flange. With air pressure at 15 pounds, repeat test for air leaks, using light engine oil. If pressure decreases gradually, leak at wheel bearing oil seal is evident. If leaks were evident at other points, such as housing outer end seal, etc., the universal joint and steering knuckle assembly must be disassembled and resealed at various points (fig. 130). If no leaks exist in steering knuckle assembly, and test indicates that leak exists at inner wheel bearing oil seal, this seal must be replaced (par. 214).

Front Axle

c. Removal. Key letters in following steps refer to figure 133.

(1) REMOVE WHEEL. With front axle jacked up on side to be serviced, remove wheelhouse skirt, and wheel and tire assembly (par. 212c.).

(2) DISCONNECT WHEEL CYLINDER AND TIE ROD. Close front brake shut-off cock, then unhook flexible hose spring, and remove hose at hull and at wheel cylinder (par. 193*b*.). Disconnect tie rod yoke from steering knuckle support.

(3) REMOVE SEALS AND STEERING KNUCKLE TRUNNIONS. Remove 12 seal retainer cap screws and lock washers. Remove inner retainers (A), seal retainers (B), spring seal retainers (C), and dust seal (D). Remove oil seal (F), gasket (E), outer retainer (G), and gasket (H) from steering knuckle support.

(4) REMOVE UPPER AND LOWER TRUNNIONS. The steering arm holds upper trunnion at left-hand side. Sufficient flexibility exists in drag link ball joints to permit removal of arm without disconnecting link. Remove four nuts and lock washers from studs, and lift upper trunnion (steering arm at left-hand side) off studs. Mark and tie each set of shims so they can be installed in original position. Remove either right or left lower trunnion in the same manner.

Figure 134—Hub and Drum, Steering Knuckle Support, and Axle Shaft Assembly Removal

Maintenance Instructions

(5) REMOVE STEERING KNUCKLE SUPPORT, HUB AND DRUM, AND AXLE SHAFT ASSEMBLY. Steering knuckle support, hub and drum, and axle shaft are removed as an assembly. Pull assembly straight out and away from outer end of axle housing (fig. 134). Remove dust seal (D) and gasket (H) from axle housing.

d. Cleaning. Clean steering knuckle support thoroughly with dry-cleaning solvent. Clean axle housing outer end in the same manner. Clean trunnion bearings thoroughly, then lubricate each bearing (Lubrication Order No. 9-802). Clean spherical surface with flint paper if rusted or pitted.

e. Installation. Key letters in following steps refer to figure 133.

(1) INSTALL GASKET AND DUST SEAL. Install new gasket (H) and dust seal (D) over outer end of axle housing. The beveled edge of dust seal must face outer end of axle housing.

(2) INSTALL STEERING KNUCKLE SUPPORT, HUB, DRUM, AND AXLE SHAFT ASSEMBLY. Make certain that axle shaft universal joint is properly lubricated (par. 173c.), then insert axle shaft into housing, carefully pushing assembly inward. Before pushing steering knuckle support in place, install upper and lower trunnion bearings in position. Rotate assembly slowly while pushing so as to match axle shaft and differential side gear splines until assembly is in place.

(3) INSTALL STEERING KNUCKLE TRUNNIONS. Clean each set of shims thoroughly, then cover each shim with a thin coating of light rust preventive compound (14-C-349-880). Install the shims in place in exactly the same position as they were removed. Install upper trunnion on right-hand side or steering arm and trunnion on left-hand side. Install nuts and lock washers and tighten firmly. Install lower trunnion in the same manner.

(4) INSTALL OUTER END SEAL. Coat gaskets, retainers, and seals with a thin film of light rust preventive compound (14-C-349-880) before installing parts in place in following sequence:

(a) Install Gasket, Outer Retainer, and Oil Seal. Position outer retainer (G) to knuckle support gasket (H). Install oil seal (F) in outer retainer (G) with felt side of seal out, and the seal joint horizontal. Position seal (F) and retainer (G) on steering knuckle support with retainer joint at top. Coat ends of split gasket (E) with cement (52-C-644), or compound (52-C-3115). Lock ends of gasket, then install on top of oil seal (F).

(b) Install Dust Seal and Retainers. Install dust seal spring retainer (C) on dust seal (D), then position dust seal. Secure dust seal (D) with retainer (B), joint on top. Aline and install lower half of inner retainer (A) with lock washers and cap screws turned finger-tight. Adjust seal retainer (B) so it will just fit inside of outer retainer (G). This adjustment must be made carefully to prevent scoring of spherical surface. Install upper half of inner retainer (A) with cap screws and lock washers. Tighten all retainer cap screws alternately and firmly.

(5) INSTALL BRAKE HOSE AND TIE ROD. Install flexible brake hose and hook suspension spring (par. 193*b.*), then open front brake

Front Axle

shut-off cock. Bleed front wheel cylinders (par. 187). Install tie rod on steering knuckle support. Lubricate front axle universal joint and steering knuckle bearings (Lubrication Order No. 9-802).

(6) INSTALL WHEEL AND WHEELHOUSE SKIRT. Install wheel and tire assembly and wheelhouse skirt as described in paragraph 212*d*.

175. FRONT AXLE REMOVAL.

a. Jack Up Vehicle. The vehicle must be placed on a level surface and rear wheels blocked to prevent rolling. Hull must be jacked up and supported with blocks behind front axle at each side. Place dolly under axle, making certain axle is secure on dolly. Remove wheelhouse skirts and wheel and tire assemblies (par. 212*c*.).

b. Disconnect Flexible Hoses and Drag Link. Close front brake shut-off cock under floor board at right-hand side of driver's compartment; then unhook wheel cylinder flexible hose spring, and remove hose at each side of hull (par. 193*b*.). Loosen clips and free axle breather hose (G501-0127837 or G501-7001967) on axle housing. Disconnect breather hose from axle housing fitting. Disconnect drag link from steering arm ball stud by removing cotter pin and backing plug out far enough to lift drag link off of ball stud.

c. Disconnect Axle Propeller Shaft Housing and Shaft. Disconnect propeller shaft housing seal at differential end of housing [par. 182*c*.(2) and (3)]. Disconnect propeller shaft at drive pinion propeller shaft flange [par. 182*c*.(4) through (6)].

d. Remove Axle. Remove nuts from U-bolts, then remove U-bolts, shock absorber eye bolt brackets, and spring bumper blocks. Lower dolly and withdraw from underneath vehicle.

176. FRONT AXLE INSTALLATION.

a. Position and Install Axle Assembly to Spring. Make certain the area under vehicle is cleared of tools, etc., then place axle assembly in position under springs. Raise axle assembly into place against springs. Make certain spring center bolts aline with recesses in spring pads. Install spring U-bolts, spring bumper blocks, and shock absorber eye bolt brackets. Tighten U-bolt nuts with torque wrench to 175 to 185 foot-pounds.

b. Connect Flexible Hoses and Drag Link. Connect wheel cylinder flexible hoses at hull (par. 193*b*.). Clean ball stud and install drag link on steering arm ball stud. Install breather hose on axle housing fitting, and attach hose in clips on housing. Make certain protective loom is in place to protect breather hose.

c. Install Propeller Shaft and Propeller Shaft Housing. Attach propeller shaft to axle drive pinion propeller shaft flange and connect propeller shaft housing seal [par. 183*b*.(7) through (10)].

d. Install Wheels and Wheelhouse Skirts. Install wheels and wheelhouse skirts (par. 212*d*.). Remove block supporting hull.

Maintenance Instructions

e. Check Lubrication, Toe-in, and Bleed Brake System. Check lubrication (Lubrication Order No. 9-802). Check front wheel toe-in and adjust as required (par. 170). Replace filler plug (G122-03-40400) and gasket (G058-31-05800) if damaged. Also check condition of axle housing cover gasket (G085-31-05760). Open front brake shut-off cock and bleed front wheel cylinders (par. 187).

f. Record Replacement. Record replacement of front axle assembly on W.D., A.G.O. Form No. 478, MWO and Major Unit Assembly Replacement Record.

Section XXXIII

Rear Axles

177. GENERAL.

a. Description. The rear axle unit consists of two banjo-type, single reduction, spiral-bevel, full-floating driving axles (fig. 135). Torque rods, three between each axle and hull bottom, absorb driving and braking load. Vehicle weight and load are supported by inverted semi-elliptic slipper type springs. The springs are attached to the spring seats with U-bolts, and spring ends rest free on each axle housing.

b. Data.

```
Housing ............................................... Banjo-type
Drive ........................................ Spiral bevel hypoid
Gear ratio ................................................ 6.66 to 1
Axle shafts ........................................... Full-floating
```

c. Repair. Repair operations for rear axle components are described in TM 9-1802B.

178. AXLE SHAFTS.

a. Removal.

(1) PRIOR TO CHASSIS SERIAL NO. 2006. With vehicle placed on level surface and front wheels blocked to prevent vehicle rolling, remove wheelhouse skirt and jack up axle on side to be serviced. If lock plates are used under axle shaft flange bolt heads, pry plate tangs away from bolts. If not, remove eight bolts and lock washers. Install two axle shaft flange bolts into tapped holes in axle shaft flange (fig. 136). Tighten bolts alternately until flange is free of hub. Remove axle shaft and gasket (G085-31-06160) from housing.

(2) AFTER CHASSIS SERIAL NO. 2005. Remove tire inflating device [par. 212*c*.(1)]. Remove five axle shaft flange bolts and lock washers. Before removing the three tire inflating device to hub locking bolts, note if hub and wheel bolts are marked as described in paragraph 211.

Rear Axles

A REAR BRAKE HOSE ASSEMBLIES
B PILLOW BLOCK ASSEMBLY
C INTERMEDIATE AXLE ASSEMBLY
D LOWER TORQUE ROD ASSEMBLY
E TRUNNION BRACKETS
F BRAKE HOSE SUSPENSION SPRING
G REAR AXLE ASSEMBLY
H TRUNNION CROSS SHAFT ASSEMBLY
I UPPER TORQUE ROD ASSEMBLY

RA PD 337146

Figure 135—Rear Axle Assemblies Prepared for Installation

Remove the three locking bolts and lock washers. Remove axle shaft and gasket as described in step (1) above.

b. Installation.

(1) PRIOR TO CHASSIS SERIAL NO. 2005. Shaft splines, flange, and hub surface must be clean. Coat new gasket evenly with grease and place over splined end of axle shaft. Insert splined end of shaft into housing and into splined differential side gear. Position gasket on hub and aline axle shaft flange on top of gasket. Attach shaft flange to hub with eight bolts and new lock washers. Tighten bolts with torque wrench to 70 to 80 foot-pounds.

(2) AFTER CHASSIS SERIAL NO. 2005. Axle shaft is installed and attached in the same manner as described in step (1) above, except that three tire inflating device to hub locking bolts must be installed as described in paragraph 211**c**. Tighten bolts and locking bolts with torque wrench to 70 to 80 foot-pounds. Install tire inflating device [par. 212**d**.(2)].

Maintenance Instructions

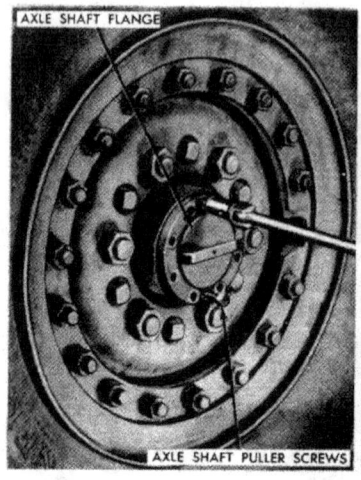

Figure 136—Axle Shaft Removal

179. AXLE REMOVAL.

a. General. The intermediate and rear axles, spring seats and springs, cross shaft and trunnions, torque rods, pillow block, and wheels comprise a "bogie" unit which can be removed as an assembly. This will provide a quick method of removing either or both axles, a salvage operation on a wrecked vehicle, or the replacement of any of the components which comprise this assembly.

b. Removal of "Bogie" Unit. Place vehicle on level surface and block front wheels securely. Raise rear of vehicle and support each side with blocks. Remove tire inflating devices from axle hubs [par. 212**c.**(1)]. Loosen wheel nuts on axle which is to be replaced.

(1) DISCONNECT HOUSINGS AND PROPELLER SHAFTS. Disconnect intermediate and rear axle propeller shaft housings from bulkhead seals [par. 182**c.**(2) and (3)]. Be sure shafts are alined as described in paragraph 182**b.** Disconnect intermediate and rear axle propeller shaft housings and propeller shafts at intermediate axle and at pillow block [par. 182**c.**(4) through (6)].

(2) DISCONNECT PILLOW BLOCK AND AXLE HOUSING BREATHER HOSES. Remove clamps which attach pillow block and intermediate axle breather hoses on torque rod. Disconnect breather hose from pillow block and intermediate axle. Remove bolts which attach breather hose clamps on rear axle housing differential cover. Remove clamps which attach breather hose on torque rod and disconnect hose fitting from axle housing.

(3) DISCONNECT FLEXIBLE BRAKE HOSE ASSEMBLIES. Disconnect brake hose suspension springs from hull. Disconnect brake hoses at hull (par. 193**b.**).

Rear Axles

(4) DISCONNECT UPPER TORQUE RODS. Remove nuts and lock washers from both upper torque rods at hull brackets only. Using a forked pry bar (fig. 171), pry torque rod pin out of hull bracket, at the same time strike bracket with a hammer sharply to assist loosening pin in bracket if necessary.

(5) DISCONNECT CROSS SHAFT TRUNNIONS. Place jacks under each cross shaft trunnion to support trunnion cross shaft assembly. Remove six nuts and lock washers from studs which attach trunnions to brackets at each side, then carefully lower jacks until trunnions are free of studs.

(6) REMOVE "BOGIE" UNIT FROM UNDER VEHICLE. Make certain that all disconnections have been made and tools, jacks, etc., are cleared of wheels; then raise hull sufficiently to clear wheels and roll "bogie" out from under vehicle.

c. "Bogie" Unit Disassembly. The removal of either or both of the rear or intermediate axles from "bogie" unit is performed in the following manner:

(1) REMOVE REAR AXLE (FIG. 135). Remove brake hose assembly from each wheel cylinder. Disconnect propeller shaft at drive pinion propeller shaft flange by removing four nuts and lock washers from two universal joint U-bolts; then remove U-bolts and disconnect universal joint. Tape bearings on universal joint to prevent loss. Disconnect torque rods from axle housing brackets as described in subparagraph *b.*(4) above. Support axle and remove wheel and tire assemblies (par. 212*c.*).

(2) REMOVE INTERMEDIATE AXLE (FIG. 135). Remove four bolts and lock washers which attach pillow block to bracket. The torque rods are removed as described in subparagraph *b.*(4) above. Remove brake hose assembly from each wheel cylinder, then support axle and remove wheel and tire assemblies (par. 212*c.*).

180. AXLE INSTALLATION.

a. "Bogie" Unit Assembly.

(1) INSTALL REAR AXLE (FIG. 135). Place rear axle in position so that end of each spring is inserted through bracket at each side of housing. Make certain that torque rod pins and holes in torque rod brackets on axle housing are cleaned thoroughly. Insert torque rod pins in place and attach with hex nuts and lock washers. Tighten nuts firmly. Install a brake hose assembly on each wheel cylinder. Attach propeller shaft universal joint with U-bolts. Tighten nuts firmly. Install a wheel and tire assembly on each hub (par. 212*d.*). Tighten wheel nuts.

(2) INSTALL INTERMEDIATE AXLE (FIG. 135). The intermediate axle is installed in the same manner as described in step (1) above, except install pillow block assembly on bracket with four bolts and lock washers.

b. "Bogie" Unit Installation. Make certain that area under vehicle is cleared of tools, loose blocks, etc., then roll "bogie" in place under vehicle.

TM 9-802
180-181

Maintenance Instructions

(1) ATTACH CROSS SHAFT TRUNNIONS. Lower vehicle and at the same time aline trunnion bracket studs with holes in cross shaft trunnions. When holes and studs are in alinement, jack trunnion cross shaft assembly up in place and attach with 12 nuts and lock washers. Tighten nuts firmly.

(2) ATTACH TORQUE RODS TO HULL BRACKETS. Clean torque rod pins and hull brackets thoroughly. Insert each pin into bracket and attach with hex nut and lock washer, tightened firmly.

(3) ATTACH BREATHER HOSES ON AXLE HOUSINGS AND PILLOW BLOCK. Inspect breather hoses for deterioration, cracks, damage, and clogged condition. Clean or replace as required. Attach rear axle housing breather hose (G501-7001967 or G501-0217837) to fitting on rear axle housing and tighten connection firmly. Install loom on hose and attach on axle housing cover with clamps. Tighten bolts firmly. Attach breather hose to upper torque rod with two clamps, bolts, lock washers, and nuts. Attach breather hose (G501-70-01968) and (G501-70-02247) to pillow block and at intermediate axle housing. Tighten connections securely. Attach pillow block and intermediate axle breather hoses on upper torque rod with two clamps, bolts, lock washers, and nuts. Tighten clamp bolts securely.

(4) CONNECT PROPELLER SHAFTS AND HOUSINGS. Install upper and lower propeller shafts and housings, and attach seals [par. 183*b*.(6) through (10)]. Lubricate universal joints (Lubrication Order No. 9-802).

(5) INSTALL FLEXIBLE BRAKE HOSE ASSEMBLIES. Attach brake hose assemblies and suspension springs to hull (par. 193*b*.). Bleed brakes (par. 187). Tighten wheel nuts firmly, then install tire inflating devices on hubs [par. 212*d*.(2)]. Install wheelhouse skirts.

(6) CHECK AXLE LUBRICANT LEVELS. Examine lubricant level in rear axles (Lubrication Order No. 9-802). Remove supports, etc., from beneath hull and blocks away from front wheels.

(7) RECORD OF REPLACEMENT. Record the replacement on W.D., A.G.O. Form No. 478, MWO and Major Unit Assembly Replacement Record.

Section XXXIV

Propeller Shafts, Housings, and Pillow Block

181. GENERAL.

a. General Description. Power is transmitted from the transmission to the transfer case, then to the front, intermediate, and rear axles by universal joints and tubular type propeller shafts (fig. 137). The propeller shafts connecting the axle transfer case to the front axle, intermediate axle, and pillow block are enclosed in individual housings, the ends of which are sealed with bellows type seals to prevent water leaking into the hull during water operations.

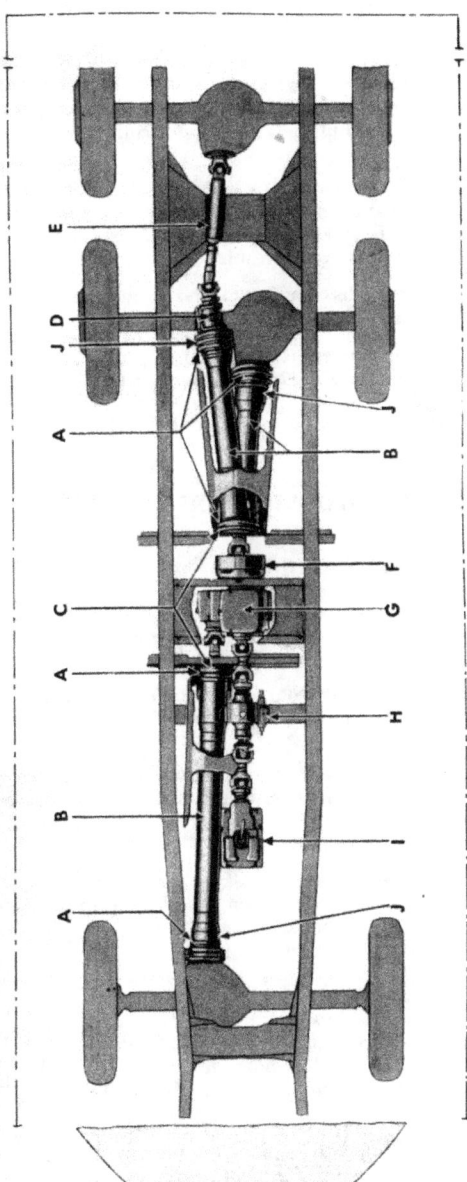

Figure 137—Propeller Shaft and Housing Arrangement

A PROPELLER SHAFT HOUSING SEAL
B PROPELLER SHAFT HOUSING
C HULL BULK HEADS
D PILLOW BLOCK
E PROPELLER SHAFT ASSEMBLY
F HAND BRAKE
G MAIN TRANSFER CASE
H WATER PROPELLER TRANSFER CASE
I TRANSMISSION
J HOUSING DRAIN PLUGS

b. Housings and Seals.

(1) HOUSINGS. Propeller shaft housings enclose shafts from axle transfer case to front and intermediate axles, and from transfer case to pillow block. These housings are metal tubular type. Each housing is equipped with a hinged support at hull bulkhead and a rigid support at axle end.

(2) SEALS. Seals at each end of housings are synthetic rubber bellows type equipped with reinforcement rings. Seals at hull bulkhead each contain two rings, while seals at axles and pillow block contain only one ring each. These rings are not interchangeable.

c. Repair.
The repair of propeller shafts, universal joints, housings, and pillow block is described in TM 9-1802B.

d. Housings and Seals Replacement.
Removal of propeller shaft housings and seals also necessitate the removal of their propeller shafts. If necessary to replace housings, seals, or shafts, operations listed in the following paragraphs (182 and 183) must be accomplished for the particular shaft to be serviced.

182. PROPELLER SHAFT, HOUSING, AND SEAL REMOVAL.

a. NOTE: *The removal procedures listed in following subparagraphs (c. through e.) include operations necessary to remove all shafts, housings, and seals. When necessary to remove any one of the shafts, housings, or seals, reference must be made to the applicable subparagraph as follows:*

(1) Propeller shaft, housing, and seal from axle transfer case to front or intermediate axle, and from transfer case to pillow block (subpar. **c.** below).

(2) Propeller shaft from pillow block to rear axle (subpar. **d.** below).
(3) Propeller shaft from transmission to water propeller transfer case, and from water propeller transfer case to axle transfer case (subpar. **e.** below).

b. Universal Joint Lubrication Fitting Alinement.
On vehicles after chassis serial No. 3427, indicators have been added to axle transfer case crossmember (H, fig. 138), and on bulkhead (C, fig. 138) where front axle propeller shaft enters hull. A groove is cut into shoulder on forward side of hand brake drum. The indicator attached on crossmember and the groove (I, fig. 138) on hand brake drum are used to aline lubrication fittings in universal joints with drain holes in propeller shaft housings. This facilitates lubrication of universal joints on rear axle propeller shafts and also of the pillow block to rear axle propeller shaft. When indicator attached on front bulkhead (C, fig. 138) is in alinement with mark (D, fig. 138) on front axle propeller shaft, the universal joint lubrication fitting will be in alinement with drain hole in front axle propeller shaft housing. On these vehicles, the indicators and markings must be in alinement before propeller shafts are removed,

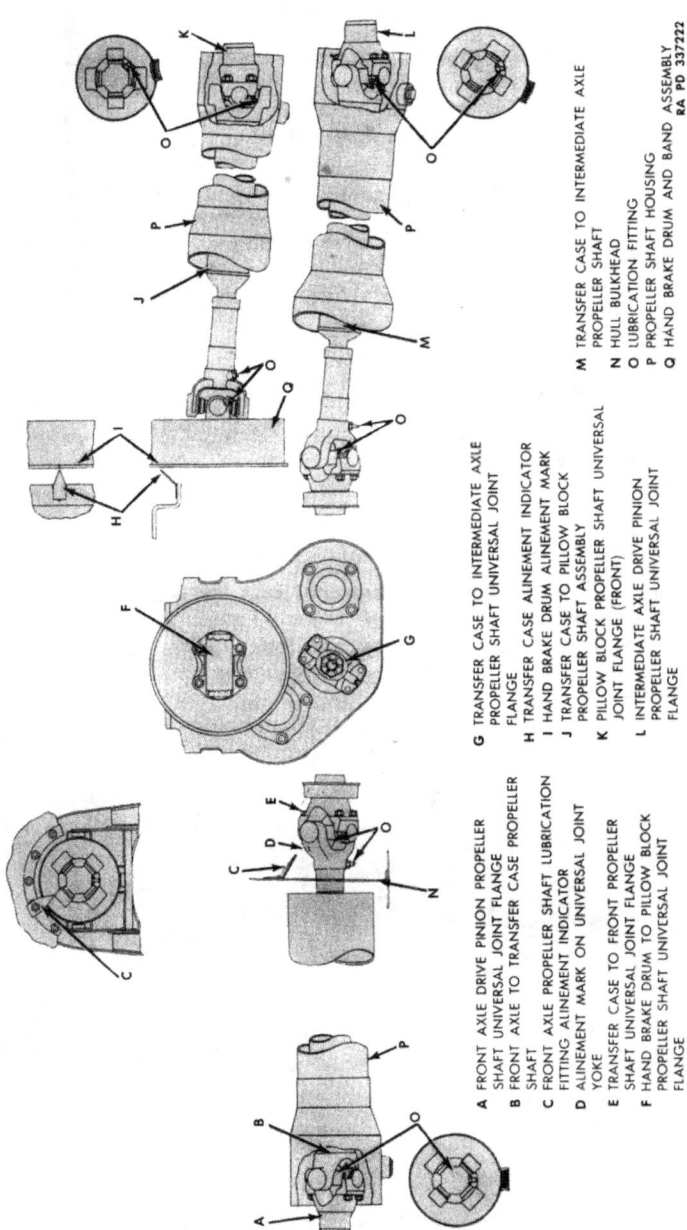

Figure 138—Alinement of Universal Joint Lubrication Fittings

A FRONT AXLE DRIVE PINION PROPELLER SHAFT UNIVERSAL JOINT FLANGE
B FRONT AXLE TO TRANSFER CASE PROPELLER SHAFT
C FRONT AXLE PROPELLER SHAFT LUBRICATION FITTING ALINEMENT INDICATOR
D ALINEMENT MARK ON UNIVERSAL JOINT YOKE
E TRANSFER CASE TO FRONT PROPELLER SHAFT UNIVERSAL JOINT FLANGE
F HAND BRAKE DRUM TO PILLOW BLOCK PROPELLER SHAFT UNIVERSAL JOINT FLANGE
G TRANSFER CASE TO INTERMEDIATE AXLE PROPELLER SHAFT UNIVERSAL JOINT FLANGE
H TRANSFER CASE ALINEMENT INDICATOR
I HAND BRAKE DRUM ALINEMENT MARK
J TRANSFER CASE TO PILLOW BLOCK PROPELLER SHAFT ASSEMBLY
K PILLOW BLOCK PROPELLER SHAFT UNIVERSAL JOINT FLANGE (FRONT)
L INTERMEDIATE AXLE DRIVE PINION PROPELLER SHAFT UNIVERSAL JOINT FLANGE
M TRANSFER CASE TO INTERMEDIATE AXLE PROPELLER SHAFT
N HULL BULKHEAD
O LUBRICATION FITTING
P PROPELLER SHAFT HOUSING
Q HAND BRAKE DRUM AND BAND ASSEMBLY

RA PD 337222

TM 9-802

Maintenance Instructions

and when propeller shafts are installed, universal joint lubrication fittings must point in downward position while marks are alined with indicators.

(1) ALINE MARKS WITH INDICATORS. Key letters in following steps *(a)* and *(b)* below refer to figure 138.

(a) Front Axle Propeller Shaft. Remove air intake grille from the aisleway behind driver's seat. Move vehicle backward or forward as required until mark on front axle propeller shaft to transfer case universal joint (D) is alined with indicator attached on bulkhead (C).

(b) Intermediate and Rear Axle. Remove air intake grille from the aisleway behind driver's seat. Move vehicle forward or backward as required until mark on hand brake drum (I) is alined with indicator attached on axle transfer case crossmember (H).

c. Axle Transfer Case to Front Axle, Intermediate Axle, and Pillow Block Propeller Shafts Removal. The procedures which follow, steps (1) through (10), apply at front axle, intermediate axle, and pillow block unless otherwise stated.

(1) DISCONNECT PROPELLER SHAFTS FROM TRANSFER CASE.

(a) Front and Intermediate Axles (fig. 137). Remove four nuts and lock washers from the two U-bolts which attach universal joint journal to transfer case flange. Disconnect universal joint and tape bearings on journal to prevent loss of bearings.

(b) Rear Axle. Remove four nuts and lock washers which attach universal joint flange to hand brake drum mounting bolts, then remove flange from mounting bolts.

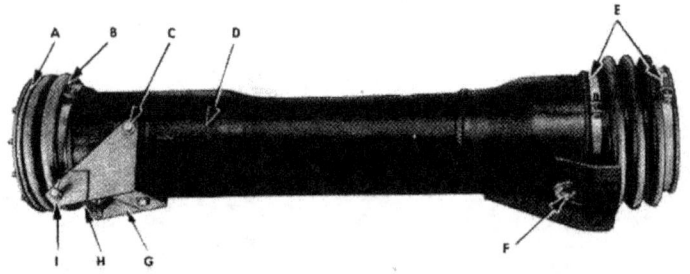

A SEAL RETAINING RING
B HOUSING SEAL
  HOUSING TO BULKHEAD (G501-03-82800)
  HOUSING TO PILLOW BLOCK (G501-03-82802)
  HOUSING TO FRONT AXLE AND INTERMEDIATE AXLE (G501-03-82801)
C HINGE CAP SCREW AND LOCK WASHER
D PROPELLER SHAFT HOUSING
E SEAL CLAMP RINGS
F DRAIN PLUG
G HINGE ASSEMBLY
H HINGE PIN
I COTTER PIN

RA PD 333193

Figure 139—Housing and Seal Installation

Propeller Shafts, Housings, and Pillow Block

(2) DISCONNECT HOUSING HINGE ASSEMBLY (FIG. 139. Remove three bolts (C) and lock washers (one at each side of housing and one at bottom) which attach hinge (G) to propeller shaft housing; then remove the four cotter pins which hold hinge pin (H) in place. Remove hinge pin and two flat washers from hinge and brackets.

(3) REMOVE SEAL CLAMP FROM BULKHEAD TO HOUSING SEAL. Using a cross-recessed screwdriver, loosen and disconnect clamp screw and remove clamp.

(4) DISCONNECT SEAL FROM AXLE OUTER BEARING OIL SEAL RETAINER. Loosen and remove seal clamp as described in step (3) above. Pry seal clear of oil seal retainer. NOTE: *At pillow block to housing seal, loosen and remove both seal clamps {step (3) above}; then slide seal toward rear of pillow block.*

(5) DISCONNECT UNIVERSAL JOINT.

(a) Front Axle. Raise right-hand side of axle with jack until wheel is clear of ground. Insert a bar through universal joint to prevent turning (fig. 145) and remove two universal joint U-bolt nuts and lock washers. Turn universal joint with bar until opposite U-bolt nuts are accessible then remove nuts and lock washers in the same manner. Pry journal away from flange and tape bearings onto journal.

(b) Intermediate Axle. Disconnect universal joint at drive pinion propeller shaft flange [step *(a)* above].

(c) Rear Axle. Raise rear axle with jack at right-hand side until wheel is clear of ground. Turn wheel until universal joint U-bolts are accessible through opening in pillow block front housing support, then remove nuts and lock washers from U-bolts. Remove universal joint journal from flange and tape bearings onto journal.

FRONT AXLE UNIVERSAL READY FOR REMOVAL

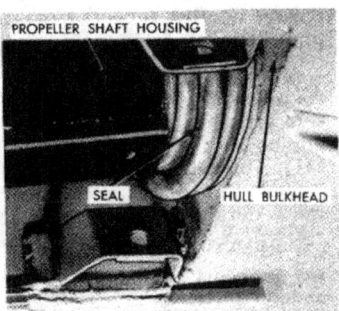
PROPELLER SHAFT HOUSING PUSHED INTO BULKHEAD

RA PD 337284

Figure 140—Propeller Shaft Housing and Shaft Prepared for Removal or Installation

Maintenance Instructions

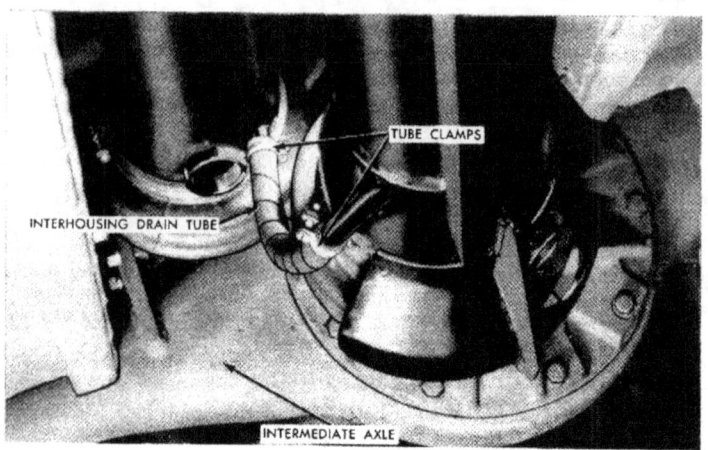

Figure 141—Interhousing Drain Tube Installed

(6) REMOVE HOUSING SUPPORTS FROM OUTER BEARING OIL SEAL RETAINER.

(a) Front and Intermediate Axles (fig. 140). Loosen and remove seal clamp which is used to attach seal on propeller shaft housing. Stretch and pull end of seal over top of drain plug and away from axle. Push propeller shaft housing through bulkhead seal sufficiently to furnish clearance at oil seal retainer; then remove four bolts and lock washers which attach housing support on oil seal retainer. After removing bolts, remove housing support from oil seal retainer and push support into propeller shaft housing.

(b) Rear Axle. The rear axle propeller shaft housing is supported at the pillow block by the pillow block propeller shaft front housing support assembly. On late vehicles, an interhousing drain tube connects this housing with the intermediate axle propeller shaft housing (fig. 141). This tube must be disconnected from both housings. Loosen two clamp bolts and clamps, then remove tube. After pillow block to housing seal is disconnected, push propeller shaft housing into bulkhead seal.

(7) REMOVE HOUSING AND PROPELLER SHAFT. Pull housing and propeller shaft assembly out of bulkhead seal and remove from under vehicle.

(8) REMOVE SEALS FROM BULKHEAD. Remove 12 nuts and lock washers (nuts are accessible at inside of hull) which attach seal retainer ring and seal to bulkhead, then remove seal and retainer ring.

(9) REMOVE SEAL FROM HOUSING. Remove seal clamp screw and clamp from end of housing, then remove seal.

TM 9-802
182-183

Propeller Shafts, Housings, and Pillow Block

(10) REMOVE SEAL FROM PILLOW BLOCK. Damaged seal is removed from pillow block by cutting seal off pillow block propeller shaft housing support.

d. Pillow Block to Rear Axle Propeller Shaft Removal.

(1) DISCONNECT UNIVERSAL JOINT. Remove the four nuts and lock washers from the two U-bolts which hold universal joint journal and bearing to flange on pillow block, then carefully drive U-bolts out of place. Disconnect universal joint U-bolts at rear axle propeller shaft universal joint flange in the same manner.

(2) REMOVE PROPELLER SHAFT ASSEMBLY. Pry universal joint journal and bearings out of propeller shaft universal joint flange at rear of pillow block. Wrap tape around journals to hold universal joint bearings in place. Remove universal joint journal and bearings from axle pinion propeller shaft universal joint flange in the same manner.

e. Transmission to Water Propeller Transfer Case, and Water Propeller Transfer Case to Axle Transfer Case Propeller Shaft Removal.

(1) DISCONNECT UNIVERSAL JOINT FLANGE. Remove floor boards from driver's compartment, and remove grille from aisleway behind driver's seat. Disconnect universal joint flange from companion flange by removing four nuts, lock washers, and bolts from universal joint flange at each end of propeller shaft assemblies.

(2) REMOVE PROPELLER SHAFT ASSEMBLIES. Separate propeller shaft universal joint flanges from companion flanges by pushing propeller shafts together at slip joint. Lift propeller shaft assemblies out of vehicle.

183. PROPELLER SHAFT, HOUSING, AND SEAL INSTALLATION.

a. NOTE: *(Refer to paragraph 238 for cleaning and painting propeller shafts, housings, and pillow block.) The installation procedures listed in following subparagraphs (b. through d.) include operations necessary to install all shafts, housings, and seals. When necessary to install any one of the shafts, housings, or seals, reference must be made to the applicable subparagraph as follows:*

(1) Propeller shaft, housing, and seal from axle transfer case to front or intermediate axle, and from transefer case to pillow block (subpar. **b.** below).

(2) Propeller shaft from pillow block to rear axle (subpar. **c.** below).

(3) Propeller shaft from transmission to water propeller transfer case, and from water propeller transfer case to axle transfer case (subpar. **d.** below).

b. Axle Transfer Case to Front Axle, Intermediate Axle, and Pillow Block Propeller Shaft Installation. The procedures which follow [steps (1) through (10)] apply at front axle, intermediate axle,

TM 9-802
183

Maintenance Instructions

and pillow block unless otherwise stated. To facilitate installation of seals on propeller shaft housings and on pillow block front housing support, apply a small quantity of general purpose grease on the inside of seal lip so that seal will slide into place on housings and pillow block housing support, and also act as a seal when seal clamps are tightened. A small amount of general purpose grease must also be applied on the inside diameter of seal clamps to permit clamps to slide on surface of seal when clamps are being tightened. Grease should be applied in the same manner on the outer circumference of the front and intermediate axle pinion outer bearing oil seal retainers. This must be done to prevent seals from "creeping" when seal clamps are being tightened.

(1) INSTALL REINFORCEMENT RINGS IN SEALS. When new seals are installed, reinforcement rings in damaged seals are to be removed and installed in new seals. Be sure that rings will not damage or cut seals after installation. Install one side of ring in seal, then with a thin bar, force ring into seal (fig. 142). Note that two rings are used in each bulkhead to propeller shaft housing seal, while only one ring is used in each axle to housing seal and pillow block to housing seal.

(2) INSTALL SEAL ON PILLOW BLOCK. Position pillow block assembly in a vise (fig. 144). Anchor a suitable bar between propeller shaft universal joint flange and propeller shaft housing support, place small end of seal over end of bar, then with a screwdriver stretch seal sufficiently to catch over end of housing support (fig. 144) and proceed to work end of seal onto housing support, alining as shown in figure 143. After seal is installed, remove pillow block from vise.

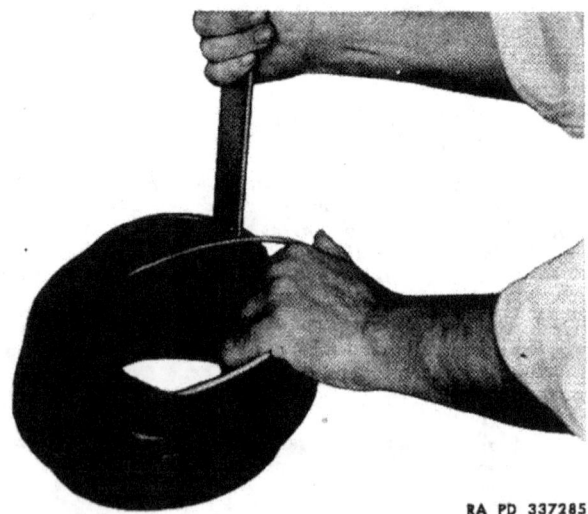

RA PD 337285

Figure 142—Method of Installing Reinforcement Ring in Propeller Shaft Housing Seals

Propeller Shafts, Housings, and Pillow Block

Figure 143—Method of Seal Alinement on Pillow Block

(3) INSTALL SEAL ON BULKHEAD. Make certain that outer surface of bulkhead is cleaned thoroughly. Coat mating face of seal with compound (52-C-3086-200). Position seal in place on bulkhead, then place seal retainer ring over end of seal. Insert retainer ring studs through seal and bulkhead; then attach ring in place with 12 nuts and lock washers installed on studs which are accessible from inside hull. Tighten nuts alternately and firmly.

(4) INSTALL SEAL ON PROPELLER SHAFT HOUSING.

(a) Front Axle. Install propeller shaft housing to front axle seal over end of housing. Stretch end of seal sufficiently so that seal extends over drain plug opening in housing. Seal must be pushed over end of housing far enough so that seal will not interfere with universal joint assembly in manner shown in figure 140.

(b) Intermediate Axle. Install housing to intermediate axle seal on end of housing. Secure seal in place with seal clamp. Before tightening seal clamp, make certain that clamp is correctly alined along edge of seal, then tighten clamp bolt firmly.

(5) INSTALL HOUSING SUPPORTS AND PROPELLER SHAFT IN HOUSING.

(a) Front and Intermediate Axles. Insert propeller shaft and universal joint assembly into housing, then insert housing support over end of propeller shaft.

(b) Rear Axle. Insert pillow block to transfer case propeller shaft universal joint assembly in housing.

(6) POSITION PROPELLER SHAFT HOUSING, SHAFT, AND SUPPORT.

(a) Front Axle. Insert propeller shaft housing and propeller shaft assembly into bulkhead housing seal. Be sure that housing support does not drop out front of housing.

Maintenance Instructions

RA PD 337192

Figure 144—Method of Installing Seal on Pillow Block Front Propeller Shaft Housing Support

(b) Intermediate and Rear Axle. Install the intermediate axle to transfer case propeller shaft assembly, housing, and support in the same manner as described in step *(a)* above. NOTE: *The pillow block to transfer case propeller shaft universal joint assembly and housing are positioned in the same manner.*

(7) INSTALL HOUSING SUPPORTS (FRONT AND INTERMEDIATE AXLES). Push propeller shaft housing towards transfer case as far as it will go. Aline housing support on pinion outer bearing oil seal retainer, then, using four bolts and new lock washers, attach support to retainer. Make certain that housing support is installed so that universal joint can be lubricated after assembling operation is completed. The lower portion of housing support ring is bent and should be positioned down when support is installed.

(8) CONNECT UNIVERSAL JOINT.

(a) Front and Intermediate Axles. Place universal joint journal in front axle propeller shaft universal joint flange. Make certain that lubrication fitting in journal is in down position (fig. 138) and insert universal joint U-bolts which attach journal to front axle universal joint propeller shaft flange. Install nuts and lock washers on U-bolts and tighten finger-tight. Insert a bar in universal joint (fig. 145) and tighten nuts firmly.

(b) Rear Axle. Aline universal joint journal in pillow block propeller shaft universal joint flange so that lubrication fitting in journal will be accessible through drain plug opening. Install U-bolts in place and

Propeller Shafts, Housings, and Pillow Block

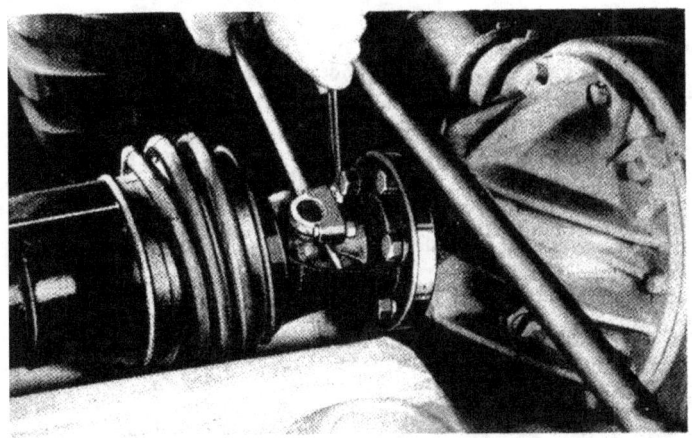

Figure 145—Method of Tightening Universal Joint U-Bolts

attach with four nuts and new lock washers. Mark universal joint flange at rear of pillow block to show position of lubrication fitting in front of pillow block universal joint. This must be done to aline lubrication fittings so that all are accessible and can be lubricated without moving vehicle. It is necessary to revolve shaft in order to tighten universal joint U-bolts, which are accessible through an opening provided in pillow block front propeller shaft housing.

(9) ATTACH PROPELLER SHAFT HOUSING TO BULKHEAD SEAL AND HOUSING HINGE ASSEMBLY. Pull housing out of seal to approximate correct position and install seal clamp temporarily in place on edge of seal. The seal clamp screw threads into ear of seal clamp at an angle so that end of clamp will slide on seal while screw is being tightened. Position clamp and screw so that screw can be final tightened after hinge assembly is installed. Attach hinge to propeller shaft housing with three bolts and new lock washers, then tighten bolts firmly. Install hinge pin in hinge and hull brackets. Make certain that a flat washer is installed between hinge and hull brackets (one at each side of hinge). After hinge pin is installed, install four cotter pins in hinge pin and secure ends of cotter pins. Tighten seal clamp screw firmly.

(10) INSTALL HOUSING SEAL ON OUTER BEARING OIL SEAL RETAINER.

(a) Front and Intermediate Axles. Position seal on pinion outer bearing oil seal retainer and on housing. End of seal on oil seal retainer must be flush with edge furthest away from propeller shaft housing. Make certain that end of seal is alined on propeller shaft housing. Install both seal clamps (one on oil seal retainer end of seal and one on oppo-

335

site end of seal). Seal clamps must be positioned close to rolled edge of seal. Tighten seal clamp screws, and at the same time make certain that ends of seals do not "creep" under seal clamp while clamp screw is being tightened. Tighten clamp screw firmly.

(b) Rear Axle. Position pillow block support to housing seal over end of housing. Make certain that small end of seal on pillow block housing support is pulled away from block on support without stretching seal; then position small seal clamp in place close to edge of seal and tighten clamp screw firmly. Install clamp which is used to attach seal on propeller shaft housing close to edge of seal and tighten clamp screw firmly. Install clamps on drain tube, then install drain tube on housing nipples (fig. 148) and tighten clamp screws firmly.

c. Pillow Block to Rear Axle Propeller Shaft.

(1) INSPECT PROPELLER SHAFT ASSEMBLY. Make certain that slip joint on propeller shaft is free and has not "frozen." If slip joint is "frozen," unscrew and slide cap, steel washer, and cork seal away from sleeve, exposing ends of splines. Lubricate slip joint (Lubrication Order No. 9-802) until lubricant appears at pressure relief valve and at ends of splines. If lubricant does not penetrate to ends of splines, disassemble slip joint. Clean splines in slip joint sleeve and on propeller shaft thoroughly; then assemble slip joint. Make certain that joint is free and lubricate slip joint (Lubrication Order No. 9-802).

(2) POSITION PROPELLER SHAFT ASSEMBLY. Remove tape or metal strip which holds universal joint journal bearings in place and position journal in pillow block propeller shaft universal joint flange. At the same time make certain that lubrication fittings on universal joint are in down position and in alinement with lubrication fittings on pillow block to transfer case propeller shaft universal joints (fig. 138). This may be checked by removing propeller shaft housing drain plug and note position of lubrication fitting in universal joint journal. Attach propeller shaft universal joint journal to rear axle pinion propeller shaft universal joint flange with two U-bolts, four nuts, and new lock washers at each universal joint. Position journal in each flange, then install U-bolts in position with nuts and lock washers. Tighten nuts alternately and firmly.

d. Transmission to Water Propeller Transfer Case, and Water Propeller Transfer Case to Axle Transfer Case Shaft Installation.

(1) INSPECT PROPELLER SHAFT ASSEMBLIES. Examine propeller shaft assembly slip joint in shaft. Note if alinement marks (fig. 146) on shaft slip joint are evident. If alinement marks are not evident, make certain that shaft slip joint is assembled so that universal joint yokes at each end of assembly are in the same plane, then install new markings on slip joint and shaft.

(2) INSTALL SHAFT ASSEMBLY. Place shaft in position between companion flanges on transmission and water propeller transfer case, or main transfer case and water propeller transfer case; slip joint and lubrication fitting should be toward the front of the vehicle. Insert

TM 9-802
183-184

Propeller Shafts, Housings, and Pillow Block

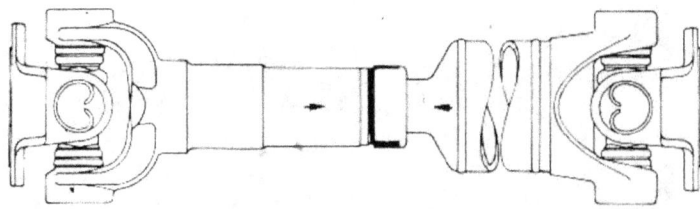

RA PD 16187

Figure 146—Propeller Shaft Alinement Marks

four bolts through each companion flange and universal joint flange. Install nuts and new lock washers. Tighten nuts alternately and firmly.

(3) REPLACE FLOOR BOARDS AND GRILLE. Install floor boards in driver's compartment and attach with screws. Install grille in aisleway behind driver's seat.

184. PILLOW BLOCK.

a. General. The pillow block assembly is mounted on a bracket which is integral with the intermediate axle housing and connects the propeller shaft assemblies between the rear axle and axle transfer case. The pillow block contains a separate shaft mounted in roller type bearings. Shaft and roller bearings are enclosed in a watertight housing.

b. Removal Procedure.

(1) PRELIMINARY INSTRUCTIONS. Jack rear of vehicle and block securely. Raise right-hand wheel of rear axle until wheel is clear of ground.

(2) DISCONNECT PILLOW BLOCK REAR UNIVERSAL JOINT. Remove four nuts and lock washers which secure two universal joint U-bolts to pillow block rear propeller shaft flange. Disconnect propeller shaft and tape bearings on journal to hold bearings in place.

(3) DISCONNECT INTERHOUSING DRAIN TUBE (ON LATE VEHICLES). Loosen clamp screws and remove drain tube from upper and lower propeller shaft housing nipples (fig. 141).

(4) DISCONNECT HINGE ASSEMBLY AND SEALS. Remove three cap screws and lock washers which attach hinge assembly to rear axle upper propeller shaft housing. Remove seal clamp from front of seal at front of housing, then loosen seal on housing. Remove both seal clamps and free both ends of pillow block to housing seal, then slide seal toward rear of pillow block.

(5) DISCONNECT PILLOW BLOCK UNIVERSAL JOINT. Jack up right-hand side of intermediate axle until wheel is clear of ground. Remove nuts and lock washers from universal joint U-bolts. The nuts are accessible through opening in pillow block propeller shaft housing support. Revolve intermediate axle wheel that is raised off ground as required in order to gain access to universal joint U-bolts.

TM 9-802

Maintenance Instructions

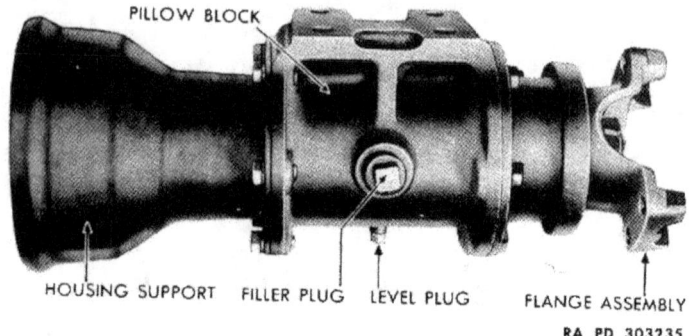

Figure 147—Pillow Block Assembly Installation

(6) DISCONNECT PILLOW BLOCK. Disconnect pillow block breather hose assembly from pillow block. Remove four bolts and lock washers which attach pillow block to intermediate axle housing bracket.

(7) REMOVE PILLOW BLOCK ASSEMBLY. Pry universal joint journal and bearings out of flange, then remove pillow block from under vehicle. Tape bearings on journal to prevent loss of bearings.

(8) INSPECT PILLOW BLOCK ASSEMBLY. Examine pillow block for indication of lubricant leak around propeller shaft flange retaining nuts at either end of pillow block. Note if lubricant leaks exist around inner edge of pillow block front housing support oil seal. If lubricant leak is evident at retainer nuts, midship propeller shaft keyway cork seals (G501-3002102) must be replaced. If lubricant leaks exist at inner edge of pillow block front housing support oil seal and rear cover oil seal, replace with new oil seal (H13-05-00145). Replace pillow block housing front support and rear cover gaskets (G501-01-94022).

c. Installation Procedure.

(1) INSTALL PILLOW BLOCK ON BRACKET. Position pillow block on intermediate axle housing bracket (fig. 147), aline bolt holes in pillow block and bracket, and attach with four bolts and new lock washers. Tighten bolts firmly.

(2) CONNECT UNIVERSAL JOINT AT REAR OF PILLOW BLOCK. Remove tape from bearing and position universal joint journal in place on pillow block universal joint flange. While doing this, make certain that pillow block to transfer case propeller shaft universal joint lubrication fittings are in a downward position (fig. 138) and in alinement with lubrication fittings on pillow block to rear axle propeller shaft assembly. Install universal joint U-bolts, then attach U-bolts with four nuts and new lock washers. After universal joint is positioned, turn intermediate axle wheel that is raised off the ground as required, in order to tighten U-bolt nuts through opening in pillow block front propeller shaft housing support. After this operation is completed, check lubrication fitting alinement through drain holes on intermediate axle

Propeller Shafts, Housings, and Pillow Block

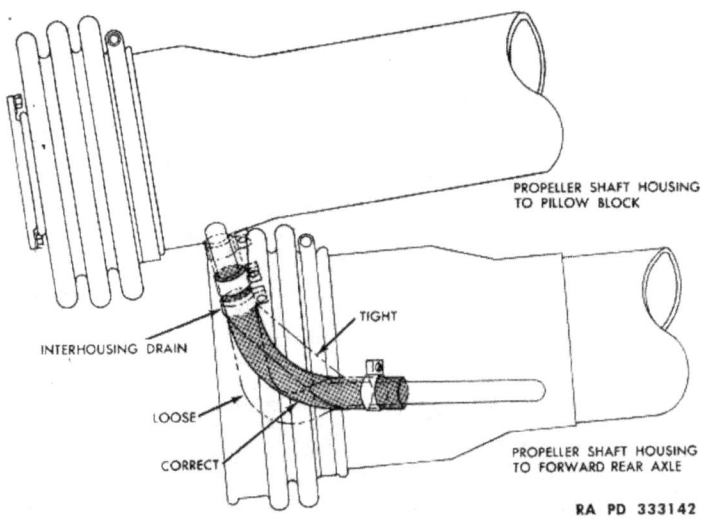

Figure 148—Interhousing Drain Tube Installation

propeller shaft housing. Lubrication fittings on the intermediate axle to transfer case propeller shaft, the pillow block to transfer case propeller shaft, and pillow block to rear axle propeller shaft are all in a downward position and can all be lubricated from underneath without moving vehicle (fig. 138).

(3) ATTACH HINGE ASSEMBLY AND SEALS. Position propeller shaft housing on pillow block front housing support. Aline end of bulkhead seal on propeller shaft housing. Apply a small amount of general purpose grease on the inside of the seal clamps. Aline seal clamp on seal near edge of seal. Tighten seal clamp bolt finger-tight, with clamp positioned so that bulkhead seal clamp bolt is accessible after hinge is installed. Attach hinge assembly to propeller shaft housing with three bolts and new lock washers. Tighten bolts firmly, then proceed to tighten seal clamp bolts firmly. Make certain that seal does not "creep" while bolt is being tightened.

(4) INSTALL INTERHOUSING DRAIN TUBE (ON LATE VEHICLES). Install tube clamps on ends of drain tube, then install drain tube on nipples extending from each of the propeller shaft housings (fig. 148). Tighten tube clamps securely. Make certain that drain tube is of the proper length and that tube does not have a sag in it, or is stretched too tight. A sag in the tube will form a pocket and in cold weather operation, water accumulation will freeze, while tube installed without sufficient "sweep" will cause tube to be pulled off of nipples.

d. Pillow Block Modification. After chassis serial No. 7801, pillow block assemblies are modified to permit lubrication with general purpose

Maintenance Instructions

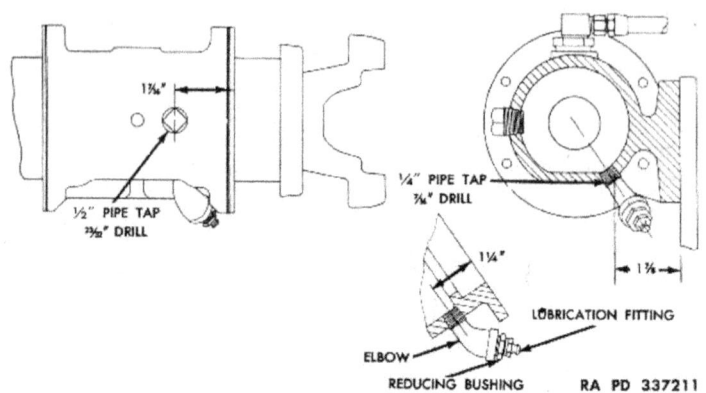

Figure 149—Pillow Block Modification

grease (Lubrication Order No. 9-802) instead of gear oil. The pillow blocks lubricated with gear oil may be modified in the following manner.

(1) INSTALL ½-INCH PIPE PLUG. The present ⅛-inch plug which is beneath connections must be left in place. Measure $1\tfrac{7}{16}$ inches from rear flange of pillow block housing and in line with present ⅛-inch plug (fig. 149). Drill a $\tfrac{23}{32}$-inch hole and tap with ½-inch pipe tap. Install ½-inch pipe plug (Item Stock No. H006-03-83915, piece mark C.P.M. IBD).

(2) INSTALL LUBRICATION FITTING. Measure $1\tfrac{7}{8}$ inches from pillow block face as shown (fig. 149). Measure $1\tfrac{1}{4}$ inches from rear flange of housing; then drill a $\tfrac{7}{16}$-inch hole and tap with a ¼-inch pipe tap. Install elbow (Item Stock No. H006-02-65505, piece mark C.P.B. X6BA) into housing. Install reducing bushing (Item Stock No. H006-02-100-10030, piece mark C.P.H. XIBA) and lubrication fitting (Item Stock No. H002-05-04208, piece mark CLDX6).

(3) ASSEMBLE PILLOW BLOCK. Hand pack bearings with general purpose grease (Lubrication Order No. 9-802). Adjust pillow block bearings as described in TM 9-1802B. Install pillow block assembly (subpar. *c*, above).

Section XXXV
Service Brake System

185. GENERAL.

a. Description. The service brake system is a foot-controlled, vacuum-assisted, hydraulic-operated brake system used to force brake shoes into contact with brake drums at each wheel. The foot pedal, mounted

Service Brake System

on the clutch and brake pedal shaft, is connected to the master cylinder piston push rod by a rod, lever shaft, and levers. Master cylinder, mounted on left-hand frame side rail under driver's compartment floor board, is hydraulically connected to Hydrovac slave cylinder and relay valve by a metal brake tube. Hydrovac, mounted inside right-hand frame side rail under front center cargo compartment floor board, is connected to wheel cylinders by metal brake tubes and flexible hoses, and to engine intake manifold by vacuum lines, hoses, and a vacuum check valve. Wheel cylinders are mounted on brake flange plate between upper ends of brake shoes at each wheel.

b. Operation (fig. 150). When the driver depresses the brake pedal, movement of pedal is transmitted through linkage to the master cylinder piston. Movement of piston in master cylinder barrel forces brake fluid into the tube leading to the Hydrovac and wheel cylinders. When hydraulic pressure from the master cylinder reaches a predetermined point, the relay valve at the Hydrovac brings the Hydrovac into action. The action of the Hydrovac adds to the manually created pressure forcing brake fluid through the tubes into the wheel cylinders. Fluid entering the wheel cylinders forces the wheel cylinder pistons outward. Movement of pistons is transferred to the brake shoes, forcing shoes outward against the brake drums. When the driver releases the brake pedal, pressure is removed from the brake fluid, the various units are returned to released position by their return springs, and brake fluid returns through the tubes to the master cylinder reservoir.

c. Data.

```
Front brake size ........................................14 in. x 2 in.
Lining width ...........................................2 in.
Lining thickness ....................................0.265 in. to 0.272 in.
Rear brake size ......................................16 in. x 3 in.
Lining width ..........................................3 in.
Lining thickness ....................................0.265 in. to 0.272 in.
```

Brake drums:

```
Front—Prior to chassis serial No. 3006...........Nondemountable type
       After chassis serial No. 3005 .................Demountable type

Rear—Prior to chassis serial No. 3004...........Nondemountable type
      After chassis serial No. 3003..................Demountable type
```

d. Repair. Repair procedures for components of the service brake system are described in TM 9-1802B.

186. BRAKE SYSTEM TESTS.

a. General. The following tests should be made at regular intervals to check the general condition and operation of the vacuum-hydraulic brake system, and to localize the cause of any deficiencies which might be found.

b. System Performance Tests.

(1) With engine running at slow idle, depress brake pedal with about as much foot pressure as required for normal application. Measure

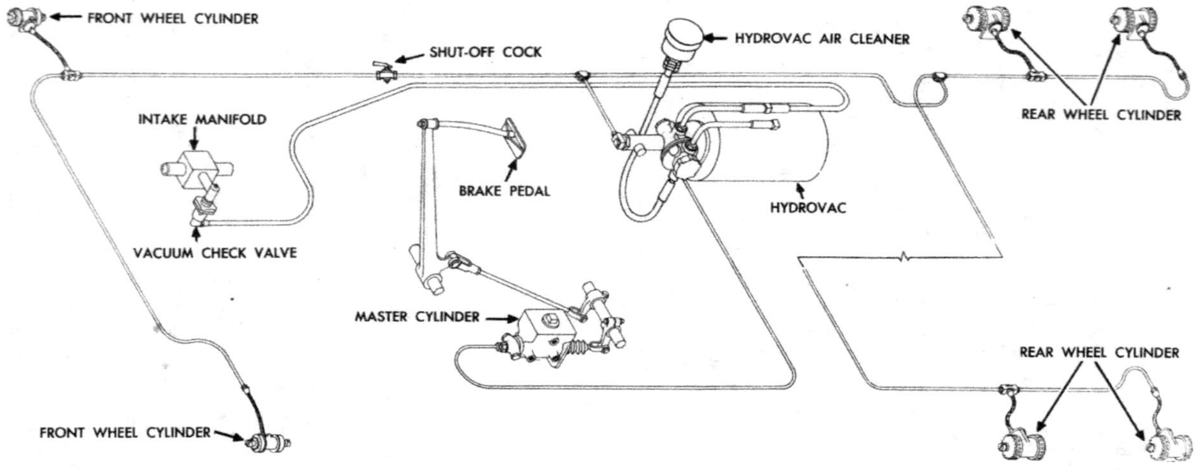

Figure 150—Schematic Diagram of Service Brake System

Service Brake System

distance between pedal pad and toeboard and note the foot pressure required to hold pedal in this position. Remove foot from pedal and stop engine.

(2) With engine stopped, depress brake pedal two or three times to approximate position noted in step (1) above. If the vacuum system is operating, the first application with engine stopped will not be noticeably different than with engine running. Succeeding applications will require noticeably greater pressure, since the vacuum was destroyed during the first application. If no difference is noted in brake applications with engine running and with engine stopped, the vacuum system is not operating properly.

(3) After destroying vacuum in system by making two or three brake applications with engine stopped, depress brake pedal and hold foot pressure on pedal. If pedal gradually "falls away" under foot pressure, the hydraulic system is leaking and an immediate check and correction must be made. If the brake pedal pad travels to within two inches of the toeboard, there is not enough brake pedal reserve and a brake shoe adjustment is required.

(4) Road-test the vehicle by making a brake application at about 20 miles per hour and note whether vehicle stops evenly and quickly. If the brake pedal has a "spongy" feel when the brakes are applied, it is an indication that there is air in the hydraulic system and the entire system must be bled (par. 187).

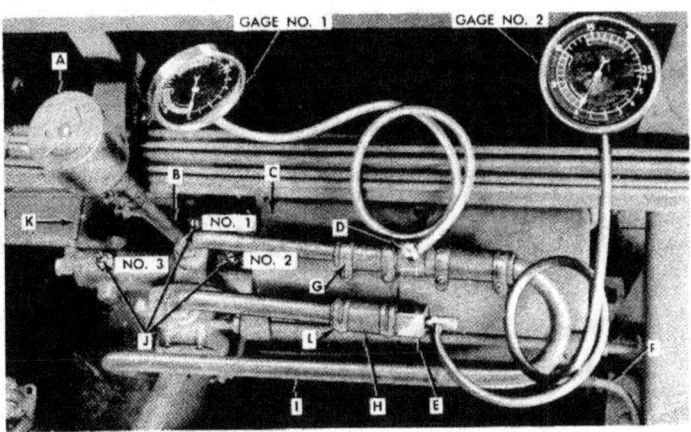

A AIR CLEANER
B AIR CLEANER TUBE
C HYDROVAC (G501-01-45861)
D TEE
E ELBOW
F MASTER CYLINDER TO HYDROVAC TUBE
G HOSE CLAMP (H006-01-00340)
H HOSE (G122-02-17432)
I VACUUM LINE
J BLEEDER SCREWS
K HYDRAULIC BRAKE TUBE
L HOSE CLAMP (G133-01-378154)

RA PD 333209

Figure 151—Hydrovac and Air Cleaner Installed

Maintenance Instructions

c. Vacuum Tests. Two vacuum gages, installed as shown in figure 151, are required for making these tests. Gages are termed gage No. 1 and gage No. 2.

(1) BRAKES RELEASED.

(a) Start the engine and leave the brake pedal in the released position. Note the reading on both vacuum gages. They should register engine manifold vacuum (at least 14 in.) and should be exactly alike. If the reading is below manifold vacuum, a leak exists in the Hydrovac or in the vacuum lines from the manifold check valve.

(b) Stop the engine and remove gage No. 1 from the Hydrovac center plate tee. Disconnect the vacuum line from the rear side of the center plate tee and connect gage No. 1 to the vacuum line. Start the engine and note the reading on gage No. 1. If the gage does not register manifold vacuum (at least 14 in.), the leak is in the vacuum lines from the check valve. Tighten all hose clamps and connections in vacuum lines or replace lines as necessary.

(c) After repairing or replacing vacuum lines, reinstall gage No. 1 in the Hydrovac center plate tee, connect the vacuum line to the rear side of the center plate tee, and repeat test *(a)* above.

(d) If the gages still register less than manifold vacuum, the leak exists in the Hydrovac. A leak in the Hydrovac can be caused by leaky gaskets, loose connections, or improper seating of the atmospheric relay valve. Any of these conditions would allow atmosphere to enter and break the vacuum sufficiently to cause the gage readings to be below manifold vacuum.

(2) BRAKES APPLIED.

(a) If both gages register manifold vacuum with the engine running and the brake pedal released, depress the brake pedal and hold in the applied position. Note the reading on both gages. Gage No. 1 should continue to register manifold vacuum, while gage No. 2 should drop to zero.

(b) If gage No. 1 does not continue to register manifold vacuum, it may be attributed to conditions within the Hydrovac which necessitate replacement of the complete unit.

187. BLEEDING SYSTEM.

a. General. The hydraulic brake system must be bled to expel any air which may have entered in the event any of the brake tubes have been broken or disconnected. The need of bleeding system is generally indicated by a springy, spongy pedal action.

b. Equipment. Hydraulic system can be bled manually or with a pressure tank. When the manual method is used, two persons are required to accomplish the operations; one to maintain a constant supply of fluid in the master cylinder reservoir and to pump the brake pedal, the other to accomplish bleeding operations at the Hydrovac and wheel cylinders. When a conventional pressure tank is used, the tank main-

Service Brake System

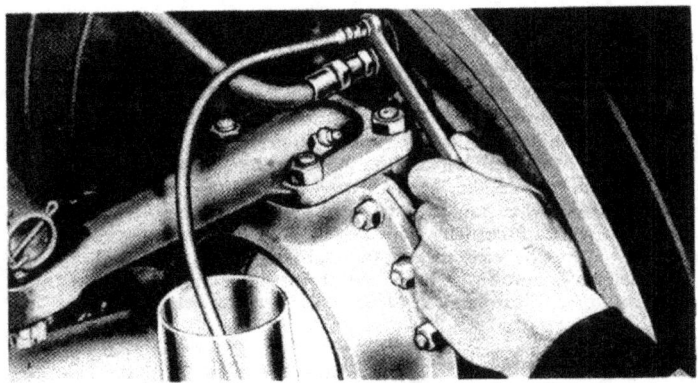

Figure 152—Bleeding Wheel Cylinder

tains a constant supply of fluid in master cylinder reservoir and contains sufficient air pressure to force the fluid through the brake tubes.

c. Bleeding Operations.

(1) CONNECT PRESSURE TANK (IF USED). Remove filler cap from master cylinder and connect pressure tank hose to filler cap opening. The pressure tank should contain 10 to 20 pounds of air pressure and sufficient hydraulic brake fluid to maintain a constant level in the master cylinder reservoir.

(2) BLEED HYDROVAC. The Hydrovac must be bled before bleeding the wheel cylinders and must be bled in sequence shown in figure 151. Remove screw and lock washer from bleeder screw No. 1 and install bleeder tube in bleeder screw. Place opposite end of bleeder tube in a container with sufficient brake fluid to cover end of tube. While pumping brake pedal, or using air pressure in pressure tank, open bleeder screw by turning it three-quarters of a turn counterclockwise and observe flow of fluid from end of bleeder tube. Close bleeder screw firmly as soon as air bubbles stop and fluid flows out of tube in a solid stream. Remove bleeder tube and install screw and lock washer in bleeder screw. Repeat this operation at bleeder screws No. 2 and No. 3.

(3) BLEED WHEEL CYLINDERS. Wheel cylinder bleeder valves are located at inner side of brake flange plate at each wheel (fig. 152). Bleed each wheel cylinder in same manner as directed for bleeding Hydrovac in step (2) above, replenishing brake fluid in master cylinder reservoir before bleeding each cylinder if manual method is being used.

188. SYSTEM ADJUSTMENTS FOR NORMAL WEAR.

a. General. Brake system adjustments to compensate for normal wear are confined to adjustments at the brake shoes. Other adjustments,

TM 9-802

Maintenance Instructions

such as pedal to toeboard clearance and master cylinder linkage adjustments are not required except when linkage has been disconnected or has become distorted.

b. Front Brake Shoe Adjustment. Jack up wheel and check wheel bearing adjustment (par. 214**b**.). Remove two adjusting hole covers from brake flange plate at each side of brake hose connection. Insert a screwdriver through adjusting hole until it engages notches in gear on wheel cylinder cover (fig. 153). Turn wheel cylinder cover in a clockwise direction (when looking at end of cylinder) until there is a slight drag as wheel is turned by hand. Back off wheel cylinder cover four notches to provide clearance between brake lining and brake drum. Perform this operation at both ends of wheel cylinder at each front wheel, making adjustments as uniform as possible at each wheel.

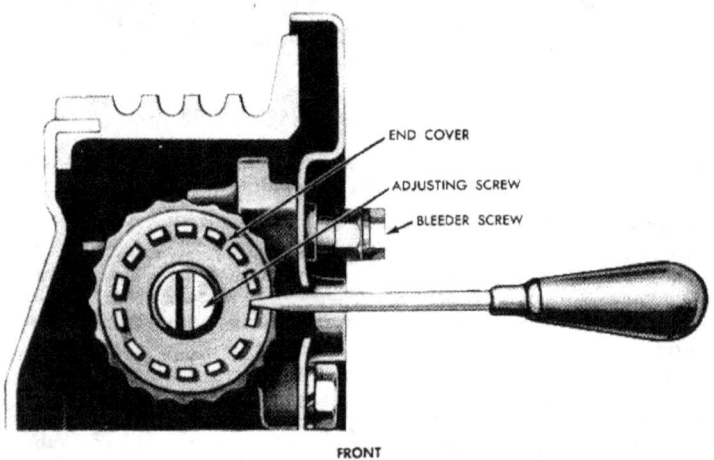

FRONT

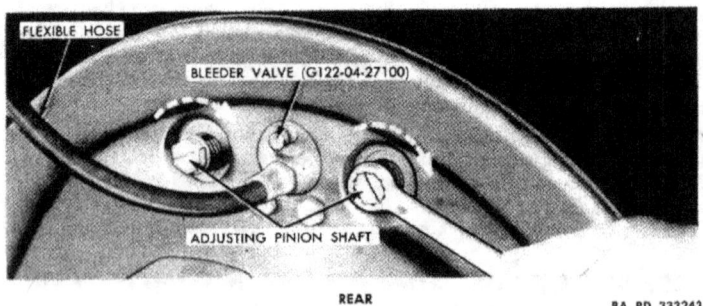

REAR

RA PD 333243

Figure 153—Adjusting Brake Shoes

TM 9-802
188-189

Service Brake System

c. Rear Brake Shoe Adjustment. Jack up wheel and check wheel bearing adjustment (par. 215**b**.). Rear brake shoe adjustments are made by using a wrench on the adjusting pinion shaft as shown in figure 153. Turn shaft in a clockwise direction as indicated by arrows on illustration, until there is a slight drag as wheel is turned by hand. Back off shaft three-quarters of a turn to provide clearance between brake lining and brake drum. Perform this operation at both pinion shafts at each rear wheel, making adjustments as uniform as possible at all wheels.

189. HYDROVAC.

a. General. The Hydrovac unit is a combined hydraulic-vacuum power unit utilizing vacuum and atmospheric pressure for its operation. The Hydrovac is so constructed that in the event the vacuum system fails, brake fluid can still flow through the slave cylinder, permitting manual application of the brakes. The Hydrovac air cleaner is vertically mounted as shown in figure 151.

b. Air Cleaner Service. Remove screw and washer attaching air cleaner assembly to stem and remove cover, fibre washer, and air cleaner shell with screens and hair from stem. Remove outer screen, hair, and inner screen from shell. Service air cleaner as described on Lubrication Order No. 9-802. Position shell over stem and install inner screen, hair, and outer screen in shell. Place fibre washer on top of stem, install cover, and attach with screw and washer.

c. Hydrovac Removal (fig. 151).

(1) DISCONNECT HOSES AND TUBES. Loosen hose clamps on hose connecting vacuum line to rear of center plate tee and slide hose back onto vacuum line. Swing vacuum line in toward center of vehicle. Loosen hose clamps on hose connecting air cleaner tube to air cleaner and slide hose down onto tube. Loosen upper hose clamp attaching air cleaner tube to bottom of relay valve and push hose down off relay valve fitting. Remove air cleaner tube with hoses. Disconnect master cylinder to Hydrovac tube from bottom of slave cylinder, and disconnect tube from front end of slave cylinder.

(2) DISCONNECT MOUNTINGS. Remove nut and lock washer from both ends of outer cylinder studs. Remove two bolts attaching front support bracket to frame side rail. Move front support bracket forward far enough to permit pulling Hydrovac ahead until outer cylinder studs will clear rear support bracket. Lift Hydrovac assembly up out of vehicle.

d. Hydrovac Installation (fig. 153).

(1) POSITION UNIT AND CONNECT MOUNTINGS. Position Hydrovac inside frame side rail with rear ends of outer cylinder studs inserted through holes in rear support bracket. Move front support bracket back over front ends of outer cylinder studs and attach bracket to frame side rail, using two bolts, lock washers, and nuts. Install nut and lock washer on both ends of outer cylinder studs and tighten firmly.

(2) CONNECT HOSES AND TUBES. Swing vacuum line into position and slide hose onto rear side of center plate tee. Tighten hose clamps

TM 9-802
189-190

Maintenance Instructions

firmly. Position air cleaner tube and slide hoses up onto fitting under relay valve and onto bottom of air cleaner stem. Tighten hose clamps firmly. Connect master cylinder to Hydrovac tube to bottom of slave cylinder and connect tube to front of slave cylinder. Tighten tube nuts firmly.

(3) BLEED BRAKES. Bleed entire brake system (par. 187).

190. VACUUM CHECK VALVE.

a. General. The vacuum check valve is vertically mounted at the engine intake manifold as shown in figure 154. The check valve seals vacuum in the vacuum lines and Hydrovac when engine is stopped, providing sufficient vacuum for one complete brake application.

b. Removal (fig. 154). Unscrew vacuum line nut from elbow at bottom of check valve and unscrew elbow from valve. Remove check valve by unscrewing valve from manifold fitting.

c. Service Operations (fig. 154). Remove four screws attaching valve cap to valve body and separate cap and body. Lift valve stem out of valve body. Discard cap to body gasket. Inspect valve seat in body for evidence of pitting or corrosion. Slight imperfections may be removed with fine steel wool. Inspect rubber seat at valve stem and replace stem if deterioration is evident. Check fit of valve stem in valve stem guides. Stem must be free in guides. Place *new* gasket on body, position valve cap on body, and attach with four screws and lock washers.

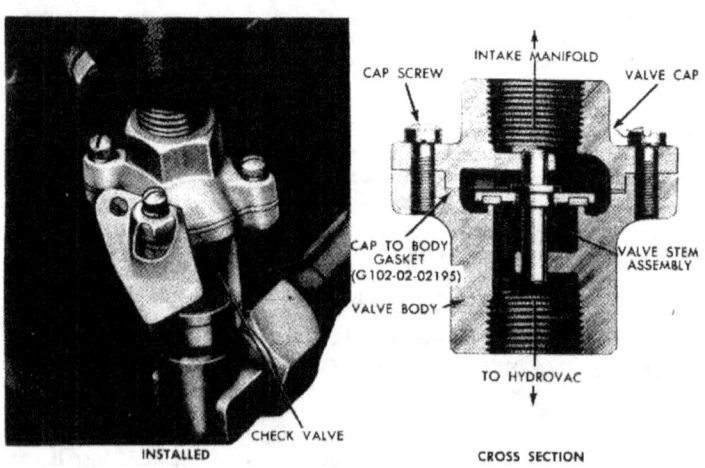

Figure 154—Vacuum Check Valve

TM 9-802
190-191
Service Brake System

d. Installation (fig. 154). Coat threads of manifold fitting with mica base antiseize compound, then thread check valve onto fitting and tighten firmly. Coat male threads of elbow with mica base antiseize compound, then thread elbow into bottom of check valve and tighten firmly. Connect vacuum line to elbow, tightening vacuum line nut firmly.

191. BRAKE PEDAL AND LINKAGE.

a. General (fig. 155). Brake pedal, mounted on clutch and brake pedal shaft, is connected to master cylinder shaft inner lever by an adjustable pull rod. Brake pedal return spring, attached to rear end of pull rod, holds the brake pedal in released position.

b. Removal (fig. 155). Remove screws attaching toeboard lower closure plate to toeboard and remove closure plate. Lift left-hand floor board out of driver's compartment. Remove cotter pin and clevis pin from each end of pedal pull rod. Remove clutch pedal (par. 154). Remove clamp bolt from shaft bracket and drive shaft toward outside of vehicle until it clears brake pedal. Lift brake pedal up out of vehicle.

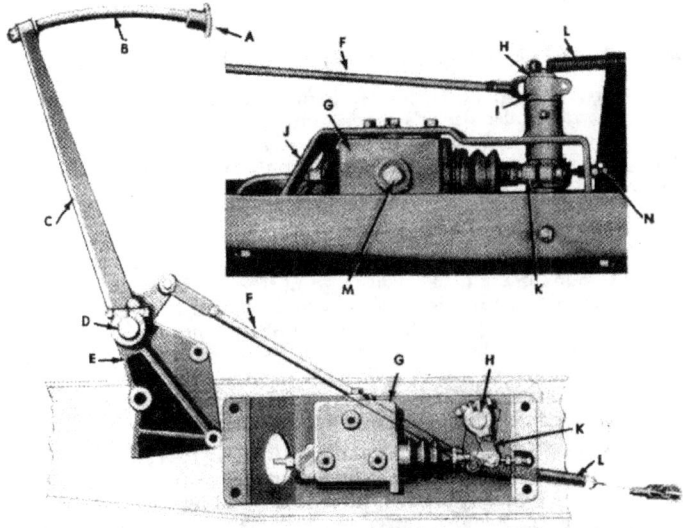

A PEDAL PAD
B PEDAL ROD
C PEDAL LEVER
D CLUTCH AND BRAKE PEDAL SHAFT
E PEDAL SHAFT BRACKET
F PEDAL TO MASTER CYLINDER ROD
G MASTER CYLINDER ASSEMBLY (G501-01-45860)
H MASTER CYLINDER LEVER SHAFT
I MASTER CYLINDER SHAFT INNER LEVER
J MASTER CYLINDER BRACKET
K MASTER CYLINDER SHAFT OUTER LEVER
L BRAKE PEDAL RETURN SPRING (G501-03-89794)
M MASTER CYLINDER FILLER CAP (G067-06-01480) AND GASKET (G085-31-05820)
N STOP SCREW

RA PD 337158

Figure 155—Brake Pedal, Master Cylinder, and Linkage Installation

349

c. Installation (fig. 155).

(1) INSTALL BRAKE PEDAL AND PULL ROD. Position brake pedal in clutch and brake pedal shaft bracket and drive shaft in through brake pedal until groove in shaft is alined with clamp bolt holes in bracket. Install clamp bolt, lock washer, and nut and tighten firmly. Install clutch pedal (par. 154). Install brake pedal pull rod with adjustable yoke at front, and connect rod to brake pedal and master cylinder shaft inner lever, using cotter pins and clevis pins.

(2) ADJUST PEDAL TO TOEBOARD CLEARANCE. Before adjusting brake pedal to toeboard clearance, check master cylinder linkage adjustment and make necessary corrections [par. 192c., steps (3) and (4)]. Remove clevis pin attaching adjustable yoke to brake pedal and loosen lock nut behind adjustable yoke. Turn yoke onto or off of pull rod as necessary to obtain one-half to one inch clearance between brake pedal and under side of toeboard. Connect rod to brake pedal, using a clevis pin and cotter pin, then tighten lock nut behind adjustable yoke. Install toeboard lower closure plate and install left-hand floor board in driver's compartment.

192. MASTER CYLINDER AND LINKAGE.

a. General (fig. 155). Master cylinder is mounted inside left-hand frame side rail under driver's compartment left-hand floor board. Brake pedal movement, transmitted to piston in master cylinder bore through linkage, causes piston to displace fluid into the brake tubes to the Hydrovac and wheel cylinders.

b. Removal (fig. 155).

(1) DISCONNECT. Remove driver's compartment left-hand floor board. Unhook brake pedal return spring from clevis pin in master cylinder shaft inner lever, then remove cotter pin and clevis pin attaching brake pedal pull rod to master cylinder shaft inner lever. Disconnect master cylinder to Hydrovac brake tube by unscrewing tube nut from fitting at front end of master cylinder. Disconnect wires from stop light switch under master cylinder. Unscrew lubrication fitting pipe nipple which extends down through frame side rail into lever shaft bushing.

(2) REMOVE MASTER CYLINDER, BRACKET, AND LINKAGE. Remove bolts attaching master cylinder bracket to frame side rail and remove master cylinder, bracket, lever shaft, and levers as an assembly from the vehicle. Remove cotter pin and clevis pin attaching master cylinder rod to outer lever. Remove six cap screws and lock washers attaching master cylinder to bracket and lift master cylinder out of bracket.

c. Installation (fig. 155).

(1) ASSEMBLE MASTER CYLINDER TO BRACKET AND LINKAGE. Position master cylinder in bracket and install six bracket to master cylinder cap screws and lock washers, three in each side. Connect master cylinder rod to outer lever, using clevis pin and cotter pin.

Service Brake System

(2) INSTALL MASTER CYLINDER, BRACKET, AND LINKAGE. Position master cylinder, bracket, and linkage assembly inside frame side rail and attach with four bolts. Tighten bolts firmly. Connect master cylinder to Hydrovac brake tube to front end of master cylinder, tightening tube nut firmly. Install wires on stop light switch terminals. Insert lubrication fitting pipe nipple down through frame side rail and thread into lever shaft outer bushing. Connect brake pedal pull rod to inner lever, using clevis pin and cotter pin.

(3) ADJUST PISTON PUSH ROD. Remove cotter pin and clevis pin attaching pull rod adjustable yoke to brake pedal. Loosen lock nut on outer lever to master cylinder rod. With one wrench on lock nut and another wrench on hex end of master cylinder piston push rod, turn push rod until rear of piston contacts stop plate in master cylinder. Turn push rod one additional turn (until it is loose in piston), then tighten lock nut.

(4) ADJUST STOP SCREW. Move linkage toward applied position until push rod contacts rear of master cylinder piston. While holding linkage in this position, adjust stop screw behind inner lever to provide a 0.020-inch clearance between lever and stop screw. Tighten lock nuts on stop screw.

(5) ADJUST PEDAL TO TOEBOARD CLEARANCE. Hook brake pedal return spring into eye in pull rod to inner lever clevis pin. Connect pull rod to brake pedal, adjusting pedal to toeboard clearance as directed in paragraph 191c.

(6) BLEED SYSTEM. Fill master cylinder with hydraulic brake fluid and bleed entire system (par. 187).

193. LINES AND CONNECTIONS.

a. General. Installation of hydraulic and vacuum lines is shown in figure 156. Key letters in figure 156 refer to figure 157 for close-up cutaway views of the connections. All hydraulic lines inside the hull are metal tubes, securely clipped to frame side rails and crossmembers. Hydraulic lines from hull connections to wheel cylinders are flexible hoses, supported by springs attached to wheelhouse side panels. The vacuum line from the check valve to the Hydrovac consists of two metal tubes, with a flexible hose connecting the two metal tubes between the clutch housing and frame side rail.

b. Flexible Hose Replacement. Two types of flexible hose to brake tube connections are used as shown in C and D, figure 157. Replacement instructions for each type are described separately in steps (1) and (2) below.

(1) TEE CONNECTION (C, FIG. 157).

(a) Removal. Unscrew bolt attaching tee fitting to flexible hose fitting. Hold flexible hose fitting with wrench at outside of hull and remove nut and lock washer from hose fitting inside frame side rail. Pull hose fitting out of hull and unscrew hose from wheel cylinder at brake flange plate.

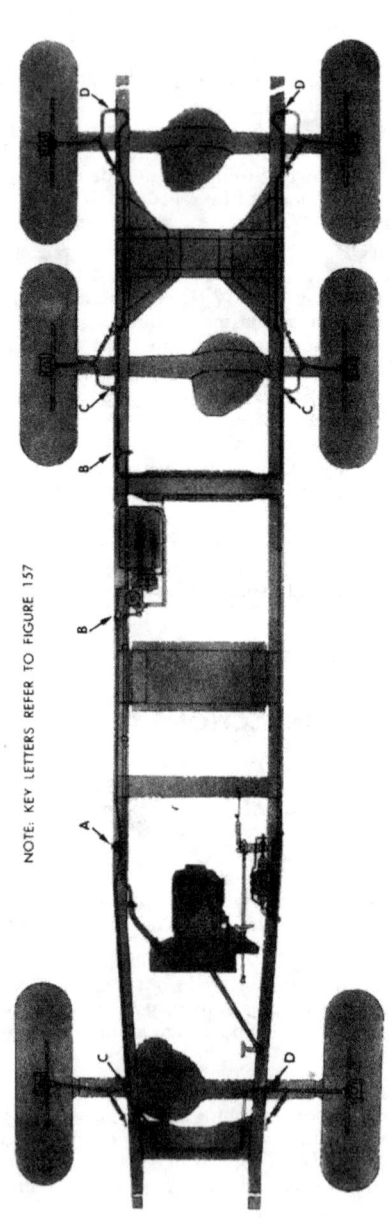

Figure 156—Hydraulic and Vacuum Lines Installation

TM 9-802
Service Brake System

(b) Installation. Reverse procedure in step *(a)* above to install flexible hose, observing the following precautions: Caulking compound (52-C-3086-200) must be generously applied between hull and flat washer; make sure all gaskets and washers are in place as shown in illustra-

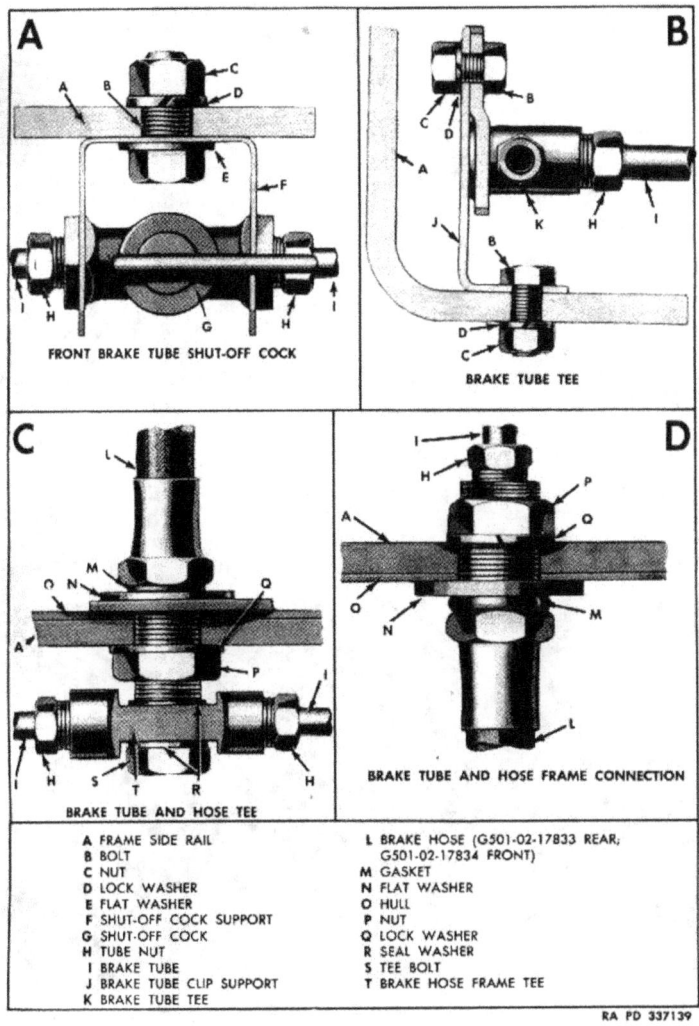

Figure 157—Hydraulic Line Fittings and Mountings

TM 9-802
193-194

Maintenance Instructions

tion; hold flexible hose fitting at outside of hull when tightening nut inside frame side rail to prevent twisting hose.

(2) STRAIGHT CONNECTION (D, FIG. 157).

(a) Removal. Unscrew tube nut from flexible hose fitting inside frame side rail. Hold flexible hose fitting with wrench at outside of hull and remove nut and lock washer from fitting inside frame side rail. Pull flexible hose fitting out of hull and frame side rail and unscrew hose from wheel cylinder at brake flange plate.

(b) Installation. Reverse procedure in step *(a)* above to install flexible hose, observing the following precautions: Caulking compound (52-C-3086-200) must be generously applied between flat washer and hull; make sure gasket and washers are in place as shown in illustration; be sure and hold hose fitting at outside of hull with wrench while tightening nut inside frame side rail.

c. Metal Tube Replacement. Replacement of metal tubes consists of unscrewing the tube nut at each end of tube, removing clips attaching tube to frame side rail or crossmember, and removing tube. When installing tube, make sure that all tube nuts are tightened firmly and that all clips are replaced. Refer to figure 156 for location of tubes. When replacing front brake shut-off cock or brake tube tees, refer to A or B, figure 157, for correct installation.

194. WHEEL CYLINDERS.

a. General. One wheel cylinder is mounted on brake flange plate between upper ends of brake shoes at each wheel. As hydraulic brake fluid enters wheel cylinders under pressure, the wheel cylinder pistons are forced apart, forcing the brake shoes outward against the brake drum.

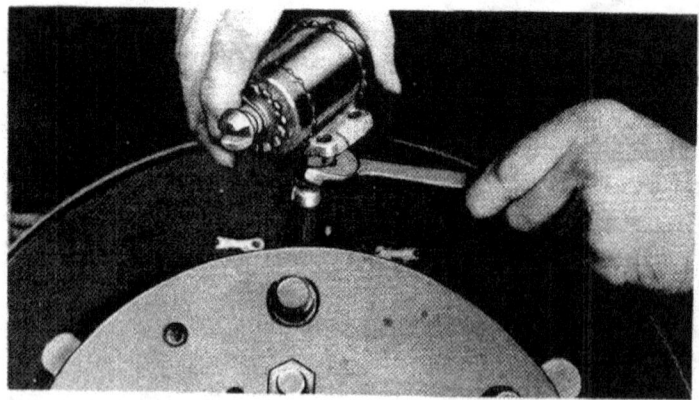

RA PD 333234

Figure 158—Removing Wheel Cylinder

354

Service Brake System

b. Removal. On vehicles equipped with demountable brake drums, remove wheel and brake drum to gain access to wheel cylinder. On early vehicles not equipped with demountable brake drums, it is necessary to remove wheel, hub, and drum. When removing front wheel cylinders, close front brake tube shut-off cock. Unhook brake hose suspension spring (G102-52-14539). Install clamp or wire on wheel cylinder and remove brake shoe return spring, then swing shoes outward away from wheel cylinder. Remove two bolts and lock washers attaching wheel cylinder to brake flange plate and pull wheel cylinder away from brake flange plate. Hold flexible hose connection with wrench and turn wheel cylinder off from hose connection (fig. 158). *Do not twist flexible hose.*

c. Treatment of Wheel Cylinders. Refer to paragraph 198.

d. Installation. Insert flexible hose through brake flange plate and, while holding hose connection with wrench, screw wheel cylinder onto hose connection (fig. 158). *Do not twist flexible hose.* Position wheel cylinder on brake flange plate and attach with two bolts and lock washers. Place upper ends of brake shoes in notches in wheel cylinder adjusting screws and install brake shoe return spring. Remove clamp or wire from wheel cylinder. Hook suspension spring into clip on hose. Install brake drum and wheel (late vehicles), or hub, drum, and wheel (early vehicles). Open front brake tube shut-off cock and bleed brake system (par. 187). NOTE: *If only the front wheel cylinders were removed and the front brake tube shut-off cock was closed, it is only necessary to bleed the front wheel cylinders.* Adjust brake shoes (par. 188).

RA PD 333212

Figure 159—Removing Brake Drum (Demountable Type)

TM 9-802
195

Maintenance Instructions

195. BRAKE DRUMS.

a. General. Brake drums on late vehicles (after chassis serial No. 3005 front; after chassis serial No. 3003 rear) are demountable type, that is, they may be removed without removing the hub. On early vehicles (prior to the above chassis serial numbers), brake drums are secured to the inner sides of the hub flanges by the wheel bolts, and the hub and drum must be removed as an assembly.

b. Demountable Type Drums (fig. 159).

(1) REMOVAL. Remove tire inflating device and wheel (par. 212**c.**) and remove wheel spacer (rear only). NOTE: *Before removing wheel spacer, stamp a number 6 on hub adjacent to stud in wheel spacer marked No. 6* (fig. 172). Remove three screws attaching drum to hub. Apply a few drops of penetrating oil through each hole in drum and permit it to seep in between drum and hub. Scrape excess paint off hub and wheel bolts next to brake drum. After penetrating oil has had time to loosen rust and corrosion, position a block of wood in groove in brake drum and drive drum off from hub (fig. 159). Alternately drive on opposite sides of drum to prevent cocking drum on wheel bolts.

(2) INSTALLATION. Make sure mating surfaces of hub and brake drum are clean and smooth. Refer to paragraph 198 for corrosion treatment. Position drum on hub and drive into place, using a wooden block against drum. Install three drum to hub screws. If old screws were damaged at removal and new screws are not available, screws may be left out. Install wheel spacer (rear only) with stud marked No. 6 alined with No. 6 on hub. Install wheel and tire inflating device (par. 212**d.**).

c. Nondemountable Type Drums (fig. 160).

(1) REMOVAL. Remove hub and drum assembly (par. 214 or 215). Position hub and drum assembly so that bolt heads are accessible. Mark the *exact center* of the bolt heads with a center punch, then drill a hole

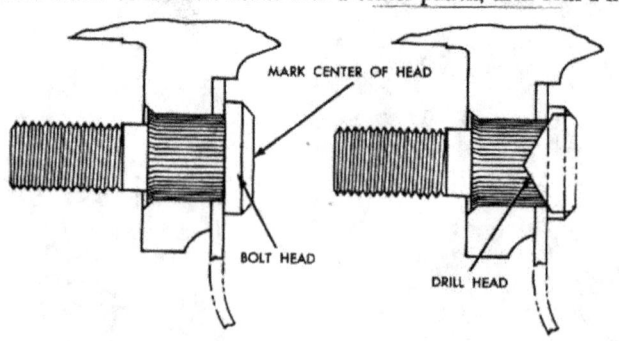

RA PD 333182

*Figure 160—Removal of Wheel Bolts
(Nondemountable Type Drums)*

in each bolt head to approximate depth shown in figure 160, using a ⅞-inch drill. Be sure drill is correctly alined, and drill only deep enough to sever bolt head from bolt. Drive bolts out of hub and drum, using a blunt drift in drilled holes, and separate hub and drum.

(2) INSTALLATION. Refer to paragraph 198 for corrosion treatment.

(a) Front. Position drum on hub and aline wheel bolt holes. Drive or press wheel bolts into place, being sure that serrations on bolt and in hub are alined. Wheel bolts must be a tight press fit.

(b) Rear. Position drum on hub and install gasket and oil deflector. Aline holes in oil deflector, gasket, drum, and hub, with the small hole in gasket alined with oil relief hole in brake drum. Insert wheel bolts through oil deflector, gasket, brake drum, and hub, making sure serrations on bolts and in hub are alined. Drive or press wheel bolts into place. Wheel bolts must be a tight press fit.

196. FRONT BRAKE SHOES.

a. General (fig. 161). The brake shoe assemblies are connected to an anchor plate with articulating links and an anchor pin. Guide plates, riveted to anchor plate near upper ends of shoes, hold each shoe in alinement. The upper end of each shoe rests in slots in outer ends of adjusting screws which are threaded into wheel cylinder end covers. On vehicles equipped with demountable drums, it is only necessary to remove the wheel and drum to gain access to brake shoes. On early vehicles not equipped with demountable drums, it is necessary to remove the wheel, hub, and drum.

b. Removal (fig. 161). Jack up wheel to be serviced and remove wheel and brake drum, or wheel, hub, and drum on early vehicles. Install clamp or wire on wheel cylinder to prevent end covers from coming off and remove brake shoe return spring. Remove anchor pin lock with screwdriver and remove anchor pin. Remove brake shoes with links attached by swinging them clear of guides on anchor plate. Remove friction pin locks, springs, and pins. Remove link pin locks and remove link pins.

c. Installation (fig. 161).

(1) INSPECT AND TREAT PARTS. Refer to paragraph 198.

(2) ASSEMBLE LINKS TO SHOES. Assemble links to shoes and install link pins and new link pin locks. Reverse shoe links have a slight offset near each end and must be installed so that the offsets provide a wide opening at the anchor pin end, permitting them to be installed over the forward shoe links. Install friction pins, springs, and new locks.

(3) INSTALL SHOES AND LINKS. Position shoes in guides on anchor plate and install anchor pin and new anchor pin lock. Check fit of shoes in guides. Shoes should be free without excessive side play. Position upper ends of shoes in slots in adjusting screws and install brake shoe return spring.

(4) NOTE: *Several types of brake shoe return springs have been used on these vehicles, all of which were serviced under the same part num-*

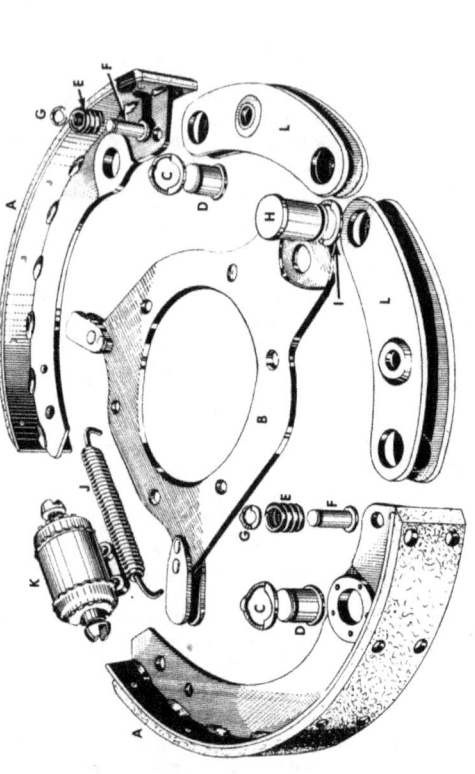

A BRAKE SHOE AND LINING ASSEMBLY (G501-01-25841)
B ANCHOR PLATE
C LINK PIN LOCK (G085-31-08200)
D LINK PIN
E PIN SPRING
F PIN
G PIN LOCK (G085-31-08120)
H ANCHOR PIN
I ANCHOR PIN LOCK (G081-31-08200)
J BRAKE SHOE RETURN SPRING (G085-31-13900)
K WHEEL CYLINDER (G501-01-45862)
L LINK

Figure 161—Front Brake Shoe Assembly—Installed and Disassembled

RA PD 33323

Service Brake System

ber. *The latest type should be installed and may be identified by the diameter of the hook at each end of the spring. Diameter of hook on latest type is 0.162 inch, while on the early types the diameter of the hook is 0.148 inch.*

(5) INSTALL BRAKE DRUM AND WHEEL. Remove wheel cylinder clamp or wire. Install brake drum and wheel, or hub, drum, and wheel on early vehicles. Adjust brakes (par. 188).

197. REAR BRAKE SHOES.

a. General (fig. 162). Brake shoe assemblies are connected to anchor plate with articulating links and two anchor pins at the bottom. Guide plates, riveted to anchor plate near upper ends of shoes, hold each shoe in alinement. The upper end of each brake shoe rests in slots in outer ends of adjusting screws which are threaded into wheel cylinder end covers. On vehicles equipped with demountable brake drums, it is only necessary to remove the wheel and drum to gain access to the brake shoes. On early vehicles not equipped with demountable drums, it is necessary to remove the wheel, hub, and drum.

b. Removal (fig. 162). Jack up the wheel to be serviced and remove wheel and brake drum, or wheel, hub, and drum on early vehicles. Install a clamp or wire on wheel cylinder to prevent end covers from coming off and remove brake shoe return spring. Remove anchor pin locks, using a screwdriver, and remove anchor pins. Remove brake shoes with links attached by swinging them clear of guides on anchor plate. Remove friction pin locks, springs, and pins. Remove link pin locks and remove link pins.

c. Installation (fig. 162).

(1) INSPECT AND TREAT PARTS. Refer to paragraph 198.

(2) ASSEMBLE LINKS TO SHOES. Assemble links to both shoes by installing link pins and locks, and friction pins, springs, and locks. Use new locks on link pins and friction pins.

(3) INSTALL SHOES AND LINKS. Position shoes at anchor plate and install anchor pins and new anchor pin locks. Check fit of shoes in guides. Shoes should be free without excessive side play. Position upper ends of shoes in slots in adjusting screws and install brake shoe return spring. (See "NOTE" in par. 196c.).

(4) INSTALL BRAKE DRUM AND WHEEL. Remove clamp or wire from wheel cylinder. Install brake drum and wheel, or hub, drum, and wheel on early vehicles. Adjust wheel bearings (par. 215), then adjust brakes (par. 188).

198. CORROSION TREATMENT OF BRAKE PARTS.

a. Wheel Cylinders. To prevent corrosion and freezing of wheel brake cylinders, treat cylinders as follows: Clean and paint wheel cylinders according to instructions in paragraph 238. Thoroughly mix one part of basic carbonate white lead pigment (52-P-19990-5) to two parts

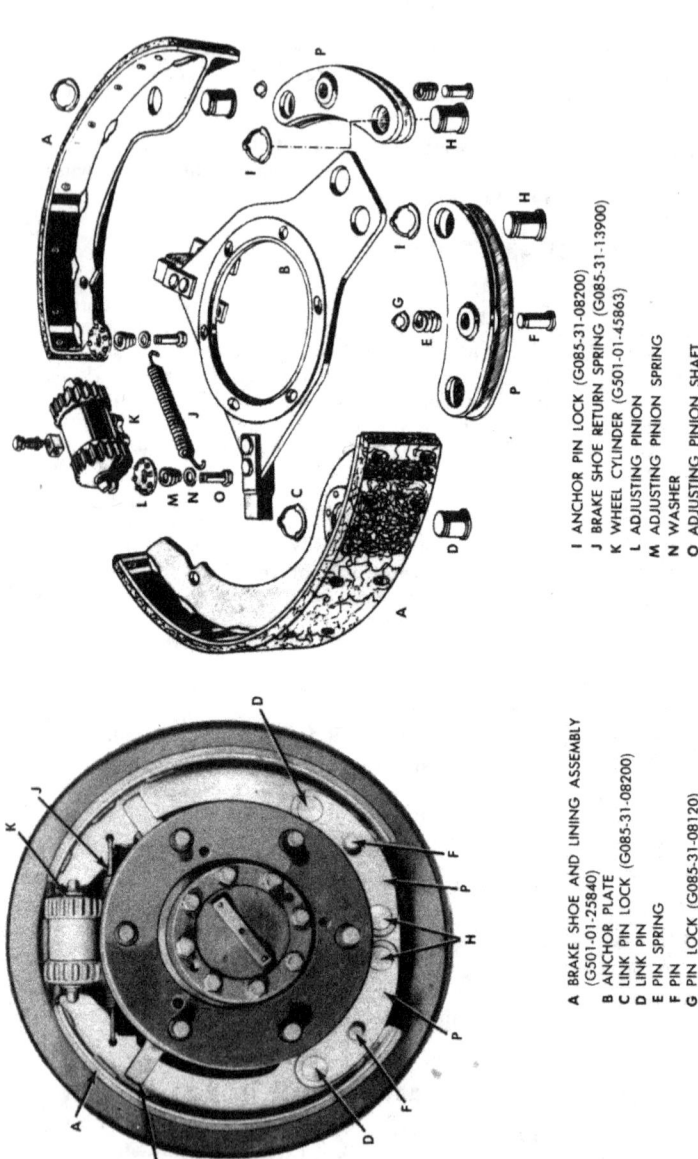

A BRAKE SHOE AND LINING ASSEMBLY
(G501-01-25840)
B ANCHOR PLATE
C LINK PIN LOCK (G085-31-08200)
D LINK PIN
E PIN SPRING
F PIN
G PIN LOCK (G085-31-08120)
H ANCHOR PIN
I ANCHOR PIN LOCK (G085-31-08200)
J BRAKE SHOE RETURN SPRING (G085-31-13900)
K WHEEL CYLINDER (G501-01-45863)
L ADJUSTING PINION
M ADJUSTING PINION SPRING
N WASHER
O ADJUSTING PINION SHAFT
P LINK

Figure 162—Rear Brake Shoe Assembly—Installed and Disassembled

of asbestos grease (14-G-588). If asbestos grease is not available, use water pump grease. Apply a coating (not excessive) of this mixture to inside of wheel cylinder covers, outer ends of pistons, adjusting screw threads, and exterior surface of cylinder contacted by the covers. After installing covers, apply an additional coating of asbestos grease and white lead pigment mixture to exterior of cylinder at edge of cover and to outer adjusting screw threads.

b. Plated Parts. The following parts are zinc or cadmium plated in production: anchor plate, brake shoes, anchor and link pins, and oil deflector. When servicing the brakes, these parts must be replaced with new parts if it is evident that corrosion has affected their functioning. Nonfriction surfaces of these parts that are new or in good condition should be protected by a thin coating of thin film rust preventive compound (41-C-507). Care must be exercised when applying compound to prevent it from reaching a friction surface which would prevent proper operation of brakes.

c. Painted Parts. The following parts are painted in production: brake drum (except braking surface), brake flange plate (inside only), anchor plate spacer, and brake shoe return spring. When servicing the brakes, these parts must be repainted if it is evident that corrosion has affected their functioning. Follow the same surface preparation and painting instructions as outlined in paragraph 238, with the exception that when metal conditioner phosphoric acid is used, this acid should be used on disassembled parts only, and parts should be painted with metal primer only. No olive drab lusterless enamel is to be used.

d. Metal Brake and Air Lines.

(1) METAL BRAKE LINES. Two coats of zinc chromate primer (52-P-20624) or one coat of thin film rust preventive compound (41-C-507 or Navy Spec. 52C18 Grade 1) should be applied to cleaned metal brake lines.

(2) METAL AIR AND WATER LINES. Apply a coat of thin film rust preventive compound (41-C-507) to metal air lines and to tire pump metal water lines.

Section XXXVI

Hand Brake System

199. GENERAL.

a. Description (fig. 163). Manually operated hand brake lever at right of driver is connected by a rod and levers to an external-contracting band type brake, mounted at rear of axle transfer case. Brake band assembly is anchored to the transfer case on supports integral with rear

TM 9-802
199

Maintenance Instructions

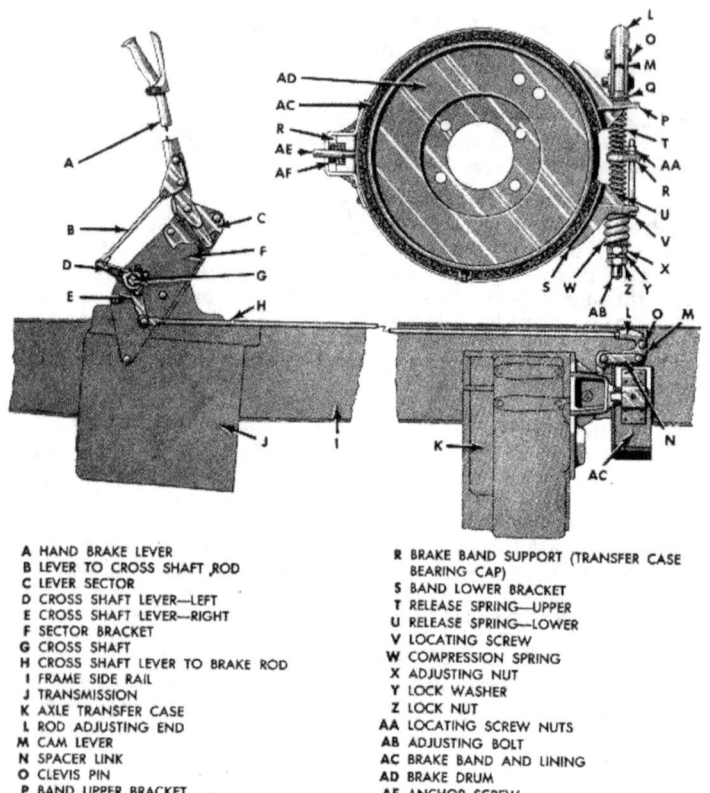

- A HAND BRAKE LEVER
- B LEVER TO CROSS SHAFT ROD
- C LEVER SECTOR
- D CROSS SHAFT LEVER—LEFT
- E CROSS SHAFT LEVER—RIGHT
- F SECTOR BRACKET
- G CROSS SHAFT
- H CROSS SHAFT LEVER TO BRAKE ROD
- I FRAME SIDE RAIL
- J TRANSMISSION
- K AXLE TRANSFER CASE
- L ROD ADJUSTING END
- M CAM LEVER
- N SPACER LINK
- O CLEVIS PIN
- P BAND UPPER BRACKET
- Q CAM SHOE
- R BRAKE BAND SUPPORT (TRANSFER CASE BEARING CAP)
- S BAND LOWER BRACKET
- T RELEASE SPRING—UPPER
- U RELEASE SPRING—LOWER
- V LOCATING SCREW
- W COMPRESSION SPRING
- X ADJUSTING NUT
- Y LOCK WASHER
- Z LOCK NUT
- AA LOCATING SCREW NUTS
- AB ADJUSTING BOLT
- AC BRAKE BAND AND LINING
- AD BRAKE DRUM
- AE ANCHOR SCREW
- AF ANCHOR SPRING

RA PD 337173

Figure 163—Hand Brake Components Installed

bearing retainer. Brake drum is bolted between transfer case rear axle propeller shaft flange and propeller shaft universal joint flange.

b. Operation (fig. 163). As hand brake lever is pulled back, brake rod is pulled forward, applying pressure to cam levers and adjusting bolt at brake band. Movement of cam levers and adjusting bolt draws ends of band and lining together, bringing lining into contact with drum. As hand brake lever is moved forward, brake rod moves to rear, removing pressure from cam levers and adjusting bolt. Ends of band are forced apart by release springs to restore operating clearance between lining and drum.

c. Repair. Repair procedures for components of the hand brake system are described in TM 9-1802B.

Hand Brake System

200. ADJUSTMENTS FOR NORMAL WEAR.

a. General. Hand brake is in need of adjustment when hand brake lever reserve travel is less than one-half of the sector range. Adjustment operations must be performed in the sequence given in subparagraph *b.* below. Hand brake is accessible after removing cargo compartment front center floor board.

b. Adjustment Procedure (fig. 164).

(1) DISCONNECT BRAKE ROD. Block wheels to prevent vehicle from rolling, then place hand brake lever in fully released (forward) position. Remove cotter pin and clevis pin attaching brake rod adjusting end to cam levers.

(2) ADJUST AT ANCHOR. Remove lock wire from anchor screw slot. Adjust anchor screw to obtain a clearance of 0.010 to 0.015 inch between lining and drum. Insert lock wire through anchor bracket and slot in anchor screw, then twist ends of wire together to lock anchor screw in adjusted position.

(3) ADJUST AT BOTTOM. Loosen lock nut on locating screw. Hold locating screw with screwdriver and turn locating screw nut with wrench to obtain a clearance of 0.020 inch between lining and drum. Tighten lock nut on locating screw.

(4) ADJUST AT TOP. Loosen lock nut at lower end of adjusting bolt. Turn adjusting nut as necessary to obtain a clearance of 0.020 inch between lining and drum. Tighten lock nut firmly.

(5) ADJUST AND CONNECT BRAKE ROD. Loosen lock nut ahead of brake rod adjusting end. Turn rod end as necessary to permit free installation of clevis pin through cam levers and rod end. Secure clevis pin with cotter pin and tighten lock nut ahead of rod end. Check hand brake operation, install cargo compartment floor board, then remove block from wheels.

201. HAND BRAKE BAND.

a. Removal (fig. 163).

(1) REMOVE FLOOR BOARD. Block wheels to prevent vehicle from rolling. Place hand brake lever in fully released (forward) position. Remove cargo compartment front center floor board.

(2) REMOVE ADJUSTING BOLT. Remove cotter pins and clevis pins attaching spacer links to brake support and adjusting bolt. Remove lock nut, lock washer, adjusting nut, flat washer, and compression spring from lower end of adjusting bolt. Lift adjusting bolt straight up, removing two release springs and cam shoe as bolt is removed.

(3) REMOVE LOCATING SCREW AND ANCHOR SCREW. Remove two nuts from locating screw and remove screw. Remove anchor screw lock wire, then unscrew anchor screw from anchor bracket and brake support.

TM 9-802
201

Maintenance Instructions

Figure 164—Hand Brake Band Adjustments

(4) REMOVE BRAKE BAND AND LINING ASSEMBLY. Pull brake band and lining straight to rear off from brake drum and brake support. Anchor spring will be removed with band. Spread ends of band and pull band off from propeller shaft.

b. Installation (fig. 163).

(1) POSITION BRAKE BAND AND LINING ASSEMBLY. Position anchor spring in brake support as brake band and lining assembly is moved forward over brake drum and support.

(2) INSTALL ANCHOR SCREW AND LOCATING SCREW. Thread anchor screw through anchor bracket and anchor spring, and

Hand Brake System

into brake support. Insert locating screw through holes in brake band lower bracket and brake support. Thread two nuts onto locating screw finger-tight.

(3) INSTALL ADJUSTING BOLT. Install cam shoe on adjusting bolt. Insert threaded end of adjusting bolt down through brake band upper bracket, upper release spring, brake support, lower release spring, and brake band lower bracket. Install compression spring, flat washer, adjusting nut, lock washer, and lock nut on lower end of adjusting bolt.

(4) CONNECT SPACER LINKS. Insert clevis pin through spacer links, cam levers, and eye in top of adjusting bolt. Connect spacer links to brake support with clevis pin. Install cotter pins in both clevis pins.

(5) ADJUST BRAKE. Adjust brake as directed in paragraph 200*b*.

202. HAND BRAKE DRUM.

a. Removal (fig. 163).

(1) REMOVE BRAKE BAND. Remove brake band and lining assembly (par. 201*a*.).

(2) DISCONNECT PROPELLER SHAFT. Brake drums on late vehicles have a groove cut in shoulder on forward side of drum. When this mark is alined with pointer on transfer case crossmember, propeller shaft lubrication fittings are accessible through propeller shaft housing drain plugs. To maintain correct relationship between this mark and propeller shaft when brake drum is installed, aline mark on drum with pointer on transfer case crossmember before disconnecting propeller shaft. Remove nuts and lock washers from four bolts attaching propeller shaft and brake drum to transfer case flange. Telescope propeller shaft to permit removal of brake drum.

(3) REMOVE BRAKE DRUM. Remove brake drum from transfer case flange, using a soft hammer or wooden block to loosen drum from flange.

b. Installation (fig. 163).

(1) CLEAN AND INSPECT DRUM. Thoroughly clean brake drum, using dry-cleaning solvent, and wipe dry with a clean cloth. Examine drum and replace with a new part if cracked, broken, or deeply scored or grooved.

(2) INSTALL DRUM AND CONNECT PROPELLER SHAFT. Position brake drum on transfer case flange with mark alined with pointer on transfer case crossmember, and insert bolts through transfer case flange and drum. Connect propeller shaft (par. 183*b*.). If a new unmarked drum is installed, place a mark on shoulder of drum, after installing, in alinement with pointer on transfer case crossmember. NOTE: *Before marking drum, refer to paragraph 182b. to make sure propeller shaft lubrication fittings are in correct position.*

(3) INSTALL BRAKE BAND. Install brake band and lining assembly (par. 201*b*.) and adjust brake (par. 200*b*.).

203. HAND BRAKE LEVER AND LINKAGE.

a. Removal (fig. 163).

(1) REMOVE LEVER TO CROSS SHAFT ROD, AND LEVER. Block wheels to prevent vehicle from rolling and place hand brake lever in released position. Remove driver's compartment floor boards and cargo compartment front center floor board. Remove two cotter pins and clevis pins attaching lever to cross shaft rod to hand brake lever and cross shaft lever. Remove two bolts attaching sector to bracket and remove hand brake lever and sector assembly, and two sector to bracket spacers.

(2) DISASSEMBLE HAND BRAKE LEVER AND SECTOR. Remove cotter pin, flat washer, and clevis pin attaching pawl to lever and swing pawl out of lever. Remove cotter pin attaching pawl to lever rod and remove pawl. Remove cotter pin, nut, and bolt securing sector in hand brake lever and remove sector from lever.

(3) REMOVE CROSS SHAFT AND LEVERS. Remove cotter pin and clevis pin attaching brake rod to cross shaft right-hand lever. Loosen clamp bolts attaching right- and left-hand levers to cross shaft and remove levers and Woodruff keys from cross shaft. Pull cross shaft out of sector bracket and cross shaft bracket.

(4) REMOVE CROSS SHAFT BRACKET. Remove two bolts and one stud nut attaching cross shaft bracket to right-hand side of transmission and remove bracket.

(5) REMOVE SECTOR BRACKET. Remove three bolts attaching sector bracket to left-hand side of transmission. Pull sector bracket out from between clutch and brake pedal shaft bracket and transmission.

b. Installation (fig. 163).

(1) INSTALL SECTOR BRACKET. Position sector bracket between clutch and brake pedal shaft bracket and transmission. Install three bolts and lock washers attaching bracket to transmission, with spacers between bracket and transmission on two upper bolts.

(2) INSTALL CROSS SHAFT BRACKET. Position cross shaft bracket at right-hand side of transmission, install bracket to transmission rear bolt and lock washer, and install nut and lock washer on stud at bottom of bracket. Make sure surface of bracket around forward bolt hole is clean and free from paint, then install bracket to transmission forward bolt with engine ground strap and flat washer under lock washer and bolt head.

(3) INSTALL CROSS SHAFT AND LEVERS. Insert cross shaft through sector bracket and cross shaft bracket. Install short lever (3-inch hole centers) on left-hand end of shaft, using Woodruff key, clamp bolt, lock washer, and nut. Install long lever ($3\frac{1}{2}$-inch hole centers) on left-hand end of shaft, using Woodruff key, clamp bolt, lock washer, and nut.

(4) ASSEMBLE HAND BRAKE LEVER AND SECTOR. Install sector in hand brake lever and attach with bolt, nut, and cotter pin. Install

TM 9-802
203-205

Spring Suspension

pawl on lever rod and attach with cotter pin. Position pawl between lower ends of lever and install clevis pin, flat washer, and cotter pin.

(5) INSTALL HAND BRAKE LEVER. Position hand brake lever and sector assembly at top of sector bracket and attach with two bolts, nuts, and lock washers, with spacers on bolts between sector and bracket.

(6) INSTALL RODS. Install hand brake lever to cross shaft rod and attach with clevis pins and cotter pins. Use a spacer on each side of rod eye between adapters on hand lever. Connect brake rod to cross shaft right-hand lever, using clevis pin and cotter pin. Adjust brake (par. 200*b*.).

Section XXXVII
Spring Suspension

204. GENERAL.

a. Description. The front spring system consists of two semi-elliptic springs shackled at the front and pivoted to brackets at the rear. The springs are mounted directly on the axle housings with U-bolts. Shock absorbers are used with front springs only. The rear spring system consists of inverted semi-elliptic type springs, mounted on roller bearing spring seats with U-bolts. Slipper type spring ends contact brackets on the forward and the rearward rear axles. The ends of the springs are free to slide forward or backward to permit springs to lengthen and retract under load compression and rebound action. Torque rods, three at each axle, interconnect the forward rear axle and the rearward rear axle with the trunnion brackets.

b. Repair. Repair procedures for spring suspension components are described in TM 9-1802B.

205. FRONT SPRINGS.

a. Description. The front springs are semi-elliptic type mounted to the hull with shackles at front and stationary brackets at rear (figs. 165 and 166). The top leaf of each spring has an eye formed at each end into which a bronze bushing is pressed. The third leaf is also partially wrapped around the eye. A center bolt is used to aline and hold spring leaves together. Rebound clips, two at each side of center bolt, are used to prevent leaves from spreading apart and at the same time hold spring leaves in alinement during rebound action.

b. Front Shackle.

(1) REMOVAL.

(a) Raise Front of Vehicle. Jack up or lift front of vehicle until spring tension is completely relieved. Block wheels to prevent vehicle from rolling. Remove wheelhouse skirt.

TM 9-802
205

Maintenance Instructions

A FRONT SPRING FRONT BRACKET PIN
B FRONT SPRING ASSEMBLY (G501-03-89828)
C SHOCK ABSORBER LINK
  (G501-02-76565 DUKW-353-474 PRIOR TO)
  SHOCK ABSORBER LINK
  (G501-02-76565-DUKW-353-474 AND AFTER)
D FRONT SPRING BUMPER
E FRONT BRAKE HOSE
F U-BOLTS
G FRONT SPRING REAR PIN (G501-03-38699)
H SHACKLE PIN CLAMP BOLT
I FRONT SPRING FRONT SHACKLE PIN
  (G501-03-38710)
J FRONT SPRING SHACKLE ASSEMBLY

RA PD 337195

Figure 165—Front Spring and Shock Absorber Installation

(b) Remove Shackle. Remove shackle pin clamp bolts, nuts, and lock washers (fig. 166). Remove lubrication fittings from shackle pins. Install puller (41-P-2951-85) to shackle pin and pull pin from shackle and spring. After pins are removed, remove spring shackle.

(2) INSTALLATION.

(a) Install Shackle Pin. Clean shackle pins thoroughly. Make certain lubricant channel in each shackle pin is not clogged. Position shackle and aline with holes in bracket and spring eye, then using a soft faced hammer, drive shackle pins into place (fig. 166). Make certain that clamp bolt holes in bracket and shackle are in alinement with grooves in shackle pins.

(b) Install Clamp Bolts and Lubrication Fittings. Clean lubrication fittings thoroughly before installing in shackle pin. Apply a small amount of engine oil on clamp bolts, then insert clamp bolts in bracket and in shackle and attach with nuts and new lock washers. Tighten nuts firmly.

c. Front Spring Removal.

(1) REMOVE U-BOLTS AND BUMPER BLOCK. Raise and support front end of vehicle to relieve spring tension. Block rear wheels to pre-

TM 9-802
205

Spring Suspension

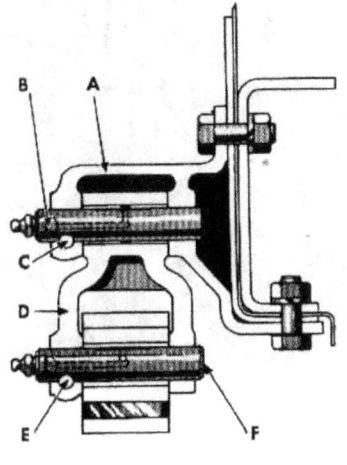
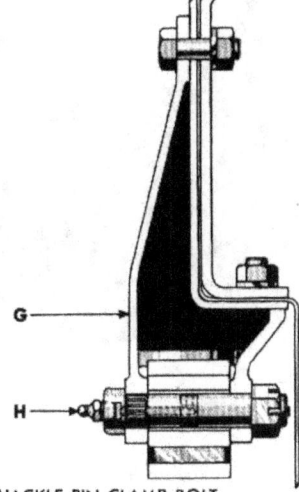

A FRONT SPRING FRONT BRACKET
B FRONT SPRING FRONT SHACKLE PIN
C SHACKLE PIN CLAMP BOLT
D FRONT SPRING SHACKLE AND BUSHING

E SHACKLE PIN CLAMP BOLT
F FRONT SPRING FRONT SHACKLE PIN
G FRONT SPRING REAR BRACKET
H FRONT SPRING REAR PIN

RA PD 16194

Figure 166—Front Spring Shackle and Pin Installation

vent vehicle from rolling. Remove nuts from U-bolts which attach bumper block and shock absorber link bracket. This operation will permit removal of bumper block and free shock absorber link bracket.

(2) REMOVE SHACKLE PIN AND REAR BRACKET PIN. Remove lower shackle pin. Remove cotter pin and slotted hex nut from rear front spring bracket pin. Remove lubrication fitting, then remove pin. Free front spring shackle from spring by swinging shackle toward front of vehicle and remove spring assembly.

d. Front Spring Installation.

(1) POSITION SPRING ASSEMBLY. Make certain that spring center bolt recess on top of axle housing is clean. Clean bracket pin lubrication channel thoroughly. Examine pin and, if excessively worn or grooved, replace with new pin. Position spring on top of axle. Make certain center bolt is in recess. Aline spring eye in rear bracket and in shackle.

(2) INSTALL BRACKET PIN. Insert bracket pin into bracket through spring eye. Make certain that serrations on bracket pin are in alinement with serrations in bracket, then drive bracket pin into place, using soft faced hammer. Install slotted hex nut on inner end of pin. Draw nut up as firmly as possible, then back nut off one-half turn, and at the same

TM 9-802
205-206

Maintenance Instructions

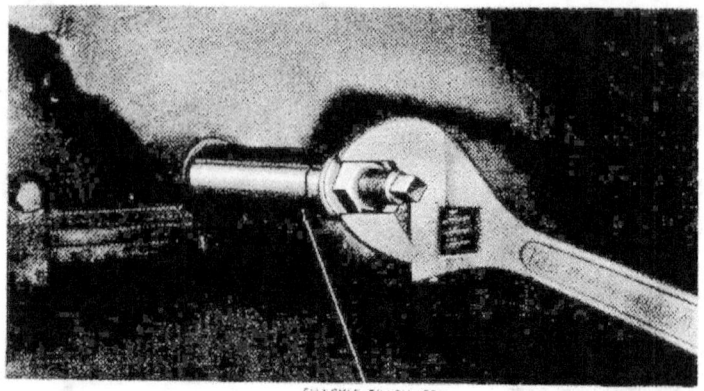

Figure 167—Shackle Pin Removal with Puller (41-P-2951-85)

time aline slots in nut with cotter pin hole in pin. This must be done to prevent spring binding in bracket. There must be no noticeable end play of spring on pin, but spring eye must be free to oscillate on pin without binding. Install new cotter pin full size of hole in end of bracket pin, then lock cotter pin on nut in adjusted position. Install lubrication fitting in outer end of bracket pin (fig. 167).

(3) INSTALL SHACKLE PIN AND U-BOLTS. Position shackle over end of spring and install shackle pin and clamp bolt [subpar. **b.**(2) above]. Place spring bumper block on top of spring. Position U-bolts, then install shock absorber link bracket over end of U-bolts. Install U-bolt nuts and tighten nuts with torque wrench to 170 to 185 foot-pounds. Lower vehicle to the ground. Lubricate spring shackle and bracket pin (Lubrication Order No. 9-802) and install wheelhouse skirt.

206. SHOCK ABSORBERS.

a. Description. The double-acting hydraulic type shock absorbers are attached to front axle with links.

b. Filling Shock Absorbers.

(1) CHECK ACTION OF SHOCK ABSORBER. Disconnect shock absorber link at front axle link bracket. Pull shock absorber arm down. If arm drops easily part way, then stops and continues moving down slowly the balance of the distance, there is not enough liquid in shock absorber.

(2) CLEAN AND FILL SHOCK ABSORBER. Clean exterior of shock absorber thoroughly with dry-cleaning solvent. Remove filler cap, fill shock absorber with hydraulic fluid (51-F-364-15), then replace filler

Spring Suspension

cap. Move shock absorber arm up and down several times to work fluid into piston cylinder. Add additional fluid to fill reservoir. To provide sufficient air space in shock absorber, allow fluid to escape until fluid level is even with bottom edge of filler plug hole before replacing filler cap. Install new gasket on filler cap if necessary. Shock absorber packing washers which have been operating with fluid below proper level may become worn and cause leaks around shaft. Leaks of this nature can only be corrected by installing a new shock absorber assembly.

c. Assembly Removal. Remove wheelhouse skirt, position jack under front axle, then raise axle until wheel is clear of ground. Remove wheel (par. 212*c.*). Disconnect link from shock absorber arm, then remove nuts and lock washers from bolts which attach shock absorber to hull. Remove shock absorber.

d. Assembly Installation. Apply cement (52-C-685) around bolt holes and bolts in hull. Install bolts. Position shock absorber over ends of bolts. Install nuts and new lock washers, then tighten nuts firmly. Connect shock absorber link to shock absorber arm. Lubricate front spring shackle and bracket pins (Lubrication Order No. 9-802). Install wheel (par. 212*d.*). Lower and remove jack, then install wheelhouse skirt.

207. REAR SPRINGS.

a. Description. The rear springs are of the inverted semi-elliptic slipper type. Leaves are held together with a center bolt. Four spring clips are provided, two at each side of center bolt, to hold spring leaves in alinement and limit spring leaf separation during rebound action. The spring assembly is attached to spring seat with U-bolts (fig. 168).

b. Removal.

(1) RAISE VEHICLE. Remove wheelhouse skirt, then place jack under cross shaft to frame bracket and raise vehicle high enough to relieve spring tension on side to be serviced. Place jack under intermediate axle and raise axle until wheel clears ground. Repeat operation at rear axle. Remove tire inflating device (if used) and wheel (par. 212*c.*).

(2) REMOVE SPRING FROM SEAT. Remove nuts from U-bolts, then remove U-bolts and spacer. Loosen spring seat clamp bolts, then with a suitable pry bar, force spring off of seat. Slide spring back in its seat until front end of spring can be lifted out of bracket on intermediate axle. Pull spring forward until rear end of spring clears bracket on rear axle (fig. 168).

c. Installation.

(1) POSITION SPRING. Insert end of spring in intermediate axle spring bracket, then slide spring forward in its seat until rear end of spring clears bracket on rear axle. Slide spring toward rear axle until center bolt drops into recess in spring seat. Be sure that spring assembly is resting solidly on spring seat. Place spacer in position on top leaf of spring (fig. 168).

TM 9-802
207-208

Maintenance Instructions

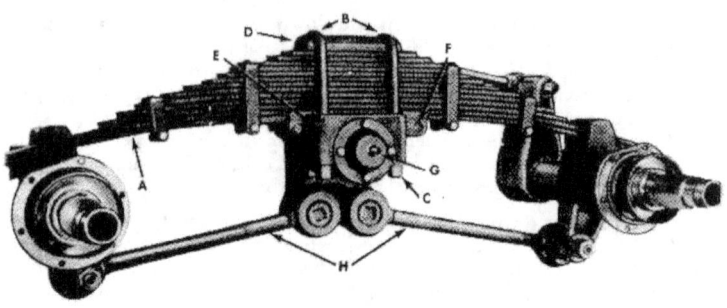

A REAR SPRING ASSEMBLY
B U-BOLTS
C U-BOLT NUTS
D U-BOLT SPACER
E SPRING SEAT
F SPRING SEAT CLAMP BOLT
G SPRING SEAT CAP
H LOWER TORQUE ROD

RA PD 333215

Figure 168—Rear Spring Installation

(2) ATTACH SPRING ASSEMBLY TO SPRING SEAT. Install two U-bolts and aline on spacer and in spring seat. Install nuts on U-bolts and tighten with torque wrench to 200 to 220 foot-pounds. Tighten spring seat clamp bolts firmly. Install wheel and tire inflating device (if used) (par. 212*d*.). Remove blocks, jacks, etc. Check tightness of U-bolt nuts after spring is under load. Install wheelhouse skirt.

208. REAR SPRING SEAT.

a. Description. The rear spring seats are supported on the trunnion cross shaft by tapered roller bearings (fig. 169) which must be lubricated at intervals specified on Lubrication Order No. 9-802, and disassembled and inspected at intervals indicated in paragraph 60.

b. Checking Spring Seat Bearings.

(1) REMOVE TIRE INFLATING DEVICE AND WHEEL. Raise each axle until tire is clear of ground and place support blocks under axle housing. Position jack under rear spring trunnion bracket and raise vehicle to relieve weight on spring. Remove wheelhouse skirt. Remove tire inflating devices and wheels (par. 212*c*.).

(2) DISCONNECT SPRING. Loosen two spring seat clamp bolts. Remove nuts from two spring clips. Remove spring clips and spacer. Lower jack under rear spring trunnion bracket until spring seat is free of spring.

(3) CHECK BEARING ADJUSTMENT. Oscillate spring seat in both directions while pulling and pushing on seat. If seat oscillates smoothly without noticeable end play or side shake, no further inspection is required and spring can be reassembled. If end play or side shake is noticed or if oscillation is jerky, spring seat and bearings must be removed for further inspection.

372

Spring Suspension

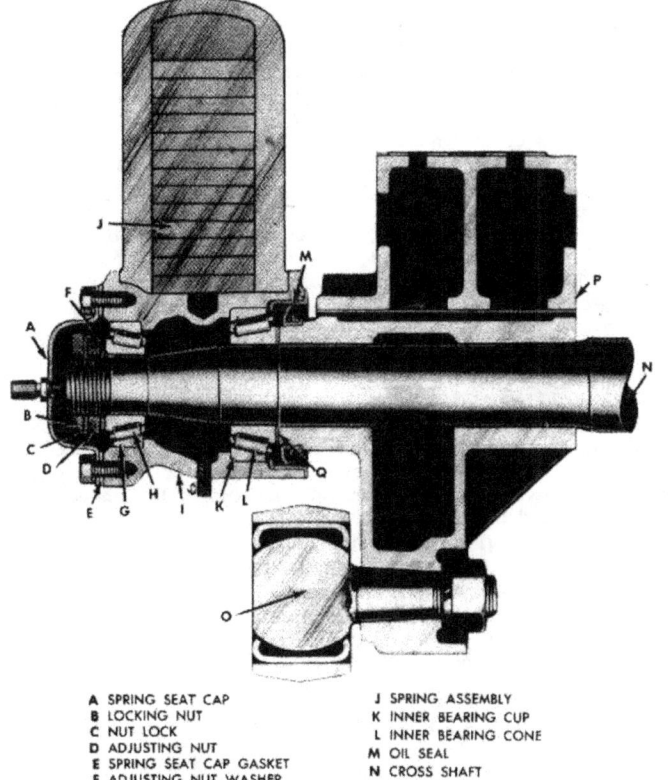

A SPRING SEAT CAP
B LOCKING NUT
C NUT LOCK
D ADJUSTING NUT
E SPRING SEAT CAP GASKET
F ADJUSTING NUT WASHER
G OUTER BEARING CUP
H OUTER BEARING CONE
I SPRING SEAT
J SPRING ASSEMBLY
K INNER BEARING CUP
L INNER BEARING CONE
M OIL SEAL
N CROSS SHAFT
O TORQUE ROD
P FRAME TRUNNION BRACKET
Q SPACER

RA PD 333210

Figure 169—Rear Spring Seat Cross Section

c. Spring Seat Removal.

(1) REMOVE SPRING SEAT CAP. Perform operations in subparagraph **b.**, steps (1) and (2) above. Remove spring seat cap by taking out four cap screws and lock washers. Remove cap and gasket.

(2) REMOVE SPRING SEAT. Straighten tangs of adjusting nut lock, then remove lock nut, nut lock, adjusting nut, and adjusting nut washer. Remove spring seat together with outer bearing assembly. After chassis serial No. 4201, an oil seal flange (fig. 169) is used and is also removed with spring seat assembly. Lift outer bearing assembly from spring seat.

373

Maintenance Instructions

(3) CLEAN AND INSPECT BEARINGS AND CUPS. Wash bearing cone and roller assemblies and cups thoroughly with dry-cleaning solvent, wipe bearings and cups dry, and inspect them carefully. If surfaces of cups or bearing rollers are pitted, they should be replaced. A pitted surface is one in which small particles have broken out, leaving jagged depressions. Bearings used in spring seats roll back and forth as vehicle passes over uneven terrain, but bearing rollers always return to same relative position in cups. In fact, bearing rollers rest in this one position most of the time. Polished lines appear on bearing cups showing "resting" position of rollers and should not be confused with pitting. These lines are spaced according to distance between line of contact of each roller. These lines are not harmful and bearings should not be replaced unless rough or jerky condition can be felt by rotating bearing roller assembly in race, or if surfaces of cups are actually pitted or broken. If bearing cups or cones are damaged, replace with new parts. On vehicles after chassis serial No. 4201, wash seal flange thoroughly. Wipe dry and inspect flange for pitted or worn condition. Check tightness of flange in spring seat.

(4) REMOVE BEARING CUPS AND SEAL. Drive bearing cups out of spring seat, using punch and hammer. Be careful not to "cock" cups during removal to prevent damaging the seat. Before removing inner bearing cup on vehicles prior to chassis serial No. 4202, remove oil seal retainer, felt, and washer.

(5) REMOVE INNER BEARING AND SEAL. Disconnect intermediate axle to cross shaft bracket torque rod at bracket (fig. 170). Use suitable puller (41-P-2905-60) and remove inner bearing assembly from cross shaft. On vehicles prior to chassis serial No. 4202, remove oil seal retainer, felt, and washer or after chassis serial No. 4201 remove lip type oil seal assembly from cross shaft.

d. Spring Seat Installation.

(1) Two types of oil seals have been used on these vehicles. Type used prior to chassis serial No. 4202 consists of a felt, retainer, and washer. Type used after chassis serial No. 4201 is a lip type used with a seal flange. Whenever the spring seat is removed, replace the felt type seal with a new lip type seal, if available. Instructions are also given for installing felt type seal in the event the lip type seal is not available.

(2) INSTALL SEAL AND INNER BEARING.

(a) Lip Type Seal. Apply a small amount of cement (52-C-685) to seal shoulder of cross shaft frame bracket and drive seal against end of shoulder. Be sure that cupped side of rubber seal is toward frame. Install bearing spacer on cross shaft. Install bearing cone and roller assembly. If seal flange was removed, coat outside of flange sparingly with cement (52-C-685) and press into spring seat after inner bearing cup has been installed.

(b) Felt Type Seal. Install seal washer, felt, and retainer on cross shaft bracket. Make sure that retainer flange is under felt away from bearing. Install inner bearing cone and roller assembly.

(3) INSTALL SPRING SEAT. Fill cavity between inner seal and bearing with lubricant and apply a small amount of lubricant on seal

Spring Suspension

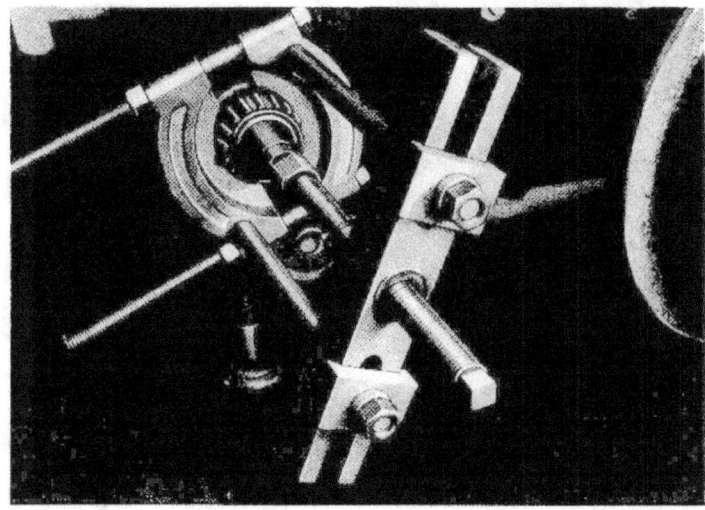

RA PD 337162

Figure 170—Pulling Inner Spring Seat Bearing

contacting surfaces. Use lubricator or hand pack method to thoroughly lubricate race and rollers of bearing cone assembly (see Lubrication Order No. 9-802). Position spring seat on cross shaft end and install outer bearing.

(4) INSTALL ADJUSTING NUT AND WASHER. Place adjusting nut washer and adjusting nut (inner) over end of cross shaft. Draw adjusting nut up to approximate adjustment. Spring seat should be oscillated while tightening to prevent grease from being squeezed out from under bearing rollers.

(5) ADJUST BEARINGS. Tighten adjusting nut until slight increase in bearing drag over original drag of bearing seal is noticed when seat is oscillated. Lubricate bearings with pressure gun as directed on Lubrication Order No. 9-802.

(6) INSTALL BEARING CAP. When adjusting nut is tightened properly, replace adjusting nut lock and locking nut (outer). Tighten locking nut securely. Test adjustment once more to see that it has not been changed and correct if necessary. Bend portion of nut lock over flats of adjusting nut and lock nut. Install the bearing cap and new gasket. Install and tighten the four cap screws and lock washers.

(7) ATTACH SPRING TO SPRING SEAT. Using jack under rear spring trunnion bracket, raise vehicle until spring seat contacts spring. Attach seat to spring [par. 207c.(2)]. Install wheels and tire inflating devices (par. 212d.). Remove jacks and install wheelhouse skirt.

Maintenance Instructions

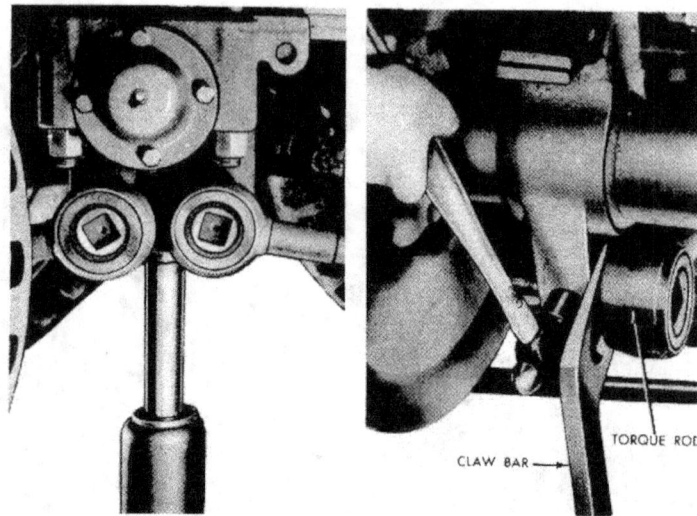

METHOD OF RAISING AT REAR

REMOVING TORQUE ROD

RA PD 333208

Figure 171—Raising Rear End and Disconnecting Torque Rods

209. TORQUE RODS.

a. Description. Torque rods, three on each side of trunnion cross shaft, connect the rear axle and intermediate axle to hull brackets and trunnion cross shaft brackets. The lower rods connect the axle to cross shaft brackets, whereas the upper torque rods extend from the axle housing brackets to the brackets which are bolted through the hull and trunnion crossmember. Both ends of torque rods are mounted in special bearings, or rubber bushed ball pins.

b. Removal. Jack up rear end of vehicle with jacks placed under trunnion cross shaft brackets as shown in figure 171. Remove nuts and washers from torque rod pins. Force torque rod pins out of brackets by inserting a claw bar between bracket and hub of torque rod (fig. 171). Strike bottom of bracket sharply with a heavy hammer and at the same time apply considerable force in prying with claw bar. Remove upper ends of torque rods in the same manner.

c. Installation. Clean torque rod pins thoroughly with dry-cleaning solvent. Make certain that bushings are clean and in good condition. The lower torque rods must be installed before upper torque rods are installed. Install torque rod pins to axle brackets, then to trunnion cross shaft bracket or hull brackets. Force torque rod pin in firmly, using a block of wood and a heavy hammer. Install lock washers and nuts and tighten securely. Lower vehicle and remove jacks.

Section XXXVIII
Wheels, Tires, and Hubs

210. GENERAL.

a. Description. Single disk-type wheels are mounted on hubs at each axle. Hubs are mounted on opposed roller bearings. Tires are military desert type equipped with hinged metal bead locks. The purpose of the bead locks is to secure the tire to the wheel rim when tires are deflated to low pressure for sand operation. Spare wheel and tire assembly is mounted on rear deck.

b. Data.

Wheels

Type	Disk
Size	18 x 8 in.
Wheel offset	3½ in.

Rim Type

Prior to chassis serial No. 406	"L"—with lock ring
After chassis serial No. 405	"CV"—with side ring

Wheel Bearings—Front

Inner cone and roller assembly	Tim-33275
Inner cup	Tim-33472
Outer cone and roller assembly	Tim-399A
Outer cup	Tim-394A

Wheel Bearings—Rear

Inner cone and roller assembly	HY-KD-12051
Inner cup	HY-12051-Z
Outer cone and roller assembly	HY-KB-11786
Outer cup	HY-11786-Y

Tires

Size	11.00-18
Number of plies	10

c. Repair. Repair procedures for wheels and hubs are described in TM 9-1802B.

211. MARKING OF HUBS AND WHEEL STUDS (FOR VEHICLES EQUIPPED WITH CENTRAL TIRE PRESSURE CONTROL SYSTEM).

a. General. A fixed relation must be maintained between tire valve stem, wheel mounting studs or bolts, and three tire inflating device to hub locking bolts. The instructions which follow do not include any removal or installation procedures. These instructions are specifically for the marking of the hub and wheel studs before removing wheel, axle shaft, drive flange, hub, or rear wheel spacer to facilitate reassembling these parts in correct position; the instructions are also necessary to locate the proper positions of these parts when assembling new unmarked parts, parts which have been removed without marking, or parts on which the markings have become obliterated.

TM 9-802

Maintenance Instructions

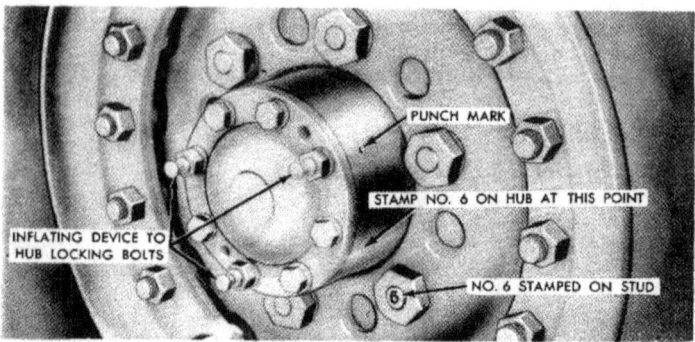

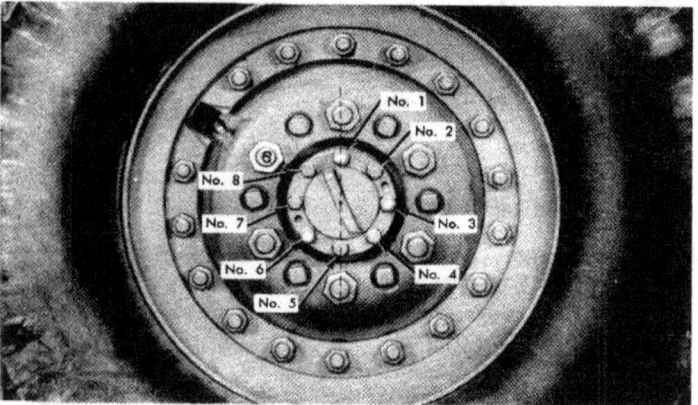

Figure 172—Marking of Hubs and Wheel Studs

b. Hub and Stud Marking (fig. 172). Late vehicles have a number "6" stamped on wheel mounting stud or bolt adjacent to tire valve stem. Hubs are marked with a prick punch adjacent to each of the three tire inflating device to hub locking bolts. Check for these markings, and if they are not readily visible, they should be made so before removing wheel, axle shaft, hub, etc. A number "6" should also be stamped on rear hubs adjacent to the wheel stud marked "6" (fig. 172) before removing rear wheel spacer. This will maintain correct relationship between this stud and the three inflating device to hub locking bolts.

c. Location of Inflating Device to Hub Locking Bolts in Unmarked Hubs (fig. 172). The hub (and wheel spacer at rear) must be installed before correct position of inflating device to hub locking bolts can be determined. Locate two axle shaft or drive flange bolts (or bolt holes) which are in a straight line with two wheel mounting bolts or studs. Starting with one of these axle shaft or drive flange bolts (or holes) as No. 1, number the bolts (or holes) clockwise around the flange. Tire inflating device to hub locking bolts must be installed in holes Nos. 1, 3, and 6. Mark hub (not flange) adjacent to these points with a prick punch.

d. Location of Tire Valve Stem (fig. 172). When installing a wheel on a hub which does not have a number "6" stamped on one of the wheel mounting studs or bolts, first locate No. 1 axle shaft or drive flange bolt (subpar. c. above). Stamp a number "6" on first wheel mounting bolt or stud counterclockwise from No. 1 flange bolt. Also stamp a number "6" on rear hub adjacent to wheel stud marked "6." Wheel is then installed with valve stem adjacent to stud or bolt marked "6."

212. WHEELS.

a. General. Front wheels are attached directly to the hubs by wheel hub bolts and wheel nuts. Rear wheels are attached to wheel spacers by studs and wheel nuts. The wheel spacers are attached to hub by hub bolts and wheel spacer to hub nuts. Right- and left-hand wheel nuts and wheel spacer to hub nuts are not interchangeable. Nuts for right-hand side are marked "right" and nuts for left-hand side are marked "left." In procedures which follow, disregard instructions pertaining to tire inflating devices when servicing vehicles prior to chassis serial No. 2006.

b. Wheel Nut Tightening Procedure. Remove wheelhouse skirts and tire inflating devices [subpar. c.(1) below]. Tighten front and rear wheel nuts as described in steps (1) and (2) below, using wheel nut wrench furnished with vehicle.

(1) FRONT. Alternately tighten wheel nuts as tightly as possible without using added extension on wrench handle. Turn right-hand nuts (3500-2202032) clockwise and left-hand nuts (3500-2202033) counterclockwise to tighten. After tightening, install tire inflating devices and wheelhouse skirts [subpar. d.(2) below].

(2) REAR. Tighten wheel spacer to hub nuts (square head) first, then with opposite end of wrench, tighten wheel nuts (hex head). Tighten nuts as tightly as possible without using added extension on wrench handle. Turn right-hand nuts clockwise, and left-hand nuts counterclockwise. After tightening, install tire inflating devices and wheelhouse skirts [subpar. d.(2) below].

c. Wheel Removal.

(1) REMOVE WHEELHOUSE SKIRT AND TIRE INFLATING DEVICE. Remove wheelhouse skirt by removing cotter pins and clevis pins attaching skirt to hull, then pull skirt off. Remove inflating device to valve stem hose cover by removing two cotter pins and pushing clevis pins in. *Do not lose pins.* Unscrew hose from valve stem, then loosen lock nuts on three tire inflating device lock bolts and back out lock bolts.

Maintenance Instructions

REMOVING INFLATING DEVICE

INFLATING DEVICE REMOVED

RA PD 333241

Figure 173—Tire Inflating Device Removal

Pull inflating device straight off from hub (fig. 173). Hang inflating device on hanger plate (fig. 173) if vehicle is so equipped. Install valve core in valve stem. On vehicles not equipped with hanger plates, lay inflating device to one side, being sure that tire inflating hose can not be damaged. NOTE: *Tire inflating device hanger plates (fig. 173) should be made up and installed locally on vehicles not so equipped.*

(2) REMOVE WHEEL. Before removing wheel from vehicles equipped with central tire pressure control system, make sure that wheel bolt (front) or wheel spacer stud (rear) adjacent to tire valve stem is stamped with the number "6" (fig. 172). Raise wheel off ground, using jack under axle, and remove six nuts (hex) attaching wheel to hub bolts (front) or to wheel spacer studs (rear). CAUTION: *Do not loosen side ring nuts.* Turn right-hand nuts counterclockwise and left-hand nuts clockwise to remove. Slide wheel and tire assembly off from hub.

d. Wheel Installation.

(1) INSTALL WHEEL. Make sure that mating surfaces of wheel and hub (wheel spacer at rear) are clean. Before installing rear wheels, refer to subparagraph e. below. Place wheel and tire assembly on hub, aline tire valve stem with bolt or stud marked "6," then push wheel into place. Install six wheel nuts and tighten, using wheel nut wrench furnished with vehicle. Before tightening rear wheel nuts, make sure that wheel spacer to hub nuts are tight. Wheel nuts must be tightened daily during first 500 miles of operation after wheel has been installed.

(2) INSTALL TIRE INFLATING DEVICE AND WHEELHOUSE SKIRT. Install tire inflating device on hub (fig. 173), and tighten three lock bolts and lock nuts. CAUTION: *Make sure valve core is removed from valve stem.* Connect hose to valve stem, tightening connection with

Wheels, Tires, and Hubs

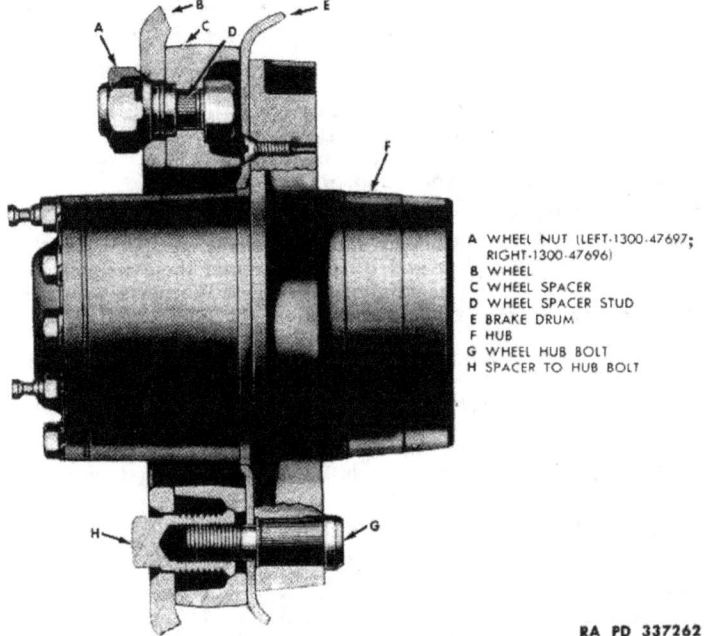

A WHEEL NUT (LEFT-1300-47697; RIGHT-1300-47696)
B WHEEL
C WHEEL SPACER
D WHEEL SPACER STUD
E BRAKE DRUM
F HUB
G WHEEL HUB BOLT
H SPACER TO HUB BOLT

RA PD 337262

Figure 174—Rear Wheel Spacer Installation

fingers; do not use pliers. Install hose cover with outer end hooked under wheel rim, and attach to inflating device with two clevis pins and cotter pins.

e. Rear Wheel Spacers (fig. 174). Whenever rear wheels are removed (subpar. **c.** above), examine rear wheel spacer studs for damaged or corroded threads and for looseness in spacer. On vehicles after chassis serial No. 5695, except 6601 through 7057, serrations have been added to wheel spacer studs to prevent studs turning in spacer when removing wheel nuts. When replacing rear wheel spacer studs, studs having serrations must be used.

(1) REMOVE WHEEL SPACER. On vehicles equipped with central tire pressure control system, make sure hub is stamped with number "6" adjacent to wheel spacer stud stamped "6" (fig. 172) before removing spacer. Remove six spacer to hub nuts (square head) and pull spacer off hub.

(2) REPLACE STUDS. Remove nuts attaching studs to wheel spacer and press studs out of spacer. Press new serrated studs into spacer, being sure to aline flat portion of stud shoulder with annular groove in spacer.

381

TM 9-802
212-213

Maintenance Instructions

Make sure studs are bottomed against spacer, then install and tighten nuts on studs. Tack-weld nuts to studs after tightening.

(2) INSTALL WHEEL SPACER. Install wheel spacer on hub and attach with six spacer to hub nuts. On vehicles equipped with central tire pressure control system, stud marked "6" must be adjacent to number "6" stamped on hub (fig. 172). If stud marked "6" has been replaced, or if marking on hub is not visible, install spacer in any position, then refer to paragraph 211*d*. for location of No. "6" stud.

f. Wheel Balance Weights. All wheels are balanced to assure steering stability and prevent shimmy. Balance weights are spot welded on inside of wheel rim. Rust and corrosion around these weights may loosen them and in time the weights may be lost. Whenever wheels are removed, balance weights should be examined for loose condition. Loose weights should be arc welded at each end to wheel rims, being careful not to use excessive metal at the welds. If balance weights are missing, the outline of the weight is generally impressed on the rim. Weight of the same length and width as impression and same thickness as on other wheels can be made and welded to rim. If no impression of missing weight is legible and no facilities are available to properly balance, wheel, the unbalanced wheel should be used on the rear axles only.

213. TIRES AND RIMS.

a. General. Tires are pneumatic type equipped with hinged metal bead locks between the wheel rims and the tubes. On vehicles prior to chassis serial No. 406, tires are held on wheel rim by a lock ring. After chassis serial No. 405, tires are held in place by side rings which are secured to the wheel rim by bolts and nuts. Front and rear tires are the same size and are interchangeable.

b. Tire Rotation. The tires on a vehicle receive different wear because of such factors as load distribution, power and brake application, and steering. The spare tire will deteriorate if not used for long periods. Rotating tires will equalize wear and extend their usefulness. Diagram in figure 175 shows the correct procedure for rotating tires. Start with spare tire, marked No. 1, and move wheel and tire assemblies to positions indicated in figure 175. Refer to paragraph 212***c.*** and ***d.*** for removal and installation instructions.

c. Tire Removal—Side Ring Type Wheels (fig. 176).

(1) REMOVE WHEEL AND TIRE ASSEMBLY. Remove wheel and tire assembly (par. 212***c.***) and lay assembly on floor with outside of wheel up.

(2) REMOVE SIDE RING. Observe warning stamped on side ring— WARNING: *Deflate tire before removing nuts.* After making sure tire is completely deflated, remove side ring nuts using wrench furnished with vehicle. Drive tire iron or pry bar in between tire bead and side ring at several points to loosen bead from ring, then remove side ring. It may be necessary to pry side ring up to top of bolts, place blocks

Wheels, Tires, and Hubs

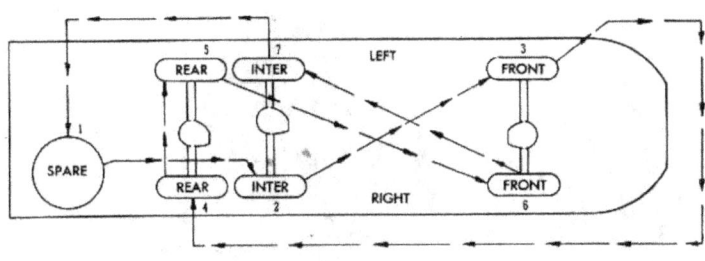

RA PD 337182

Figure 175—Tire Rotation Diagram

between side ring and bolting flange on wheel rim, and drive tire bead down away from side ring.

(3) REMOVE WHEEL FROM TIRE AND BEAD LOCK. Turn tire and wheel assembly over and drive a tire iron or pry bar in between tire bead and wheel rim at several points to loosen bead from rim. Again turn tire and wheel assembly over, and block the assembly off the floor with blocks under tire close to, but not touching rim. Place heavy block on wheel and drive wheel down out of tire and bead lock assembly, using a heavy hammer. It may be necessary to block the assembly up under a vehicle frame and use a jack between the wheel and vehicle frame to force wheel out.

(4) REMOVE BEAD LOCK AND TUBE. Force a pry bar between tire bead and bead lock at a point about eight inches from the bead lock hinge on the side away from the valve stem. Pry bead lock in away from tire beads to collapse bead lock. Pivot bead lock in tire at valve stem until bead lock is at right-angles to tire, then roll bead lock out of tire and off from valve stem. Pull tube out of tire.

d. Tire Installation—Side Ring Type Wheels (fig. 176).

(1) INSTALL TUBE AND BEAD LOCK. Install tube in tire with valve stem next to red dot balance mark on tire. Install valve core in valve stem and inflate tube enough to remove wrinkles, and to spread tire beads to width of bead lock. Collapse bead lock and, holding bead lock at right-angles to tire, insert the valve stem through the hole in bead lock and push bead lock half-way through tire. Swing bead lock around into position in tire, then place foot on bead lock between hinge and valve stem and jerk up on top of bead lock to snap hinge closed. Make sure bead lock is properly centered between tire beads with lug on bead lock directly under horizontal portion of valve stem. Remove valve core from valve stem to deflate tube.

(2) INSTALL TIRE AND BEAD LOCK ON WHEEL. Place wheel on floor with side ring bolts up. Lift tire horizontally with valve stem pointing up, and lower over wheel with valve stem alined with valve stem slot in wheel rim. Make sure tire is straight on wheel and force down until tire is against outer flange of wheel rim.

TM 9-802
213

Maintenance Instructions

Figure 176—Tire and Wheel Disassembled, and Method of Installing Bead Lock (CV Type Rim)

(3) INSTALL SIDE RING. Place side ring over side ring bolts, with valve slot inside ring alined with valve slot in wheel rim. Force side ring down enough to start nuts on bolts, then tighten nuts alternately and evenly, using wrench furnished with vehicle. CAUTION: *Make sure side ring nuts are tightened before attempting to inflate tire.*

(4) INSTALL WHEEL AND TIRE ASSEMBLY. Install wheel and tire assembly, and install tire inflating device on vehicles so equipped (par. 212d.). Inflate tire to proper pressure (par. 32).

e. Tire Removal—Lock Ring Type Wheels (fig. 177).

(1) REMOVE WHEEL AND TIRE ASSEMBLY. Remove wheel and tire assembly (par. 212c.) and lay on floor with outside of wheel up. Remove valve core from valve stem to completely deflate tire. CAUTION: *Tire must be completely deflated before attempting to remove lock ring.*

(2) REMOVE LOCK RING. Using lock ring removing bar furnished with vehicle, insert straight end of bar in notch in wheel rim near split

Wheels, Tires, and Hubs

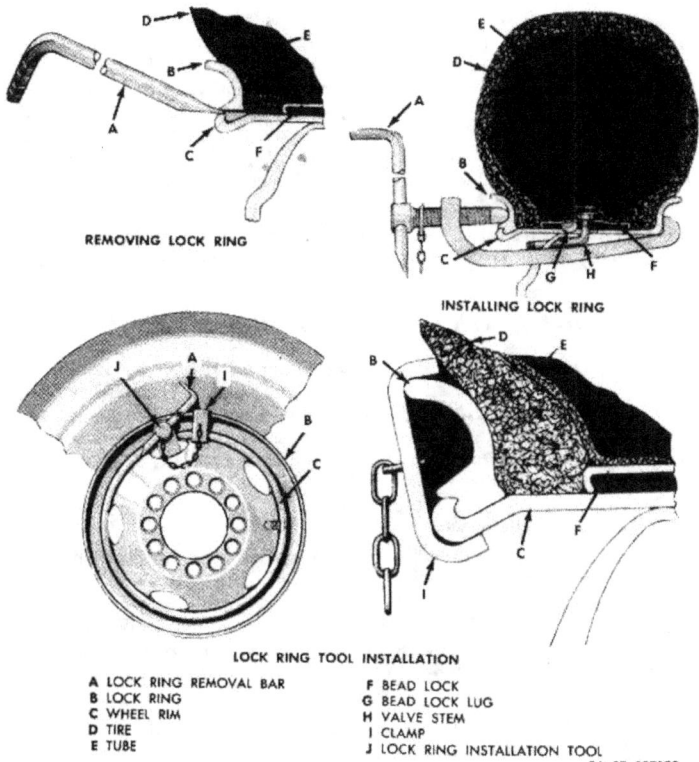

REMOVING LOCK RING

INSTALLING LOCK RING

LOCK RING TOOL INSTALLATION

A LOCK RING REMOVAL BAR
B LOCK RING
C WHEEL RIM
D TIRE
E TUBE
F BEAD LOCK
G BEAD LOCK LUG
H VALVE STEM
I CLAMP
J LOCK RING INSTALLATION TOOL

RA PD 337190

Figure 177—Removal and Installation of Lock Ring (L Type Rim)

in lock ring. Pry lock ring out of rim, then insert hooked end of bar between rim and lock ring and work lock ring out of rim.

(3) REMOVE WHEEL AND BEAD LOCK FROM TIRE. This procedure is the same as for side ring type wheels. Refer to subparagraph *c.*, steps (3) and (4) above.

f. Tire Installation—Lock Ring Type Wheels (fig. 177).

(1) ASSEMBLE TIRE, TUBE, AND BEAD LOCK. This procedure is the same as for side ring type wheels. Refer to subparagraph *d.*, steps (1) and (2) above.

(2) INSTALL LOCK RING. Install lock ring tool through hole in wheel disk so that hooked end of tool engages inside flange of wheel rim (fig. 177). Place end of lock ring on wheel rim with split in ring

near screw end of tool. Place end of tool screw against lock ring and force lock ring into place in rim by tightening screw. Use lock ring removing bar as a handle for turning screw (fig. 177). Place lock ring clamp (on chain attached to screw) over rim and ring to hold ring in position, then back off screw and move tool to next hole in wheel disk. Force lock ring into position at this point and move clamp to a position close to screw. Repeat these operations all around wheel until lock ring is fully seated all around the wheel rim. CAUTION: *Make sure lock ring is fully seated before attempting to inflate tire.*

(3) INSTALL WHEEL AND TIRE ASSEMBLY. Install wheel and tire assembly (par. 212*d*.) and inflate tire to proper pressure (par. 32).

214. FRONT HUBS AND BEARINGS.

a. General (figs. 178 and 179). Each front hub is mounted on steering knuckle on opposed tapered roller bearings. Hub and bearings are retained on steering knuckle by inner and outer adjusting nuts, with a "star" type lock between the two nuts. A bearing washer is used between outer bearing and inner adjusting nut. An oil seal is pressed into inner end of each hub.

b. Bearing Adjustment.

(1) CHECK ADJUSTMENT. Jack up wheel to be checked until tire clears ground and remove wheelhouse skirt. Check sideways "shake" of wheel by grasping tire and pulling back and forth, or by using a long bar under tire. If bearings are properly adjusted, movement of brake drum in relation to brake flange plate will be just noticeable with wheel turning freely. If movement is excessive, adjustment is required [steps (2) through (4) below].

(2) REMOVE TIRE INFLATING DEVICE AND DRIVE FLANGE. Remove tire inflating device (if used) [par. 212*c*.(1)], and remove drive flange [par. 173*b*.(2)].

(3) ADJUST BEARINGS. Bend tangs of nut lock away from adjusting nuts, then remove outer adjusting nut, using wrench furnished with vehicle. Remove nut lock. While rotating wheel, tighten inner adjusting nut until wheel binds, then back off nut about one-eighth turn. Check adjustment. Install a new nut lock on steering knuckle and bend a short tang on lock nut into a slot in inner adjusting nut. It may be necessary to turn adjusting nut slightly to aline slot with tang on lock. Install outer adjusting nut and tighten firmly, again check adjustment, then bend long tang of lock into slot in outer adjusting nut.

(4) INSTALL DRIVE FLANGE AND TIRE INFLATING DEVICE. Install drive flange [par. 173*d*.(5)], then install tire inflating device (if used) and wheelhouse skirt [par. 212*d*.(2)].

c. Hub and Bearings Removal (figs. 178 and 179).

(1) REMOVE WHEEL, BRAKE DRUM (LATE VEHICLES), AND DRIVE FLANGE. Remove wheel (par. 212*c*.). On vehicles equipped

Wheels, Tires, and Hubs

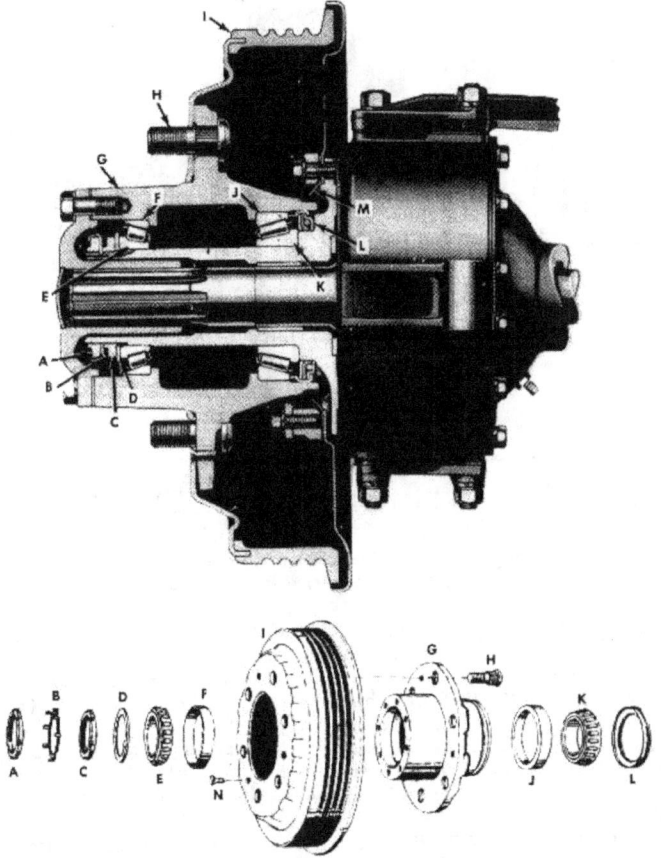

A ADJUSTING NUT (OUTER)
B ADJUSTING NUT LOCK (G085-31-08140)
C ADJUSTING NUT INNER
D BEARING WASHER
E OUTER BEARING CONE AND ROLLERS (H012-61-0312)
F OUTER BEARING CUP (H012-62-02450)
G HUB
H WHEEL BOLT
I BRAKE DRUM
J INNER BEARING CUP (H012-62-25100)
K INNER BEARING CONE AND ROLLERS (H012-61-63480)
L INNER OIL SEAL (H013-05-00200)
M OIL DEFLECTOR
N DRUM TO HUB SCREW

RA PD 337263

Figure 178—Front Hub and Bearings (After Chassis Serial No. 3005)

with demountable brake drums, remove drum (par. 195*b*.). Remove drive flange [par. 173*b*.(2)].

Maintenance Instructions

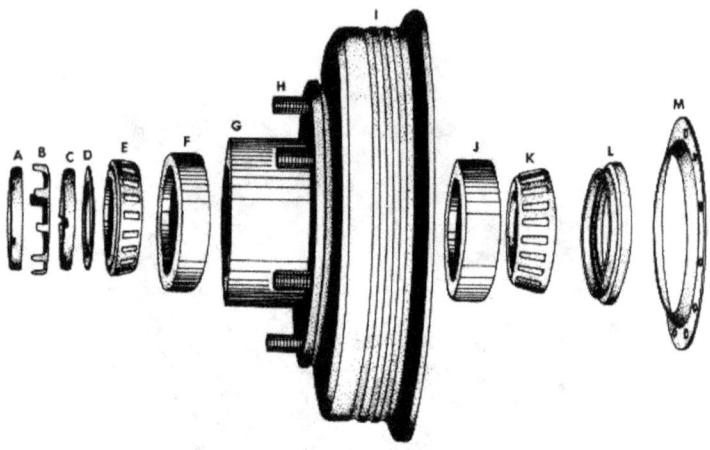

A ADJUSTING NUT (OUTER)
B ADJUSTING NUT LOCK
C ADJUSTING NUT (INNER)
D BEARING WASHER
E OUTER BEARING CONE AND ROLLERS
F OUTER BEARING CUP
G HUB
H WHEEL BOLT
I BRAKE DRUM
J INNER BEARING CUP
K INNER BEARING CONE AND ROLLERS
L INNER OIL SEAL
M OIL DEFLECTOR

RA PD 333194

Figure 179—Front Hub and Bearings
(Prior to Chassis Serial Number 3006)

(2) REMOVE HUB (AND BRAKE DRUM ON EARLY VEHICLES). Bend tangs of nut lock away from adjusting nuts, then remove outer adjusting nut, nut lock, and inner adjusting nut, using wrench furnished with vehicle. Pull hub (late vehicles), or hub and drum assembly (early vehicles) straight off from steering knuckle. Bearing washer, inner and outer bearing cone and roller assemblies, inner and outer bearing cups, and inner oil seal will come off steering knuckle with hub. Remove bearing washer and outer bearing cone and roller assembly from hub with fingers.

(3) REMOVE INNER BEARING, CUP, AND OIL SEAL. Remove inner bearing cone and roller assembly, bearing cup, and oil seal by driving against the outer edge of cup with a brass drift inserted through outer end of hub. Alternately drive against opposite sides of cup. Cup will force bearing cone and roller assembly and oil seal out of hub.

(4) REMOVE OUTER BEARING CUP (IF NECESSARY). Clean outer bearing cup in hub, using dry-cleaning solvent and clean rags. Examine cup for pitted or excessively worn condition. If cup is in good condition, do not remove. If damaged, remove cup by driving against inner edge of cup with a brass drift inserted through inner end of hub. Alternately drive against opposite sides of cup.

d. Cleaning, Inspection, and Lubrication of Bearings. Clean, inspect, and lubricate bearings, hub, and steering knuckle as instructed in paragraph 53.

Wheels, Tires, and Hubs

e. Hub and Bearings Installation (figs. 178 and 179).

(1) INSTALL BEARING CUPS. Install inner and outer bearing cups in hub with wide side of each cup toward center of hub. Cups may be driven into hubs with a brass drift and hammer. Alternately drive on opposite sides of cup to prevent cocking cup in hub. Make sure cups are fully seated against shoulders in hub.

(2) INSTALL INNER BEARING AND OIL SEAL. Place inner bearing cone and roller assembly in hub. Coat outside circumference of new oil seal with joint and thread compound (52-C-3115) or cement (52-C-644), whichever is available. Install seal with flexible portion of seal toward bearing, using a block of wood and hammer to drive seal into place.

(3) INSTALL HUB (AND BRAKE DRUM ON EARLY VEHICLES). Install hub (late vehicles) or hub and drum assembly (early vehicles) on steering knuckle. Install outer bearing cone and roller assembly, bearing washer, and inner adjusting nut.

(4) INSTALL BRAKE DRUM (LATE VEHICLES) AND WHEEL. Install brake drum on vehicles equipped with demountable drums (par. 195*b*.), then install wheel [par. 212*d*.(1)].

(5) ADJUST BEARINGS. Adjust bearings and complete the installation as directed in subparagraph *b*.(3) and (4) above.

215. REAR HUBS AND BEARINGS.

a. General (figs. 180 and 181). Each rear hub is mounted on axle housing on opposed barrel type roller bearings. Hub and bearings are retained on axle housing by an inner adjusting nut and an outer adjusting nut and oil seal assembly, with a "star" type lock between the two nuts. An inner adjusting nut washer is used between inner adjusting nut and outer bearing. An oil seal is pressed into inned end of hub.

b. Bearing Adjustment. Adjustment procedure for rear wheel bearings is the same as for front wheels (par. 214*b*.) except that in step (2) the axle shaft must be removed (par. 178*b*.) instead of the drive flange.

c. Hub and Bearings Removal (figs. 180 and 181).

(1) REMOVE WHEEL, BRAKE DRUM (LATE VEHICLES), AND AXLE SHAFT. Remove wheel (par. 212*c*.) In vehicles equipped with demountable brake drums, remove drum (par. 195*b*.). Remove axle shaft (par. 178*b*.).

(2) REMOVE HUB (AND BRAKE DRUM ON EARLY VEHICLES). Bend tangs of nut lock away from adjusting nuts, then remove outer adjusting nut and oil seal assembly, nut lock, and inner adjusting nut, using wrench furnished with vehicle. Pull hub (late vehicles) or hub and drum assembly (early vehicles) straight off from axle housing. Inner and outer bearing cone and roller assemblies, inner and outer bearing cups, inner adjusting nut washer, and inner oil seal will come off with hub. Remove inner adjusting nut washer and inner bearing cone and roller assembly from hub with fingers.

- A AXLE SHAFT FLANGE BOLT
- B LOCK WASHER
- C AXLE SHAFT
- D GASKET
- E OUTER ADJUSTING NUT AND OIL SEAL ASSEMBLY
- F ADJUSTING NUT LOCK (G085-31-08180)
- G INNER ADJUSTING NUT
- H INNER ADJUSTING NUT WASHER
- I OUTER BEARING CONE AND ROLLERS (G501-01-39901)
- J OUTER BEARING CUP (G501-01-43547)
- K BEARING RETAINING RING
- L HUB
- M WHEEL HUB BOLT
- N BRAKE DRUM
- O INNER BEARING CONE AND ROLLERS (G501-01-39902)
- P INNER BEARING CUP (G501-01-43548)
- Q OIL DEFLECTOR
- R INNER OIL SEAL (H013-05-00194)
- S DRUM TO HUB SCREW
- T SPACER TO HUB NUT (LEFT—1300-47699) RIGHT—1300-47698)
- U WHEEL SPACER STUD
- V WHEEL SPACER

RA PD 337264

Figure 180—Rear Hub and Bearings (After Chassis Serial No. 3003)

390

Wheels, Tires, and Hubs

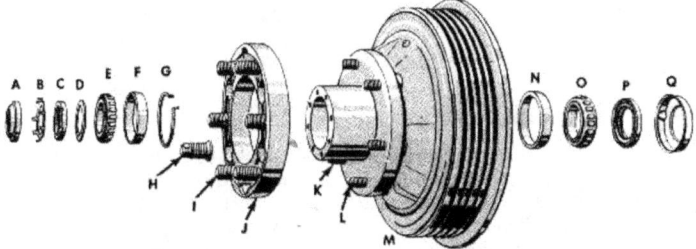

- A OUTER ADJUSTING NUT AND OIL SEAL ASSEMBLY
- B ADJUSTING NUT LOCK
- C INNER ADJUSTING NUT
- D INNER ADJUSTING NUT WASHER
- E OUTER BEARING CONE AND ROLLERS
- F OUTER BEARING CUP
- G BEARING RETAINING RING
- H SPACER TO HUB NUT
- I WHEEL SPACER STUD
- J WHEEL SPACER
- K HUB
- L WHEEL HUB BOLT
- M BRAKE DRUM
- N INNER BEARING CUP
- O INNER BEARING CONE AND ROLLERS
- P INNER OIL SEAL
- Q OIL DEFLECTOR

RA PD 337163

Figure 181—Rear Hub and Bearings (Prior to Chassis Serial No. 3004)

(3) REMOVE INNER BEARING, CUP, AND OIL SEAL. This procedure is the same as for front hubs [par. 214c.(3)].

(4) REMOVE OUTER BEARING CUP (IF NECESARY). Follow same instructions as for front hubs [par. 214c.(4)]. Be sure drift is against bearing cup and not against snap ring. Do not remove snap ring unless it is damaged.

d. Cleaning, Inspection, and Lubrication of Bearings. Clean, inspect, and lubricate bearings and hub as directed in paragraph 53.

e. Hub and Bearings Installation (figs. 180 and 181).

(1) INSTALL BEARING CUPS, INNER BEARING, AND OIL SEAL. Installation of these parts is the same as for front hubs. Refer to paragraph 214e.(1) and (2).

(2) INSTALL HUB (AND BRAKE DRUM ON EARLY VEHICLES). Install hub (late vehicles) or hub and drum assembly (early vehicles) on axle housing. Install outer bearing cone and roller assembly, inner adjusting nut washer, and inner adjusting nut.

(3) INSTALL BRAKE DRUM (LATE VEHICLES) AND WHEEL. Install brake drum on vehicles equipped with demountable drums (par. 195b.), then install wheel [par. 212d.(1)].

(4) ADJUST BEARINGS. Adjust bearings and complete the installation as directed in subparagraph b.(3) and (4) above, except that in step (4), the axle shaft must be installed (par. 178b.) instead of drive flange.

Section XXXIX
Steering System

216. GENERAL.

a. Description. The steering system includes a conventionally mounted steering gear assembly which is interconnected to front axle steering knuckles through a Pitman arm, drag link, and tie rod. A cable, wound on spool attached to steering gear worm shaft, operates linkage to turn marine rudder at rear of vehicle. Movement of steering wheel is transmitted to front wheels and to rudder simultaneously. Rudder control linkage on early vehicles differs from that used on late vehicles and the peculiarities of each type are fully covered in paragraphs 222 and 223 respectively.

b. Data.

Steering Gear Assembly
Type .... Recirculating ball
Make .... Saginaw Steering Gear
Model 565-D-5
Ratio .... 25.6 to 1
Mounting .... Flange type

c. Repair. Operations necessary for repair of steering gear assembly and rudder control linkage are described in TM 9-1802C.

217. STEERING GEAR ASSEMBLY ADJUSTMENTS.

a. Sequence of Adjustments. There are two adjustments provided at steering gear to compensate for normal wear. One adjustment, for eliminating end play in worm shaft, is made by changing thickness of shim pack at housing end cover. The second adjustment, for controlling lash between rack teeth on worm nut and teeth on sector shaft, is made by lash adjuster screw in housing side cover. A third adjustment can be made to prevent binding in steering gear mountings. Worm bearing adjustment must *always* precede sector lash adjustment. Adjustments may be made with steering gear assembly installed in vehicle; however, if the steering gear is out of the vehicle, adjustments should be made on bench prior to installation as adjustment points are more readily accessible at that time. CAUTION: *Approach end of gear travel cautiously with linkage disconnected to prevent damage to worm nut assembly.*

b. Worm Bearing Adjustment (fig. 182). The following instructions cover worm bearing adjustment with steering gear in vehicle. If assembly is out of vehicle, omit steps (1), (2), and (3) below.

(1) CHECK STEERING GEAR MOUNTINGS. Remove bolt attaching steering column to brace extending from instrument panel, then make sure flange to frame bolts are tight.

(2) LOOSEN RUDDER CABLE. Remove rudder cable center guide pulley from mounting in stern compartment, thereby providing slack in

Steering System

Figure 182—Steering Gear Adjustments

cable. Turn steering wheel to right and left extremes to pull cable slack into engine compartment.

(3) DISCONNECT DRAG LINK. Loosen plug in end of drag link sufficiently to permit removal of drag link from Pitman arm ball stud.

Figure 183—Checking Steering Gear Adjustments with Tension Gage

Maintenance Instructions

(4) CHECK WORM BEARING ADJUSTMENT (FIGS. 182 AND 183). Loosen sector gear lash adjuster screw a few turns to relieve any load imposed on worm bearings by close meshing of rack teeth and sector teeth. Tighten end cover screws firmly. Measure pull required to keep wheel in motion by using tension gage as illustrated in figure 183. Take scale reading with gage at right angle to wheel spoke. If pull required to keep wheel in motion is not between $1\frac{3}{4}$ and $2\frac{1}{4}$ pounds, the worm bearings require adjustment [steps (5) and (6) below].

(5) ADJUST WORM BEARINGS (FIG. 182). Place receptacle under steering gear assembly to catch lubricant; then remove end cover screws and remove end cover. Add or remove shims as necessary to produce correct gage reading [step (4) above] when cover is installed and screws fully tightened. Shims are available in thicknesses of 0.002, 0.010, or 0.030 inch. Lubricate steering gear as directed on Lubrication Order No. 9-802 when worm bearing adjustment has been completed.

(6) CHECK FOR "LUMPY" ACTION. Turn steering wheel gently from extreme right to extreme left, meanwhile noting action. If lumpy or uneven action is noted, bearings are damaged. Notify higher authority.

c. Sector Gear Lash Adjustments (fig. 182). As sector gear lash adjustment must follow worm bearing adjustment, the lash adjuster screw will have been backed off before worm bearing adjustment was made [subpar. **b.**(4)].

(1) TIGHTEN SIDE COVER SCREWS. Check and tighten side cover screws (fig. 182) if necessary prior to making sector gear lash adjustment.

(2) LOCATE CENTER OF STEERING WHEEL ROTATION. Turn steering wheel gently from extreme right to extreme left position, counting the number of revolutions. Turn wheel back exactly half way. This places the steering gear in correct position for driving vehicle straight ahead. On late vehicles, the markers (fig. 183) will be at top of steering wheel. A piece of tape may be used to mark this position if wheel does not have markers.

(3) ADJUST SECTOR GEAR LASH (FIGS. 182 AND 183). Turn lash adjuster screw clockwise until all gear backlash is removed, then tighten lock nut. Check adjustment, using tension gage as described in subparagraph **b.**(4), except that gage reading should now be betwen $2\frac{3}{4}$ and $3\frac{1}{4}$ pounds as wheel is pulled through center position. Readjust if necessary to obtain correct gage reading. When worm bearing and sector lash adjustments have been completed, the steering gear column must be attached to brace below instrument panel. Adjustment check described above should then be repeated and if gage reading has increased, mounting adjustment described in subparagraph **d.** below must be made.

d. Steering Gear Mounting Adjustment.

(1) REMOVE STEERING GEAR TO FRAME CLAMP PLATE. Remove Pitman arm (par. 218**b.**). Remove nuts from steering gear to frame

Steering System

and hull mounting bolts and remove clamp plate (fig. 186). Scrape off all hardened caulking compound from clamp plate and hull side.

(2) REPLACE CLAMP PLATE AND POSITION STEERING GEAR AT MOUNTINGS. Coat inner side of clamp plate with caulking compound (52-C-3086-200); then place plate in position against hull side and loosely install steering gear to frame and hull bolts. Raise steering column into position at instrument panel brace and loosely install steering column clamp to brace bolt.

(3) TIGHTEN MOUNTING BOLTS FIRMLY. Tighten nuts on steering gear to frame and hull mounting bolts. Upper front bolt should be tightened last as this bolt acts as pivot to properly position steering gear. Install lock nuts on mounting bolts and firmly tighten mounting bolt at column clamp and brace. Check pull at steering wheel with tension gage after all mounting bolts are tight. If pull exceeds limits ($2\frac{3}{4}$ to $3\frac{1}{4}$ lb.), binding is indicated and cause must be located and corrected.

(4) CONNECT STEERING GEAR LINKAGE. Install Pitman arm, then connect drag link (par 220*d*.).

218. PITMAN ARM REPLACEMENT.

a. General. Pitman arm fits onto serrations on outer end of sector shaft. A flat spot in serrations makes it impossible to install arm incorrectly. Ball at lower end of arm is not removable.

b. Pitman Arm Removal.

(1) DISCONNECT DRAG LINK FROM PITMAN ARM. Remove cotter pin at arm end of drag link and back out screw plug until drag link can be lifted off ball stud on arm.

(2) REMOVE PITMAN ARM. Place socket wrench on arm nut and remove nut. Install special puller (41-P-2951-35) over arm as illustrated

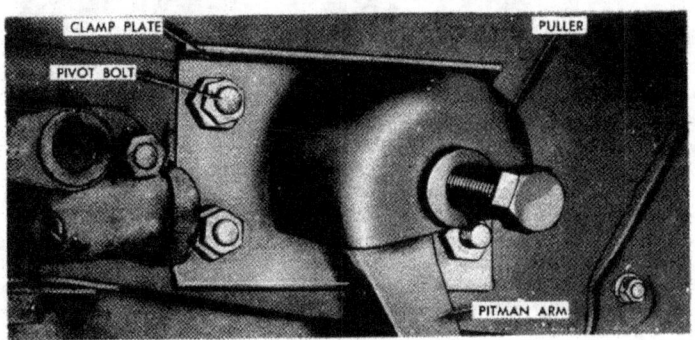

RA PD 337152

Figure 184—Removing Pitman Arm (Puller 41-P-2951-35)

in figure 184. Tighten screw of puller until arm is off splines of shaft and withdraw arm and puller.

c. Pitman Arm Installation.

(1) INSPECT SPLINES ON PITMAN ARM AND SHAFT. Inspect splines on arm and shaft to see that there are no burrs or nicks which might prevent assembly of arm to shaft.

(2) POSITION ARM ON SHAFT. Start arm on shaft, making sure that flat spot in arm and shaft serrations are alined. Install arm nut on shaft and tighten nut until arm has moved far enough to permit installation of lock washer. Remove nut, install new lock washer, and reinstall nut. Tighten arm nut securely, using a socket and a handle having sufficient leverage to fully tighten nut. Assemble drag link socket on Pitman arm ball stud and adjust (par. 220*b*.).

219. STEERING GEAR ASSEMBLY REPLACEMENT.

a. Steering Gear Assembly Removal.

(1) REMOVE STEERING WHEEL. Remove two screws attaching horn button retainer to steering wheel, then remove retainer, horn button, contact, insulator, and spring. Remove steering wheel retaining nut and

RA PD 337205

Figure 185—Removing Steering Wheel with Puller (41-P-2954) and Special Adapter (41-A-18-251)

Steering System

horn terminal plate. Assemble puller (41-P-2954) and special adapter (41-A-18-251) on steering wheel as shown in figure 185. Turn puller screw clockwise to pull steering wheel off worm shaft.

(2) DISCONNECT STEERING COLUMN FROM MOUNTING AND REMOVE CABLE FROM HORN CONNECTOR. Remove clamp to brace bolt and remove steering column clamp and antisqueak. On vehicles prior to chassis serial No. 1151 only, remove horn cable from connector on steering column.

(3) LOOSEN TOEBOARD ASSEMBLY. Remove three closure plates from around steering column. Remove clevis pin from lower end of starter pedal rod to disconnect rod. Remove cotter pin from end of accelerator idler lever to bell crank rod and remove rod from lever. Remove all toeboard retaining screws. Lift lower edge of toeboard away from support angle and lower toeboard to horizontal position.

(4) REMOVE CLUTCH PEDAL. Remove clutch pedal rod nut, and drive pedal rod out of clutch pedal lever. Remove lever to link clevis pin. Remove retainer spring from end of clutch and brake pedal cross shaft. Slide pedal lever off cross shaft and remove from vehicle.

(5) REMOVE PITMAN ARM. Disconnect steering drag link from Pitman arm by removing cotter pin and loosening screw plug at drag link end, and lifting drag link off Pitman arm ball stud. Remove Pitman arm (par. 218*b*.).

(6) DISCONNECT RUDDER CONTROL CABLE. Enter stern compartment and remove cable from thimble. Pull disconnected cable end

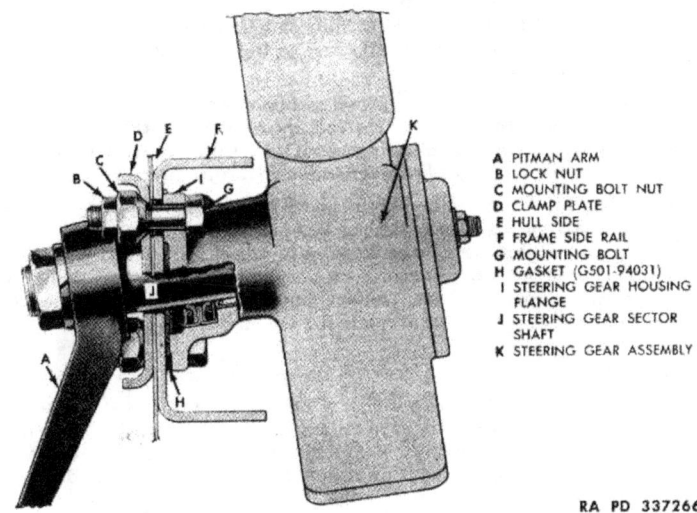

A PITMAN ARM
B LOCK NUT
C MOUNTING BOLT NUT
D CLAMP PLATE
E HULL SIDE
F FRAME SIDE RAIL
G MOUNTING BOLT
H GASKET (G501-94031)
I STEERING GEAR HOUSING FLANGE
J STEERING GEAR SECTOR SHAFT
K STEERING GEAR ASSEMBLY

RA PD 337266

Figure 186—Steering Gear Mounting at Frame

through loom at side of vehicle and into engine compartment. Remove two cap screws attaching cable clamp to rudder cable spool and unwind cable from spool.

(7) WITHDRAW STEERING GEAR ASSEMBLY (FIG. 186). Remove nuts and bolts attaching steering gear housing flange to frame. Remove steering gear assembly to frame clamp plate. Lift assembly away from frame, move steering column to left, and turn assembly as necessary to raise it past frame side rail. Lift the assembly out through opening in toeboard and remove from vehicle. Clean off any caulking compound or old gasket which may remain on frame side rail.

b. Steering Gear Assembly Installation. Key letters in steps (1) through (7) below refer to figure 186.

(1) REMOVE CAULKING COMPOUND. Remove all dry or hardened portions of gasket and caulking compound from inner side of frame side rail before installing steering gear assembly.

(2) POSITION STEERING GEAR ASSEMBLY IN VEHICLE. Place a new cork gasket (H) around sector shaft and against housing flange (F). Coat flange and gasket with caulking compound (52-C-3086-200). Lower the assembly through driver's compartment and into position against frame side rail (I). Insert four mounting bolts (G) through housing flange, then tighten mounting and connect linkage [par. 217d., steps (2), (3), and (4)].

(3) INSTALL RUDDER CABLE. Attach rudder cable to spool, thread cable through loom (par. 221c.), and connect and adjust rudder linkage as directed in paragraph 222b. or 223b.

(4) INSTALL CLUTCH PEDAL. Slide clutch pedal lever on cross shaft and install retainer spring. Install lever to link clevis pin. Install pedal rod and retain with nut.

(5) INSTALL TOEBOARD. Move toeboard into position and install retaining screws. Install three closure plates around steering column. Connect starter pedal to rod using clevis pin. Connect accelerator idler lever to bell crank rod at idler lever and install cotter pin.

(6) INSTALL STEERING WHEEL. Make sure that steering column upper bearing spring is in place and key is installed in worm shaft key slot. Install steering wheel with keyway in wheel hub alined with key; then place terminal plate in center of wheel and install wheel retaining nut. Install spring, insulator, contact, button, and retainer in steering wheel and install two screws to retain the assembly.

220. DRAG LINK.

a. Description. The drag link is a tubular link with ball sockets at each end. These ball sockets have an automatic adjusting feature which incorporates a pair of opposed wedge blocks and spring (fig. 187). The position of the wedge blocks is indicated by a round head pin projecting from the side. Whenever the wedge blocks have reached the end of their travel, they must be returned to their original position by tightening the screw plug at the end of the socket.

Steering System

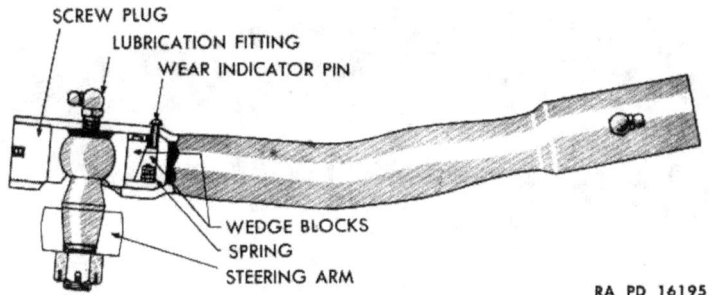

Figure 187—Steering Gear Drag Link

b. Drag Link Adjustment (fig. 187).

(1) CHECK POSITION OF WEAR INDICATOR PINS. The head of the wear indicator pin is flush with side of socket whenever wedge blocks are in position as shown in figure 187. Pin projects out from side of socket as sockets wear. Manual adjustment is required whenever pin head projects $\frac{3}{8}$ inch, measured between socket body and under side of pin head.

(2) ADJUST BALL SOCKETS. Remove cotter pin which retains screw plug in socket end. Force wear indicator pin in as far as possible, then screw the plug tightly into socket. Back off screw plug $\frac{1}{2}$ to 1 turn and install new cotter pin. Perform operation at each end of drag link.

c. Drag Link Removal (fig. 187).
Remove cotter pin from both ends of drag link. Back out end plugs as far as possible without removing them. Turn steering wheel in both directions to loosen ball studs in drag link ends, then pull drag link off steering arm ball stud and Pitman arm ball stud. NOTE: *Drag link can be disconnected at one end only if so desired for replacing Pitman arm or steering arm.*

d. Drag Link Installation (fig. 187).
Position drag link over ball studs on Pitman arm and steering arm; then adjust as described in subparagraph *b.*(2) above. Lubricate drag link as described on Lubrication Order No. 9-802.

221. RUDDER CABLE, SPOOL, AND SHEAR PIN.

a. General. Linkage between steering gear and rudder linkage in stern compartment consists of a $\frac{1}{8}$-inch steel cable which is guided by pulleys and loom as shown in figures 191, 192, and 193. The cable spool is attached to and turns with steering gear worm shaft. Cable is clamped in position at spool while ends are attached to tiller arm (early vehicles) or to tiller lever (late vehicles) by means of cable clamps (fig. 189). In the event rudder or linkage becomes jammed, the cable spool shear pin will shear, thereby preventing breakage of cable and also permitting steering of front wheels.

TM 9-802
221

Maintenance Instructions

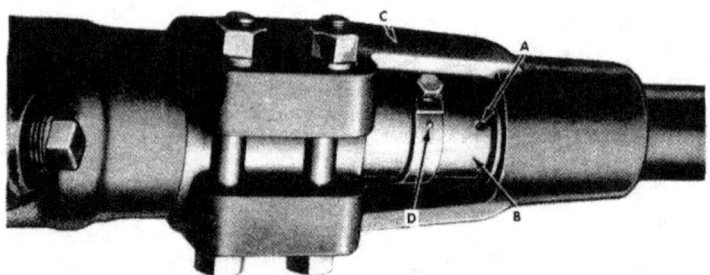

SHEAR PIN AND LOCATING HOLE

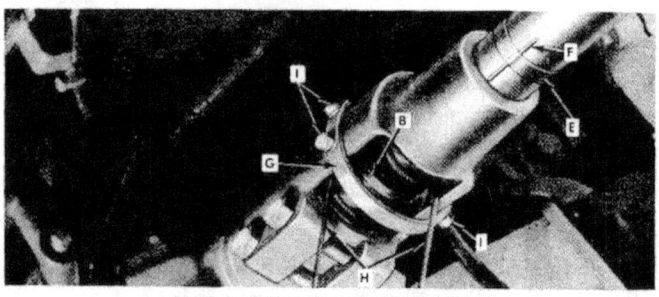

CABLE INSTALLATION AT STEERING COLUMN
A LOCATING HOLE
B CABLE SPOOL
C SPOOL HOUSING
D SHEAR PIN
E CLAMP
F SPARE SHEAR PIN
G CABLE GUARD
H RUDDER CABLE
I CABLE GUARD SCREWS

RA PD 333216

Figure 188—Rudder Cable, Spool, and Shear Pin Installation

b. Rudder Control Cable Removal. The same operations are necessary to remove rudder control cable on both early and late type rudder linkage, except as noted in text.

(1) DISCONNECT CABLE FROM RUDDER LINKAGE. Remove four cable clamps used to hold cable at tiller upper arm (fig. 191) or tiller lever (fig. 192), then pull cable off thimbles.

(2) REMOVE CABLE FROM CABLE SPOOL. Pull cable into engine compartment, then remove cable guard and cable clamp (G and E, fig. 188). Unwind cable from spool and remove cable from vehicle.

c. Rudder Control Cable Installation. Prior to installing rudder control cable it is important that steering gear assembly is adjusted properly; also, that spring to axle U-bolts are tight and that no looseness exists at drag link sockets or Pitman arm.

(1) PREPARE CABLE FOR INSTALLATION. Lay out full length of cable in a straight line to be sure there are no kinks or twists. Double one end back to within eight feet of the other end and mark the center of the loop.

TM 9-802
221

Steering System

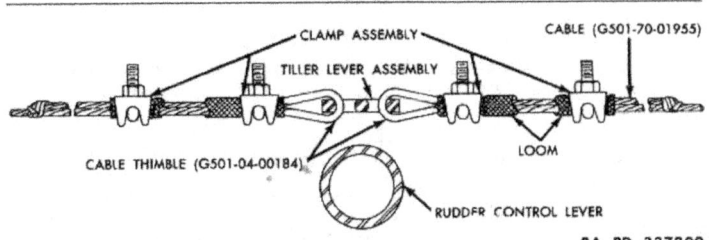

Figure 189—Rudder Control Cable Clamp Installation

(2) WIND CABLE ON SPOOL. Place front wheels in straight-ahead position, then enter engine compartment. Insert the long end of cable in spool housing under steering post and at top of spool. Wind cable around steering post 3¾ turns to notch in spool. Insert cable in notch in spool at point where cable is marked. Place clamp over cable, insert the cap screws and tighten firmly. After tightening clamp, wind 3¾ turns of cable around steering post at bottom of spool and out over top of steering post.

(3) INSTALL CABLE GUARD. Install cable guard, using hex head screws as shown in figure 188. NOTE: *Whenever installing cable guard, hex head cap screws (¼-20 x ½, cadmium or zinc plated) should be used even though cross-recessed head screws may have been used originally. Due to limited space, hex head screws may be installed more readily.*

(4) INSERT CABLE ENDS IN LOOM AT LEFT SIDE OF VEHICLE (FIG. 190). Start long length of cable through flap at side of hull and place cable in upper pulley. Slide through upper loom to stern compartment pulley. Place short end of cable over lower pulley and pass through lower loom to pulley in stern compartment.

(5) ATTACH CABLE TO RUDDER LINKAGE (FIGS. 189, 191, and 192). Pass long end of cable around pulleys—one in front center of stern compartment and one at right-hand side. Place loom (fig. 189) on each cable end, then pass cable around thimbles and back through loom. With cable adjusted as described in paragraph 222*b*.(3) or paragraph 223*b*.(1), install four cable clamps with nuts on top and loom under clamp U-bolt. Clamps must be installed according to foregoing instructions to prevent interference with rudder control lever during operation of linkage. This is especially true on vehicles after chassis serial No. 1505.

d. Cable Spool Shear Pin Replacement. One spare shear pin is clamped to steering column jacket just above cable spool housing (fig. 188). Key letters in steps (1) through (4) below refer to figure 188.

(1) REMOVE CABLE GUARD. Remove cable guard (G). Turn steering wheel until wheels are in extreme right turn position and swing rudder to extreme right turn position. This will unwind cable from upper part of spool, thereby uncovering locating hole in spool.

TM 9-802
221-222

Maintenance Instructions

(2) ALINE SPOOL AND SHAFT. Insert alining punch (approximately $3/16$ inch diameter) which will fit snugly into locating hole (A) in cable spool. Have assistant turn steering wheel alternately to right and left as necessary so that punch can be forced into mating hole in steering gear worm shaft. This will hold shear pin holes in cable spool and worm shaft in alinement during shear pin replacement.

(3) REMOVE BROKEN SHEAR PIN. Shear pin hole in spool is $3/8$ inch in diameter at side of spool opposite locating hole (fig. 188), while hole in opposite side of spool is approximately same size as shear pin. Remove portion of broken pin from large hole first; then with a $3/32$-inch diameter drift, drive out remaining portions of shear pin. Be careful to remove pieces of pin which may drop into spool housing when driven out of spool

(4) INSTALL NEW SHEAR PIN. Drive a new shear pin into place through spool and shaft. Ends of shear pin must be flush with outside of spool.

222. RUDDER AND LINKAGE (EARLY TYPE).

a. **Description.** Rudder and linkage used on early vehicles (prior to chassis serial No. 1506) is illustrated in figures 190 and 191. Rudder

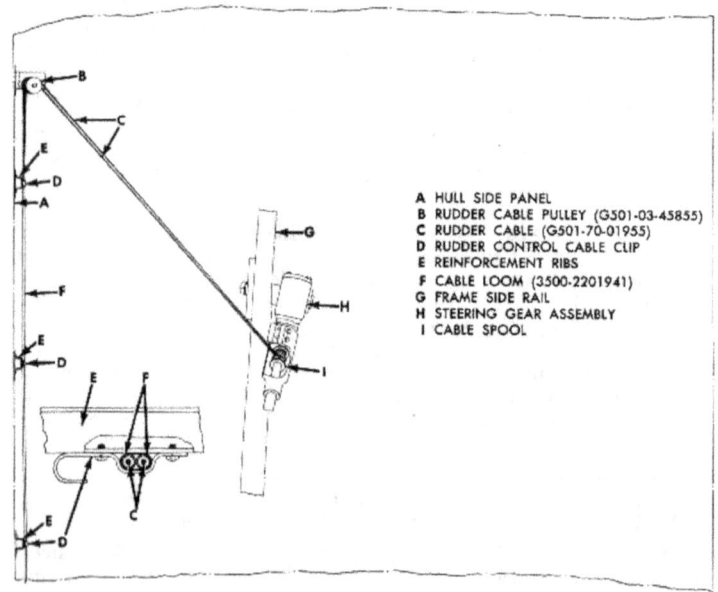

Figure 190—Rudder Forward Linkage RA PD 337206

Steering System

control is affected through use of steering wheel, the movement of which is transferred to rudder by cable and rudder linkage. Rudder and rudder shaft are integral. Rudder linkage, located in vehicle stern compartment, consists of tiller shaft and arm assembly, rudder control lever, and an adjustable rod interconnected with tiller arm and rudder control arm.

b. Linkage Adjustment and Inspection. Cable or linkage adjustment is required whenever cable sags or rudder does not have proper amount of movement to right or left of straight-ahead position. Key letters in steps (1) through (4) below refer to figure 191.

(1) POSITION FRONT WHEELS STRAIGHT AHEAD. Ascertain straight-ahead position by sighting, or by driving straight on a level surface; then accurately mark steering wheel so that wheel can be readily returned to straight-ahead position after it has been turned for checking purposes.

(2) ADJUST LINKAGE IN STERN COMPARTMENT. Measure length of connecting rod (I) between rudder control lever (R) and tiller shaft lower arm (J). If distance between centerlines of ball sockets at each end of rod is not 21¾ inches, loosen lock nuts behind ball socket assemblies and turn rod until this dimension is obtained.

(3) ADJUST CABLE AND LINKAGE POSITION. With steering wheel set in straight-ahead position, main portion of rudder blade must be in parallel with centerline of vehicle. Adjust cable ends inside stern compartment to secure rudder position while holding steering wheel at straight-ahead position. Cable tension must be snug, and cable ends clamped securely at tiller arm.

(4) CHECK RUDDER LINKAGE FOR DISTORTION. When marine steering linkage has been adjusted as described in steps (1), (2), and (3) above, the tiller arm should point directly toward the rudder shaft. Also, the rudder stop arm (F) on rudder shaft should move between stops as steering wheel is turned each way as far as possible. If for any reason tiller upper arm position varies or rudder stop arm hits hard against stop when turning steering wheel, distortion between upper arm exists. Parts must be straightened to original alinement (123 degrees 35 minutes angle between arms) or parts replaced.

c. Rudder and Linkage Removal. Key letters in steps (1) through (5) below refer to figure 191.

(1) DISCONNECT LINKAGE. Withdraw cotter pin, then remove screw plug from forward end of rod (I) and lift rod from rudder control lever (R).

(2) LOOSEN STOP LEVER AND RUDDER CONTROL LEVER. Remove clamp bolts from rudder control lever (R) and stop lever (F), and drive levers downward until keys are exposed, then remove keys.

(3) DISCONNECT AND REMOVE RUDDER. Loosen lock nut, and back off packing nuts, then remove packing. Remove access plate (C) from deck plate (D), then remove nut and flat washer from upper end of rudder shaft. Withdraw rudder and shaft assembly from under vehicle.

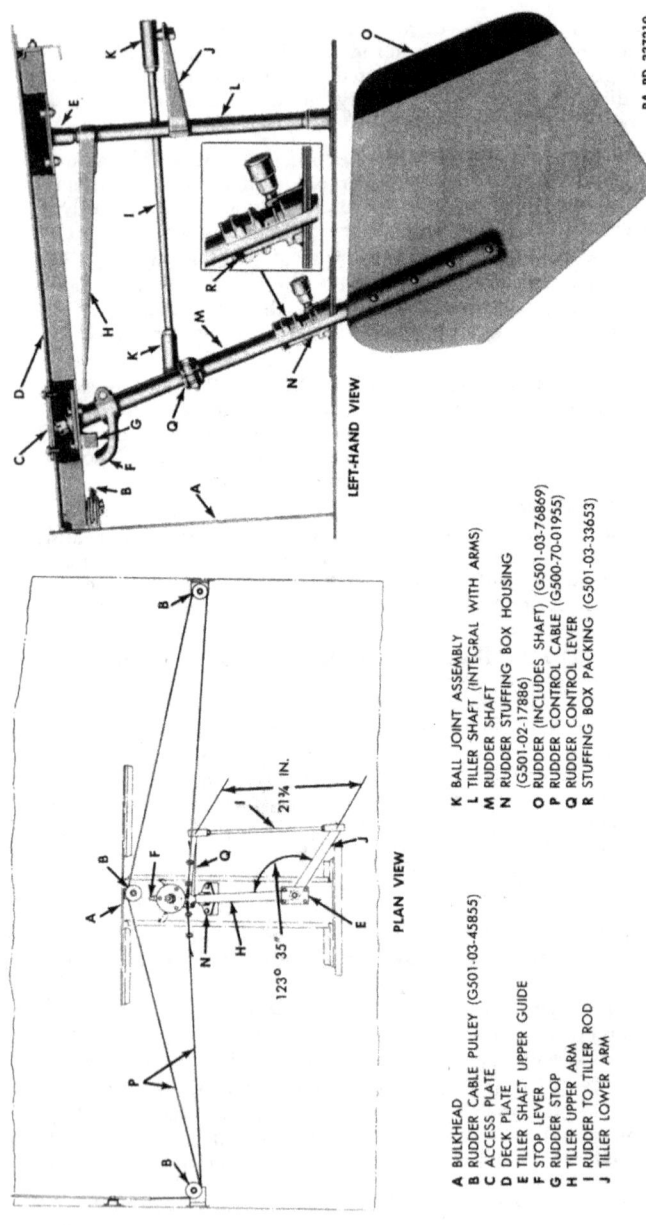

Figure 191—Rudder and Rear Linkage (Prior to Chassis Serial No. 1506)

Steering System

(4) REMOVE CONNECTING ROD. Remove screw plug from rearward end of rudder to tiller connecting rod (I), then lift rod off tiller arm ball.

(5) REMOVE TILLER SHAFT. Disconnect cable from tiller upper arm (H) by removing clamps and pulling out of thimbles. Remove bolts attaching tiller shaft upper guide, raise guide assembly, and remove tiller shaft from vehicle.

d. Rudder and Linkage Installation. Key letters in steps (1) through (6) below refer to figure 191.

(1) INSTALL TILLER SHAFT. Set lower end of tiller shaft into lower guide, position upper guide assembly on upper end of tiller shaft, then install bolts which attach guide assembly (E).

(2) INSTALL RUDDER. Insert end of rudder shaft through rudder stuffing box housing (N). Drop gland nut over end of shaft, then position rudder control lever (R) and stop lever (F) on shaft adjacent to respective Woodruff key slots. Insert upper end of rudder shaft through support bearing, and install flat washer and nut. Tighten nut fully, then back off to next cotter pin hole. Install cotter pin and access plate (C).

(3) POSITION RUDDER CONTROL LEVER AND STOP LEVER. Tap Woodruff keys into slots, then drive the rudder control lever (R) and stop lever (F) into place. Tighten clamp bolt in each lever.

(4) INSTALL CONNECTING ROD. Position connecting rod (I) over ball studs at rudder control lever (R) and tiller lever lower arm (J), then install screw plugs in end of rod and secure plugs with cotter pins. Adjust rudder linkage as described in subparagraph ***b.*** above.

(5) PACK AND ADJUST RUDDER STUFFING BOX. Install rudder stuffing box packing and adjust packing gland as described in paragraph 224.

(6) CONNECT RUDDER CONTROL CABLE. Connect rudder control cable as described in paragraph 221c.(5).

223. RUDDER AND LINKAGE (LATE TYPE).

a. Description. Information and instructions contained in this paragraph apply to rudder and linkage used on vehicles after chassis serial No. 1505, illustrated in figures 192 and 193.

b. Linkage Adjustment and Inspection (fig. 192). Correct relationship between front wheel position and rudder positions must be maintained to attain proper operation of the steering system. Loose or slack sables contribute to shear pin failure and damage to cable. Pulleys should rotate freely and pulleys and cables at pulleys should always be properly lubricated. To retard corrosion, coat cables with thin film rust preventive compound (14-C-507).

(1) RUDDER CABLE ADJUSTMENT (FIG. 192). Inside the stern compartment, adjust steering cable in end of tiller shaft so that with

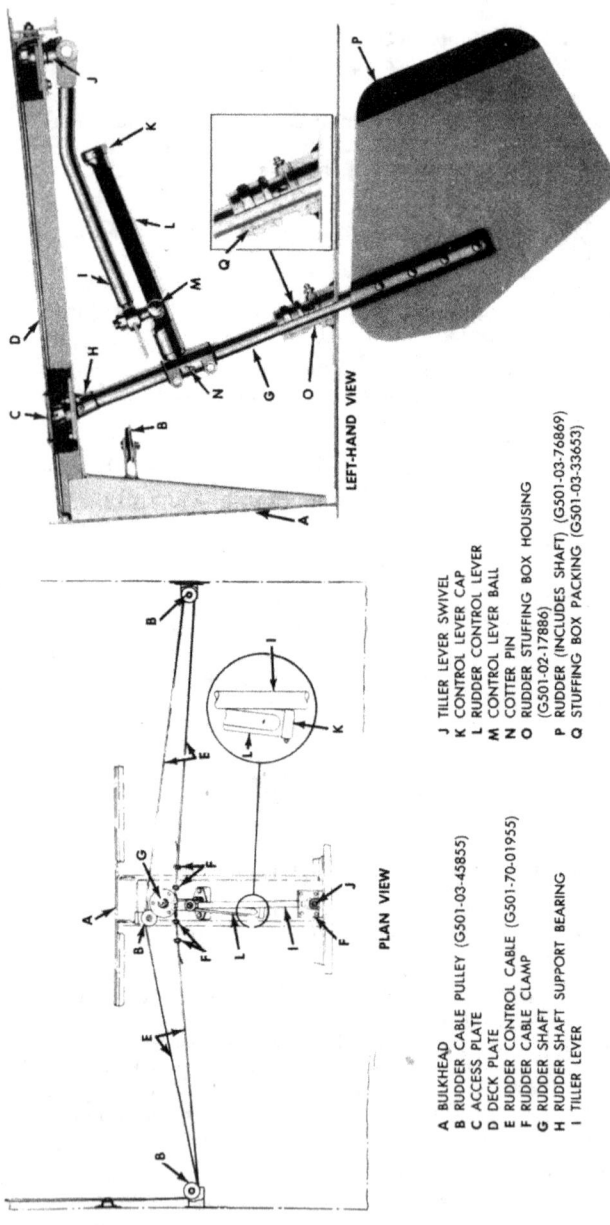

PLAN VIEW

LEFT-HAND VIEW

A BULKHEAD
B RUDDER CABLE PULLEY (G501-03-45855)
C ACCESS PLATE
D DECK PLATE
E RUDDER CONTROL CABLE (G501-70-01955)
F RUDDER CABLE CLAMP
G RUDDER SHAFT
H RUDDER SHAFT SUPPORT BEARING
I TILLER LEVER
J TILLER LEVER SWIVEL
K CONTROL LEVER CAP
L RUDDER CONTROL LEVER
M CONTROL LEVER BALL
N COTTER PIN
O RUDDER STUFFING BOX HOUSING (G501-02-17886)
P RUDDER (INCLUDES SHAFT) (G501-03-76869)
Q STUFFING BOX PACKING (G501-03-33653)

RA PD 337216

Figure 192—Rudder and Rear Linkage (After Chassis Serial No. 1505)

Steering System

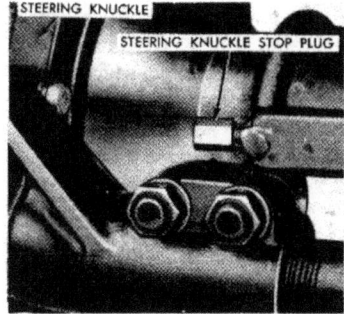 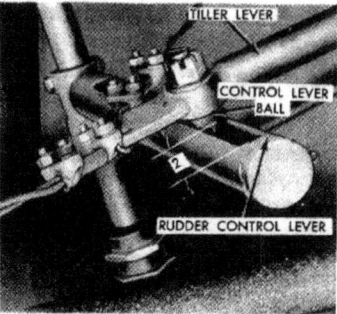

RA PD 337267

Figure 193—Rudder Control Position and Steering Knuckle Stop Plug

steering wheel accurately in straight-ahead position and cables tight, right-hand rear corner of rudder control lever assembly will be directly below the left-hand side of tiller lever assembly (inset, fig. 192). In this position, main body of rudder should at the same time be parallel to the centerline of the vehicle. If it is not, rudder linkage may be distorted. Parts should be carefully checked for alinement, and replaced if necessary. CAUTION: *When making cable adjustment, be sure cable clamp U-bolts are installed with ends upward to prevent interference with rudder control lever assembly. Refer to figure 189.*

(2) RUDDER TRAVEL ADJUSTMENT (FIG. 193). Reserve travel of rudder control lever ball in control lever assembly must be maintained to prevent rudder from binding, thereby causing shear pin breakage. Check rudder travel and adjust as described below.

(a) Check Control Lever Ball Travel. Two men are required to accomplish this test accurately—One is needed to turn steering wheel while other observes action of steering linkage. Make this check with front end of hull lifted high enough to allow front axle to be suspended from springs—same as when vehicle is afloat. When control lever ball is 2 inches from end of slot in rudder control lever, the steering knuckle at left front wheel should just contact stop plug (fig. 193). If clearance exists between stop plug and steering knuckle, one of the methods of adjustment given in steps *(b)* and *(c)* below must be employed to correct the condition.

(b) Readjust Stop. Break weld which retains stop plug. Adjust the plug until head contacts steering knuckle, then reweld.

(c) Weld Stop. Build up head of plug by welding until plug is long enough to contact steering knuckle.

Maintenance Instructions

c. Rudder and Linkage Removal. Key letters in steps (1) through (3) below refer to figure 192.

(1) DISCONNECT LINKAGE. Remove cable clamps which attach control cable to tiller lever; detach cable ends from thimbles (fig. 189).

(2) REMOVE RUDDER. Loosen lock nut, back off packing nut, and remove packing from stuffing box. Loosen clamp bolts from rudder control lever (L). Remove cotter pin (N) (when used) from lever hub and drive lever downward, then remove Woodruff key from slot in rudder shaft (G). Remove access plate (C) from deck plate (D), and remove nut and flat washer from upper end of rudder shaft. Withdraw rudder and shaft assembly from under vehicle. NOTE: *Drive upward on rudder control lever in stern compartment while rudder assembly is being removed from under vehicle.*

(3) REMOVE RUDDER CONTROL ARM AND TILLER LEVER. Remove cap screws which attach tiller lever swivel (J) to channel. Remove rudder control lever, tiller lever, and swivel from the vehicle as an assembly. Remove nut from control lever ball (M) and separate tiller lever (I) from ball. Ball (I) may be removed from rudder control lever after removing cap (K).

d. Rudder and Linkage Installation. Key letters in steps (1) through (6) below refer to figure 192.

(1) INSTALL RUDDER. Insert upper end of rudder shaft (G) through stuffing box housing. Drop stuffing box packing nut over upper end of rudder shaft. Tap Woodruff key into slot in rudder shaft, then install rudder control lever (L) on shaft (G) with key in keyway in lever hub. Raise rudder into operating position with upper end of shaft (G) entered in support bearing (H); then install flat washer and nut on upper end of shaft. Draw nut up firmly, then back off nut far enough to allow rudder shaft to turn freely in support bearing. Install cotter pin. Be sure support bearing attaching bolts are tight, then install access plate (C).

(2) INSTALL TILLER LEVER. With swivel assembly (J) installed on tiller lever (I), attach the rearward end of the assembly to channel, using four cap screws. Insert control lever ball (M) through end of rudder control lever, and install cap (K) and retain with cotter pin. Place control lever ball stud through hole in tiller lever (I), and install nut.

(3) CLAMP RUDDER CONTROL LEVER TO RUDDER SHAFT. Some late vehicles have a hole drilled through control lever hub and rudder shaft. On these vehicles, install $\frac{1}{8}$-inch cotter pin through hole, then install and tighten lever clamp bolts. On earlier vehicles, determine correct location of rudder control lever on rudder shaft by swinging the rudder control lever (L) directly below tiller lever (I), then moving lever (L) up or down as necessary to make the two levers parallel, and at the same time, being sure that rear end of control lever passes tiller lever without interference.

Steering System

(4) PACK AND ADJUST RUDDER STUFFING BOX. Install rudder stuffing box packing, and adjust packing gland as described in paragraph 224.

(5) CONNECT RUDDER CONTROL CABLE. Attach rudder control cable to tiller lever as described in paragraph 221c.(5).

(6) LUBRICATE RUDDER CONTROL LINKAGE. Lubricate rudder control linkage as described on Lubrication Order No. 9-802.

224. RUDDER STUFFING BOX.

a. General. Rudder stuffing box is used to prevent leakage at point where rudder shaft passes through hull. A gasket is used between stuffing box and hull water propeller tunnel. A braided rawhide packing in an adjustable gland forms seal around rudder shaft.

b. Rudder Stuffing Box Adjustment (figs. 191 and 192). Adjustment of rudder stuffing box is necessary whenever leakage in excess of a slow drip is observed around rudder shaft. Make following adjustment with vehicle in water.

(1) TIGHTEN PACKING NUT. Be sure stuffing box is lubricated as described on Lubrication Order No. 9-802. Loosen lock nut and tighten packing nut gradually, $\frac{1}{6}$ turn at a time, until only a small amount of water seeps into hull; then tighten lock nut firmly.

(2) CHECK ADJUSTMENT. Turn steering wheel from full right to full left several times, meanwhile noting "feel" of rudder action. If binding is evident, stuffing box packing may be compressed too tightly; if such is the case, replace packing. If packing nut bottoms on housing during adjustment, back off nut until free from housing, then replace packing.

c. Stuffing Box Removal.

(1) REMOVE RUDDER. Remove rudder as described in paragraph 222c. or paragraph 223c.

(2) REMOVE STUFFING BOX. Remove two bolts which attach stuffing box housing to hull, then remove stuffing box and gasket.

d. Stuffing Box Installation.

(1) INSTALL STUFFING BOX. Coat stuffing box gasket on both sides with caulking compound (52-C-3086-200). Place stuffing box and gasket in position in vehicle stern compartment. Coat stuffing box attaching bolt threads with same compound, then install bolts finger-tight, using lock washers under bolt heads.

(2) INSTALL RUDDER. Install rudder as described in paragraph 222d. or paragraph 223d.

(3) ADJUST RUDDER STUFFING BOX. Tighten stuffing box attaching bolts firmly. With packing in place, adjust packing nut as described in subparagraph *b.* above.

Section XL
Hull, Surf Boards, Hatches, and Windshield

225. GENERAL.

a. Description. Hull is of all steel, watertight, welded construction made of plates, angles, and channels. Vehicle frame, similar to conventional truck frame, is installed inside and bolted to hull. Frame supports power plant and power train; running gear, underneath hull, is attached to both hull and frame. Hull interior is divided into compartments by bulkheads and panels. From front to rear, these compartments are: front compartment, engine compartment, driver's compartment, cargo compartment, and rear compartment. Front and engine compartments are covered by the front deck. Rear deck covers rear compartment. Access to these compartments is provided by covered hatches in decks.

b. Repair Operations. Repair operations on items covered in this section are described in TM 9-1802C.

226. HULL DRAINAGE SYSTEM.

a. General. Hull is drained by three 3-inch diameter drain plugs in hull bottom, and three 1½-inch diameter drain plugs in propeller shaft housings. In addition, vehicles after chassis serial No. 2005 are equipped with four hand-operated drain valves.

b. Hull Drain Plugs. On vehicles after chassis serial No. 2005, there is no occasion for leaving plugs out. Plugs may be removed for draining oil, or cleaning bilge, but must be immediately replaced. On vehicles not equipped with drain valves, only the plug below transfer case must be left out at time of storage or shipment. In any event, *whenever drain plugs are removed, attach plugs to steering wheel, or stow in retainers* in driver's compartment, if vehicle is so equipped. On vehicles prior to chassis serial No. 2006, hull drain plugs are not interchangeable. Plugs and rings on hull are matched and stamped to indicate position. Numeral "1" is stamped on forward ring and plug, "2" is stamped on center ring and plug, and rear ring and plug are stamped with numeral "3." Coat plug threads with grease before installing.

c. Propeller Shaft Housing Drain Plugs. A plug in each of the propeller shaft housings must be removed to drain housing after water operation, and immediately after leaving water in below freezing temperature. Replace plugs after draining, except when vehicle is to be shipped or stored. On vehicles after chassis serial No. 3620, plug in upper rear housing need not be removed for drainage, since upper housing drains through flexible tube to lower housing. *Whenever plugs are removed, attach plugs to steering wheel, or stow in retainers in driver's compartment, if vehicle is so equipped.*

d. Hull Drain Valves. Open four drain valves after leaving water. On vehicles between chassis serial Nos. 2006 to 4201, engine compart-

TM 9-802
226

Hull, Surf Boards, Hatches, and Windshield

ment valve handle is located in engine compartment, accessible after opening engine compartment hatch cover. On later vehicles, handle is located in left front corner of driver's compartment. Engine compartment drain valve is located under generator in engine compartment, and valve under driver's seat is accessible after removal of left-hand air intake grille. Rear drain valves are accessible after removal of left and right rear cargo compartment floor boards. Four plugs, for emergency use when drain valves fail to close, are carried in engine compartment. Screw plug into threaded part of drain valve seat from underneath hull. At first opportunity, remove and clean valve, or replace if necessary.

(1) REMOVAL (FIG. 194). Remove cap screw and retainer which attach handle to housing, then remove handle. Remove lock nut from guide pin, then loosen guide pin one turn. On vehicles after chassis serial No. 7802, remove drain valve screen. Remove three cap screws and lock washers which attach housing to seat. Lift housing, shut-off disk, and pressure disk from valve seat. Clean inside of seat thoroughly with dry-cleaning solvent. Examine seat carefully, and replace if badly scored or corroded. If necessary to remove seat, mark seat and hull to permit installation in same position. Remove seven cap screws which attach seat to hull, then remove gasket and seat from under side of hull.

(2) CLEANING. Remove shut-off disk, pressure disk, spring, and seal from housing. Wash all parts except gasket and seal in dry-cleaning solvent and wipe dry. Examine parts carefully, replacing any that are worn, scored, or corroded sufficiently to impair proper operation of valve. Clean and paint screen as described in paragraph 238.

(3) INSTALLATION (FIG. 194.) Apply a thin coat of caulking compound (52-C-3086-200) to both sides of gasket, using a new gasket if available. Position gasket and seat to hull, making sure seat is in same position as when removed (fig. 195). Coat seven cap screws with caulk-

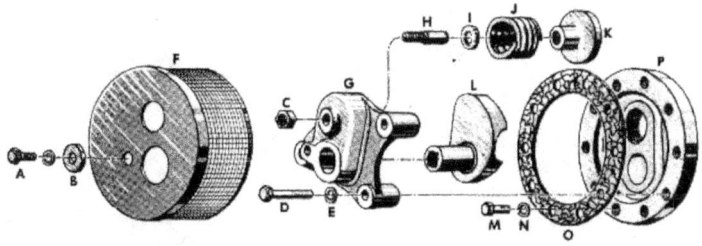

A RETAINING BOLT
B VALVE HANDLE RETAINER (G501-70-02264)
C GUIDE PIN NUT
D HOUSING TO VALVE SEAT BOLT
E LOCK WASHER
F SCREEN
G HOUSING
H GUIDE PIN

I PRESSURE DISK SEAL (G501-70-02266)
J SPRING
K PRESSURE DISK
L SHUT-OFF DISK
M BOTTOM PANEL TO SEAT BOLT
N LOCK WASHER
O GASKET (G501-70-02000)
P VALVE SEAT

RA PD 337268

Figure 194—Disassembled View of Hull Drain Valve

411

TM 9-802
226

Maintenance Instructions

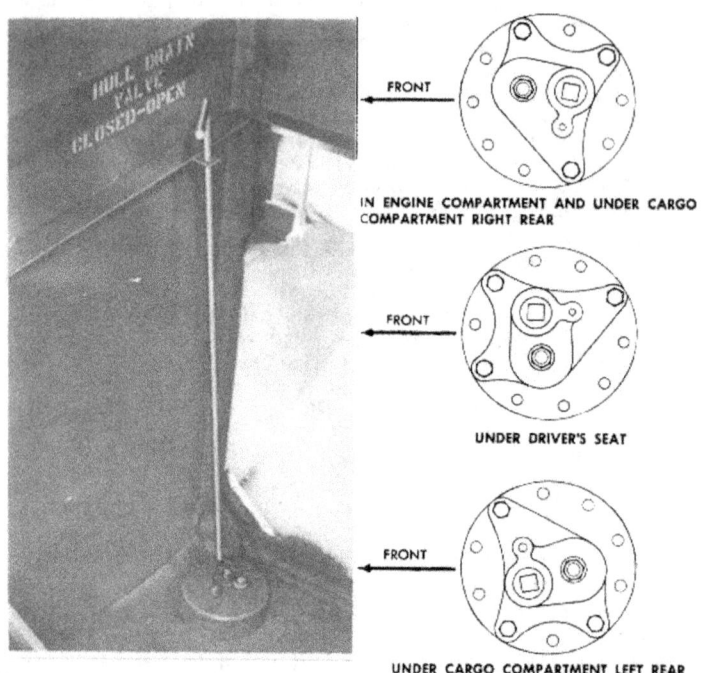

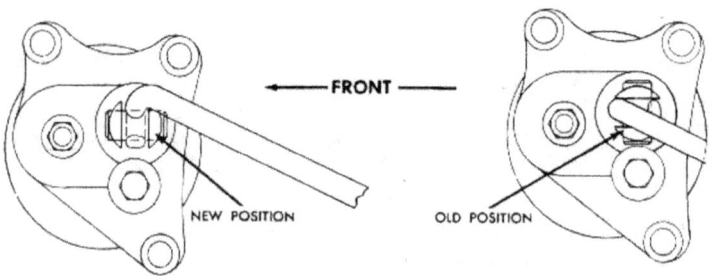

Figure 195—Hull Drain Valve

ing compound (52-C-3086-200), then install screws and lock washers. Assemble seal, spring, pressure disk, and shut-off disk in housing, lubricate parts with engine oil, then position assembly on valve seat. Housing must be in correct position as shown in figure 195. Coat three cap screws with caulking compound (52-C-3086-200), then install cap screws and washers, tightening screws evenly and firmly. Position screen over housing, if vehicle is so equipped. Connect handle to valve, then install handle retainer and cap screw. Tighten guide pin while operating valve handle, until a slight drag is felt on handle. Back off guide pin slightly, then install lock nut.

(4) ENGINE COMPARTMENT VALVE JOINT POSITION. Unless engine compartment valve joint is in correct position, angularity is such that parts are subjected to an excessive amount of strain when valve is operated. On vehicles with handle in driver's compartment, inspect position of joint with valve closed. If pin is perpendicular to centerline of vehicle, as shown in "Old Position" in figure 195, valve joint must be repositioned. Remove cap screw and retainer from valve housing. Disconnect joint from housing and rotate valve handle clockwise one-quarter turn. Connect joint to valve, then install retainer and cap screw. From inside engine compartment, hold handle rod with pipe wrench immediately above clevis and pin. Using a short length of pipe, twist handle to aline with stencils on floor board.

227. SURF BOARDS.

a. General. Three types of surf boards are in use. All vehicles are equipped with a front surf board hinged to front of hull. Vehicles prior to chassis serial No. 2006 are equipped with a windshield surf board

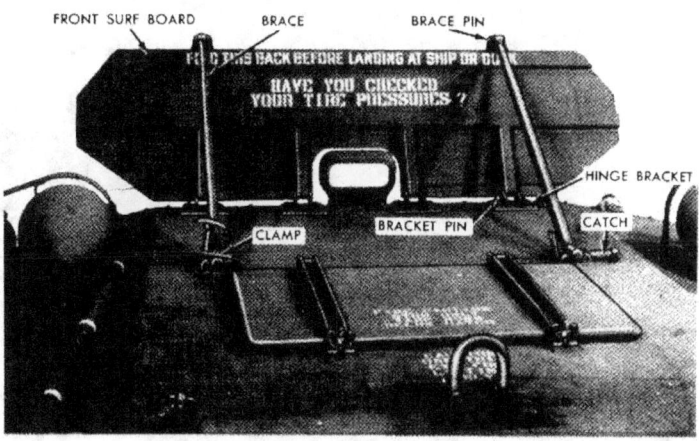

Figure 196—Front Surf Board

Maintenance Instructions

hinged to engine hatch cover. Rear surf board, used on vehicles prior to chassis serial No. 4202, is hinged to rear cargo bulkhead upper extension. Check condition of surf boards regularly, particularly after operation in rough water. Keep hinges, braces, clamps, and catches lubricated in accordance with Lubrication Order No. 9-802 to prevent corrosion and seizing of movable parts.

b. Front Surf Board (fig. 196).

(1) REMOVAL. Disengage brace catches and swing clamps free from braces. Remove cotter pins from hinge bracket pins. Remove hinge bracket pins, then lift surf board from vehicle.

(2) INSTALLATION. Position surf board to hinge brackets on front deck. Install hinge bracket pins, securing each pin with a cotter pin. Raise and lower surf board to make sure all hinges operate freely. Position braces in brace brackets, swing clamps over braces, then engage catches.

c. Windshield Surf Board (fig. 197).

(1) REMOVAL. Loosen wing nuts on surf board hold-down bolts and disenegage bolts. Remove cotter pins from surf board hinge pins, then remove hinge pins. Lift surf board off engine hatch cover, and remove from vehicle.

(2) INSTALLATION. Position surf board on engine hatch cover. Install hinge pins, securing each pin with a cotter pin. Raise surf board to windshield. Make sure slots in surf board fit over windshield brackets, with windshield in vertical position. Straighten windshield sectors if necessary. Lower surf board to hatch cover, engage hold-down bolts, then tighten wing nuts.

d. Rear Surf Board (fig. 198).

(1) REMOVAL. Remove cotter pins from surf board wing pins. Dis-

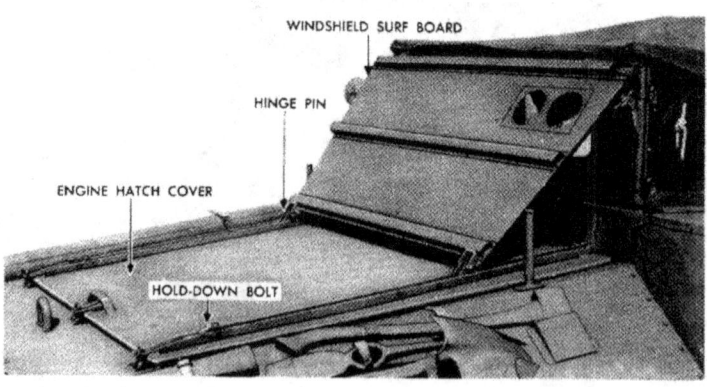

Figure 197—Windshield Surf Board

Hull, Surf Boards, Hatches, and Windshield

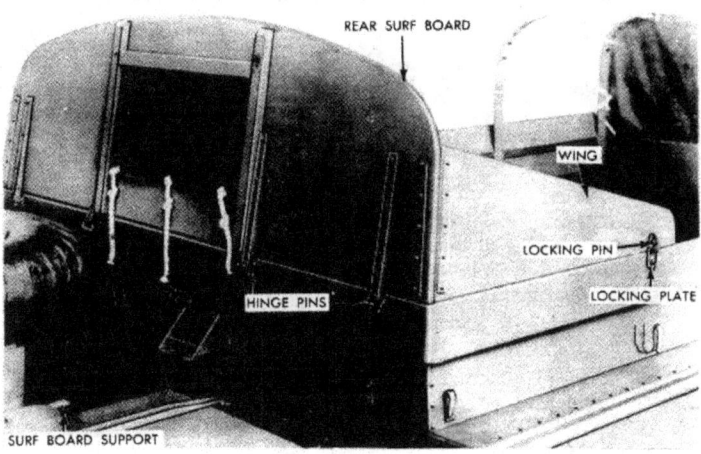

Figure 198—Rear Surf Board

engage locking plates by swinging wings into cargo compartment. Remove cotter pins from four hinge pins. Support surf board while removing hinge pins, then remove surf board and wings from vehicle.

(2) INSTALLATION. Position surf board and wings vertically on vehicle, with hinge pin holes alined. Install four hinge pins, securing each pin with cotter pin. Engage wings with locking plates and install cotter pins.

228. HATCH COVERS AND SEALS.

a. General. Hatch covers are used over front deck hatch, engine hatch, and rear deck hatch. In addition, very early vehicles have a small tool compartment hatch cover in left rear deck. This hatch cover should be permanently fastened in place as described in subparagraph *e.* below. Vehicles are equipped with an auxiliary air intake door in rear of engine hatch cover. Vehicles after chassis serial No. 5670 (except Nos. 6602 to 7135 inclusive) have door fastened permanently to engine hatch cover, and all operating mechanism is omitted. It is recommended that door be permanently fastened as described in subparagraph *f.* below.

b. Seal Felts. All hatch cover seals are removed and installed in same manner.

(1) REMOVAL. Raise hatch cover, then using a screwdriver or similar tool, raise one end of felt out of channel (fig. 199). Note manner in which ends of felt are jointed. Pull seal from channel by hand.

(2) INSTALLATION. Feed felt strip into retaining channel by first inserting one edge, then pinching other edge into place with thumb and

Maintenance Instructions

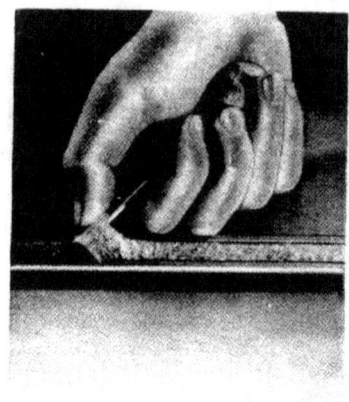
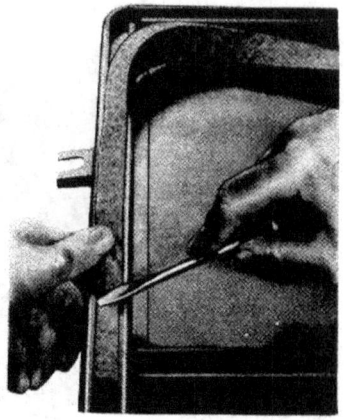

REMOVAL INSTALLATION

RA PD 303156

Figure 199—Hatch Cover Seal Removal and Installation

screwdriver (fig. 199). Complete installation of felt, then apply thin film rust preventive compound (14-C-507) to felt seal to prevent adhesion of felt to paint on hatch.

c. Hatch Covers. All hatch covers are hinged and clamped in same way; removal and installation operations are same for all hatches.

(1) REMOVAL. Loosen wing nuts on lock bolts and disengage bolts from hatch cover. Remove two cotter pins from each hinge pin, then remove pins. Lift hatch cover off deck, disengaging prop from rear hatch as cover is lifted off.

(2) INSTALLATION. Position hatch cover to deck with hinges alined. On rear cover, engage prop as cover is placed on deck. Install hinge pins, then secure each hinge pin with two cotter pins.

d. Rear Deck Hatch Cover Hinge Bolt Installation. Installation of bolts to prevent distortion of deck plate (fig. 200) is recommended on vehicles prior to chassis serial No. 7251 (except Nos. 5952 through 6601)

(1) Remove rear deck hatch cover as described in subparagraph **c.** above.

(2) In center of each deck hinge bracket, drill a $9/32$-inch diameter hole through bracket, deck plate, and deck support (fig. 200).

(3) Apply caulking compound (52-C-3086), then install hex-head bolt (HI-54-52301—$1/4$-28 x $5/8$), lock washer ($1/4$), and nut (HI-41-67521—$1/4$-28) at each bracket.

(4) Install rear deck hatch cover (subpar. **c.** above).

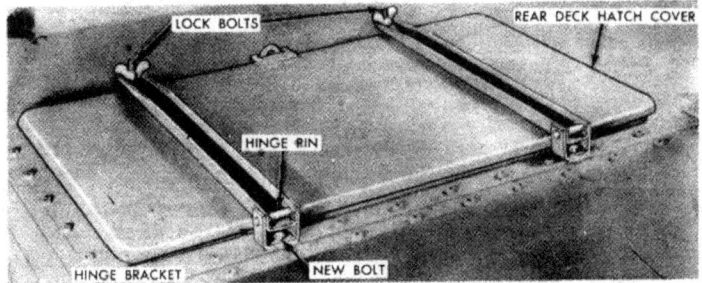

HINGE BRACKET BOLTS INSTALLED

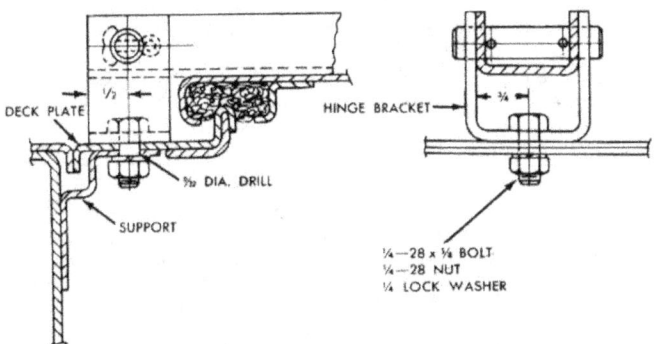

SECTIONAL VIEWS OF HINGE BRACKET BOLT INSTALLATION

Figure 200—Rear Deck Hatch Cover

e. Tool Compartment Hatch Cover. The small hatch cover on left rear deck on vehicles prior to chassis serial No. 613 is easily damaged at shipside. Cover should be permanently closed as follows:

(1) Remove tools, then drill four $1/2$-inch diameter drain holes in rear corners of compartment shelf.

(2) Thoroughly clean and paint hull sides and shelf inside compartment.

(3) Close cover and permanently fasten, preferably by welding.

f. Auxiliary Air Intake Door (fig. 201). Additional cooling advantage by use of auxiliary air intake is offset by danger of stalling engine by shipping water through door. Therefore, it is recommended that door be permanently closed on vehicles prior to chassis serial No. 7136 (except Nos. 5671 through 6601) as follows:

(1) Raise engine compartment hatch cover. Remove entire auxiliary

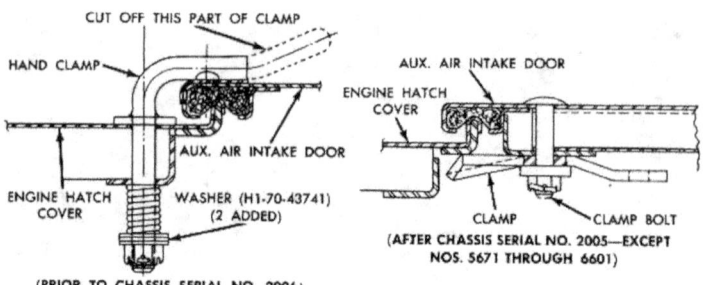

Figure 201—Auxiliary Air Intake Door Permanently Closed

air intake door operating mechanism including screen. Do not remove latches.

(2) Cover hole in upper toeboard with any suitable metal plate, attaching plate with screws. Remove "Auxiliary Cooling Air Intake" instruction plate from vehicle.

(3) Inspect air scoop door seal (G501-03-82791) and make any necessary repairs or replacements to insure a watertight seal.

(4) At under side of engine hatch cover, remove nuts, cotter pins from latch bolts. With latch in locked position, install 3/8-inch lock washer, install nut and cotter pin, and tighten securely to permanently close door. On vehicles with hand clamps (prior to chassis serial No. 2006), remove nuts. Install two additional 3/8-inch flat washers (HI-70-4371) on each bolt, then install nut. Make sure clamps are in proper position to lock hatch cover, then firmly tighten nuts to fully compress springs and secure with cotter pins. On vehicles prior to chassis serial No. 2006, cut off ends of clamps. Tack-weld clamps to door, using shielded arc. Avoid heating door sufficiently to burn seal.

229. HULL AND DECKS.

a. General. After water operation, particularly in salt water, pump out or drain bilge, then wash and rinse inside of hull thoroughly with fresh clean water to prevent corrosion. It is important to keep inside of hull clean and free from trash, dirt, leaves, etc., to prevent clogging bilge pump and drain valve strainers and screens. Keep hull free from corrosion by cleaning and painting as described in paragraph 238.

b. Hull Leaks. Check interior of hull immediately after water operation to determine extent and cause of leakage. Correct points of leakage, or mark for later repair. Bolts are used to attach frame, front spring, rear axle trunnion bracket, and reinforcing plates to hull. Keep these bolts tight; if leakage at bolts cannot be stopped by tightening bolts, remove bolts, coat with caulking compound (52-C-3086-200), then install bolts.

TM 9-802
229

Hull, Surf Boards, Hatches, and Windshield

c. Front Deck (fig. 202). All units under front deck can be serviced or replaced without removal of deck. Front deck should be removed only if damaged sufficiently to necessitate replacement.

(1) REMOVAL.

(a) Remove front surf board (par. 227*a*.), then remove windshield surf board (par. 227*c*.) if vehicle is so equipped.

(b) Remove front deck and engine hatch covers (par. 228*c*.).

(c) Remove headlights, blackout lights, and horn as described in paragraphs 131*e*., 132*d*., and 150*b*. respectively.

(d) Remove pioneer tools, boat hook, hand pump, and other equipment stowed on deck.

(e) From inside front and engine compartments, remove bolts and screws which attach air duct panels, radiator supports, and front surf board hinges to deck. Remove bolts attaching lifting eye braces to angle. Disconnect lighting and horn wiring harnesses.

(f) From top side, remove cap screws which attach deck to hull and windshield lower panel. Remove cap screws from front surf board hinge brackets and remove brackets.

A AIR SCOOP DOOR
B ENGINE COMPARTMENT HATCH COVER
C HAND BILGE PUMP
D HEADLIGHT
E BLACKOUT MARKER LIGHT
F FRONT SURF BOARD
G MIRROR HEAD (G501-02-11420)
H AX
I SHOVEL
J BOAT HOOK
K FRONT DECK HATCH COVER
L BLACKOUT DRIVING LIGHT

RA PD 337217

Figure 202—Front Deck (After Chassis Serial No. 2005)

TM 9-802
229

Maintenance Instructions

(g) Pry front deck free from hull, raise upward to clear supports, then remove from vehicle by tipping and sliding off front of hull.

(2) INSTALLATION.

(a) Position deck against front of hull with front edge of deck on ground. Spread caulking compound (52-C-3086-200) on top rail of hull, deck plate support angle attached to windshield lower extension, and on under side of deck around outer edges.

(b) Slide deck into position on hull, making sure air duct panels are in correct position in relation to support angles. Fill seam between deck and hull with caulking compound (52-C-3086-200).

(c) Coat under side of front surf board hinge brackets with caulking compound (52-C-3086-200), then position brackets on deck. Install cap screws attaching deck to hull. Tighten cap screws evenly and firmly, alternating to insure proper sealing of deck to hull. If new deck is being installed, trim off edges; then flange edges down to hull.

(d) Install bolts attaching air duct side panel, radiator supports, and front surf board hinge brackets to deck. Install bolts attaching lifting eye braces to angle.

(e) Install headlights, blackout lights, and horn (pars. 131**f.**, 132**e.**, and 150**c.** respectively). Connect lighting and horn wiring harnesses.

(f) Install front deck and engine hatch covers (par. 228**c.**). Install windshield surf board (par. 227**c.**) if vehicle is so equipped, then install front surf board (par. 227**b.**).

(g) Install pioneer tools and other equipment on front deck.

d. Rear Deck. Rear deck front plate must be removed to replace fuel tank.

(1) REMOVAL (FIG. 203).

(a) Remove spare tire and anchor from rear deck.

(b) Remove rear deck hatch cover (par. 228**c.**).

(c) Remove tarpaulin hooks from rear surf coaming.

(d) Remove fuel tank filler cap and chain assembly from fuel tank filler neck.

(e) Remove six screws attaching filler neck seal retainer to deck and remove retainer. Remove seal (G501-03-82803) from around filler neck.

(f) Remove nuts and washers from bolts which attach front and rear anchor brackets, and rear surf board support bracket to rear deck. Remove assemblies.

(g) Remove two nuts and lock washers from tire hold-down eyes and remove eyes.

(h) Remove self-tapping screws in deck at rear lifting eye.

(i) Remove self-tapping screws which attach deck to hull and supports.

(j) Lift deck plate straight up to clear fuel tank filler neck, and remove from vehicle.

Hull, Surf Boards, Hatches, and Windshield

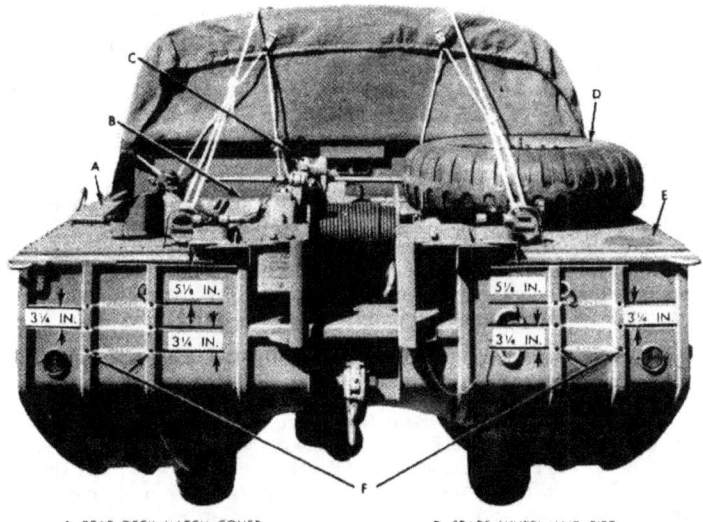

A REAR DECK HATCH COVER
B REAR DECK FRONT PANEL
C ANCHOR
D SPARE WHEEL AND TIRE
E REAR DECK REAR PANEL
F LOAD GUIDE MARKING HOLES

*Figure 203—Rear View of Vehicle
(After Chassis Serial No. 2005)*

(2) INSTALLATION (FIG. 203).

(a) Spread caulking compound (52-C-3086-200) on hull rails and deck supports. Also spread compound around plate on lifting eye.

(b) Lower rear deck front plate into position, being careful to avoid damage to fuel tank filler neck.

(c) Fill seams and joints between deck plates and between deck plates and hull with caulking compound (52-C-3086-200).

(d) Install all attaching self-tapping screws to deck plate and at lifting eye.

(e) Install spare tire hold-down eyes, coating well with caulking compound (52-C-3086-200).

(f) Install anchor brackets and rear surf board support bracket to deck plate, applying caulking compound (52-C-3086-200) to mounting bolts.

(g) Install seal to fuel tank filler neck, and position retainer, installing six retainer screws. When retainer with sheared flat is used on vehicles with fuel tank mounted on right-hand side, flat may be placed in any position.

(h) Install retainer, chain, and fuel tank cap.

(i) Install anchor in brackets, then position and securely clamp spare tire in place.

Maintenance Instructions

(j) Install hatch cover as described in paragraph 228c.

e. Load Guide Markings (fig. 203). Rubbing action of rope fenders in water operation necessitates frequent renewal of load guide markings. To facilitate renewal of markings, drill locating holes (fig. 203) on vehicles prior to chassis serial No. 4899. Drill a $3/16$-inch diameter hole through each end of each marking into rub rails (not into hull) as shown in figure 203.

f. Reflectors. Eight reflectors are installed on sides and rear of vehicle. Amber reflector (G085-33-01836) is mounted on sides at front and amidships, while red reflector (G085-33-01835) is mounted on rear and on sides at rear. Each reflector is attached to hull with two self-tapping screws and lock washers. When installing reflector, coat back of reflector with caulking compound (52-C-3086-200).

g. Rear View Mirror. Mirror head (G501-02-11420) is attached to mirror arm by means of a nut and washer.

h. Air Intake Center Grille Reinforcement. Visually inspect center grille for reinforcement which extends from front to rear of grille, $11 3/8$ inches from right-hand end. All vehicles not so equipped should have grille reinforced. Make reinforcement from $3/16$-inch by 1-inch strip steel or hand iron, $16 1/2$ inches long. Position reinforcement $11 3/8$ inches from right-hand end of grille, then weld reinforcement to grille frame. Using shielded arc, weld both sides of each end of reinforcement to grille frame with a $1/8$-inch fillet, 1 inch long. Remove welding slag and burned paint, then clean and paint (par. 238) to prevent corrosion.

230. HULL BULKHEADS.

a. General. Three bulkheads are used, serving to divide hull into functional sections, as well as to reinforce hull structure. These bulkheads are: bow bulkhead, between front and engine compartments; front cargo bulkhead, serving as front wall of cargo compartment; and rear cargo bulkhead, between cargo and rear compartments. Front cargo bulkhead is the only bulkhead necessary to remove for access to units in the hull.

b. Front Cargo Bulkhead.

(1) REMOVAL. Remove cargo compartment front floor boards, then remove air intake grilles. Remove nuts, washers, and bolts which attach floor support angles to bulkhead. Remove nuts, washers, and bolts which attach bulkhead to gun mount left rear bracket. Remove nuts, washers, and bolts which attach bulkhead to surf coaming and retaining plate at each end of bulkhead. Lift bulkhead straight up to remove from vehicle.

(2) INSTALLATION. Position bulkhead in vehicle. Install bolts, washers, and nuts attaching bulkhead to retaining plate and surf coaming at each side of vehicle, leaving nuts loose. Install all bolts with bolt heads in cargo compartment to avoid snagging cargo. Install bolts, washers, and nuts attaching bulkhead to gun mount left rear bracket, leaving

TM 9-802
230-231

Hull, Surf Boards, Hatches, and Windshield

nuts loose. Install bolts, washers, and nuts attaching floor support angles to bulkhead. Tighten all bulkhead attaching bolts and nuts firmly. Install air intake grilles and cargo compartment front floor boards.

231. PINTLE HOOK AND TOWING SHACKLES.

a. General. Pintle hook is mounted at rear of vehicle below winch. Pintle hook must be properly lubricated (Lubrication Order No. 9-802) to insure proper operation, and to prevent corrosion and seizing of parts. Pintle hook attaching parts are accessible inside rear compartment. Removal and installation of pintle hook necessitates an assistant outside vehicle to prevent hook turning.

b. Pintle Hook.

(1) REMOVAL (FIG. 204). Remove six cap screws which attach pintle hook end cap to pintle box, then remove end cap and gasket. Remove cotter pin, nut, and washer from pintle hook. Remove retainer, gasket, sleeve, spring, and sleeve. Pull pintle hook straight back to remove from vehicle.

(2) INSTALLATION (FIG. 204). Coat all parts, except outer part of pintle hook, with medium lubricating preservative oil, using sufficient oil to thoroughly coat parts. Insert pintle hook through hull from rear of

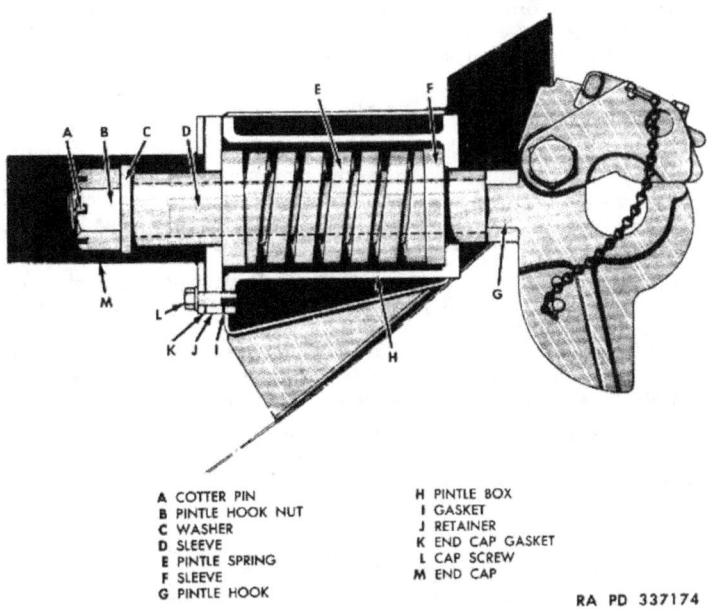

A COTTER PIN
B PINTLE HOOK NUT
C WASHER
D SLEEVE
E PINTLE SPRING
F SLEEVE
G PINTLE HOOK
H PINTLE BOX
I GASKET
J RETAINER
K END CAP GASKET
L CAP SCREW
M END CAP

RA PD 337174

Figure 204—Pintle Hook

423

TM 9-802
231-233

Maintenance Instructions

Vehicle. Install sleeve, spring, and sleeve on pintle shaft. Do not reverse sleeves; positioning must be as shown in figure 204. Install gasket and retainer, then install washer and nut on pintle hook. Tighten nut sufficiently to slightly compress spring, then install cotter pin. Partly fill end cap with medium lubricating preservative oil, then install gasket and cap. Install six cap screws and lock washers, tightening screws firmly. Pintle hook must have no end play, yet must be loose enough to turn by hand. Remove cap and adjust nut if necessary.

(3) PINTLE HOOK POSITIONING. To prevent damage to landing craft ramps and injury to personnel, anchor pintle hook in horizontal position with ropes tied to winch supports. Permanent modification of pintle can be made to obviate necessity for horizontally positioning pintle. With cutting torch, cut off projecting lug on under side of pintle on same radius as the existing rib.

c. Tow Hook Shackles. Three tow hook shackles (G501-03-84510) are attached to bow bottom by means of pins and cotter pins on vehicles prior to chassis serial No. 4167. Due to possibility of shearing cotter pins and spreading shackles when pulling sideways, replacement of pins with bolts and nuts as on late vehicles is recommended. Use one each of bolt (G501-70-01951), nut (G501-70-01950), and cotter pin (H101-137233) for each shackle. Keep pins or bolts properly lubricated to prevent corrosion. If bolts and nuts are not available, remove cotter pins, and weld original washers to each end of shackle pin. Use shielded arc and weld a 1/8-inch fillet around entire circumference of pin, allowing slight clearance between washer and shackle.

232. BILGE PUMP HEATING SYSTEM.

a. General. Heat from engine air exhaust is used to prevent freezing of bilge pumps and manifold in low temperatures. Heat is controlled by a lever, at left of driver, which opens and closes the air recirculation door in left-hand air exhaust duct. Three hoses conduct heated air from bottom of left-hand air exhaust duct to bilge pumps and manifold.

b. Hose Removal. Remove cargo compartment left front floor board and enter bilge. Remove hose clamps attaching hose to hot air tube, and at other end of tube, if used. Remove clamps attaching hose to hull, if used, then remove hose from vehicle. All hoses are removed in same manner, including forward bilge pump and manifold hoses (G501-02-17825) used prior to chassis serial No. 4202.

c. Hose Installation. Position hose in vehicle and attach to hot air tube with hose clamp. Install hose clamp at exhaust end of tube, if used. Install clamps attaching hose to hull, if used. Install cargo compartment left front floor board.

233. WINDSHIELD (EARLY TYPE).

a. General. Windshield used prior to chassis serial No. 2006, consists of windshield frame and glass, hinged at top to tubing frame. Tub-

Hull, Surf Boards, Hatches, and Windshield

- A TUBING FRAME
- B FRAME AND GLASS
- C ADJUSTING ARM SCREW
- D ADJUSTING ARM CLAMP KNOB
- E ADJUSTING ARM
- F SECTOR PIVOT SCREW
- G END PIN LOCK SCREW
- H SECTOR
- I END PIN

RA PD 337168

Figure 205—Windshield Assembly (Early Type)

ing frame is hinged at bottom to windshield lower panel by means of end pins.

b. Frame and Glass. Frame and glass can be removed without removing tubing frame from vehicle.

(1) REMOVAL (FIGS. 205 AND 206). Disconnect hose from windshield wiper motor. Open windshield, remove two screws which attach adjusting arms to brackets on windshield frame, and disengage arms from brackets. Using screwdriver, pry open one end of hinge strip at upper corner of windshield. Swing windshield to horizontal position, then slide windshield frame endwise sufficiently to completely disengage interlocking hinge strips.

(2) INSTALLATION (FIGS. 205 AND 206). Hold windshield frame horizontally, engage end of hinge strip with strip on tubing frame, then slide frame into position. Bend end of hinge strip closed to lock windshield in lateral position. Engage adjusting arms with brackets on windshield frame, then install connecting screws, tightening screws firmly. Connect hose to windshield wiper motor.

c. Windshield Assembly (fig. 206). Complete windshield can be removed as an assembly.

(1) REMOVAL. Remove driver's compartment doors, then remove driver's compartment top cover. Disconnect windshield wiper hose at

TM 9-802
233-234

Maintenance Instructions

RA PD 303236

Figure 206—Windshield Frame and Glass Removal

windshield bottom. Remove two cap screws and washers which lock end pins in place. Screw a long 1/4-20 cap screw into threaded hole in end of each end pin, then pull on cap screws to remove end pins. Use end pin locking cap screws if longer cap screws are not available. Support windshield, then remove sector pivot screws from tubing frame brackets. Disengage sectors from brackets, then remove windshield assembly from vehicle.

(2) INSTALLATION. Inspect condition of frame bottom weatherstrip and replace if necessary. Position windshield assembly on vehicle, then install two end pins, alining holes in windshield lower tube with lock screw holes in pins. Install cap screws and washers to lock end pins in place. Engage sectors with windshield brackets, then install and tighten sector pivot screws. Connect windshield wiper hose at windshield bottom.

234. WINDSHIELD (LATE TYPE).

a. General. Windshield used after chassis serial No. 2006 is composed of three sections, each of heavy glass in metal frames. Center section is hinged at bottom to lower windshield extension. Triangular-shaped wings are hinged to center section, serving as supports as well as side windows.

(1) REMOVAL (FIG. 207). Remove driver's compartment cover. Disconnect windshield wiper hose from tube at lower center of windshield. Remove 13 screws and lock washers which attach windshield to lower windshield extension. Loosen windshield wing clamp knob on each wing, then fold wings into windshield while tilting windshield forward. Remove windshield assembly from vehicle.

Hull, Surf Boards, Hatches, and Windshield

RAISED POSITION

LOWERED POSITION

A HOLD-DOWN CATCH
B WINDSHIELD HINGE
C WINE SHIELD GLASS
D WING GLASS
E CLAMP KNOB

F LOWER WINDSHIELD EXTENSION
G WIPER HOSE
H WING LATCH
I WIPER MOTOR

RA PD 337154

Figure 207—Windshield Assembly (Late Type)

(2) INSTALLATION (FIG. 207). Inspect condition of windshield to lower extension felt. Replace felt if necessary, applying rubber cement (52-C-1452) and pressing into place. Position windshield on vehicle with wings opened. Install 13 screws and lock washers attaching windshield hinge to lower windshield extension. Connect windshield wiper hose to tube at lower center of windshield.

235. WINDSHIELD WIPERS.

a. General. Each vehicle is equipped with two windshield wipers. One vacuum-operated wiper and one hand-operated wiper are used on vehicles prior to chassis serial No. 2006. After chassis serial No. 2005, vehicles are equipped with two air-operated windshield wipers. Inspect

Maintenance Instructions

hoses and connections if windshield wiper motors fail to operate properly. Use a soap and water solution on air lines to detect leaks. Lubricate motor shaft at windshield frame sparingly with engine oil if any binding is evident. Replace blades when blades fail to wipe windshield properly.

b. Windshield Wiper Blade. Removal and installation of blades is same for both vacuum windshield wiper and air-operated wiper blades.

(1) REMOVAL. Pull wiper arm away from windshield with one hand. With other hand, swing lower end of blade outward and upward toward nut on motor shaft until metal back of blade contacts arm. Pull blade straight away from motor shaft to remove air wiper blade (H017-500811), or vacuum wiper blade (G501-01-22200) from vehicle.

(2) INSTALLATION. With hook on blade pointing to motor shaft, and with metal part of blade in contact with forward side of arm, engage hook by pushing blade toward shaft. Hold lower end of arm away from windshield with one hand; with the other hand, swing blade end near motor outward and downward into position.

c. Hand-operated Wiper.

(1) REMOVAL. Remove nut and washer from wiper shaft at rear of windshield, then remove handle. Pull wiper arm and blade free from front of windshield to remove from vehicle.

(2) INSTALLATION. Insert shaft on wiper arm through windshield frame from front side. Position wiper handle on end of shaft from rear side of windshield and attach with washer and nut.

d. Vacuum-operated Motor.

(1) REMOVAL. Pull connection hose from windshield wiper motor. Remove blade as described in subparagraph **b.** above. Unscrew nut from wiper arm, then remove arm. Remove two screws and washers which attach wiper motor to windshield frame. Pull motor from rear of windshield and remove from vehicle. Examine the three connection hoses (G501-02-17819) and replace if necessary.

(2) INSTALLATION. Insert motor shaft through windshield frame from rear of windshield. Attach motor to windshield with two screws and lock washers. Position wiper arm on motor shaft and install attaching nut. Install wiper blade as described in subparagraph **b.** above. Connect hose to wiper motor.

e. Air-operated Motor.

(1) REMOVAL. Unscrew tubing nut and disconnect tube from wiper motor. Remove wiper blade as described in subparagraph **b.** above. Unscrew nut from wiper shaft, then remove wiper arm (G508-7000650). Remove two screws which attach motor to windshield frame. Pull motor (G501-02-95850) free from rear of windshield to remove from vehicle. Inspect windshield wiper lower to upper tube hose (G501-70-02151) and replace if necessary.

(2) INSTALLATION. Insert motor shaft through windshield frame from rear of windshield, and install two attaching screws and lock washers. Position wiper arm on motor shaft and install attaching nut. Install wiper blade as described in subparagraph *b.* above. Position tube to wiper motor, then connect to motor with tubing nut.

236. SEATS.

a. General. Separate driver's and co-pilot's seats are mounted on seat bases which are an integral part of driver's compartment. Driver's seat is adjustable by lifting rear edge of seat and moving forward or back as desired. Co-pilot's seat is not adjustable; however, both seat back and seat bottom are hinged. Seat bottom may be raised to permit gunner to stand on floor, or seat back may be folded down on seat bottom to provide a raised platform for gunner. Cushions from both seats can be used as life preservers.

b. Seat Cushions. Seat cushion removal and installation operations are same for both seats.

(1) REMOVAL. Pull bottom of seat back cushion forward, then slide cushion to side to disengage bead on back cushion flap from metal channel in seat back. Remove seat back cushion. Remove seat cushion by lifting out of seat bottom.

(2) INSTALLATION. Position end of flap bead in seat back cushion in end of metal channel in seat back frame. Slide cushion sideways into place. Lay seat cushion in seat bottom frame.

c. Seat Frames.

(1) DRIVER'S SEAT REMOVAL. Remove seat cushion, then remove hole cover. Through opening in seat bottom, remove two cap screws which attach and guide seat. Lift seat off seat base and remove from vehicle.

(2) DRIVER'S SEAT INSTALLATION. Position seat on seat base. Install two cap screws and washers attaching seat to base. Lift rear edge of seat and adjust forward and back to make sure seat operates freely. Install hole cover and seat cushion.

(3) CO-PILOT'S SEAT REMOVAL. Raise seat bottom, then remove nut, washer, and bolt which attach sector arm to seat bottom. Remove six nuts and washers which attach seat to base. Remove two nuts, washers, and bolts which attach chains to seat base. Lift seat assembly straight up to remove from vehicle.

(4) CO-PILOT'S SEAT INSTALLATION. Position seat assembly on seat base, then install six attaching washers and nuts. Attach each chain to seat base with bolt, washer, and nut. Attach sector arm to seat bottom with bolt, washer, and nut.

237. TARPAULINS AND BOWS.

a. Tarpaulins, Curtains, and Covers. Keep all straps and lashing ropes properly fastened while tarpaulins, curtains, and covers are installed on vehicle. Do not permit tarpaulins, curtains, and covers to flap in the wind. When tarpaulins, curtains, and covers are to be stowed, fold carefully, and do not crumple. Do not fold or stow tarpaulins, curtains, and covers when wet. Tarpaulins, curtains, and covers can be waterproofed as described in paragraph 238*d*.

b. Tarpaulin Bows. Stow only steel bows in front compartment. Wood bows (on early vehicles) must not be stowed in front compartment due to fire hazard through contact with exhaust system. Keep bows free from corrosion, and paint when necessary, as described in paragraph 238.

238. CLEANING, PAINTING, AND WATERPROOFING.

a. General. Corrosion occurs very readily in salt water operation; therefore, more attention must be given to corrosion prevention than under other operating conditions. Metal parts such as hull, bilge pump tubes (exterior surfaces), large mesh bilge screens, suspension springs, brake hose support springs, wheels, axle housings, transmission cases, etc., must be properly treated as outlined in this paragraph. Following general rules apply to cleaning and painting operations:

(1) Do not apply multiple coats of paint without removing old paint. Painting over old paint and building up numerous coatings increases fire hazard and weight.

(2) Surfaces must be clean and free from rust before repainting. Paint will not properly adhere to corroded, greasy, dirty surfaces, or old loose paint. Steam clean if equipment is available. CAUTION: *Do not steam clean forward propeller and winch drive shaft bearings.*

(3) Two normal coats of enamel or primer applied evenly and permitted to dry thoroughly between coats is preferred to a single thick coat.

b. Cleaning. Remove corrosion, using wire brush, flint paper, or steel wool. Mix one part of metal conditioner phosphoric acid (51-A-1303) or (51-A-1302) to two parts of water, wire brush solution on surface, and allow to soak. While wet, loosen all foreign matter with wire brush or steel wool, then immediately wipe surface clean with cloth. CAUTION: *Do not remove white film that forms upon drying.* Remove all excess acid in cracks with alcohol, water, or dry-cleaning solvent. If metal conditioner acid is not available, use dry-cleaning solvent or synthetic enamel thinner undiluted to clean surfaces after rust has been removed. Allow cleaned surfaces to dry thoroughly before applying primer.

c. Painting. Apply three coats of primer evenly by spraying or brushing, allowing 2 to 8 hours drying time between coats, depending upon atmospheric conditions. Primers in order of preference are: lead chromate primer (ES-359b), zinc chromate primer (52-P-20624), and rust inhibitive synthetic primer (41-P-20467). Apply one or two normal coats of lustreless synthetic olive drab enamel (52-E-4171-15) or other material as required, such as white enamel (52-E-6022-240) inside com-

Forward Bilge Pump System (Oberdorfer Type) (Prior to Chassis Serial No. 4202)

partments and red glyptal paint (52-P-8057-710) under battery. To outer surfaces of hull decks only, apply one coat of non-skid, olive drab, lustreless enamel (52-E-5750) over primer. Use spray gun or brush, applying material to a minimum of $1/32$ inch thick. CAUTION: *Do not apply non-skid enamel inside of hull.*

d. Waterproofing.

(1) CLEANING. Waterproofing compound may be applied to all duck and canvas used on vehicle, such as tarpaulin, cover, curtains, etc. Canvas and duck must be thoroughly clean. Stretch canvas taut, suspended with seams vertical. Remove mud and dirt with a clean dry brush, scrubbing with brush and clear water, if necessary. Mildew is best removed with dry brush. Water must not be used until mildew has been removed. Remove oil and grease by scrubbing with soap and water, then rinsing with clean water. *Do not use gasoline or dry-cleaning solvent to remove oil or grease.* Allow canvas to dry thoroughly before applying compound.

(2) APPLICATION. NOTE: *Waterproofing compound (51-C-1580) is inflammable.* Avoid proximity of open flame during application and until compound has dried thoroughly. Use respirator when spraying, and protect hands with cotton gloves or protective cream. Stir compound thoroughly, then treat only one side of canvas—the weather or outer side. Using a closely confined spray, apply in quick, horizontal strokes, one panel at a time. Work from top to bottom, applying a sufficient quantity to keep a moderate flow running down the surface. Remove stop marks by brushing before compound is dry. Compound can also be applied by brushing, using a 4-inch flat paint brush. Keep brush full, applying in vertical strokes from top to bottom, one panel at a time. Make sure compound is worked well into seams, particularly when using brush. Allow at least 24 hours drying time before using treated canvas.

e. Life Preservers. Canvas or cloth cover material on life preservers can be treated as described in subparagraph **d.** above, or can be coated with fire, water, and weather resistant preservative compound [Navy Spec. 52 C26 (INT)].

Section XLI

Forward Bilge Pump System (Oberdorfer Type)

(Prior to Chassis Serial No. 4202)

239. GENERAL.

a. Description. The Oberdorfer type forward bilge pump system is superseded by the Gould type system after chassis serial No. 4201 (pars. 245 through 249). The Oberdorfer gear type pump, belt driven from a pulley on the water propeller transfer case, draws water from four points in the hull through a system of tubes and strainers (fig. 208). Four manifold valves, operated by rods in floor board at front of driver's seat, control pumping from the various points (par. 36*b*.). For cold weather operation, hot air from engine air exhaust is conveyed to bilge pumps and manifold by a system of hoses. Pump assembly, reservoir, valves, and manifold are accessible by removing cargo compartment left front floor board, then entering bilge. Removal of air intake grilles and driver's compartment floor boards permits maximum accessibility for certain operations.

b. Repair Operations. Repair operations on Oberdorfer forward bilge pump system are described in TM 9-1802C.

240. BILGE PUMP DRIVE.

a. Drive Belt Adjustment (fig. 208). Apply moderate thumb pressure to belt at a point midway between pulleys. If belt deflection is less than $\frac{1}{2}$ inch or more than $\frac{3}{4}$ inch, adjust belt in following manner:

(1) ALINE PULLEYS. Enter right-hand bilge, then visually check pulley alinement by sighting along belt across driving pulleys. Pulleys must be in same plane, and must not be cocked in relation to each other. Driven pulley replacement is described in paragraph 241***c***. Refer to paragraph 255 for removal and installation of driving pulley. Working from left-hand bilge, loosen driven pulley set screws, move pulley toward or away from pump to aline with driving pulley, then tighten set screws firmly.

(2) ADJUST BELT TENSION (FIG. 208). Loosen two adjusting bolt nuts, then slide pump bracket toward or away from driving pulley to obtain proper belt tension. Tighten adjusting bolt nuts firmly while holding pump and bracket in proper position. Again check belt tension and pulley alinement, and readjust if not correct. When new belt is installed, check tension after two hours operation, and again after six hours. Readjust, if necessary, to compensate for stretching of new belt.

b. Drive Belt Removal.

(1) DISCONNECT TIRE PUMP MOUNTING.

(a) Prior to Chassis Serial No. 906. Remove adjusting bolt at front of tire pump support, remove hinge pin from rear end of tire pump support, then move tire pump support forward sufficiently to pass belt between pump support and water propeller transfer case upper support member.

(b) Between Chassis Serial Nos. 905 and 2006. Remove two cap screws and washers which attach tire pump support hinge bracket to water propeller transfer case upper support member (fig. 208). Swing hinge bracket downward to provide clearance before removing belt.

(2) DISCONNECT SHIFTER SHAFTS. Disconnect *single* shifter shaft at water propeller transfer case on vehicles prior to chassis serial No. 2506. Disconnect *two* shifter shafts at water propeller transfer case, on vehicles after chassis serial No. 2505.

TM 9-802
240-241

Forward Bilge Pump System (Oberdorfer Type) (Prior to Chassis Serial No. 4202)

(3) REMOVE DRIVE BELT (ALL VEHICLES). Loosen two bilge pump adjusting bracket bolt nuts (fig. 208), slide pump and bracket toward driving pulley, then remove belt from pulleys.

c. Drive Belt Installation.

(1) INSTALL DRIVE BELT (ALL VEHICLES). Position drive belt on pulleys, then adjust drive belt as described in subparagraph *a*. above.

(2) CONNECT SHIFTER SHAFTS. Connect single shifter shaft at water propeller transfer case on vehicles prior to chassis serial No. 2506. Connect two shifter shafts at water propeller transfer case on vehicles after chassis serial No. 2505.

(3) CONNECT TIRE PUMP MOUNTING.

(a) Prior to Chassis Serial No. 906. Install hinge pin which attaches tire pump support to water propeller transfer case upper support member. Install adjusting bolt at front of tire pump support. Adjust tire pump drive chain as described in paragraph 260.

(b) Between Chassis Serial Nos. 905 and 2006. Install two cap screws and washers which attach tire pump support hinge bracket to water propeller transfer case upper member (fig. 208).

241. BILGE PUMP ASSEMBLY.

a. Accessibility. Remove cargo compartment left front floor board, then enter bilge for access to pump assembly.

b. Packing Adjustment (fig. 208). Whenever leakage is evident, adjust pump packing. NOTE: *A small amount of leakage (or seepage) is necessary to prevent overheating and scoring shaft.* After loosening lock nut a few turns with a suitable wrench, tighten packing nut until leakage is reduced, but not entirely stopped. Tighten lock nut against packing nut firmly. Examine pump for leakage after a short period of use. Adjustment is correct if leakage has not increased.

c. Packing Replacement (fig. 208). When leakage cannot be reduced by tightening packing nut, repack pump. Pump may be packed while mounted in vehicle; however, operation is considerably facilitated by removing pump from vehicle (subpars. *d.* and *e.* below).

(1) REMOVAL. Using suitable wrench, loosen two pulley set screws. With a suitable puller, remove pulley and key from shaft. Loosen packing nut lock nut, then remove packing nut and packing gland from pump. Remove old packing (G508-7000791) with a suitable pick or wire.

(2) INSTALLATION. Wind new packing around pump shaft, pressing it into packing recess, then install packing gland and packing nut. Make sure pulley fits freely on shaft, then install key and pulley, tightening pulley set screws only slightly.

(3) ADJUSTMENT. Tighten packing nut while rotating pump shaft by hand until a slight drag is felt on shaft. Tighten lock nut firmly against packing nut. For final adjustment in vehicle, refer to subparagraph *b.* above.

Maintenance Instructions

PRIOR TO CHASSIS SERIAL NO. 2006

BETWEEN CHASSIS SERIAL NOS. 2005 AND 4202

A PACKING NUT LOCK NUT
B PACKING NUT
C DRIVEN PULLEY
D DRIVE BELT (G501-01-18254)
E TIRE PUMP SUPPORT
F DRIVE PULLEY
G WATER PROPELLER TRANSFER CASE
H HINGE BRACKET CAP SCREWS
I TIRE PUMP HINGE BRACKET
J ADJUSTING BRACKET BOLTS
K ADJUSTING BRACKET
L PUMP MOUNTING BOLTS
M PUMP ASSEMBLY (G501-03-45878)
N INLET NIPPLE

RA PD 337214

Figure 208—Bilge Pump and Drive (Oberdorfer Type)

Forward Bilge Pump System (Oberdorfer Type) (Prior to Chassis Serial No. 4202)

d. Bilge Pump Assembly Removal (fig. 208). Loosen four hose clamp bolts above and below pump, then disconnect outlet and inlet hoses from pump. Slide pump toward driving pulley after loosening two adjusting bracket bolts. Remove two nuts, washers, and bolts mounting pump to adjusting bracket, then remove pump.

e. Bilge Pump Assembly Installation (fig. 208). Attach pump to adjusting bracket with two bolts, washers, and nuts. Sight across pulleys to make sure pump driven pulley is in vertical alinement with driving pulley, then tighten nuts firmly. Attach inlet and outlet hoses to pump, tightening hose clamp bolts firmly. After moving pulley on pump shaft to aline with driving pulley, tighten pulley set screws firmly. Position belt on pump pulley, then adjust belt as described in paragraph 240*a*.

242. CONTROL VALVES AND MANIFOLD.

a. General. Four bilge pump valves and a drain cock are attached to bilge pump manifold which is mounted in bilge below driver's floor board. Maximum accessibility to valves and manifold is obtained by removal of driver's floor board, left-hand air intake grille, and cargo compartment left front floor board.

b. Bilge Pump Valves (fig. 209). Adjustment, removal, cleaning, and installation operations are same for all valves.

(1) ADJUSTMENT. Adjust valve whenever valve fails to remain open when placed in open position. Adjustment is made by tightening valve packing gland sufficiently to overcome tendency of valve to close under the weight of control rod and due to action of pump.

(2) REMOVAL. Before removing valve, study positioning of valve so that valve can be installed in same position. Disconnect valve control lever by removing cotter pin and washer from control rod. Loosen two hose clamp bolts, then disconnect hose from valve nipple. Using suitable wrench, unscrew from manifold. Remove valve and nipples as an assembly from vehicle.

(3) DISASSEMBLY. Remove valve cap and gasket after removing two cap screws. Examine valve disks and seats for scoring, to determine necessity of further disassembly for cleaning. If necessary to further disassemble valve, proceed as follows:

(a) Remove Lever. Position valve in soft-jaw vise. Drive out lever retaining pin with small punch, then tap lever lightly to remove from stem.

(b) Remove Stem and Disks. Unscrew packing gland. Remove packing with a suitable pick. Pull stem out of valve body, then invert body to permit disks to drop out.

(c) Clean Valve. If oil or grease is present, wash all valve parts, except packing and gasket, in dry-cleaning solvent. Wire-brush parts to remove scale and sediment.

(4) ASSEMBLY. Install disks in valve body, making sure disks seat properly. Position stem and washer in body, then install packing (new,

Maintenance Instructions

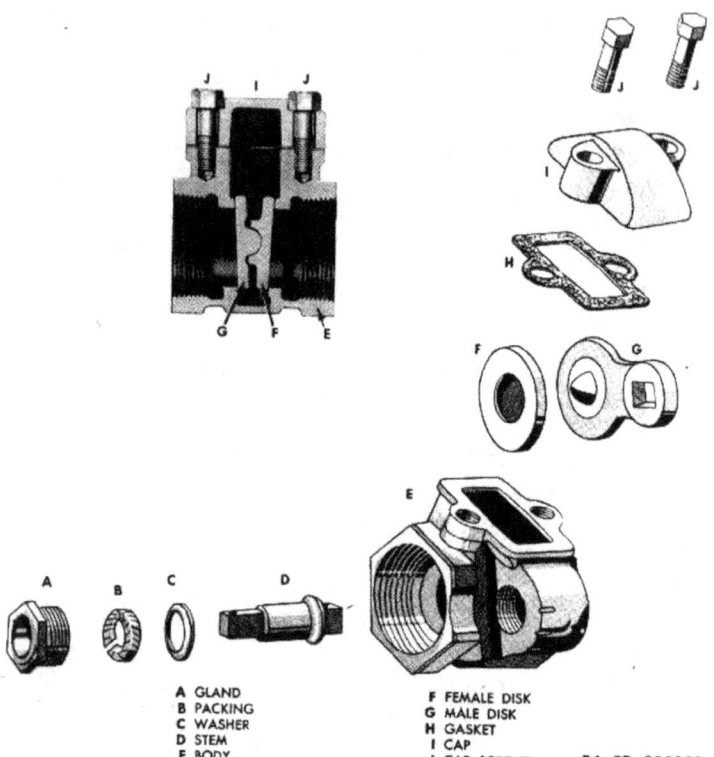

A GLAND
B PACKING
C WASHER
D STEM
E BODY
F FEMALE DISK
G MALE DISK
H GASKET
I CAP
J CAP SCREWS

RA PD 333200

Figure 209—Disassembled and Sectional Views of Valve

if available) around stem. Install packing gland on stem, and screw into valve body. Install lever on stem, install retaining pin in stem, and bend pin slightly at each end to hold in place. Tighten packing gland until packing is tight enough to hold up weight of lever. Position gasket (new, if available) on valve body, and install cap, tightening cap screws firmly.

(5) INSTALLATION. Coat pipe threads with white lead pigment (52-P-19990). Screw valve to manifold in proper position with a suitable wrench. Connect valve control rod to valve lever, install washer, then secure with cotter pin. Make sure valve can be fully opened and closed by rod, and that valve lever does not closely approach "dead-center" in either extreme position. With wrench, turn valve as necessary to insure proper valve operation. With valve correctly installed, control rod handle will be level with other handles. Connect hose to valve nipple, tightening hose clamp bolts firmly.

TM 9-802

Forward Bilge Pump System (Oberdorfer Type) (Prior to Chassis Serial No. 4202)

c. Drain Cock.

(1) REMOVAL. Remove cotter pin and washer from drain cock control rod. After disconnecting rod from drain cock lever, unscrew cock from manifold.

(2) DISASSEMBLY. Remove cotter pin, washer, spring, and notched washer from stem, then remove stem from body. Examine stem and seat carefully for scale, corrosion, and scoring. Badly scored parts necessitate replacement of drain cock. Thoroughly clean parts, using dry-cleaning solvent if parts are oily or greasy.

(3) ASSEMBLY. Apply a thin coat of petrolatum or water pump grease to stem, then install in body. Install notched washer, spring, and plain washer in stem. Compress spring sufficiently to install cotter pin in stem.

(4) INSTALLATION. Coat pipe threads with white lead pigment (52-P-19990). Screw drain cock into manifold, tightening firmly into proper position. Connect control rod to drain cock and secure with washer and cotter pin.

d. Bilge Pump Manifold.

(1) REMOVAL. Remove cotter pin from lower ends of drain cock control rod and four valve control rods, then disconnect and remove rods. Loosen hose clamp bolts and disconnect five hoses from valve nipples. Remove two pump manifold mounting nuts, washers, and bolts. Remove manifold and valves as an assembly from vehicle.

(2) DISASSEMBLY. Unscrew valves, nipples, and drain cock from manifold. Clean manifold thoroughly, removing all rust and scale. Examine manifold carefully for cracks, breaks, and damage to threads.

(3) ASSEMBLY. Coat pipe threads with white lead pigment (52-P-19990) and install nipples, valves, and drain cock in manifold, tightening firmly into position.

(4) INSTALLATION. Position manifold and valves, as an assembly, in vehicle, then mount manifold with two bolts, washers, and nuts. Attach five hose connections to valve and manifold nipples, tightening hose clamp bolts firmly. Connect drain cock control rod and four valve control rods to valve levers, install washers, then secure with cotter pins.

243. STRAINERS AND SCREENS.

a. General. Cup type intake strainers are located in engine compartment, left rear compartment, and right rear compartment. Basket type strainer is located amidships in hull. Cup type strainer is now used for replacement of basket type. A system of pipes connects strainers to valves and manifold (fig. 210). Two cylindrical strainers, enclosed in a watertight box located under and accessible at rear of driver's seat, are interposed in system between reservoir and forward bilge pump (figs. 210 and 211). Discharge line leads from pump to discharge outlet in side coaming at driver's left. Pump is primed through a bleeder line connecting to bleeder strainer in left side of hull below water line.

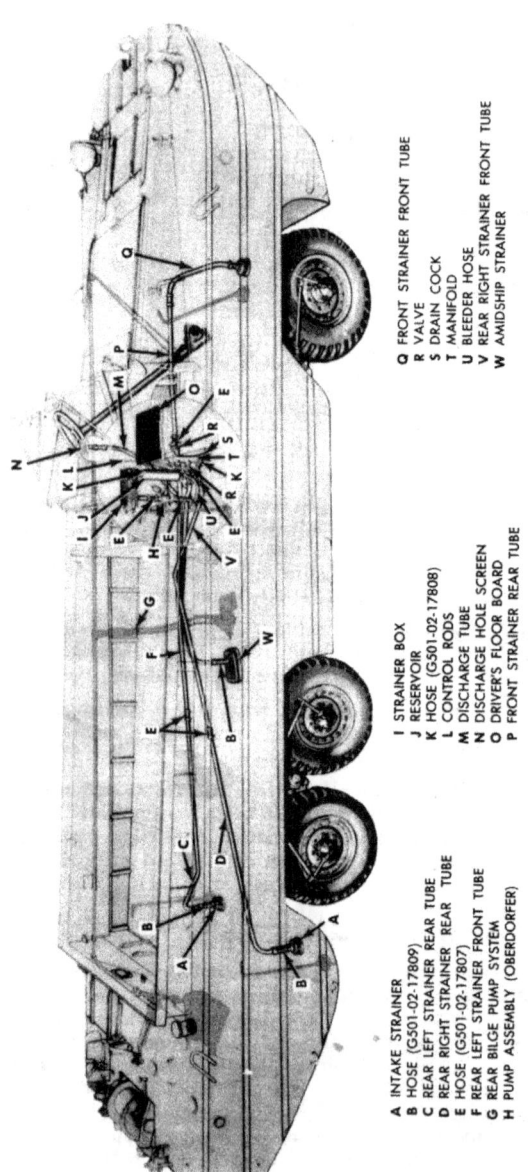

A INTAKE STRAINER
B HOSE (G501-02-17809)
C REAR LEFT STRAINER REAR TUBE
D REAR RIGHT STRAINER REAR TUBE
E HOSE (G501-02-17807)
F REAR LEFT STRAINER FRONT TUBE
G REAR BILGE PUMP SYSTEM
H PUMP ASSEMBLY (OBERDORFER)
I STRAINER BOX
J RESERVOIR
K HOSE (G501-02-17808)
L CONTROL RODS
M DISCHARGE TUBE
N DISCHARGE HOLE SCREEN
O DRIVER'S FLOOR BOARD
P FRONT STRAINER REAR TUBE
Q FRONT STRAINER FRONT TUBE
R VALVE
S DRAIN COCK
T MANIFOLD
U BLEEDER HOSE
V REAR RIGHT STRAINER FRONT TUBE
W AMIDSHIP STRAINER

RA PD 337272

Figure 210—Forward Bilge Pump System (Oberdorfer Type)

TM 9-802
243

Forward Bilge Pump System (Oberdorfer Type) (Prior to Chassis Serial No. 4202)

b. Strainers—In Hull (fig. 210).

(1) REMOVAL. Loosen hose clamp bolt at strainer, disconnect strainer from hose, then remove strainer from vehicle. Engine compartment strainer is more easily removed by disconnecting front tube from rear tube at hose connection, then removing front tube and strainer as an assembly from the vehicle. Front strainer can then be disconnected from front tube at hose connection.

(2) CLEANING AND PAINTING. Wash strainer thoroughly, using dry-cleaning solvent if strainer is greasy or oily. Wipe strainer dry, then examine carefully for clogging, rust spots, chipped paint, or other evidences of corrosion, to determine necessity for replacing or painting strainer. Clean and paint strainer as described in paragraph 238.

(3) INSTALLATION. Connect strainer to hose, tightening hose clamp bolt firmly. Early type strainers must be positioned 2 inches above hull bottom with spacers, if necessary. Late type strainers are supported by spacers which should rest on hull bottom. Connect engine compartment strainer to hose attached to front tube, tightening hose clamp bolt firmly. Position assembly of strainer and front tube in vehicle, then attach front tube to rear tube hose connection.

c. Strainer and Box Assembly (figs. 210 and 211).

(1) STRAINER REMOVAL. At back of driver's seat, loosen wing nut and latch screw, then swing cover aside. Remove strainers by pulling on ring in strainer.

(2) STRAINER CLEANING. Wash strainers thoroughly in clean fresh water. Use dry-cleaning solvent if greasy or oily. If screens are clogged,

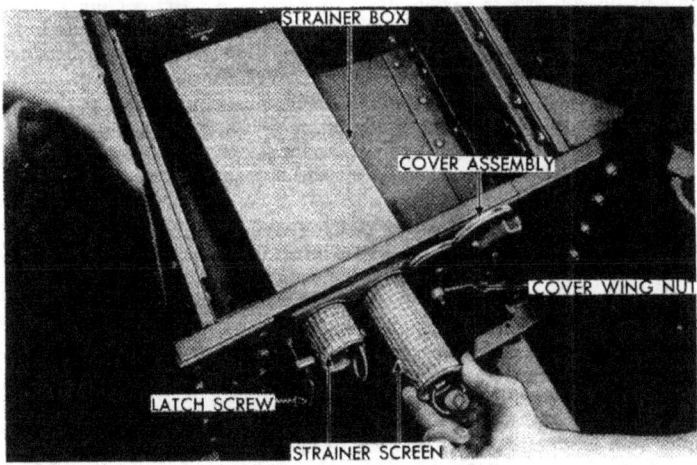

RA PD 303238

Figure 211—Removing Strainers from Strainer Box

Maintenance Instructions

use compressed air, or scrub with damp, firm sand, usually found near water's edge. Replace strainers if impossible to clean.

(3) STRAINER INSTALLATION. Examine leather gaskets (early type) on strainer caps. Cement gaskets to caps if necessary and work a small amount of chassis grease into each gasket to keep leather from hardening and to insure a good seal. Late type gasket of synthetic rubber is now supplied as replacement for leather gasket. Rubber gasket is not cemented, being designed to fit around cap. Keep grease away from rubber gasket. Position strainers in box, making sure strainer caps center properly over openings. Tighten cover wing nut and latch screw firmly.

(4) STRAINER BOX REMOVAL. Remove driver's seat as described in paragraph 236. Disconnect inlet and outlet hose connections underneath box inside base of driver's seat. Remove two mounting nuts, washers, and bolts, then lift front of box to remove from seat base.

(5) STRAINER BOX CLEANING AND PAINTING. Remove and clean strainers as described in steps (1) and (2) above. Wash strainer box thoroughly, using dry-cleaning solvent if box is greasy or oily. Remove all rust and corrosion with wire brush, flint paper, or steel wool. Paint as described in paragraph 238.

(6) STRAINER BOX INSTALLATION. Position strainer box in seat base; then install two mounting bolts, washers, and nuts, tightening nuts firmly. Connect inlet and outlet hoses to box, tightening hose clamp bolts firmly. Install driver's seat as described in paragraph 236.

d. Bleeder Line Strainer.

(1) REMOVAL. Disconnect bleeder hose from strainer in left side of hull by loosening hose clamp, and pulling hose off strainer inner half. Remove six nuts, washers, and bolts from strainer. Strainer inner half, inner screen, outer screen, and gasket, can then be removed. Strainer outer body, being welded to hull, is not removable.

(2) CLEANING AND PAINTING. Clean screens thoroughly, using dry-cleaning solvent to remove any oil or grease. Examine screens carefully and replace screens if badly corroded. Remove all rust and corrosion from strainer halves. Paint halves and large-mesh screen as described in paragraph 238.

(3) INSTALLATION. Position gasket (new, if available) to flange of strainer body; position screens and strainer inner half to body; install six bolts, nuts, and washers. Tighten nuts evenly and firmly. Connect bleeder hose to strainer, tightening hose clamps firmly.

e. Discharge Hole Screen or Cover.
A hinged-type screen or cover is installed over bilge pump discharge hole in surf coaming at left of driver on vehicles after chassis serial No. 3005. Screen or cover prevents entry of foreign material into discharge lines with possible resultant damage to pump. Screens or covers should be obtained and installed over both front and rear bilge pump outlets on all vehicles not so equipped. Cover hinge is attached to vertical coaming by means of two screws, washers, and nuts. Hinge must operate freely and must be maintained in that condition.

TM 9-802

Forward Bilge Pump System (Oberdorfer Type) (Prior to Chassis Serial No. 4202)

244. RESERVOIR AND TUBES.

a. Reservoir Removal (fig. 210). Disconnect bleeder hose at bottom of reservoir. Disconnect hoses and remove curved pipe connecting manifold to reservoir. Disconnect reservoir to strainer box hose, then remove reservoir from vehicle. Thoroughly wash reservoir, using drycleaning solvent if greasy or oily. Remove all exterior rust spots by using wire brush, flint paper, or steel wool. Paint as described in subparagraph *c.*(3) following.

b. Reservoir Installation. Position reservoir in vehicle, then connect hose to strainer box and reservoir. Connect curved pipe to manifold and reservoir with hoses. Connect bleeder hose to bottom of reservoir. Tighten all hose clamp bolts firmly.

c. Tubes and Hoses (fig. 210). Bilge pump tubes and hoses are accessible in bilges after removal of cargo compartment floor boards, air intake grilles, and driver's compartment floor boards. One discharge tube hose connection is accessible in left-hand air exhaust duct. Forward intake line is accessible through engine hatch. Discharge and bleeder tubes and hoses are accessible through left-hand bilge. Removal and installation of bilge pump heater hoses are described in paragraph 232.

(1) TUBE AND HOSE REMOVAL. Bilge pump tubes are removed by loosening hose clamps on connecting hoses, disconnecting hoses, then removing U-bolts, clamps, or clips attaching tubes to hull. Examine hoses and discard any that have deteriorated.

(2) TUBE CLEANING. Tap tube lightly with hammer to dislodge scale. With long handled wire brush, remove all rust, sediment, and corrosion from inside of tube. Suspend tube in vertical position over a suitable container, with lower end plugged. Fill tube with a mixture of one part of metal conditioner phosphoric acid (51-A-1302) and two parts of water. Allow mixture to remain in tube for five minutes, then remove plug, allowing mixture to drain into container. Flush tube with water, then wipe dry with a clean cloth.

(3) TUBE PAINTING. Paint exterior of tube as described in paragraph 238. Suspend tube in vertical position over a suitable container to coat interior of tube. Plug lower end of tube with wooden plug, cork, or wadded cloth. Fill tube with coating material, then remove plug, allowing material to drain into container. Material drained from tube can be re-used, but only for coating tubes. Allow coating to dry with tube in vertical position. Allow sufficient time for thorough drying between coats, and after final coat. Various materials may be used, as follows:

(a) Prime Coat. Apply two coats of lead chromate primer (ES-359b), or zinc chromate primer (52-P-20624), or rust inhibitive synthetic primer (41-P-20467).

(b) Finish Coat. Follow with coating of red synthetic paint (glyptal, 52-P-8057-710), or lustreless synthetic olive drab enamel (52-E-4171-15), or any other available enamel.

(c) Optional Coat. If paint is not available, a coating of thin film rust preventive compound (14-C-507) may be applied in place of the above primer and enamel coats.

Maintenance Instructions

(4) TUBE INSTALLATION. Position tubes in vehicle, then install connecting hoses, tightening hose clamp bolts firmly. Make sure all connections are tight, as an intake line leak can materially reduce efficiency of pump, or make pump inoperative.

Section XLII

Forward Bilge Pump System (Gould Type) (After Chassis Serial No. 4201)

245. GENERAL.

a. Description. The Gould type forward bilge pump supersedes the Oberdorfer system (pars. 239 through 244) after chassis serial No. 4201. The Gould centrifugal type pump, chain driven from a sprocket on water propeller transfer case, draws water from three points in the hull through a system of pipes and strainers (fig. 214). Three manifold valves, operated by levers projecting through front of driver's seat base, control pumping from the various compartments (par. 36**b.**). A system of hoses conveys hot air from engine air exhaust to bilge pump, manifold, and valves for cold weather operation.

b. Accessibility. Pump assembly is accessible by removing cargo compartment front floor boards, then entering bilge. Valves and manifold are accessible by removing driver's seat cushion and hole cover. Maximum accessibility for certain operations is obtained by removing air intake grilles and driver's compartment floor boards.

c. Repair Operations. Repair operations on Gould forward bilge pump system are described in TM 9-1802C.

246. BILGE PUMP DRIVE.

a. Drive Chain Adjustment (fig. 212). Apply moderate thumb pressure to chain at a point midway between sprockets. If chain deflection is more or less than $\frac{1}{2}$ inch, adjust chain.

(1) ALINE SPROCKETS. Enter right-hand bilge, then visually check sprocket alinement by sighting along chain sprockets. Sprockets must be in same plane and must not be cocked in relation to each other, nor wobble. Replace defective sprockets. Driven sprocket is removed by loosening set screw, then pulling sprocket and key off shaft. Whenever driven sprocket is removed, or as soon as available, install the new $\frac{5}{8}$-inch brass key in place of the $1\frac{1}{2}$-inch steel key. Brass key prevents damage to pump by shearing when pump jams or freezes. Position key on shaft, install sprocket, and tighten set screw. Paragraph 255**b.** describes the removal and installation of driving sprocket. Loosen driven sprocket set screw, move sprocket toward or away from pump to aline with driving sprocket, then tighten set screw firmly. Sprocket alinement can be

TM 9-802

Forward Bilge Pump System (Gould Type) (After Chassis Serial No. 4201)

- A PUMP INLET
- B PUMP OUTLET
- C FRAME LEFT SIDE RAIL
- D PUMP HANGER BRACKET
- E COTTER PIN
- F SUPPORT PIN
- G ADJUSTING YOKE INNER NUT
- H ADJUSTING YOKE
- I DRIVE CHAIN
- J SPROCKET SET SCREW
- K DRIVEN SPROCKET
- L DRIVE SPROCKET
- M PUMP ASSEMBLY
- N WATER PROPELLER TRANSFER CASE

RA PD 333237

Figure 212—Bilge Pump and Drive (Gould Type)

checked accurately with a straightedge and C-clamps. Straightedge must be at least $5/16$ inch thick, and of proper length to contact full surfaces of sprockets without interference from chain. Clamp straightedge to driven sprocket, then adjust driven sprocket to bring straightedge into full contact with face of driving sprocket.

(2) ADJUST CHAIN TENSION (FIG. 212). Loosen lock nut on adjusting yoke at outside of frame left side rail, then increase or decrease chain tension to proper amount by turning the two adjusting nuts. Tighten both adjusting nuts against frame side rail, then tighten lock nut firmly against outer nut. Again check tension and sprocket alinement, and readjust if not correct.

b. Drive Chain Removal (fig. 212). Loosen lock nut on adjusting yoke, then remove lock nut and outer nut from adjusting yoke. Swing pump toward sprocket sufficiently to disengage drive chain from driven

TM 9-802
246-247

Maintenance Instructions

sprocket. It may be necessary to loosen hose clamp on bleeder hose to permit swinging pump. Disengage chain from driving sprocket and remove from vehicle. Chain may be opened at connecting link, if necessary, as described in paragraph 251*b*. and *c*.

c. **Drive Chain Installation (fig. 212).** Position chain on driving and driven sprockets, then insert adjusting yoke through frame side rail. Install outer adjusting nut on adjusting yoke. Adjust chain tension by means of the two adjusting nuts (subpar. *a*, above). When correct adjustment has been obtained, tighten adjusting nuts against frame side rail, then install and tighten lock nut firmly.

247. BILGE PUMP ASSEMBLY.

a. **Accessibility.** Remove cargo compartment left front floor board, then enter bilge for access to pump assembly.

b. **Packing Adjustment (fig. 213).** Whenever leakage is evident, adjust pump packing. NOTE: *A small amount of leakage (seepage) is necessary to prevent overheating and scoring shaft.* Tighten both gland nuts alternately until leakage is reduced but not entirely stopped. CAUTION: *Nuts must be tightened evenly to avoid cocking gland and scoring shaft.* Check pump for leakage after a short period of use. Adjustment is correct if leakage has not increased.

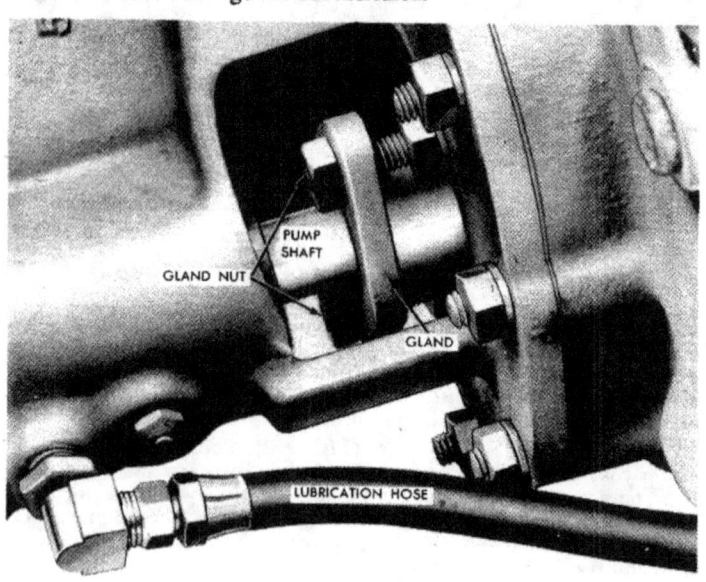

RA PD 337149

Figure 213—Bilge Pump Stuffing Box Gland

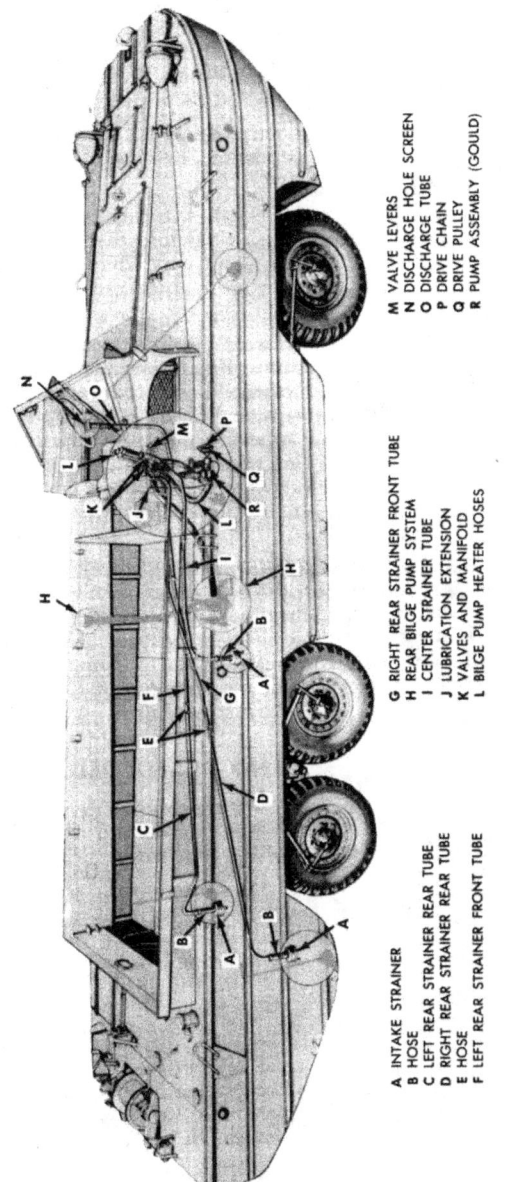

A INTAKE STRAINER
B HOSE
C LEFT REAR STRAINER REAR TUBE
D RIGHT REAR STRAINER REAR TUBE
E HOSE
F LEFT REAR STRAINER FRONT TUBE
G RIGHT REAR STRAINER FRONT TUBE
H REAR BILGE PUMP SYSTEM
I CENTER STRAINER TUBE
J LUBRICATION EXTENSION
K VALVES AND MANIFOLD
L BILGE PUMP HEATER HOSES
M VALVE LEVERS
N DISCHARGE HOLE SCREEN
O DISCHARGE TUBE
P DRIVE CHAIN
Q DRIVE PULLEY
R PUMP ASSEMBLY (GOULD)

RA PD 337273

Figure 214—Forward Bilge Pump System (Gould Type)

TM 9-802
247-248

Maintenance Instructions

c. Packing Replacement (fig. 213). When leakage cannot be reduced by tightening stuffing box gland nuts, repack pump. Repacking operation is facilitated by removal of pump from vehicle, although it is possible to pack pump while mounted in vehicle. Refer to subparagraphs ***d.*** and ***e.*** below for removal and installation of pump assembly.

(1) PACKING REMOVAL. Remove two stuffing box gland nuts, then slide gland back on shaft as far as possible. Remove old packing with a suitable pick or wire.

(2) PACKING INSTALLATION. Install five packing rings, one at a time, using stuffing box gland to push rings into place. Position gland on studs, then install nuts. Tighten gland nuts alternately until gland starts to compress packing, then further tighten each gland nut one-sixth turn.

d. Bilge Pump Assembly Removal (fig. 212). Disconnect inlet and outlet hoses from pump after loosening hose clamps. Loosen bleeder line hose clamps below pump, then disconnect bleeder line hose at pump. Disconnect lubrication extension hose at pump if vehicle is so equipped. Remove lock nut and adjusting nut from adjusting yoke at outside of frame left side rail. Swing pump toward driving sprocket and disengage drive chain from driven sprocket. Remove cotter pin from support pin at hanger bracket, remove support pin, then remove pump from vehicle.

e. Bilge Pump Assembly Installation (fig. 212). Position pump to hanger bracket, install support pin and secure with cotter pin. Connect chain to driven sprocket, then position adjusting yoke through frame rail. Install outer adjusting nut and lock nut, then adjust chain (par. 246*a.*). Connect inlet and outlet hoses to pump, then connect bleeder line hose. Tighten all hose clamp bolts firmly. Connect lubrication extension hose to pump if vehicle is so equipped.

248. CONTROL VALVES AND MANIFOLD.

a. General. Three bilge pump valves are attached to manifold which is mounted under driver's seat (fig. 215). Valves and manifold are accessible after removal of seat cushion and hole cover.

b. Bilge Pump Valves (fig. 215). Adjustment, cleaning, packing, and replacement operations are same for all valves. Valves can be adjusted, repacked, and cleaned without removal from vehicle. Replacement, however, necessitates removal of complete valve and manifold assembly from vehicle.

(1) ADJUSTMENT. Adjust valve whenever leakage is evident, or whenever valve fails to remain open when placed in open position. Vehicles after chassis serial No. 9213 (except Nos. 11879 to 12778 inclusive) are equipped with friction springs to hold handles in open or closed positions. Adjust valve by tightening valve packing gland sufficiently to stop leak or to hold valve lever in position.

(2) PACKING REPLACEMENT. Repack valve whenever further tightening of packing gland fails to stop leaks or produce desired fric-

Forward Bilge Pump System (Gould Type) (After Chassis Serial No. 4201)

tional effect on lever. With a small punch, drive out lever retaining pin, then remove lever from stem. Unscrew and remove packing gland, then remove packing, using a suitable pick. Install new packing on stem, then screw packing gland into valve body. Position lever on stem, then install retaining pin in stem, bending ends of pin sufficiently to hold in place. Tighten packing gland until packing is tight enough to hold up weight of lever.

(3) CLEANING. Remove valve cap and gasket after removing two cap screws. Remove lever, packing gland, and packing as described in step (2) above. Turn stem to lift valve disks from seats. Hold disks with one hand, then pull stem out of body with other hand. Remove all scale and sediment from valve parts. Replace entire valve if disks or seats are deeply scored. Install disks in body, then position stem and washer in body. Wind packing around stem, using new packing if available. Install packing gland, tightening sufficiently to slightly compress packing. Install lever on stem, then install retaining pin in stem, bending ends of pin sufficiently to hold in place. Position cap on gasket, then install attaching cap screws.

(4) VALVE REPLACEMENT. Remove assembly of manifold and valves from vehicle, then remove valve from manifold [subpar. c.(2) below]. Install new valve on manifold, then install assembly of valves and manifold in vehicle [subpar. c.(4) below].

c. Bilge Pump Manifold (fig. 215).

(1) REMOVAL. Remove driver's seat as described in paragraph 236c. Unhook spring and spring extension from clip on valve linkage. Remove nut and washer which attach lower ball joint to valve lever. Loosen hose clamps and disconnect four hoses from manifold. Remove four nuts and washers from manifold U-bolts, remove two U-bolts, and remove manifold and valve from vehicle.

(2) DISASSEMBLY. Carefully note positions of valves and elbows relative to manifold to permit ready assembly in same positions. Using a vise and pipe wrench, or two pipe wrenches, unscrew three nipples, elbows, and valves from manifold. Using a wire brush and dry-cleaning solvent, remove all traces of sediment, scale, and corrosion and wipe parts dry. Examine parts carefully for damaged threads, cracks, and other damage, replacing all seriously damaged parts. Clean and paint interior of manifold, elbows, and nipples as described in paragraph 238.

(3) ASSEMBLY. Coat male threads with white lead pigment (52-P-19990). Using vise and pipe wrench, screw three valves onto manifold, positioning valves as shown in figure 215. Screw elbows into valves, positioning elbows as shown in figure 215. Screw nipples into elbows.

(4) INSTALLATION. Remove all corrosion from exterior of manifold and valve assembly, and from valve linkage. Clean and paint as described in paragraph 238. Avoid getting paint in joints of moving parts. Position assembly of manifold and valves in vehicle, then install two U-bolts, four washers, and nuts. Connect lower ball joint to valve

TM 9-802
248-249

Maintenance Instructions

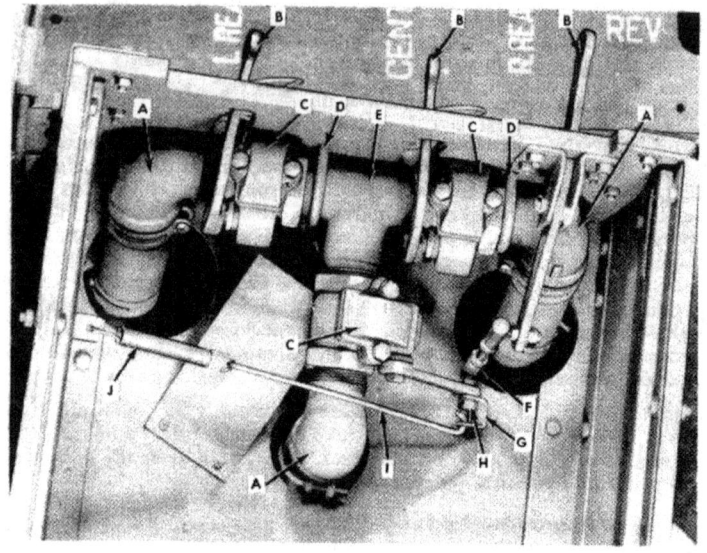

A ELBOW
B VALVE LEVER
C VALVE
D U-BOLT
E MANIFOLD
F LOWER BALL JOINT
G CLIP
H LOWER BALL JOINT NUT
I SPRING EXTENSION
J SPRING

RA PD 333236

Figure 215—Manifold and Valves

lever, install clip, and install washer and nut. Check operation of valves, making sure valves can be completely opened and closed. Connect four hoses to manifold, tightening hose clamps firmly. Hook spring and spring extension to clip at lower ball joint. Lubricate parts according to Lubrication Order No. 9-802.

249. STRAINERS AND TUBING.

a. General (fig. 214). Three cup-type strainers, located in left rear compartment, right rear compartment, and amidships, are used on later vehicles with Gould bilge pump system. Earlier vehicles were equipped with a basket-type amidship strainer, now replaced by cup-type. A system of tubes and hoses conducts flow of water from intake strainers to manifold valves. Outlet from manifold is connected by tube and hoses to inlet of pump. Pump discharges through tubing and hoses to discharge outlet in surf coaming at driver's left. Bleeder line, which serves to both prime pump and drain pump system, connects bleeder strainer in side of hull to bottom of pump.

b. Strainers—In Hull (fig. 214). Strainers used with Gould bilge pump system are same as those used in same relative positions in the Oberdorfer system (par. 243). Removal, cleaning and painting, and installation of strainers are described in paragraph 244.

c. Bleeder Line Strainer. Bleeder strainer, being welded to hull, is not removable. Design of system provides a self-cleaning action; however, bleeder strainer can be flushed out by pouring a large quantity of clean water through discharge outlet with all manifold valves closed. Any sediment remaining in bleeder line or strainer can be removed by disconnecting bleeder line hoses and removing tubing. Paint strainer and screen as described in paragraph 238.

d. Discharge Hole Screen or Cover. Hinged-type screen or cover over discharge outlet is attached to vertical surf coaming with two screws, washers, and nuts. Hinge must operate freely. Paint screen or cover when necessary, as described in paragraph 238.

e. Tubes and Hoses (fig. 214). Bilge pump tubes and hoses are accessible in bilges after removal of cargo compartment floor boards, air intake grilles, and driver's compartment floor boards. One discharge tube hose connection is accessible in left-hand air exhaust duct. Removal and installation of bilge pump heater hoses are described in paragraph 232. With the exception of engine compartment intake line, the tubes used with the Gould pump are removed, cleaned, painted, and installed in same manner as those in the Oberdorfer system. Lead coated tubes on later vehicles, however, need not have interiors painted. Refer to paragraphs 238 and 244.

Section XLIII

Rear Bilge Pump System (Higgins)

250. GENERAL.

a. Description. The Higgins centrifugal type bilge pump is mounted on frame left side rail under cargo compartment. Pump is chain driven from a sprocket on the water propeller drive shaft and operates whenever water propeller is engaged. Vertical adjustment of pump is provided for proper chain tension. Intake strainer is attached directly to pump and discharge tubes convey water from pump to discharge outlet in left side surf coaming.

b. Pump Types. On vehicles prior to chassis serial No. 2006, a single link chain drives the small pump ($1\frac{3}{4}$-in. water outlet). Later vehicles

Maintenance Instructions

are equipped with a larger capacity pump (2¾-in water outlet), driven by a double link chain. Small pump on early vehicles can be replaced by the larger pump, if available. For this purpose, a kit (GM-2206456) is available, which contains all necessary parts and full instructions for installation. All operations, removal, installation, assembly, etc., are same for both pumps and drives.

c. Accessibility. Pump assembly, drive, strainer, tubing, and hoses are accessible in bilge after removal of cargo compartment left front and front center floor boards.

d. Repair Operations. Repair operations on rear bilge pump system are described in TM 9-1802C.

251. BILGE PUMP DRIVE.

a. Drive Chain Adjustment (fig. 216). Apply moderate thumb pressure to chain midway between sprockets. If chain deflection is more or less than ½ inch, adjust chain.

(1) ALINE SPROCKETS. Stand in right side of cargo compartment, then visually check sprocket alinement by sighting along chain across sprockets. Loosen driven sprocket set screws, move sprocket toward or away from pump as necessary to aline with driving sprocket, then tighten set screws firmly. Sprockets must be in same plane, must not be cocked in relation to each other, nor wobble while rotating. Replace defective driving (par. 257**b.**) and driven sprockets (subpars. **e.** and **f.** below). Vehicles after chassis serial No. 4801 (except Nos. 6602 to 6801 inclusive) are equipped with two sprocket alinement guides to aid in vertical alinement of sprockets. Guides are steel strips bolted to frame left side rail on each side of bilge pump mounting bracket. Keep guide bolts tight. If guide bolts become loose, first aline pump, move guides into contact with pump mounting bracket, then tighten guide bolts firmly. Sprocket alinement can be checked accurately with a straightedge and C-clamps. Straightedge must be at least $5/16$ inch thick, and of proper length to contact full surfaces of sprockets without interference from chain. Clamp straightedge to driven sprocket then adjust driven sprocket to bring straightedge into full contact with face of driving sprocket. If face of driving sprocket is not parallel with straightedge, loosen pump alinement guides, if vehicle is so equipped, then adjust pump. Tighten pump mounting bolts, then move alinement guides into contact with pump mounting bracket and tighten bolts firmly.

(2) ADJUST CHAIN TENSION. Loosen two hose clamps on pump to discharge tube hose. Loosen four nuts on bolts which attach pump mounting bracket to frame side rail. Slide pump downward to tighten chain, or upward to loosen chain. When proper adjustment has been obtained, tighten mounting bolt nuts firmly. Again check tension and sprocket alinement, and readjust if not correct. Tighten two pump to discharge hose clamps firmly. Rotate water propeller drive shaft by hand to make sure pump operates freely. Lubricate chain according to Lubrication Order No. 9-802.

TM 9-802

Rear Bilge Pump System (Higgins)

A DISCHARGE TUBE CLAMP
B LOWER DISCHARGE TUBE
C FRAME LEFT SIDE RAIL
D INTAKE STRAINER
E PUMP (G501-03-45887)
F HOSE (G501-02-17806)
G WATER PROPELLER DRIVE SHAFT
H DRIVE CHAIN (G501-01-35400)
I DRIVE SPROCKET
J DRIVEN SPROCKET

RA PD 337220

Figure 216—Rear Bilge Pump and Drive

b. Drive Chain Removal. Loosen two pump to discharge tube hose clamps. Loosen four nuts on bolts which attach pump mounting bracket to frame side rail. Move pump upward sufficiently to disengage drive chain from driven sprocket. Separate chain at connecting link after removing two cotter pins, then remove chain from driving sprocket.

c. Drive Chain Installation. Position chain around driving sprocket. Connect ends of chain with connecting link, install link plates, and cotter pins. Raise pump sufficiently to engage drive chain on sprocket. Adjust chain tension and aline sprockets as described in subparagraph *a.* above.

252. BILGE PUMP ASSEMBLY.

a. Packing Adjustment (fig. 217). Whenever leakage exceeds the small amount necessary to prevent overheating and scoring shaft, adjust packing nut. Loosen packing nut lock screw on vehicles prior to chassis serial No. 2006. Adjust packing nut, using a suitable tool. Do not completely stop leakage.

b. Packing Replacement (fig. 217). When leakage cannot be satisfactorily educed by tightening packing nut, repack pump. Although pump can be repacked while mounted in vehicle, operation is considerably facilitated by removal of pump from vehicle. Refer to subparagraphs c. and d. below for removal and installation of pump assembly.

(1) PACKING REMOVAL. Remove packing nut lock screw and nut on vehicles prior to chassis serial No. 2006. On later vehicles, remove lock screw, nut, and packing nut lock. Unscrew packing nut, then slide packing nut and packing gland back on shaft. Using suitable pick or wire, remove old packing. If pump is mounted in vehicle, loosen two hose clamps and four mounting bolts, then disengage drive chain from driven sprocket.

Figure 217—Rear Bilge Pump Assembly (Higgins)

(2) PACKING INSTALLATION. Install, successively, one moulded packing ring, four rope-type rings, and one moulded ring. Install rings one at a time, pushing each ring in place with packing gland. Avoid distorting moulded rings during installation. Position packing gland and nut in stuffing box, then tighten packing nut while rotating shaft by hand until a slight drag is felt on shaft. Install lock screw and nut, with screw engaged in slot in packing nut on vehicles prior to chassis serial No. 2006. On later vehicles, install lock screw, lock, and nut, with lock engaged in slot in packing nut. If pump is mounted in vehicle, connect drive chain to driven sprocket, then adjust chain tension as described in paragraph 251a.

c. Bilge Pump Assembly Removal (fig. 217). Loosen two hose clamps, then disconnect hose from pump outlet. Remove four pump to frame nuts, washers, and bolts. Disengage driven sprocket from drive chain, then lift assembly of pump and intake strainer from vehicle. Inspect pump drain hole. Vehicles after chassis serial No. 9233 have countersunk hole to aid in locating hole when cleaning. Countersink hole, if pump is not so equipped, using a 1/4-inch diameter drill ground to a 120-degree angle.

d. Bilge Pump Assembly Installation (fig. 217). Position pump on frame side rail, then install four pump to frame bolts, washers, and nuts, leaving nuts loose. Raise pump assembly and engage drive chain on driven sprocket. Connect discharge tube hose to pump outlet, leaving hose clamp bolts loose. Adjust chain tension and sprocket alinement as described in paragraph 251a.

e. Driven Sprocket Removal (fig. 217). If pump is mounted in vehicle, loosen two hose clamps and four pump to frame bolt nuts, and move pump upward sufficiently to disengage chain. Loosen two sprocket set screws, then pull sprocket and key off of pump shaft.

f. Driven Sprocket Installation (fig. 217). Position sprocket and key to pump shaft, then engage drive chain. Do not tighten set screws until sprockets are alined. If pump is mounted in vehicle, adjust chain tension and aline sprockets (par. 251a.).

253. STRAINERS AND TUBING.

a. Intake Strainer. Intake strainer is mounted directly on inlet of pump.

(1) REMOVAL (FIG. 218). Loosen intake strainer set screw, then pull strainer from pump. Straighten ends of screen retaining wires, withdraw wires, and remove screen from strainer.

(2) CLEANING. Thoroughly clean strainer, removing all dirt and sediment, then remove all traces of corrosion, using steel wool or flint paper. Examine screen carefully, and replace if screen is distorted or corroded sufficiently to impair its efficiency. Clean and paint as described in paragraph 244.

(3) INSTALLATION (FIG. 218). Position screen in strainer and insert retaining wires. Bend both ends of wires to secure in place. On

Maintenance Instructions

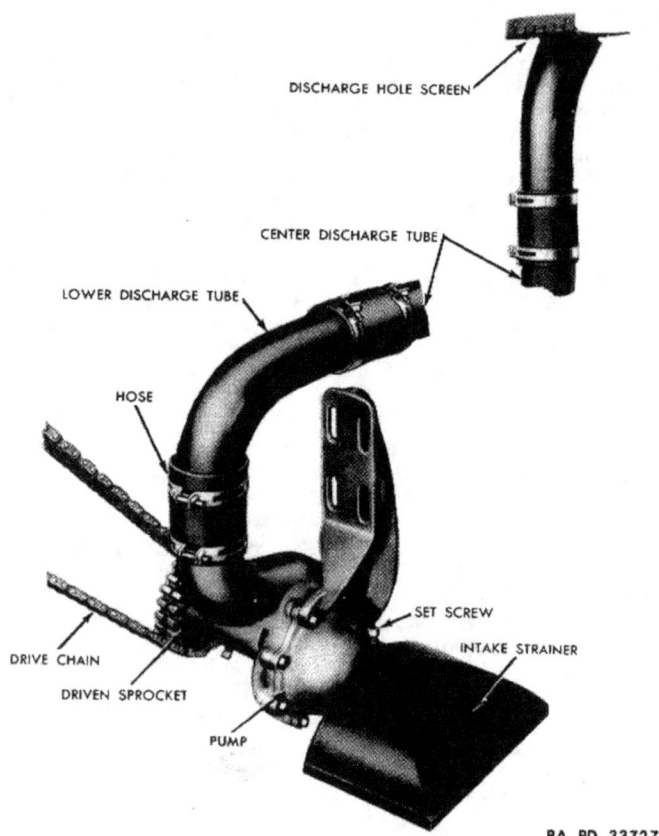

Figure 218—Rear Bilge Pump System

vehicles prior to chassis serial No. 2006, screens are sometimes distorted by being drawn up into strainer by suction of pump. Drill eight holes in lower edge of strainer and attach screen to strainer with wires through these holes (fig. 219). Position strainer on pump, tightening set screw firmly.

b. Discharge Hole Screen or Cover (fig. 218). Discharge screen or cover installed on vehicles after chassis serial No. 3005, is identical with screen used on Oberdorfer pump discharge. Installation of screens or covers on earlier vehicles should be made at first opportunity. Refer to paragraph 243e.

Rear Bilge Pump System (Higgins)

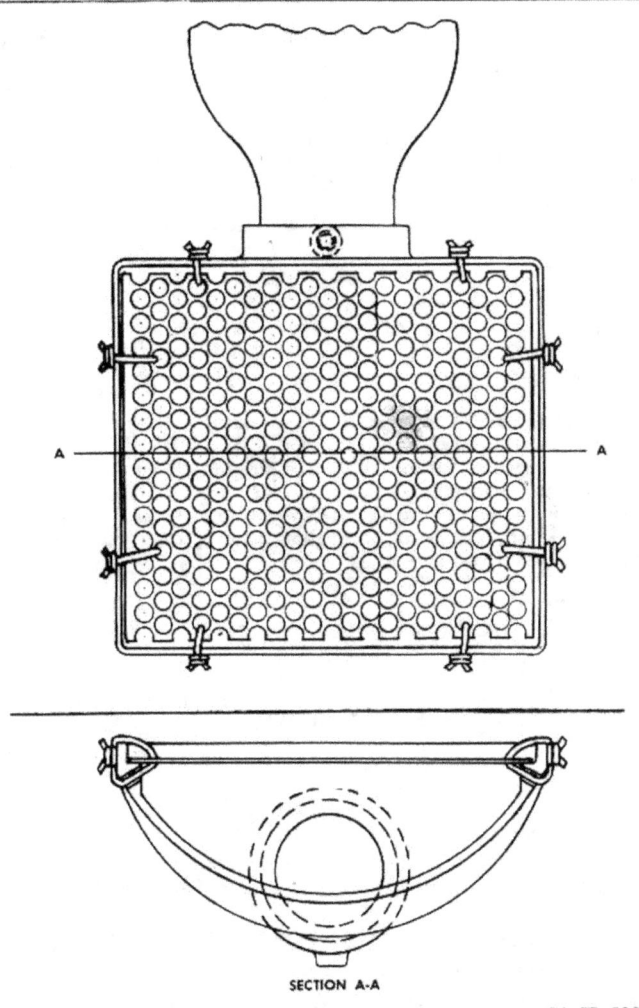

SECTION A-A

Figure 219—Early Type Intake Screen Wired in Place

c. Tubes and Hoses (fig. 218).

(1) REMOVAL. Remove nuts and washers from clamp which attaches lower discharge tube to frame, then remove clamp. Loosen hose clamps, disconnect hoses, then remove tubes.

(2) CLEANING. Clean and paint interior of tubes as described in paragraph 244, except that lead coated tubes used on late vehicles need not be painted internally. Clean and paint exterior of tubes as described in paragraph 238.

(3) INSTALLATION. Position tubes in vehicle, then connect hoses. Tighten hose clamp bolts firmly. Position clamp around lower discharge tube and through frame, then install washers and nuts.

Section XLIV
Water Drive System

254. GENERAL.

a. Description. The drive for the water propeller is from a water propeller transfer case. This transfer case is connected to the transmission through a short propeller shaft. Transmission speeds used in water operation are transmitted through water propeller transfer case, then to water propeller by a drive line consisting of three drive shafts (fig. 220). Two types of water propeller transfer cases have been used, single-speed and two-speed.

b. Data.

(1) PRIOR TO CHASSIS SERIAL NO. 2506.

```
Type ....................................................... 1-speed
Make ........................................................ G.M.
Gear ratio ........................................... 1.3448 to 1
```

(2) AFTER CHASSIS SERIAL NO. 2505.

```
Type ....................................................... 2-speed
Make ........................................................ G.M.
Gear ratios
    Forward ........................................... 1.3448 to 1
    Reverse (overdrive) ............................. 2.5789 to 1
```

c. Repair. Operations necessary for repairing the various units comprising the water drive system are described in TM 9-1802C.

255. WATER PROPELLER TRANSFER CASE AND CONTROLS.

a. General. The water propeller transfer case used on vehicles prior to chassis serial No. 2506 is a single-speed unit which is controlled by a lever extending upward from cross shaft mounted at rear of transmission. A two-speed unit is used on vehicles after chassis serial No. 2505. The control lever and shift linkage used on the latter type is mounted directly to the top of the water propeller transfer case (fig. 223). A bilge pump drive pulley (fig. 223) or sprocket (fig. 222) is installed on forward end of transfer case countershaft. Mounting is similar for either the single-speed or two-speed unit.

Water Drive System

A WATER PROPELLER
B STRUT
C JOURNAL AND OIL SEAL ASSEMBLY
D STUFFING BOX (G501-01-24530)
E THRUST BEARING ASSEMBLY
F CENTER DRIVE SHAFT BEARING AND BRACKET ASSEMBLY
G BILGE PUMP DRIVE SPROCKET
H WATER PROPELLER TRANSFER CASE
I SHIFT LEVER AND LINKAGE
J TRANSMISSION
K WATER PROPELLER REAR DRIVE SHAFT
L WATER PROPELLER CENTER DRIVE SHAFT
M WATER PROPELLER FRONT DRIVE SHAFT
N TRANSFER CASE TO TRANSMISSION SHAFT
O WATER PROPELLER TRANSFER CASE TO AXLE TRANSFER CASE SHAFT
P BILGE PUMP DRIVE PULLEY (EARLY MODELS) SPROCKET (LATE MODELS)

RA PD 337223

Figure 220—Water Propeller and Drive Installation (After Chassis Serial No. 2505)

TM 9-802
255

Maintenance Instructions

A AXLE PROPELLER SHAFT
B FORWARD WATER PROPELLER SHAFT
C LOWER MOUNTING BOLT
D UPPER MOUNT CAP SCREW
E LOWER SUPPORT MEMBER
F UPPER SUPPORT MEMBER
G TRANSFER CASE
H BILGE PUMP PULLEY AND BELT

RA PD 337185

Figure 221—Water Propeller Transfer Case Installation (Prior to Chassis Serial No. 2506)

b. Forward Bilge Pump Drive Pulley or Sprocket Replacement. Vehicles prior to chassis serial No. 4202 have one of two types of bilge pump drive pulleys mounted on forward end of water propeller transfer case countershaft. A sprocket attached to hub (fig. 222) mounted on transfer case countershaft is used on later vehicles having a chain driven bilge pump. Replacement of pulley or sprocket may be accomplished without removing water propeller transfer case from vehicle.

(1) PULLEY REPLACEMENT (FIG. 223).

(a) Removal. Remove bilge pump drive belt as described in para-

graph 240**b.** Remove cotter pin and pulley retaining nut. Withdraw pulley from end of shaft, then remove key. Pulley has tapped holes to accommodate puller screws.

(b) Installation. Install key in slot in transfer case shaft and drive pulley into place. Install pulley retaining nut and secure with cotter pin. Install and adjust drive belt as described in paragraph 240**c.**

(2) SPROCKET AND HUB REPLACEMENT (FIG. 222).

(a) Removal. Remove bilge pump drive chain as described in paragraph 246**b.** Withdraw cotter pin from hole through sprocket hub and countershaft; then remove hub retaining nut from end of transfer case countershaft. Remove hub and sprocket from countershaft as an assembly, and remove key from countershaft slot. Separate sprocket and hub by removing lock wire and sprocket to hub cap screws. NOTE: Sprocket *may be removed from hub without removing hub from transfer case if so desired.*

(b) Installation. Mount sprocket on hub, installing four cap screws through sprocket and into tapped holes in forward face of hub. Secure cap screws by threading lock wire through cap screw heads. Tap key into keyway in countershaft, then place hub and sprocket assembly on countershaft and install retaining nut. Insert long cotter pin through holes in hub and countershaft to secure hub retaining nut. Install and adjust drive chain as described in paragraph 246**c.**

c. Water Propeller Transfer Case Removal. Removal procedure for single and two-speed units is same except as noted in text.

(1) REMOVE BILGE PUMP DRIVE BELT OR CHAIN. Remove bilge pump drive belt or chain as described in paragraph 240**b.** or paragraph 246**b.**

(2) REMOVE CONTROL LINKAGE (AFTER CHASSIS SERIAL NO. 2505 ONLY) (FIG: 223). Remove four cap screws attaching shift lever support to water propeller transfer case, then lift control assembly from vehicle.

(3) DISCONNECT PROPELLER SHAFTS FROM WATER PROPELLER TRANSFER CASE. Disconnect propeller shafts (N and O, fig. 220) from water propeller transfer case by removing U-joint to flange bolts, then moving shafts away from transfer case.

(4) REMOVE WATER PROPELLER FRONT DRIVE SHAFT. Remove water propeller front drive shaft as described in paragraph 257**b.**(1).

(5) REMOVE WATER PROPELLER TRANSFER CASE (FIGS. 221 AND 222). Remove two bolts and nuts attaching transfer case to lower support and remove cap screw which attaches transfer case to upper support. Remove upper support to side rail bolts at right-hand end of support. Pry upper support upward to allow removal of transfer case; then lift the assembly out of vehicle through air intake grille opening.

d. Water Propeller Transfer Case Installation. Same operations are necessary for installation of either the single-speed or two-speed units except as noted in text.

TM 9-802
255

Maintenance Instructions

FRONT VIEW
A MOUNTING BOLTS
B LOWER SUPPORT MEMBER
C UPPER SUPPORT MEMBER

REAR VIEW
D MOUNTING CAP SCREW
E BILGE PUMP DRIVE CHAIN
F BILGE PUMP DRIVE SPROCKET

RA PD 333222

Figure 222—Water Propeller Transfer Case Mountings (Late Vehicles)

(1) MOUNT WATER PROPELLER TRANSFER CASE AT SUPPORT MEMBER (FIGS. 221 AND 223). Lower the water propeller transfer case through air intake grille opening and move unit into place between upper and lower support members with mounting bolt holes alined. Install two mounting bolts at lower support member and one cap screw at upper support member. Attach right-hand end of upper support to frame side rail, using bolts with lock washers.

(2) CONNECT PROPELLER SHAFTS TO WATER PROPELLER TRANSFER CASE. Position propeller shaft flanges at flanges on water propeller transfer case with bolt holes alined; then install flange bolts with lock washers. Tighten flange bolts firmly and tighten dust cap at each slip joint. Install water propeller front drive shaft as described in paragraph 257*b*.(2).

(3) INSTALL CONTROL LINKAGE (AFTER CHASSIS SERIAL NO. 2505 ONLY) (FIG. 223). Position control linkage assembly at top of water propeller transfer case, then install four mounting cap screws.

(4) INSTALL BILGE PUMP DRIVE BELT OR CHAIN. Install and adjust bilge pump drive belt or chain as described in paragraph 240*c*. or 246*c*.

Water Drive System

e. Control and Linkage Replacement (Prior to Chassis Serial No. 2506).

(1) REMOVAL.

(a) Remove Shifter Shaft Control Rod. Unhook shift lock spring. Disconnect control rod at shifter shaft and cross shaft shift lever by removing cotter pins and clevis pins, then remove rod.

(b) Remove Cross Shaft and Control Lever. Loosen clamp bolt in control lever and move lever toward center of vehicle far enough to expose key in shaft. Remove key and shaft retainer springs at inner and outer sides of right-hand bracket; then remove cross shaft and control lever.

(c) Disconnect Power Plant Stabilizer Rod. Disconnect power plant stabilizer rod at cross shaft left-hand bracket by removing clevis pin.

(d) Remove Winch Control Lever. Disconnect winch control lever from link at power take-off shifter arm by removing cotter pin and clevis pin. Remove cotter pin at end of winch control lever to transmission stud and remove lever and stud.

(e) Remove Cross Shaft Brackets. Remove nut attaching left-hand bracket to transmission and slide bracket off stud. Remove two nuts attaching right-hand bracket to transmission, loosen hand brake cross shaft bracket cap screws, and remove water propeller cross shaft bracket.

(2) INSTALLATION.

(a) Install Cross Shaft Brackets. Place right-hand bracket over forward stud under hand brake cross shaft bracket and install stud nuts. Install left-hand bracket and secure to transmission with nut on forward stud and winch control lever to transmission stud.

(b) Install Winch Control Lever and Power Plant Stabilizer Rod. Place winch control lever over stud and attach to link at power take-off with clevis pin and cotter pin. Install new cotter pin in hole at end of winch control lever stud. Attach power plant stabilizer rod to left-hand bracket with clevis pin and cotter pin.

(c) Install Cross Shaft. Start shaft through right-hand bracket with keyway end of shaft toward center of vehicle. Insert key in shaft, install control lever and insert shaft in left-hand bracket. Install cross shaft retainer springs in grooves at right-hand end of shaft. Tighten clamp bolt in lever when lever is centered over Woodruff key.

(d) Install Shifter Shaft Control Rod. Position control rod between shifter shaft at transfer case and short arm on control lever at cross shaft. Attach rod using clevis pins. Install shift lock spring.

f. Control and Linkage Replacement (After Chassis Serial No. 2505).

(1) REMOVAL. Remove center section of driver's compartment floor, remove one clevis pin and flat washer from end of each water propeller transfer case shift shaft, remove four shift lever assembly support to transfer case cap screws and lock washers, then lift the complete assembly out and remove from vehicle.

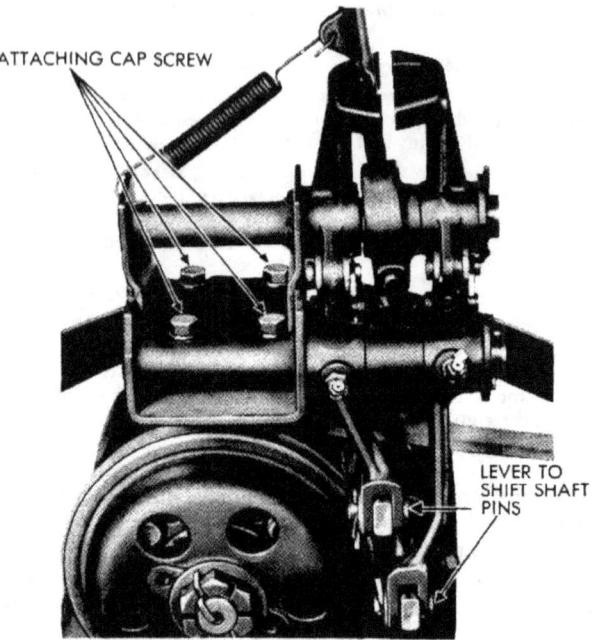

Figure 223—Water Propeller Transfer Case Control Linkage (After Chassis Serial No. 2505)

(2) INSTALLATION. Position linkage assembly at water propeller transfer case with mounting cap screw holes alined. Attach linkage support bracket, using cap screws with lock washers.

256. WATER PROPELLER DRIVE SHAFT STRUT AND BEARING.

a. General. Water propeller rear drive shaft is supported at rearward end by a strut attached to hull at water propeller tunnel. Vehicles prior to chassis serial No. 2506 have a strut bearing of poured babbitt construction, while on vehicles after chassis serial No. 2505, a replaceable spherical journal type strut bearing is used. The latter type bearing incorporates seals which prevent dirt from entering the bearing and also retain lubricant. A sand slinger is installed just ahead of strut bearing on all vehicles to deflect sand and other foreign material away from bearing. The replaceable type bearing may be installed on early vehicles by replacing the babbitted strut with strut and cap illustrated in figure 225. Instructions for replacing strut are described in TM 9-1802C.

Water Drive System

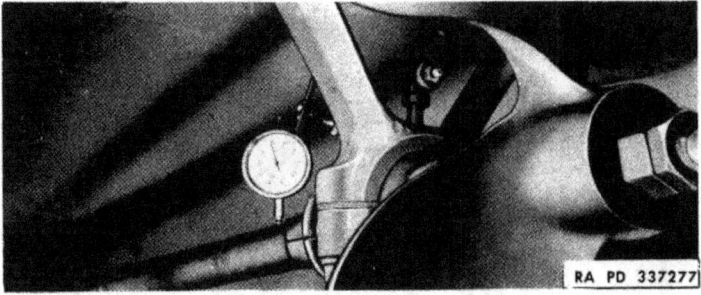

Figure 224—Checking Wear at Strut Bearing

b. Inspection (fig. 224). The clearance between water propeller rear shaft and strut bearing should be checked at inspection intervals. The following method is recommended; however, if a dial indicator is not available, excessive play may be detected by a hand-feel inspection.

(1) ATTACH DIAL INDICATOR. Attach a dial indicator similar to that illustrated in figure 224 to the strut with the indicator point resting on top of the drive shaft.

(2) CHECK CLEARANCE. Exert force upward by lifting on water-propeller blades, at the same time noting indicator reading. If shaft can be moved more than 0.010 inch, a new strut bearing should be installed.

c. Strut Bearing Replacement. If the vehicle is one prior to chassis serial No. 2506 on which the bearing and strut are integral, refer to TM 9-1802C for procedure necessary to pour a new bearing, or to replace strut as desired. Perform operation given below to replace strut bearing on vehicles equipped with new type strut and bearing.

(1) REMOVAL.

(a) Remove Water Propeller. Remove water propeller as described in paragraph 257**e.**(1).

(b) Remove Lubrication Fitting. Remove lubrication fitting elbow and nipple from journal.

(c) Remove Strut Journal Assembly (fig. 225). Remove lock wire, then remove cap screws attaching cap to strut. Remove cap and slide journal off rear end of drive shaft.

(d) Remove Sand Slinger. Loosen set screw in sand slinger (one-piece type) or remove the two screws used to assemble the halves of two-piece type and remove sand slinger. NOTE: *Whenever a one-piece sand slinger is removed from water propeller rear drive shaft, it is recommended that the two-piece slinger shown in figure 225 be installed to replace one-piece type.* Both types have same part number.

(2) INSTALLATION.

(a) Install Sand Slinger. If one-piece sand slinger is to be used, it must be installed on drive shaft prior to installation of journal assem-

TM 9-802
256

Maintenance Instructions

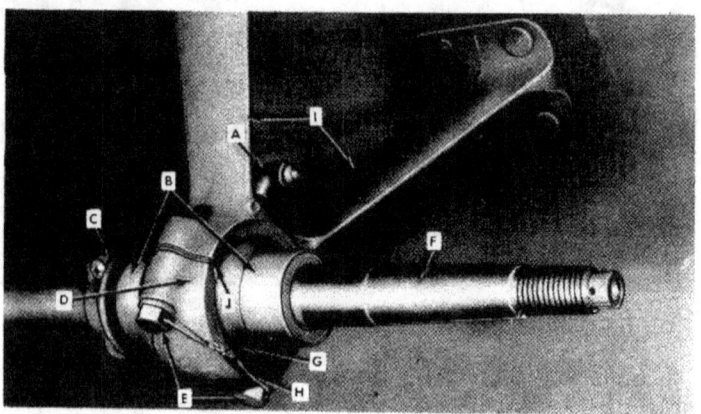

JOURNAL AND SAND SLINGER INSTALLED

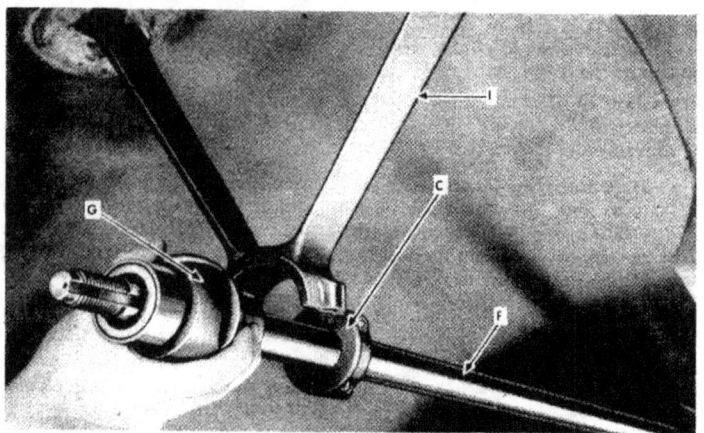

REMOVING JOURNAL AND OIL SEAL ASSEMBLY

A LUBRICATION FITTING
B JOURNAL OIL SEAL
C SAND SLINGER
D STRUT CAP
E CAP SCREWS
F WATER PROPELLER REAR DRIVE SHAFT
G JOURNAL
H LOCK WIRE
I STRUT
J SHIMS

RA PD 333249

Figure 225—Water Propeller Drive Shaft Journal

bly. However, installation of two-piece slinger may be deferred until step *(d)* below. Place slinger on propeller rear drive shaft, leaving screws loose until journal is installed.

Water Drive System

(b) Position Journal on Shaft. Clean rear portion of drive shaft to remove all old lubricant and abrasive material which may be present. Coat bearing surface and oil seals with lubricant to facilitate journal installation. Carefully guide journal past threaded section and keyway in propeller shaft. Slide journal onto shaft until it fits into strut as shaft is lifted upward. NOTE: *Be sure that tapped hole in journal is alined with hole in strut so that lubrication fitting can be installed.*

(c) Install Strut Cap (fig. 225). Coat threads of strut cap attaching screws with joint and thread compound (52-C-3115), then with journal assembly seated at strut, install screws with lock washers to attach cap, using shims between cap and strut. Use same thickness of shims at each side of cap and check to be sure that cap seats against shims and at same time seizes journal firmly. NOTE. *Cut shims from sheet metal or shim stock if regulation shims are not available.* Install lock wire through holes in cap screw heads. If cap screws do not extend to top of tapped hole in strut, fill remaining portion of hole with caulking compound (52-C-3086-200) and apply olive-drab lusterless enamel (52-E-4171-15) over compound.

(d) Position Sand Slinger. Move sand slinger toward strut bearing and tighten strut bearing, and tighten slinger screws to locate sand slinger with $1/16$ inch clearance between slinger and strut bearing.

(e) Install Water Propeller. Install water propeller as described in paragraph 257e.(2).

257. WATER PROPELLER AND DRIVE SHAFTS.

a. General. Three drive shafts (fig. 220) are used to drive the water propeller. Front and center drive shafts are tubular type, while rear shaft is of solid construction. The drive shafts are connected by universal joints. A hand crank wheel, used as an auxiliary means for starting the engine, is welded onto forward end of front drive shaft tube. A bilge pump drive sprocket is mounted between water propeller front and center drive shafts. Rear drive shaft is tapered at rear end to accommodate water propeller.

b. Front Drive Shaft Replacement (fig. 220).

(1) REMOVAL. Remove rear bilge pump drive chain as described in paragraph 251*b.*; then remove bolts attaching U-joint on front shaft to center drive shaft flange. Raise hand crank wheel cover. Force front drive shaft forward to separate front and center shafts: then remove bilge pump drive sprocket. Pull front drive shaft away from water propeller transfer case.

(2) INSTALLATION. Inspect machined suface on drive shaft U-joint front yoke to be certain it is free from nicks or scores which would impair efficiency of transfer case oil seal. Place yoke over splines of transfer case countershaft and move shaft forward as far as possible. Position rear bilge pump drive sprocket at flange on forward end of center drive shaft. Sprocket must be positioned on flange with toothed portion toward front of vehicle. Move front shaft U-joint into aline-

ment with holes in sprocket and install bolts. Place hand crank wheel cover over wheel. Install rear bilge pump drive chain (par. 251c.).

c. Center Dive Shaft Replacement (fig. 220).

(1) REMOVAL. Disconnect front shaft from center shaft as described in subparagraph b.(1) above. Remove bolts which attach bearing bracket to crossmember. Remove drive shaft guard by removing nuts at underside of support angles on trunnion crossmember, then lifting guard out of place. Remove bolts attaching center drive shaft U-joint to flange at forward end of rear drive shaft, then lift center drive shaft out of vehicle. Bearing and bracket assembly may be pulled off front end of shaft after flange has been removed (refer to paragraph 258b.).

(2) INSTALLATION (FIG. 220).

(a) Position Center Drive Shaft in Vehicle. With bearing and bracket assembly and center drive shaft flange installed on front end of shaft, place center shaft in vehicle with shaft U-joint toward rear of vehicle.

(b) Connect Center Drive Shaft into Drive Line. Attach U-joint at rearward end of center drive shaft to flange on rear drive shaft, using four bolts. Place guard over center shaft with ends extending through holes in support angle at trunnion crossmember, then install nuts on lower ends of guard. Attach center drive shaft bearing bracket to crossmember with two bolts, being sure to use spacer between bracket and crossmember. Connect center drive shaft to front drive shaft U-joint as described in subparagraph b.(2) above.

d. Rear Drive Shaft Replacement.

(1) REMOVAL.

(a) Remove Water Propeller. Remove water propeller as described in subparagraph e.(1) below.

(b) Loosen Sand Slinger (fig. 225). Loosen screws in sand slinger to allow slinger to slide off shaft during shaft removal.

(c) Separate Center and Rear Shafts (fig. 228). Remove guard retaining nuts from underside of trunnion crossmember and remove center drive shaft guard. Remove four bolts attaching center drive shaft U-joint to flange at forward end of rear drive shaft; then move rear end of center drive shaft to one side to allow removal of rear drive shaft.

(d) Detach Thrust Bearing from Frame Crossmember (fig. 228). Loosen packing nut at stuffing box. Also loosen clamp bolt which secures stuffing box hose to tunnel tube and move hose forward away from tunnel tube. Remove four thrust bearing housing to crossmember bolts. On replaceable type, remove cap from strut, then remove journal from shaft, using care to prevent damage to seals.

(e) Remove Rear Drive Shaft. Pull rear drive shaft, thrust bearing and stuffing box forward as an assembly. Station mechanic at strut bearing to remove sand slinger as soon as end of shaft clears strut bearing. Remove rear drive shaft assembly from vehicle and slide stuffing box and hose assembly off rear end of shaft.

Water Drive System

(f) Remove Flange and Thrust Bearing Assembly. Remove flange and thrust bearing assembly from rear drive shaft as described in paragraph 258c.(1).

(2) INSTALLATION.

(a) Install Flange and Thrust Bearing Assembly. Install thrust bearing assembly and flange on front end of rear drive shaft as described in paragraph 258c.(2).

(b) Position Rear Drive Shaft and Thrust Bearing Assembly in Vehicle. Be sure drive shaft is absolutely clean, then slide stuffing box assembly onto rear end of shaft and along shaft to within six inches of collar (fig. 230). Hose with clamps must be in position at stuffing box, and tunnel tube plug, as illustrated in figure 230, must be in place before succeeding operations are performed. Insert rear end of drive shaft through plug in tunnel tube. On early vehicles on which the strut bearing is integral with strut, it will be necessary to have an assistant at rear of vehicle to place sand slinger on shaft and guide rear end of drive shaft through strut bearing. If vehicle is equipped with replaceable type strut bearing, install sand slinger, journal, and strut cap as instructed in subparagraph c.(2) above.

(c) Connect Center and Rear Drive Shafts and Install Guard. Move center drive shaft U-joint into alinement with flange on rear drive shaft and install four bolts through flange and U-joint. Place center drive shaft guard over shaft and install nuts at ends of guard below support crossmember.

(d) Attach Thrust Bearing and Stuffing Box Hose (fig. 230). Install thrust bearing mounting bolts, then move stuffing box hose over tunnel tube and tighten clamp bolt. Adjust stuffing box as described in paragraph 258d.

(e) Install Water Propeller and Position Sand Slinger. Move sand slinger as necessary to provide $1/16$ inch clearance between sand slinger and strut bearing; then tighten slinger retaining screws. Install water propeller as described in subparagraph e.(2) below. CAUTION: *Before operating vehicle, be sure to lubricate strut bearing, thrust bearing, and stuffing box as instructed on Lubrication Order No. 9-802.*

e. Water Propeller Replacement.

(1) REMOVAL (FIG. 226).

(a) Remove Propeller Retaining Nut. Withdraw cotter pin at end of shaft and remove lock nut and retaining nut.

(b) Remove Propeller. Assemble puller (41-P-2951-48) on propeller as illustrated in figure 226; then tighten the three nuts at puller plate alternately one turn at a time until propeller has been withdrawn from shaft. It may be necessary to strike puller plate with hammer to start propeller off shaft if it does not begin to move when a reasonable tension is applied by tightening puller bolts. Propeller hub may be heated if necessary to facilitate removal. Remove key from keyway in shaft.

TM 9-802
257-258

Maintenance Instructions

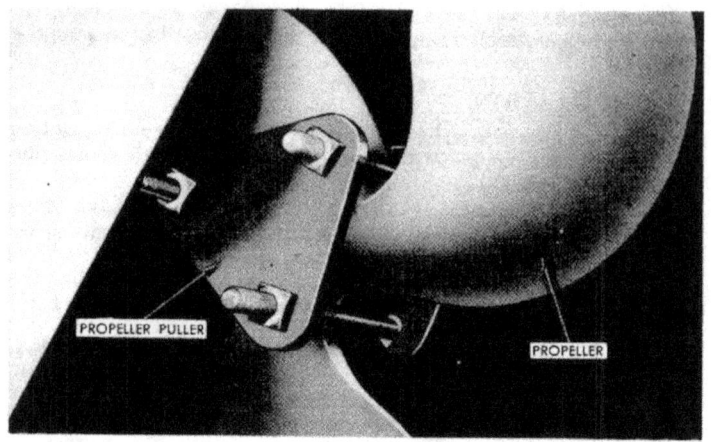

Figure 226—Water Propeller Removal

(2) INSTALLATION.

(a) Check Fit of Propeller Key. See that propeller key is a slip fit in keyways in shaft and propeller hub. Measure distance key extends out of shaft and depth of keyway in propeller hub. There should be not less than 0.010 inch clearance between top of key and bottom of hub keyway to make sure propeller seats on shaft and not on the key.

(b) Install Propeller. Start water propeller over end of shaft with keyways in shaft and in hub alined, then slide propeller on shaft as far as possible. Insert key in keyway and move key and propeller into position by installing retaining nut. Tighten nut until propeller is seated on tapered portion of shaft and install lock nut and cotter pin.

258. WATER PROPELLER DRIVE SHAFT BEARINGS AND STUFFING BOX.

a. General. Two ball bearing assemblies are used to support the water propeller drive shaft in addition to the babbitted bearing at the strut. A single row ball bearing mounted in a support bracket is installed on forward end of center drive shaft, and a thrust bearing (double row ball type) is installed on forward end of rear drive shaft. Driving force of water propeller is transmitted to vehicle through thrust bearing which is mounted in a spherical shaped chamber in thrust bearing housing. Bearing on center shaft is sealed type which does not require service during life of the bearing, while thrust bearing must be lubricated periodically through the lubrication fitting installed in housing. A stuffing box with replaceable rawhide packing in an adjustable gland is used at

Water Drive System

point where drive shaft passes through hull. Stuffing box is attached to hull tunnel tube by a hose, clamped in position.

b. Center Drive Shaft Bearing Replacement. Following procedure is for replacement of bearing and bracket assembly without removing drive shaft from vehicle.

(1) REMOVAL (FIG. 227).

(a) Separate Front Drive Shaft from Center Drive Shaft. Remove rear bilge pump drive chain as described in paragraph 246**b.**; then remove bolts attaching U-joint on front shaft to center drive shaft flange. Force front drive shaft forward to separate front and center shafts, then remove bilge pump drive sprocket.

(b) Remove Center Drive Shaft Flange. Remove flange retaining nut and washer, then drive flange off splines on forward end of shaft. If flange is equipped with grease retainer guard, inspect part and replace if damaged.

(c) Remove Bearing and Bracket Assembly. Remove bolts which attach bearing bracket to crossmember. Lift bracket away from crossmember and remove spacer. Remove bearing and bracket assembly from end of center drive shaft. If grease retainer guard is used on end of drive shaft, inspect part and replace if damaged.

(2) CENTER DRIVE SHAFT BEARING AND BRACKET DISASSEMBLY AND ASSEMBLY. Vehicles prior to chassis serial No. 14789 not equipped with grease retainer at center drive shaft bearing have a spacer assembled at each side of ball bearing assembly, while the bearing used on vehicles after above number have grease retainers installed in place of spacers. Steps necessary to replace bearing in bracket are given below. The term "early type" in text refers to bearing without grease retainers, while "late type" has reference to bearing equipped with grease retainers. Key letters in text refer to figure 227.

(a) Disassembly.
  1. Support drive shaft bearing bracket (E) in arbor press. Apply pressure at bearing cushion ring (F) and force ring and bearing (H) out of bracket.
  2. Cushion ring is formed from rubber stock and can be stretched to allow removal of bearing. Pull ring off bearing, then separate bearing (H) from spacers (early type) or grease retainers (D) and dust washers (I) (late type).

(b) Assembly.
  1. Locate spacer (early type), or grease retainer (D) and dust washers (I) (late type) on each side of bearing (N); then install the assembly in cushion ring (F).
  2. Place bearing support bracket (E) on press plate with beveled side of hole up. Apply hydraulic brake fluid on outside of cushion ring; then press bearing and cushion ring assembly into bracket. When late type assembly is being assembled, be careful not to damage or distort grease retainers (D).

TM 9-802
Maintenance Instructions

A FLANGE NUT
B CENTER DRIVE SHAFT FLANGE
C GREASE RETAINER GUARD
D GREASE RETAINER
E BEARING SUPPORT BRACKET
F CUSHION RING
G CENTER DRIVE SHAFT
H BALL BEARING ASSEMBLY
I DUST WASHER
J GREASE CAVITY   RA PD 337279

Figure 227—Water Propeller Center Drive Shaft Bearing

(3) CENTER DRIVE SHAFT BEARING INSTALLATION (FIG. 227).

(a) Install Bearing and Bracket Assembly. Center drive shaft bearing used on vehicles after serial No. 14789 are equipped with a grease retainer as illustrated in figure 227. Bearings on vehicles prior to above chassis serial No. may be modified to incorporate the grease retainer. Step 1 below covers the installation of bearing without grease retainer, while step 2 covers installation with grease retainer. Key letters in text refer to figure 227.

TM 9-802

Water Drive System

1. Mount bearing and bracket assembly on forward end of center drive shaft with bearing inner race against shoulder on shaft. Place flange on splined section of shaft, then install retaining nut and secure with cotter pin.
2. Pack cavity (J) in grease retainer (D) at each side of bearing (H) with general purpose grease, No. 2; then with retainer guard (C) in place on drive shaft (G), install bearing assembly (N) on shaft with dust washer (I) located at each side of bearing inner race. Install drive shaft flange (B) with grease retainer guard (C) in position as shown in figure 227. Install washer and nut on end of drive shaft, then tighten flange retaining nut (A) firmly and retain with cotter pin.

(b) Bolt Bearing Bracket to Crossmember. Bolt bearing bracket (E) to crossmember with two bolts, using spacer between base of bracket and crossmember.

c. Thrust Bearing and Oil Seals Replacement. Water propeller rear drive shaft thrust bearing may be replaced without removing the rear drive shaft from vehicle; however, if the drive shaft is to be replaced at same time, the thrust bearing and drive shaft should be removed from vehicle as an assembly and the bearing replacement performed on bench.

(1) THRUST BEARING AND OIL SEALS REMOVAL. Key letters in text refer to figure 228.

(a) Separate Center and Rear Drive Shafts. Perform step *(c)* in paragraph 257**d.**(1).

(b) Remove Thrust Bearing. Remove nut (M) at forward side of flange (C). Remove flange with suitable puller. Remove four thrust bearing housing mounting bolts, then drive bearing and housing assembly off end of shaft.

(c) Disassemble Thrust Bearing. Remove screw (H), turn cap (I) counterclockwise, and remove from housing (J). Remove retainer bolt (E). Lift retainers (Q) and bearing (O) out of housing. Separate retainers (Q) and remove from bearing (O), using a screwdriver to pry retainers apart. NOTE: *If oil seals require replacement, perform inspection and repair operations described in TM 9-1802C.*

(2) THRUST BEARING AND OIL SEAL INSTALLATION. Assembly and installation of thrust bearing components must be performed together to prevent damage to oil seals. Be sure oil seals are properly installed in retainers and are in good condition before performing operations described below. Key letters in text refer to figure 229 unless otherwise stated.

(a) Position Bearing Cap. Place bearing cap over rear drive shaft with set screw notches facing toward rear.

(b) Install Rear Oil Seal Retainer Assembly. Place retainer and oil seal assembly (C) on replacer (A), then position tool over end of drive shaft as illustrated in figure 229, and slide retainer and oil seal onto rear drive shaft collar (B).

THRUST BEARING MOUNTING

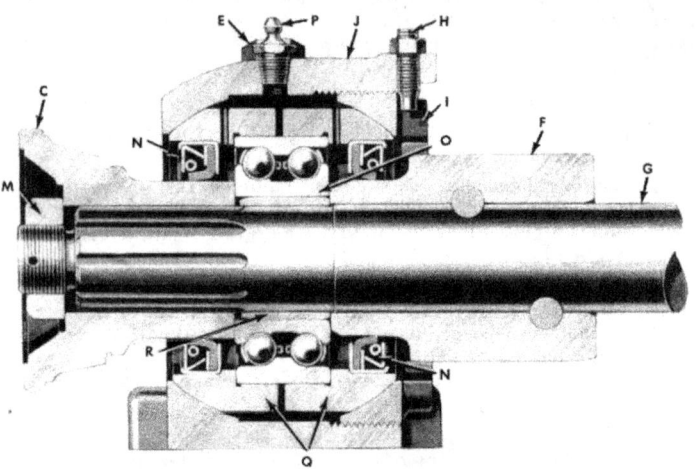

SECTIONAL VIEW OF THRUST BEARING INSTALLED

A WATER PROPELLER CENTER DRIVE SHAFT
B UNIVERSAL JOINT ASSEMBLY
C DRIVE SHAFT FLANGE
D THRUST BEARING HOUSING MOUNTING BOLTS
E RETAINER BOLT
F REAR DRIVE SHAFT COLLAR
G REAR DRIVE SHAFT
H HOUSING TO CAP LOCK SCREW
I THRUST BEARING OIL SEAL CAP
J THRUST BEARING HOUSING
K FRAME CROSSMEMBER
L CENTER DRIVE SHAFT GUARD
M FLANGE RETAINING NUT
N OIL SEAL (501-03-82829)
O THRUST BEARING ASSEMBLY
P LUBRICATION FITTING
Q THRUST BEARING RETAINER
R BEARING COLLAR
S UNIVERSAL JOINT BEARING GASKET
 (G102-03-02425)

RA PD 337278

Figure 228—Water Propeller Drive Shaft Thrust Bearing

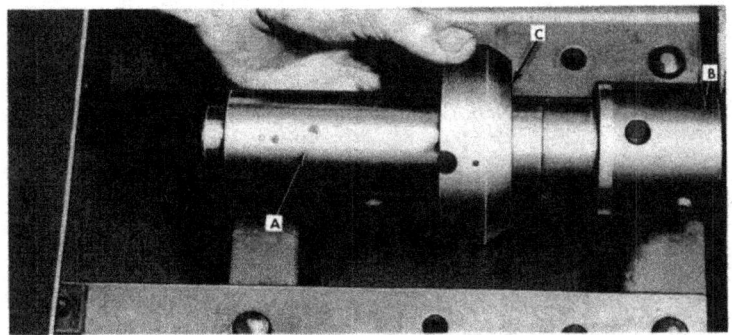

INSTALLING RETAINER AND OIL SEAL ON DRIVE SHAFT COLLAR

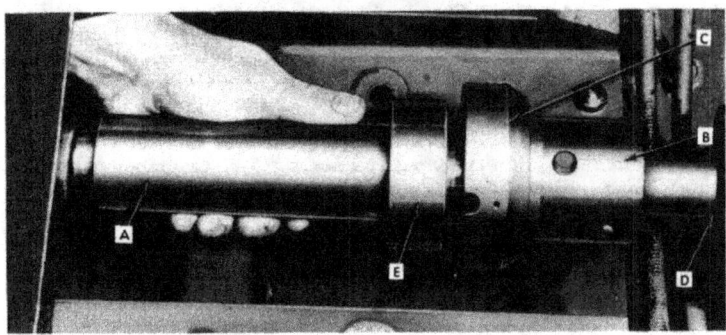

INSTALLING BEARING ON REAR DRIVE SHAFT

INSTALLING RETAINER AND OIL SEAL ON FLANGE

A SEAL REPLACER
B DRIVE SHAFT COLLAR
C THRUST BEARING RETAINER AND OIL SEAL ASSEMBLY
D CAP
E THRUST BEARING ASSEMBLY
F THRUST BEARING HOUSING
G DRIVE SHAFT FLANGE

RA PD 337187

Figure 229—Assembling Water Propeller Rear Drive Shaft Thrust Bearing (Replacer 41-R-2395-32)

Maintenance Instructions

(c) Install Thrust Bearing Assembly. Pack bearing with lubricant (Lubrication Order No. 9-802), then drive bearing onto forward end of drive shaft, using special driver illustrated in figure 229. CAUTION: *Thrust bearing must be installed with bearing face which bears number and nomenclature toward front of vehicle and outer race of bearing must fit into retainer (C).*

(d) Place Forward Oil Seal on Flange. Set flange (G) on bench and place bearing housing (F) around flange in relative position shown in figure 229. Place retainer and oil seal assembly on replacer (A), then with replacer in position at flange (fig. 229), slide retainer and seal off replacer and onto flange.

(e) Position Flange and Housing at Bearing. While holding housing (F) and flange (G) together, start flange onto splines at forward end of drive shaft. Aline cutouts in forward and rear retainers so that retainer bolt (E) will enter cutouts when bolt is installed. Drive flange into place on shaft and install flange retaining nut. Tighten nut firmly and retain with cotter pin. Install and tighten retainer bolt (E). Aline mounting holes in thrust bearing housing with holes in support angles and install four mounting bolts.

(f) Install and Adjust Thrust Bearing Oil Seal Cap. Screw bearing cap (I) into housing (J) to pull retainers (Q) into place on bearing outer race. Tap sharply with a soft hammer to seat retainers in housing. Adjust bearing cap by tightening firmly and then backing off to next notch. Install housing to cap lock screw (H) with end of screw engaging notch in cap. Tighten lock nut on screw.

(g) Connect Center and Rear Drive Shafts. Connect center drive shaft U-joint to flange on rear drive shaft as described in paragraph 257**d.** (2)(d).

d. Stuffing Box Adjustment. Initial adjustment of water propeller rear drive shaft stuffing box may be made with vehicle on land, but final adjustment must be made with vehicle in water. Key letters in text refer to figure 230.

(1) TIGHTEN PACKING NUT. If an excessive amount of water enters vehicle through stuffing box gland, adjust packing nut (A) as follows:

(a) Initial Adjustment (Vehicle Out of Water). Loosen check nut. Tighten packing nut gradually one-sixth turn at a time, meanwhile noticing when packing produces drag on shaft, then tighten check nut (B).

(b) Final Adjustment. With vehicle in water and water propeller shaft turning slowly, notice amount of water which enters bilge past stuffing box gland. Adjustment is normal if small amount of water seeps past gland. If no water is observed leaking at this point, loosen packing nut to prevent possible overheating. If water in excess of slight seepage enters bilge through stuffing box, tighten packing nut as described in step *(a)* above.

Water Drive System

STUFFING BOX INSTALLED

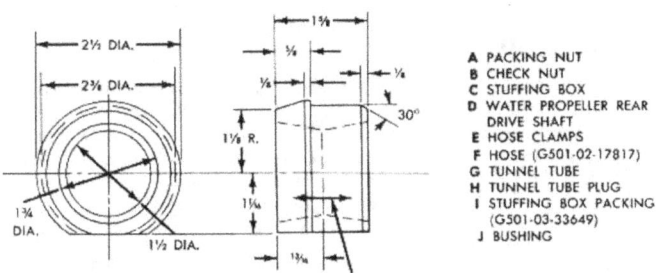

SECTIONAL VIEW OF STUFFING BOX AND TUNNEL TUBE PLUG INSTALLATION

TUNNEL TUBE PLUG DIMENSIONS

A PACKING NUT
B CHECK NUT
C STUFFING BOX
D WATER PROPELLER REAR DRIVE SHAFT
E HOSE CLAMPS
F HOSE (G501-02-17817)
G TUNNEL TUBE
H TUNNEL TUBE PLUG
I STUFFING BOX PACKING (G501-03-33649)
J BUSHING

RA PD 333201

Figure 230—Water Propeller Drive Shaft Stuffing Box and Tunnel Tube Plug

e. Stuffing Box Replacement. Key letters in text refer to figure 230.

(1) REMOVAL. Remove water propeller rear drive shaft as described in paragraph 257*d*.(1). Remove hose clamps (E) and separate hose (F) from stuffing box. Remove packing nut (A) and check nut (B) from stuffing box housing. Remove packing from gland (I).

Maintenance Instructions

(2) TUNNEL TUBE PLUG MODIFICATION.

(a) Inspect Rear Shaft Tunnel Tube Plug. Vehicles prior to chassis serial No. 8,900, and from 11,179 through 12,312 inclusive, are built with old style tunnel plug which did not have a shoulder to hold it in position. Whenever water propeller rear drive shaft and stuffing box are removed, the style of tunnel plug should be observed and new style plug installed, if this modification has not previously been made. The new style plug is not furnished for service; however, by referring to dimensional drawing of plug (fig. 230), the plug can readily be fashioned from material obtained locally.

(b) Tunnel Tube Plug Installation. Install tunnel tube plug (H) in tunnel tube with shoulder on plug contacting edge of tube and flat section of plug at bottom of tube.

(3) INSTALLATION. Place hose (F) at stuffing box housing and secure with clamp (E). Place remaining clamp on hose with clamp bolt loose. With water propeller rear drive shaft on bench, place packing nut on drive shaft and then move stuffing box assembly to position. Wrap new rawhide packing (I) around shaft (D) and start packing nut onto stuffing box housing. Install water propeller rear drive shaft as described in paragraph 257**d**.(2).

Section XLV

Tire Pump System (Early Type)

259. GENERAL.

a. Description. Tire pump (fig. 231) is mounted on an adjustable bracket which is attached to the vehicle frame below the driver's seat and is driven from the power take-off by chain and sprocket. The tire pump is engaged by a shift lever located near the right rear corner of the driver's seat. Removal procedures for either the air-cooled or water-cooled pump are similar, with differences noted in text.

b. Data.

(1) AIR-COOLED TIRE PUMP (CHASSIS SERIAL NO. 006 TO 905).

Two-cylinder, single or double chain drive.
Maximum permissible engine speed .... 1350 rpm

(2) WATER-COOLED TIRE PUMP (CHASSIS SERIAL NO. 906 TO 2005).

Maximum permissible engine speed .... 2500 rpm

(3) STORAGE TANK.

Capacity .... ¾ cu ft

c. Repair. For repair instructions on tire pump components, refer to TM 9-1802C.

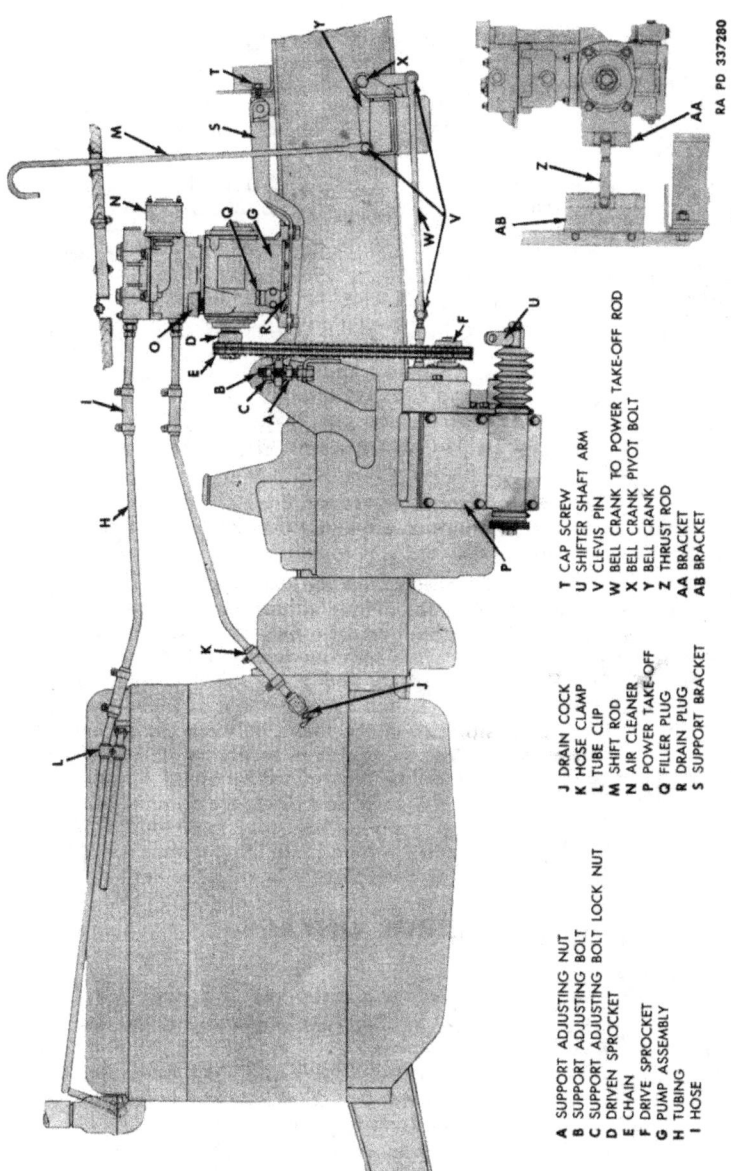

Figure 231 — Water-cooled Tire Pump Installation

A SUPPORT ADJUSTING NUT
B SUPPORT ADJUSTING BOLT
C SUPPORT ADJUSTING BOLT LOCK NUT
D DRIVEN SPROCKET
E CHAIN
F DRIVE SPROCKET
G PUMP ASSEMBLY
H TUBING
I HOSE
J DRAIN COCK
K HOSE CLAMP
L TUBE CLIP
M SHIFT ROD
N AIR CLEANER
P POWER TAKE-OFF
Q FILLER PLUG
R DRAIN PLUG
S SUPPORT BRACKET
T CAP SCREW
U SHIFTER SHAFT ARM
V CLEVIS PIN
W BELL CRANK TO POWER TAKE-OFF ROD
X BELL CRANK PIVOT BOLT
Y BELL CRANK
Z THRUST ROD
AA BRACKET
AB BRACKET

477

260. DRIVE CHAIN AND SPROCKETS.

a. Chain Removal. Working in bilge compartment, loosen support bracket adjusting bolt nuts at front end of support. Disassemble chain connecting link by removing two cotter pins, then remove chain from sprockets.

b. Sprocket Removal. Remove cotter pin from driven sprocket retaining nut, then remove nut and shims (water-cooled tire pump only). With a $5/16$-inch hex wrench, remove two or four set screws, as case may be, which retain drive and driven sprocket to shaft. With a brass drift and hammer, drive sprockets and shaft keys from shaft. Remove the remaining shims and spacers.

c. Sprocket Installation. Install shaft key (GM-066383) instead of Woodruff type, then install drive sprocket on power take-off shaft. Carefully drive sprocket squarely on shaft. Install set screws and tighten firmly with hex wrench. Install spacer and two shims on pump driven shaft, then install shaft key and sprocket squarely on shaft. Install two shims, sprocket retaining nut, and cotter pin. Tighten nut firmly. NOTE: *Shims and retaining nut are not used to secure driven sprocket on air-cooled tire pump.*

d. Chain Installation. Place chain around drive and driven sprocket, then install connecting link in such a manner that link side plate cotter pin will be toward tire pump.

e. Sprockets Alinement and Chain Adjustment. Sprockets must be in the same plane (A, fig. 232). Three adjustments are provided to attain this plane. The tire pump support adjusting bolt maintains tension on chain. Shims at driven sprocket hub, on water-cooled pump only, adjust the sprocket longitudinally (D and E, fig. 232). No shims are used on air-cooled pump sprocket hub as sprocket is adjusted longitudinally by changing its position on shaft. Shims between tire pump and support adjust the angular position of driven sprockets (B and C, fig. 232). Alinement of sprockets may be determined by use of a chalk line (A, fig. 232). Bearing in mind that each time shims are changed between pump and support, the pump support adjusting bolt must also be changed to maintain the proper tension on chain. No attempt is made to give a step by step procedure as operations will vary for each vehicle.

261. TIRE PUMP CONTROL LINKAGE.

a. Removal.

(1) REMOVE SHIFT ROD. Remove cotter pin and clevis pin from bell crank upper arm. Shift rod can then be removed through driver's compartment floor board.

(2) REMOVE BELL CRANK TO POWER TAKE-OFF ROD. Remove cotter pins and clevis pins from lower bell crank arm and power take-off auxiliary shift shaft. Remove rod from bilge compartment.

(3) REMOVE BELL CRANK. Remove nut from bell crank pivot bolt, then remove bolt and washer. Bell crank can then be removed from bracket.

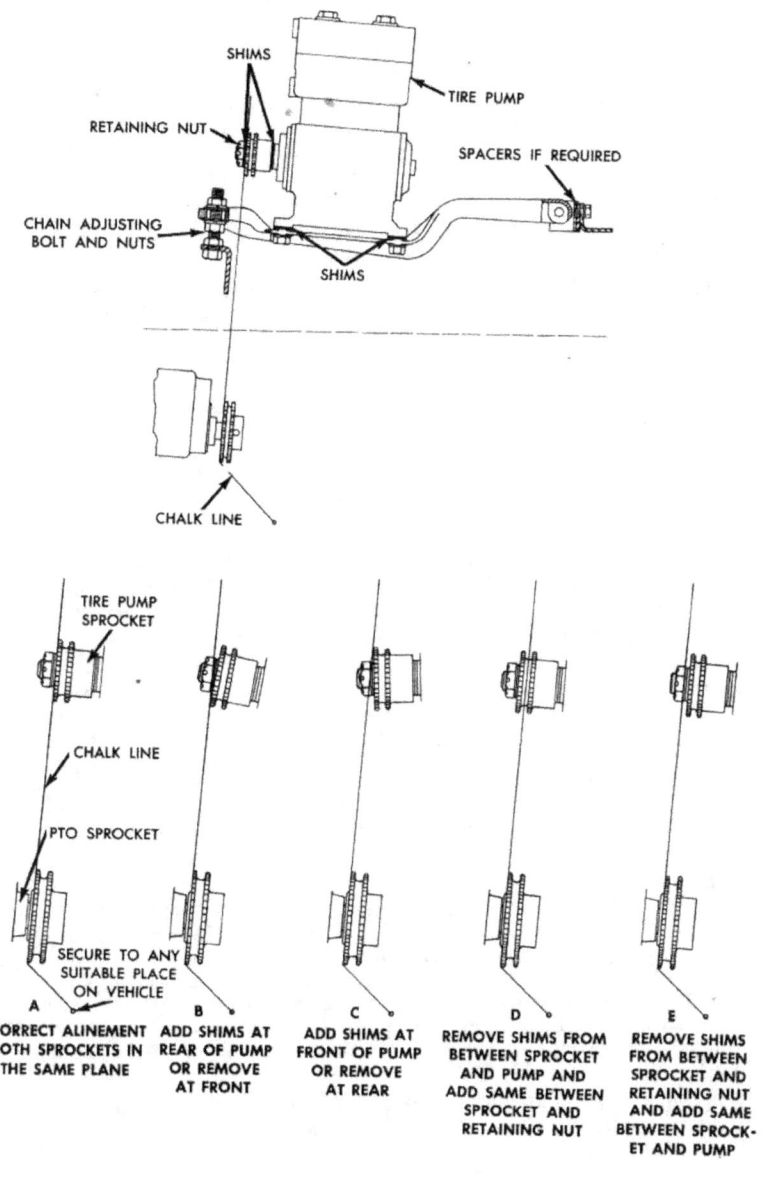

Figure 232—Tire Pump Sprocket Alinement

Maintenance Instructions

b. Installation.

(1) INSTALL BELL CRANK. Position bell crank to bell crank bracket with long arm pointing forward and short arm downward. Install bell crank pivot bolt through bell crank bracket and bell crank. Secure with nut and cotter pin.

(2) INSTALL BELL CRANK TO POWER TAKE-OFF ROD. Position rod to bell crank lower arm and power take-off auxiliary shift shaft, then secure with cotter pins and clevis pins.

(3) INSTALL SHIFT ROD. Install shift rod through hole in driver's compartment floor boards and secure to bell crank upper arm with cotter pin and clevis pin.

262. TIRE PUMP REPLACEMENT.

a. Removal.

(1) DISCONNECT AIR LINES AND COOLING LINES. Disconnect air and water line connections, depending upon type of pump.

(2) REMOVE CHAIN AND ADJUSTING BOLT. Remove chain (par. 260a.). Remove nuts, lock washers, plain washers, and adjusting bolt.

(3) REMOVE PUMP AND SUPPORT BRACKET. Remove cotter pin and clevis pin at frame bracket end of thrust rod on water-cooled pump only. Loosen and remove two bolts, lock washers, and flat washers from hinge to pump support bracket to rear of pump and remove pump from vehicle.

(4) REMOVE SUPPORT BRACKET AND THRUST ROD FROM PUMP. Remove four nuts, lock washers, and bolts from pump support bracket, then remove bracket. On water-cooled pump only, remove two nuts and lock washers from thrust rod bracket at front bearing cap, then remove thrust rod from bracket. Remove cotter pin and clevis pin from thrust rod and bracket, then remove thrust rod from bracket. Remove the cotter pin and clevis pin from hinge, then remove hinge from support.

b. Installation.

(1) INSTALL SUPPORT BRACKET AND THRUST ROD BRACKET. One water-cooled pump only, place thrust rod bracket on pump front bearing cap and install two nuts and lock washers. Place pump support bracket on bottom of pump and install three hex head bolts and one flathead bolt, flat washers (three at each corner of pump), nuts, and lock washers. Flathead bolt must be in left front corner of support bracket to allow clearance between bracket and master cylinder. Position hinge on support bracket, and install clevis pin and cotter pin.

(2) INSTALL PUMP AND SUPPORT BRACKET. Position pump and support bracket assembly in vehicle. Line up front of support bracket with adjusting bolt bracket. Before installing hinge bracket bolts, insert the flat washers, if necessary, on either right or left side of hinge bracket as required to line up pump support with adjusting bolt bracket. Refer to figure 231. Install bolts and lockwashers and tighten securely.

Tire Pump System (Early Type)

(3) INSTALL CHAIN. Install chain (par. 260**d**.).

(4) INSTALL ADJUSTING BOLT AND ADJUST CHAIN. Place adjusting bolt through pump support brackets and install nuts, plain washers, and lock washers. Adjust chain for proper tension by loosening or tightening adjusting bolt nuts. However, before adjusting chain, it is imperative that sprocket be alined (par. 260**e**.). Refer to figure 232.

(5) INSTALL THRUST ROD (WATER-COOLED PUMP ONLY). Install thrust rod between brackets on pump and frame. Install clevis pin at pump end of rod, turn adjustable yoke at frame end of rod until clevis pin is slip fit in yoke and bracket, then install cotter pins in both clevis pins.

(6) INSTALL AIR AND COOLING LINE CONNECTIONS. Connect air and water lines to pump. Tighten connections firmly.

263 AIR TANK AND LINES.

a. General. The air tank is located on support brackets at the right side of the hull under and to the right of the driver's seat. The tank is held in place by U-bolts with spacers between the supports and tank. The inlet line, extending from the tire pump to the tank, is of the metal type, securely clipped to the hull. The outlet lines extend from both ends of the tank or from the center to the right and left inflation hose assemblies. The tank is equipped with a drain cock to remove condensation and a safety valve to prevent damage caused by over pressure.

b. Air Tank.

(1) REMOVAL. Open drain cock and allow all air to exhaust from tank, then disconnect outlet and inlet lines at tank and tire inflation hoses. Remove lines from vehicle. Remove nuts from two U-bolts, then withdraw tank through cargo compartment.

(2) INSTALLATION. Position tank in place on supports and spacers and install two U-bolts. Tighten all bolt nuts securely. Connect outlet and inlet lines at tank and tire inflation hoses. Tighten air line connections securely.

c. Safety Valve.

(1) REMOVAL. Unscrew safety valve from air storage tank.

(2) INSTALLATION. Apply gasket cement (52-C-685) on valve thread before installing valve in air storage tank. Screw valve into storage tank and tighten securely.

(3) SAFETY VALVE ADJUSTMENT. Prior to chassis serial No. 2006, some safety valves were set to release at 150 pounds pressure. All safety valves must be set to release at 50 pounds pressure as outlined in steps *(a)* through *(e)*.

(a) Remove Drain Cock. Remove drain cock (H006-01-00805) from bottom of air storage tank and install a tee. Install an air gage (41-G-124) in one arm of tee and the drain cock in the opposite arm of tee. Use pipe fittings as necessary to adapt air gage and drain cock.

(b) Operate Tire Pump. Operate tire pump until air gage registers 50 pounds of air pressure in storage tank. Tank pressure can be decreased by opening drain cock. Regulate tank pressure until it is stable at 50 pounds gage reading.

(c) Adjust Safety Valve. Adjust safety valve to release at 50 pounds pressure. Loosen lock nut at end of safety valve and turn adjusting screw clockwise to increase release pressure, or counterclockwise to decrease release pressure. When final adjustment is obtained, tighten lock nut.

(d) Check Adjustment. After setting the valve, decrease air tank pressure by opening drain cock and again bring air pressure up to 50 pounds to check safety valve release action.

(e) Remove Tee Fitting. When satisfied with valve adjustment, remove air gage drain cock and tee from air tank. Coat threads on drain cock with gasket cement (52-C-685) and install in original position in air tank, tightening firmly to prevent leaks.

Section XLVI
Central Tire Pressure Control System

264. GENERAL.

a. System Description and Operation. Location of each component of the central tire pressure control system is shown in figure 233. Tire pump, mounted in front compartment and driven directly by the engine crankshaft, maintains air pressure in the air tank. Air pressure in air tank is piped to the tire inflation and deflation control valves assembly. When tire inflating control lever is placed in "INFLATE" position, air pressure passes through the control valve to the air line manifold and valves, thence to each tire through individual air lines and tire inflating devices.

b. Data.

Tire Pump
- Make .... Midland Steel Products (MSP)
- Model MSP-N-5048B
- Type .... Two-cylinder, water-cooled, self-lubricated
- Cylinder size .... 2¼ in. x 1⅝ in.
- Capacity .... 9 cu ft per min.

Tire Pump Governor
- Model MSP-N-2426

Governor Setting
- Cut-in .... 50 lb
- Cut-out (approximately) .... 75 lb

Air Tank Safety Valve
- Set to blow off at .... 100 to 105 lb

c. Repair. Repair procedures for components of the central tire pressure control system are described in TM 9-1802C.

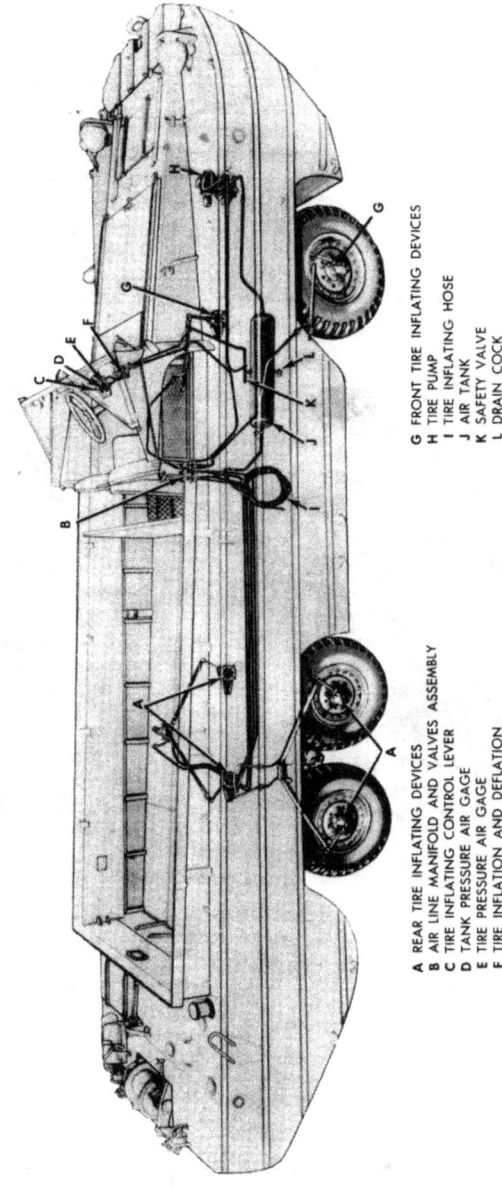

A REAR TIRE INFLATING DEVICES
B AIR LINE MANIFOLD AND VALVES ASSEMBLY
C TIRE INFLATING CONTROL LEVER
D TANK PRESSURE AIR GAGE
E TIRE PRESSURE AIR GAGE
F TIRE INFLATION AND DEFLATION CONTROL VALVES
G FRONT TIRE INFLATING DEVICES
H TIRE PUMP
I TIRE INFLATING HOSE
J AIR TANK
K SAFETY VALVE
L DRAIN COCK

RA PD 333220

Figure 233—Location of Central Tire Pressure Control System Components

TM 9-802
265

Maintenance Instructions

265. TIRE PUMP GOVERNOR.

a. General. Tire pump governor is mounted on top of tire pump as shown in figure 236. Governor automatically limits air tank pressure to a predetermined range by holding inlet valves open and stopping compression when air tank pressure is built up to maximum pressure limit, and by releasing inlet valves and starting compression when air tank pressure drops to minimum pressure limit. Figure 234 shows governor in cut-in (compressing) position. Cut-in setting is adjusted by increasing or decreasing tension on diaphragm spring. Trigger stop, (I, fig. 234), was not installed on vehicles prior to chassis serial No. 2740.

b. Cut-in Pressure Adjustment (fig. 235). Governor should be adjusted so that compression begins when tank pressure gage reading is

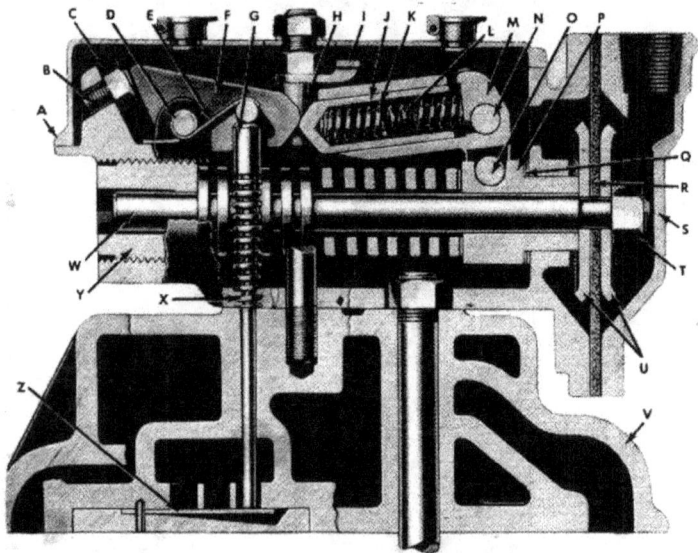

A COVER
B TRIGGER STOP SCREW
C LOCK NUT
D TRIGGER TO BASE PIN
E TRIGGER SPRING
F TRIGGER
G INLET VALVE RELEASE PLUNGER
H SPACER
I TRIGGER STOP
J DISENGAGING PLUNGER
K DISENGAGING PLUNGER SPRING (OUTER)
L DISENGAGING PLUNGER SPRING (INNER)
M DISENGAGING PLUNGER HOUSING
N HOUSING TO BASE PIN
O HOUSING TO PISTON PIN
P PISTON
Q SHIMS
R DIAPHRAGM
S END COVER
T DIAPHRAGM GUIDE ROD NUT
U DIAPHRAGM PLATES
V TIRE PUMP CYLINDER HEAD
W DIAPHRAGM GUIDE ROD
X INLET VALVE RELEASE PLUNGER SPRING
Y ADJUSTING SCREW
Z INLET VALVE

RA PD 333221

Figure 234—Cross Section of Tire Pump Governor (Cut-in Position)

Central Tire Pressure Control System

RA PD 337171

Figure 235—Adjusting Governor Cut-In Pressure

at 50 pounds. With compression beginning at 50 pounds, governor should assume cut-out position and stop compression when tank pressure gage reading is approximately 75 pounds; however, governor should always be set at 50-pound cut-in point. Adjustment is made by turning the external adjusting screw (fig. 235), which varies the tension on the diaphragm spring. Turn adjusting screw clockwise to increase cut-in pressure, or counterclockwise to decrease cut-in pressure.

c. Governor Removal (fig. 236). Disconnect air tank to governor cooling coil from governor by unscrewing cooling coil tube nut from elbow in governor end cover. Remove two nuts and internal-toothed lock washers attaching governor cover to governor and lift cover off. Remove two nuts, trigger stop (if used), and two spacers from governor attaching studs and lift governor assembly off from tire pump cylinder head.

d. Governor Installation (fig. 236).

(1) Before installing governor, lift inlet valve release plungers and springs out of cylinder head and examine them for bent plungers or broken springs. Replace with new parts if damaged. Thoroughly clean top of cylinder head and bottom of governor.

(2) Place springs on inlet valve release plungers and insert plungers down through holes in cylinder head. Carefully place governor over governor attaching studs, at the same time guiding inlet valve release plungers and springs through holes in bottom of governor. Install two spacers, trigger stop (if used), and two nuts on governor attaching studs and tighten nuts firmly. Install governor cover on governor and attach with two nuts and internal-toothed lock washers. Coat threads of air tank to governor cooling coil tube nut with joint and thread compound (52-C-3115) and thread nut into elbow in governor end cover. Tighten tube nut firmly.

(3) Lubricate governor as instructed on Lubrication Order No. 9-802. Adjust governor to correct cut-in setting (subpar. **b.** above).

TM 9-802
266

Maintenance Instructions

266. TIRE PUMP.

a. General. Tire pump is a two-cylinder, water-cooled, self-lubricated air compressor mounted in front compartment ahead of engine radiator (fig. 236). The tire pump drive shaft connects the tire pump crankshaft directly to the engine crankshaft; therefore, the tire pump is driven constantly while the engine is running. Compression of air is automatically started and stopped by the tire pump governor, mounted on top of tire pump cylinder head.

b. Air Cleaner. Two types of tire pump air cleaners have been used (fig. 237). Both are oil-wetted hair element type filters with the same internal construction, the difference being in external construction. Operations necessary for servicing air cleaners are as follows: Remove air cleaner from air cleaner adapter, using wrench on reducing bushing. Remove nuts and lock washers (or snap ring) attaching air cleaner cover to shell and remove cover. Lift air cleaner tube, hair, and baffles out of shell. Service air cleaner as instructed on Lubrication Order No. 9-802. Install air cleaner tube, hair, and baffles in shell, positioning parts as shown in figure 237. Install air cleaner cover and attach with nuts and lock washers or with snap ring, as the case may be. On type "1" (fig. 237), prick punch bolt threads after tightening nuts to prevent nuts from working loose.

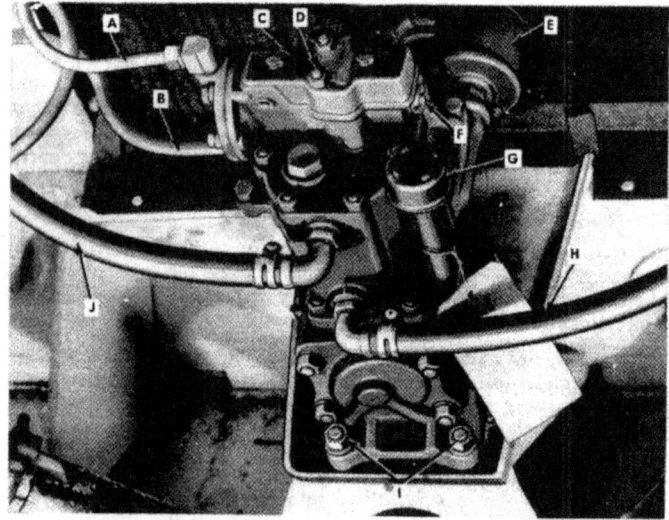

A AIR TANK TO GOVERNOR COOLING COIL
B PUMP DISCHARGE TO TANK COOLING COIL
C TIRE PUMP GOVERNOR (G501-70-01933)
D GOVERNOR ATTACHING STUDS
E TIRE PUMP AIR CLEANER
F ADJUSTING SCREW
G CRANKCASE BREATHER
H WATER INLET HOSE
I TIRE PUMP TO SUPPORT BOLTS
J WATER RETURN HOSE

RA PD 33324

Figure 236—Tire Pump Installed

TM 9-802

Central Tire Pressure Control System

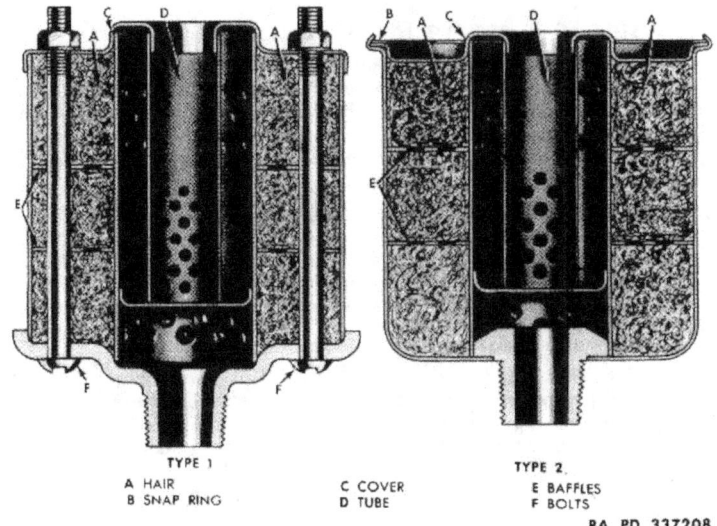

TYPE 1
A HAIR
B SNAP RING
C COVER
D TUBE

TYPE 2
E BAFFLES
F BOLTS

RA PD 337208

Figure 237—Tire Pump Air Cleaner

c. Crankshaft Front (Drive End) Bearing Cap Seal Replacement.

(1) REMOVAL. Disconnect drive shaft and remove tire pump (subpar. *d.* below). Remove cotter pin and nut attaching drive coupling to tire pump crankshaft and, using a suitable puller, pull coupling off from end of crankshaft. Remove Woodruff key from crankshaft. Remove nuts and lock washers from four studs attaching bearing cap to crankcase and remove bearing cap and oil seal assembly. Remove oil seal (G501-03-82799) from bearing cap.

(2) INSTALLATION.

(a) Thoroughly clean oil seal seat in bearing cap. Coat outside circumference of new oil seal with joint and thread compound (52-C-3115), and press or drive seal into bearing cap with lip of seal toward inner face of cap. Make sure seal is fully seated in cap.

(b) Clean all particles of gasket from bearing cap and crankcase and position new gasket over studs. Position bearing cap and oil seal assembly over end of crankshaft and, using a piece of shim stock to guide lip of seal over shoulder on crankshaft, push cap and seal assembly into place. Remove shim stock, then install four nuts and lock washers on studs and tighten firmly.

(c) Install Woodruff key in keyseat in crankshaft, then install drive coupling on crankshaft. Install nut on end of crankshaft and tighten firmly, then install cotter pin. Install tire pump and connect drive shaft (subpar. *e.* below).

487

d. Tire Pump Removal (fig. 236).

(1) DISCONNECT WATER AND AIR LINES. Drain cooling system until level of cooling liquid is below tire pump connections. Loosen hose clamps attaching hoses to elbows in cylinder block and cylinder head and pull hoses off elbows. Disconnect air tank to governor cooling coil and tire pump discharge to tank cooling coil from tire pump by unscrewing tube nuts.

(2) DISCONNECT DRIVE SHAFT AND REMOVE TIRE PUMP. Remove four bolts and lock washers attaching drive shaft body to drive coupling and push drive shaft body back away from coupling. Remove nuts and lock washers from four tire pump to support bolts and remove bolts. Lift tire pump off from support and out of front compartment.

e. Tire Pump Installation (fig. 236).

(1) INSTALL TIRE PUMP AND CONNECT DRIVE SHAFT. Position tire pump on support in front compartment and attach with four tire pump to support bolts, nuts, and lock washers. Make sure tire pump seats solidly on support. Any unevenness of support may be compensated for by using $7/16$-inch flat washers as shims between tire pump base and support. Connect drive shaft to drive coupling, using four bolts and lock washers.

(2) CONNECT WATER AND AIR LINES. Slide hoses over fittings in elbows and tighten hose clamps firmly. Coat threads of tube nuts on air cooling coils with joint and thread compound (52-C-3115) and thread nuts into fittings at tire pump. Refer to figure 236 for location of hoses and air line cooling coils. Fill cooling system (par. 117a.).
NOTE: *Observe instructions on caution tag attached to tire pump.*

267. TIRE PUMP DRIVE SHAFT.

a. General. Tire pump drive shaft connects tire pump crankshaft directly to engine crankshaft as shown in figure 238. Front (universal joint) end of drive shaft is bolted to drive coupling on tire pump crankshaft. Rear end of drive shaft is bolted to the flexible drive coupling disk, which is bolted to the engine crankshaft balancer.

b. Drive Shaft Removal. Remove three cotter pins, nuts, flat washers, corrugated washers, and bolts attaching engine end of drive shaft to drive coupling disk. At front end, remove four bolts and lock washers attaching drive shaft body to drive coupling on tire pump. With drive shaft free at both ends, remove it from the engine compartment, carefully working it back out of the opening in radiator from the right-hand side of the engine. Turn fan as necessary to permit drive shaft to pass between fan blades.

c. Drive Shaft Universal Joint Inspection and Packing. Mount drive shaft in a vise in a vertical position with the universal joint end up. Pry grease cover tangs away from drive shaft body and remove cover and gasket. Push body down, telescoping dust cover, until universal joint is exposed. Wipe grease off exposed parts and check balls for

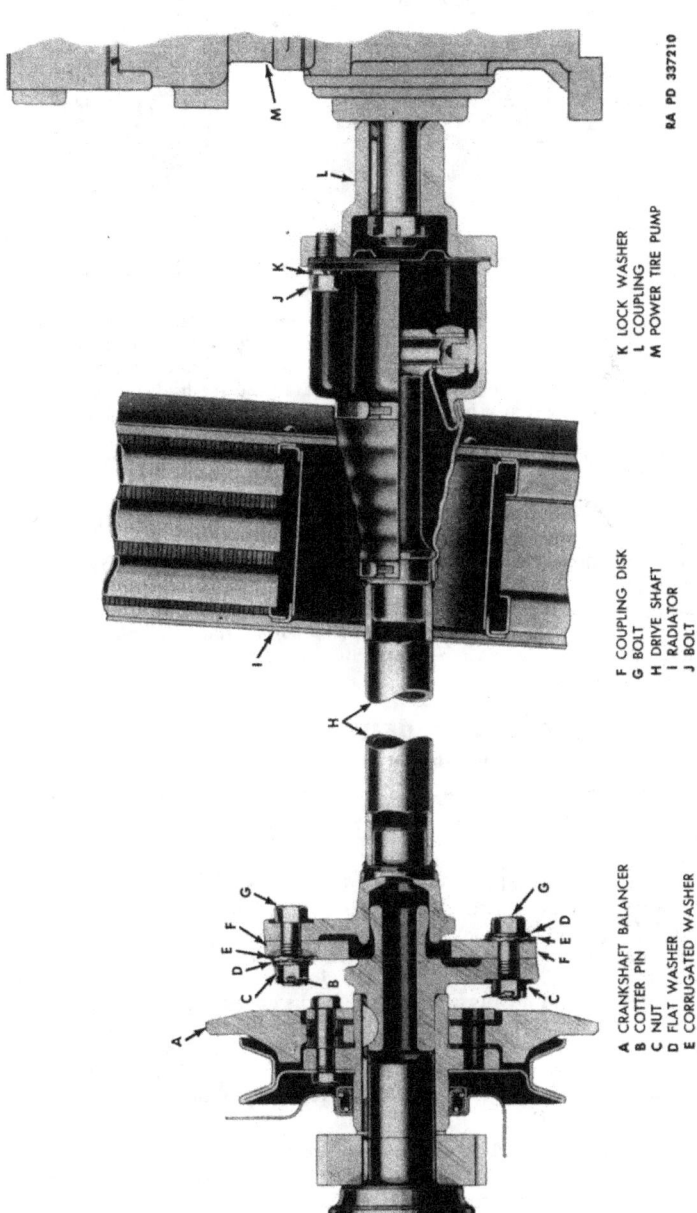

Figure 238—Tire Pump Drive Shaft

A CRANKSHAFT BALANCER
B COTTER PIN
C NUT
D FLAT WASHER
E CORRUGATED WASHER
F COUPLING DISK
G BOLT
H DRIVE SHAFT
I RADIATOR
J BOLT
K LOCK WASHER
L COUPLING
M POWER TIRE PUMP

RA PD 337210

TM 9-802
267-268

Maintenance Instructions

Figure 239—Method of Packing Drive Shaft Universal Joint

looseness on trunnion pin. Pull body up in operating position, grip body in both hands, and attempt to twist the body in both directions to check for looseness. Inspect lubricant in joint for contamination. If wear is evident or if lubricant is contaminated, notify higher authority. If no wear is evident and lubricant is in good condition, pack additional lubricant (Lubrication Order No. 9-802) into joint as shown in figure 239. Install gasket and grease cover, and bend cover tangs down over drive shaft body.

d. Drive Shaft Installation. Position drive shaft in vehicle, guiding universal joint end through opening in radiator from right-hand side of engine. Connect drive shaft to coupling disk at engine, using three bolts, corrugated washers, flat washers, nuts, and cotter pins. The corrugated washers must be installed next to the flexible disk as shown in figure 238 with the corrugations approximately radial. Tighten nuts firmly. Connect drive shaft body to coupling at tire pump, using four bolts and lock washers.

268. INFLATION AND DEFLATION CONTROL VALVES ASSEMBLY.

a. General. This assembly consists of two tire inflation and deflation control valve assemblies, one tire inflating check valve, and interconnecting fittings. The assembly is mounted on upper toeboard in engine compartment and is connected to the tire inflating control lever at the instrument panel by rods and levers. When tire inflating control lever is moved to "INFLATE" position, tire inflating control valve (C, fig. 240) is opened, permitting air pressure to pass through valve to the line valve manifold and thence to each tire. When control lever is moved to "DEFLATE" position, tire deflating control valve (D, fig. 240) is opened and air pressure in tires backs up through the line valve manifold and exhausts from the open port in the deflating control valve. The following procedures cover removal and installation of tire inflation and deflation control valves as a unit assembly. Replacement of any individual unit of this assembly is a repair operation (refer to par. 264c.).

b. Control Valves Assembly Removal (fig. 240).

(1) DISCONNECT UPPER ROD AND AIR LINES. Remove cotter pin and clevis pin connecting upper rod to lever on tire inflating valve.

Central Tire Pressure Control System

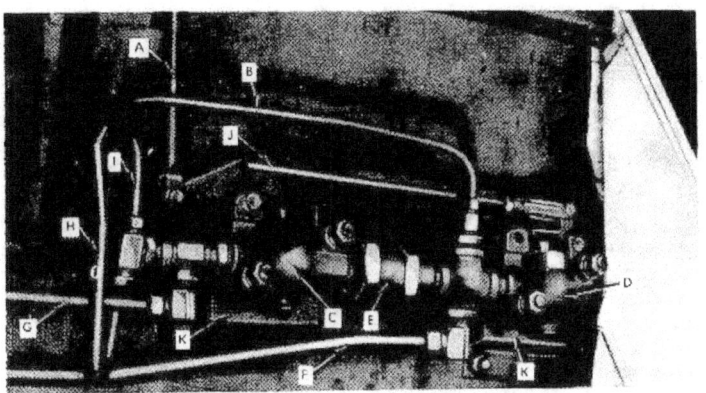

A UPPER ROD
B TIRE PRESSURE GAGE LINE
C TIRE INFLATING CONTROL VALVE (G501-70-01969)
D TIRE DEFLATING CONTROL VALVE (G501-70-01969)
E TIRE INFLATING CHECK VALVE
F CONTROL VALVE TO LINE VALVE MANIFOLD LINE
G AIR TANK TO CONTROL VALVE LINE
H WINDSHIELD WIPER LINE
I AIR TANK PRESSURE GAGE LINE
J LOWER ROD
K CONTROL VALVE BRACKETS

RA PD 333206

Figure 240—Inflation and Deflation Control Valves Installed

Disconnect five air lines from the assembly by unscrewing the air line nuts from connections.

(2) REMOVE ASSEMBLY. Remove four nuts and lock washers (two at each bracket) attaching control valve brackets to upper toeboard and lift control valves and brackets as an assembly from the toeboard.

c. Control Valves Assembly Installation (fig. 240).

(1) INSTALL ASSEMBLY. With four bracket to toeboard bolts inserted up through upper toeboard, position valves and brackets assembly on toeboard with bolts extending through holes in brackets. Install nut and lock washer on each bolt and tighten firmly.

(2) CONNECT AIR LINES. Coat threads of each air line nut with joint and thread compound (52-C-3115). Refer to figure 240 for identification and location of each line and thread line nuts into connections. Tighten nuts firmly.

269. TIRE INFLATING LINE VALVES AND MANIFOLD ASSEMBLY.

a. General (fig. 241). Air line valves and manifold assembly, consisting of six line valves installed on a single manifold, provides the driver with a means of controlling flow of air pressure to each individual tire. The assembly is attached to the inner side of the left-hand riser of the co-pilot's seat by two U-bolts, with the valve hand-wheels extend-

TM 9-802
269-270

Maintenance Instructions

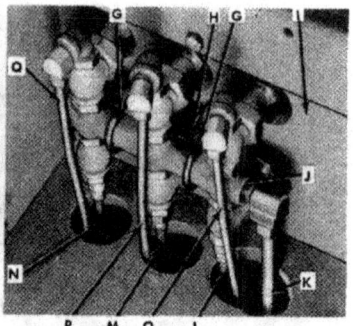

VIEWED FROM DRIVER'S SEAT

VIEWED FROM UNDER CO-PILOT'S SEAT

A RIGHT FRONT TIRE LINE VALVE*
B RIGHT FRONT REAR TIRE LINE VALVE*
C RIGHT REAR REAR TIRE LINE VALVE*
D LEFT FRONT TIRE LINE VALVE*
E LEFT FRONT REAR TIRE LINE VALVE*
F LEFT REAR REAR TIRE LINE VALVE*
G MANIFOLD TO SEAT RISER U-BOLTS
H MANIFOLD SPACER
*G501-70-02119

I CO-PILOT'S SEAT RISER
J TIRE INFLATING LINE VALVE MANIFOLD
K CONTROL VALVE TO MANIFOLD LINE
L LEFT FRONT TIRE LINE
M LEFT FRONT REAR TIRE LINE
N LEFT REAR REAR TIRE LINE
O RIGHT FRONT TIRE LINE
P RIGHT FRONT REAR TIRE LINE
Q RIGHT REAR REAR TIRE LINE

RA PD 337145

Figure 241—Air Line Valves Installed

ing through the seat riser where they are accessible to the driver. The following procedures cover removal and installation of the line valves and manifold as a unit assembly. Replacement of any individual unit of this assembly is a repair operation (refer to par. 264c.).

b. Line Valves and Manifold Assembly Removal (fig. 241). Disconnect six tire lines and one control valve to manifold line by unscrewing line nuts from elbows. Remove four nuts and lock washers from two U-bolts attaching manifold to seat riser and remove U-bolts. Lift line valves and manifold assembly away from seat riser.

c. Line Valves and Manifold Assembly Installation (fig. 241). Position line valves and manifold assembly at seat riser with handwheels inserted through holes in seat riser and with spacer in place between manifold and riser. Install two manifold to seat riser U-bolts, install four nuts and lock washers, and tighten firmly. Coat threads of air line nuts with joint and thread compound (52-C-3115). Refer to figure 241 for identification and location of air lines and thread air line nuts into elbows in valves and manifold. Tighten nuts firmly.

270. TIRE INFLATING DEVICES.

a. General. One tire inflating device (hub device) (fig. 242) is mounted on each wheel hub. Inflating device is an airtight rotary joint which provides a connection between the air supply line and the tire. The inner part (base) of the inflating device rotates with the wheel

TM 9-802

Central Tire Pressure Control System

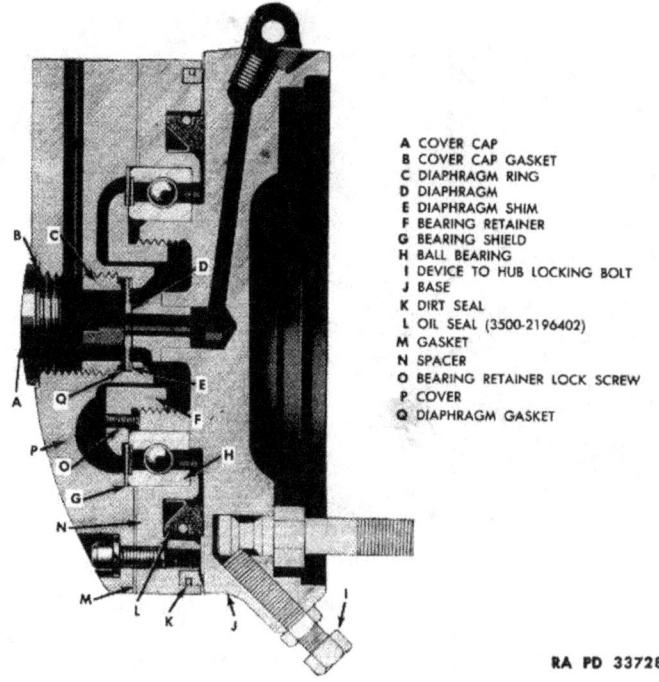

A COVER CAP
B COVER CAP GASKET
C DIAPHRAGM RING
D DIAPHRAGM
E DIAPHRAGM SHIM
F BEARING RETAINER
G BEARING SHIELD
H BALL BEARING
I DEVICE TO HUB LOCKING BOLT
J BASE
K DIRT SEAL
L OIL SEAL (3500-2196402)
M GASKET
N SPACER
O BEARING RETAINER LOCK SCREW
P COVER
Q DIAPHRAGM GASKET

RA PD 337283

Figure 242—Tire Inflating Device

hub, while the outer part (cover) is held stationary by a swivel ended strut attached to the hull. Tire inflating hose, which is clipped in the channel of the strut, delivers air pressure from the air line at the hull connection to the inflating device. Air pressure is delivered from the inflating device to the tire through the inflating device to valve stem hose. Inflating device is attached to wheel hub by three inflating device to hub locking bolts and three lock bolts. NOTE: *The instructions given in subparagraphs* **b.** *and* **c.** *below are for removing inflating device for repairs, or for replacing it with a new unit. For instructions covering removal and installation of inflating device when servicing wheels, brakes, etc., refer to paragraph* 212**c.**(1) *and* **d.**(2).

b. Inflating Device and Hose Removal (fig. 243 or 244).

(1) REMOVE INFLATING DEVICE. Close line valve on side of copilot's seat (fig. 26). Remove two bolts and lock washers attaching hose to inflating device line to inflating device cover and swing strut and line assembly to one side. Remove two cotter pins and clevis pins attaching hose cover to inflating device and remove cover. Disconnect hose from valve stem and install valve core in valve stem. Loosen lock nuts

Maintenance Instructions

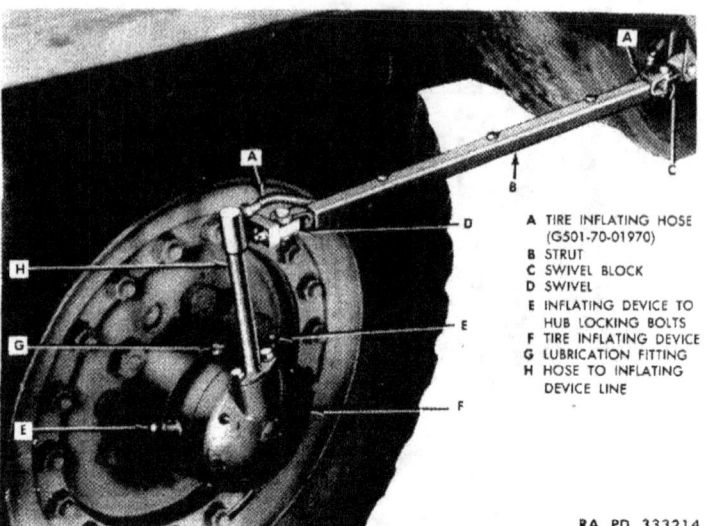

A TIRE INFLATING HOSE (G501-70-01970)
B STRUT
C SWIVEL BLOCK
D SWIVEL
E INFLATING DEVICE TO HUB LOCKING BOLTS
F TIRE INFLATING DEVICE
G LUBRICATION FITTING
H HOSE TO INFLATING DEVICE LINE

RA PD 333214

Figure 243—Front Tire Inflating Device Installed

on three inflating device lock bolts and back out lock bolts. Pull inflating device off from hub.

(2) REMOVE HOSE AND STRUT (IF NECESSARY). Remove nuts and lock washers from three bolts attaching hose clips to strut. Pull hose out of strut and remove clips. At front, remove cotter pin and clevis pin at each end of strut and remove strut. At rear, remove strut by removing nut and lock washer from ball stud at each end of strut. Hold hose with wrench on fitting and unscrew hose to inflating device line from hose, then unscrew hose from connection at hull.

c. Inflating Device Installation (fig. 243 or 244).

(1) INSTALL HOSE AND STRUT (IF REMOVED). Coat threads on fitting at each end of hose with joint and thread compound (52-C-3115). Thread hose fitting into connection at hull and tighten firmly. Thread hose to inflating device line onto fitting at other end of hose and tighten firmly, holding hose fitting with wrench to prevent twisting hose. Place hose clips on hose and attach clips to strut with bolts, nuts, and lock washers, then bend clips and hose into channel of strut. Connect strut at each end using clevis pins and cotter pins (front), or nuts and lock washers (rear).

(2) INSTALL INFLATING DEVICE. Position inflating device on hub with three locking bolts in hub inserted in holes in inflating device base. Make sure device is fully seated against hub, then tighten three lock bolts and lock nuts. Remove valve core from stem, connect inflating device to valve stem hose to valve stem, then install hose guard and

Central Tire Pressure Control System

A REAR TIRE INFLATING HOSE (G501-70-01971)
B STRUT
C INFLATING DEVICE TO VALVE STEM HOSE COVER
D HOSE TO INFLATING DEVICE LINE
E TIRE INFLATING DEVICE
F INFLATING DEVICE TO HUB LOCKING BOLTS
G LUBRICATION FITTING

RA PD 333232

Figure 244—Rear Tire Inflating Device Installed

attach with two clevis pins and cotter pins. Position hose to inflating device line on inflating device cover, using a new gasket between line and cover, and attach with two bolts and lock washers. Tighten bolts firmly. Open line valve.

d. Inflating Device Diaphragm Replacement.

(1) REMOVAL. This operation can be performed with inflating device installed, however it can be more readily accomplished with the assembly removed from the hub. Remove inflating device as described in subparagraph **b.** above. Place assembly in a vise, with the vise jaws gripping the inflating device cover. CAUTION: *Do not tighten vise jaws excessively.* Using tool supplied with vehicle, remove cover cap and diaphragm ring as shown in figure 245. Lift diaphragm gasket, diaphragm, and shims out of cover.

(2) INSTALLATION.

(a) Install Shims. Thoroughly clean shim seat and shims. Place original quantity of shims in cover, then insert plug gage on inflating device tool into cover as shown in figure 245. NOTE: *Gage must be clean and free from rust and corrosion, and plunger must be free in gage.* Make sure gage is fully seated against shims and that plunger in gage is against diaphragm seat, then check position of plunger in relation to

TM 9-802
270

Maintenance Instructions

REMOVING COVER CAP

REMOVING DIAPHRAGM RING
RA PD 337172

Figure 245—Cover Cap and Diaphragm Ring Removal

top surface of gage, using a straightedge across top of gage (fig. 246). Top of plunger must be flush with top of gage. Add or remove shims as necessary to obtain this condition. Shims are available in thicknesses of 0.001 inch and 0.003 inch.

   (b) Install Diaphragm, Diaphragm Ring, and Cover Cap. Daub a small amount of general purpose grease on diaphragm seat and on diaphragm boss, and install diaphragm in cover. Make sure diaphragm is evenly seated on shims. Place a new diaphragm gasket on extended portion of diaphragm ring and coat outer surface of gasket with general purpose grease. Thread diaphragm ring and gasket assembly into cover and tighten snugly. Install a new gasket on inflating device cover cap. Install cap in cover, and tighten firmly. Install inflating device (subpar. **c.** above).

   (c) NOTE: *After replacing inflating device diaphragm, slight leakage may occur. Leakage should stop after a few miles of operation, since the rotation of the diaphragm seat against the diaphragm will "wear in" the diaphragm and form a good seal. If leakage does not stop after a reasonable period, it is an indication of dirt between diaphragm and seat or a defective diaphragm. Leakage can often be corrected by reversing diaphragm in assembly. If leakage cannot be stopped by reversing diaphragm, replace diaphragm.*

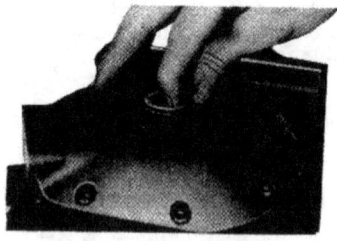
PLACING SHIMS IN COVER

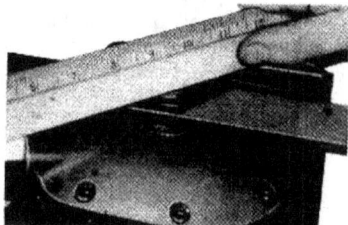
CHECKING SHIM THICKNESS

RA PD 337177

Figure 246—Installing Diaphragm Shims

TM 9-802

Central Tire Pressure Control System

271. AIR TANK AND LINES.

a. General (fig. 247). Air tank is mounted inside the hull on the right-hand side under the driver's compartment. In addition to air lines connecting the air tank to the tire pump, tire pump governor, and inflation and deflation control valves, the air tank is equipped with a drain cock, safety valve, and outlet fittings for connecting tire inflating hose (manual).

b. Air Tank Safety Valve. Safety valve is installed on air tank to prevent overloading the air pressure system in the event the tire pump governor fails to cut-out (stop compression). Safety valve is set to blow-off at 100 to 105 pounds pressure. Test and adjust safety valve setting in the following manner:

(1) Open drain cock and exhaust air from tank, then close drain cock. Remove safety valve from air tank by unscrewing valve from tee fitting on top of air tank.

(2) Connect safety valve to an outside air pressure supply having 100 pounds or more pressure, with an air gage installed in the supply line to indicate pressure at which safety valve releases.

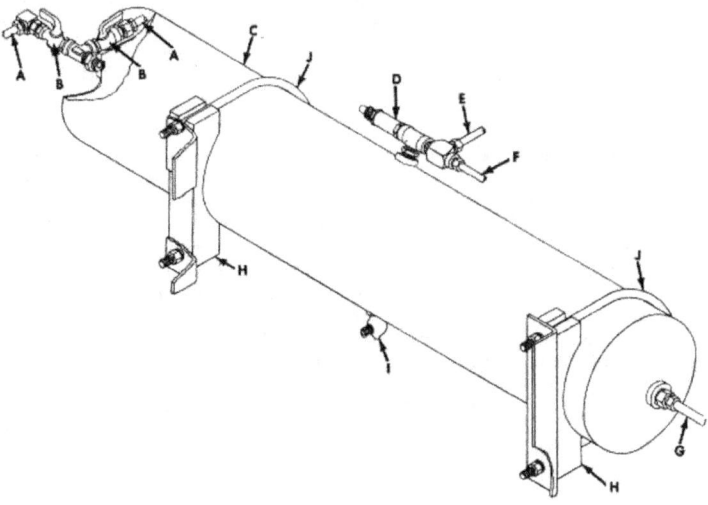

A TANK TO INFLATING HOSE (MANUAL) LINE
B SHUT-OFF COCKS
C AIR TANK
D SAFETY VALVE
E TANK TO GOVERNOR LINE
F TANK TO CONTROL VALVE LINE
G TIRE PUMP TO TANK LINE
H TANK SPACERS
I DRAIN COCK
J U-BOLTS

RA PD 337151

Figure 247—Air Tank Installed

Maintenance Instructions

(3) Open valve in air supply line and observe gage reading when safety valve releases. Valve should release at 100 pounds pressure.

(4) Loosen lock nut at end of safety valve and turn adjusting screw clockwise to increase release pressure, or counterclockwise to decrease the release pressure. Tighten lock nut on safety valve when correct adjustment is obtained.

(5) Coat threads of safety valve with joint and thread compound (52-C-3115) and install in tee fitting on air tank.

c. Air Tank Removal (fig. 247). Open drain cock to exhaust air pressure from tank. Disconnect all air lines from tank by unscrewing air line nuts. Remove four nuts and lock washers from two U-bolts attaching air tank to support brackets. Remove two U-bolts, air tank, and tank spacers from side of hull. If new tank is to be installed, remove drain cock, tee fitting and safety valve assembly, and inlet and outlet fittings for installation in new tank.

d. Air Tank Installation (fig. 247).

(1) INSTALL FITTINGS. Coat threads of drain cock, tee fitting, and inlet and outlet fittings with joint and thread compound (52-C-3115) and install in tank in positions shown in figure 247.

(2) INSTALL TANK. Position U-bolts and spacers around tank, then place the assembly in the vehicle with U-bolts through holes in support brackets. Install nuts and lock washers on U-bolts and tighten firmly.

(3) CONNECT AIR LINES. Coat threads of all air line nuts with joint and thread compound (52-C-3115) and connect lines to tank. Refer to figure 247 for identification and location of air lines. Close drain cock at bottom of tank, and close shut-off cocks at rear end of tank.

e. Air Lines Replacement. Air lines and connections are accessible in engine compartment, under driver's compartment, and under cargo compartment floor boards. Air lines from line valves to hull connections are in sections to facilitate replacement. Removal of any air line is accomplished by unscrewing the line nut from fitting or connection at each end and removing clips attaching line to vehicle. When installing air lines, coat threads of line nuts with joint and thread compound (52-C-3115), thread the nut into its respective fitting or connection, and secure line to vehicle with clips and bolts. Treat air lines to prevent corrosion as described in paragraph 198d.

Section XLVII
Winch and Controls

272 GENERAL.

a. Description (fig. 248). The winch is a worm driven horizontal drum type, mounted in the pocket of the stern compartment. Power for operating the winch is supplied by the vehicle engine through a power

Winch and Controls

A L.H. SUPPORT ANGLE
B R.H. SUPPORT ANGLE
C A-FRAME BRACKET
D ROPE GUARD SUPPORT
E ROPE GUARD
F WINCH CABLE (3500-2198218)

RA PD 337176

Figure 248—Winch Installed on Vehicle

take-off and winch drive shaft. The winch controls consist of a winch power take-off control lever, located in the driver's compartment, and a sliding clutch shift yoke at the winch. The winch is equipped with a drag brake which works in conjunction with the sliding clutch to prevent the drum from overrunning the cable when cable is pulled from the drum. The drum flange lock also works in conjunction with the sliding clutch to prevent the drum from being turned by the motion of the vehicle, thereby unwinding the cable. The winch brake acts on the winch worm shaft to hold the load when the power supply has been cut off.

b. Data.

Type	Worm driven—horizontal drum
Drive	From power take-off
Capacity	10,000 lb
Make	Gar Wood
Model	42Y3212

c. Repair. For repair procedures on winch components, refer to TM 9-1802C.

273. ADJUSTMENT AND SERVICE ON VEHICLE.

a. Adjustment Tests.

(1) TEST DRAG BRAKE OPERATION. Disengage sliding jaw clutch. Take hold of cable and begin to pull cable off drum. Drum should cease to revolve as soon as pull is stopped. If drum overruns cable, the drag brake requires adjustment.

Maintenance Instructions

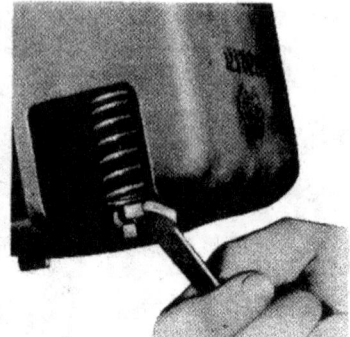

DRAG BRAKE ADJUSTMENT　　　WINCH BRAKE ADJUSTMENT

RA PD 337150

Figure 249—Winch Adjustments

(2) TEST WINCH BRAKE OPERATION.

(a) Manual. With winch power take-off lever and winch sliding clutch in the disengaged position, turn winch drive shaft by hand. When turning drive shaft in "lifting" direction, a slight drag should be noticeable. When turning drive shaft in "lowering" direction, drag must be about twice the drag encountered when turned in "lifting" direction.

(b) Operating Winch. Using an A-frame, raise a load of 2½ tons with the winch. Lower the load a short distance with the winch, then depress clutch pedal, disengaging clutch. Winch brake must stop and hold load. If it does not, need for winch brake adjustment is indicated. CAUTION: *Brake may become warm even though it is properly adjusted; however, if hand cannot be held on brake cover on account of heat, this indicates that brake is too tight and should be loosened.* Brake is designed to hold load, and if properly adjusted, will not become overheated. Excessive heat indicates that brake band should be relined or the brake band assembly replaced.

b. Drag Brake Adjustment (fig. 249).

(1) DISENGAGE SLIDING JAW CLUTCH. Lift poppet knob and move shift yoke to disengage sliding clutch.

(2) ADJUST DRAG BRAKE LINK. Insert screwdriver or wedge between end of tension bolt and drag brake shoe. Force tension bolt away from shift yoke to permit use of wrenches on adjusting nut and lock nut. Loosen lock nut and back off adjusting nut one full turn, then remove wedge and check adjustment [subpar. *a.*(1) above]. Repeat above process if necessary, to obtain satisfactory brake operation. When correct adjustment is obtained, turn lock nut up tight against adjusting nut. In the event a satisfactory adjustment cannot be obtained, it will be necessary to reline brake or replace drag brake shoe assembly.

c. Winch Brake Adjustment (fig. 249).

(1) ADJUST BRAKE BAND SPRING TENSION. Back off lock nut, then tighten adjusting nut one-half turn and reset lock nut against adjusting nut.

(2) TEST ADJUSTMENT. Accomplish procedure for winch brake test [subpar. *a.*(2) above]. Repeat step (1) above if necessary to obtain correct adjustment. NOTE: *If brake will not hold load after adjustment, or if it overheats when properly adjusted as indicated by test, it will be necessary to replace the brake band assembly.*

d. Winch Brake Replacement.
For operations necessary to replace winch brake, refer to TM 9-1802C.

e. Corrosion Prevention of Winch Brake.

(1) REMOVE WINCH BRAKE COMPONENTS. Disassemble and remove brake components as directed in TM 9-1802C.

(2) REMOVE CORROSION AND PAINT PARTS. Remove corrosion from all non-friction surfaces of brake disk, band, and internal surface of case. Paint these surfaces with two coats of zinc chromate primer, permitting first coat to dry before applying second coat.

(3) INSTALL AND ADJUST WINCH BRAKE. Install winch brake components as described in TM 9-1802C; then test and adjust as described in subparagraphs *a.*(2) and *c.* above.

(4) APPLY RUST PREVENTIVE TO THREADS. When adjustments have been completed, coat anchor nuts, adjusting nuts, and threaded ends of brake band with a thin film of rust preventive compound.

274. SHEAR PIN AND WINCH CABLE REPLACEMENT.

a. Shear Pin.
In the event a shear pin should be sheared, or pin shows signs of distortion or partial shearing when inspection is made by removal of pin after winching operation, replacement of pin is made as follows:

(1) MOVE STOP COLLAR OR REMOVE STOP CLAMP. Open stern compartment hatch cover and enter stern compartment. Raise stop collar (snap ring at rear drive shaft) from its groove in shaft splines, and move it toward rear of vehicle as far as it will go. If stop clamp is used instead of stop collar, remove screw, then remove clamp from around shaft (fig. 250).

(2) REMOVE SHEAR PIN. Move drive shaft rear universal joint forward on shaft splines until shear pin hole in winch worm shaft is exposed. Using a suitable punch, drive portions of shear pin from worm shaft and from universal joint yoke. Inspect holes in yoke and worm shaft for enlargement and replace parts as necessary.

(3) GREASE END OF WORM SHAFT. Coat end of worm shaft and inside of U-joint yoke with general purpose grease to prevent corrosion and seizing of yoke on worm shaft.

(4) POSITION DRIVE SHAFT. Rotate drive shaft so that shear pin hole in universal joint yoke lines up with shear pin hole in winch worm

TM 9-802
274-275

Maintenance Instructions

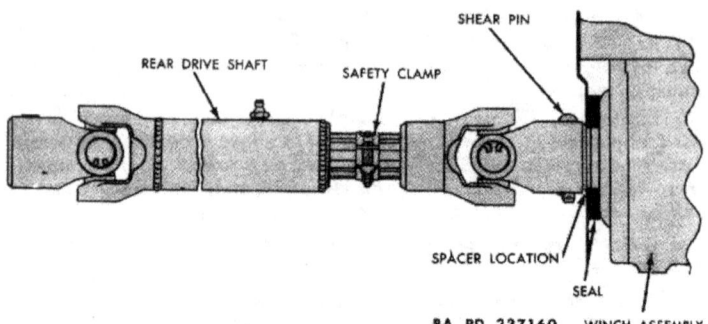

Figure 250—Shear Pin and Safety Clamp Installation

shaft. Move universal joint rearward so that shear pin may be installed through universal joint yoke and worm shaft.

(5) INSTALL SHEAR PIN. Dip shear pin in medium preservative lubricating oil, then install pin and secure with cotter pin. Check end play of yoke on worm shaft. If necessary, install spacer washers between yoke and winch to eliminate end thrust. Move stop collar into position in groove in shaft splines. If stop clamp is used instead of stop collar, fit clamp around shaft, locate clamp to provide 5/8-inch clearance between front edge of clamp and rear end of shaft tube and tighten clamp screw to lock clamp in place (fig. 250). Close stern compartment hatch cover.

(6) CAUTION: *Always use one of the shear pins furnished. Never use a substitute; use of a substitute may result in expensive replacement of parts. Spare shear pins are located in a special mounting bracket in stern compartment near end of winch worm shaft.*

b. Winch Cable.

(1) REMOVE CABLE FROM DRUM. Disengage sliding clutch and unlock drum flange lock, then pull cable straight out from winch by hand. Loosen two cable clamp nuts at outer side of right-hand drum flange, then pull cable out of clamp.

(2) INSTALL CABLE ON DRUM. Insert end of cable through clamp at inner side of right-hand drum flange, then tighten clamp nuts firmly. Wind cable on drum evenly and compactly, using hand cranking lever to guide as shown in figure 23.

275. WINCH WORM SHAFT OIL SEALS AND BEARINGS.

a. Removal.

(1) REMOVE WINCH. Remove winch from vehicle (par. 277).

(2) REMOVE GEAR CASE FROM WINCH. Remove four bolts and

Winch and Controls

lock washers attaching gear case cover to gear case and separate gear case and cover from winch drum shaft. Remove gear case with worm to bench.

(3) REMOVE WINCH BRAKE CASE. Remove two bolts and lock washers attaching brake case to gear case. Pull brake case straight away from gear case so that brake band will slide off brake disk.

(4) REMOVE BRAKE DISK. Remove bolt and disk retaining washer from end of worm shaft. Assemble a suitable puller on disk and pull disk off worm shaft. Do not lose key.

(5) REMOVE WORM. Remove bolts and lock washers which attach worm shaft bearing caps to gear case, then withdraw bearing caps. Force worm with bearings out of gear case as an assembly.

(6) REMOVE BEARING FROM WORM SHAFT. Use a suitable bearing puller or arbor press and remove bearing (H012-13-01045 or G012-03-12045) from each end of worm shaft.

(7) REMOVE OIL SEALS FROM BEARING CAPS. Hold worm shaft bearing cap in vise equipped with soft jaws, and drive oil seal (H720-05-00094) out of each bearing cap.

b. Installation.

(1) INSTALL OIL SEALS IN BEARING CAPS. Coat oil seal seat in each bearing cap with cement (52-C-685) and press new oil seal, with seal lip toward inside of cap, into each bearing cap. Be sure seal is pressed in squarely and is not cocked or bent during installation.

(2) INSTALL BEARINGS ON WORM SHAFT. Press bearings, with side of bearing which bears trade name and number away from worm thread, onto worm shaft tight against shoulder on shaft. Bearing number ND-H-20309 must be installed at brake end of shaft and bearing number ND-1309 at joint end.

(3) INSTALL WORM IN GEAR CASE. Use a lead hammer and drive worm shaft and bearings into position in gear case. Coat seal wiping surface at each end of worm shaft, also lip of oil seals with general purpose grease. Place a new bearing cap gasket (G501-01-93969) in position at each end of gear case and install bearing cap with oil seal. Guide oil seal over end of worm shaft, being careful not to damage seal. Install bearing cap bolts and lock washers and tighten firmly.

(4) INSTALL BRAKE DISK. Tap brake disk key into keyway in worm shaft. Support the assembly at joint end of worm shaft and drive brake disk on end of worm shaft far enough to permit installation of disk retaining washer and bolt. Tighten bolt to draw disk into position against shoulder on worm shaft.

(5) INSTALL WINCH BRAKE CASE. Assemble brake band over brake disk, and move brake case into position against gear case. Install two brake case to gear case bolts and lock washers.

(6) ASSEMBLE GEAR CASE AND COVER ON WINCH. Assemble gear case with worm, gasket (G162-12-87711), and gear case cover to

winch drum shaft, being certain that dowel pins in gear case fit into dowel holes in bushings. Install four cover to gear case bolts and lock washers and tighten firmly.

(7) INSTALL WINCH. Install winch in vehicle (par. 278).

276. DRIVE SHAFT AND UNIVERSAL JOINTS.

a. Description. Four tubular drive shafts are utilized in transmitting power from the power take-off to the winch assembly. The shafts are supported by three ball bearing assemblies, each set in rubber and securely mounted to the vehicle frame. The drive shafts are coupled together by universal joint assemblies. A slip joint is provided at the forward end of the front drive shaft and also at the rear end of the rear drive shaft to allow for lengthwise movement. The winch rear drive shaft incorporates a stop collar or a clamp, located at the rearward end, which prevents the shaft from sliding forward and off the winch worm shaft if and when the shear pin is sheared off. The shear pin is a special type pin located in the yoke of the universal joint which is attached to the winch worm shaft. The shear pin passes through the universal joint yoke and winch worm shaft and acts as a safety device to prevent breakage or damage in case the winch is loaded beyond capacity.

b. Drive Shaft Removal Procedure (figs. 250 and 251). Drive shafts should be removed progressively starting at winch and working forward. To provide maximum accessibility for mechanic, open stern compartment hatch cover and remove cargo compartment center and left front floor boards, also driver's compartment center and left front floor boards.

(1) MOVE STOP COLLAR OR REMOVE STOP CLAMP AND REMOVE SHEAR PIN (FIG. 250). Lift stop collar (snap ring at rear drive shaft slip joint) from its groove in shaft splines and move it along splines, toward rear of vehicle, as far as it will go. If stop clamp is used instead of stop collar, remove clamp from around shaft. Remove shear pin cotter pin and drive shear pin out of yoke, using a suitable punch.

(2) DISCONNECT DRIVE SHAFT FROM WINCH. Telescope or collapse slip joint at rear drive shaft until universal joint yoke is removed from end of winch worm shaft.

(3) REMOVE REAR CENTER DRIVE SHAFT REAR YOKE. Loosen set screw holding universal joint yoke to rear end of rear center shaft and drive yoke from shaft. Yoke is keyed to shaft. Do not lose key.

(4) REMOVE REAR DRIVE SHAFT. Withdraw rear shaft forward through clearance hole in rear bulkhead, and remove from vehicle through cargo compartment floor board opening.

(5) REMOVE REAR CENTER DRIVE SHAFT. Loosen set screw holding universal joint yoke to front end of rear center shaft, then remove two nuts and lock washers from rear bearing to support bolts and remove bolts. Remove rear center shaft with rear bearing from

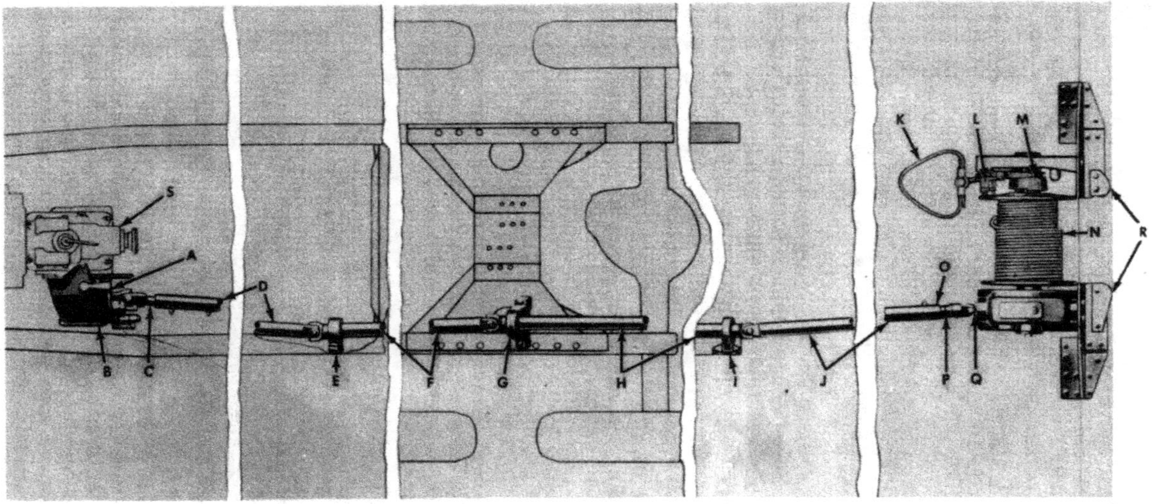

A WINCH POWER TAKE-OFF LEVER
B POWER TAKE-OFF
C FRONT SLIP JOINT
D FRONT DRIVE SHAFT
E DRIVE SHAFT BEARING (FRONT)
F FRONT CENTER DRIVE SHAFT
G DRIVE SHAFT BEARING (CENTER)
H REAR CENTER DRIVE SHAFT
I DRIVE SHAFT BEARING (REAR)
J REAR DRIVE SHAFT

K CLUTCH SHIFTING ROPE
L DRAG BRAKE
M SLIDING CLUTCH
N WINCH CABLE (3500-2198218)
O REAR SLIP JOINT
P STOP CLAMP
Q SHEAR PIN LOCATION
R SUPPORT BRACKETS AND ROPE GUARD
S TRANSMISSION

RA PD 337189

Figure 251—Winch System

505

vehicle. Center bearing and universal joint yoke will remain in vehicle. Yoke is keyed to shaft. Do not lose key.

(6) REMOVE CENTER BEARING. Remove center bearing to frame bolt nuts, lock washers, and spacers and remove bolts; then remove bearing and upper spacer from vehicle. This will provide room for removal of front center shaft.

(7) REMOVE FRONT CENTER DRIVE SHAFT. Loosen set screw holding universal joint to front end of front center shaft and remove yoke from shaft. Yoke is keyed to shaft. Do not lose key. Remove shaft from vehicle.

(8) REMOVE FRONT BEARING. Remove two nuts and lock washers from bearing to frame bolts and remove bolts and spacers. Then remove bearing from vehicle.

(9) REMOVE FRONT DRIVE SHAFT. Move front shaft toward rear, pulling shaft off front universal joint splines. Remove shaft from vehicle through cargo compartment floor board opening.

(10) REMOVE FRONT UNIVERSAL JOINT. Loosen set screw holding universal joint yoke to power take-off shaft and remove universal joint from shaft. Yoke is keyed to shaft. Do not lose key.

(11) REMOVE REAR BEARING FROM SHAFT. In the event rear center shaft is replaced by new part, bearing may be pressed or driven from shaft.

c. Drive Shaft Installation Procedure (figs. 250 and 251). Drive shafts should be installed progressively in reverse order to removal. Begin at power take-off and work toward rear of vehicle. When installing winch drive shaft bearings equipped with neoprene cushion rings, apply a coating of asbestos grease around the outside of bearing to prevent early bearing failure due to water coming in contact with bearing assembly.

(1) INSTALL FRONT UNIVERSAL JOINT. Place key in keyway and install front universal joint yoke on power take-off shaft. Tighten yoke set screw securely.

(2) INSTALL FRONT DRIVE SHAFT. Assemble front shaft over splines of front universal joint in such a manner that universal joint yokes on either end of shaft will be in the same plane.

(3) PLACE FRONT BEARING. Place front center bearing in position but do not attach to frame.

(4) INSTALL FRONT INTERMEDIATE DRIVE SHAFT. Place front center shaft in position, inserting front end through frame crossmember, and install front bearing on shaft. Then place key in keyway on shaft and install universal joint yoke on shaft in such a manner that universal joint yokes on both ends of shaft will be in same plane. Tighten yoke set screw securely.

(5) ATTACH FRONT BEARING TO FRAME. Assemble spacers over bolts, then insert bolts through bearing bracket and frame. Position

spacers so bearing will be at proper angle to line up shaft and install bolts, lock washers, and nuts. Tighten nuts securely.

(6) INSTALL REAR CENTER DRIVE SHAFT. Press center bearing and rear bearing on rear center drive shaft and place drive shaft in position and install shaft in universal joint yoke. Tighten set screw securely.

(7) ATTACH CENTER AND REAR BEARINGS TO FRAME. Install two center bearing to frame bolts in bearing bracket; position long spacer over bolts so bearing will be at proper angle, and insert bolts through frame. Install two spacers, lock washers, and nuts to bolts and tighten nuts securely. Install two rear bearing to frame bolts through bearing bracket and support and install lock washers and nuts. Tighten nuts securely.

(8) INSTALL REAR DRIVE SHAFT. Place rear drive shaft in position through cargo compartment rear bulkhead opening. Place key in keyway in rear end of rear center shaft and drive rear shaft front universal joint yoke on shaft. Universal joint yokes on both ends of shaft must be in same plane.

(9) ASSEMBLE REAR UNIVERSAL JOINT TO WINCH. Grease universal joint and worm shaft, position universal joint on worm shaft, and install shear pin [par. 274a., steps (3), (4), (5), and (6)].

277. WINCH ASSEMBLY REMOVAL.

a. Attach Chain Fall. Attach chain fall or a suitable hoist to winch so that it may be suspended during removal of mounting parts and lifted clear of vehicle after mounting parts are removed.

b. Remove Left-hand Rope Guard. Remove two left-hand support angle to winch worm shaft housing bolts and lock washers. Remove left-hand rope guard to lower support nut, lock washer, and bolt. Remove four A-frame bracket and left-hand support angle to bracket nuts, lock washers, and bolts, and remove A-frame bracket, left-hand rope guard, and support angle from vehicle (fig. 248).

c. Remove Right-hand Rope Guard. Remove right-hand support angle to winch end frame nut, lock washer, and bolt. Remove right-hand rope guard to lower support nut, lock washer, and bolt. Remove four A-frame bracket and right-hand support angle to bracket nuts, lock washers, and bolts and remove A-frame bracket, right-hand rope guard, and support angle from vehicle (fig. 248).

d. Remove Shear Pin (fig. 250). Enter stern compartment and remove cotter pin from winch worm shaft to drive shaft shear pin, then drive out shear pin.

e. Disconnect Drive Shaft (fig. 250). Lift stop collar from its groove in rear drive shaft splines and slide it toward rear of vehicle on shaft splines as far as it will go. (If stop clamp is used instead of stop collar, remove clamp screw and remove clamp from around shaft). Move drive shaft rear universal joint forward to telescope slip joint and remove joint yoke from end of winch worm shaft.

Maintenance Instructions

f. Remove End Frame to Hull Bolt. Remove nut and lock washer from winch end frame to hull bolt, then remove bolt.

g. Remove Hull to Worm Shaft Housing Bolts and Remove Winch. Remove two hull to winch worm shaft housing bolts and lock washers and lift winch assembly from vehicle. (Do not lose felt seal or drive shaft spacers, if used, at worm shaft).

278. WINCH ASSEMBLY INSTALLATION.

a. Place Winch in Vehicle. Coat both sides of winch worm shaft to winch box felt seal with caulking compound (52-C-3086-200), then install felt seal over winch worm shaft (fig. 250). Using chain fall or a suitable hoist, place winch assembly into position in vehicle.

b. Install Left-hand Rope Guard. Place left-hand rope guard, support angle, and A-frame bracket in position and install four A-frame bracket and left-hand support angle to bracket bolts, lock washers, and nuts. Install left-hand rope guard to lower support bolt, lock washers, and nut. Install two left-hand support angle to winch worm shaft housing bolts and lock washers (fig. 248).

c. Install Right-hand Rope Guard. Place right-hand rope guard support angle and A-frame bracket in position and install four A-frame bracket and right-hand support angle to support bolts, lock washers, and nuts. Install right-hand rope guard to lower support bolt, lock washer, and nut. Install right-hand support angle to winch end frame bolt, lock washer, and nut.

d. Install End Frame to Hull Bolt. Install winch end frame to hull bolt, lock washer, and nut. Enter stern compartment for access to inner end of bolt for tightening nut.

e. Install Hull to Worm Shaft Housing Bolts. Install two hull to winch worm shaft housing bolts and lock washers from inside stern compartment.

f. Connect Drive Shaft. From inside stern compartment, grease universal joint and worm shaft, position universal joint on worm shaft, and install shear pin [par. 274***a.***, steps (3), (4), (5), and (6)].

Section XLVIII

A-Frame Assembly

279. GENERAL.

a. The A-frame consists of two frame tube assemblies, two stay cables, one stay rod, one pulley, shaft, and snap rings (fig. 252). These parts are stowed on the cargo floor when not in use. Operation of A-frame is covered in paragraph 38.

TM 9-802
280

A-Frame Assembly

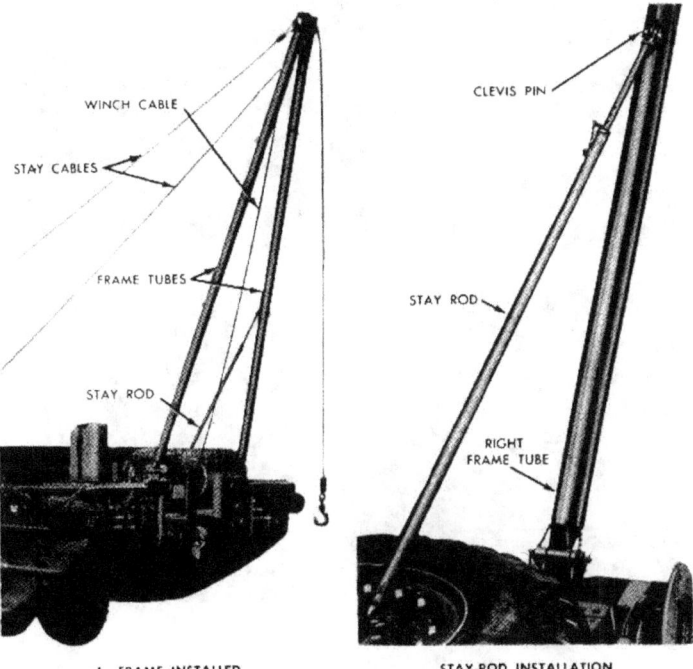

A FRAME INSTALLED 　　　STAY-ROD INSTALLATION
RA PD 337140

Figure 252—A-Frame Installed

280. ASSEMBLY AND INSTALLATION.

a. Remove Tarpaulin and Rear Curtain (If Necessary). A-frame can be installed without removing tarpaulin, rear curtain or rear surf board, if the A-frame tubes are supported in manner to prevent crushing the bows and curtains.

b. Install Frame Tube Assemblies (fig. 253). Lay upper ends of tubes over cargo space. Install lower ends to brace brackets at rear, inserting pins attached to tubes. Insert cotter pin.

c. Install Pulley (fig. 253). Install pulley on shaft with snap ring at each side of pulley. Unwind about 25 feet of cable from winch drum (par. 29). If short chain and hook are assembled to cable end, attach extra hook and shackle to cable eye. Position cable into pulley sheave, then install pulley and shaft into upper ends of frame tubes. Install tie pin to attach the two tubes together.

509

TM 9-802
280

Maintenance Instructions

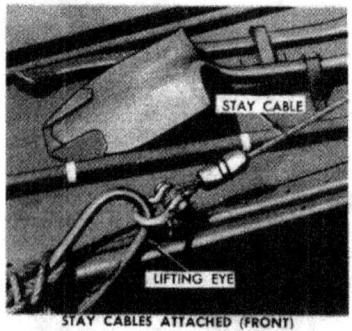

RA PD 333245

Figure 253—A-Frame Attachments

d. Attach Stay Cables (fig. 253). Place eye end of stay cables over lugs at pulley. Shackle opposite ends of stay cables to front lifting eyes.

e. Install Stay Rod Assembly (fig. 252). Insert upper end (telescope end) of stay rod over lug on tube. Install clevis pin and secure with cotter pin.

f. Raise A-Frame into Operating Position. Raise A-frame until cables support it. Install lower end of stay rod in spare wheel stud hole (fig. 252). Select a hole to the rear as far as possible. Push A-frame tubes toward rear as far as possible, then install pin in nearest available hole.

g. Travel Position. A-frame may be temporarily folded forward by removing stay rod. If vehicle is to be moved for any distance, the A-frame should be stowed. For short moves, disconnect stay rod from spare wheel stud hole, fold A-frame forward, then place lower end of stay rod into hole in center rear cargo floor board (fig. 254), or if floor is covered, lash free end to mooring eyes.

TM 9-802
281-282
Compass

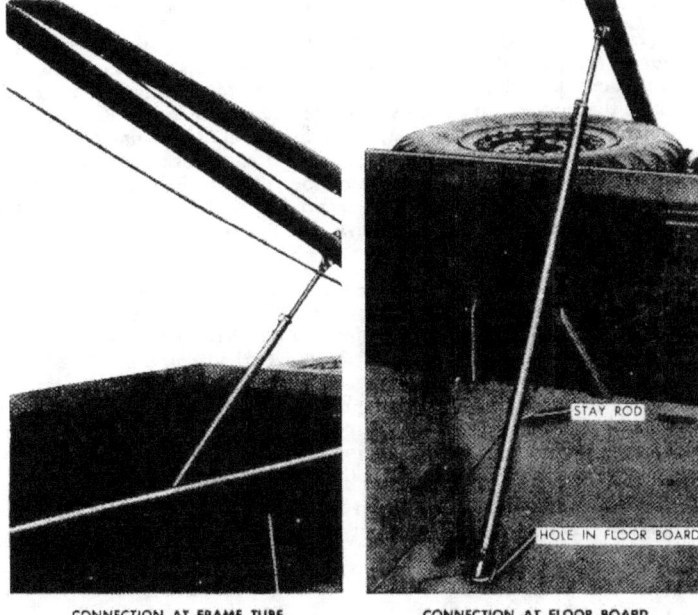

CONNECTION AT FRAME TUBE   CONNECTION AT FLOOR BOARD
RA PD 337178

Figure 254—Stay Rod Connection with A-Frame Folded Forward

281. REMOVAL.

a. Remove Stay Rod Assembly. Push frame tubes to the rear, then remove upper stay rod adjusting pin. Remove lower end of stay rod from spare wheel. Lower A-frame.

b. Remove Stay Cables. Remove stay cables at both ends.

c. Remove Tubes from Brackets. Pull brace bracket pins. Push A-frame "legs" or tubes together as far as possible, then stow on cargo floor.

Section XLIX

Compass

282. GENERAL.

a. Compass Equipment. One of four types of compasses are used, Hull, Pioneer, Sherrill AEG or AEG-1, and Sherrill M-6. Each type can be identified by reference to figures 256, 257, 258, and 259.

283. INITIAL COMPENSATING OF COMPASS.

a. Upon receipt of vehicle, equipped with a compass, or when installing a compass, the instrument must be compensated according to instructions included with each instrument. Manufacturer's instructions state that a compass course should be laid out, marking all cardinal and mid-cardinal points. Further, cardinal and mid-cardinal points can be determined by an accurate magnetic compass (pocket compass satisfactory). In addition to this information, it is further advisable that the compass course be laid out on terrain that is as level as possible, being free from small hills and valleys, rocks or other obstacles causing an uneven terrain.

b. Compensating Conditions. Before starting the compensating procedure as outlined in manufacturer's instructions, it is further necessary that a definite conclusion should be arrived at on the compliments, such as tools, guns and other firing power that would be normally used on the vehicle. If the vehicle is to carry a fifty (50) caliber machine gun over the co-driver's seat, the gun should be mounted and the barrel should be extended in a carrying position as it would normally be carried when not in use. In addition to the normal equipment, as would be used with the vehicle, the following instructions should be used.

(1) When taking a reading on cardinal and mid-cardinal points, the engine should be operating at approximately 2300 revolutions per minute.

(2) Emergency brake should be in the "full off" position.

(3) Co-driver's seat should be in the "upright" position.

(4) All tools that are to be carried with the vehicle should be in the tool box. Oilcan on late model vehicles should be in its bracket as it normally would be carried. The glove compartment should be examined for any metal articles, such as screw drivers, pliers, etc., that would cause a magnetic attraction of the compass. Anything not normally carried should be removed.

(5) If it is desired that the compass be compensated for mostly night operation where the lights would be used, it is advisable to have the lights in a "full on" position while compensating the compass; otherwise, if the compass is to be used mostly for daily operations, the compass should be compensated with the lights in the "off" position. However, in this case, the driver should be familiar with the constant error caused with the lights burning and notation should be made of this error for night operation with lights in use.

(6) The windshield as used on late model vehicles must be in an "upright" position and firmly clamped in place during the compensating procedures. Lowering windshield affects compass.

(7) It can be assumed that operators, when in actual operation, will wear helmets and other field equipment as issued by the Commanding Officer. Personnel compensating the compass should also be dressed and equipped in the same manner. Tools of any kind should be removed from pockets of clothing.

TM 9-802
283

Compass

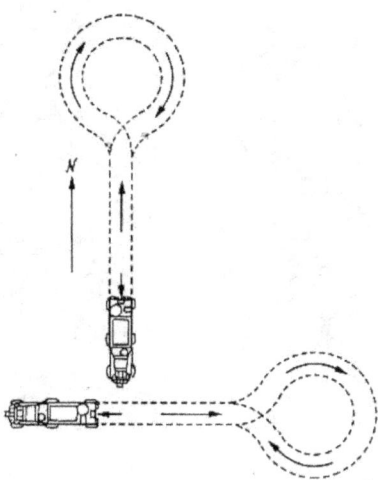

Figure 255—Method of Driving Vehicle During Daily Compass Check

(8) It is further suggested that selected personnel perform all compensating procedure in operation. The driver should not attempt to compensate the compass. After the compensation is completed, it is a duty of the driver to perform the daily check of the compass.

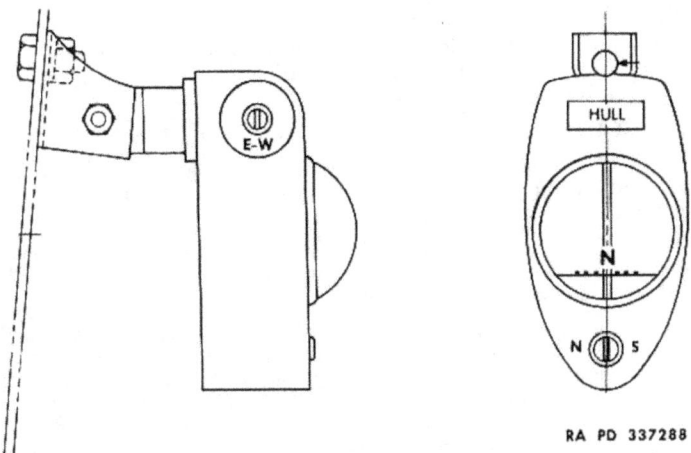

Figure 256—Hull Compass Installed

TM 9-802
283

Maintenance Instructions

A SIDE PLATE
B LAMP ROD AT CONNECTOR
C MOUNTING BRACKET
D LOCK NUT

E FLAT WASHER
F NON-MAGNETIC SCREW DRIVE
G N. S. COMPENSATING SCREW
H E. W. COMPENSATING SCREW

RA PD 337291

Figure 257—Pioneer Compass Installed

c. Daily Check. Compass should be checked daily in the following manner. Methods are the same for all compasses with exceptions noted:

(1) Head the vehicle North (0°) as indicated on the vehicle compass. Drive approximately 200 feet direct North (fig. 255).

(2) Turn the vehicle in opposite direction and drive same distance, *paralleling the tracks made when headed North.* If compass does not read South (180°), note the deviation.

(3) NORTH AND SOUTH DEVIATION ADJUSTMENT.

(a) Hull Compass (fig. 256). With a *brass* screw driver or a copper coin, adjust north and south screw *one-half* the deviation noted in step (2) above.

(b) Pioneer Compass (fig. 257). Using brass screw driver (mounted on side of instrument), adjust North and South screw *one-half* the deviation noted in step (2) above.

(c) Sherrill Compass (figs. 258 and 260). On AEG and AEG-1 models, remove upper thumb at top of compass. It may be necessary to loosen the side knobs, then tilt the instrument forward to remove the cover. Remove the front half of compensation cover. On M-6 model, remove compensation cover screws and lift cover off unit. Adjust the North and South compensator screw one-half the deviation noted in step (2) above.

Compass

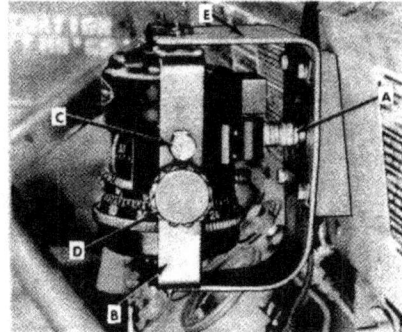

A LIGHT SOCKET CONNECTION NUT
B COMPASS FRAME
C COMPASS TO FRAME MOUNTING CAP SCREWS
D COMPASS TO FRAME SIDE KNOB
E MOUNTING BRACKET
F FRAME TO BRACKET MOUNTING BOLT
G RUBBER INSULATOR
H FLAT WASHERS
I LOCK NUT
J COMPENSATING COVER
K BOTTOM KNOB
L UPPER THUMB NUT
M N. S. THUMB COMPENSATOR SCREW
N E. W. THUMB COMPENSATOR SCREW

RA PD 337289

Figure 258—Sherrill Compass Installed (Model AEG)

(4) Head the vehicle East (90°) as indicated on the *vehicle compass*. Drive approximately 200 feet directly East (90°).

(5) Turn the vehicle in opposite direction and drive same distance, paralleling the tracks made when heading East. If compass does not read West (270°), note the deviation.

(6) EAST AND WEST DEVIATION ADJUSTMENT.

(a) Hull Compass (fig. 256). Adjust the E.W. screw one-half the deviation noted in step (5) above.

(b) Pioneer Compass (fig. 257). With brass screw driver, adjust the E.W. screw one-half the deviation noted in step (5) above.

(c) Sherrill Compass (figs. 258 and 260). Turn the E.W. compensator screw one-half the deviation noted in step (5) above.

515

TM 9-802
284

Maintenance Instructions

284. COMPASS REPLACEMENT.

a. Hull (fig. 256).

(1) REMOVAL. Remove nut attaching compass mounting bracket to lower panel of windshield.

(2) INSTALLATION. Install mounting bolt through front of lower windshield panel. Place mounting bracket over bolt, then nut and lock washer. Before tightening nut, position compass to maintain vehicle alinement with center line of hull. It may be necessary to loosen bolt which supports rubber mounting base to bracket.

b. Pioneer (fig. 257).

(1) REMOVAL. Remove side plates. Remove lamp socket. Remove mounting screws, nuts, washers, and screws.

RA PD 337293

Figure 259—Sherrill Compass (Model M-6) Assembled

Compass

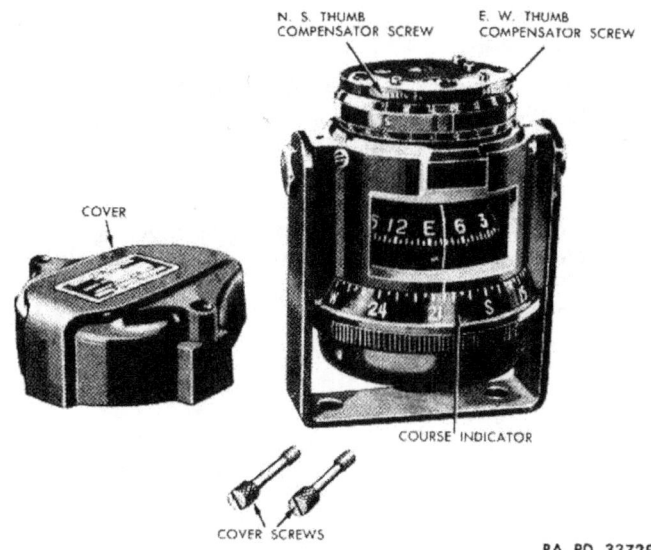

Figure 260—Sherrill Compass (Model M-6) with Cover Removed

(2) INSTALLATION.

(a) Remove side plates. Remove lamp socket connector, then remove socket. Remove wire retainer by loosening two terminal screws. Place connector over wires, then connect wires to plug.

(b) Position compass in mounting bracket. Install four mounting screws, working frame inside of compass frame. Install screws through rubber mountings and threaded holes in mounting bracket.

(c) Install flat washers and nuts. Position light plugs in socket, then tighten connector.

(d) Do not install side plates until compass has been compensated.

c. Sherrill (AEG Models) (fig. 258).

(1) REMOVAL. Remove light socket connector nut, then withdraw plug. Remove mounting bracket bolt nuts, lock washers, and bolts.

(2) INSTALLATION.

(a) Remove light connector nut, then light plug. Place nut over wiring harness. Solder ends of wires to plug terminals.

(b) Place compass in compass frame. Install compass to frame mounting cap screws. Install compass to frame side knobs and tighten.

(c) Install compass and frame assembly to mounting bracket. Install the frame to mounting bracket bolts through rubber insulators, then install flat washers and lock nuts. Tighten light socket connector nut.

d. Sherrill (Model M-6) (figs. 259 and 260).

(1) REMOVAL. Remove light connections at rear of compass. Remove compass from bracket.

(2) INSTALLATION.

(a) Remove compass from mounting bracket.

(b) Attach bracket to dash, using tapped holes provided.

(c) Mount compass in bracket so that compass card or dial is level (vehicle must be level).

(d) Connect light wires at rear of compass.

PART FOUR
AUXILIARY EQUIPMENT

Section L
General

285. SCOPE.

a. As no auxiliary equipment is furnished with this vehicle, no information can be supplied in this part.

APPENDIX

Section LI
Shipment and Limited Storage

286. GENERAL INSTRUCTIONS.

a. Preparation for domestic shipment of the vehicle is the same as preparation for limited storage. Preparation for shipment by rail includes instructions for loading and unloading the vehicle, blocking necessary to secure the vehicle on freight cars, clearance, weight, and other information necessary to properly prepare the vehicle for rail shipment. For more detailed information and for preparation for indefinite storage refer to AR 850-18 and FM 9-25.

287. PREPARATION FOR LIMITED STORAGE OR DOMESTIC SHIPMENT.

a. A vehicle to be prepared for limited storage or domestic shipment is one temporarily out of service for less than 30 days, or a vehicle that must be ready for operation on call. If the vehicle is to be indefinitely stored after shipment by rail, it will be prepared for such storage at its destination.

b. If the vehicle is to be placed in limited storage, take the following precautions.

(1) LUBRICATION. Completely lubricate the entire vehicle, except the engine (par. 53). For preparation of the engine, see step (8) below.

(2) BATTERY. Check battery and terminals for corrosion and, if necessary, clean and thoroughly service battery (par. 130).

Appendix

(3) COOLING SYSTEM. If freezing temperature may normally be expected during the limited storage or shipment period, test the coolant with a hydrometer and add the proper quantity of antifreeze compound to afford protection from freezing at the lowest temperature anticipated during the storage or shipping period. Completely inspect the cooling system for leaks.

(4) TIRES. Clean, inspect tires and inflate them to 40 pounds pressure. Replace with serviceable tires, all tires requiring retreading or repairing. Do not store vehicles on floors, cinders, or other surfaces which are soaked with oil or grease. Wash off immediately any oil, grease, gasoline, or kerosene which comes in contact with the tires under any circumstances.

(5) ROAD TEST. The preparation for limited storage will include a road test of at least 5 miles, after the battery and lubrication services, to check on general condition of the vehicle. Correct any defects noted in the vehicle operation, before the vehicle is stored or note on a tag attached to the steering wheel, stating the repairs needed or describing the condition present. A written report of these items will then be made to the officer in charge.

(6) FUEL IN TANKS. It is not necessary to remove the fuel from the tanks during temporary storage or shipment within the United States, nor to label the tanks under Interstate Commerce Commission Regulations. Leave fuel in the tanks except when storing in locations where fire ordinances or other local regulations require removal of all gasoline before storage. If vehicles are to be maintained ready for operation on call in excess of 30 days, the following precautions against gum formation must be taken:

(a) The fuel system must be free from accumulated gum. Unless the vehicle is entering its first storage and has never been issued for use, inspect and clean the fuel pump; carbureter accelerator pump plunger, venturi tube, choke and throttle valves, float mechanism; fuel lines; fuel tanks; fuel filters; fuel shut-off cocks; and screens.

(b) If gum is present in the above parts, it can best be removed by benzol, acetone, alcohol, or a mixture of these solvents. Deposited gum is not readily soluble in fresh gasoline. When gum has dried, it may be necessary to resort to mechanical means to remove it.

(c) Parts which cannot be thoroughly cleaned and freed from the gum deposit without damage should be replaced.

(d) After cleaning and reassembling, fill fuel tank half full of fresh gasoline which has not been long in storage.

(e) Add two containers (8 oz) of gum-preventive compound to fuel tank.

(f) Fill the fuel tank to capacity and operate the vehicle for at least 5 minutes.

(7) EXTERIOR OF VEHICLES. Wash down and flush the hull and hatches with fresh water. If practicable, remove rust appearing on the vehicle exterior with flint paper. Repaint painted surfaces whenever necessary to protect wood or metal. Coat exposed polished metal sur-

Shipment and Limited Storage

facs susceptible to rust with light rust preventive compound. Close firmly all doors, hatches, and vision slots. Make sure paulins are in place and firmly secured. Leave rubber mats, such as floor mats, where provided, in an unrolled position on the floor, and not rolled or curled up. Equipment such as pioneer tools and fire extinguishers will remain in place in the vehicle. For treatment of small arms carried on or within vehicles refer to the pertinent technical manuals.

(8) ENGINE.

(a) Remove spark plugs and spray into tops of cylinders with preservative engine oil, SAE 30 (grade II), while slowly rotating engine. Replace spark plugs.

(b) If spark plugs cannot be removed, spray preservative oil into air intake with engine running at a fast idle until smoke comes from exhaust pipe. CAUTION: *Preservative oil should never be poured through carbureter.* After spraying preservative oil into air intake, shut off engine and allow to cool for about 15 minutes. Start engine and again spray preservative oil into air intake for several minutes only. The second spraying is necessary in order to coat exhaust valves. Do not run engine for more than several minutes as exhaust valves will become so hot that preseravtive oil will not adhere properly. Perform this treatment when further running of the engine is not necessary.

(c) If it becomes necessary to run the engine after treatment, it should not be operated at over 1,600 revolutions per minute. Hold operation to a minimum, and spray cylinders again after operation.

(9) INSPECTION. Make a systematic inspection, just before shipment or temporary storage, to insure all above steps have been covered and that the vehicle is ready for operation on call. Make a list of all missing or damaged items and attach it to the steering wheel. Refer to "Before-operation Service" (par. 56).

(10) BRAKES. Release brakes and chock the wheels.

c. Inspections in Limited Storage. When vehicle is placed in limited storage, inspect the battery weekly. If water is added to the battery when freezing weather is anticipated, recharge the battery with a portable charger or remove it for recharging. Do not attempt to charge the battery by running the auxiliary generator. Remove any rust from vehicle with flint paper.

288. LOADING AND BLOCKING FOR RAIL SHIPMENT.

a. Preparation. In addition to the preparation described in paragraph 287, when Ordnance vehicles are prepared for domestic shipment, the following preparation and precautions will be taken.

(1) EXTERIOR. Cover the body of the vehicle with a canvas cover ordinarly supplied as an accessory.

(2) BATTERY. Disconnect the battery to prevent its discharge by vandalism or accident. This may be accomplished by disconnecting the

positive lead, taping the end of the lead, and tying it back away from the battery.

(3) MARKING CARS. All cars containing Ordnance vehicles must be placarded "DO NOT HUMP."

b. Placing Vehicle on Car.

(1) TYPES OF CARS. Ordnance vehicles may be shipped on flat cars, end door box cars, side door cars, or drop end gondola cars, whichever type is the most convenient.

(2) FACILITIES FOR LOADING. Whenever possible, load and unload vehicle from open cars, using permanent end ramps and spanning platforms. Movement from one flat car to another along the length of the train is made possible by crossover plates or spanning platforms. If no permanent end ramp is available, an improvised ramp can be made from railroad ties. Vehicle may be loaded in a gondola car without drop ends by using a crane.

(3) BRAKE WHEEL CLEARANCE. If a flat car is used, position the vehicle with a railroad brake wheel clearance of at least 6 inches (A, fig. 261). When more than one vehicle is loaded on car, locate vehicle on the car in such a manner as to prevent the car from carrying an unbalanced load. Apply the brakes and place the transmission in low gear.

c. Securing Vehicles.
In securing or blocking a vehicle, three motions, lengthwise, sidewise, and bouncing must be prevented. The following is an approved method of blocking and securing these vehicles on freight cars:

(1) Locate eight blocks (B, fig. 261), one each against front and rear of front wheels, in front of intermediate wheels and in back of rear wheels. Nail heel of block to car floor with three 40-penny nails and toe-nail that portion under tire to car floor with two 40-penny nails. Locate eight blocks (C, fig. 261) one each to upper end of blocks "B" and lower end of car floor and nail upper end to blocks "B" with three 30-penny nails and lower end to car floor with three 30-penny nails. Locate eight blocks (D, fig. 261) one each against blocks "C" and nail to car floor with three 30-penny nails. Using suitable material, such as waterproof paper, burlap or equivalent, locate bottom portion under cleats "F," top portion to extend 2-in. above cleats "F." Locate 12 cleats (F, fig. 261), two each against the outside of each wheel, securing material "E" under lower cleat so that material extends 2-in. above upper cleat. Nail lower cleat to floor with four 30-penny nails and top cleat to the one below with four 30-penny nails. Locate over front and both rear axles (G, fig. 261) 4 strands No. 8 gage black annealed wire, or wires of equivalent strength. Pass over axle, underneath and around cleats (H, fig. 261) and twist taut after cleats "H" have been nailed in place, lengthwise of car and nailed down with four 30-penny nails. Pass through towing clevises at front of vehicle, four strands, No. 8 gage black annealed wire, or wires of equivalent strength (J, fig. 261). Locate wires underneath and around cleats (H, fig. 261) and twist taut

TM 9-802
288

Shipment and Limited Storage

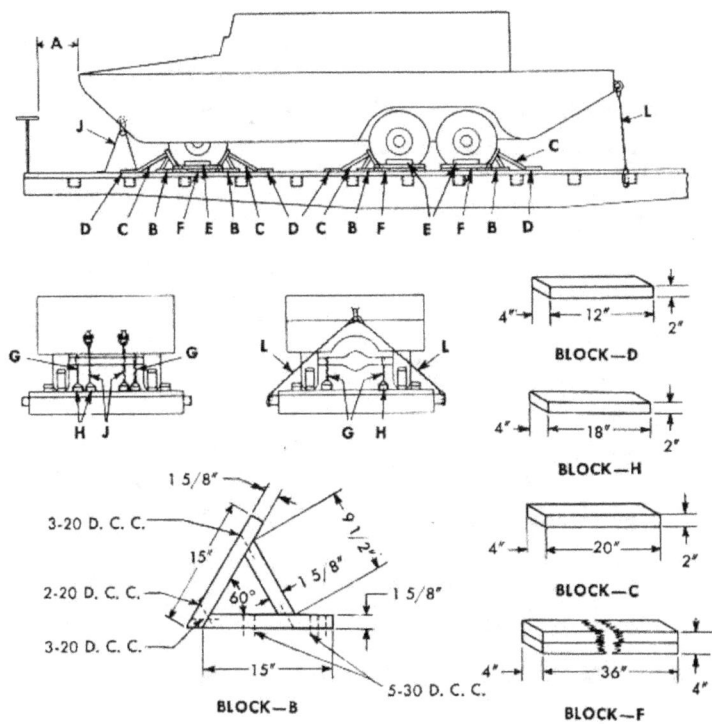

RA PD 346536

Figure 261—Blocking requirements for Rail Shipment

after cleats "H" have been nailed to the floor lengthwise of the car with four 30-penny nails. At the rear of the vehicle loop four strands No. 8 gage black annealed wire, or wires of equivalent strength around towing hook and through opposite stake pockets (L, fig. 261) and twist taut with rod or bolt at both sides of hook.

d. Shipping Data.

Length, over-all	31 ft
Width, over-all	98 in.
Height, over-all	9 ft 2¼ in.
Area of car floor occupied per vehicle	253 sq ft
Volume occupied per vehicle	2,325 cu ft
Shipping weight per vehicle	14,880 lb

523

Appendix

Section LII
References

289. PUBLICATIONS INDEXES.

a. The following publications indexes should be consulted frequently for latest changes to or revisions of the publications given in this list of references and for new publications relating to materiel covered in this manual:

Introduction to Ordnance Catalog (explains SNL system)	ASF Cat. ORD-1 IOC
Ordnance publications for supply index (index to SNL's)	ASF Cat. ORD-2 OPSI
Index to Ordnance Publications (lists FM's, TM's, TC's, and TB's of interest to Ordnance personnel, MWO's, OPSR's, BSD, S of SR's, OSSC's and OFSB's. Includes alphabetical listing of Ordnance major items with publications pertaining thereto)	OFSB1-1
List of publications for training (lists MTP's, TR's, TC's, FM's, TM's, WDTB's, firing tables and charts, lubrication orders, changes, recisions, cancelations and supersessions)	FM 21-6
List of miscellaneous publications (lists MP's, MWO's, SB's, RR's, and War Department Pamphlets)	WD Pamphlet 12-6
List of training films, film strips and film bulletins (lists TF's, FS's, and FB's by serial number and subject)	FM 21-7
Military training aids (lists graphic training aids, models, devices, and displays)	FM 21-8

290. STANDARD NOMENCLATURE LISTS.

a. Vehicular.

Truck, 2½-ton, 6x6, amphibian (GMC Model DUKW-353) SNL G-501

b. Maintenance.

ORD 5, Antifriction bearings and related items	SNL H-12
ORD 5, Cleaning, preserving, and lubrication materials, recoil fluids, special oils, and miscellaneous related items	SNL K-1
ORD 5, Elements, oil filter	SNL K-4
ORD 5, Lubricating equipment, accessories, and related dispensers	SNL K-3
ORD 5, Miscellaneous hardware	SNL H-2
ORD 5, Soldering, brazing and welding materials, gases and related items	SNL K-2
ORD 5, Standard hardware	SNL H-1
ORD 5, Tires, tubes, tire valves and patches, etc.	SNL H-14
Tools, maintenance, for repair of automotive and semiautomotive vehicles:	
ORD 6, Tool-sets (special) automotive and semiautomotive	SNL G-27 (Section 1)
ORD 6, Tool-sets (common) specialists' and organizational	SNL G-27 (Section 2)

References

291. EXPLANATORY PUBLICATIONS.

a. Fundamental Principles.

Automotive brakes	TM 10-565
Automotive electricity	TM 10-580
Automotive power transmission units	TM 10-585
Basic maintenance manual	TM 38-250
Chassis, body, and trailer units	TM 10-560
Driver's manual	TM 10-460
Driver selection and training	TM 21-300
Electrical fundamentals	TM 1-455
Fuels and carburetion	TM 10-550
Fuels, lubricants, cleaners, and preservatives	TM 9-2835
Military motor vehicles	AR 850-15
Motor vehicle inspections and preventive maintenance service	TM 9-2810
Precautions in handling gasoline	AR 850-20
Radio fundamentals	TM 11-455
Sheet metal work, body, fender, and radiator repairs	TM 10-450
Standard military motor vehicles	TM 9-2800

b. Maintenance and Repair.

Cleaning, preserving, lubricating and welding materials and similar items issued by the Ordnance Department	TM 9-850
Maintenance and care of pneumatic tires and rubber treads	TM 31-200
Ordnance Maintenance: Carburetors (Zenith)	TM 9-1826C
Ordnance Maintenance: Electrical equipment (Delco-Remy)	TM 9-1825A
Ordnance Maintenance: Fuel Pumps	TM 9-1828A
Ordnance Maintenance: Hull and water drive for 2½-ton, 6x6, amphibian truck, (GMC DUKW-353)	TM 9-1802C
Ordnance, Maintenance: Power plant for 2½-ton amphibian truck 6x6, (GMC DUKW-353) and 2½-ton truck (GMC)	TM 9-1802A
Ordnance Maintenance: Power train for 2½-ton amphibian truck, 6x6 (GMC DUKW-353)	TM 9-1802B
Ordnance Maintenance: Speedometers, tachometers, and recorders	TM 9-1829A
Ordnance Maintenance: Vacuum brake systems (Bendix B-K)	TM 9-1827B
Ordnance Service in the Field	FM 9-5

c. Protection of Materiel.

Camouflage	FM 5-20
Decontamination	TM 3-220
Decontamination of armored force vehicles	FM 17-59
Defense against chemical attack	FM 21-40
Explosives and demolitions	FM 5-25

d. Storage and Shipment.

Ordnance company, depot	FM 9-25
Ordnance storage and shipment chart—Group G— major items	OSSC-G
Registration of motor vehicles	AR 850-10
Rules governing the loading of mechanized and motorized army equipment, also major caliber guns, for the United States Army and Navy, on open top equipment published by Operations and Maintenance Department of Association of American Railroads	
Storage of motor vehicle equipment	AR 850-18

INDEX

A

A-frame
- Description...................508
- Installation....................509
- Operation..................... 82
- Removal......................511

Accelerator.....................215

After-operation and weekly service........................125

Air circulation................. 76

Air cleaner, engine..............208

Air cleaner, tire pump..........486

Ammeter
- Operation..................... 40
- Replacement..................280

Antifreeze table................. 90

At-halt service..................123

Axle, front
- Axle shaft and universal joint .312
- Data..........................307
- Description...................307
- Housing outer end seal.......315
- Installation....................319
- Removal......................319
- Steering arm..................311
- Tie rod.......................309
- Toe-in adjustment............308
- Trouble shooting.............162

Axles, rear
- Axle shafts....................320
- Data..........................320
- Description...................320
- Installation....................323
- Removal......................322
- Trouble shooting.............162

Axle shaft and universal joint....312

Axle shafts, rear................320

Axle transfer case—see "Transfer case, axle"

B

Battery
- Cold weather protection...... 92
- Hot weather maintenance..... 94
- Service.......................250

Battery and lighting system
- Battery and cables............250
- Blackout driving light........255
- Blackout marker lights........256
- Corrosion prevention and waterproofing...............250
- Description...................249
- Headlights....................253
- Radio noise suppression......274
- Stop and taillight.............257
- Trouble shooting.............157

Battery cables...................250

Before-operation service........118

Belt, bilge pump (Oberdorfer)..432

Belt, fan........................234

Bilge pump, Gould..............444

Bilge pump, Higgins............452

Bilge pump, Oberdorfer........433

Bilge pumps
- Controls...................... 37
- Forward system (Gould type)..442
- Heating system...............424
- Forward system (Oberdorfer type).........................431
- Rear system (Higgins type)...449

Bilge pump systems
- Cold weather precautions..... 86
- Operation..................... 79
- Trouble shooting.............168

Bilge pump system (Gould type)
- Bilge pump...................444
- Control valves and manifold...446
- Description...................442
- Pump drive...................442
- Strainer and tubing...........448

Bilge pump system (Higgins)
- Bilge pump...................452
- Description...................449
- Pump drive...................450
- Strainer and tubing...........453

INDEX

B—Cont'd

Bilge pump system (Oberdorfer type)
  Bilge pump.................433
  Control valves and manifold...435
  Description.................431
  Pump drive..................432
  Reservoir and tubes.........441
  Strainers and screens.......437

Blackout driving lights.........255

Blackout marker lights..........256

Bleeding brakes.................344

Brake drums.....................356

Brake, hand
  Adjustment..................363
  Brake band..................363
  Brake drum..................365
  Control..................... 35
  Description.................362
  Lever and linkage...........366
  Operation...................362

Brake shoes, front
  Adjustment..................346
  Replacement.................357

Brake shoes, rear
  Adjustment..................347
  Replacement.................359

Brakes, service
  Bleeding system.............344
  Brake drums.................356
  Brake shoes, front..........357
  Brake shoes, rear...........359
  Controls.................... 36
  Corrosion treatment.........359
  Data........................341
  Hydrovac....................347
  Lines and connections.......351
  Master cylinder.............350
  Pedal and linkage...........349
  System adjustments..........345
  System description..........340
  System operation............341
  System tests................341
  Trouble shooting............163
  Vacuum check valve..........348
  Wheel cylinders.............354

C

Carburetor
  Adjustment..................212
  Cleaning fuel bowl..........212
  Controls.............36 and 213
  Description.................209

Central tire pressure control system
  Air tank and lines..........497
  Data........................482
  Description.................482
  Inflating devices...........492
  Inflation and deflation control valves.....................490
  Tire inflating line valves and manifold..................491
  Tire pump...................486
  Tire pump drive shaft.......488
  Tire pump governor..........484

Check valve, vacuum.............348

Cleaning, painting, and waterproofing....................430

Clutch
  Control..................... 35
  Data........................288
  Description.................287
  Installation................291
  Pedal and linkage...........288
  Pedal free-travel adjustment...288
  Removal.....................290
  Trouble shooting............159

Coil, ignition..................207

Cold weather fuel and lubricants. 87

Cold weather precautions....... 86

Compass
  Daily check.................514
  Initial compensation........512
  Replacement.................516

Condenser, distributor..........205

Controls and instruments....... 33

Cooling system
  Cold weather protection..... 90
  Data........................230
  Description.................230

INDEX

C—Cont'd

Drive belt.................234
Fan and water pump.........236
Hot weather maintenance.....93
Overflow tank..............240
Radiator...................239
Servicing..................231
Thermostat.................237
Trouble shooting...........155

Corrosion prevention and waterproofing
Battery and lighting system....250
Brakes.....................359
Generator..................247
Ignition coil..............207
Instrument and gage panels...275
Spark plugs................207
Starting system............241

Crankcase ventilation.........184

Cranking, hand................44

Curtains, tarpaulins, and lashings 68

Cylinder head and gasket, engine 177

D

Deck, front..................419

Deck, rear...................420

Demolition to prevent enemy use 95

Destruction of material in event of imminent capture..........94

Dimmer switch—see "Switch, dimmer"

Distributor..................202

Distributor condenser........205

Distributor points...........204

Drag link....................398

Drive shaft, tire pump.......488

Drive shafts, water propeller...465

Drive shafts, winch..........504

Driver maintenance...........117

D—Cont'd

Driving controls..............33
Driving in water..............56
Driving on coral..............53
Driving on land...............50
Driving on sand...............52
Driving on soft mud...........53
During-operation service.....121

E

Engine
Crankcase ventilation system..184
Cylinder head and gasket.....177
Data.........................16
Description and data........172
Installation................192
Manifold....................175
Oil filter..................183
Oil pan.....................181
Oil pump....................182
Removal.....................187
Starting.....................43
Stopping.....................44
Trouble shooting............144
Tune-up.....................173
Valve clearance and adjustment....174
Warm-up......................44

Entering water................56

Equipment.....................21

Exhaust pipes................226

Exhaust system
Description.................226
Exhaust pipes...............226
Muffler and tail pipe.......228
Trouble shooting............154

F

Fan..........................236

Fan belt.....................234

Fender lashing................73

TM 9-802

INDEX

F—Cont'd

	Page No.
Filter, fuel	221
Filter, oil	183
Fire extinguishers	82

Fuel and air intake system
- Air cleaner 208
- Carbureter 209
- Carbureter controls 213
- Cold weather fuels 87
- Controls 36
- Data 208
- Fuel filter 221
- Fuel pump 219
- Fuel tank 222
- Fuel tubes 225
- Governor 217
- Manifold heat control 208
- Operation 207
- Trouble shooting 152

Fuel filter 221

Fuel pump 219

Fuel tank 222

Fuel tubes 225

G

Gage, air tank pressure
- Operation 39
- Replacement 283

Gage, gas
- Operation 39
- Replacement 280

Gage, oil pressure
- Operation 39
- Replacement 280

Gage, thermo
- Operation 39
- Replacement 279

Gage, tire pressure
- Operation 39
- Replacement 283

Generating system
- Data 244

G—Cont'd

- Description 244
- Generator 245
- Generator regulator 247
- Radio noise suppression 273
- Trouble shooting 156

Generator 245

Generator regulator 247

Governor, engine 217

Governor, tire pump 484

H

Hand brake—see "Brake, hand"

Hand cranking 44

Hatch covers 415

Headlights 253

Headlight switch—see "Switch, lighting"

Horn and button 286

Hot weather operation 93

Hubs—see "Wheels, tires, and hubs"

Hull
- Bilge pump heating system ... 424
- Bulkheads 422
- Deck, front 419
- Deck, rear 420
- Description 410
- Drainage .... 37, 80, and 410
- Drain plugs .... 80 and 410
- Drain valves 410
- Hatch covers 415
- Pintle hook 423
- Seats 429
- Surf boards 413
- Tarpaulin and bows 429
- Towing shackles 424
- Windshield (early type) 424
- Windshield (late type) 426

Hydrovac 347

INDEX

I

	Page No.
Ignition coil	207
Ignition timing	199

Ignition switch—see "Switch, ignition"

Ignition system
- Data.........................199
- Description..................197
- Distributor..................202
- Distributor condenser........205
- Distributor points...........204
- Ignition coil................207
- Manual advance...............202
- Radio noise suppression......270
- Spark plugs..................206
- Timing.......................199
- Trouble shooting.............152

Instruments
- Compass...................... 40
- Ammeter...................... 40
- Tachometer................... 39
- Speedometer.................. 39

Instruments and gages	38
Instruments, gages, and switches	275
Introduction	5

L

Landing from water	58
Lashing instructions	73

Lights
- Blackout driving.............255
- Blackout marker..............256
- Headlights...................253
- Instrument panel.............282
- Signal.......................286
- Stop light...................257
- Taillight....................257

Litter stops	84

Lubrication
- Cold weather lubricants...... 87
- Detailed instructions........ 99

Lubrication order	98

M

	Page No.
Maintenance instructions	97
Maintenance of vehicles during cold weather	91
Manifold, bilge pump (Gould)	446
Manifold, bilge pump (Oberdorfer)	435
Manifold, engine	175
Manifold heat control	208
Manifold, tire inflating valve	491
Master cylinder	350
Miscellaneous controls	36
Muffler, exhaust	228

O

Oil filter	183
Oil pan, engine	181
Oil pump, engine	182
Operating instructions	26
Operation of auxiliary equipment	60
Operation on sand, mud, and coral	52
Operation under ordinary conditions	42
Operation under unusual conditions	85
Organizational maintenance	129
Overflow tank	240

P

Pillow block
- Installation.................338
- Modification.................339
- Removal.....................337

Pitman arm	395
Pintle hook	423

TM 9-802

INDEX

P—Cont'd

Plugs, spark.....................206

Polarizing generator............247

Power take-off
   Controls and linkage.........300
   Description..................300
   Installation....................306
   Oil seals......................303
   Removal......................306
   Trouble shooting.............160

Preventive maintenance services.116

Propeller, water.................465

Propeller shafts, housings, and seals
   Description...................324
   Drainage......................82
   Installation....................331
   Removal......................326
   Trouble shooting.............162

Propeller shaft pillow block....337

Protection of cooling system.... 90

Pump, fuel......................219

Pump, oil.......................182

Pump, water....................236

R

Radiator overflow tank..........240

Radiator........................239

Radio noise suppression system...............158 and 269

Records......................... 5

Regulator cover.................249

Regulator, generator............247

Rudder and linkage (early type).402

Rudder and linkage (late type).405

Rudder cable....................399

Rudder stuffing box.............409

S

Seats...........................429

Service upon receipt of equipment....................... 26

Shear pin, rudder cable.........401

Shear pin, winch...............501

Shifting gears................... 45

Shipment and limited storage...519

Shock absorbers................370

Spare parts..................... 24

Spark plugs....................206

Special tools................... 97

Speedometer
   Cable replacement............284
   Operation..................... 39
   Replacement.................280
   Shaft replacement............284

Spring seat, rear................372

Springs, front..................367

Springs, rear...................371

Spring suspension
   Description...................367
   Shock absorbers.............370
   Spring seat, rear..............372
   Springs, front................367
   Springs, rear.................371
   Torque rods..................376
   Trouble shooting.............165

Starter.........................241

Starter controls.................244

Starter switch.................. 40

Starting system
   Description...................241
   Radio noise suppression......274
   Starter.......................241
   Starter controls...............244
   Trouble shooting.............155

Steering arm...................311

INDEX

S—Cont'd

Steering gear
   Adjustments...................392
   Installation....................398
   Removal......................396

Steering system
   Data..........................392
   Description...................392
   Drag link.....................398
   Gear adjustments.............392
   Gear installation.............398
   Gear removal.................396
   Pitman arm...................395
   Rudder and linkage (early type).........................402
   Rudder and linkage (late type).405
   Rudder cable, spool, and shear pin...........................399
   Rudder stuffing box...........409
   Trouble shooting.............167

Stop light switch—see "Switch, stop light"

Strut bearing...................463

Stuffing box, rudder............409

Stuffing box, water propeller drive shaft...................468

Surf boards....................413

Switch, blackout driving light
   Operation..................... 41
   Replacement..................281

Switch, dimmer
   Operation..................... 42
   Replacement..................285

Switch, ignition
   Operation..................... 40
   Replacement..................281

Switch, instrument light
   Operation..................... 41
   Replacement..................280

Switch, lighting
   Operation..................... 40
   Replacement..................281

Switch, starter................. 40

S—Cont'd

Switch, stop light
   Operation..................... 42
   Replacement..................285

T

Tachometer
   Operation..................... 39
   Replacement..................283
   Shaft replacement............284

Tank, fuel......................222

Tank, overflow.................240

Tarpaulin......................429

Tarpaulin bows................430

Thermostat....................237

Throttle control...............215

Tie rod, front axle.............309

Tire inflating devices..........492

Tire pressures.................. 67

Tire pressure control system (after chassis serial No. 2005)
   Controls...................... 37
   Operation..................... 65
   Trouble shooting............170

Tire pump (after chassis serial No. 2005)
   Air cleaner...................486
   Drive shaft...................488
   Governor.....................484
   Installation...................488
   Oil seal replacement.........487
   Removal......................488

Tire pump (prior to chassis serial No. 2006).................480

Tire pump system (prior to chassis serial No. 2006)
   Air tank and lines............481
   Control linkage..............478
   Controls...................... 36
   Data..........................476
   Description...................476

INDEX

T—Cont'd

Drive chain and sprockets.....478
Operation.....................64
Tire pump....................480
Trouble shooting.............170

Tire pump system (late type)—see "Central tire pressure control system"

Tires
  Deflating....................67
  Inflating....................66
  Pressures....................68
  Replacement.................382

Tires and rims................382

Toe-in adjustment.............308

Tools, on vehicle..............17

Tools, parts, and accessories..17

Tools, special.................97

Torque rods...................376

Towing shackles...............424

Towing vehicle.................59

Transfer case, axle
  Controls.....................33
  Controls and linkage........294
  Data........................294
  Description.................294
  Installation................298
  Removal.....................298
  Shifting.....................48
  Trouble shooting............161

Transfer case, water propeller
  Controls.....................33
  Controls and linkage replacement.....................461
  Data........................456
  Description.................456
  Installation................459
  Pulley or sprocket replacement 458
  Removal.....................459

Transmission
  Controls.....................33
  Description.................293
  Installation................293

T—Cont'd

  Removal.....................293
  Shifting.....................45
  Trouble shooting............160

Trouble shooting
  Axle transfer case..........161
  Battery and lighting system..157
  Bilge pump systems..........168
  Brake system................163
  Clutch......................159
  Cooling system..............155
  Engine......................144
  Exhaust system..............154
  Front and rear axles........162
  Fuel and air intake system..152
  General.....................144
  Generating system...........156
  Ignition system.............152
  Propeller shafts............162
  Radio noise suppression system.........................158
  Spring suspension...........165
  Starting system.............155
  Steering system.............167
  Tire inflation systems......170
  Transmission and power take-off.........................160
  Water drive system..........169
  Wheels, tires, and hubs.....166
  Winch.......................172

V

Valve adjustment, engine......174

Valve, crankcase ventilator...184

Vehicle
  Characteristics...............7
  Cold weather maintenance....91
  Description...................7
  Difference in design.........14
  Identification...............13
  Maximum utilization..........14
  Run-in test..................30
  Tabulated data...............15
  Tools, parts, and accessories..17

INDEX

W

Water drive system
  Data........................456
  Description.................456
  Drive shafts................465
  Propeller...................465
  Propeller drive shaft bearings and stuffing box............468
  Propeller drive shaft strut and bearing.....................462
  Trouble shooting.............169
  Water propeller transfer case and controls................456

Water operation................ 53

Water propeller
  Operation..................... 54
  Replacement.................465

Water propeller transfer case—see "Transfer case, water propeller"

Water pump, engine............236

Wheel cylinders, brake.........354

Wheel spacers..................381

Wheels........................379

Wheels, tires, and hubs
  Bearing adjustment, front.....386
  Bearing adjustment, rear......389
  Data........................377
  Hubs and bearings, front......386
  Hubs and bearings, rear.......389
  Marking of hub and wheel studs......................377

W—Cont'd

  Tires and rims...............382
  Trouble shooting.............166
  Wheels......................379

Winch
  Adjustment..................499
  Cable.......................502
  Control lever lock location...302
  Controls...............36 and 62
  Controls and linkage installation.......................302
  Controls and linkage removal.301
  Data........................499
  Description.................498
  Drive shafts and U-joints.....504
  Installation.................508
  Oil seals and bearings.......502
  Operation.................... 60
  Removal.....................507
  Shear pin...................501
  Trouble shooting............172
  Winding cable............... 64

Windshield (after chassis serial No. 2005)
  Operation.................... 75
  Replacement.................426

Windshield (prior to chassis serial No. 2006)
  Operation.................... 75
  Replacement.................424

Windshield wipers
  Controls..................... 37
  Replacement.................427

Wiring, harnesses, and circuits...258

IN HIGH DEFINITION
NOW AVAILABLE!

COMPLETE LINE OF WWII AIRCRAFT FLIGHT MANUALS

WWW.PERISCOPEFILM.COM

Also Now Available!

Visit us at:

www.PeriscopeFilm.com

TM 9-879
WAR DEPARTMENT MANUAL
~~RESTRICTED~~

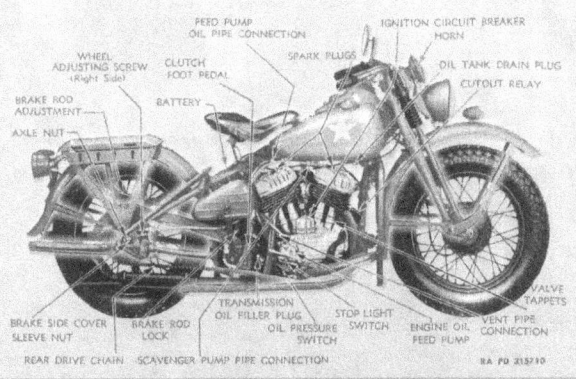

MOTORCYCLE, SOLO
HARLEY-DAVIDSON MODEL WLA
TECHNICAL MANUAL

by WAR DEPARTMENT
PERISCOPE FILM LLC

©2012 PERISCOPE FILM LLC
ALL RIGHTS RESERVED
ISBN #978-1-937684-87-7
WWW.PERISCOPEFILM.COM